INTERNATIONAL MARKETING STRATEGY

FIFTH EDITION

INTERNATIONAL MARKETING STRATEGY

ANALYSIS, DEVELOPMENT AND IMPLEMENTATION

ISOBEL DOOLE

ROBIN LOWE

SOUTH-WESTERN
CENGAGE Learning™

Australia • Canada • Mexico • Singapore • Spain • United Kingdom • United States

SOUTH-WESTERN
CENGAGE Learning™

International Marketing Strategy, 5th Edition
Isobel Doole and Robin Lowe

Publishing Director: John Yates

Publisher: Jennifer Pegg

Development Editor: Lucy Mills

Production Editor: Leonora Dawson-Bowling

Manufacturing Manager: Helen Mason

Senior Production Controller: Maeve Healy

Marketing Manager: Angela Lewis

Typesetter: Newgen, India

Cover design: Adam Renvoize

Text design: Design Deluxe, Bath, UK

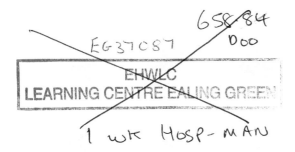

For product information and technology assistance, contact
emea.info@cengage.com.

For permission to use material from this text or product,
and for permission queries, email
clsuk.permissions@cengage.com

Products and services that are referred to in this book may be either trademarks and/or registered trademarks of their respective owners. The publishers and author/s make no claim to these trademarks.

British Library Cataloguing-in-Publication Data
A catalogue record for this book is available from the British Library.

ISBN: 978-1-84480-763-5

Cengage Learning EMEA
High Holborn House, 50-51 Bedford Row
London WC1R 4LR

Cengage Learning products are represented in Canada by
Nelson Education Ltd.

For your lifelong learning solutions, visit
www.cengage.co.uk

Purchase e-books or e-chapters at:
http://estore.bized.co.uk

Printed by Seng Lee Press
1 2 3 4 5 6 7 8 9 10 – 10 09 08

To Andrew and Sylvia

and to our children;

Rob, Libby and Will,

Catherine and Jonathan

BRIEF CONTENTS

CONTENTS

LIST OF FIGURES, TABLES, ILLUSTRATIONS AND DILEMMAS

LIST OF FIGURES

LIST OF TABLES

LIST OF ILLUSTRATIONS

LIST OF DILEMMAS

PREFACE

Introduction

Markets and marketing are becoming ever more international in their nature and managers around the world ignore this fact at their peril. To achieve sustainable growth in markets that are becoming increasingly global, or merely to survive in domestic markets that are increasingly attacked by international players, it is essential that organisations understand the complexity and diversity of international marketing and that their managers develop the skills, aptitudes and knowledge necessary to compete effectively around the globe.

This new and completely revised edition of *International Marketing Strategy* continues to meet the needs of the international marketing student and practitioner in an up to date and innovative manner. It recognises the increasing time pressures of both students and managers and so strives to maintain the readability and clarity of the previous editions, as well as providing a straightforward and logical structure that will enable them to apply their learning to the tasks ahead.

The book continues to incorporate new, significant and relevant material with learning innovations that ensure its continued status as the best-selling UK text on international marketing strategy.

Structure of the book

As in previous editions, the book is divided into three main subject areas – analysis, strategy development and implementation – each of which has four chapters. For each chapter the learning objectives for the reader are stated at the outset and these lead to the key themes of the chapter, which are explored in the text. Illustrations of the key issues are provided along with examples of the kind of practical dilemmas faced by international marketing managers.

Success in international marketing is achieved through being able to integrate and appreciate the interaction between the various elements of the international marketing strategy development process and this is addressed in two ways. First, at the end of each chapter a case study is included. Whilst the main focus of the chapter case study is on integrating a number of the themes of the chapter, the reader should also draw on their learning from the chapters that have gone before to give a complete answer. Second, at the end of each part there is a more comprehensive integrative learning activity for the reader that focuses on international marketing strategy development. At the end of Part 1 this activity is concerned with analysis, at the end of Part 2 with strategy development and at the end of Part 3 with implementation. The format for these learning activities is similar so that the three integrative learning activities, when added together, integrate all the learning from the book and provide a practical and comprehensive exercise in international marketing strategy development for the reader.

New to this edition

A number of chapters have been revised and updated to ensure the inclusion of the latest developments in international marketing. Each chapter now has a case study that encourages further reflection and discussion on the key themes of the chapter.

In Chapter 1 we have included a full section introducing international marketing planning. The chapters (5 and 6) on international marketing in SMEs and global firms have been expanded to include the management and planning implications of the strategy development issues highlighted within the chapter.

In this new edition Chapter 12 focuses on how technology not only supports and enables the international marketing process in areas such as customer relationship management, value and supply chain management, but is also changing the process by which the future strategies of organisations in international markets are being formulated.

The majority of the case studies, illustrations and dilemmas are new or updated. Material is used from around the world and includes a number of cases and illustrations from Asia, Latin America, Eastern Europe and Ireland. The authors have endeavoured to cater for the needs of readers who are developing their international marketing skills in Europe, the Americas, Asia, Australasia or other parts of the world. Each illustration and dilemma has a question highlighting a specific issue that should be considered.

The Integrative Learning Activity is an innovative section at the end of each part with the objective of encouraging readers to integrate their learning from the chapters and the parts. By obtaining and analysing data through secondary sources, typically through the Internet, the reader is able to proceed through the steps of the international marketing strategy process, thus acquiring further knowledge and using this opportunity to practise a number of their international marketing skills.

How to study using this book

The aim of the book is for readers to have an accessible and readable resource for use both as a course book and for revision. The text is also recommended reading for students of the CIM qualifications.

It has a clear structure which is easy to use and easy for the reader to follow, thus making it ideal for incorporation into a course delivered in a 12-week teaching semester. Its geocentric view of international marketing, with examples of good practice in competing internationally from around the globe, makes it ideal for use with courses with multicultural students.

International Marketing Strategy has been developed to help the reader learn, understand and practise a number of elements of the international marketing strategy process. The process involves the analysis of a situation, development of a strategy against a background of a number of strategic options and the implementation of the chosen option. It is important to recognise that there is not one 'right' strategy, because success is ultimately determined by many factors and, besides, it will usually take a number of years before the strategy can be seen finally as a success or failure. Therefore, this book provides a framework, within the parts and chapter structure, in which to understand and evaluate the factors that should be taken into account (and which should be dismissed too) in building an international marketing strategy.

Structure of the book

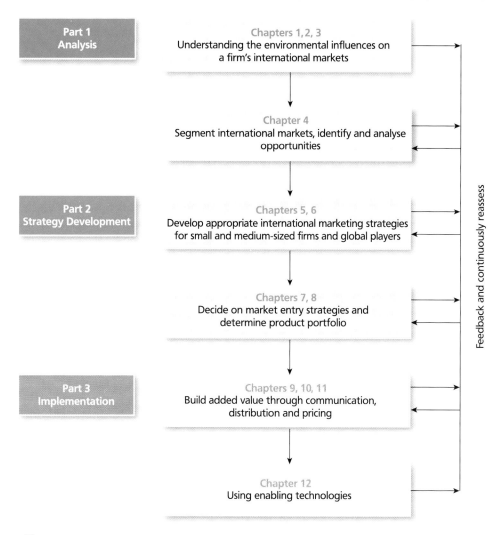

Parts

The three parts focus on the topics of analysis, strategy development and implementation. Each part contains an introduction to the four chapters that have been grouped together.

PART 1 ANALYSIS

Part 1 focuses on analysing the international marketing environment. It provides an introduction to how the international marketing environment influences how firms operate. It explores the changing nature of the environment and explains the structures that support and control international trade. Also considered are the social and cultural influences on customer buying behaviour in international markets.

Frameworks and processes that provide the means to systematically identify and evaluate marketing opportunities and carry out market research across the world are explained.

CASE STUDIES AT THE END OF EACH CHAPTER

PART 1 ANALYSIS

Chapter 1

Flatbread goes round the world explores the success and the reasons behind the success of a Mexican flour product company expanding throughout America, Europe and Asia.

Chapter 2

Should governments support domestic companies investing in foreign markets? This case examines the role of government support agencies in assisting and advising companies trading and investing overseas.

Chapter 3

Leapfrogging the banking system investigates the mobile phone banking revolution taking place in Africa.

Chapter 4

Segmenting the global mobile phone gaming market addresses the issues arising from Cometa Wireless Gaming Systems' attempt to sell mobile phone games to a global market.

Integrative Learning Activity

Li Ning analyses the opportunities in the domestic and global market for the leading sports supplier in China.

PART 2 STRATEGY DEVELOPMENT

Chapter 5

Ebac – dipping their toes further into the water looks at the options and measures taken by a dehumidifier company to combat similar, cheaper Asian imports

Chapter 6

Conglomerate breaks out from India focuses on Tata Sons group's approach to becoming more competitive and global.

Chapter 7

When joint ventures go wrong. Unforeseen factors cause major problems in promising mergers between companies from developed and developing countries.

Chapter 8

Lego explores the toymaker's attempts at diversification in the face of declining sales and profits, and the outcomes of this diversification.

Integrative Learning Activity

Future Global Players examines the different starting points and means used by newcomers from developing economies to cultivate global brands.

PART 3 IMPLEMENTATION

Chapter 9

Google to dominate online ads? This case looks at bigger corporations taking over more independent networking sites and the ensuing issues (legal, advertising and user-related).

Chapter 10

Merry Management Training presents the problems arising when a Western management training consultancy and a small Dubai consultancy firm enter into a friendly informal agreement.

Chapter 11

Beta Automotive explores the strengths and weaknesses of a Singaporean entrepreneur looking to exploit the grey market in auto parts on an international basis.

Chapter 12

India showing IBM the way? This case touches on former and current means of internationalisation and assesses IBM's history and future as a 'globally integrated enterprise'.

Integrated Learning Activity

Microsoft attempts to market its newest products, competing with other companies as well as its own earlier software.

PART 2 STRATEGY DEVELOPMENT

Part 2 explains the international marketing strategy options available for small and medium-sized firms and also the largest organisations that will enable them to compete effectively in global markets. The factors that affect the choice of strategy are considered as well as the challenges that are posed to the managers of these strategies.

A key decision for most organisations is which market entry method to use to exploit the market opportunities from the many options available. This is then followed by the selection and development of the products and service strategy that determine the portfolio that will be offered to customers.

PART 3 IMPLEMENTATION

Part 3 deals with the international communication, distribution and pricing strategies that support the introduction and development of the business in the various worldwide markets. The different local market factors that affect implementation are considered. These factors may allow the associated implementation programmes and processes to be standardised across different markets but, frequently, it is necessary to adapt the strategies to suit local needs.

Finally, technology plays a key enabling role in international marketing strategy implementation. It supports the programme and process delivery and also provides opportunities for creativity that allow innovative firms to gain competitive advantage.

Readers should realise that these groupings of chapter topics within parts are primarily to provide a clear structure and layout for the book. In practice, however, there is considerable overlap between analysis, strategy development and implementation topics. For example, product strategy and market entry are considered by organisations in some situations to be implementation issues, and technology might be used to support analysis, set the overall international marketing strategy or support implementation.

Chapters

After a brief introduction to each chapter the learning objectives for the chapter are set out: these should provide the focus for study. To help to reinforce the learning and encourage the reader to explore the issues more fully the chapters contain a number of additional aids to learning.

Illustrations

The illustrations that have been provided are not present just to reinforce a key issue or learning point that has been discussed within the chapter: the questions that have been added are intended to enable the reader to reflect upon the deeper and broader implications too and thus provide a further opportunity for discussion. Our aim is that the settings for the illustrations be as diverse as possible, geographically, culturally, by business sector, size and type of organisation, in order to try to help the reader consider the situations described from alternative perspectives.

Dilemmas

The dilemmas included emphasise the point that there are few simple and straightforward management decisions in international marketing. Organisations and managers often face difficult problems that require a decision. The dilemmas within a chapter provide the opportunity for the reader to identify those factors that should be taken into account in coming to the decision and, hopefully, consider rather more creative ideas that lead to decisions and solutions that add greater value.

Case studies

The case studies provide the opportunity for the reader to carry out more comprehensive analysis of key chapter topics before deciding what strategic decisions or plans should be made. These short cases provide only limited information and, where possible, readers should obtain more information on the case study subject from appropriate websites in order to complete the tasks. The reader should start with the questions that have been supplied in order to help guide the analysis or discussion. After this, however, the reader should think more broadly around the issues raised and decide whether these are indeed the right questions to ask and answer. International markets change fast and continuously and new factors that have recently emerged may completely alter the situation.

Integrative learning activities

At the end of each of the three parts of the book we have included an Integrative Learning Activity. Their purpose is to integrate the four chapters that make up each of the parts. More importantly, however, is that as a whole the three activities provide a framework for planning an international marketing strategy and give the opportunity for readers to consider the practical issues involved in developing, planning and implementing an outline international marketing strategy. The objective of these activities is to provide a vehicle through which the reader is able to develop practical skills in research, analysis, evaluation and strategy development. In completing these activities you will need to synthesise the various strands and themes explored throughout the book and apply them to a practical situation.

Web support

The textbook is fully supported by the accompanying website that can be found at www.cengage.co.uk/doole5. This enables students and lecturers to access a number of resources in order to explore the subject further. Lecturers can use the site to access valuable online teaching resources, including a full set of PowerPoint slides to accompany the text and hints and tips on how to use the case studies, illustrations etc. in a classroom situation. Students are able to access learning resources to accompany the textbook and hotlinks to other websites that may be useful in exploring the cases and illustrations in the text.

ID, RL

ACKNOWLEDGEMENTS

Inevitably, in the task of writing this textbook we have had help, support and valuable contributions from many people. We would especially like to thank our colleagues from Sheffield Hallam University and other univerisities who have contributed a number of case studies and illustrations.

We are indebted to our students from many countries, the managers of many businesses in South Yorkshire, who have freely given their time to share their expert knowledge of international niche marketing, and managers in many larger companies, including IBM and Shell, who have discussed with us the challenges they face in global marketing. Over the years they have all helped to shape and influence our view of international marketing strategy.

The team at Cengage Learning have always encouraged us and we are grateful for their professionalism in turning the manuscript into its finished form.

Every effort has been made to obtain permission from the copyright holders for material reproduced in this book. Any rights not acknowledged here will be acknowledged in subsequent printings if due notice is given to the publisher.

WALK THROUGH TOUR

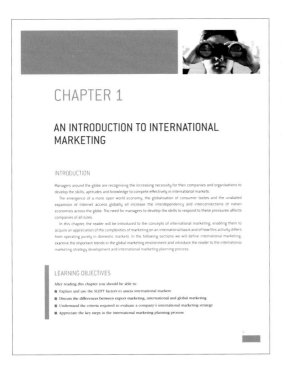

Learning objectives Listed at the start of each chapter, highlighting the key concepts covered in that chapter.

Dilemmas International marketing dilemmas and associated questions are located throughout the text and provide a forum for classroom and tutorial discussion.

Summary Featured at the end of every chapter, the summary captures the key issues in each chapter, helping you to assess your understanding and revise key content.

Keywords Highlighted throughout the book where they first appear, and alerting you to core concepts and techniques. Listed at the end of every chapter and emboldened within the text.

Illustrations Illustrative real-life examples are featured throughout the text, showing international companies' marketing strategies, accompanied by a question.

Case studies A longer and in-depth case study is provided at the end of every chapter. They draw upon real-world companies and help to demonstrate theory in practice. Each case is accompanied by questions to test the reader's understanding.

Discussion questions Short discussion questions appear at the end of every chapter. This feature encourages readers to review and/or critically assess their understanding of the main topics covered in the chapter.

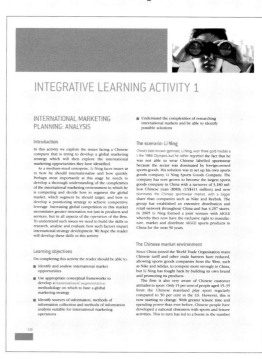

Integrative learning activities A series of in-depth learning activities is presented at the end of each part. Each one integrates the four chapters of the associated part.

ACCOMPANYING WEBSITE

Visit the International Marketing Strategy accompanying website at **www.cengage.co.uk/doole5** to find further teaching and learning material including:

FOR STUDENTS

- Internet projects
- Multiple choice questions for each chapter
- Case Studies and accompanying questions from the text
- Related weblinks

FOR LECTURERS

- Instructor's Manual – including teaching notes, how to use the text and answers to the questions within the text
- Downloadable PowerPoint slides
- Case Study teaching notes to accompany cases within the text
- Additional Case Study Material from the fourth edition with full commentaries to use as a teaching aid – ideal for classroom and tutorial discussion
- Cases and notes from the previous edition

PART 1 ANALYSIS

AIMS AND OBJECTIVES

Knowledge and an understanding of the markets in which companies operate are important for all business activities. In international markets, because of geographical distances and the complexities of operating in a number of disparate markets where risk and uncertainty are high, the need for knowledge and understanding becomes of paramount importance. It is this issue that is central to Part 1 of this book. The chapters in this section concentrate on helping the reader generate a greater understanding of the concepts of the international marketing process and the international environment within which companies operate. It aims to extend the range of understanding in order to enable the reader to deal with international marketing situations and to develop the skills to analyse and evaluate non-domestic markets, which in turn will enable their firms to compete effectively in world markets.

In Chapter 1 we focus on the international marketing environment. The book uses the SLEPT approach to understanding the complexities of the environmental influences on international marketing, thus enabling the reader to acquire an appreciation of the complexities of marketing on an international basis. We examine what is meant by international marketing and introduce the reader to the international market planning process. We also examine the reasons for success and failure in international marketing strategies and the characteristics of best international marketing practice.

In Chapter 2 the focus is on gaining an understanding of the international trading environment. We first examine, at a macro level, the development of international trading structures and the changes in trading patterns, as well as reviewing the major international bodies formed to foster world trade. The evolution of trading regions is analysed and the implications to international marketing companies assessed.

In Chapter 3 we take a fairly detailed look at the social and cultural influences in international marketing. The components of culture are

1 An introduction to international marketing

2 The international trading environment

3 Social and cultural considerations in international marketing

4 International marketing research and opportunity analysis

examined together with the impact of these components on international marketing. We then look at how cultural influences impact on buyer behaviour across the globe both in consumer markets and in business-to-business markets and discuss methods that can be used to analyse cultures both within and across countries.

In Chapter 4 the focus is on the identification and evaluation of marketing opportunities internationally. Segmentation of international markets is discussed, and how to prioritise international opportunities. The marketing research process and the role it plays in the development of international marketing strategies are also examined. The different stages in the marketing research process are discussed, with particular attention being paid to the problems in carrying out international marketing research in foreign markets and coordinating multi-country studies.

CHAPTER 1

AN INTRODUCTION TO INTERNATIONAL MARKETING

INTRODUCTION

Managers around the globe are recognising the increasing necessity for their companies and organisations to develop the skills, aptitudes and knowledge to compete effectively in international markets.

The emergence of a more open world economy, the globalisation of consumer tastes and the unabated expansion of Internet access globally all increase the interdependency and interconnections of nation economies across the globe. The need for managers to develop the skills to respond to these pressures affects companies of all sizes.

In this chapter, the reader will be introduced to the concepts of international marketing, enabling them to acquire an appreciation of the complexities of marketing on an international basis and of how this activity differs from operating purely in domestic markets. In the following sections we will define international marketing, examine the important trends in the global marketing environment and introduce the reader to the international marketing strategy development and international marketing planning process.

LEARNING OBJECTIVES

After reading this chapter you should be able to:

- Explain and use the SLEPT factors to assess international markets
- Discuss the differences between export marketing, international and global marketing
- Understand the criteria required to evaluate a company's international marketing strategy
- Appreciate the key steps in the international marketing planning process

THE STRATEGIC IMPORTANCE OF INTERNATIONAL MARKETING

Last year's international trade in merchandise exceeded US$10.5 trillion and world trade in services is estimated at around US$2.4 trillion. Whilst most of us cannot visualise such huge amounts, it does serve to give some indication of the scale of international trade today.

This global marketplace consists of a population of 6.6 billion people which is expected to reach 10 billion by 2050 according to the latest projections prepared by the United Nations.

Global wealth is increasing and this is reflected in higher demand. Increasing affluence and commercial dynamism has seen nations across Asia, Central and Eastern Europe emerge as high growth economies. Increasing affluence and demand simply means that consumers will actively seek choice, with the result that globally competition is intensifying as companies compete to win the battle for disposable income.

Population growth and increased affluence together have helped create a 'global youth culture' – teenagers now account for 30 per cent of the population globally. In many countries, more than half the population is pre-adult, creating one of the world's biggest single markets, the youth market. Everywhere adolescents project worldwide cultural icons, Nike, Coke, Gap and Sony Walkman, as well as Sega, Nintendo and the Sony Playstation. When 'virtual reality' is commonplace, the one-world youth culture market will exceed all others as a premier global market segment. Parochial, local and ethnic growth products may face difficult times.

Older consumers are also increasingly non-national in their identity, if not in their personal identity then from the perspective of the consumable fabric of their lives. They drive international cars, take foreign holidays, watch international programmes on television, use international hardware and software. On the supply side, multinational and global corporations are increasing in size and embracing more global power. The top 500 companies in the world now account for 70 per cent of world trade and 80 per cent of international investment. Total sales of multinationals are now in excess of world trade, which gives them a combined gross product of more than some national economies.

To strategically position themselves for global competitiveness, companies are consolidating through mergers, acquisitions and alliances to reach the scale considered necessary to compete in the global arena. At the same time, there is a trend towards global standardisation, as companies strive for world standards for efficiency and productivity. In Europe last year mergers and acquisitions were worth US$ 1.59 trillion, in the USA $1.54 trillion. The Indian company Tata took over Corus making them the world's largest steel producer, overtaking Mittal (Dutch) who in the same year took over Aecelor of Luxembourg. In Germany e.ON bid for Endesa of Spain. GSK have a number of global alliances in the pharmaceutical market, creating the world's largest research-based pharmaceutical company. Such trends can also be seen in the service sector. In the US, Morgan Stanley and Dean Witter merged to offer global investment as well as global private banking and credit card services. There has also been an increase in the number of joint ventures and international strategic alliances to compete in mature markets. Xerox entered into a joint venture with Fuji to consolidate their global position and the Siemens and Fujitsu joint venture is now the only computer hardware company in Europe following the global consolidation of that sector.

The global marketplace is no longer the summation of a large number of independent country markets but much more multilateral and interdependent, economically, culturally and technically. Information moves anywhere in the world at the speed of light, the ease of transmission being facilitated by the convergence of long distance telecoms, cuts in the cost of electronic processing and the exponential growth in Internet access.

The combination of all these forces has meant that all companies need to develop a marketing orientation which is international in nature and that companies need managers who have the skills to analyse, plan and implement strategies across the globe. It is for these reasons that international marketing has become such a critical area of study for managers and an important component of the marketing syllabus of business faculties in universities.

So perhaps now we should turn our attention to examining exactly what we mean by international marketing.

What is international marketing?

Many readers of this textbook will have already followed a programme of study in marketing but, before explaining what we mean by international marketing, let us reflect for a few moments on our understanding of what is meant by marketing itself. The Chartered Institute of Marketing defines marketing as the 'Management process responsible for identifying, anticipating and satisfying customer requirements profitably'. Thus marketing involves:

- focusing on the needs and wants of customers
- identifying the best method of satisfying those needs and wants
- orienting the company towards the process of providing that satisfaction
- meeting organisational objectives.

In this way, it is argued, the company or organisation best prepares itself to achieve competitive advantage in the marketplace. It then needs to work to maintain this advantage by manipulating the controllable functions of marketing within the largely uncontrollable marketing environment made up of SLEPT factors: i.e. Social, Legal, Economic, Political and Technological.

How does the process of international marketing differ? Within the international marketing process the key elements of this framework still apply. The conceptual framework is not going to change to any marked degree when a company moves from a domestic to an international market; however, there are two main differences. First, there are different levels at which international marketing can be approached and, second, the uncontrollable elements of the marketing environment are more complex and multidimensional given the multiplicity of markets that constitute the global marketplace. This means managers have to acquire new skills and abilities to add to the tools and techniques they have developed in marketing to domestic markets.

International marketing defined

At its simplest level, international marketing involves the firm in making one or more marketing mix decisions across national boundaries. At its most complex, it involves the firm in establishing manufacturing/processing facilities around the world and coordinating marketing strategies across the globe. At one extreme there are firms that opt for 'international marketing' simply by signing a distribution agreement with a foreign agent who then takes on the responsibility for pricing, promotion, distribution and market development. At the other extreme, there are huge global companies such as Ford with an integrated network of manufacturing plants worldwide and who operate in some 150 country markets. Thus, at its most complex, international marketing becomes a process of managing on a global scale. These different levels of marketing can be expressed in the following terms:

- Domestic marketing, which involves the company manipulating a series of controllable variables such as price, advertising, distribution and the product/service attributes in a largely uncontrollable external environment that is made up of different economic structures, competitors, cultural values and legal infrastructure within specific political or geographic country boundaries.

- International marketing, which involves operating across a number of foreign country markets in which not only do the uncontrollable variables differ significantly between one market and another, but the controllable factors in the form of cost and price structures, opportunities for advertising and distributive infrastructure are also likely to differ significantly. It is these sorts of differences that lead to the complexities of international marketing.

- Global marketing management, which is a larger and more complex international operation. Here a company coordinates, integrates and controls a whole series of marketing programmes into a substantial global effort. Here the primary objective of the company is to achieve a degree of synergy in the overall operation so that by taking advantage of different exchange rates, tax rates, labour rates, skill levels and market opportunities, the organisation as a whole will be greater than the sum of its parts.

This type of strategy calls for managers who are capable of operating as international marketing managers in the truest sense, a task which is far broader and more complex than that of operating either in a specific foreign country or in the domestic market. In discussing this, Sarathy *et al.* (2006) comment that 'the international marketing manager has a dual responsibility; foreign marketing (marketing within foreign countries) and global marketing (co-ordinating marketing in multiple markets in the face of global competition)'.

Thus, how international marketing is defined and interpreted depends on the level of involvement of the company in the international marketplace. International marketing could therefore be:

- Export marketing, in which case the firm markets its goods and/or services across national/political boundaries.

- International marketing, where the marketing activities of an organisation include activities, interests or operations in more than one country and where there is some kind of influence or control of marketing activities from outside the country in which the goods or services will actually be sold. Sometimes markets are typically perceived to be independent and a profit centre in their own right, in which case the term multinational or multidomestic marketing is often used.

- Global marketing, in which the whole organisation focuses on the selection and exploitation of global marketing opportunities and marshals resources around the globe with the objective of achieving a global competitive advantage.

The first of these definitions describes relatively straightforward exporting activities, numerous examples of which exist. However, the subsequent definitions are more complex and more formal and indicate not only a revised attitude to marketing but also a very different underlying philosophy. Here the world is seen as a market segmented by social, legal, economic, political and technological (SLEPT) groupings.

In this textbook we will incorporate the international marketing issues faced by firms, be they involved in export, international or global marketing.

For all these levels the key to successful international marketing is being able to identify and understand the complexities of each of these SLEPT dimensions of the international environment and how they impact on a firm's marketing strategies across their international markets. As in domestic marketing, the successful marketing company will be the one that is best able to manipulate the controllable tools of the marketing mix within the uncontrollable environment. It follows that the key problem faced by the international marketing manager is that of coming to terms with the details and complexities of the international environment. It is these complexities that we will examine in the following sections.

THE INTERNATIONAL MARKETING ENVIRONMENT

The key difference between domestic marketing and marketing on an international scale is the multidimensionality and complexity of the many foreign country markets a company may operate in. An international manager needs a knowledge and awareness of these complexities and the implications they have for international marketing management.

There are many environmental analysis models which the reader may have come across. For the purposes of this textbook, we will use the SLEPT approach and examine the various aspects and trends in the international marketing environment through the social/cultural, legal, economic, political and technological dimensions, as depicted in Figure 1.1.

Social/cultural environment

The social and cultural influences on international marketing are immense. Differences in social conditions, religion and material culture all affect consumers' perceptions and patterns of buying behaviour. It is this area that determines the extent to which consumers across the globe are either similar or different and so determines the potential for global branding and standardisation.

A failure to understand the social/cultural dimensions of a market are complex to manage, as McDonald's found in India. It had to deal with a market that is 40 per cent vegetarian, had an aversion to either beef or pork among meat-eaters

FIGURE 1.1

The environmental influences on international marketing

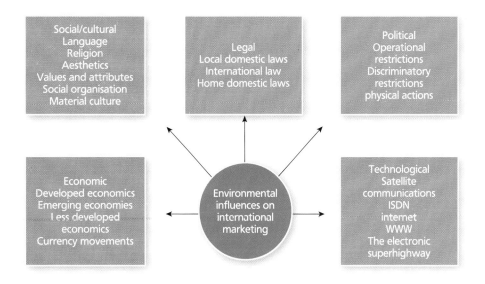

and a hostility to frozen meat and fish, but with the general Indian fondness for spice with everything. To satisfy such tastes, McDonald's discovered it needed to do more than provide the right burgers. Customers buying vegetarian burgers wanted to be sure that these were cooked in a separate area in the kitchen using separate utensils and sauces like McMasala and McImli were developed to satisfy the Indian taste for spice. Interestingly however, these are now innovations they have introduced into other markets.

Cultural factors

Cultural differences and especially language differences have a significant impact on the way a product may be used in a market, its brand name and the advertising campaign.

Initially, Coca-Cola had enormous problems in China as Coca-Cola sounded like 'Kooke Koula' which translates into 'A thirsty mouthful of candle wax'. They managed to find a new pronunciation 'Kee Kou Keele' which means 'joyful tastes and happiness'.

Other companies who have experienced problems are General Motors whose brand name 'Nova' was unsuccessful in Spain ('no va' in Spanish means 'no go'). Pepsi Cola had to change its campaign 'Come Alive With Pepsi' in Germany as, literally translated, it means 'Come Alive Out of the Grave'. In Japan McDonald's character Ronald McDonald failed because his white face was seen as a death mask. When Apple launched the iMac in France they discovered the brand name mimicked the name of a well established brand of baby laxative – hardly the image they were trying to project.

Operating effectively in different countries requires recognition that there may be considerable differences in the different regions. Consider northern Europe versus Latin Europe, the northwest of the USA versus the south or Bejing and Taipei. At the stage of early internationalisation it is not unusual for Western firms to experience what appear to be cultural gaps with their counterparts in Latin America and Asian countries as well as in different regions of those countries. A campaign by Camay soap which showed a husband washing his wife's back in the bath was a huge success in France but failed in Japan, not because it caused offence, but because Japanese women viewed the prospect of a husband sharing such a time as a huge invasion of privacy.

On the other hand, some commentators argue there are visible signs that social and cultural differences are becoming less of a barrier. The dominance of a number of world brands such as Microsoft, Intel, Coca-Cola, McDonald's, Nike etc., all competing in global markets that transcend national and political boundaries, are testimony to the convergence of consumer needs across the globe. However, it is important not to confuse globalisation of brands with the homogenisation of cultures. There are a large number of global brands but even these have to manage cultural differences between and within national country boundaries.

There are also a number of cultural paradoxes which exist. For example, in Asia, the Middle East, Africa and Latin America there is evidence both for the westernisation of tastes and the assertion of ethnic, religious and cultural differences. There are more than 600 000 Avon ladies now in China and a growing number of them in Eastern Europe, Brazil and the Amazon (see Illustration 1.1).

In northern Kenya you may find a Sambhuru warrior who owns a cellular telephone. Thus, whilst there is a vast and, sometimes, turbulent mosaic of cultural differences, there are commentators who believe there is evidence that a global village is potentially taking shape which, as Kenichi Ohmae (2005) says, 'will be a nationless state marked by the convergence of customer needs that transcends political and cultural boundaries'.

The social/cultural environment is an important area for international marketing managers and we will return to this subject in a number of chapters where we examine the various aspects of its strategic implications. Chapter 3 is devoted to a full examination of the social and cultural influences in international marketing. In Chapter 5 we will examine the forces driving the global village and its strategic implication to companies across the world.

Social factors

Growth and movement in populations around the world are important factors heralding social changes. Eighty per cent of the world's population live in developing countries; by 2025 this is likely to reach 85 per cent. Two out of every five people live in China and India. However, whilst world population is growing dramatically, the growth patterns are not consistent around the world.

Over the next half century, Africa's population will almost treble. China's population will rise much more slowly from 1.2 billion to 1.5 billion. With a population of 1.53 billion people, India will have more inhabitants than China in 50 years' time. Europe is the only region where the population is expected to decline; any increase in population in high income countries is entirely due to migration.

There are also visible moves in the population within many countries, leading to the formation of huge urban areas where consumers have a growing similarity of needs across the globe. By 2010, 50 per cent of the world's population will live in urban areas: the world is moving into gigantic conurbations. The population of greater Tokyo is soon to be close to 30 million and Mexico City 20 million. Cities such as Lagos, Buenos Aires and Djakarta will soon outstrip cities such as Paris, London and Rome. In the year 2015, no European city will be in the top

ILLUSTRATION 1.1

The beautification of the ageing baby boomers

Analysts at Goldman Sachs estimate that the global beauty industry is worth about 100 billion US dollars a year and is growing at up to 7 per cent a year, more than twice the rate of the developed world's GDP. This growth is being driven by richer, ageing baby-boomers and increased discretionary income in the West, and by the growing middle classes in developing

countries. China, Russia and South Korea and Brazil are turning into huge markets. In India, sales of anti-ageing creams are growing by 40 per cent a year. Avon is expanding rapidly in Eastern Europe and Russia as well as in South America. Brazil now has more than 900 000 Avon ladies.

Global competition in the market is becoming increasingly intense. Unilever and Procter and Gamble, facing maturity in many of their traditional businesses, are devoting more resources to developing global beauty brands. Luxury product manufacturers such as Dior, Chanel and Yves St Laurent are moving into mainstream beauty products and many of the global giants are growing by buying up smaller brands. Japan's Kao have gone into the hair dye market by buying John Frieda while Estée Lauder has acquired Stila, MAC and Bobbi Brown, all of which are innovative and growing make-up brands.

The traditional global beauty brands established by such companies as L'Oréal, Elizabeth Arden and Helena Rubenstein are now having to fight hard in a global market where traditionally they have earned huge margins and enjoyed continuous growth for many years.

QUESTION *Outline the reasons for the changing structure of the global beauty market.*

30 and 17 of the world's mega cities of 10 million plus will be in emerging markets. This has powerful implications for international marketing. These cities will be markets in themselves. Urban dwellers require similar products (packaged conveniently and easy to carry). Similarly, they demand services, telephones and transportation of all kinds and modern visual communications. It also means, for the incoming company, that customers are accessible. They are identifiable and firms can communicate with them efficiently via supermarkets, advertising and other marketing communication tools. Table 1.1 shows the ten mega cities in the world forecast for 2015.

Legal environment

Legal systems vary both in content and interpretation. A company is not just bound by the laws of its home country but also by those of its host country and by the growing body of international law. Firms operating in the European Union are facing ever-increasing directives which affect their markets across Europe. This can affect many aspects of a marketing strategy – for instance advertising – in the form of media restrictions and the acceptability of particular creative appeals (see Illustration 1.2). Product acceptability in a country can be affected by minor regulations on such things as packaging and by more major changes in legislation. In the USA, for instance, the MG sports car was withdrawn when the increasing difficulty of complying with safety legislation changes made exporting to that market unprofitable. Kraft Foods sell a product called Lifesavers, which are very similar to the Nestlé Polo brand, in many countries. Using EU law, Nestlé attempted to stop the sale of Lifesavers in the EU purely to protect their market share.

It is important, therefore, for the firm to know the legal environment in each of its markets. These laws constitute the 'rules of the game' for business activity. The legal environment in international marketing is more complicated than in

TABLE 1.1 The world's ten mega cities in 2015

City	Country	Population (millions)
Tokyo	Japan	26.4
Mumbai	India	26.1
Lagos	Nigeria	23.2
Dhaka	Bangladesh	21.1
Sao Paulo	Brazil	20.4
Karachi	Pakistan	19.2
Mexico City	Mexico	19.2
New York	USA	17.4
Jakarta	Indonesia	17.3
Calcutta	India	17.3

SOURCE: UNITED NATIONS

domestic markets since it has three dimensions: (1) local domestic law; (2) international law; (3) domestic laws in the firm's home base.

■ *Local domestic laws.* These are all different! The only way to find a route through the legal maze in overseas markets is to use experts on the separate legal systems and laws pertaining in each market targeted.

■ *International law.* There are a number of international laws that can affect the organisation's activity. Some are international laws covering piracy and hijacking, others are more international conventions and agreements and cover items such as the International Monetary Fund (IMF) and World Trade Organisation (WTO) treaties, patents and trademarks legislation and harmonisation of legal systems within regional economic groupings, e.g. the European Union.

■ *Domestic laws in the home country.* The organisation's domestic (home market) legal system is important for two reasons. First, there are often export controls which limit the free export of certain goods and services to particular marketplaces, and second, there is the duty of the organisation to act and abide by its national laws in all its activities, whether domestic or international.

It will be readily understandable how domestic, international and local legal systems can have a major impact upon the organisation's ability to market into

ILLUSTRATION 1.2

SOURCE: ADAPTED FROM *THE ECONOMIST*, 21 MAY 2003 AND 'ASDA SLAMS "HAM-FISTED" PARMA RULING' *BBC NEWS* 20 MAY, 2003

PHOTO CREDIT: CUBOIMAGES SRL/ALAMY

When is a Parma ham not a Parma ham?

The European Court of Justice has decided that it is illegal for the world-famous Parma ham to be sliced and packaged outside the Italian region that gives Parma ham its name. The ruling was a victory for the 200 or so producers of Parma ham who had launched their legal action against Asda, a UK food retailer. The case hinged on the court's interpretation of geographical indications – EU-protected trademarks that recognise the importance of products closely associated with a particular place, whether it be Parma ham, French champagne, Spanish sherry or Stilton cheese from Britain. The Parma producers argued that slicing the ham was an important process that had to be done locally. Asda argued they should be free to slice and pack the ham where they chose in order to cut costs and reduce the price to consumers. The court showed it was more concerned with the protection of the ham producers' rights than market efficiency. However strangely Asda can still use the Parma name when the meat is sliced on a delicatessen counter in front of shoppers?

The question is, how will the world view the decision? Some commentators use such examples to question the commitment of the European Union to freeing trade and becoming more competitive.

QUESTION *Do you think the court decision protects local market diversity across European markets, or does it act as a restrictive trade practice?*

particular overseas countries. Laws will affect the marketing mix in terms of products, price, distribution and promotional activities quite dramatically. For many firms, the legal challenges they face in international markets are almost a double-edged sword. Often firms operating internationally face ethical challenges in deciding how to deal with differing cultural perceptions of legal practices.

In many mature markets they face quite specific and, sometimes, burdensome regulations. In Germany, for instance, environmental laws mean a firm is responsible for the retrieval and disposal of the packaging waste it creates and must produce packaging which is recyclable, whereas in many emerging markets there may be limited patent and trademark protection, still evolving judicial systems, non-tariff barriers and an instability through an ever-evolving reform programme.

China earned notoriety in the past for allowing infringements of copyright and blatant piracy. However, this is now changing. Some governments are reluctant to develop and enforce laws protecting intellectual property partly because they believe such actions favour large, rich, multinationals. Anheuser Busch (USA) and Budvar (Czech Republic) have been in constant litigation over the right to use the name Budweiser in the European Union and both companies have recently been legally deemed the right to use it.

Piracy in markets with limited trademark and patent protection is another challenge. Bootlegged software constitutes 87 per cent of all personal computer software in use in India, 92 per cent in Thailand and 98 per cent in China, resulting in a loss of US$8 billion for software makers each year.

India is regarded by many firms as an attractive emerging market beset with many legal difficulties, bureaucratic delay and lots of red tape. For example, shoes cannot be imported in pairs but have to be imported one at a time – which causes huge problems for shoe manufacturers who need to import shoes as production samples. The way many of them overcome the problem is by importing the left shoe via Madras and the right shoe via Mumbai. Companies such as Mercedes Benz, Coca-Cola and Kellogg have found the vast potential of India's market somewhat hard to break into. Its demanding consumers can be difficult to read and local rivals can be surprisingly tough. Political squabbles, bureaucratic delays and infrastructure headaches are also major obstacles.

Economic environment

It is important that the international marketer has an understanding of economic developments and how they impinge on the marketing strategy. This understanding is important at a world level in terms of the world trading infrastructure such as world institutions and trade agreements developed to foster international trade, at a regional level in terms of regional trade integration and at a country/ market level. Firms need to be aware of the economic policies of countries and the direction in which a particular market is developing economically in order to make an assessment as to whether they can profitably satisfy market demand and compete with firms already in the market.

Amongst the 194 countries in the world, there are varying economic conditions, levels of economic development and Gross national income (GNI) per capita. Gross national income in the world is US$62 trillion (purchasing power parity [ppp]); however, it is not shared equitably across the world. The United Nations classes 75 per cent of the world's population as poor, that is, they have a per capita income of less than US$3470, and only 11 per cent of the population as rich, meaning they have a per capita income of more than US$8000. Perhaps more startling is the UN claim that the richest 50 million people in the world share the same amount of wealth as the poorest 3000 million. Such disparities of incomes set particular challenges for companies operating in international markets in terms of seeking possible market opportunities, assessing the viability of potential markets as well as identifying sources of finance in markets where opportunities are identified but where there is not capacity to pay for goods.

Another key challenge facing companies is the question as to how they can develop an integrated strategy across a number of international markets when there are divergent levels of economic development. Such disparities often make it difficult to have a cohesive strategy, especially in pricing.

The Economist 'Big Mac' Index (Figure 1.2) is a useful tool which illustrates the difficulties global companies have in trying to achieve a consistent pricing strategy across the world. It provides a rough measure of the purchasing power of a currency. UBS, a bank in the USA, uses the price of the Big Mac burger to measure the purchasing power of local wages around the world. It divides the price of a Big Mac by the average net hourly wage in cities around the world. A worker from Jakarta must work for almost $1\frac{1}{2}$ hours to buy a Big Mac, but a Moscow wage buys the burger in 25 minutes and a Tokyo salary buys one in just ten. This causes problems for McDonald's in trying to pursue a standard product image across markets. Priced in US dollars, a Big Mac in Switzerland would cost US$5.21, whereas in China it would be US$1.31.

In order to examine these challenges further we divided the economies into developed economies and less developed economies.

The developed economies

The developed economies of the North American Free Trade Area (NAFTA), European Union (EU) and Japan account for 80 per cent of world trade. For many firms this constitutes much of what is termed the global market. Even though many companies call themselves global, most of their revenues and profits will be earned from these markets. In the European Union nearly 70 per cent of the international goods traded are traded within the European Union; in NAFTA, 50 per cent of goods exported are to other members of NAFTA. This leads some commentators to argue that most competition, even in today's global market-place, is more active at a regional level than a global level. It is from these developed economies that the global consumer with similar lifestyles, needs and desires emanates. However, emerging markets are now becoming more economically powerful and moving up the ranks, especially such countries as Brazil, Russia, India and China.

FIGURE 1.2
The Big Mac index

SOURCE: ©THE ECONOMIST NEWSPAPER LIMITED, LONDON (AUGUST 31ST 2006)

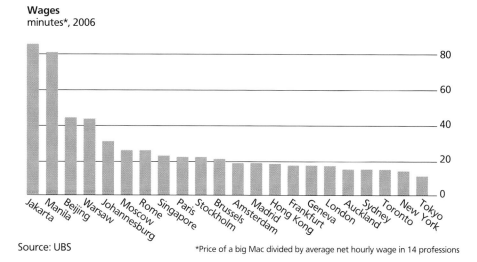

Wages
minutes*, 2006

Source: UBS   *Price of a big Mac divided by average net hourly wage in 14 professions

The emerging economies

In countries such as Brazil, Russia, India and China, (the BRIC economies) there is a huge and growing demand for everything from automobiles to cellular phones and all are viewed as key growth markets where there is an evolving pattern of government-directed economic reforms, lowering of restrictions on foreign investment and increasing privatisation of state-owned monopolies. All these emerging economies herald significant opportunities for the international marketing firm.

Such markets often have what is termed as a 'dual economy'. Usually there tends to be a wealthy urban professional class alongside a poorer rural population. Income distribution tends to be much more skewed between the 'haves' and the 'have nots' than in developed countries. From negligible numbers a few years ago, China now has a middle class of 100 million which is forecast to grow to 500 million in the next century. Brazil and Indonesia have middle classes of 25 million each.

Less developed countries

This group includes underdeveloped countries and less developing countries. The main features are a low GDP per capita, a limited amount of manufacturing activity and a very poor and fragmented infrastructure. Typical infrastructure weaknesses are in transport, communications, education and healthcare. In addition, the public sector is often slow-moving and bureaucratic.

It is common to find that less developed countries (LDCs) are heavily reliant on one product and often on one trading partner. In many LDCs this product is the main export earner. In Angola, for instance, the sole export is oil and in the Sudan oil accounts for 99 per cent of their exports. In addition, three-quarters of LDCs depend on their main trading partner for more than one-quarter of their export revenue. The risks posed to the LDC by changing patterns of supply and demand are great. Falling commodity prices can result in large decreases in earnings for the whole country. The resultant economic and political adjustments may affect exporters to that country through possible changes in tariff and non-tariff barriers, through changes in the level of company taxation and through restrictions on the convertibility of currency and the repatriation of profits. In addition, substantial decreases in market sizes within the country are probable.

A wide range of economic circumstances influences the development of the less developed countries in the world. Some countries are small with few natural resources and for these countries it is difficult to start the process of substantial economic growth. Poor health and education standards need money on a large scale, yet the pay-off in terms of a healthier, better-educated population takes time to achieve. At the same time, there are demands for public expenditure on transport systems, communication systems and water control systems. Without

---

DILEMMA 1.1

How do you sell to subsistence farmers in Africa ?

KickStart International is a non-profit organisation that sells irrigation systems to subsistence farmers in Africa. The customers are hard to reach. They live hours from major cities and many are illiterate. Even though they are a non-profit organization, KickStart needs to build brand loyalty which is difficult in a market where there is a lack of trust in a foreign US company .The other dilemma is given the levels of illiteracy, how do they educate the farmers to use the equipment and how do KickStart get their message across given the small budget they have for such activities?

QUESTION *How should KickStart approach this market?*

real prospects for rapid economic development, private sources of capital are reluctant to invest in such countries. This is particularly the case for long-term infrastructure projects and, as a result, important capital spending projects rely heavily on world aid programmes. Marketing to such countries can be problematic, as in the case of KickStart in Dilemma 1.1.

Currency risks

Whilst we have examined economic factors within markets, we also need to bear in mind that in international marketing transactions invariably take place between countries, so exchange rates and currency movements are an important aspect of the international economic environment. On top of all the normal vagaries of markets, customer demands, competitive actions and economic infrastructures, foreign exchange parities are likely to change on a regular if unpredictable basis. World currency movements, stimulated by worldwide trading and foreign exchange dealing, are an additional complication in the international environment. Companies that guess wrongly as to which way a currency will move can see their international business deals rendered unprofitable overnight. Businesses that need to swap currencies to pay for imported goods, or because they have received foreign currency for products they have exported, can find themselves squeezed to the point where they watch their profits disappear.

In Europe, the formation of the European Monetary Union (EMU) and the establishment of the Single European Payments Area (SEPA) has led to greater stability for firms operating in the market. The formation of the European Monetary Union and the introduction of the single currency across Europe has had important implications for company strategies which we will discuss in Chapter 2, when we examine regional trading agreements, and in Chapter 11, when we look at pricing issues in international marketing.

Political environment

The political environment of international marketing includes any national or international political factor that can affect the organisation's operations or its decision making. Politics has come to be recognised as the major factor in many international business decisions, especially in terms of whether to invest and how to develop markets.

Politics is intrinsically linked to a government's attitude to business and the freedom within which it allows firms to operate. Unstable political regimes expose foreign businesses to a variety of risks that they would generally not face in the home market. This often means that the political arena is the most volatile area of international marketing. The tendencies of governments to change regulations can have a profound effect on international strategy, providing both opportunities and threats. The invasions of Afghanistan and Iraq have brought market development opportunities for some but market devastation for others and higher political risk in neighbouring markets for all. The instability in the Middle East and the continued threat of global terrorism have served to heighten firms' awareness of the importance of monitoring political risk factors in the international markets in which they operate. Lesser developed countries and emerging markets pose particularly high political risks, even when they are following reforms to solve the political problems they have. The stringency of such reforms can itself lead to civil disorder and rising opposition to governments, as has been seen recently in Indonesia, Venezuela, Brazil and Argentina.

Political risk is defined as a risk due to a sudden or gradual change in a local political environment that is disadvantageous or counter productive to foreign firms and markets.

The types of action that governments may take which constitute potential political risks to firms fall into three main areas:

- *Operational restrictions*. These could be exchange controls, employment policies, insistence on locally shared ownership and particular product requirements.

- *Discriminatory restrictions*. These tend to be imposed on purely foreign firms and, sometimes, only firms from a particular country. The USA has imposed import quotas on Japan in protest at non-tariff barriers which they view as being imposed unfairly on US exporters. They have also imposed bans on imports from Libya and Iran in the past. Such barriers tend to be such things as special taxes and tariffs, compulsory subcontracting, or loss of financial freedom.

- *Physical actions*. These actions are direct government interventions such as confiscation without any payment of indemnity, a forced takeover by the government, expropriation, nationalisation or even damage to property or personnel through riots and war. In 2001 the Nigerian government claimed ownership of Shell's equipment and machinery without any prior warning.

Investment restrictions are a common way governments interfere politically in international markets by restricting levels of investment, location of facilities, choice of local partners and ownership percentage. When Microsoft opened its Beijing office, it planned to use its Taiwan operations to supply a Mandarin language version of Windows. The government not only wanted such an operating system to be designed in China but also insisted on defining the coding standards for Chinese characters' fonts, something Microsoft had done independently everywhere else in the world. In a flurry of meetings with officials, Bill Gates argued that the marketplace, not the government, should set standards. But the Chinese electronics industry threatened to ban Windows and president Jiang Zemin personally admonished Gates to spend more time in China and 'learn something from 5000 years of Chinese history'. Gates sacked the original management team and promised to cooperate with Beijing.

The World Trade Organisation has led negotiations on a series of worldwide agreements to expand quotas, reduce tariffs and introduce a number of innovative measures to encourage trade amongst countries. Together with the formation of regional trading agreements in the European Union, North and South America and Asia, these reforms constitute a move to a more politically stable international trading environment. An understanding of these issues is critical to the international marketing manager, which is why in Chapter 2 we examine in some detail the patterns of world trade, the regional trading agreements and the development of world trading institutions intended to foster international trade. In Chapter 4 we will examine in some detail the procedures, tools and techniques which can help the analysis and evaluation of opportunities across such markets.

The political and economic environments are greatly intertwined and, sometimes, difficult to categorise. It is important, however, that a firm operating in international markets assesses the countries in which it operates to gauge the economic and political risk and to ensure they understand the peculiarities and characteristics of the market they wish to develop. Illustration 1.3 examines Cadbury's, who caused huge offence by their misreading of political sentiments in India.

Technological environment

Technology is a major driving force both in international marketing and in the move towards a more global marketplace. The impact of technological advances can be seen in all aspects of the marketing process. The ability to gather data on markets, management control capabilities and the practicalities of carrying out the business function internationally have been revolutionised in recent years with the advances in electronic communications.

Satellite communications, the Internet and the World Wide Web, client–server technologies, ISDN and cable as well as email, faxes and advanced telephone networks have all led to dramatic shrinkages in worldwide communications.

Shrinking communications means, increasingly, that in the international marketplace information is power. At the touch of a button we can access information on the key factors that determine our business. News is a 24 hours a day service. Manufacturers wanting to know the price of coffee beans or the relevant position of competitors in terms of their share price or new product activity have it at their immediate disposal.

As wireless technology renders land cables and telephone lines redundant, developing countries are abandoning plans to invest in land-based communication. They are bypassing terrestrial communication systems, enabling them to catch up

ILLUSTRATION 1.3

SOURCE: ADAPTED FROM *THE ECONOMIST*, 22 AUGUST 2002 AND *BBC NEWS ONLINE* 7 OCTOBER 2002

PHOTO CREDIT: BARRY LEWIS/ALAMY

Cadbury's in political faux pas

The Indian division of Cadbury-Schweppes suffered embarrassment around the world and incensed large swathes of Hindu society by running a newspaper advertisement comparing its Temptations chocolate to the war-torn region of Kashmir. The ad carried the tagline:

> 'I'm good. I'm tempting. I'm too good to share. What am I? Cadbury's Temptations or Kashmir?'.

To make sure nobody missed the point, the ad's creators laid the 'too good to share' catch-line over a map of Kashmir.

The ad caused a national outcry. Arguments over Kashmir have taken India and Pakistan to the brink of nuclear war: using them to sell chocolate was perhaps not the wisest thing to do. Indian politicians were shocked at the very mention of sharing the territory and threatened nationwide protests. To add insult to injury the advertisement was timed to appear on 15 August, India's Independence Day. Cadbury's British roots may have made the ad even harder to swallow. It was British colonial rulers who, at partition in 1947, drew the boundary line between India and Pakistan that the two nations have battled over ever since.

Though Cadbury India has apologised, it does show that in global markets, multi-nationals can't hide their blunders for long.

QUESTION *What are the dangers of a company making such blunders when it operates globally?*

with and, in some cases, overtake developed countries in the marketplace. In emerging economies consumers are jumping from no telephone to the latest in global communications technology. Wireless application protocol (WAP) technology allows online services to be available to mobile phone users on the move, wherever they happen to be in the world. The use of Global System for Mobile Communications (GSM) technology enables mobile phone operators to determine the location of a customer globally to send them relevant and timely advertising messages.

British Airways operates its worldwide online operations from Mumbai: everything from ticketing to making an 'exceptional request' facility, such as wheelchair assistance needed for a passenger can be managed from the centre in Mumbai. Increasingly companies are using India as a centre for their global online customer service operations. The ease of hiring computer-literate graduates by the hundred, who are intelligent, capable, keen and inexpensive to hire, as is local property to rent, makes India an attractive location (see Illustration 1.4).

THE INTERNET AND THE WORLD WIDE WEB (WWW)

The Internet and the access gained to the World Wide Web has revolutionised international marketing practices. Airlines such as EasyJet and RyanAir have helped completely change the way we book our airline reservations. EToys, a virtual company based in the US, has no retail outlets but a higher market capitalisation than Toys'R'Us. Firms ranging from a few employees to large multinationals have realised the potential of marketing globally online and so have developed the facility to buy and sell their products and services online to the world.

ILLUSTRATION 1.4

Indian brands emerge from the shadows

FLEXCUBE is the world's best-selling banking-software product. For many years Indian technicians have been beavering away writing code to be sold as an American or European brand. Now India's own brands are starting to fight in the global markets in their own right. Indian marketing professionals have been arguing for some time that IT exports would be more secure if they relied less on outsourcing and were 'products', where the Indian

PHOTO CREDIT: FREDRIK RENANDER/ALAMY

seller owns the intellectual property, not just the brainpower for hire. Mixing his metaphors wildly, Rajesh Hukku, the founder and chairman of i-flex, argues that Indian firms otherwise risk being doomed forever to providing 'the cheap labour at the bottom of the food chain'.

At a time when there has been a protectionist backlash in America and Europe against the outsourcing of IT jobs to India and fears of decline in the industry as margins and costs are being further reduced, Indian software firms are emerging from the shadows and fighting in the global market under their own brand names.

Last year, Nasscom, the Indian industry's lobby group, estimated that India captured just 0.2 per cent of a global market of US$180 billion for software products. It expects that to increase, but recognises the obstacles. The product business depends on heavy investment in sales, marketing and branding and the ability to market globally against fierce and rich competitors.

A recent success has been the tie up with Financial Services Inc. (FSI) in the USA to launch FLEXICUBE as a hosted offering to community banks in the US. FLEXCUBE will help community banks in the USA to compete with large banks and financial institutions on an equal footing.

QUESTION *How should new brands in developing countries compete against established US global brands?*

SOURCE: ADAPTED FROM *THE ECONOMIST*, 8 MAY 2003 AND HTTP://WWW.THEHINDUBUSINESSLINE.COM I-FLEX TO LAUNCH CORE BANKING SOLUTION 15 NOVEMBER 2006

An estimated 1.2 billion people – some 17 per cent of the global population – now have access to the Internet. However, for many this will be through public-based Internet services in cafes etc. The United Nations estimate that global e-business is now worth more than US$10 trillion, most of which is business-to-business (B2B), not business-to-consumer (B2C) purchases.

The Internet has meant huge opportunities for small and medium-sized enterprises (SMEs) and rapid internationalisation for many. It has enabled them to substantially reduce the costs of reaching international customers, reduce global advertising costs and made it much easier for small niche products to find a critical mass of customers. Because of the low entry costs of the Internet it has permitted firms with low capital resources to become global marketers, in some cases overnight. There are, therefore, quite significant implications for SMEs which will be examined further in Chapter 5, where we discuss in some detail the issues in international marketing pertinent to SMEs.

For all companies, the implications of being able to market goods and services online have been far reaching. The Internet has led to an explosion of information to consumers, giving them the potential to source products from the cheapest supplier in the world. This has led to the increasing standardisation of prices across borders or, at least, to the narrowing of price differentials as consumers become more aware of prices in different countries and buy a whole range of products via the net. In B2C marketing this has been most dramatically seen in the purchase of such things as flights, holidays, CDs and books. The Internet, by connecting end-users and producers directly, has reduced the importance of traditional intermediaries in international marketing (i.e. agents and distributors) as more companies have built the online capability to deal direct with their customers, particularly in B2B marketing. To survive, such intermediaries have begun offering a whole range of new services, the value added element of their offering no longer being principally in the physical distribution of goods but rather in the collection, collation, interpretation and dissemination of vast amounts of information. The critical resource possessed by this new breed of 'cybermediary' is information rather than inventory. The Internet has also become a powerful tool for supporting networks both internal and external to the firm. Many global firms have developed supplier intranets through which they source products and services from preferred suppliers who have met the criteria to gain access to their supplier intranets. It has become the efficient new medium for conducting worldwide market research and gaining feedback from customers.

Thus the Internet produces a fundamentally different environment for international marketing and requires a radically different strategic approach affecting all aspects of the marketing process. Not all forays into Internet marketing have been successful. Many early dotcom high growth companies became 'dot.bombs' when they failed to sustain their early promise. Levi Strauss stopped its Internet selling operation after finding the cost of servicing returned goods was greater than the revenue generated from new sales.

The dual technological/cultural paradox

On one hand commentators view technological advancement and shrinking communications as the most important driving force in the building of the global village where there are global consumers who have similar needs. On the other hand, to access this global village a person invariably needs a command of the English language and access to a whole range of equipment. In many markets we stumble against the paradox that whilst in some countries there is a market of well-educated and computer-literate people, in other countries the global electronic highway completely bypasses them.

Despite all that has been said in previous sections, many developing and emerging markets are characterised by poor, inadequate or deteriorating infrastructures. It is estimated that only 10 per cent of the world's population has direct access to a PC and only 7 per cent have direct access to the Internet. Essential services required for commercial activity, ranging from electric power to water supplies, from highways to air transportation and from phone lines to banking services are often in short supply or unreliable. There are also major disparities in the cost of accessing the Internet. In the USA, accessing the Internet for 20 hours per month would cost 1 per cent of a person's average income; in Mexico it would cost 15 per cent of a person's average income. However, in Bangladesh the same amount of access is equivalent to 278 per cent of the average income and in Madagascar 614 per cent, hardly making access to the Internet feasible for the average person, even if it is technically available.

The huge population shifts discussed earlier have also aggravated the technical infrastructure problems in many of the major cities in emerging markets. This often results in widespread production and distribution bottlenecks, which in turn raises costs. 'Brown outs', for instance, are not uncommon in the Philippines, even in the capital city Manila, where companies and offices regularly lose electric power and either shut down in those periods or revert to generators. Fragmented and circuitous channels of distribution are a result of lack of adequate infrastructure. This makes market entry more complicated and the efficient distribution of a product very difficult. Pepsi Cola in Eastern Europe have a large number of decentralised satellite bottling plants in an attempt to overcome the lack of a distribution infrastructure.

The reader will find that we will examine the impact of the Internet on the relevant marketing practices and processes as we move through the chapters of the book. Chapter 12 of this edition is devoted to examining the implications for the international marketing strategies of companies of such trends in the technology environment.

DIFFERENCES BETWEEN INTERNATIONAL AND DOMESTIC MARKETING

As we have seen in the previous sections, there are many factors within the international environment which substantially increase the challenge of international marketing. These can be summarised as follows:

1 *Culture*: often diverse and multicultural markets

2 *Markets*: widespread and sometimes fragmented

3 *Data*: difficult to obtain and often expensive

4 *Politics*: regimes vary in stability – political risk becomes an important variable

5 *Governments*: can be a strong influence in regulating importers and foreign business ventures

6 *Economies*: varying levels of development and varying and sometimes unstable currencies

7 *Finance*: many differing finance systems and regulatory bodies

8 *Stakeholders*: commercial, home country and host country

9 *Business*: diverse rules, culturally influenced

10 *Control*: difficult to control and coordinate across markets.

The international competitive landscape

A major difference for managers operating on international markets is the impact all these currents and cross-currents have on the competitive landscape. Wilson and Gilligan (2003) define marketing as 'getting the competitive advantage and keeping it'. The task of achieving this in a competitive environment where firms are subject to local, regional and global competition can be immensely challenging. This is especially so if indigenous local competitors are supported by the government of the country.

Across international markets, advanced countries are seeing significant competition from both emerging markets and less developed countries who are exploiting modern technology and their own low labour costs to compete in markets no longer so protected by tariff walls.

The complexity of competition is also heightened by the strategic use of international sourcing of components by multinationals and global firms to achieve competitive advantage.

Given the nature of the challenges and opportunities identified above and the speed of change within the international environment, this means that substantially different pressures are being placed upon management than if they were purely operating in domestic markets. It follows from this that the manager of international marketing needs a detailed knowledge and understanding of how particular environmental variables impact on a firm's international marketing operations.

Perlmutter (1995) identified nine cross-cultural management incompetencies which led to failure across a spread of country markets. He defined these core incompetencies as 'the bundle of activities and managerial skills that are mis-matched in a great variety of countries where firms do business'.

The first three are interrelated and relate to the failure to be market driven.

1 Inability to find the right market niches.

2 Unwillingness to adapt and update products to local needs.

3 Not having unique products that are viewed as sufficiently higher added value by customers in local markets.

4 A vacillating commitment. It takes time to learn how to function in countries such as Japan.

5 Assigning the wrong people. Picking the wrong people or the wrong top team in an affiliate.

6 Picking the wrong partners. There is a list of difficulties in building alliances; a main limitation is picking partners who do not have the right bundle of capabilities to help reach the local market.

7 Inability to manage local stakeholders. This includes incompetence in developing a satisfactory partnership relationship with unions and governments.

8 Developing mutual distrust and lack of respect between HQ and the affiliates at different levels of management.

9 Inability to leverage ideas developed in one country to other countries worldwide.

If such mistakes are not to be made in your marketing strategies it is essential to ensure that the company has a robust and rigourous approach to its international marketing plannning processes. Approaches to achieving this will be discussed in the following sections.

THE INTERNATIONAL MARKET PLANNING PROCESS

In international marketing the very complexity of handling the diverse range of factors that must be considered make planning and control a difficult activity to carry out satisfactorily. For large global companies, the problem becomes one of how to structure the organisation so that its increasingly complex and diverse activities around the world can be planned and managed effectively, its goals can be achieved and its stakeholders' expectations satisfied.

In this section we look at the international marketing planning and control process and consider how managers can respond to the challenges posed in the previous sections by ensuring they have robust strategy development and market planning processes.

The planning process

The planning process is the method used by the management of the firm to define in detail how it will achieve its current and future strategic aims and objectives. In doing this, it must evaluate the current and future market opportunities, assess its own current and potential capabilities and attempt to forecast how those changes over which it has no control might help or hinder its efforts to reach its objectives.

The international planning process must allow the company to answer the following three marketing questions.

1 Where is the company now?
2 Where does it want to go?
3 How might it get there?

These questions are fundamental for the majority of businesses whether they are large or small, simple or complex, and they emphasise the firm's need to prepare for the future to ensure its own survival and growth within the increasingly competitive international environment. There is an implication in these questions that the future is likely to be significantly different from the past, so planning is inevitably about forecasting and implementing change which determines the very nature and future direction of the organisation.

The starting point of the planning process for any company is to set long-term goals and objectives which reflect its overall aspirations. These goals cannot be set in isolation, however, as the company's history and current levels of success in its different country markets are usually major determinants of its future. Other factors, too, over which the company has little control in international markets, such as the economic and political situation of the countries in which it is operating, the response of the competition and the diverse background, behaviour and expectations of its customers, all have a major impact upon the company's operations and will have a significant effect on determining whether or not it will meet its goals.

Too many firms, particularly smaller ones, fail to prepare contingency plans to cope with the unexpected and, in some cases, even the predictable events in international markets: they are often surprised and unprepared for success too. When unexpected events occur, many companies too easily ignore the plan and develop new strategies as they go along. Whilst it may be possible to survive in a relatively uncomplicated domestic environment by reacting rapidly to new situations as they arise, it is impossible to grow significantly in international markets, as an overly reactive management style is usually wasteful of opportunities and resources.

In international markets, planning and control is essential for both day to day operations and the development of long-term strategies in order to manage the differences of attitudes, standards and values in the extended parts of the organisation and avoid the problems of poor coordination and integration of the diverse activities. The plans which are developed must be sufficiently flexible to cope with unfamiliar cultures, rapidly changing political, economic and competitive environments, and the effects of unexpected events which affect global companies in one way or another throughout the world on an almost daily basis.

As a company moves into international markets, having previously been marketing solely to domestic markets, the processes of planning and control remain largely the same, but the complexity of the process increases dramatically. In a domestic situation misunderstandings between different departmental managers can be relatively quickly sorted out with a face to face discussion, but in the international situation this is much harder and often impractical. More impersonal communications, along with longer lead times, different cultures and the use of different languages, results in seemingly inconsistent and often negative attitudes in international managers.

Major evolutionary stages of planning

As most companies move gradually into international markets they go through the major evolutionary stages of planning: the unplanned stage, the budgeting stage, the annual business planning and the strategic planning stage (see Illustration 1.5).

ILLUSTRATION 1.5

Divine Chocolate Ltd

Kuapa Kokoo is a cooperative of small-scale cocoa farmers in Ghana, who set up Divine Chocolate Ltd (formerly the Day Chocolate Company). The company buys all its cocoa at fair trade prices which means the farmers receive a guaranteed minimum price of US$1600 per tonne of cocoa, plus a social premium of US$150 per tonne which they invest in farm and community development projects. Divine Chocolate have two brand names, Divine and Dubble, which carry the Fairtrade Mark licensed by the international Fairtrade Labelling Organisation (FLO).

PHOTO CREDIT: DIVINE CHOCOLATE LTD

The mission of Divine Chocolate is to bring fair trade chocolate to the mainstream world markets. Their milk chocolate recipe was developed with UK tastes in mind, and both Divine and Dubble were created to a quality standard and designed to compete with major brands. Prices also matched those of equivalent products already available on the market.

In July 2006 the Body shop donated their shares in Divine Choclate Ltd to Kuapa Kokoo, which now owns 45 per cent of the company. With this very special farmer–ownership model for the business and two successful Fairtrade brands, Divine has a strong appeal to today's more conscientious consumer.

Armed with a delicious product and a compelling story, and the clout of supporting charities such as Comic Relief (UK) and Christian Aid, Divine Chocolate has succeeded in getting both Divine and Dubble listed in all the top UK supermarkets, as well as many independents. They also supply chocolate for own label products in the Co-op and Starbucks in the UK. The company now has the USA and other European markets in their sights. However, given their limited resources, can they build on their UK success and take their message to new countries and new cultures with very different consumer behaviour patterns and varying attitudes to the importance of fairtrade?

QUESTION *How can the Divine Chocolate Company develop a marketing plan to help them develop into new international markets?*

The unplanned stage: In its early stages of international marketing, the company is likely to be preoccupied with finding new export customers and money to finance its activities. Frequently business is very unpredictable and is consequently unplanned, so that a short-term 'crisis management' culture emerges.

The budgeting stage: As the business develops, a system for annual budgeting of sales, costs and cash flow is devised, often because of pressure from external stakeholders such as banks. Being largely financial in nature, budgets often take little account of marketing research, product development or the longer term potential of international markets.

Annual business planning: Companies begin to adopt a more formalised annual approach to planning by including the whole of the business in the planning review process. One of three approaches to the process of international market planning generally emerge at this stage:

1 *Top-down planning*: this is by far the simplest approach, with senior managers setting goals and developing quite detailed plans for middle and senior staff to implement. To be successful, this clearly requires the senior managers to be closely in touch with all their international markets and for the business to be relatively uncomplicated in the range of products or services offered. It has the advantage of ensuring that there is little opportunity for misinterpretation by local managers, but the disadvantage of giving little opportunity for local initiative. Most of the strategic decisions at McDonald's and Coca-Cola are taken in the US, and by Sony in Japan.

2 *Bottom-up planning*: in this approach the different parts of the company around the globe prepare their own goals and plans and submit them to headquarters for approval. Whilst this encourages local initiative and innovation, it can be difficult to manage as the sum of the individual parts that make different demands on resources, financial returns and marketing profiles rarely add up to a feasible international development plan.

3 *Goals down, plans up*: in an attempt to benefit from the positive elements of the first two approaches, this third approach is based upon senior management assessing the firm's opportunities and needs, setting corporate global objectives and developing broad international strategies. Financial goals are then set for each part of the company, which has the responsibility for developing individual strategies and plans to achieve these targets. For this approach to work effectively the senior management generally allows considerable flexibility in the way that the goals are achieved by the component parts of the firm around the globe. This approach is adopted particularly by companies that have a very diverse portfolio of businesses and products.

The strategic planning stage: So far, the stages discussed have been concerned with relatively short-term planning (one to two years), but for many aspects of international marketing such as new market entry, growth strategies and brand management, much longer-term planning is essential. By developing strategies for a five year timescale, it is possible to avoid short-term, highly reactive and frequently contradictory and wasteful activity. The annual marketing plan then becomes a more detailed version of the five year strategic plan which can be rolled forward year on year.

The obvious benefits of strategic planning are that all staff can be better motivated and encouraged to work more effectively by sharing a vision of the future. There are, however, potential dangers too. Long-term strategic plans often fail to cope with the consequences of unexpected events, either environmental or political. There is often confusion between managers over what are strategic issues and what are operational tactics. What a manager in a foreign subsidiary might consider to be a strategic issue, such as achieving a substantial market share increase in the country, might be regarded as an operational matter by a senior manager at the headquarters, which does not consider success in that particular country a priority for the company.

The international marketing planning process

There are a number of elements in the international marketing plan, as detailed in Figure 1.3.

STAKEHOLDER EXPECTATIONS

The complexities of the international marketing environment mean another major difference for companies competing on international markets is that the company has many more organisations and people who have a stake in how they conduct their business and so consequently many more stakeholders whose differing expectations they have to manage. The ability of a company to pursue its chosen marketing strategy is determined to a large degree by the aims and expectations of the stake-holders, who directly or indirectly provide the resources and support needed to implement the strategies and plans. It is important to clearly identify the different stakeholder groups, understand their expectations and evaluate their power, because it is the stakeholders who provide the broad guidelines within which the firm operates. Figure 1.4 identifies the typical stakeholders of a multinational enterprise. Body Shop, the environmentally conscious UK toiletries retailer, is always likely to have problems balancing the widely differing pricing and profit expectations and environmental concerns of its franchisees, customers and shareholders.

Whilst the senior management of the firm aim usually to develop and adopt strategies which do not directly oppose these stakeholder expectations, they do, of course, frequently widen or alter the firm's activities due to changes in the market and competition. Moreover, a wide range of stakeholders influence what multinational enterprises (MNEs) do by giving greater attention to the political, commercial and ethical behaviour of the organisations as well as taking more interest in the actual operation of the business and the performance and safety of the products. As a result of this, companies need to explain their strategies and

FIGURE 1.3

Aspects of international marketing planning

Stakeholder expections

- Shareholders, customer, host government, employees in each country, pressure groups

Situation analysis

- Evaluation of the environment and individual markets

Resources and capabilities

- Individual small business unit strengths and weaknesses analysis
- Capability to deal with threats and opportunities

Corporate aims and objectives

- Financial, market, area, brand and mix objectives

Marketing strategies

- Growth strategies
- Standardisation and adaptation

Implementation of the plan

- Individual SBU and marketing mix plans
- Regional, global or multidomestic integration

Control and feedback

- Setting relevant standards, measuring performance, correcting deviations

plans to shareholders through more detailed annual reports, to staff through a variety of briefing methods and to pressure groups and the community in general through various public relations activities, particularly when their activities have an impact on the local environment or economy. In international marketing it is particularly important that the firm addresses the concern of its host country stake-holders, who may be physically and culturally very distant from the headquarters.

Particular attention should be paid to the different expectations of the stakeholders and their power to influence the firm's strategic direction. Given the different expectations of the firm's stakeholders it is inevitable that conflicts will occur. For example, shareholders usually want a high return on their invest-ment and may expect the firm to find countries with low production costs, but the workers in these countries want an adequate wage on which to live. It is often the firm's ability to manage these potential conflicts that leads to success or failure in international marketing.

International pressure groups are another important stakeholder MNEs have to manage. Global communications and the ability of the Internet to draw together geographically dispersed people with shared interests have led to the growing power of globally based pressure groups. Such has been the success of a number of these, it is now the case that pressure-groups are seen by many global operators as one of the key stakeholders to be considered in international strategy decision making. The role of pressure groups in global markets tends to be to raise aware-ness of issues of concern. Among those that have received wide press coverage affecting international marketing strategies are:

■ the Greenpeace efforts to raise awareness to threats on the environment

■ the anti-globalisation lobby demonstrating against the perceived dark global forces they see manifested in the World Trade Organisation

■ the anti-child labour movement.

Gap, the clothes manufacturer and retailer, responded to a revelation that companies who had a licence to produce their products were using child labour by applying the employment guidelines and dismissing the 'child'. This only exacerbated the anger of the pressure groups. Levi, another target of the anti-child

FIGURE 1.4
Some typical stakeholders of multinational enterprises

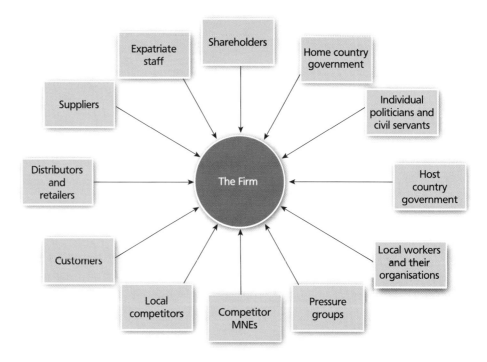

labour movement, finding themselves exposed to the same bad publicity, dismissed the child but agreed to fund the child's education up to the point when they would be eligible to seek employment. This pacified the pressure group in the short term, but one is left wondering what Levi would do if they subsequently discovered that there were another few thousand under-age employees across other factories they use, or if there was a sudden influx of employees that were recruited and then declared themselves under age in order to seek educational support.

One of the main roles of international public relations is to try to manage the expectations and aspirations of pressure groups and all the stakeholders of a company. In international marketing one of the key responsibilities is to establish good practice to respond to publicity generated by pressure groups on issues where they have been seen not to meet stakeholder expectations.

As the international business environment becomes more competitive, dynamic and complex, there is a greater need for individual managers to be aware not simply of their immediate situation, but also of the possible impact of changes taking place in surrounding areas too.

Situation analysis

Situation analysis is the process by which the company develops a clear understanding of each individual market and then evaluates its significance for the company and for other markets in which the business operates. As the international business environment becomes more competitive, dynamic and complex, there is a greater need for individual managers to be aware not simply of their immediate situation, but also of the possible impact of changes taking place in surrounding areas too. Individual national markets can be both surprisingly similar and surprisingly dissimilar in nature, and it is important to understand these linkages and the implications of the changes which take place. Chapters 2 and 3 give the reader a detailed insights onto the factors to consider in carrying out a situational analysis of the international marketing environment.

The processes and procedures for segmenting international markets and carrying out the necessary research to build the situational analysis are examined in some depth in Chapter 4.

A detailed analysis of each of these factors as they affect both the local and international market environments is necessary in order to forecast future changes. The most frequently adopted approach by firms is to extrapolate past trends. However, with so many factors to consider and the increasing frequency with which unexpected events seem to occur, it may be extremely difficult and misleading to build up one all-embracing vision of the future. Firms are responding to this uncertainty by developing a series of alternative scenarios as the basis of the planning process. An effective, robust strategy needs to contain contingency plans to deal with a variety of situations in which the company might find itself.

Resources and capabilities

In stressing the need to analyse and respond to external forces over which even global companies have little control, there can be a temptation amongst some managers to believe that the current capabilities of the organisation are inadequate when facing the future. A more thorough analysis of the firm's situation is needed and the SWOT framework (analysing the firm's strengths, weaknesses, opportunities and threats) is appropriate for this purpose. It is important therefore to audit not just the most obvious company weaknesses but also the strengths of the company, which are often taken for granted but which are really its source of competitive advantage. This is particularly important in international markets as, for example, customer and brand loyalty may be much stronger in certain markets than others, and products which may be at the end of their life in the domestic market may be ideal for less sophisticated markets. SWOT analysis should, therefore, be carried out separately on each area of the business by function, product or market and focus upon what action should be taken to exploit the opportunities and minimise the threats that are identified in the analysis. This will lead to a clearer evaluation of the resources that are available or which must be acquired to ensure the necessary actions are carried out.

Knowledge management

The increasing globalisation of business, particularly because it is being driven by information technology, has led many firms to re-examine what contributes to their global competitive advantage. They have recognised the fact that it is the pool of personal knowledge, skills and competencies of the firms' staff that provides its development potential and they have redefined themselves as 'knowledge-based' organisations. Moreover, these firms have acknowledged that they must retain, nurture and apply the knowledge and skills across their business if they wish to be effective in global markets. The growth potential can only be exploited if the firm becomes a learning organisation in which the good practice learned by individual members of staff can be 'leveraged', transferred and built upon throughout its global activity.

Corporate objectives

Having identified stakeholder expectations, carried out a detailed situation analysis and made an evaluation of the capabilities of the company, the overall goals to be pursued can be set. It is important to stress that there is a need for realism in this, as too frequently corporate plans are determined more by the desire for short-term credibility with shareholders than with the likelihood that they will be achieved. The objectives must be based on realistic performance expectations rather than on a best case scenario. Consideration must also be given to developing alternative scenarios so that realistic objectives can be set and accompanied by contingency plans in case the chosen scenario does not materialise.

   The process adopted for determining long-term and short-term objectives is important and varies significantly depending on the size of the business, the nature of the market and the abilities and motivation of managers in different markets. At an operational level, the national managers need to have an achievable and detailed plan for each country, which will take account of the local situation, explain what is expected and how performance will be measured. For most companies the most obvious international strategic development opportunities are either in increasing geographical coverage and/or building global product strength. This is discussed in much further detail in Chapter 5 from the viewpoint of the SME and in Chapter 6 from the viewpoint of globally based organisations. Dilemma 1.2 helps you consider this question from the viewpoint of a government trying to sell the strategic presence of a city.

Marketing strategies

Having set the objectives for the company, both at corporate and the subsidiary level, the company will develop detailed programmes of the marketing strategies and activities which will achieve the objectives. Decisions will need to be made as to how the company will segment and target its international markets? How will it position itself in different international markets. How will it add value to its efforts through its product portfolio, communications, distribution and pricing strategies? It is this that is at the heart of the following chapters of this book as we take the reader through the detailed considerations in developing an international marketing strategy. A central consideration in marketing strategy development for international markets is the dilemma facing all international managers as to how far they can standardise marketing strategies in different country markets. This essential question will be examined as we go through different aspects of international marketing strategy development and implementation.

Implementation of the marketing plan

Having agreed the overall marketing strategy, plans for implementation are required at a central and local subsidiary level. Firms usually allocate resources to individual subsidiaries on a top-down basis, but this needs to be modified to include the special allocations made to enable foreign subsidiaries to resource specific market opportunities or difficulties encountered in particular markets. Agreement is reached through a process of discussion between the operating department and management levels. Detailed budgets and timescales can then be set for all areas of marketing including those outside agencies (such as marketing researchers, designers and advertising agencies) in order to ensure that their contributions are delivered on time and within the budget. Some allowance must be made for those activities which might be more difficult to estimate in terms of cost or time, such as research and development of new products.

We have, so far, emphasised the need for careful, detailed and thorough preparation of the plan, but it is essential that the plan is action oriented and contains programmes designed to give clear direction for the implementation, continuous evaluation and control of all the firm's marketing activity. The plan must therefore be: *strategic*, by fulfilling the corporate and marketing objectives and coordinating the individual strategic business unit (SBU) plans, *tactical*, by focusing upon individual SBU marketing activities in each country, and *implementable*, by detailing the individual activities of each department within the SBU.

The control process

The final stage of the planning process is setting up an effective system for obtaining feedback and controlling the business. Feedback and control systems should be regarded as an integrated part of the whole planning process, and they are essential in ensuring that the marketing plans are not only being implemented but are still appropriate for the changing international environment.

DILEMMA 1.2

How does a city sell itself internationally?

Ontario in Canada has set expanding the city's international strategic presence as a major priority. They view this strategy as essential to attracting job-creating investments to the province, which will also connect Ontario's companies with the contacts and information they need to succeed in a global economy. It already has a number of international marketing centres located within the Canadian embassies in places such as New York, Munich, Tokyo and New Delhi. However, it now wishes to ensure a more strategic presence in three key regions – the Euro Zone, China and Central America – and is trying to decide whether it should take a different approach to setting up its centres and where such centres should be located in these regions.

QUESTION *How would you advise the Ontario ministry to solve this dilemma?*

There are three essential elements of the control process:

1 *Setting standards*: the standards that are set need to be relevant to the corporate goals such as growth and profits reported by financial measures, return on capital employed and on sales, and non-financial indicators, e.g. market share. Intermediate goals and individual targets can be set by breaking the plan down into measurable parts which when successfully completed will lead to the overall objectives being achieved. The standards must be understandable, achievable and relevant to each local country situation.

2 *Measuring performance against standards*: to obtain measurements and ensure rapid feedback of information, firms use a variety of techniques, including reports, meetings and special measurements of specific parts of the marketing programme, such as cost–benefit analysis on customers, product lines and territories or marketing audits for a thorough examination of every aspect of marketing in a particular country. They also use benchmarking, which allows comparisons of various aspects of the business, such as efficiency of distribution, customer response times, service levels and complaints, with other companies that are not necessarily from the same business sector.

3 *Correcting deviations from the plan*: perhaps the most difficult decisions that must be made are to determine when performance has deviated sufficiently from the plan to require corrective action to be taken either by changing the plan or the management team charged with the responsibility of carrying out the plan.

A checklist of the essential elements of the international marketing plan is summarised in Figure 1.5.

FIGURE 1.5
Essential elements of the international marketing plan

Does the plan contain:

International analysis

- assumptions about the world economy and the environment trends in the principal markets?
- details of historical performance (sales, cost, profitability)?
- forecast of future performance based on (a) an extrapolation of the past (b) alternative scenarios?
- identified opportunities and threats?

Company capability assessment

- analysis of the company strengths, weaknesses and future capabilities in comparison with local and international competition?

International mission statement with:

- long-term aims and objectives and the strategies to achieve them?
- one year marketing objectivies and individual strategies (for example, budgets, brand objectives and development of personnel)?

Operational plans

- detailed country by country forecasts and targets?
- detailed country by country plans for all marketing activities and coordination with other functions (for example, manufacturing)?
- an explanation of how country plans will be integrated regionally or globally if appropriate?

Contingencies and controls

- a summary of the critical factors for success?
- an assessment of the likely competitor response?
- a contingency component for when things do not go to plan?
- a control process for feedback, evaluation and taking corrective action?

Reasons for success

Hamel and Prahalad (1996) suggest the firms operating globally that succeed are those that perceive the changes in the international environment and are able to develop strategies which enable them to respond accordingly. The firms that will do well will base their success largely on the early identification of the changes in the boundaries of markets and industries in their analysis of their international marketing environment. Management foresight and organisational learning are therefore the basis of a sustainable competitive advantage in global markets.

The increasing globalisation of business, particularly because it is being driven by information technology, has led many firms to re-examine what contributes to their global competitive advantage. They have recognised the fact that it is the pool of personal knowledge, skills and competencies of the firm's staff that provides its development potential and they have redefined themselves as 'knowledge-based' organisations. Moreover, these firms have acknowledged that they must retain, nurture and apply the knowledge and skills across their business if they wish to be effective in global markets. The growth potential of international markets can only be exploited if the firm becomes a learning organisation in which the good practice learned by individual members of staff in one market can be leveraged and built upon throughout its global activity.

However, firms are increasingly vulnerable to losing these valuable personal assets, because of the greater mobility of staff, prevalence of industrial espionage and the security risks and abuse associated with the Internet. Moreover, with the increase in communications it is becoming more difficult to store, access and apply the valuable knowledge that exists amongst the huge volume of relatively worthless data that the company deals with. Consequently, effective knowledge management is now critical for success. This means having Web-enabled database systems that facilitate effective data collection, storage in data warehouses and data mining (the identification of opportunities from patterns that emerge from detailed analysis of the data held).

Successful global operators use the knowledge gained to assess their strengths and weaknesses in light of their organisational learning and ensure they have the company capability and resources to respond to their learning in order to sustain their competitive advantage. This is particularly important in international markets as, for example, customer and brand loyalty may be much stronger in certain markets than others, and products that may be at the end of their life in the domestic market may be ideal for less sophisticated markets. In the dynamic international markets, therefore, if a firm is to succeed it must develop the ability to think, analyse and develop strategic and innovative responses on an international, if not global scale, perhaps such as Mrs Lofthouse did for the Fishermans Friend in Illustration 1.6.

Characteristics of best practice in international marketing

It is apparent, therefore, that firms and organisations planning to compete effectively in world markets need a clear and well-focused international marketing strategy that is based on a thorough understanding of the markets which the company is targeting or operating in. International markets are dynamic entities that require constant monitoring and evaluation. As we have discussed, as markets change so must marketing techniques. Innovation is an important competitive variable, not only in terms of the product or service but throughout

ILLUSTRATION 1.6

Fisherman's Friend

Fisherman's Friend lozenges were initially developed for sailors and Fleetwood fishermen who were working in the severe weather conditions of the North Atlantic fishing grounds. For an entire century the company made around 14lb of lozenges a month which were only sold in the local area. However, when Doreen Lofthouse joined the company she set about expanding the market by selling into towns throughout Lancashire and Yorkshire. Distribution then spread throughout the UK, before expanding overseas. Norway was a logical starting point and it is now the market with the highest sales per head of population. Surprisingly, the lozenge was a success in many hot countries too. Italy was the largest export market at one point before being overtaken by Germany. Although the lozenge needs no adaptation – a cough needs no translation – promotion of Fisherman's Friend differs greatly from country to country. The traditional concept has been the centre of advertising in the UK, but overseas promotional themes are quite different. An Italian TV commercial showed a girl who breathed so deeply after eating a lozenge that the buttons pop off her blouse to reveal her cleavage; in Denmark a man breathes fire; in the Philippines butterflies flutter against pastel shades accompanied by gentle music. Fisherman's Friend is now available in over 100 countries worldwide and in many it is seen as a strong sweet, not as medicated confectionery. Exports now account for over 95 per cent of the company's total production.

QUESTION *What are the reasons for the success of Fisherman's Friend?*

the marketing process. Countertrading, financial innovations, networking and value-based marketing are all becoming increasingly important concepts in the implementation of a successful international strategy.

The challenge, then, of international marketing is to ensure that any international strategy has the discipline of thorough research and an understanding and accurate evaluation of what is required to achieve the competitive advantage. Doole (2000) identified three major components to the strategies of firms successfully competing in international markets:

- A clear international competitive focus achieved through a thorough knowledge of the international markets, a strong competitive positioning and a strategic perspective which was truly international.

- An effective relationship strategy achieved through strong customer relations, a commitment to quality products and service and a dedication to customer service throughout international markets.

- Well-managed organisations with a culture of learning. Firms were innovative and willing to learn, showed high levels of energy and commitment to international markets and had effective monitoring and control procedures for all their international markets.

SUMMARY

- In this chapter we have discussed the growing strategic importance of international marketing and examined the issues associated with successfully competing in international markets. The chapter examines the main differences between domestic and international marketing, the different levels at which international marketing can be approached and the more complex and multidimensional uncontrollable elements of the international marketing environment.

- We have examined the major aspects of the SLEPT factors in the international marketing environment. The environments in which international companies must operate is typically characterised by uncertainty and change – factors which, taken together, increase the element of risk for international marketing managers.

- It has been suggested that marketing managers need to have a properly planned approach to any international activity because, without this, the costs and likelihood of failure are likely to increase. We examined the international marketing planning and control process and considered how managers can respond to the challenges posed in the international marketing environment by ensuring they have robust strategy development and market planning processes.

- The reasons for success and failure on international markets were examined and it was suggested the firms operating globally that succeed are those that perceive the changes in the international environment and are able to develop strategies which enable them to respond accordingly. Management foresight and organisational learning are therefore the basis of a sustainable competitive advantage in global markets.

- The reader has been introduced to many of the concepts that are important to the international marketing management process and will have gained an understanding of the issues to be addressed. All the various aspects of the international marketing strategy process introduced in this chapter will be examined in more detail in the following chapters. In Chapter 2 the international trading environment and the trends and developments in trading patterns will be examined.

KEYWORDS

Cross-currents
Cultural paradoxes
Currents
Emerging economics
European Union
Export marketing
Global marketing

Global youth culture
Globalisation
Gross national income
International marketing
International trade
Less developed economies

Multinational enterprise
North American Free
    Trade Area
Piracy
Purchasing power parity
World trade
World Trade Organisation

CASE STUDY

Flatbread goes round the world

Gruma S.A.B. de C.V is located near Monterrey, Mexico, and produces corn flour and other flour products, which it processes into tortillas and related snacks for markets worldwide. Its brand names include Maseca, Mission, and Guerrero. Its customers include supermarkets, mass merchandisers, smaller independent stores, restaurant chains, food service distributors and schools. The company began operations in 1949. In the early 1970s, Gruma launched its product on the Central American markets, specifically in Costa Rica. In 1976 it expanded to the

PHOTO CREDIT: REPRODUCED WITH PERMISSION FROM WWW.GRUMA.COM

United States and in 1987 it began expanding its operations across the globe, opening plants in Honduras, El Salvador, Guatemala and Venezuela. It now has plants in Europe and most recently China.

The Asian market presents a very exciting development for Gruma. The company established their presence on continental China in the first instance and then gradually expanded their penetration of markets across Asia to the Middle East. It has already established distributorships in Japan, Korea, Singapore, Hong Kong, Thailand, the Philippines, Taiwan and India.

How has a Mexican company with a niche food product like cornflour succeeded so well in international markets? According to Martinez and Haddock, the answer lies in the fact that many of the markets they have focused on are emerging markets which tend to follow the same path of development. These emerging markets exhibit a natural life cycle – a predictable pattern of consumer demand that is evident in steel, wheat, consumer products, and every other major economic sector. What Gruma are following in their international expansion is the tried and tested method of leveraging the similarities across from market to market and growing their company accordingly. The root of the success of Gruma has been their ability to observe the life cycle of emerging markets around the world and expertly time their entry into these markets.

However, the other key factor has been their ability to adapt their products to local market tastes. Their key competitive advantage in international markets is based not on their product but the ability to roll any kind of flour, from corn to wheat to rice, into saleable flatbread. Most people from India do not eat corn tortillas, but they do eat a flatbread called naan, made from wheat, which Gruma sells in the United Kingdom and plans to sell in India. The Chinese don't eat many corn tortillas, but they buy wraps made by Gruma for Peking duck.

Gruma also follow a policy of deploying a senior 'beachhead' team to enter the new market in which they are building a presence. In China, the beachhead team had skills honed through many years of experience in Latin America and was already primed to develop the necessary market

SOURCE: ADAPTED FROM WWW.GRUMA.COM AND MARTINEZ AND HADDOCK (2007) 'THE FLATBREAD FACTOR', STRATEGY AND BUSINESS, SPRING

insights to feed into their marketing campaign. Thus, observed trends in China such as a decrease in home cooking among dual-career professionals, increasing penetration of fast food chains, an increase in cold storage in supermarkets and rapid improvements in the logistics and distribution channels were all utilised in thinking through the Gruma market-building strategy in China.

QUESTIONS

1 Evaluate the reasons behind the success of Gruma S.A.B. de C.V.

2 What environmental factors can be monitored to help decision makers recognise when it is the optimum time to enter a market?

DISCUSSION QUESTIONS

1 What are the major environmental influences which impact on international marketing? Show how they can affect international marketing strategies.

2 Using examples, examine the reasons why marketing strategies fail in international markets.

3 Identify three major global pressure groups. Examine how they have influenced the international marketing strategies of particular firms.

4 What skills and abilities are necessary requirements for an effective international marketing manager? Justify your choices.

5 How can marketing managers accommodate the multiplicity of international markets into a cohesive international marketing strategy and plan?

References

Dicken, P. (2007) *Global shift-mapping the changing contours of the world economy*, 5th edn. Sage.

Doole, I. (2000) 'How SMEs Learn to Compete Effectively on International Markets', Ph.D.

El-Kahal, S. (2006) *Introduction to international business*. McGraw-Hill.

Economist, The (2006) ' "The new titans":a survey of the world economy', 16 September.

Haliburton, C. (1997) 'Reconciling global marketing and one to one marketing – A global individualism response', in Doole, I. and Lowe, R. (eds), *International marketing strategy – contemporary readings*, ITP.

Hamel, G. and Prahalad, C.K. (1996) *Competing for the future*. Harvard Business School Press.

Hofstede, G. (2003) *Culture's consequences: comparing values, behaviours, institutions and organisations across nations international differences in work-related values*, 2nd edn. Sage.

Kotabe, M.and Helsen, K. (2008) *Global marketing management*, 4th edn. J. Wiley and Sons.

Ohmae, K. (2005) *The next global stage: the challenges and opportunities in our borderless world*. Pearson Education.

Perlmutter, M.V. (1995) 'Becoming globally civilised, managing across culture', Mastering Management Part 6, *Financial Times*, 1 December.

Porter, M.C. (1990) *The competitive advantage of nations*. Macmillan.

Quelch, J. and Deshpande. R. (2004) *The global market: developing a strategy to manage across borders* .Wiley and Sons.

Rugimbana, R. and Nwankwo, S. (2003) *Cross cultural marketing*. Thomson Learning.

Sarathy, R., Terpstra, V. and Russow, L.C (2006) *International marketing*, 9th edn. Dryden Press.

Wilson, R. and Gilligan, C. (2003) *Strategic marketing management: planning implementation and control*, 3rd edn, Butterworth-Heinemann.

CHAPTER 2

THE INTERNATIONAL TRADING ENVIRONMENT

INTRODUCTION

International marketing takes place within the framework of the international trading environment. If the reader is to have the skills necessary to develop international marketing strategies, some understanding of the parameters of the international trading environment in which they operate is needed.

In this chapter we examine the development of international trade in recent years. We will analyse the growth and changing pattern of international trade and discuss the institutions that aim to influence international trade.

We will also look at the changing regional trading blocs and the implications these have on trading structures around the globe.

LEARNING OBJECTIVES

After reading this chapter the reader should be able to:

- Discuss the effects and implications of the factors impacting on world trade
- Explain the key trends in the major regional trading blocs around the globe
- Understand the role of the major world institutions that foster the development of multilateral free trade across the world

WORLD TRADING PATTERNS

The world economy consists of over 194 nations with a population of 6.6 billion and a gross domestic product (GDP) output totalling US$61 trillion purchasing power parity (ppp), last year global GDP grew by 3.9 per cent. International trade in merchandise totals US$10.5 trillion and trade in services is currently estimated by the World Trade Organisation (WTO) to be about US$2.4 trillion. However, this may be well below the true figure.

Together, East Asia, North America and the European Union account for 86 per cent of world trade and the world gross GDP. Figure 2.1 highlights the major trade flows between the three points of what has become known as Ohmae's triad (2005) after the Japanese writer who first coined the phrase.

However, such figures mask the potential future reality; that 85 per cent of the world's population lives in emerging markets and at market exchange rates their share of the world economy accounts for only 30 per cent. Measured in ppp terms it is now over 50 per cent. It is anticipated that by 2050 the combined GNP of emerging economies will eclipse that of the developed countries. The International Monetary Fund (IMF) estimate that in the next five years emerging economies as a whole will grow at about 7 per cent per annum compared to a rate of less than 3 per cent by developed countries.

Brazil, Russia, India and China are the four biggest emerging economies (now known as BRICS after being grouped together under the acronym by Goldman Sachs).

Economies such as China (10.4 per cent GDP growth) and India (9.2 per cent), are obvious stars and there is much debate as to which one will achieve future dominance. However, according to *The Economist* (2006) Brazil and Russia both

FIGURE 2.1
Global trade flows

SOURCE: ADAPTED FROM P. DICKENS, 2007. GLOBAL SHIFT-MAPPING; THE CHANGING CONTOURS OF THE WORLD ECONOMY. 5TH ED SAGE.

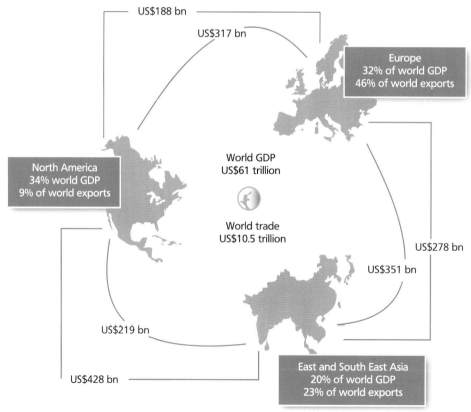

actually produce more than India at present. In market exchange rate terms only China and Brazil rank in the world's top ten economies.

In international trade emerging economies are also becoming major players; their share of world exports has jumped from 20 per cent in 1970 to 43 per cent. Again, China is having the biggest impact. It is soon expected to account for 10 per cent of world trade, up from 4 per cent in 2000 and 7.3 per cent at current figures (see Table 2.1). Rising exports give countries more money to spend on imports. Over the next decade it is expected that one billion new consumers willenter the global marketplace as incomes in emerging countries rise further and households start to have more disposable income to spend on non-essential goods.

As Table 2.1 demonstrates, Germany is the the world's biggest exporter, followed closely by the USA. The USA, however, is the biggest exporter of commercial services, accounting for 15 per cent of this traffic which puts it far in front of any other competitors. The UK, the next largest supplier of services, has only 8 per cent of world exports followed by Germany with 6 per cent. France and Japan have approximately a 5 per cent share each.

In merchandise exports China continues to move up the rankings and is now the third-largest exporter, moving up from sixth place since the last edition of this text was written in 2003 (it was not even in the top ten in 2001).

The UK's share of global merchandise exports has declined appreciably over the past 30 years. Compared with a 7.5 per cent share in the mid-1960s, the UK currently accounts for only 3.7 per cent of global merchandise exports. The pattern of change over the period is very similar to that of US exports, with a sizable decline in the ten years to the mid-1970s followed by relative stability since. German exports, by contrast, have grown, and now take pole position from the USA as the world's leading exporting nation.

TABLE 2.1 Top 10 world exporters in merchandise, 2007

Country	Percentage share
Germany	9.3
United States	8.7
China	7.3
Japan	5.7
France	4.4
Netherlands	3.9
Britain	3.7
Italy	3.5
Canada	3.4
Belgium	3.9

SOURCE: WTO.ORG

Future prospects

World trade volume continues to grow year on year, growing last year by 6 per cent while world GDP last year grew by just under 4 per cent. Table 2.2 examines the annual percentage change in GDP and consumer prices (inflation). China and India have the leading growth rates in terms of GDP, however, Argentina, Malaysia, Russia and Venezuela all have growth growth rates in excess of 5 per cent per annum. For Venezuela this is a huge turnaround: only two years ago the Venezuelan economy contracted by 16 per cent. In Table 2.3, China, Japan, Russia and Germany all exhibit an exceptionally strong and healthy

TABLE 2.2 Percentage change on previous year in real GDP/GNP and consumer prices

Country	Growth rate (%)	Inflation rate (%)
Argentina	6.3.	9.8
Australia	2.9	2.8
Belgium	2.1	1.8
Brazil	3.3	3.7
Canada	2.4	2.0
China	10.4	2.1
Czech Republic	4.8	3.3
Euro zone	2.0	2.0
France	2.0	1.4
Germany	1.6	1.4
Hong Kong	5.0	2.5
India	9.2	6.1
Ireland	3.4	5.3
Italy	1.2	1.9
Japan	1.9	0.4
Malaysia	5.2	3.4
Mexico	3.2	3.8
Netherlands	2.3	1.7
Poland	4.7	2.5
Russia	6.5	9.2
Singapore	5.0	1.0
South Africa	4.2	5.6
South Korea	4.2	2.3
Spain	3.0	2.7
Taiwan	3.9	1.5
Thailand	4.3	3.6
Turkey	4.0	8.6
UK	2.4	2.2
USA	2.2	2.2
Venezuela	5.5	17.0

SOURCE: ADAPTED FROM *THE ECONOMIST* (2007), WWW.IMF.ORG (2007), WWW.WORLDBANK.ORG/DATA (2007), AND NATIONAL STATISTICS OFFICES AND CENTRAL BANKS

balance of payment surpluses. The US, however, is still forecast to have a huge trade deficit (US$837 billion), as does the UK. In Chapter 1 we discussed the difficulties of marketing to countries with high inflation rates. According to Table 2.2 firms are likely to have difficulties in such markets as Venezuela, Russia, Argentina and Turkey, where inflation is in excess of 8 per cent. Latin America is a particular area of concern given the economic and political challenges facing countries like Argentina, Brazil, Venezuela and Colombia.

TABLE 2.3 Trade balances in merchandise trade

Country	US$ billion
Argentina	+12.4
Australia	−9.4
Brazil	+46.1
China	+177.5
Euro zone	−15.7
Germany	+203
Hong Kong	−17.9
India	−51.7
Ireland	+29.3
Japan	+79.6
Mexico	−5.8
Malaysia	+28.6
Netherlands	+39.4
Poland	−4.1
Russia	+140.8
Spain	−112.8
Taiwan	+21.3
Turkey	−53.2
UK	−152.2
USA	−837.2
Venezuela	+36.8

SOURCE: WORLD BANK (2007) WORLD DEVELOPMENT INDICATORS

THE REASONS COUNTRIES TRADE

International trade is a vital part of world economic activity but it is not a new phenomenon. Whilst the growth of international trade has accelerated in the past 40 years, it goes back far beyond then and has been developing throughout the ages since the time when barter was used.

The great growth period for trade was in the eighteenth and nineteenth centuries when many of today's important trading links were forged and developed.

A major source of many of the conflicts in the nineteenth century was the desire by nations to win the right to trade in foreign markets. One of the reasons why Great Britain went to war with Napoleon was to open the French markets to our newly industrialised nation. The colony of Hong Kong and the associated New Territories returned to China in 1997 were acquired by the UK in the early nineteenth century for trading purposes.

The reasons nations trade are many and varied: the two key explanations of why nations trade, however, are based on the theory of comparative advantage and the international product life cycle.

The theory of comparative advantage

The rationale for world trade is based largely upon Ricardo's theory of comparative advantage. At its simplest level, the theory suggests that trade between countries takes place because one country is able to produce a product at a lower price than is possible elsewhere. An illustration of this is provided by the way in which Japanese companies such as Sony and Hitachi came to dominate the European television market. Their strategy was based upon higher product quality, better design and, more importantly for our purposes here, the lower prices that were made possible by far greater economies of scale and better manufacturing technology than was currently being achieved by the European producers.

It is this notion of relative cost that underpins world trade; in other words, countries concentrating upon producing products in which they have a comparative advantage over their foreign competitor countries.

How comparative advantage is achieved

A comparative advantage can be achieved in a variety of ways:

- ▪ Sustained period of investment. This may well lead to significantly lower operating costs.
- ▪ Lower labour cost. A firm operating internationally may locate a manufacturing plant in an emerging economy to take advantage of the lower labour costs there. The average hourly wage in the USA is US$20, in China US$3.40, in India US$2.90 and in Indonesia US$1.89. In the Phillipines it is only US$1.37! Many developed countries complain of the disadvantage this creates for them in trying to compete in international markets. This competitive disadvantage is further compounded by the government subsidies and support given in such countries. However, as Illustration 2.1 points out, such countries are not just competing on low labour costs but emerging as global players in the technology markets.
- ▪ Proximity to raw materials. This is another way to achieve comparative advantage as has been the case with Australia's reserves of coal and mineral ores.

■ Subsidies to help native industries. When the US announced increased wheat subsidies to US farmers, they outraged the Australian and Canadian wheat farmers who saw it as a direct attack on their international markets. Without comparable government support, they felt they were unable to compete with US wheat in these markets.

■ Building expertise in certain key areas. This is another way to achieve comparative advantage. The Japanese identified biotechnology as a key area where they have comparative strength and so have targeted it as a priority research area.

Some countries use international trade to buy in a comparative advantage, buying in highly developed products and so speeding up their development. Porter (1990) suggests that countries can build a national advantage through four major attributes:

■ Factor conditions: the nation's position in factors of production such as skilled labour or infrastructure necessary to compete.

■ Demand conditions: the nature of demand in the home country.

■ Related and supporting industries: the presence or absence of supplier industries and related industries that are internationally competitive.

■ Firm strategy, structure and rivalry: the conditions in the nation governing how companies are created, organised and managed and the nature of domestic rivalry.

ILLUSTRATION 2.1

The comparative advantage of China and India

SOURCE: ADAPTED FROM 'THE TECHNOLOGY INDUSTRY: DIFFERENT STROKES', THE ECONOMIST, 7 OCTOBER 2006 AND 'CHINA–IND A, THE CHALLENGE', BUSINESS WEEK, AUGUST 2005

In a report published 2006 by the OECD listing the world's 250 largest technology firms, measured by revenue, companies from China, Hong Kong and India appeared for the first time and the number from Taiwan more than trebled. The figures for China mask the fact that many Western companies have operations there, which is why they are now the world's largest exporter of technology goods. Domestically, China is now the sixth-biggest buyer of hi-tech goods and services in the world;

PHOTO CREDIT: KEVIN FOY/ALAMY

by 2010 it will be in third place, behind America and Japan. China and India make an interesting contrast in their technological development. They have roughly the same population, but China spends 2.5 times as much on technology as India does. It is the world's largest mobile phone market, and the second-largest market for PCs. China had around 110 million Internet users compared with 51 million in India, and China has 430 million mobile phone users, versus 120 million in India. The two countries are adopting technology at different paces and in different ways.

A further difference is that China's manufacturing strength means hi-tech gear is available locally at low cost, whereas India must import it. India has focused more on software and services, which can be delivered via networks without bureaucratic interference, unlike China which has focused on competing in physical goods. However, India is seen as playing an invaluable role in the global innovation chain. Motorola, Hewlett-Packard, Cisco Systems, Google and other tech giants now rely on their Indian teams to devise software platforms and the tech hubs in such places as Bangalore. These companies are spawning companies producing their own chip designs, software, and pharmaceuticals at an exhilarating pace of innovation.

QUESTION *Compare and contrast the alternative strategies of China and India to build a comparative advantage.*

The international product life cycle

The theory of comparative advantage is often used as the classic explanation of world trade. Other observers, however, believe that world trade and investment patterns are based upon the product life cycle concept. Writing from an American perspective, Vernon and Wells (1968) suggested that on an international level, products move through four distinct phases:

1 US firms manufacture for the home market and begin exporting.
2 Foreign production starts.
3 Foreign products become increasingly competitive in world markets.
4 Imports to the USA begin providing significant competition.

This cycle begins with the product being developed and manufactured, for example, in the USA for high-income markets, subsequently being introduced into other markets in the form of exports. The second phase begins to emerge as the technology is developed further and becomes more easily transferable. Companies in other countries then begin manufacturing and, because of lower transportation and labour costs, are able to undercut the American manufacturers in certain markets.

The third phase is characterised by foreign companies competing against US exports which, in turn, leads to a further decline in the market for US exports. Typically, it is at this stage that US companies either begin to withdraw from selected markets or, in an attempt to compete more effectively, begin investing in manufacturing capacity overseas to regain sales.

The fourth and final stage begins when foreign companies, having established a strong presence in their home and export markets, start the process of exporting to the US and begin competing against the products produced domestically.

It is these four stages, Vernon suggests, that illustrate graphically how American automobile firms have found themselves being squeezed out of their domestic markets having enjoyed a monopoly in the US car market originally.

Although the product life cycle provides an interesting insight into the evolution of multinational operations, it should to be recognised that it provides only a partial explanation of world trade as products do not inevitably follow this pattern. First, competition today is international rather than domestic for all goods and services. Consequently, there is a reduced time lag between product research, development and production, leading to the simultaneous appearance of a standardised product in major world markets. Second, it is not production in the highly labour-intensive industries that is moving to the low labour-cost countries but the capital-intensive industries such as electronics, creating the anomalous situation of basing production for high-value, high-technology goods in the countries least able to afford them. Nor does the model go very far in explaining the rapid development of companies networking production and marketing facilities across many countries. Thus global business integration and sharing of R&D, technological and business resources is seen as a more relevant explanation of today's world trade.

BARRIERS TO WORLD TRADE

Marketing barriers

Whilst countries have many reasons for wishing to trade with each other, it is also true to say that all too frequently an importing nation will take steps to inhibit the inward flow of goods and services.

One of the reasons international trade is different from domestic trade is that it is carried on between different political units, each one a sovereign nation exercising control over its own trade. Although all nations control their foreign trade, they vary in terms of the degree of control. Each nation or trading bloc invariably establishes trade laws that favour their indigenous companies and discriminate against foreign ones.

Thus, at the same time as trade has been developing worldwide, so has the body of regulations and barriers to trade. WTO list the technical barriers to trade that countries use in their attempts to protect their economy from imports. The main protagonists are seen as the USA, Italy, France and Germany.

However, the major barriers to trade are becoming increasingly covert, i.e. non-tariff barriers which are often closely associated with the cultural heritage of a country and very difficult to overcome. The complex distribution patterns in Japan are one such example. Thus, whilst Japan is seen not to have many overt barriers, many businesses experience great difficulties when trying to enter the Japanese market. In Russia recently 167,500 Motorola handsets were seized at a Moscow airport. They were alleged to have been smuggled, to be counterfeit, to violate a Russian patent and to be a danger to public health. As a result some 50,000, it was claimed, were destroyed by the Interior Ministry but suprisingly, a large number of Motorola phones appeared on the Russian black market. Whatever the rights and wrongs of the intentions, trade distortion practices can provide nightmare scenarios for the international marketer. It is thus important to be aware of the practices of the countries being targeted and the types of barriers companies face. Trade distortion practices can be grouped into two basic categories: **tariff** and **non-tariff barriers,** as illustrated in Figure 2.2.

TARIFF BARRIERS

Tariffs are direct taxes and charges imposed on imports. They are generally simple, straightforward and easy for the country to administer. Whilst they are a barrier to trade, they are a visible and known quantity and so can be accounted for by companies when developing their marketing strategies.

Tariffs are used by poorer nations as the easiest means of collecting revenue. The Bahamas for example has a minimum import tax of 30 per cent on all goods, and some products are taxed even higher. Tariffs are also imposed to protect the

FIGURE 2.2
Market entry barriers

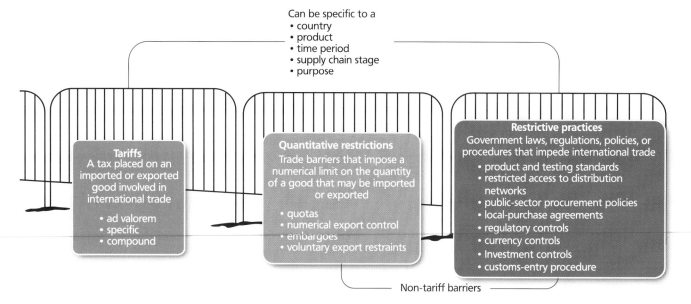

Can be specific to a
• country
• product
• time period
• supply chain stage
• purpose

Tariffs
A tax placed on an imported or exported good involved in international trade
• ad valorem
• specific
• compound

Quantitative restrictions
Trade barriers that impose a numerical limit on the quantity of a good that may be imported or exported
• quotas
• numerical export control
• embargoes
• voluntary export restraints

Restrictive practices
Government laws, regulations, policies, or procedures that impede international trade
• product and testing standards
• restricted access to distribution networks
• public-sector procurement policies
• local-purchase agreements
• regulatory controls
• currency controls
• Investment controls
• customs-entry procedure

Non-tariff barriers

home producer, as in the US and Australia. Both of these countries have high tariff walls for certain industries they wish to protect – for example, cars and agricultural products. The trend towards the lowering of tariff barriers across the globe in recent years (the average tariff is now 5 per cent whereas in 1945 it was 45 per cent), together with the opening up of new markets to foreign investment, notably Asia and Eastern Europe, has greatly complicated the decision for many companies as to where to place manufacturing facilities.

These trends have made global production much more possible, but it has also reduced the need for many overseas plants. Markets that previously demanded local production facilities because tariff levels made importing prohibitive can now be supplied from non-domestic sources.

A good example of these dynamics can be seen in Australia in the automotive sector. Tariffs on imported cars have fallen from 57.5 per cent to 15 per cent and it is planned they will fall to 5 per cent in 2010. Japanese manufacturers therefore found they no longer needed to have plants in Australia to serve the market.

Tariffs can take many forms, as can be seen in Figure 2.2. The most common, however, are:

■ *Specific*: charges are imposed on particular products either by weight or volume and usually stated in the local currency.

■ *Ad valorem*: a straight percentage of the import price.

■ *Discriminatory*: in this case the tariff is charged against goods coming from a particular country, either where there is a trade imbalance or for political purposes.

Non-tariff barriers

In the past 40 years, the world has seen a gradual reduction in tariff barriers in most developed nations. However, in parallel to this, non-tariff barriers have substantially increased. Non-tariff barriers are much more elusive and can be more easily disguised. The effect can, however, be more devastating because they are an unknown quantity and are much less predictable.

Non-tariff barriers take many different forms:

■ Increased government participation in trade is one that is gaining more dominance and which is used by nations to gain competitive advantage, as in the case of the US wheat subsidy previously discussed.

■ Customs entry procedures can also impede trade. These take many forms: administrative hold-ups, safety regulations, subsidies and differing technical standards are just a few. In Angola enforcing a contract involves 47 procedures and takes over 1000 days. A World Bank study of non-tariff barriers showed that out of the 35 least business-friendly countries in the world, 27 were in Sub-Saharan Africa.

The need for customs modernisation and harmonisation has become a priority for companies who find their operations severely hampered by administrative delays at borders and which stand to be disadvantaged even more as economic globalisation gathers pace.

Clearly the extent of customs delays and red tape varies enormously from country to country but everywhere there is a need for governments to take account of business needs for simple, transparent, coordinated and harmonised customs procedures.

■ Quantitative restrictions such as quotas are another barrier. These are limits on the amount of goods that may enter a country. An import quota can be more restrictive than a tariff as there is less flexibility in responding to it. The Japanese car industry faced quotas both in Europe and the US and so developed manufacturing capacity in these markets as a means of overcoming the barriers. The US also imposes quotas on imports from China. However, China, according to the US, has been transshipping products through other ports such as Hong Kong in order to circumvent the quotas.

■ Financial controls were last seen in the UK in the mid-1970s but are used today in Mexico and Eastern Europe where high inflation and lack of hard currency require stringent monetary control. This is probably the most complete tool for the regulation of foreign trade as it gives the government a monopoly of all dealings in foreign exchange. A domestic company earning foreign exchange from exporting must sell it to the national bank and, if goods from abroad need to be bought, a company has to apply for foreign exchange. Thus foreign currency is scarce. The International Monetary Fund has placed stringent controls on several countries, in particular Indonesia, Brazil and Argentina. The latter countries especially have huge external debts which are viewed as unsustainable.

Countries practising exchange controls tend to favour the import of capital goods rather than consumer goods. The other major implication to companies operating in foreign markets is the restrictions on repatriating profits in foreign currency, requiring either countertrade dealings or the use of distorted transfer prices to get profits home (see Chapter 11 on pricing issues).

Non-tariff barriers become much more prevalent in times of recession. In the US and Europe we have witnessed the mobilisation of quite strong political

ILLUSTRATION 2.2

To protect or not protect?

Protectionism first became a global issue in the 1930s when the US President Herbert Hoover used the notorious 'Smoot Hawley' tariff to increase the cost of agricultural imports to the USA. This opened the floodgates to tariffs being imposed on many products. The bi-partisan policies by successive govern-ments across the world that grew from this caused global trade to decline by two-thirds in just five years.

PHOTO CREDIT: FRANCIS LI/ALAMY

Today the same policies are practised – it is just the targets that are different. Despite the USA and Canada being members of the North American Free Trade Area, the US lumber industry tried to stop Canadian softwood lumber exports getting into the US market. The USA accused them of unfair trade practices, especially government subsidies, and so imposed a tariff duty averaging 27 per cent on Canadian softwood lumber export. In 2006 there were 12 bills in the US congress to punish China for successfully exporting to the USA. Europe also threatened the imposition of tariffs on China over cheap shoe exports which they viewed as being supported by the government in Bejing.

In Europe, despite being members in the same Economic Union the French government backed the merger of the state controlled Gaz de France and Suez to protect the latter from takeover by the Italian firm Enel. This sent a clear message to foreign firms to keep out of the French energy market. This was despite the French energy firm EDF successfully building a profile in the European countries it expanded into which did not impose the same restrictions.

QUESTION *Compare the benefits and drawbacks of governments protecting their home industries from foreign competition.*

lobby groups, as indigenous industries which have come under threat, lobby their governments to take measures to protect them from international competition.

The last major era of protectionism was in the 1930s. During that decade, under the impact of the most disastrous trade depression in recorded history, countries around the world adopted high tariffs and abandoned their policies of free trade. Even today a number of governments impose different types of restrictions on imports to protect their home industries as Illustration 2.2 shows. In 1944 there was a reaction against the high tariff policy of the 1930s and significant efforts were made to move the world back to free trade. In the next section we will look at the world institutions that have been developed since that time to foster international trade and provide a trade climate in which such barriers can be reduced.

THE DEVELOPMENT OF WORLD INSTITUTIONS TO FOSTER INTERNATIONAL TRADE

In the 1930s international trade was at low ebb, protectionism was rife and economies were strangling themselves. Several initiatives were born, primarily out of the 1944 Bretton Woods conference, to create an infrastructure that fostered trading relations. These initiatives fell into three areas:

- Need for international capital: the International Bank for Reconstruction and Development (IBRD).
- International liquidity: International Monetary Fund.
- Liberalisation of international trade and tariffs: General Agreement of Trade and Tariffs/World Trade Organisation.

International Bank for Reconstruction and Development

The World Bank, officially called the International Bank for Reconstruction and Development, was founded together with the International Monetary Fund (IMF) in 1944. The World Bank began operating in June 1946 and membership of the Bank is open to all members of the IMF. Currently, there are 150 member countries. The Bank is owned and controlled by its member governments. Each member country subscribes to shares for an amount relative to its economic strength. The largest shareholder in the World Bank at the moment is the United States.

The primary purpose of the Bank is to provide financial and technical help for the development of poorer countries. Currently it lends about £15 billion a year to help raise the standard of living in poorer countries.

The scope of the Bank's operations has increased phenomenally during the past two decades. It now provides more than five times as much financial help to developing countries than in any year since the 1960s. The Bank provides support for a wide variety of projects related to agriculture, education, industry, electricity, rural development, tourism, transportation, population planning, urban development, water supply and telecommunications. The Bank lends money only for productive purposes and gives serious consideration to the prospects of repayment before granting the loan.

Whilst the countries who are members subscribe to the share capital of the World Bank, it relies mainly on private investors for its financial resources through borrowing in various capital markets. In this way, private investors become involved in the development efforts of developing countries. Since the IBRD obtains most of its funds on commercial terms, it charges its borrowers a commercial rate of interest. Loans are usually repayable over a 20-year period.

This has led to what has been euphemistically termed the 'debt crisis'. Many of the poor developing countries, recipients of large capital loans, are finding it impossible to meet the burden of debt facing them. Some of this debt is unpayable when the interest on the debt is greater than what the country produces. However in some cases this is what is known as 'Odious debt', debt incurred by undemocratic countries and misspent. It is estimated that developing countries owed US$1.2 trillion to the world's richest nations. Table 2.4 illustrates the heavy burden of debt that some countries may face. The problems of countries in Africa are well documented but the countries identified in this table are interesting in that they are all countries competing in world markets. Turkey, Phillipines, Indonesia and Bulgaria are all growing emerging economies, however in all cases their external debt is more than 80 per cent of their GDP. There is now international agreement that international reforms are needed in order to achieve more sustainable debt platforms and many campaigns are fighting for the debts of many countries, particularly in Africa, to be written off completely.

TABLE 2.4 The heavy burden of debt

	Debt US$ billion	% GDP
Argentina	168.0	102
Brazil	235.0	54
Bulgaria	13.0	86
Chile	43.0	67
China	193.0	13
India	113.5	19
Indonesia	134.0	82
Mexico	140.0	25
Nicaragua	6.0	40
Phillipines	63.0	80
Poland	95.0	48
Russia	175.0	52
Thailand	52.0	41
Turkey	145.0	81

SOURCE: WORLD TRADE ORGANISATION (2006) WORLD DEVELOPMENT INDICATORS

International Development Association

In the 1950s it became obvious that many of the poorer countries needed loans on much easier terms than the World Bank could provide. The International Development Association (IDA) was established in 1960 to help meet this need. It was made an affiliate of the World Bank and was to be administered in accordance with the Bank's established methods.

The IDA makes soft loans of about US$7 billion annually. Almost all are granted for a period of fifteen years without interest, except for a small charge to cover administrative overheads. Repayment of loans does not start until after a ten-year period of grace. Both the IDA and the IBRD lay down stringent requirements that have to be met before any loans are granted. In many cases this has meant that in order to be granted the investment the countries have had to make quite hard political decisions in order to achieve the balanced budget required. In some cases this has led to severe hardship and social disorder, for which the institutions have been severely criticised.

International Monetary Fund (IMF)

The objective of the IMF was to regain the stability in international exchange rates that had existed under the gold standard. Although the system of pegged rates failed to keep up with the growth in international trade, the functions of the IMF have continued to develop.

The main function is to provide short-term international liquidity to countries with balance of payments deficit problems enabling them to continue to trade internationally. The IMF, with its 150 members, provides a forum for international monetary cooperation enabling the making of reciprocal agreements amongst countries and the monitoring of the balance of payments positions of countries. Thus it serves to lessen the risk of nations taking arbitrary actions against each other, as happened in the 1930s, and can also sound a warning bell for nations with potential liquidity problems.

The IMF's seal of approval is, for emerging markets, essential to attract foreign investment and finance. It is also a precondition of financial assistance from the Fund. Indonesia, Brazil, Argentina and Turkey have all been recent recipients of IMF funding. Brazil and Argentina were recipients of the Fund's largest-ever loans. Both countries posed huge risks for the IMF. Several prominent economists argued that Brazil's huge foreign-debt burdens were unsustainable and that the loan would only add to their burden. Argentina's current external government debt stands at US$168 billion, Brazil's is US$235 billion and Indonesia's US$134 billion, but all three have repaid the short-term loans from the IMF.

Turkey now accounts for two-thirds of the outstanding debts to the IMF and has recieved repeated help, in spite of the government's persistent failure to stick to its policy obligations and the criticism of the IMF for that failure.

As countries have looked for other means of defending their economies in times of financial crisis the IMF is now lending less than previously, and its role is starting to change as it takes on the global role of examining policies that underpin prosperity and poverty and tries to guide nations to the former.

The World Trade Organisation

The predecessor of the World Trade Organisation was the General Agreement on Tariffs and Trade (GATT). Established in January 1948, it was a treaty not an organisation, with the signatories being contracting parties. Prior to the

Doha Round which commenced in 2001 there had been a series of eight trade liberalization 'rounds'. These entailed tens of thousands of tariff concessions on industrial goods and covered trade flows worth hundreds of billions of dollars. Twenty-three countries participated in the 1948 opening round when 45 000 tariff concessions were agreed covering US$10 billion worth of trade. Under the first eight GATT rounds, the average tariff on manufactured products in the industrial world fell from around 45 per cent in 1947 to under 5 per cent. This has been an important engine of world economic growth which, in turn, has stimulated further increases in world trade. Signatories to these treaties account for well over 90 per cent of world trade.

The last round of negotiations to be completed was the Uruguay Round with 107 participants. It was widely seen as the most complex and ambitious round ever attempted. This was due to the sheer volume of its coverage – fifteen sectors and US$1 trillion worth of trade. An important part of the treaty was the formation of the World Trade Organisation, which commenced in 1995 and replaced GATT. The WTO currently has 150 members and another 29 countries who have observer status. The latest member to join was Vietnam in January 2007.

The WTO preaches a gospel of multilateral trade and most-favoured-nation status which obliges each signatory to the treaties to grant the same treatment to all other members on a non-discriminatory basis. It has evolved regulations which it has tried to enforce through its adjudicatory disputes panels and complaints procedures. The WTO has been the final arbitrator in a number of trade disputes, most notably between the USA and China in disputes over copyright, piracy and the use of brand names and between the USA and the European Union. The USA considers the EU's refusal to approve genetically modified (GM) foods illegal under the WTO trade rules and launched a formal complaint against them. Barring US producers from exporting GM crops to the EU is estimated to cost US producers several hundred million dollars a year. Interestingly, however, the WTO has recently allowed the EU to impose up to US$4 billion of tariffs against America as recompense for a US foreign tax sales break which the WTO has deemed an illegal subsidy.

The main aim of the WTO is to promote a free market international trade system. It promotes trade by:

- working to reduce tariffs
- prohibiting import/export bans and quotas
- eliminating discrimination against foreign products and services
- eliminating other impediments to trade, commonly known as non-tariff barriers.

The latest round of negotiations is called the Doha Round, In this round members of the WTO are attempting to liberalise trading rules in a number of areas, including agricultural subsidies, textiles and clothing, services, technical barriers to trade, trade-related investments and rules of origin.

Over three-quarters of the WTO members are developing countries. The Doha Round has been dubbed the Development Round as it specifically aims to ease trading restrictions for these countries. It is estimated that developing countries face trade barriers four times those applied by rich countries to each other. These barriers reduce export earnings by US$100 billion per annum. Two of the main problem areas for negotiators are the international trading of textiles and agriculture, which accounts for 70 per cent of developing countries' exports. Average tariffs for textiles are 15–20 per cent compared to an average of 3 per cent for industrialised goods. In the European Union and the USA agricultural subsidies amount to US$1 billion per day, six times the annual amount spent on aid by these two regions.

In 2006 the Doha Round of talks were seriously stalled and many thought the objectives of the round would not be achieved, the main problem being the USA's unease due to the developing countries refusal to open up markets to the extent demanded. Of equal concern to the developing countries was the refusal by the USA to reduce the trade-distorting subsidies which developing countries viewed as leading to the unlawful dumping of produce from the USA onto global markets. Of equal concern was the EU's refusal to reduce the agricultural tariffs which block developing countries from EU markets. Hopefully a compromise solution will be found with the proposal that if the USA cap their trade distorting farm subsidies to US$17 billion the EU may cut their agricultural tariffs by 54 per cent and open the door to successful negotiations on the rest of the Doha agenda.

THE DEVELOPMENT OF WORLD TRADING GROUPS

It is believed by some that during the 50 years of global economic expansion under the auspices of GATT, despite the long-term commitments to multilateral trade, there has been an unstoppable momentum of the creation of giant trading blocs.

The formation of the European Monetary Union in 1999 was, perhaps, the most significant of these. When the Single European Market was formed in 1993, the United States effectively became the second largest market in the world. Given the rise of the economies of China and India, who will dominate the international markets of the twenty-first century? This question interests many observers of the global competitive battles now being fought. There is a fear that the world economy may divide into three enormous trading blocs dominated by the world's major trading regions, the EU, NAFTA and China/East Asia, rather than a world of multilateral free trade, particularly if the DOHA round of WTO talks do fail to achieve their ambitious objectives. Some commentators argue that national economies are becoming vulnerable to the needs of the trading blocs within which trade is free, currencies are convertible, access to banking is open and contracts are enforceable by law. Whilst this scenario may be a long way from the present position, we are already seeing the growing strength of trading blocs such as the North American Free Trade Association (NAFTA), Association of South East Asian Nations (ASEAN) and the formation of the European Monetary Union.

In this section we will examine in detail the regional trading blocs that are emerging, but first let us examine different forms of trade agreements.

Forms of market agreement

There are nine levels of market association ranging from limited trade cooperation to full-blown political union (see Table 2.5). At the lower level of association, agreements can be purely for economic cooperation in some form, perhaps a decision to consult on or coordinate trade policies. At the next level of cooperation, there will be the development of trade agreements between countries on either a bilateral or multilateral basis. Often these are for a particular sector – for example the multi-fibre agreement on textiles. Sometimes such agreements, especially trade preference ones, will act as a forerunner to closer ties. As far as formal trade groupings are concerned, there are five major forms: free trade areas, customs unions, common markets, economic unions and political unions.

TABLE 2.5 Main types of trade associations

Type	Description	Degree of policy harmonisation amongst members	Common external tariff	Free movement of capital and people	Example
Economic cooperation	Broad agreement for consultations on and possible coordination of economic trade policies	None/very low	No	No	Canada–EC framework agreement, APEC
Bilateral or multilateral trade treaty	Trade regulation and often, but not necessarily, liberalisation in one or more specified sector(s)	Low	No	No	The Peru, Chile accord
Sectoral free trade agreement	Removal of internal tariffs in a specified sector may include non-tariff barrier reduction	Medium (within Specified sector(s))	No	No	The multi-fibre agreement
Trade preference agreement	Preferred trade terms (often including tariff reduction) in all or most sectors, possibly leading to free trade area	Low/medium	No	No	South African Development Cone (SADC)
Free trade area (or agreement)	Removal of internal tariffs and some reduction of non-tariff barriers in all or most sectors	Medium	No	No	ASEAN, NAFTA, Mercosur
Customs union	Free trade area but with a common external tariff, harmonisation of trade policy toward third countries	Medium/high	Yes	Possibly	Economic Community of West African States, ANCOM, CACM
Common market	Customs union, but with provisions for the free movement of capital and people, removal of all trade barriers, elaborate supranational institutions, significant harmonisation of internal market structure and external policies				European single market
Economic union	Common market, but with integration of monetary policies, possibly common currency, significant weakening of national powers of member states	Very high	Yes	Yes	European Monetary Union
Political	Full or partial federalism, including sharing of powers between supranational institutions and national governments	Highest	Yes	Yes	Would resemble federal states (e.g. US, Canada, Germany)

SOURCE: UNKNOWN

Free trade area

The free trade area type of agreement requires different countries to remove all tariffs amongst the agreement's members. Let us assume that there are three nations – A, B and C – that agree to a free trade area agreement and abolish all tariffs amongst themselves to permit free trade. Beyond the free trade area A, B and C may impose tariffs as they choose. The EEA (European Economic Area) formed between the EU and EFTA (European Free Trade Area) and the LAFTA (Latin American Free Trade Area) illustrate the free trade area type of agreement, as does NAFTA, the agreement between the USA, Canada and Mexico, and the Asian Free Trade Area (AFTA).

Customs union

In addition to requiring abolition of internal tariffs amongst the members, a customs union further requires the members to establish common external tariffs. To continue with the example (countries A, B and C), under a customs union agreement B would not be permitted to have a special relationship with country X – A, B and C would have a common tariff policy towards X. Prior to 1993, the EC was, in reality, a customs union. The objective of Mercosur is to form a customs union. Their cooperative effort started as a free trade area and now they have developed into a customs union.

Common market

In a common market type of agreement, not only do members abolish internal tariffs amongst themselves and levy common external tariffs, they also permit free flow of all factors of production amongst themselves. Under such an agreement, countries A, B and C would not only remove all tariffs and quotas amongst themselves and impose common tariffs against other countries such as country X, but would also allow capital and labour to move freely within their boundaries as if they were one country. This means that, for example, a resident of country A is free to accept a position in country C without a work permit.

The European Union is essentially a common market, with full freedom of movement of all factors of production. Similarly the Andean nations in South America have formed ANCOM, the Central American nations have grouped themselves as CACM and the Carribbean community have formed CARICOM.

Economic union

Under an economic union agreement, common market characteristics are combined with the harmonisation of economic policy and member countries are expected to pursue common fiscal and monetary policies. Ordinarily this means a synchronisation of money supply, interest rates, regulation of capital market and taxes. In effect, an economic union calls for a supranational authority to design an economic policy for an entire group of nations. This is the objective of the European Monetary Union.

Political union

This is the ultimate market agreement amongst nations. It includes the characteristics of economic union and requires, additionally, political harmony amongst the members. Essentially, it means nations merging to form a new political entity: Germany and the USA are perhaps the closest examples historically. Yugoslavia, which was created after the First World War, was a political union, as was the Soviet Union, although neither of these still exist.

Figure 2.3 shows the major trading regions to have developed significantly in the past decade, together with their member countries. In the following sections we will examine these major trading groups and the developments they have undergone.

THE EUROPEAN UNION

Since 1987 and the signing of the Single European Act, Europe has undergone momentous changes, the key amongst these being:

- the creation of the EU and its single market
- formation of the European Monetary Union (EMU)
- the expansion of the European Union (EU) to include members of the European Economic Area (EEA) and central, eastern and southern Europe.

The Single European Market

The formation of the European Union meant that the EU became the largest trading bloc in the world with a population of 460 million people in 2007, making it a powerful competitive force in the global markets. This, of course, was the key

FIGURE 2.3
Regional trading areas of the world

NAFTA
Canada
Mexico
United States

FTAA
An agreement to create a free-trade area among 34 countries in North and South America

MERCOSUR
Argentina
Brazil
Paraguay
Uruguay
Venezuela

ASSOCIATE MEMBERS
Peru
Bolivia
Chile
Equador
Colombia

EU
Austria
Belgium
Britain
Cyprus
Czech
  Republic
Denmark
Estonia
Finland
France
Germany
Greece
Hungary
Ireland
Italy
Latvia
Lithuania
Luxembourg
Malta
Netherlands
Poland
Portugal
Slovakia
Spain
Sweden

APEC
Australia
Brunei
Canada
Chile
China
Hong Kong
Indonesia
Japan
Malaysia
Mexico
New Zealand
P.N.G
Philippines
Singapore
Korea
Taiwan
Thailand
United States
Russia
Vietnam

AFTA
Brunei
Indonesia
Malaysia
Philippines
Singapore
Thailand
Vietnam
Laos
Myanmar
Cambodia

objective of the moves towards unification and the formation of the single market across the union. In the early 1980s it was recognised that if European companies were to compete successfully in the increasingly interdependent and global economy, a free and unbridled large internal market was necessary. This would enable companies to develop the critical mass needed to compete globally. The highly fragmented and restricted European market was seen as a major barrier to the ability to compete in global markets.

The EU was formed as a result of the signing of the Single European Act in 1987 which created, within Europe, 'an area without internal priorities in which the free movement of goods, personal services and capital is ensured in accordance with the provision of the Treaty of Rome'.

The key changes were:

- *Removal of tariff barriers*: a single customs check at all intra-EU borders enabling goods and services to move freely across Europe.

- *Removal of technical barriers*: a major impediment to trade was the differing and complex standards required in each country. Harmonisation of these standards has paved the way for product standardisation throughout Europe.

- *Public procurement*: public procurement amounts to 15 per cent of EU GNP, only 2 per cent of which went to foreign suppliers. By opening up the market to all European suppliers and by ensuring its enforcement, it is estimated that 17.5 billion euros are saved per annum.

- *Free movement of labour and workers' rights*: nationals of member states now have the right to work in other member states.

- *Opening up of professions*: through mutual recognition of qualifications, professionals in certain categories have their qualifications recognised by other member states.

- *Financial services*: the opening up of banking, insurance and investment services through the introduction of a single banking licence and the harmonisation of banking conditions.

- *Transport, haulage and coastal cabotage*: road haulage permits and quotas have been abolished. A more competitive air transport industry is also being pursued, as is unlimited cabotage for transport through the EU. Trucks are now allowed to pick up goods in any EU country and drop them off where required without the bureaucracy of permits and border documentation.

- *Company law*: several European developments in the area of company law are taking place in the fields of takeover bids, health and safety, cross-border merger, etc. The road to greater control from Brussels is now becoming especially apparent in this area.

- *Fiscal barriers*: there are many EU variations of fiscal policies, e.g. VAT. The UK has a standard rate of 17.5 per cent whereas France has six rates varying from 2.1 to 33.33 per cent. Moves are being made to reduce these disparities.

- *The environment*: the European Environment Agency was established to try to provide an integrated and Europe-wide policy for environmental protection.

Most analysts agree that the formation of the EU has greatly enhanced market opportunities for European companies. Since its formation it is estimated to have created about 2.5 million jobs and generated prosperity equivalent to 1 trillion euros. As a result of its formation, there is a potential home market of 460 million consumers for companies within its walls. Intra-regional trading amongst EU members accounts for 75 per cent of all trade. With such interdependency, it is little wonder that so much effort has been put into completing the unification. However, fifteen or so years on, whilst most goods are now crossing Europe's national borders with little or no hindrance, the liberalisation of trade in services has not made the same progress. Europe's service providers are hindered by all sorts of petty bureaucratic rules, often justified on health, safety or consumer-protection grounds, which discourage them from entering new European markets. In some cases, the European Commission has itself hampered progress by granting certain industries exemptions from the normal rules of fair competition, although these exemptions are starting to be undone. One of the most famous cases is that of new cars. British motorists have long been outraged that the prices in their local showrooms are so much higher than on the continent. Their attempts to buy cars more cheaply across the Channel have often been frustrated because of restrictions that the car makers were allowed to impose on dealers. However since 2005, car makers have no longer been able to threaten to stop supplying, for example, a Belgian car dealer who advertises directly to British motorists and sets up a delivery service in Britain.

European Monetary Union

The idea of a single European currency had been around since the early 1960s. As trade between member countries increased, various attempts were made to stabilise exchange rates. Previous systems such as the Exchange Rate Mechanism (ERM) attempted to create monetary stability through a system of fixed and floating exchange rates. This proved, however, to be incapable of coping with capital flows, which resulted in problems for sterling and the lira in September 1992, with the remaining currencies also facing problems the following year. Pressure for further integration in the Community resulted in the move to monetary union and a single European currency. This created the Economic and Monetary Union (EMU), sometimes called the Euro zone as countries within the zone all use the Euro as a domestic currency.

Whilst Britain and Eastern European countries who have recently joined the EU are still not members, the firms from these countries trading in the European Union will be affected by the Euro and economic activity in the Euro zone. Companies not in the Euro zone have to convert their customer invoices and accounts, credit notes and prices into euros. Company computer systems for customer and/or supplier accounts have had to be adapted to deal with euros. The estimated conversion cost in computers, tills, packaging and billing was over US$1 billion. On the other hand, companies with customer and supplier bases largely outside the EU have faced little or no impact on their businesses.

Strategic implications

EMU was not just a monetary event, but one that has had a serious impact on the real economy. Prices and wages became transparent; consumers now shop around for the best deals; middlemen try to exploit any prevailing regional price differences and margins everywhere are now coming under pressure.

The competitive environment is viewed by many as being tougher under EMU. The change has affected companies both inside and outside the EMU zone, but companies operating inside the Euro zone have had to adjust more quickly than companies operating outside it.

In some cases, it has taken outsiders longer to sense the changes EMU has brought. By the time the UK eventually joins EMU, UK companies might find that their competitors are significantly ahead in their logistical and strategic operations.

Global European companies such as Hewlett Packard, BMW, Daimler-Benz and Siemens for example, use Euro zone pricing policies. Pharmaceutical companies introduce new drugs across the EU at a single pan-European price. Marks and Spencer quote all prices in euro as well as the local currencies.

The question is, which industries do commentators expect to be winners in the new competitive landscape and which have lost from the introduction of the euro? The banks have been significant losers in terms of the business of buying and selling European currencies. The formation of the Single European Payments Area (SEPA), discussed in Chapter 11 is likely to have a further impact on the margins previously achieved by European banks. The biggest difference, however, has not been between industries but between efficient, flexible companies and those that have stuck to their old national ways and found it difficult to compete in the new open and competitive landscape.

Companies that have concentrated on their national markets have been particularly vulnerable to takeover or extinction at the hands of their more far-sighted European competitors. Those businesses already used to competing internationally have had a strong advantage. As sources of supply widen, specialisations based on national talents have developed further. French and German companies, for example, run call centres from Dublin, where multilingual Irish operators (or continental expatriates) provide advice or take orders over the telephone more cheaply and flexibly than would be possible in the companies' home countries. Another effect of the single currency has been to open the European market for those small and medium-sized companies who have previously concentrated on their domestic customers. It has been estimated that currency fluctuations and the costs of dealing with them previously deterred a third of small and medium-sized German companies from venturing abroad. Many who did export concentrated exclusively on countries where currencies were informally linked to the Deutschmark, such as Austria and the Netherlands.

Widening European membership

Enlargement of the European Union has happened at several stages of its development over the past fifty years, and there have been four previous enlargements.

In 1993 the European Council adopted the Copenhagen Criteria for admission to the EU. These require that member countries attain the following:

- Stable institutions guaranteeing democracy and the rule of law.
- A functioning market economy, as well as the capacity to cope with the competitive pressure and market forces within the EU.
- The ability to fulfil membership obligations, including adherence to the aims of political, economic and monetary union.

Ten countries from southern, central and eastern Europe joined the EU in 2004. They are Cyprus, Malta, Czech Republic, Hungary, Poland, Slovakia, Slovenia, Estonia, Latvia and Lithuania. Bulgaria, Turkey and Romania are in the application stages of accession.

The annual growth rate amongst the countries joining from Central and Eastern Europe has been between 4–6 per cent compared to 1–3 per cent among existing EU members. It is reasonable to expect such a differential to continue in the medium term and as such the new members from Central Europe may be considered a younger and faster-growing version of Western Europe. Ilustration 2.3 discusses one such example.

However, given that the EU is now a tariff free trade area, the inclusion of central Europe makes the disparities between the wealth of members more pronounced. Ireland is one of the wealthiest countries of the 25 EU members with a GDP per capita of US$47 000. This compares to a GDP per capita in Portugal of US$16 000 and Poland of US$8000. The EU average is US$31 000. Clearly this poses challenges for marketers trying to establish a consistent marketing postion across the European Union.

As the figures show, growth and opportunity has not been confined to new members. Since joining the EMU Ireland has seen vibrant growth. Its exports are now worth 84 billion euros, 62 per cent of which is to its EU partners. An essential part of their success story has been in the exporting of financial services, as Illustration 2.4 highlights.

THE FREE TRADE AREA OF THE AMERICAS

The North American Free Trade Area (NAFTA) consisting of the US, Canada and Mexico, is regarded as the world's richest single market. NAFTA has a combined population of 425 million people and produces over US$17 trillion in annual output. Together they account for 34 per cent of the world GDP.

ILLUSTRATION 2.3

Skoda has the last laugh

The Czech word *skoda* means pity or shame so on seeing a passing Skoda car, Czechs used to say 'there goes a shame' – and nobody would argue much. Today Skoda Autos (of the

PHOTO CREDIT: TIM GUTT

Czech Republic), once a butt of jokes, has now completely overhauled its image and has been voted the number one car manufacturer of 2006 by respondents of the *Top Gear* magazine in the UK. With the help of its German partner Volkswagen who have the controlling share in Skoda, its profitability continues to grow. The company employs about 4 per cent of the Czech workforce, or 150 000 people, directly or indirectly.

Productivity in its plants is higher than Western levels and labour costs are much lower than at other VW plants in Europe. Analysts reckon that Skoda is the most successful former Communist company anywhere. In 2006 alone they produced 556 000 cars and they are central Europe's largest car manufacturer. Despite a three-year recession in the Czech Republic, Skoda has continued to grow its sales, last year its sales were CZK204 billion and it made a respectable profit of CZK28 billion.

The growth has been driven by exports. Ten years ago around 30 per cent of Skodas were sold abroad; now around 80 per cent are exported. Skoda has factories and assembly plants in Russia, Poland, India and China and sells its cars across the globe. Its controlled expansion into western Europe has continued apace, especially into Germany, the firm's biggest Western market.

Volkswagen's presence in central Europe has had three advantages. First, it increased Volkswagen's leadership in Europe through the conquest of local central European markets. Second, it increased competitiveness through local manufacturing and purchases. Third, it has allowed them the possibility of using Skoda to penetrate other markets in Europe, China, India, Russia and South East Asia.

QUESTION *Evaluate the reasons for Skoda's success*

The main provisions of the NAFTA agreement aimed to:

- Eliminate tariffs on manufactured goods.
- Eliminate tariffs on 57 per cent of the agricultural produce from Mexico.
- Harmonise and streamline customs procedures and bureaucracy.
- Liberalise telecommunications, transport, textiles, banking and finance.
- Establish a NAFTA trade commission to settle trade disputes.

The attractive feature of NAFTA is that by virtue of the fact that Mexico is at a different stage of economic development from the US and Canada, the gains through specialisation have been relatively large, allowing the US to specialise in more complex products that are intensive in their use of knowledge, technology and capital equipment.

The available evidence suggests that this is precisely what has happened. US exports to Mexico of electronic goods, transport equipment and services have increased substantially. Meanwhile, most of the anecdotal evidence about US workers harmed by NAFTA comes from light manufacturing industries and agriculture.

However, it must be said that the scale of change induced by NAFTA is probably quite small relative to other factors impinging on the US economy over the last decade, such as technological change and reductions in defence spending.

For many, the creation of NAFTA was a US response to the formation of the single market in Europe. However, for others it has signalled the era of the drive

ILLUSTRATION 2.4

The Irish gem

In just 10 years, Ireland has become an owner of foreign wealth on a scale that some other countries took decades to acquire. The economy has been growing at around 7 per cent a year in real terms, or more than 10 per cent in money terms. It is now four times the size it was in 1993, having gone from annual GNP of € 38bn to € 150bn.

PHOTO CREDIT: RUSS MERNE/ALAMY

An important part of this growth has been its development as an international financial services centre. The list of international companies now operating from the Republic of Ireland reads like a 'who's who' of the international financial services market. AIG, ABN AMRO, Citigroup, Commerzbank, Depfa Bank, Hartford Life, JP Morgan Chase, ING, MBNA, Merrill Lynch, State Street and Unicredito are just a few of the big names that have been attracted there, making it a microcosm of New York and London. These companies cite the tight regulatory landscape and the availability of a highly skilled educated workforce as their key criteria for including Ireland as a location in their global operations. In the early days companies were attracted by a cheap and plentiful labour force; the industry today is characterised by highly technical and streamlined operations.

In Ireland there are now 450 international financial services companies offering cross-border services from Ireland, employing in excess of 25 000 people and making a significant contribution to the Irish economy. International financial services account for more than one third of Irish exports and large proportion of the country's net trade surplus.

QUESTION *What do you think are the reasons for Ireland's change in fortunes?*

SOURCE: ADAPTED FROM *IRISH INDEPENDENT* 22 FEBRUARY, 2007 & THE *FINANCIAL TIMES* 24 AUGUST 2006

by the US to create a free trade area across Americas. The Free Trade Area of the Americas (FTAA) is a proposed agreement to eliminate or reduce trade barriers among all nations in the American continents (except Cuba) and involves negotiations with the Central American Common Market, the Andean Community and Mercosur. However, there is opposition and Venezuela, Bolivia, Ecuador and Nicaragua have formed the Bolivarian Alternative for the Americas in opposition to the FTAA.

Discussions have also faltered over similar issues to those in the Doha round of World Trade Organisation talks. The USA and Canada endeavouring to expand trade in services and increased intellectual property rights, while the central and South American nations are seeking to end the trade distorting agricultural subsidies in the USA. Brazil has taken a leadership role among the South American nations.

Mercosur

Mercosur is the customs union linking Argentina, Brazil, Paraguay, Uruguay and Venezuela. The associate members of Bolivia, Chile, Columbia, Equador and Peru have a free trade agreement with Mercosur. This South American southern cone is the fourth largest integrated market in the world and consists of 300 million people with a combined GNP of over US$1 trillion. Geographically Mercosur is four times the size of the European Union.

The creation of Mercosur was seen as an integral part of the formula across South America to conquer inflation, expand the size of its markets and attract substantial foreign direct investment, and this has, on the whole, been successful.

As a result Mercosur itself has developed and formed its own supra Mercosur institutions which include the policy-making Common Market Council and the Common Market Group. These implement policies and monitor compliance with the council's decisions. A Mercosur parliament was inaugurated in 2006 but has advisory powers only. Its 90 members are drawn from member countries' national parliaments.

However, whilst the Customs Union has laudable and shared aims it has been riven by disputes among its members. As Brazil's car industry has become increasingly competitive, Argentina responded by imposing tariffs on Brazilian steel imports. Argentina and the union's smallest country, Uruguay, clashed over plans to build two large pulp mills along the border – the biggest foreign investments Uruguay had ever attracted. Argentina said it feared pollution and the impact on tourism and fishing. The matter went to the International Court of Justice (ICJ), which ruled in favour of Uruguay, but Argentina pledged to continue its fight against the mills.

The bloc's smaller members, Paraguay and Uruguay, complain of restricted access to markets in Argentina and Brazil and have sought to set up bilateral trade deals outside Mercosur, which the rules are supposed to forbid.

The other fear is that Mercosur is becoming politicised and moving away from its free-trade origins. Talks to secure a trade accord with the EU have stalled, with farm subsidies and tariffs on industrial goods being among the stumbling blocks. Negotiations on a planned FTAA have stalled as a result of some Mercosur leaders rejecting US ambitions for a free trade area across the whole of the Americas.

As trade barriers have fallen, especially in intra-regional trade, many multinationals have tried to bring the Mercosur countries into their worldwide strategy. For example, as part of its drive to dominate the global ice-cream industry Unilever bought Kibon, Brazil's largest ice-cream maker. However, besides the challenges described above, these companies have found there are three strategic issues they have had to face when trying to build a presence in the Mercosur markets:

■ *Infrastructural weaknesses*: although the region has achieved remarkable growth in internal trade in the past few years, its infrastructure has to be substantially improved to facilitate a more competitive flow of materials, machinery and goods. This will allow corporations to develop fully integrated regional strategies. As things stand, the inefficient infrastructure hampers companies' efforts to achieve the economies of scale needed for regional competitiveness.

■ *The need to develop industrial 'clusters'*: a nation's successful industries are usually linked through clusters of vertical and horizontal relationships. The vehicle assembly industry based in São Paulo, which has been successful for decades, illustrates how clustering of related businesses (glass, rubber, pistons and steel) is a driving force behind an industry's competitiveness. Such clusters should increase the opportunities for small and medium-sized companies – not just the big corporations – to profit from the process of regional economic integration.

■ *The business mindset*: a major obstacle to development is the business culture amongst traditional entrepreneurs. A mindset based on paternalism, centralisation of authority and casual opportunism can pose problems for carrying out business in such countries.

The development of the Southern American markets is essential if the economies of the region are to compete effectively in a much larger area – as will happen if the FTAA becomes a reality. Mercosur, the Andean Pact and other trade agreements in the region are the building blocks of potential new structures to come.

Companies in the area are becoming familiar with the complexities of the new business landscape and trying to increase their cross-border capabilities. Whether they will flourish in the larger, more integrated, global economy that will be the competitive playing ground if the USA succeeds in its aspirations for the FTAA is yet to be seen.

THE ASIAN PACIFIC TRADING REGION
Asia Pacific Economic Cooperation

The Asia Pacific Economic Cooperation (APEC) is essentially a forum amongst 21 countries who border on the Pacific. Thus it includes the NAFTA countries, Russia, China, Japan as well as the founding father Australia, New Zealand, ASEAN nations and Peru and Chile in South America. As such APEC is home to to more than 2.6 billion people and represents approximately 56 per cent of world GDP and 49 per cent of world trade.

At its inception the aim was to provide a forum to discuss ways and means to build economic and trade cooperation. Now, however, they are more ambitious and have clear objectives in three areas: (1) to develop and strengthen the multilateral trading system across APEC; (2) to increase the interdependence and prosperity of member economies; and (3) to promote sustainable economic growth in the region.

Some members of the group would like an Asia-Pacific trading bloc to emerge because they fear being excluded from traditional US markets. They now aim to reduce trade transaction costs by 10 per cent across APEC member economies by 2010. The objective is that free and open trade will be achieved by industrialised economies no later than 2010, and by developing economies no later than 2020, but this is a voluntary commitment, based on 'good faith and a pledge of best endeavour'.

Combining FTAA, East Asian and Australasian countries into one Asia-Pacific bloc would mean that nearly 70 per cent of their trade would be intra-regional. However, there is marked resistance amongst Asian members of APEC to an enhanced role of the group. The US is giving a high priority to the APEC grouping and intends to forge closer trade and investment ties across the Pacific.

The Asia Pacific region has the fastest growth in the world. Asia is the principal export region for US products. Transpacific trade is 50 per cent greater than its transatlantic trade and more than 40 per cent of US trade is now in the Asian region. To foster this growth, the United States supports a more active APEC. It is from this region too that a number of the new global brands are emerging, as discussed in Illustration 2.5.

ILLUSTRATION 2.5

The Asian blue chip tigers

According to Antoine van Agtmael, in his book 'The Emerging Markets Century, How a New Breed of World Class Companies is Overtaking the World' it is the rising Asian companies that will be the blue chips of the twenty-first century. He identifies 25 'innovative superstars' from emerging Asian economies who are developing at such a rate that they will soon dominate global markets and outsmart their Western rivals. These tigers are fighting across many sectors, steel, hi-tech gadgets, aircraft, cement and beer.

PHOTO CREDIT: IMAGEBROKER/ALAMY

Amongst them some are already well-known global brands such as Samsung, the South Korean electrical goods manufacturer with a market value of £46 billion and the global leader in memory chips and flat screens for computers and televisions. There is also Hon Hai from Taiwan, the computer and electronics manufacturer that makes products used in Nokia mobile phones, Sony Playstations and Dell computers. It is the world's largest contract-electronics maker and is now valued at £18 billion. Infosys from India is an IT services provider valued £15 billion and a leading player in global outsourcing. Embraer from Brazil, the world's fourth-largest aircraft maker, Lenovo and Tata steel are also seen as the blue chips of the future.

These companies have adopted a variety of strategies in their fight to develop a global brand. At one extreme, Samsung has built its brand from scratch; at the other, China's computer-maker Lenovo paid $1.5 billion to buy IBM's ailing PC business, partly because it wanted to gain control of the ThinkPad brand. Hon Hai made a name for itself producing components for the fledgling personal computer industry. Over the past two decades it has grown explosively, signing deals with IBM, Apple, Dell, Sony and Nokia. Others gained the strength to pull off big deals after gaining access to cheap funding. India's Tata Steel won a fierce auction to buy Corus, the Anglo-Dutch steel group, for £6.7 billion, beating off competition from Brazil's CSN.

Commentators suggest that in 20 years' time there are likely to be between 300 and 400 emerging-market companies in the Fortune 500 list of the world's biggest firms, compared with the present 58.

QUESTION *Evaluate the environmental factors that are fuelling the growth of these emerging market super brands.*

SOURCE: ADAPTED FROM SUNDAY TIMES 11 FEBRUARY, 2007, AGTMAEL, A., AND (2007) THE EMERGING MARKET CENTURY, SIMON & SCHUSTER

The ASEAN Free Trade Area

The members of the Association of South East Asian Nations (ASEAN) – Thailand, Indonesia, Singapore, Brunei, Malaysia and the Philippines, Vietnam, Myanmar, Cambodia and Laos – plan to complete the formation of the ASEAN free trade zone (AFTA) by 2015.

ASEAN is already well on the way to creating a largely tariff-free market of 550 million people, nearly one-tenth of the global population. The goal is to increase 'the region's competitive advantage as a production base geared for the world market'. The primary mechanism for achieving this is the Common Effective Preferential Tariff (CEPT) scheme, which established a schedule for phased tariff reductions to a rate between 0–5 per cent. Total trade of the AFTA members is now US$800 billion and they have a combined GDP of US$900 billion.

However, some observers are sceptical about the potential development of AFTA. Geographical distances and cultural and political disparities have meant that previous attempts at closer economic integration have failed. These nations are keenly competitive and some members have not kept to agreements to lower trading restrictions. ASEAN has also failed to support action against its rogue state of Myanmar, thus making many doubt the political will of the group. Nevertheless, the ASEAN economies are trying to pull closer together and their objective is to form an Asian Economic Region by 2020. Where EU and NAFTA integration has been based on treaties, in Asia so far it has been based on market forces, the chief of these being the region's fast rate of growth. By the year 2010, Asia should account for about a third of world production. Increasingly growth is also coming from intra-Asian trade, which recent estimates have put as high as 45 per cent. Whilst its good intentions are evident, ASEAN has still a long way to go in achieving its objective and the way this progresses may be critical to its competitive position in world markets. United they could be a powerful force to be reckoned with – divided they could be left well behind the developing Asian power houses of China and India.

BARRIERS TO DEVELOPING A COHESIVE TRADING REGION

Whilst an Asian trading bloc may never have the cohesion of either Europe or America, as the fastest-growing economic region in the world any move towards integration will be watched closely by international competitors. There are particular barriers to developing a liberalised Asian trading bloc. First, there is a huge diversity amongst the nation states, not just culturally but in historical, religious, and economic terms. Japan currently has a GDP per capita of US$23 400, Myanmar US$1 200. Politically, the countries embrace very different systems. Vietnam and Laos have communist dictatorships, Myanmar and Thailand have military juntas and Brunei is an absolute monarchy. What democratic structures there are in many of these markets fall short of European standards, e.g. in Indonesia. In a number of countries the institutions are either non-existent or too weak to ensure the economic fairness necessary to sustain the progress to regulation of markets and trust in the rule of law which is crucial to any commercial relationship. Furthermore, the geographical area is huge and there are no natural groupings of nation states. There is also uncertainty as to the role China and India will play in this region over the next decade.

CHINA

In the past decade the centre of gravity and dynamism of the Asia Pacific economy has been China and perhaps will continue to be in the decade ahead. This is a prediction that could conceivably fall flat if political conditions change. The past decade has seen a phenomenal rate of growth in China itself. China's GDP is estimated to be around US$2.3 trillion and it has a current growth rate of 9.4 per cent. Measured on a purchasing power parity (PPP) basis, in 2006 China stood as the second-largest economy in the world after the US, although in per capita terms the country is still lower middle-income and 130 million Chinese fall below international poverty lines. According to a study by China's Academy of Social Science (CASS), by 2030 it will have become the world's largest economy, surpassing even the US. Some Western studies have even estimated that China's economy will have achieved top spot a decade earlier than this. Five years ago China was not in the top ten of world exports, but it is now number three, only just behind the world economic power houses of the USA and Germany. The fact that imports and exports account for 70 per cent of its GDP gives an indication of its openness to trade and investment with the rest of the world. Chinese companies themselves are becoming much larger and the country's 500 largest companies now account for more than three-quarters of its gross domestic product.

The World Bank report *China 2020* estimates that China will achieve an annual growth rate of 6.5 per cent for the next 20 years. In 2001 China became a member of the World Trade Organisation and is now becoming increasingly integrated into the global economy and more open to Western companies. As part of the agreement to its accession to the WTO it agreed to eliminate over 70 non-tariff barriers and reduce the average tariff on goods from 17 per cent to 10 per cent.

In the past year some major contracts have been won by Western companies in the Chinese market. Alstom has two contracts for more than 350 million euros with the Chinese Ministry of Railways for the manufacture of electric freight locomotives and the electrification of a high speed line. Motorola has a US$400 million contract to build a high-speed communications network and Lucent Technologies have been contracted to supply US$427 million of network equipment. However, it is the potential market for automotives in China, set to grow at a rate of 15 per cent per annum, which is attracting most international interest. Volkswagen is reported to be investing 3 billion euro in the coming years to try and achieve a market share of 20 per cent.

Overall levels of direct investment in China remain strong. In 2006 it attracted a record US$63 billion foreign direct investment, surpassing the US to become the world's premier destination for investment flows as companies become increasingly attracted by cheap labour, robust economic growth and market deregulation: 70 per cent of foreign direct invesment goes to manufacturing. Companies that have succeeded in China include Diageo, Johnson and Johnson, Siemens, Hewlett Packard, Microsoft, Motorola and Volkswagen. Over 100 R and D centres have been established in China by leading multinationals, a clear indication that foreign direct investors are not simply interested in China as a low-cost base.

It should come as no surprise, however, that companies have faced severe difficulties in establishing themselves in China: some car manufacturers especially have suffered huge losses. The main problems they have faced centre around Chinese bureaucrats pushing for over-capacity, inconsistent regulations, red tape leading to significant increases in costs, insufficient protection of intellectual property, illegal business practices, debt collection and government taxation policies.

Finally, whilst all this investment has helped China to achieve rapid economic development, it has been spread unevenly across the country (see Dilemma 2.1). For example, the southern coastal regions of China, typified by Guangzhou Province, have grown out of all recognition compared with the rural regions.

DILEMMA 2.1

Knitted pullovers threaten the US and EU

Zhuyangxi, in China's heartland, is a typical rural township where most people earn less than US$500 annually. The closure of unprofitable state companies dealt a bitter blow and left many unemployed.

However, despite decades of political control aimed at sapping any entrepreneurial spirit, the ladies of Zhuyangxi township joined a burgeoning knitting cottage industry, producing colourful chunky pullovers for the European and American markets via Chunkichill, a British online company.

As global textile quotas were abolished on 1 January 2005, the founder Tim Wilson believed that the community could use their skills to generate much needed income and help his company profit from developing a niche market.

However, Brussels and Washington were soon taken aback by a huge surge in textile exports from China in 2006 and reintroduced the quotas on a whole host of Chinese garments – including knitted pullovers.

Now the only possible way for Chunkichill to export is via a third country and then to rework and re-export to Europe and the US.

To Brussels and Washington China is one vast entity – so it doesn't matter if the garments they view as a threat to their own industries come from a big factory near the coast or from the poor in the countryside.

QUESTION *How can such matters be resolved? Should the Zhuyangxi chunky pullovers, knitted by laid-off workers, be viewed as part of a much wider threat to Western manufacturing?*

SOURCE: ADAPTED FROM BBC NEWS: 19 DECEMBER 2006

SUMMARY

■ In this chapter we have discussed the major developments in international trade. The world economy consists of over 194 nations with a population of 6.6 billion and an output (GDP) totalling US$62 trillion (ppp), last year global GDP grew by 3.9 per cent. International trade in merchandise totals US$10.5 trillion and trade in services is currently estimated by the WTO to be about US$2.4 trillion.

■ In the last 50 years multilateral trade has flourished and a number of institutions have been developed to foster international trade. The World Bank, the IMF and the WTO all play important roles in ensuring a multilateral and fair international trading environment. It is important for the reader to have an understanding of how they may impact on the international marketing strategy of a company.

■ The major trading regions around the globe are at different stages and their continuing development has been discussed. The creation of the EU and the formation of the Economic and Monetary Union (EMU) have changed the competitive landscape across the globe radically. Other areas are now formally developing as trading regions with free trade areas emerging in Asia, the Pacific and the Americas. Some commentators believe this is moving world trade to a more regionally focused trading pattern.

■ In recent years there have been substantive changes in the global competitive structures as emerging markets strengthen their economic foundations and regional trading areas become more cohesive. The BRIC economies, Brazil, Russia, India and China are viewed as the star performers in emerging economies.

■ The centre of gravity and dynamism of the Asia Pacific economy in the past decade has been China. China is developing the potential to dwarf most countries as it continues its rapid development and speedy economic growth. Commentators are interested to see whether it is China or India that will dominate the global trading structures of the twenty-first century.

KEYWORDS

Asian Free Trade Area	Economic and Monetary Union	Mercosur
Association of South East Asian Nations	Exchange Rate Mechanism	Non-tariff barriers
	Free Trade Area of the Americas	Single European Market
Balance of payments	Hard currency	Tariff
Comparative advantage	International Development Association	Trade deficit
Copenhagen criteria	International Monetary Fund	Trading blocs
Doha Round	International product life cycle	World Bank

CASE STUDY

Should governments support domestic companies investing in foreign markets?

As well as trying to protect domestic markets, governments try to help domestic companies export to international markets. They regard this as important because companies that trade successfully on international markets tend to be more profitable and innovative. This in turn means that they generate more wealth, employ more people and pay more tax to their governments.

The UK provides support to businesses trying to trade overseas through an organisation called UK Trade and Investment (UKTI) which has offices in the UK and in embassies and Consular Offices throughout the world.

Until recently support has focused on providing subsidies to travel overseas and to attend overseas trade fairs. The staff based in UKTI offices around the world carry out market research on behalf of UK companies to identify whether there is demand in the foreign market and to provide lists of contacts, possible agents etc. They also help open doors for companies, particularly to senior politicians and senior managers in the markets being investigated.

With the advent of cheap travel, the significant amounts of information available on the internet and a rapid increase in consultants providing specialist support overseas, the focus of the support of UKTI has shifted to working with companies to build knowledge and skills so they are able to be more professional in their approach to international business and reduce the risk of costly mistakes, such as:

■ A firework company in the UK won a major contract in Hong Kong. The company employed 13 staff all year and a few more at the peak sales period just prior to the British Guy Fawkes night on 5 November where traditionally there are a lot of firework displays. The Hong Kong contract was their first overseas sale and required a major up front investment in materials by the company to fulfil the order. Rather than arrange payment in advance or ensure they got paid on delivery, they dispatched the fireworks and simply waited for the money to arrive. When it didn't they ran out of cash and were closed by the bank.

■ A major PLC was used to Letters of Credit (a way of ensuring prompt payment) taking 9 months to be paid. A chance conversation between the Finance Director and a bank manager led them to train the staff and reduce the payment to 1 month. They had £14 million in outstanding letters of credit – just think how much extra cash they now have.

■ A sausage manufacturer sent a large consignment of sausages to the USA. Sadly they hadn't received approval from the US Food and Drink Administration which controls food quality in the USA. They had to pay to have the sausages quarantined and returned.

These kind of things happen every week, all of them hugely costly to the companies and entirely avoidable.

The role of the government support agencies is therefore primarily to ensure that companies reduce *risk* in international business by being fully prepared.

Outward investment

Traditionally governments have primarily been concerned with helping companies reduce risk when trading overseas by learning the basics of international trading. The examples outlined above are problems which could be avoided with basic training. Of course once you understand the basics and you have put them into practice by trading with one country you can do the same in another.

Another very high-risk activity is when companies make investments overseas for the first time. However, public support agencies such as UKTI provide little support for this area of activity.

Investing overseas for the first time is often far more risky than trading overseas because companies are investing a lot of time and money in developing a business presence overseas, be that setting up a factory or opening an office. Whatever the proposal, they are looking at a cost of hundreds of thousands of pounds sterling, rather than the thousands a trading mistake may cost a company.

So why is so little support given by governments?

Before you read the rest of this section think about how stories of companies making foreign-based investments have been written in the newspapers of your home country. If you are in the UK it may well look like this:

400 jobs lost as mill moves production to Hungary

Just imagine how much worse it would be for the Government if the heading said:

Government helps firm make 400 jobless by helping mill move to Hungary

There is a justified concern in government circles that negative PR from providing support to companies to outwardly invest would be detrimental. This is despite the Prime Minister saying in a speech that all international business was good. Even shifting call centre jobs overseas was a good thing as the UK wanted to create well-paid high-value jobs not poorly paid ones.

Is the concern justified? Some companies have no option but to invest overseas in order to expand internationally and develop their business. Look at the list below. For the businesses listed what trading options do they have if they wish to develop their international business?

1	2	3	4
Night Club	University	Solicitor	Clothing manufacturer
Restaurant	Hairdresser	Consultant	Steel manufacturer
Shop	Fitness instructor	Builder	Food manufacturer

The answer is that all those in column 1 will probably need premises overseas. The ones in column 2 will at least need to have a visible marketing presence. Those in column 3 will probably have to employ staff overseas and so need offices. Only the businesses in column 4 have a number of options and could deliver their products from their domestic market.

The question is, how should government support agencies direct their support to domestic companies wishing to invest in foreign markets?

The answer is not straightforward. UK Trade and Investment published a route map to outward investment, a substantial guide to the process companies need to go through to successfully invest overseas. They decided, because of possible negative PR not to publicise it widely, but put it on the UKTI website as a compromise position.

There are four reasons why UKTI does not very openly support outward investment:

- Infrequency – whilst there are an increasing number of businesses investing overseas it is still a small percentage of total businesses
- Complexity – it may be difficult to offer much help beyond talking through the process with the company to ensure they have considered all the options fully
- Negative PR risk – as mentioned above
- Unfamiliarity – it is much easier to work with companies exporting products than companies like solicitors or universities selling their services.

QUESTIONS

1 Do you think UKTI and other similar government agencies should provide more support to companies investing in foreign markets?

2 How should the government support for exporting providing services vary from that provided to exporters of manufactured products?

3 How would you use the services provided by UKTI in developing a market entry plan? (hint: look at www.uktradeinvest.gov.uk)

SOURCE: MARK ROBSON, SHEFFIELD HALLAM UNIVERSITY

DISCUSSION QUESTIONS

1 Identify barriers to the free movement of goods and services. Explain how barriers influence the development of international trade.

2 What do you consider to be the macro forces impacting on the development of world trade? Show by examples how they are changing the nature of international business.

3 To what extent do you agree with the view that the open global market no longer exists but simply consists of closed trading regions within which trade now moves freely?

4 How has the emergence of China as a major global competitor impacted on global marketing?

5 Recent mega mergers in the pharmaceutical and media industry are becoming increasingly evident. What is the rationale behind such mergers and how will it lead to global competitive advantage?

References

Agtmael, A. (2007) *The emerging markets century*, Simon and Schuster.

Dicken, P. (2007) *Global shift – mapping the changing contours of the world economy*, 5th edn. Sage.

Griffin, R.W. and Pustay, M.W. (2005) *International business*, 4th edn. Pearson/Prentice Hall.

Porter, M.C. (1990) *The competitive advantage of nations*. Macmillan.

Vernon, R. and Wells, L.T. (1968) 'International trade and international investment in the product life cycle', *Quarterly Journal of Economics*, May.

World Bank, The '*China 2020: development challenges in the new century*', available at http://www.econ.worldbank.org.

Useful websites

http://www.economist.co

http://news.ft.com/home/uk/

http://www.imf.org

http://www.pwcglobal.com

http://www.oecd.org

http://www.un.org

http://www.worldbank.org/

CHAPTER 3

SOCIAL AND CULTURAL CONSIDERATIONS IN INTERNATIONAL MARKETING

INTRODUCTION

Markets in countries around the world are subject to many influences, as we saw in Chapter 1. Whilst it is possible to identify those influences common to many country markets, the real difficulty lies in understanding their specific nature and importance.

The development of successful international marketing strategies is based on a sound understanding of the similarities and differences that exist in the countries and cultures around the world. The sheer complexity of the market considerations that impinge on the analysis, strategic development and implementation of international marketing planning is a major challenge.

In this chapter we will examine the social and cultural issues in international marketing and the implications they have for strategy development.

LEARNING OBJECTIVES

After reading this chapter you should be able to:

■ Discuss and evaluate social and cultural factors impacting on an international marketing strategy

■ Understand the cross-cultural complexities of buying behaviour in different international markets

■ Assess the impact of social and cultural factors on the international marketing process

■ Carry out a cross-cultural analysis of specified international markets

SOCIAL AND CULTURAL FACTORS

Social and cultural factors influence all aspects of consumer and buyer behaviour, and the variation between these factors in different parts of the world can be a central consideration in developing and implementing international marketing strategies. Social and cultural forces are often linked together. Whilst meaningful distinctions between social and cultural factors can be made, in many ways the two interact and the distinction between the various factors is not clear-cut. Differences in language can alter the intended meaning of a promotional campaign and differences in the way a culture organises itself socially may affect the way a product is positioned in the market and the benefits a consumer may seek from that product. A sewing machine in one culture may be seen as a useful hobby: in another it may be necessary to the survival of a family.

Kotler and Keller (2005) included such things as reference groups, family, roles and status within social factors. Whilst this is a useful distinction from the broader forces of culture, social class and social factors are clearly influenced by cultural factors. Take the example of the family, which is an important medium of transmitting cultural values. Children learn about their society and imbibe its culture through many means but the family influence is strong, particularly during the early formative years of a child's life. Furthermore, the way in which family life is arranged varies considerably from one culture to another. In some cultures the family is a large extended group encompassing several generations and including aunts and uncles, whilst in other cultures the family is limited more precisely to the immediate family of procreation, and even then the unit might not be permanent and the father and mother of the children might not remain together for the entirety of the child-rearing process. Thus social and cultural influences intertwine and have a great impact on the personal and psychological processes in the consumer and buyer behaviour processes and, as such, play an integral part in the understanding of the consumer in international markets. Toys R Us found quite distinct differences in the type of toys demanded in their various international markets. Whereas the US children preferred TV- and movie-endorsed products, Japanese children demanded electronic toys, South East Asian children wanted educational toys, and the more conservative cultures of the European markets expected a choice of traditional toys.

It is not feasible to examine all the social or cultural influences on consumer and buyer behaviour in one chapter, neither is it possible to describe all the differences between cultures across the world. In the first section we will highlight the more important sociocultural influences which are relevant to buyer behaviour in international markets. In the following section we will focus on developing an understanding of the components of culture and its impact on consumer behaviour and the implications for international marketing strategies. We will then discuss the methodologies which can be used to carry out cross-cultural analyses to enable comparisons to be made across cultures, and finally we will examine business-to-business marketing and the impact of culture in these types of markets.

WHAT IS CULTURE?

Perhaps the most widely accepted definition of culture is that of Ralph Linton (1945): 'A culture is the configuration of learned behaviour and results of behaviour whose component elements are shared and transmitted by members of a particular society.' Or perhaps, more appropriately: 'The way we do things around here.' In relation to international marketing, culture can be defined as: 'The sum total of learned beliefs, values and customs that serve to direct consumer behaviour in a particular country market.'

Thus culture is made up of three essential components:

Beliefs: A large number of mental and verbal processes which reflect our knowledge and assessment of products and services.

Values: The indicators consumers use to serve as guides for what is appropriate behaviour. They tend to be relatively enduring and stable over time and widely accepted by members of a particular market.

Customs: Overt modes of behaviour that constitute culturally approved or acceptable ways of behaving in specific situations. Customs are evident at major events in one's life, e.g. birth, marriage, death and at key events in the year e.g. Christmas, Easter, Ramadan, etc.

Such components as values, beliefs and customs are often ingrained in a society, and many of us only fully realise what is special about our own culture – its beliefs, values and customs – when we come into contact with other cultures. This is what happens to firms when they expand internationally and build up a market presence in foreign markets: often the problems they face are a result of their mistaken assumption that foreign markets will be similar to their home market and that they can operate overseas as they do at home. Frequently in international markets the toughest competition a firm may face is not another supplier but the different customs or beliefs as a result of cultural differences. This means that for a company to succeed in that market they often have to change ingrained attitudes about the way they do business. The beliefs and values of a culture satisfy a need within that society for order, direction and guidance. Thus culture sets the standards shared by significant portions of that society, which in turn sets the rules for operating in that market.

Hofstede (2003) identifies a number of layers within a national culture.

Layers of culture

- A national level according to one's country which determines our basic cultural assumptions.
- A regional/ethnic/religious/linguistic affiliation level determining basic cultural beliefs.
- A gender level according to whether a person was born as a girl or as a boy.
- A generation level which separates grandparents, parents and children.
- A social class level associated with educational opportunities, a person's occupation or profession.

All of these determine attitudes and values and everyday behavioural standards in individuals and organisations.

Given such complexities, market analysts have often used the 'country' as a surrogate for 'culture'. Moreover, culture is not something granted only to citizens of a country or something we are born with, it is something we learn as we grow in our environment. Similar environments provide similar experiences and opportunities and hence tend to shape similar behaviours.

Sarathy *et al.* (2006) identify eight components of culture which form a convenient framework for examining a culture from a marketing perspective (see Figure 3.1).

The components of culture

EDUCATION

The level of formal primary and secondary education in a foreign market will have a direct impact upon the sophistication of the target customers. A simple example will be the degree of literacy. The labelling of products, especially those with possibly hazardous side-effects, needs to be taken seriously for a market that has a very low literacy rate. The UK company ICI markets pesticides throughout the world: in developed countries its main form of communication is advertising and printed matter. In developing countries they rely heavily on training and verbally based educational programmes to get their message across.

SOCIAL ORGANISATION

This relates to the way in which a society organises itself. How the culture considers kinship, social institutions, interest groups and status systems. The role of women and caste systems are easily identifiable examples – if the firm has a history of successfully marketing to 'the housewife/homemaker', life is more difficult in a culture where women have no social status at all. House ownership is another example. In Switzerland the majority of people rent rather than own their houses and expect to rent property with domestic appliances already installed, which means the banks, not individual families, are the largest purchasers of washing machines.

TECHNOLOGY AND MATERIAL CULTURE

This aspect relates not to materialism but to the local market's ability to handle and deal with modern technology. Some cultures find the idea of leaving freezers plugged in overnight, or servicing cars and trucks that have not yet broken down difficult to understand. In instances such as these the organisation is often faced with the choice of either educating the population (expensive and time-consuming) or de-engineering the product or service (difficult if you have invested heavily in product development).

FIGURE 3.1
A cultural framework

SOURCE: ADAPTED FROM SARATHY *ET AL.* (2006)

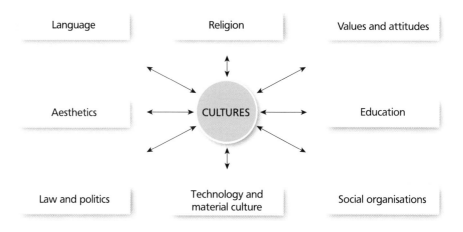

LAW AND POLITICS

The legal and political environments in a foreign market are usually regarded as consequences of the cultural traditions of that market. Legal and political systems are often a simple codification of the norms of behaviour deemed acceptable by the local culture. This aspect was dealt with in some detail in Chapter 1. **Cultural sensitivity** to political issues in international markets is of the utmost importance. Thus an advertisement for the Orange mobile phone network in Ireland with the strapline 'The future's bright, the future's orange', clearly did not have any awareness of political sensitivities in Northern Ireland.

AESTHETICS

This covers the local culture's perception of things such as beauty, good taste and design, and dictates what is acceptable or appealing to the local eye. A firm needs to ensure that use of colour, music, architecture or brand names in their product and communications strategies is sympathetic and acceptable to the local culture. For the unwary, there are many, many traps in this area. Pepsodent tried to sell its toothpaste in the far reaches of East Asia by emphasising that it 'whitens your teeth'. Unfortunately they did not realise there was a practice amongst local natives in some areas of chewing betel nuts to blacken their teeth to make them attractive. Colour can mean completely different things in different cultures and brand names sometimes do not travel well because of this, as we can see in Illustration 3.1.

VALUES AND ATTITUDES

The values consumers from different countries place on things such as time, achievement, work, wealth and risk-taking will seriously affect not only the

---

ILLUSTRATION 3.1

SOURCE: ANTHCNY GRIMES, UNIVERSITY OF HULL

Cadbury's: Lady Purple or Aunty Violet?

Like ourselves, colours may or may not be aesthetically pleasing but they all have a personality. When we look at a colour a whole spectrum of thoughts, feelings and emotions are evoked in our minds. Some of these associations are instinctive in us all, others we learn from the environment in which we live. From the passionate excitement of red to the playful happiness of yellow, colours are constantly eliciting subconscious responses in us.

For international marketers this notion is particularly pertinent. In our efforts to cue the customer into positioning our brand in a certain way, the colours used in the design, packaging and advertising of a product can send very powerful messages about the personality of our brand. However, as the meaning of colour is often derived from the cultural environment, the messages and thus the personality may fluctuate greatly across countries and cultures.

In a recent study, the Cadbury's brand was perceived very differently by UK and Taiwanese participants. Whilst in the UK Cadbury's was seen to be luxurious, stylish, expensive, classy and silkily feminine, the Taiwanese had an image of an old, warm, friendly, but essentially poor brand, low in quality and lacking in class.

In the same study, participants from the two countries were asked to discuss their perceptions of the colour purple – a colour that Cadbury's is currently attempting to register as a trademark.

Once again, the British made associations with luxury, style, sophistication, youth and femininity. The Taiwanese, on the other hand, talked of a warm, old, quiet colour, serious, a little sad but dignified. In both cultures, all the feelings, emotions and characteristics associated with the colour purple had been transferred to give very different meaning to the Cadbury's brand.

When taking colour abroad, therefore, marketers may do well to heed some of mother's most motherly advice, 'Looks aren't everything. It's the personality that counts!'

QUESTION *How can marketers ensure they understand such cultural sensitivities when entering new markets?*

products offered but also the packaging and communication activities. The methods used by a firm to motivate its personnel are also strongly influenced by the local culture and practice. Encouraging local sales forces to sell more by offering cars and more money, for example, may not work in all cultures. Values are important to marketers as they can be translated into consumption vehicles, as illustrated in Table 3.1.

RELIGION

Religion is a major cultural variable and has significant if not always apparent effects on marketing strategy. For example, the identification of sacred objects and philosophical systems, beliefs and norms as well as taboos, holidays and rituals is critical for an understanding of a foreign market. Religion, for example, will affect the food that people eat and when they eat it as well as their attitudes to a whole range of products from deodorants to alcoholic drink.

In some countries religion is the most dominant cultural force. For instance, in Islamic markets such as Saudi Arabia, no violation of religion by advertising and other promotional practices, no matter how insignificant, will go unnoticed or unpunished either by the government or the consumer. This can cause problems for advertisers. Shaving advertisements cannot be shown if the male actor shows too much of his chest. Likewise, in certain Gulf states, an advertisement where someone uses their left hand to handle food could upset local sensibilities. Major violations of religion are sometimes punished in more liberal and so-called secular markets within the Islamic world. Rules surrounding religious laws require

TABLE 3.1 Cultural values and their relevance to consumer behaviour

Value	General features	Relevance to consumer behaviour
Achievement and success	Hard work is good; success flows from hard work	Acts as a justification for acquisition of goods ('You deserve it')
Efficiency and practicality	Admiration of things that solve problems (e.g. save time and effort)	Stimulates purchase of products that function well and save time
Progress	People can improve themselves; tomorrow should be better than today	Stimulates desire for new products that fulfil unsatisfied needs; ready acceptance of products that claim to be 'new' or 'improved'
Material comfort	'The good life'	Fosters acceptance of convenience and luxury products that make life more comfortable and enjoyable
Individualism	Being oneself (e.g. self-reliance, self-interest, self-esteem)	Stimulates acceptance of customised or unique products that enable a person to 'express his or her own personality'
External conformity	Uniformity of observable behaviour, desire for acceptance	Stimulates interest in products that are used or owned by others in the same peer group
Youthfulness	A state of mind that stresses being young at heart and a youthful appearance	Stimulates acceptance of products that provide the illusion of maintaining or fostering youthfulness

SOURCE: SCHIFFMAN, L.G. AND KANUK, L.L. CONSUMER BEHAVIOUR, 9TH EDN, © 2007, P. 416 ADAPTED BY PERMISSION OF PEARSON EDUCATION, INC., UPPER SADDLE RIVER, NJ

heightened insight and empathy by international companies. Comparative ads are banned as, according to the laws of Islam, pegging one product against another diminishes the sense of unity and social community. Companies need to understand the difference between two key terms, *Haraam* and *Makruh*.

Haraam are subjects or things that are absolutely unlawful and strongly prohibited in Islam, such as alcohol and cheating. These taboo subjects are banned in advertising and other promotional activities in countries such as Saudi Arabia, Kuwait and Iran. *Makruh* are subjects which are seen as distasteful: they are discouraged in Islam but are not banned. Smoking is not forbidden in Islam but it is highly discouraged.

LANGUAGE

Language can be divided into two major elements: the spoken language of vocal sounds in patterns that have meaning, and silent language, which is the communication through body language, silences and social distance. This is less obvious but is a powerful communication tool. To many commentators language interlinks all the components of culture and is the key to understanding and gaining empathy with a different culture. In the following section we will examine the different components of language.

Language and culture

SPOKEN LANGUAGE

Spoken language is an important means of communication. In various forms, for example plays and poetry, the written word is regarded as part of the culture of a group of people. In the spoken form the actual words spoken and the ways in which the words are pronounced provide clues to the receiver about the type of person who is speaking.

Chinese is spoken as the mother tongue (or first language) by three times more people than the next largest language, English. However, Chinese is overtaken by English when official language population numbers are taken into account. However, the official language is not always spoken by the whole population of a country. For example, French is an official language in Canada but many Canadians have little or no fluency in French. English is often but by no means always the common language between business people of different nationalities.

Speaking or writing in another language can be a risky activity (see Illustration 3.2). In advertising, particular attention needs to be paid when translating from one language to another. The creative use of copy to gain attention and to influence comprehension of the target audience can result in a clever use of words. However, inadequate translation often results in clumsy errors. In Germany a General Motors advertisement mentioned a 'body by Fischer' which became 'corpse by Fischer'. This is clearly a straightforward translation error, directly resulting from the mistranslating of the word 'body'. The Hertz company strapline, 'Let Hertz put you in the driving seat', became 'Let Hertz make you a chauffeur'. Instead of communicating liberation and action as intended, this translation provided an entirely different meaning, implying a change of occupation and status. In India an advertisement for the milky drink Horlicks was translated into Tamil as 'twenty men asleep under the tree'.

LANGUAGE IN WEB MARKETING

The choice of language to use for a company website is also problematic for companies operating across many borders. Should it be multilingual, thus incurring greater costs in ensuring its sustainability, or should it be in one language? Surprisingly, whilst English is a widely spoken language throughout the world, it is only the first language of 6 per cent of the world's population, yet 96 per cent of all e-business sites are written in English.

Managers have previously assumed that English is the international language of the Internet. Whilst this was so in the early days, according to Forrester Research, web contact time is doubled on sites localised for language and culture. Japanese businessmen, for example, are three times more likely to conduct an online transaction when addressed in Japanese. The US consultancy Global Reach estimates that for every US$2 million a US site generates from domestic sales, another US$1 million is lost when non-Americans do not easily understand the website.

Obviously a preferred solution for many companies is to build the web capability to offer a multilingual website, localised to the language and cultural sensitivities of the market, as discussed in Illustration 3.3.

SILENT LANGUAGE

Silent language is a powerful means of communication and the importance of **non-verbal communication** is greater in some countries than others. In these cultures people are more sensitive to a variety of different message systems. Table 3.2 describes some of the main silent languages in overseas business.

Silent languages are particularly important in sales negotiations and other forms of business meetings. They will, in addition, influence internal communications in companies employing people from different countries and cultures.

Difficulties can arise even between cultures which are geographically close to each other but have different perceptions of language. The word *konzept* in German means a detailed plan, in French the word concept means an opportunity to discuss. Executives could meet with hugely varying expectations if a conceptual discussion was on the agenda.

ILLUSTRATION 3.2

Written language: but what does it mean?

In France the Toyota MR2, pronounced emm-er-deux, is written phonetically as merde.

The car maker AMC were confident Matador meant bullfighter, but when they launched the Matador in South America they found to their cost that it actually meant 'killer'.

Japanese hotel notice to hotel guests: 'You are invited to take advantage of the chambermaid.'

Acapulco hotel notice regarding drinking water: 'The manager has personally passed all the water served here.'

Visitors to a zoo in Budapest were asked 'Not to feed the animals. If you have any suitable food, give it to the guard on duty.'

A Bangkok dry cleaner to potential customers: 'Drop your trousers here for best results.'

A Roman laundry innocently suggested: 'Ladies leave your clothes here and spend the afternoon having a good time.'

A Hong Kong dentist claims to extract teeth 'By the latest Methodists.'

A Copenhagen airline office promises to 'Take your bags and send them in all directions.'

QUESTION *What unusual translations have you come across when reading international advertisements?*

PHOTO CREDIT: EDDIE GERALD/ALAMY

SOURCE: ADAPTED FROM BBC NEWS ONLINE AND THE *SUNDAY TIMES*

CULTURAL LEARNING

The process of enculturation, i.e. learning about their own culture by members of a society, can be through three types of mechanism: formally, through the family and the social institutions to which people belong, technically, through the educational processes, be it through schools or religious institutions, and informally, through peer groups, advertising and various other marketing-related vehicles.

This enculturation process influences consumer behaviour by providing the learning we use to shape the toolkit of labels, skills and styles from which

SOURCE: ADAPTED FROM BBC NEWS ONLINE, APRIL 2003

ILLUSTRATION 3.3

Localising Websites

Companies competing on international markets now realise that if they are going to maximise the value from their company websites they need the capability to localise the content to suit the language and cultural sensitivities of the markets they

PHOTO CREDIT: VARIO IMAGES GMBH & CO.KG/ALAMY

are targeting. Consultants called localisation outsourcers have been springing up in the USA and the UK to help companies do just this. Most use a combination of human translators and machine translation technologies to translate and edit text in a culturally sensitive way.

Localisation specialists claim they can help clients protect their brands by providing control over Web-based marketing strategies on a global basis. The concept: centralise the message, translate it, and colloquialise it. Outsourcers also examine design concerns, such as the cultural implications of colour – in many parts of Asia, for example, white is the colour death.

Further, localisation experts can point out legal and regulatory snares. In France, for instance, consumers enjoy a one-week grace period after they receive an online purchase. In Germany, comparative advertising is banned on the Web. In China, clients may become unnerved when they find out that encrypted Web sites are regulated by the Chinese government.

QUESTION *What are the dangers of standardising web pages across the globe?*

SOURCE: © 1987 BY EDWARD T. HALL AND MILDRED REED HALL

TABLE 3.2   The main silent languages in overseas business

Silent language	Implications for marketing and business
Time	Appointment scheduling. The importance of being 'on time'. The importance of deadlines.
Space	Sizes of offices. Conversational distance between people.
Things	The relevance of material possessions. The interest in the latest technology.
Friendship	The significance of trusted friends as a social insurance in times of stress and emergency.
Agreements	Rules of negotiations based on laws, moral practices or informal customs.

people construct strategies of action, e.g. persistent ways of going through the buying process.

The process of acculturation is the process international companies need to go through to obtain an understanding of another culture's beliefs, values and attitudes in order to gain an empathy with that market. As we have seen, culture is pervasive and complex and it is not always easy for someone outside a given culture to gain an empathy with that market.

Having examined the main components of culture and the various important dimensions, we will now look at how culture impacts on consumer behaviour.

CULTURE AND CONSUMER BEHAVIOUR

There are several important ways in which the various components of culture influence a consumer's perception, attitude and understanding of a given product or communication and so affect the way a consumer behaves in the buying process. Jeannet and Hennessey (2004) identify three major processes through which culture influences consumer behaviour as depicted in Figure 3.2.

Culture is seen as being embedded in elements of society such as religion, language, history and education (cultural forces). These elements send direct and indirect messages to consumers regarding the selection of goods and services (cultural message). The culture we live in determines the answers to such questions as: Do we drink coffee or juice at breakfast? Do we shop daily or on a weekly basis? and so affects the consumer decision process.

The body of theory on which our understanding of consumer behaviour is based predominantly hails from the USA. Usunier and Lee (2005) argue that the means by which international marketing managers understand consumer behaviour is flawed because the theoretical principles on which we base our understanding do not necessarily hold true across different cultures. There are some important assumptions which international marketers need to question when applying Western theroretical principles in order to understand consumer behaviour across international markets:

1 That Maslow's hierarchy of needs is consistent across cultures.
2 That the buying process in all countries is an individualistic activity.
3 That social institutions and local conventions are similar across cultures.
4 That the consumer buying process is consistent across cultures.

FIGURE 3.2
Cultural influences on buyer behaviour

SOURCE: ADAPTED FROM JEANNET
AND HENNESSEY (2004)

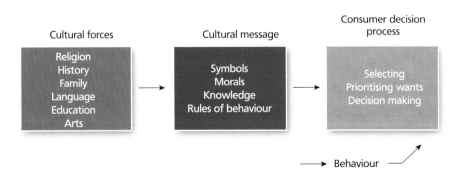

That Maslow's hierarchy of needs is consistent across cultures

Culture influences the hierarchy of needs (Maslow 1970) on two levels. First, the axiom that one need must be satisfied before the next appears is not true for every culture, and second, similar kinds of needs may be satisfied by different products and consumption types.

For example, in some less developed countries, a consumer may go without food in order to buy a refrigerator and, therefore, satisfy the dominant need of social status before physical satisfaction. A study identified that self-esteem needs were most important to Chinese consumers, and physiological needs the least important. Physiological needs include food, water, shelter, etc., self-esteem needs include prestige and success.

In building a presence in the Chinese market, companies would need to target consumers with high self-esteem needs by linking a product such as credit cards to success in business or beer to success in sporting activities.

Likewise, similar kinds of needs may be satisfied in very different ways. For example, to a Hindu the need for self-realisation does not necessarily imply material consumption, as in Western cultures, but in fact abandoning all worldly possessions.

That the buying process in all countries is an individualistic activity

Many Western buying behaviour models are primarily based on individual purchases with reference to family decision making in the context of husband and wife decisions. They assume buying decisions are focused on an individual's decision-making process. In Asia a family may be a complex structure and an individual would need to take into account all members of the family in making major purchase decisions, so the decision making is of a much more collectivist nature.

That social institutions and local conventions are similar across cultures

Institutions such as the state, the religious institutions, trade unions and the education system also influence consumer behaviour.

The UK company ROMPA, which serves the market for people with learning disabilities, found enormous cultural differences across their European market due to the varying influences the national institutions had on how charities and social institutions should be organised. In Germany the market was highly organised and strongly supported financially by the state. In Spain the state lottery was the prime benefactor through major national charities, whereas in Italy the church was the major benefactor, with very little involvement by the state.

That the consumer buying process is consistent across cultures

There are many inconsistencies in the buying processes across cultures around the globe. Three aspects which are particularly pertinent to our discussion are the differences in the level of consumer involvement, the perception of risk in a purchase and the cognitive processes of consumers.

Consumer involvement

The Chinese are seen as having a low level of involvement when purchases are for private consumption but a high level of involvement when they are buying products for their social or symbolic value. Since the Chinese greatly value social harmony and smoothness of relationships within the extended family, the social significance of products is highly important, be it to express status, gratitude, approval or even disapproval.

Perceived risk

The level of risk consumers associate with a purchase varies enormously across cultures, and as such it is an important variable in consumer behaviour. It will determine whether a consumer will go for the comfortable purchase or is willing to try new products and services. Risk incorporates three components: physical, financial and social risk.

Whereas in some countries, *physical risk* may be important (e.g. the fear of bird flu), others may be more sensitive to *social risk* and the loss of social status if a wrong buying decision is made (i.e. the Chinese fear of losing face). *Financial risk* closely relates to the level of economic development in a country. It is likely to be less in the more affluent economies where if a wrong purchase decision is made the financial hardship suffered may not be so profound.

The level of brand loyalty found in a market is also closely related to the perception of risk. There are huge variations in attitudes to brand loyalty across different cultures. In the US the standard buyer behaviour is that of disloyalty. A consumer will shift from one brand to another because it is standard behaviour to test several competitive products and so foster price competition. Thus in the US it is relatively easy for a new entrant to persuade Americans to try their product, but much harder to get them to keep buying it.

In other cultures, consumers are more fundamentally loyal, less brand-conscious and not so used to cross-product comparisons. In Australia and South East Asia buyers have a greater need for brand security, are less confident with regard to trying unknown products and so are less willing to take risks.

Cognitive style

Western consumer behaviour models assume a logical buying process with rational steps, including the formation of awareness, the searching for information, reviewing the information, evaluating alternatives and finally making a choice. Sometimes by attacking traditional cognitive styles advertisers have had surprising success, as in the case of Skoda.

Many authors argue that internationally there are many different models of the buying process. Asian consumers tend to have a quite different cognitive style to Western consumers. The Chinese as well as the Japanese have a more synthetic, concrete and contextual orientation in their thought patterns, as opposed to the Americans who tend to have a more analytical and abstract decision-making process. Thus culture not only impacts on how we behave as consumers but on the whole decision-making process. Advertisers and marketing managers need, as in the case of Skoda in Dilemma 3.1, to examine how they can exploit such nuances in building their global brands.

ANALYSING CULTURES AND THE IMPLICATIONS FOR CONSUMER BEHAVIOUR

As we have seen in previous sections, there are many social and cultural influences which determine our values, beliefs and customs and combine to form a cultural identity which in turn influences the process of decision making when buying products. All these aspects need to be examined to understand the consumer in any international market.

Blackwell *et al.* (2006) suggest the following steps should be undertaken when analysing consumer behaviour in international markets. They propose that if a company is to fully empathise with a culture they must pose a series of questions about buyer behaviour, culture and the suitability of various marketing communications approaches for that culture. These steps consist of:

- *Determine relevant motivations in the culture.* What needs are fulfilled with this product in the minds of members of the culture? How are these needs presently fulfilled? Do members of this culture readily recognise these needs?

- *Determine characteristic behaviour patterns.* What patterns are characteristic of purchasing behaviour? What forms of division of labour exist within the family structure? How frequently are products of this type purchased? Do any of these characteristic behaviours conflict with behaviour expected for this product? How strongly ingrained are the behaviour patterns that conflict with those needed for distribution of this product?

- *Determine what broad cultural values are relevant to this product.* Are there strong values about work, morality, religion, family relations and so on that relate to this product? Does this product denote attributes that are in conflict with these cultural values? Can conflicts with values be avoided by changing the product? Are there positive values in this culture with which the product might be identified?

- *Determine characteristic forms of decision making.* Do members of the culture display a studied approach to decisions concerning innovations, or an impulsive approach? What is the form of the decision process? Upon which information sources do members of the culture rely? Do members of the culture tend to be rigid or flexible in the acceptance of new ideas? What criteria do they use in evaluating alternatives?

DILEMMA 3.1

Skoda

Skoda, a subsidiary of Volkswagen, adopted a pan-European approach to building its brand profile in Europe. All advertising was developed centrally and concentrated on building the product profile. The new Skoda marketing manager questioned this approach, arguing that there was a failure in previous pan-European advertising campaigns to recognise that the brand meant something quite different in most Western European countries and, consequently, the campaigns were not connecting with the target audience. In the UK, for instance, Skoda had to put up with a fair amount of ridicule. Even having their cars endorsed by independent critics and being named Car of the Year did nothing to change the strong negative public perception of the brand. However, the European advertising budget for Skoda was very small compared to its main rivals and so economies of scale were a consideration.

QUESTION *How would you solve the dilemma?*

■ *Evaluate promotion methods appropriate to the culture.* What role does advertising occupy in the culture? What themes, words or illustrations are taboo? What language problems exist in present markets that cannot be translated into this culture? What types of sales staff are accepted by members of the culture? Are such sales staff available?

■ *Determine appropriate institutions for this product in the minds of consumers.* What types of retailers and intermediary institutions are available? What services do these institutions offer that are expected by the consumer? What alternatives are available for obtaining services needed for the product but not offered by existing institutions? How are various types of retailers regarded by consumers? Will changes in the distribution structure be readily accepted?

Self-reference criterion

As we have discussed, it is of crucial importance when examining foreign markets that the culture of the country is seen in the context of that country. It is better to regard the culture as different from, rather than better or worse than, the home culture. In this way, differences and similarities can be explored and the reasons for differences can be sought and explained. The differences approach avoids the evaluative and often superior approach based on one's own self-reference criterion.

'Self-reference criterion' (SRC) characterises our unconscious reference to our own cultural values when examining other cultures. Usunier and Lee (2005) suggests a four-step approach to eliminate SRC.

1 Define the problem or goal in terms of home country cultural traits, habits and norms.

2 Define the problems or goals in terms of the foreign culture, traits, habits and norms.

3 Isolate the SRC influence in the problem and examine it carefully to see how it complicates the problem.

4 Redefine the problem without the SRC influence and solve for the foreign market situation.

The process of enculturation to gain empathy with a foreign country market is not an easy one. It requires:

■ *Cultural empathy*: the ability to place yourself in the position of the buyer from another culture. In this way a strong attempt is made to understand the thinking approaches, the decision-making process and the interactions between this and the cultural and other forces influencing the buyer.

■ *Neutrality*: the ability to identify the differences that exist without making value judgements about 'better' or 'worse' cultures. Inevitably, self-reference will exist. If the focus is placed on differences rather than superiority, the chances of achieving accurate cross-cultural analysis are increased.

To ensure they achieve this, companies follow a number of policies. They may recruit foreign staff at their head office, collaborate with local firms when entering a new market or they may put managers through acculturation programmes. Guinness understood the importance of avoiding SRC in developing their knowledge base of the new international markets in which they were operating, so they ensured they had a management team in each market which was truly multinational, as well as including managers with a local knowledge. Perhaps this is where the US company buying a German company went wrong (see Dilemma 3.2).

CROSS-CULTURAL ANALYSIS

So far our discussions have been concerned primarily with understanding what is meant by culture, examining its components and surveying its influence on consumer behaviour and how that differs across cultures.

However, strategists and students of international marketing need to move beyond this and endeavour to develop ways to compare and contrast consumers, market segments and buyers across cultures. In today's global environment where culture is becoming increasingly de-territorialised and each culture is penetrated by the influences of other cultures, this is becoming increasingly complex as a research task. Cultural influences are much more diffuse and opaque than previously. This means that cultural analysis does not necessarily equate to country analysis and any research design must account for such complexities.

International marketers must decide the relevent cultural segments/grouping for analysis and then need appropriate frameworks or conceptual schemata to enable comparisons to be made and contrasts and similarities to be drawn across cultural groupings.

For the most part, cross-cultural classification approaches tend to be either mere lists or incredibly theoretical complex structures. There is a recognised lack of a universal, broadly generalisable framework within which to visualise cross cultural analysis. The contextual approach and the work of Hofstede (2003) are used by many researchers as the basis for methodologies of cross-cultural analysis. In the following sections we will examine how these concepts can be used by firms in attempting to analyse consumer behaviour across cultures and will then highlight some further frameworks which readers may find useful.

The high/low context approach

The main thesis of the contextual approach to analysing culture is that one culture will be different from another if it understands and communicates in

---

DILEMMA 3.2

Mittelstand vs US executives

A US company recently bought into 180-year-old family-owned Mittelstand in Germany. The US company thought the purchase would give them a good base for the European market. They were particularly interested in Germany, which they regarded as the largest and most technically sophisticated market in Europe. As a financially driven company the new US owner needed to ensure a high rate of return on its investment and so had to examine costings in the company closely and introduce efficient US working practices to cut costs. The company canteen was closed in the belief that rather than eat a full hot meal, workers could eat sandwiches whilst working. Morning cheerleader sessions were introduced to motivate staff.

Managers were addressed by their first names to build relationships. Unfortunately such practices led to a breakdown of the deal. The German managers were grossly insulted by the informal form of address. The workers took industrial action against the loss of hot midday meals and the staff refused to join cheerleader sessions. To add to the new owner's problems, they found it very difficult to extract accurate financial information because the financial side of the business had traditionally been handled by tax advisers outside the company, not by managers within it.

QUESTION *How could the new owner have avoided the breakdown of the deal? Do you think they should persevere and rectify the situation or withdraw?*

different ways. Languages are therefore seen as the most important component of culture.

The language differences between some cultures will be large and therefore there will be marked differences in their cultures. Language and value differences between the German and Japanese cultures, for instance, are considerable. There are also differences between the Spanish and Italian cultures but they are much less; both have languages based on Latin, they use the same written form of communication and have similar although not identical values and norms.

In different cultures the use of communication techniques varies. In some languages communication is based on the words that are said or written (spoken language). In others, the more ambiguous elements such as surroundings or social status of the message-giver are important variables in the transmission of understanding (silent language). Hall used these findings to classify cultures into what he referred to as 'low context cultures' and 'high context cultures'.

- *Low context cultures* rely on spoken and written language for meaning. Senders of messages encode their messages expecting that the receivers will accurately decode the words used to gain a good understanding of the intended message.

- *High context cultures* use and interpret more of the elements surrounding the message to develop their understanding of the message. In high context cultures the social importance, knowledge of the person and the social setting add extra information and will be perceived by the message receivers.

Figure 3.3 shows the contextual differences in the cultures around the world. At one extreme are the low context cultures of Northern Europe. The Swiss, in particular, have a high explicit content in their communications. At the other extreme are the high context cultures. The Japanese have subtle and complex ways of communicating with people according to their age, sex and the relative and actual social positions of the people conversing.

FIGURE 3.3

The contextual continuum of differing cultures

SOURCE: USUNIER *ET AL.* (2005)

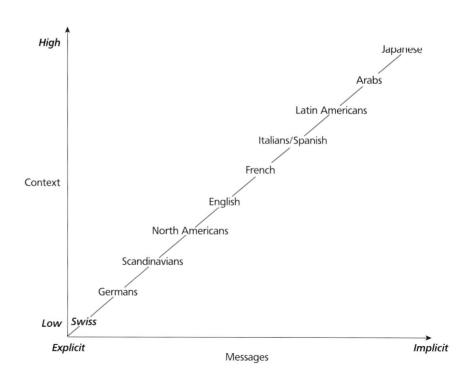

The greater the contextual difference between those trying to communicate, the greater the difficulty firms will have in achieving accurate communications.

Hofstede's cultural dimensions

Hofstede (2003) was primarily interested in uncovering differences in work-related values across countries. He identified five dimensions of culture: individualism, power distance, uncertainty avoidance, masculinity and Confucianism. These dimensions, he argued, largely account for cross-cultural differences in people's belief systems and behaviour patterns around the globe.

Individualism

Individualism (IDV) describes the relationship between an individual and his or her fellow individuals in society. It manifests itself in the way people live together, for example in nuclear families, extended families or tribes, and has a great variety of value implications. At one end of the spectrum are societies with very loose ties between individuals. Such societies allow a large degree of freedom and everybody is expected to look after his or her own self-interest and possibly that of the immediate family. Societies of this type exemplify high individualism (high IDV) and display loose integration. At the other end are societies with very strong ties between individuals. Everybody is expected to look after the interests of their in-group and to hold only those opinions and beliefs sanctioned by the in-group which, in turn, protects the individual. These 'collective' (low IDV) societies show tight integration. Hofstede identified highly individualistic countries as the USA, Great Britain and the Netherlands. Collectivist countries were Colombia, Pakistan and Taiwan. The mid-range contains countries such as Japan, India, Austria and Spain.

Power distance

Power distance (PDI) involves the way societies deal with human inequality. People possess unequal physical and intellectual capacities which some societies allow to grow into inequalities in power and wealth. However, some other societies de-emphasise such inequalities. All societies are unequal but some are more unequal than others (Hofstede 2003). The Philippines, India and France score relatively high in power distance (see Illustration 3.4). Austria, Israel, Denmark and Sweden show relatively low PDI scores, while the United States ranks slightly below midpoint.

Combining power distance and individualism reveals some interesting relationships (see Figure 3.4). Collectivist countries seem to show large power distance but individualist countries do not necessarily display small power distance. For example, the Latin European countries combine large power distance with high individualism. Other wealthy Western countries combine smaller power distance with high individualism. It is interesting to observe that in Hofstede's sample, almost all developing countries tend to rate high on both collectivism (low individualism) and power distance. Of the countries Hofstede studied, only Costa Rica combined small power distance with high collectivism (low individualism).

Uncertainty avoidance

Uncertainty Avoidance (UA) reflects how a society deals with uncertainty about the future, a fundamental fact of human existence. At one extreme, weak UA cultures socialise members to accept and handle uncertainty. People in such cultures tend to accept each day as it comes, take risks rather easily, do not work too hard and tolerate opinions and behaviour different from their own. Denmark, Sweden and Hong Kong all rated low in UA. The other extreme – strong UA

ILLUSTRATION 3.4

France: image vs reality?

France scored relatively high in power distance dimension in Hofstede's analysis, and certainly some regard it as a culture that is inherently conservative and resistant to change. It is argued

PHOTO CREDIT: MIKE GOLDWATER/ALAMY

that this is because with the characteristics of large power distance it as a blocked society with too many top-down bureaucratic rules which breed distrust amongst people and a resistance to change amongst individuals. Consequently individuals perceive innovation and risk-taking with suspicion and so will be hostile to an open global market which encourages diffusion of cross-cultural ideas and new products and services. Globscan, a polling group, found that 71 per cent of Americans agreed that the free market economy was the best system available, as did 66 per cent of the British and 65 per cent of Germans. Only 36 per cent of French respondents agreed.

Yet France boasts some of the most successful companies operating on global markets. Carrefour's empire spreads the globe and virtually in every sector there are world class French firms, cars (Renault), tyres (Michelin), cosmetics (L'Oréal), luxury goods (LVMH) and food (Danone).

QUESTION *How do you account for the contradiction in the image of France as a bureaucratic culture resistant to change and the reality of the performance of French companies on global markets?*

SOURCE: ADAPTED FROM A SURVEY OF FRANCE; *THE ECONOMIST* 28TH OCTOBER 2006

FIGURE 3.4

Power distance/individualism dimensions across cultures

SOURCE: © GEERT HOFSTED BV (2003). REPRODUCED WITH PERMISSION

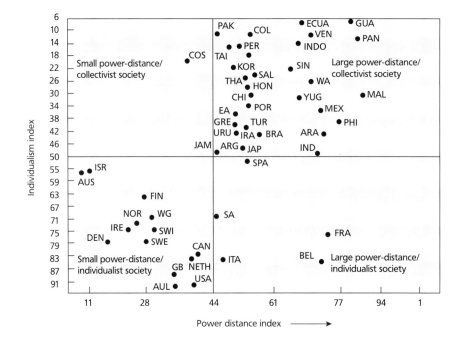

societies – fosters the need to try to beat the future, resulting in greater nervousness, aggressiveness and emotional stress. Belgium, Japan and France ranked relatively high in uncertainty avoidance while the United States scored somewhat below midpoint.

Masculinity

Masculinity (MAS) deals with the degree to which societies subscribe to the typical stereotypes associated with males and females. Masculine values stress making money and the pursuit of visible achievements: such societies admire individual brilliance and idolise the successful achiever, the superman. These traditional masculine social values permeate the thinking of the entire society, women as well as men. Hofstede's research indicated that within his sample, Japan, Austria, Venezuela and Italy ranked highest in masculinity.

In more feminine societies, both men and women exhibit values associated with traditionally feminine roles such as endurance and an emphasis on people rather than money. Societal sympathy lies with the underdog, the anti-hero rather than the individually brilliant. Sweden, Norway, the Netherlands and Denmark rank as some of the most feminine societies studied by Hofstede. The United States scored fairly high on the masculinity dimension, placing it near the top one-third.

An assertive salesperson would be better accepted in a highly masculine culture such as Austria than in Denmark's more feminine culture. The level of masculinity also explains part of the perception that business people have of each other. In feminine countries where relationships are more highly valued, the supplier–client relationship is seen much more as a partnership than in more masculine cultures. Thus the affective aspects of the business relationship are seen as of vital importance, particularly in negotiations as we will see in the section on cross-cultural negotiating later in this chapter.

Confucian dynamism

The Confucian dynamism dimension assesses cultures on the degree they are universalistic or particularistic. Universalistic cultures believe that what is true and good can be determined and defined and can be applied everywhere. Particularistic cultures evolve where 'unique circumstances and relationships are more important considerations in determining what is right and good rather than abstract rules' (Hofstede 2003). Confucian philosophy traditionally pervades Chinese culture. Its major characteristics include a strong bias towards obedience, the importance of rank and hierarchies and the need for smooth social relations. Within Confucian ethics, four relations were basic, between ruler and those ruled, father and son, husband and wife, and friend and friend. Everyone is expected to know where they stand in the hierarchy of human relations and one's place carries with it fixed standards of how one behaves towards others.

Culture/communication typologies

A number of writers have developed frameworks that can be utilised for cross-cultural analysis which have built on the above work. In this section we will discuss the communication typologies and the relationship beween the cultural dimensions identified by Hofstede and the adoption of new products.

Communication typologies

Four verbal communication typologies were suggested by Gudykunst *et al*. (2005) which can be used as a basis for cross-cultural analysis. These are as follows:

1 *Direct vs indirect* refers to the degree of explicitness of the verbal message of a culture. The Chinese use the indirect style, often hiding their real feelings and being more concerned with group harmony and the feelings of others. The use of the indirect style refers to the high context culture and Hofstede's collective dimension.

2 *Elaborative vs succinct* reflects the quantity of talk that people feel comfortable with in a particular culture. The succinct style is where quantity of talk is relatively low. This reflects high uncertainty avoidance and a high context culture. Elaborative styles may be used more in low context cultures where the spoken language is of greater importance, as in the US.

ILLUSTRATION 3.5

The use of humour in international advertising

Every culture enjoys some form of humour, but humour has difficulty crossing cultural boundaries because what is funny in one culture is often not so in another. In cultures where the desire to avoid uncertainty is high, as in Germany, humour with its inherent ambiguity is likely to be restrained in advertising. In an analysis of beer advertising across Europe, researchers found humour dominated British commercials, whereas it was used more sparingly in German or Dutch commercials.

In Europe typical examples of humorous advertising include commercials that tell a funny story, use of irony or making fun of typical situations. In Thailand, however, advertising that has made its mark in terms of creativity and popularity is primarily characterised by humour, sometimes black, sometimes slap-stick and always identifiably Thai. This is probably indicative of a trait across Asia which surprised Unilever when they found they had greatly under-utilised the use of humour when addressing women consumers. Their study showed that 83 per cent of women in Asia preferred the portrayal of humour over the traditional Western heavy-handed use of emotions in advertising.

In B2B cross-cultural advertising status is an important consideration. In some countries people may loosen up as they get promoted and be more receptive to humour, but in more hierarchical cultures, such as France, the reverse is more likely to be the case. Seniority is largely determined by intellectual achievement and academic credentials. Consequently, French executives are keen to avoid being branded lightweight. So whilst clever and sophisticated humour is acceptable, the risk of appearing foolish, with the accompanying loss of credibility and intellectual standing, tends to inhibit other forms of

PHOTO CREDIT: IMAGE COURTESY OF GUINNESS(R) ARCHIVE, DIAGEO IRELAND

humour. The self-mocking humour for which British advertising is renowned is likely to be completely misunderstood.

In international advertising it may be as well to remember the old Chinese proverb: 'You get sick by what you put in your mouth, but you can be hurt by what comes out of your mouth.'

QUESTION *Evaluate the implications of using humour in cross-cultural advertising.*

3 *Personal vs contextual* contextual style focuses on the role of the speaker and the role of relationships. The role and hierarchical relationship of the parties in conversation will be reflected in the form of address and words that are used. This type of communication reflects high power distance, collectivism and high context cultures such as Japan.

4 *Instrumental vs affective* defines the orientation of the speaker. In the affective verbal style the speaker is process orientated. There is concern that neither the speaker nor the receiver will be put in an uncomfortable position. The speaker also listens to and closely observes the receiver in order to interpret how the message is being taken. This is a reflection of a high context collective culture, such as South East Asia.

Such typologies may influence the receptiveness of consumers across cultures to humour in advertising. We explore this in Illustration 3.5

HOFSTEDE'S CULTURAL DIMENSIONS VS RATE OF PRODUCT ADOPTION

Singh (2006) suggests that particular dimensions of culture are critical in determining whether consumers of certain cultures are likely to easily adopt new products or services or not. Essentially he measured the propensity of a culture to innovate and found that cultures characterised by a small power distance, weak uncertainly avoidance and masculinity are more likely to be innovative and accept new product ideas than cultures where there was a large power distance, strong uncertainty avoidance and more feminine traits exhibited. Equally he suggested that cultural dimensions were also linked to the preferred type of communication. Individualistic cultures are more likely to be swayed by more impersonal channels, whereas collectivist cultures are more likely to be swayed by interpersonal communications. Heineken tapped into the need for social acceptance to avoid uncertainty in collectivist cultures in their innovative campaign in Asia. They built a perception of popularity by asking staff in bars selling Heineken to leave bottles on tables by not pouring full beers into glasses and not collecting the empties. Suddenly little green bottles were seen everywhere and it didn't take long for customers to start asking for that particular brand.

SOCIAL AND CULTURAL INFLUENCES IN BUSINESS-TO-BUSINESS MARKETING

Much of the discussion relating to the influences of social cultural factors on international marketing assumes a market for predominantly fast-moving consumer goods where decisions are made on either a family or individual basis. Yet a considerable proportion of exports relates to industrial goods and services where companies are primarily concerned with company-to-company or business-to-business marketing and dealing, therefore with primarily organisational or even government buyers. The question we now need to address is how relevant the social/cultural factors we have been discussing are to these types of markets.

In business-to-business marketing there are essentially two types of buyers: organisations and governments. In this section we will highlight some of the social/cultural influences on these types of buyers which are particularly relevant to international marketing. Following this we will discuss the impact of culture on cross-cultural negotiating styles and the practice of gift-giving in international business relationships.

Organisational buyers

Business buying decisions are influenced by decisions about technology, the objectives and tasks of the company, the organisational structure of the buying company and the motivations of people in the company. The technology decision is an interesting area. Some companies rely on their own internal capability to produce solutions to problems they need to solve in the areas of technology and how to manufacture the product. However, Japanese companies have encouraged their suppliers to help them by providing technological improvements. This approach is now influencing business practices across the world. The US adversarial approach of developing a precise buying specification and then challenging supplying firms to win the contract by providing the best deal is now less common.

Culture at the organisational level can play a significant part in the way in which the various roles are enacted. When it comes to international encounters, humour for instance can be a double-edged sword. The dangers of a joke backfiring are increased when the parties concerned do not share a common culture. Different cultures have different beliefs and assumptions which determine when humour is considered appropriate, what can be joked about and even who can be joked with. Attitudes to uncertainty, status and the sanctity of business influence the extent to which humour is allowed to intrude on proceedings.

There are a number of different corporate cultural characteristics in European countries which influence buyer behaviour. The French have a hierarchical system of management with a strong tendency to centralism, consequently it is often difficult for sales people to reach the top manager as that individual may well be buffered behind half a dozen assistants. Spanish and Italian decision making tends to be highly autocratic and based on the model of the family; decision making is shared, with systems that tend to be informal. The German position is influenced by earned respect for formal qualifications and technical competence. Leadership depends upon respect rather than subservience.

Government buyer behaviour

In many countries the government is the biggest buyer, far larger than any individual consumer or business buyer. Governments buy a wide range of goods and services: roads, education, military, health and welfare. The way in which governments buy is influenced by the extent to which public accountability in the expenditure of public money is thought important.

It has been estimated that 20 per cent of the gross domestic product of the European Union is controlled through the value of purchases and contracts awarded by the public sector. In the US approximately 30 per cent of the gross national product is accounted for by the purchases of US governmental units. For some companies their international business comprises government buyers in different countries. It is important, therefore, to understand the government buying processes.

Usual forms of buying procedure are the open tender and selective tender. In open bid contracts, tenders are invited against a tight specification, and contracts are usually awarded to the lowest-price bid. Selective tender contracts are offered to companies who have already demonstrated their ability in the area appropriate to the tender. Only those companies on the selective tender list will be invited to tender. As with open tender, the lowest price is often used to adjudicate the bids.

In the European Union specific rules have been drawn up in an attempt to remove the barriers between potential suppliers of government contracts from different countries of the EU. Suppliers from all EU member states should have an equal opportunity to bid for public authority contracts and public works contracts must be advertised throughout the EU.

The business-to-business buying process

In the B2B buying processes the various types of buying are classified into three different classes of buying: straight re-buy, modified re-buy and new task.

A straight re-buy represents the bulk of the business buying. The buy signal is often triggered through information systems when stock levels reach a predetermined replenishment point. The modified re-buy indicates a certain level of information search and re-evaluation of products/services and supplies before the purchase is made. The new task represents an area of considerable uncertainty in which the company needs to make decisions about what it wants, about performance standards and about supplier capabilities. The new task, particularly if the purchase is of major importance to the company, will involve senior management and might take a long time to complete.

The way in which a company manages each of the buy classes will be influenced by cultural factors. Companies with a strong ethnocentric orientation may limit their search for suppliers to suppliers from their own country. For more internationally oriented companies, the country of origin effect will distort information collection and appraisal. The influence of established relationships in cultures in which personal contacts and relationships are important will act as a barrier to companies which operate in a more formal way.

Relationship marketing is very important in business-to-business marketing, where companies may gain competitive advantage not necessarily from the product but through the added value they have built because of their relationship. This is especially important in markets such as China. The Chinese rely heavily on personal relationships in business dealings. It is important for foreign companies to understand the dynamics of these relationships (known as *guanxi*). There is a saying in Chinese, 'If you do not have a relationship you do not exist!'

Personal selling and negotiation between the buyer and seller as they go through the interaction process in order to build a business relationship which is mutually beneficial is an important part of international marketing. It is in this process of negotiation and relationship building that cultural factors have their greatest impact.

The role of culture in negotiation styles

Culture can be a major determinant in the success or failure of business negotiations. In Saudi Arabia business may look informal and slow paced, but in negotiations a businessman would be grossly insulted if they were expected to negotiate with a representative rather than the top person. Indian negotiators bargain much longer and tend to be much more competitive and persistent in trying to maximise their gains.

However, some commentators suggest that whilst a lack of understanding of the cultural differences in negotiation styles may be a major cause of negotiation failure, awareness of cultural differences may not be a major factor in negotiation success, unless that awareness is accompanied by a deeper understanding of how culture impacts on the whole negotiation process. A negotiation process can be broken down into four stages

1 Non-task discussion

2 Task-related exchange of information

3 Persuasion

4 Concession and agreement.

The first stage, *non-task discussion*, describes the process of establishing rapport between members of the negotiation teams. Japanese negotiators would spend considerable time and money entertaining foreign negotiating teams in order to establish a rapport, whereas US executives saw the delays as frustrating and the money spent as wasteful. GEC Alsthom sales executives found karaoke sessions very useful when negotiating with the North Koreans for a contract for high-speed trains between Seoul and Pusan. The firm undertstood from the outset that the first stage of negotiations needed to include a broad range of activities, such as singing, to help establish a rapport on which the relationship could be built.

The *task-related exchange of information stage* describes the exchange of information that defines the participants' needs and expectations. Well over 90 per cent of all large Japanese companies and most of the smaller ones used a decision-making process called *ringi*. The system is based on the principle that decisions are made only when a consensus is reached by the negotiating team. Proposals are circulated amongst the negotiating team and the affected individuals in the main office staff, for each to affix their own personal seal of approval. Without the group's approval, which takes a long time to acquire, no proposal will be accepted. What may appear to US negotiators as stalling tactics is often simply the different process by which the Japanese reach a decision.

The *persuasion stage* for US executives is the one that consumes time, whereas for Japanese negotiators who have previously taken the time to understand each other's expectations, it is seen as unnecessary. Japanese negotiators may, as a result, remain silent. This is not because they do not agree with the proposal but because they are either waiting for more information or for them, agreement has been reached and therefore negotiations are complete.

This often leads to misunderstanding at the *concession and agreement stage*. An extension of the Japanese preference for establishing strong personal relationships is their dislike for the formal Western-style contract. A loosely worded statement expressing mutual cooperation and trust developed between negotiating parties is much preferred. The advantage of these agreements is that they allow a great deal of flexibility in the solution of unforeseen problems, whereas Western negotiators may feel the need to bargain to the end and do not see their job as complete until they have actually obtained a signature. Table 3.3 gives an interesting summary of differences in buyer–seller negotiating styles in selected countries.

Usunier and Lee (2005) suggests a number of ways to minimise cultural impact in negotiations in order to build effective transcultural relationships.

■ *Adaptation*. In international business meetings, people who do not appear to feel the need to adapt may be considered indolent: 'Those who adapt are aware of differences, whereas those to whom others adapt remain unaware.'(Usunier and Lee (2005))

■ *Interpreters*. Be aware that interpreters influence meaning. They may translate better from one language into another than in the opposite direction. The loyalty of interpreters needs to be considered. Are they more in favour of one party than the other? Should you use your own interpreter? Should you use several interpreters to reduce stress errors and bias?

■ *Cultural blocks*. Not everything will translate – it is not possible to translate meaning exactly for all elements in an interpretation. Culture-specific elements will block some attempts at translation.

■ *The stereotype*. Avoid negative stereotyping which is likely to increase
negotiation conflicts and difficulties.

■ *Intercultural preparation*. Good prior preparation in intercultural
understanding is a necessary investment to improve international
business effectiveness.

Ethical issues in cross-cultural marketing

Cultural sensitivity is often at the heart of the ethical dilemmas that managers face
when operating in international markets. There are few, if any, moral absolutes

TABLE 3.3 Differences in buyer–seller relationships styles

International market	Climate	Importance of relationships	Process	Decision making
United States	Sometimes viewed as an aggressive or confrontational climate	Of less importance. Focus is on achieving desired results	Ordered process where each point is discussed in sequence	can be either an individual or group decision process
Canada	Positive, polite climate. Hard sell will not work here	Of less importance. Focus is on achieving desired results	Ordered process where each point is discussed in sequence	Can be either an individual or group decision process
Latin America	Positive and hospitable climate	Personal, one-on-one relationships very important	Relationship building through socialisation will precede negotiations	Decisions are usually made by a high-level individual
United Kingdom	Traditional, polite climate. Hard sell will not work here	Of less importance. Focus is on achieving desired results	Ordered process where each point is discussed in sequence	Can be either an individual or group decision process
Germany/ Austria	Rigid, sober climate	Low. Germans remain aloof until negotiations conclude	Systematic process with emphasis on contractual detail	Even the most routine decisions are made by top-level officials
France/ Belgium	Formal, bureaucratic climate. Hard sell will not work here	Formal, arm's-length relationships with attention to etiquette	French teams use argument to generate discussion	Usually a group process headed by a senior negotiator
Japan	Formal polite climate with many idiosyncratic nuances	Great importance. Long-term relationships are what matter most	First all general items are agreed on, then details are discussed	A total group process with all levels involved in the final decision
China	Bureaucratic climate with an abundance of 'red tape'	Very important. Traditional, cultural courtesies are expected	Discussions are long and repetitive. Agreements must be in writing	Usually a group process headed by a senior negotiator
Russia	Bureaucratic climate with an abundance of 'red tape'	Low. Russians will remain reserved until negotiations conclude	Cumbersome process due to bureaucratic constraints	Usually a group process headed by a senior negotiator

SOURCE: LEWIN AND JOHNSTON (1997)

and few actions for which no one can provide reasonable justification. Almost every action can be justified on the basis that it is acceptable in one particular culture. In thinking about ethics managers need to be aware that simply defining what is ethical by the standards, values and actions from their own culture may be insufficient in satisfying all the stakeholders of a multinational enterprise. What is often seen as an acceptable business practice in one culture can be seen as ethically questionable in another. The SRC effect discussed earlier is particularly relevant to the discussion of how cultural sensitivities impact on what is an ethical business practice. Managers from different cultures will always be able to challenge, for instance, the US, Indian or Japanese perspective of what is ethical.

The **ethical challenges** facing international marketing managers are many. In recent years such issues as environmental abuse, the use of child labour, poor working conditions and the low levels of pay in Third World factories have received particular attention. Western consumers choosing brands look for reassurance that the product has been produced in what they see as a socially responsible manner (see Illustration 3.6). Many sportswear brands such as Nike, Levi and Gap have suffered adverse publicity when it has been made known that child labour has been used to produce their products. Anita Roddick built the Body Shop empire on the basis of ensuring her ingredients came from authentic sources of supply which did not lead to the destruction of the environment and that the indigenous producers received a fair price for the products they sold. She has recently launched an ethical fashion chain. Her key selling points for the new range of clothes are that they are free from child slavery and that the people that make them are able to earn a proper living wage and enjoy good working conditions.

Consumers globally are becoming better informed through better education and faster and more effective communications. Increasingly, therefore, they are able to question the actions of multinational enterprises, as we saw in the discussion of the role of pressure groups in Chapter 1. For their part, whilst the largest multinationals are extending their influence within the global markets, they are becoming more vulnerable to criticism. Over the past few years quality and service have improved considerably, but now firms are increasingly expected to ensure that their behaviour is ethical and in the interests of the global community which makes up their market.

However, international marketing executives operating across cultures will find themselves facing moral and ethical dilemmas on a daily basis on a wide range of issues. Some of those currently receiving particular attention are bribery and corruption, counterfeiting and piracy.

Bribery and corruption

An integral part of conducting business internationally is the practice of gift-giving. However, in many Western countries such practice is seen as bribery/corruption and is tightly regulated and controlled. Business gift-giving – or bribery, depending on your point of view – if improperly executed, could stop sensitive negotiations and ruin new and potential business relationships. German and Swiss executives tend to feel uncomfortable accepting gifts, which they view as bribes, as they will not want to be seen as being under obligation to the other party. However, business gift-giving in many cultures is an important part of persuasion. In cultures where a business gift is expected but not given, it is an insult to the host. In China it would be virtually impossible to gain any local government approval without offering financial inducements.

Cultures that view bribery as an acceptable business practice tend to fall into the high context category. In such a culture the communication style is more implicit, non-verbal and more reliant on hidden cues in the context of personal relationships. In Japan, for example, a highly developed and affluent society, gift-giving practices are widespread in the business culture. Refusing to participate in gift-giving in such cultures can cause bad feeling and misunderstandings between business clients. In high context cultures, financial inducements are often seen as important steps in bringing a person into the inner circle of a business relationship or to strengthen the relationship between a buyer and a seller.

By contrast, people in low context cultures rely on explicit contracts, communication is more formal and explicit and negotiations based on a more legalistic orientation. Laws applying to bribery tend to be very well laid out. In some

ILLUSTRATION 3.6

How the ethical consumer makes decisions

Ethical consumerism is of course nothing new; the campaign against Nestlé's sale of baby milk into Africa and boycotts of South African products during the days of apartheid attracted widespread support.

SOURCE: ADAPTED FROM P. SELIGMAN, *FINANCIAL TIMES INFORMATION*, 11 JULY 2002

Ethical consumers have helped to raise awareness of Third World debt and, as a result, prompted government action. Clearly, they tap into a latent anti-Americanism; people love eating McDonald's but are happy to protest against them for a variety of reasons – protection of the rainforest and anti-globalisation to name but two.

Most consumers are moderate, but the issues these campaigners raise are steadily changing their expectations of corporate social responsibility and this, in turn, is influencing their purchase behaviour.

For example, concerns about animal welfare have fuelled demand for Freedom Food, organic meat and dolphin-friendly tuna, while growing environmental awareness has prompted a massive growth in organic/quasi-organic and biodynamic products. Greater social awareness has led to the development of Fair Trade products and anti-child-labour campaigns.

However, some moderate ethical consumers are highly selective about what they will boycott: many vegetarians eat non-vegetarian cheese or wear leather shoes; people who openly claim to be concerned with the environment use their cars instead of public transport; fashion conscious youngsters buy Nike trainers if that's what the fashion pack dictates and people resist paying a couple of pence extra for Fair Trade coffee even though they claim to be concerned about Third World labour exploitation.

The question is, should multinationals take note of such moderate ethically aware people? These consumers may not protest at WTO summits, but are they becoming aware of what the global pressure groups are demanding? And will they change their purchasing behaviour in the future?

International marketers need to be able to anticipate consumer demands across a range of cultural markets. So even if awareness of ethical issues has not changed actual buying behaviour, how should international marketing managers respond to such challenges?

QUESTION *How far do you think ethically aware consumers translate their beliefs into purchasing behaviour across the globe?*

cultures, all business gifts will be viewed as illegal bribes; on the other hand, other cultures view gifts, pay-offs and even bribes merely as a cost of business. Bribery and corruption are part of the commercial traditions of many parts of Asia, Africa and the Middle East. Transparency International, a global counter-corruption watchdog, ranks Indonesia as the most corrupt country, followed closely by Vietnam. They estimate in Vietnam that 20 per cent of infrastructure spending finds its way into the pockets of corrupt officials.

Piracy

Piracy has been a particular problem to the global music and software industry. According to Havocscope (http://www.havocscope.com) the piracy of software, movies and music alone amounts to nearly US$57 billion. The advent of digital technology and the ability to download from the Internet has made piracy a worldwide phenomenon in the music and software industries. Prior to the recent crackdown by the government in China it was estimated that 98 per cent of software was pirated. The music industry sees the widespread practice of downloading music from what they view as illegal Internet sites as a major cause for the decline in sales of CDs worldwide.

Some commentators question whether piracy is the cause and argue the market has simply moved to an Internet download format and the big music companies haven't kept up. Apple is perhaps one of the exceptions. Something like 75 per cent of all purchased downloaded music is through iTunes. Even amongst professionals there are differing views. Robbie Williams, a UK superstar, publicly stated that he thought there was nothing wrong with piracy and that there was very little anyone could do about it.

Different cultures have varying perspectives on piracy. The US courts take a very stringent view and prosecute offenders that are caught. In China and India views on intellectual property rights are much more difficult to define. The International Intellectual Property Alliance claims that despite now being members of the WTO piracy is still a big problem in China. Whilst officially regulations have been put in place to ban such practices, in fact very little has been done to control it.

Counterfeiting

A counterfeit is something that is forged, copied or imitated without the perpetrator having the right to do it, and with the purpose of deceiving or defrauding (whereas piracy does not attempt to defraud but openly sells as a pirated copy). In China at least US$16 billion-worth of goods sold each year inside the country are counterfeit. Procter and Gamble estimates that 10–15 per cent of its revenues in China are lost each year to counterfeit products. The Ukraine now exports counterfeit optical discs, Russia markets counterfeit software, Paraguay markets imitation cigarettes. Counterfeit pharmaceuticals are routinely marketed to countries unable to afford the expensive products of the authentic drug companies; often these are substandard, or have fake labels. It is estimated by the World Health Organisation that between 5 and 7 per cent of drugs sold are counterfeits, with potentially fatal consequences.

American industries lose US$200–250 billion a year to counterfeiting. The fact that many global manufacturers have moved their production to low-cost bases around the world is seen by some to have opened the floodgates to counterfeiting. The global brands have been able to take advantage of low labour costs but gave insufficient attention to securing intellectual property rights in such countries. In today's markets, where so much of the added value of a product is in its brand identity, counterfeiters have been able to exploit consumers' expectations of quality and service with counterfeit products. Brands such as Louis Vuitton, Nike, Microsoft, Gucci and Prada are amongst the most counterfeited of global brands. The Internet has also helped build the market for counterfeit products; it is estimated that approximately US$50 billion-worth of counterfeit goods are traded each year over the Internet.

Much of the problem stems from cultural attitudes to the rights of anyone to own intellectual property. The Chinese have argued that if all ideas were copyrighted they should be able to patent the compass, icecream, noodles and many other products they have given to the world. This has led to inadequate laws on intellectual property rights (IPR) in many countries. Since 2006, all members of the World Trade Organisation, including China, have worked to fully implement an international treaty on IPR that lays down basic rules for protection and enforcement. Known as TRIPS, the WTO's **Agreement on Trade-Related Aspects of Intellectual Property Rights** introduces intellectual property rules into the world's multilateral trading system for the very first time. Since joining the WTO China has introduced a number of laws so companies can protect their intellectual property assets. How those rights are enforced in practice remains to be seen, although there is evidence of government support for the enforcement of the new laws. Recently Starbucks won a high profile case against a Chinese company using the Chinese version of its name, the court ruling that the company had the sole right to its name in both English and Chinese. The French cognac company Hennessey also won a piracy case in China against two companies copying its brand and selling it as French cognac brandy even though it was produced and bottled in China. In Europe, the European Commission has proposed new rules to harmonise member states' legislation on IPR enforcement. This has been particularly important because the EU embraced new members from eastern Europe, where counterfeiting is a serious problem in some countries.

Although nations and organisations often provide ethical guidelines on bribery, counterfeiting etc., ultimately international managers have to make decisions based on their own personal views of what is and is not ethical. Managers need to form a view when operating across different cultures as to what constitutes ethical decision making within an organisation. In taking such a view, managers need to reflect on how their views on what constitutes ethical behaviour reflect changing societal views of acceptable behaviour, how decisions will be viewed by stakeholders and the perceived and real impact upon the organisation of making those decisions. Central to their concerns is the importance the company places on the need for an ethically responsible approach to their operations in the global markets. However, interwoven within this are the commercial concerns of the business.

Companies are increasingly of the view that organisational behaviour considered to be unethical can decrease a firm's wealth, whilst behaviour considered by stakeholders to be ethical can enhance a company's competitive advantage on global markets. Attempting to take an ethically responsible decision, though, could mean the loss of perhaps an efficient and cheap source of supply or in some cases the loss of a potential deal. Any decision would need very careful consideration.

The consequence of an ethically responsible approach would involve increased resources and attention being applied to a number of areas, such as:

- The increased need for accurate and timely information.
- Increased attention to press, public reaction and global pressure groups.
- Closer relationships with stakeholders and members of the supply chain to ensure all interests are taken into consideration.
- Being prepared, when serious risks are identified, to take positive and constructive action.

SUMMARY

■ The influence of social and cultural factors in international marketing is complex and often extremely difficult for a firm operating in foreign markets to analyse and understand. In today's global environment, where culture is becoming increasingly de-territorialised and each culture is penetrated by the influences of other cultures, the isssue of examining and understanding cultural sensitivities is becoming increasingly complex.

■ If the firm is operating across a number of markets, finding consistent methods of analysing their cross-cultural markets poses particular challenges. The cultural dimensions of Hofstede and the contextual classification of cultures are two of the frameworks used.

■ This chapter has focused on developing an understanding of the components of culture and how these components impact on consumer beliefs, values, attitudes and purchasing behaviour.

■ Culture also affects the way that business is carried out in different markets. Culture underpins the legal structure of a country and ethical attitudes to decision making and the acceptability of bribes etc. Managers need to form a view when operating across different cultures as to what constitutes ethical decision making within an organisation and what constitutes ethical behaviour.

■ Culture has a significant impact, therefore, on the international marketing strategies of firms, both in consumer and business-to-business markets. In this chapter the reader should have acquired an awareness of the possible methods that can be used to categorise differences across cultures to enable a cross-cultural analysis to be carried out. In Chapter 4 we go on to look at the methods of analysing and researching international markets.

KEYWORDS

Attitude	Enculturation	Perception of risk
Beliefs	Ethical challenges	Piracy
Consumer behaviour	High-context cultures	Self-reference criterion
Cross-cultural	Individualism	Silent language
Cultural identity	Low-context cultures	Social and cultural factors
Cultural sensitivity	Non-verbal	Spoken language
Customs	communication	Values

CASE STUDY

Leapfrogging the banking system

The roads are notorious, the infrastructure under-developed and the continent has more than its fair share of conflicts and crises but as darkness falls, and villagers huddle around paraffin lamps, neon lights come to life as they illuminate the mobile phone masts proliferating across the African landscape. Africa is in the grip of a mobile phone revolution. In the past 10 years, subscribers in sub-Saharan Africa have risen from 72 000 (excluding South Africa) to 25.5 million.

Mobile Internet technologies play a very important role in making Internet services available to many in Africa. According to Mobile Africa the number of mobile phone subscriptions far exceeds fixed-line subscriptions. The International Telecommunication Union reckon that more Africans have begun using phones since 2000 than in the whole of the previous century! Use of mobile phones has been increasing at an annual rate of 65 per cent, more than twice the global average. However, Africans are now using them for more than calling their friends and family: many are using them to do their banking. For these new banking customers both the mobile phone and the whole system of banking are new to them.

About half a million South Africans now use their mobile phones as a bank. Besides sending money to relatives and paying for goods, they check balances, buy mobile airtime and settle utility bills. Traditional banks offer mobile banking as an added service to existing customers, most of whom are quite well off. Wizzit, and to some extent First National Bank (FNB) and MTN Banking, are chasing another market: the 16 million South Africans, over half of the adult population, with no bank account. Significantly, 30 per cent of these people do have mobile phones. Previously ignored as the bottom of the pyramid and of little commercial importance to the large corporations, such customers are now being courted. Wizzit hired and trained over 2000 unemployed people, known as Wizzkids, to drum up business. It worked: eight out of ten Wizzit customers previously had no bank account and had never used an ATM.

People using advanced technology to manage their finances had until now depended on the archaic system of barter. They have leapfrogged telephony technology and jumped from dealing only in cash or barter to the world of cel-

lular finance. A simplified kind of account called *Mzansi* has been launched to reach the non-banking customers, and portable banks and ATMs have been rolled out in townships and in the countryside.

In most of Africa, only a fraction of people have bank accounts – but there is huge demand for cheap and convenient ways to send money and buy prepaid services such as airtime. In Kenya, a pilot scheme called M-Pesa is being used to disburse and pay micro-loans by phone. Meanwhile Celpay is offering platforms for banks and phone companies in Zambia and Congo. In countries like Somalia, with chaotic conditions, cash transfers by phone could be a boon.

However, there are many difficulties on the way. Not all potential consumers are ready to make the leap. Many think banking too expensive and complicated, and helping new customers become financially literate takes time. The technology remains a problem in some cases, with downloads requiring dozens of text messages. Several rival platforms are still in the fight, but so far those that emphasise simplicity and ease- of- use over state-of-the-art technology and security have made the greatest strides. A lot also hangs on putting the right laws and regulations in place. They need to be tight enough to protect vulnerable users and discourage money laundering, but open enough to allow innovative mobile banking to grow.

QUESTIONS

1 From a cross-cultural perspective, do you think the values and motivations of mobile phone consumers in Africa differ from those of their counterparts in other parts of the world?

2 From a cultural perspective, how might you develop a promotional campaign in Africa to further develop the cellular banking market?

3 What other cultural and behavioural considerations might you take into consideration when designing a strategy for the cellular banking market in Africa? What implications might these have for a firms' global marketing strategy?

PHOTO CREDIT: J MARSHALL - TRIBALEYE IMAGES/ALAMY

DISCUSSION QUESTIONS

1 Discuss the view that culture lies at the heart of all problems connected with international marketing.

2 What is culture? Is it important for international marketers to take account of it or is globalisation going to make it a thing of the past?

3 Given the cultural sensitivities to ethical dilemmas, can there ever be a global harmonisation of ethical business practices in international marketing?

4   How do social and cultural influences impact on international business negotiations? Using examples, advise a company preparing for cross-cultural negotiations.

5   It has been suggested that firms from developed countries should market to developing countries by establishing partnerships in a neighbouring developing country. Explain the reasons behind such a proposition and the implications for a firm developing a globalisation strategy.

REFERENCES

Blackwell, R.D., Minniard, P.W. and Engel, J.L. (2006) *Consumer behaviour*, 9th edn. The Dryden Press.

Graham, J.L., Hodgson, J.D. and Sano, Y. (2000) *Doing business with the new Japan*, Rowman and Littlefield Publishers.

Gudykunst, W.B. (2005) *Cross-cultural and intercultural communication*, Sage Publications.

Hawkins, D.I., Mothersbaugh, D.L. and Best, R.J. (2006) *Consumer behaviour*, 10th edn. Irwin.

Hofstede, G. (2003) *Culture's consequences: comparing values, behaviours, institutions and organisations across nations*, 2nd edn. Sage.

Jeannet, J.-P. and Hennessey, H.O. (2004) *Global marketing strategies*, 6th edn. Houghton Mifflin.

Kotler, P. and Keller, K.L. (2005) *Marketing management*, 12th edn. Pearson.

Lewin, J.E. and Johnston, W.L. (1997) 'Managing the international salesforce', *Journal of Business and Industrial Marketing*, 12 (3/4).

Linton, R. (1945) *The cultural background of personality*. Appleton Century.

Maslow, A.H. (1970) *Motivation and personality*, 2nd edn. Harper and Row.

Sarathy, R., Terpstra, V. and Russow, L.C. (2006) *International marketing*, 9th edn, Dryden Press.

Schiffman, L.G. and Kanuk, U. (2006) *Consumer behaviour*, 9th edn. Prentice Hall.

Singh, S. (2006) 'Cultural differences in and influences on consumers propensity to adopt innovations', *International Marketing Review*. 23(2) 173–91.

Welford, R. and Prescott, K. (2000) *European business*, 4th edn. FT Prentice Hall.

Usunier, J.C. and Lee, J.A. (2005) *Marketing across cultures*, 4th edn. FT Prentice Hall.

CHAPTER 4

INTERNATIONAL MARKETING RESEARCH AND OPPORTUNITY ANALYSIS

INTRODUCTION

Discussions in previous chapters have illustrated the highly risky and complex environment in which the international marketing manager operates. If a company is to survive in the international marketplace, it is important that it searches for methods to reduce the risk of making a wrong decision as far as possible.

This is why **marketing research** is so fundamentally important to the international marketing process, for whilst it cannot help a manager reduce risk to the point of zero, it can ensure that the starting point for decision-making is knowledge, rather than guesswork. Lack of knowledge of foreign markets is one of the first major barriers an international marketing manager will encounter. An effective marketing research strategy is the first step in overcoming that barrier.

The purpose of this chapter is to examine the place of marketing research in international strategy and the contribution it makes to the decision-making process. We will, therefore, be examining such concepts as the role of marketing research and opportunity analysis in international markets and the building of an international marketing information system. We will also examine some of the aspects of primary marketing research in international markets and discuss the practicalities and problems in implementing multi-country studies.

LEARNING OBJECTIVES

On completion of this chapter the reader should be able to:

■ Appreciate the key roles of marketing research in international marketing

■ Understand the concepts and techniques to identify and evaluate opportunities internationally

■ Build a market profile analysis of a foreign country market

■ Discuss the difficulties and issues that arise in developing multi-country primary research studies

THE ROLE OF MARKETING RESEARCH AND OPPORTUNITY ANALYSIS

Marketing research can be defined as the systematic gathering, recording, analysis and interpretation of data on problems relating to the marketing of goods and services.

The role of research is primarily to act as an aid to the decision maker. It is a tool that can help to reduce the risk in decision making caused by the environmental uncertainties and lack of knowledge in international markets. It ensures that the manager bases a decision on the solid foundation of knowledge and focuses strategic thinking on the needs of the marketplace, rather than the product. Such a role is, of course, necessary in all types of marketing.

In international marketing, because of the increased uncertainties and complexities in world markets, the capacity to ensure a systematic planned process in the research and the use of secondary information, prior to field research, is of paramount importance if quality information is to be obtained. The research process (Malhotra *et al*. 1997) consists of six key stages. These steps are the logical process for any research study to go through in its implementation and will be relevant for all research studies:

1 *Defining the problem*. It is important to decide what information is needed and set the objectives of the research, ensuring it is both commercially worthwhile and that the objective is feasible and achievable.

2 *Developing the approach to be taken*. The planning phase will concern itself with timescales, resources to carry out the work, the expertise required to meet the objectives and the decision as to whether a qualitative or quantitative approach is to be taken.

3 *Designing the research*. In designing the research strategy consideration will be given to the different action steps that need to be taken. Ensuring full use of secondary data sources will be important, as will the use of a pilot study to ensure the development of an effective and meaningful questionnaire.

4 *Carrying out the field work*. Decisions as to how the questionnaires will be administered (telephone, mail, personal interviews or focus groups) will be made as well as decisions as to who will do the work and what resources are required.

5 *Analysing the data*. The data analysis stage will need to take full account of the objectives of the research and the client's needs. Many researchers will argue that the methodology to be used should be decided in the first stages of the research planning as it will impact on the questionnaire design and how the interviews are administered.

6 *Preparing the report and presentation*. The report and presentation are the researcher's outputs and vital in establishing the credibility of the research methods used and the validity of the findings of the research.

THE ROLE OF INTERNATIONAL MARKETING RESEARCH

The ability for research to deliver fast and yet sensitively analysed results across a range of different countries in today's global markets is crucial for competitive success. In the past decade, we have seen the speed of business increase substantively with the global diffusion of computers, digital technologies and telecommunication devices. Instant communication has become a standard even in global markets, which means that marketing research has a critical role in feeding into decision makers time-sensitive insights and changes in market behaviours around the globe.

The development of better decision tools and decision support systems and of globally based research supplier networks have in turn led to an increase in the usage of continent-wide and worldwide surveys which transcend national boundaries. The development of specialist global niche marketing research strategies and a rapid increase in the rate and spread of product innovation with which research must keep pace have all meant that the old days of slow-moving local or national test marketing results are long gone.

There has also been an information explosion. The availability of online databases and Internet-based information sources have transformed the nature of international marketing research and the role it plays in the marketing process. Electronic data interchange networks enable companies across the globe to build the ultimate in customization strategies or 'one-to-one' marketing, As marketing research has adpated to these new technologies the importance of online research has grown. It is estimated that over half of all revenue for marketing research agencies is derived from online research. Equally the role of the marketing researcher has become much more closely aligned with the decision-making processess of organisations.

Research into international market issues can incorporate three major roles:

- **cross-cultural research**, the conducting of a research project across nation or culture groups
- foreign research, research conducted in a country other than the country of the commissioning company
- multi-country research, research conducted in all or important countries where a company is represented (Sarathy *et al.* (2006)).

This does not in any way convey the enormity of the task involved in developing an international market intelligence system which would be sufficient to provide the information necessary to make sound international marketing decisions. Such an information system would not only have to identify and analyse potential markets, but also have the capacity to generate an understanding of the many environmental variables discussed in the previous three chapters. Many levels of environmental factors will affect international marketing decisions, from macro-level economic factors to political–legal factors, as well as the micro market structures and cultural factors affecting the consumer. It is a truism of international marketing that in competing internationally uncertainty is generally greater and the difficulties in getting information are also greater. It is frequently said that it is the lack of market knowledge which is the greatest obstacle to companies succeeding on international markets, and it is access to such knowledge that makes it possible for the internationally experienced company to extend their activities to new markets.

As such, the role of the international market researcher is to provide an assessment of market demand globally, an evaluation of potential markets and of the risks and costs involved in market entries, as well as detailed information on which to base effective marketing strategies.

To achieve this the researcher has three primary functions to carry out:

1 Scanning international markets to identify and analyse the opportunities.
2 Building marketing information systems to monitor environmental trends.
3 Carrying out primary marketing research studies for input into the development of marketing strategies and to test the feasibility of the possible marketing mix options, both in foreign country markets and across a range of international markets.

In the next three sections we will examine each of these in some detail.

OPPORTUNITY IDENTIFICATION AND ANALYSIS

Scanning international markets

There are 194 countries in the world (including Taiwan and the Vatican City). Even a large multinational corporation would find it difficult to resource market development in all these countries. Thus the first task for the researcher is to scan markets to identify which countries have the potential for growth. International markets are scanned primarily at this stage to identify countries that warrant further research and analysis: thus the researcher will look for countries that meet three qualifying criteria:

1 *Accessibility*. If a company is barred from entering the market, it would be an ineffective use of resources to take research further. The scanning unit would assess such things as tariffs, non-tariff barriers, government regulation and import regulations to assess the accessibility of the market. Japan is still seen as a highly profitable market, but it is viewed by some as inaccessible due to the perception of the difficulties involved in overcoming trade barriers.

2 *Profitability*. At this level the researcher would assess factors that at a macro level could render the market unprofitable – for example, the availability of currency, the existence of exchange regulations, government subsidies to local competition, price controls and substitute products. Many countries in Africa are fully accessible, but companies question the ability of trade partners in some of these countries to pay. The extra risk of non-payment reduces the profit return calculations of those markets.

3 *Market size*. An assessment is made of the potential market size to evaluate whether future investment is likely to bear fruit.

The specific indicators a company will look for tend to be very product- and market-specific. Thus a hand tool manufacturer in the north of England specialising in tools for woodworking craftsmen looked for evidence of a hobby market (accessibility), high levels of disposable income (profitability) and large numbers of educated, middle-aged men with leisure time (market size). Flower growers are more concerned with competition (see Dilemma 4.1).

At the scanning stage the researcher is attempting to identify countries where marketing opportunities exist. Having identified those opportunities, the researcher will need to make an assessment of their viability for further investigation. In principle, there are three types of market opportunities:

1 Existing markets. Here customers' needs are already serviced by existing suppliers; therefore, market entry would be difficult unless

---

DILEMMA 4.1

Dutch flowers to the US

The dominant markets for cut flowers are Western Europe, the US and Japan. Western Europe is by far the largest market, currently three times the size of the US. Research carried out by the Dutch Flower Council, however, indicates rapid growth in the market in the US. In Europe the Dutch growers face intense competition from north and west Africa and, more recently, from south and east Africa and Israel. The main suppliers to the US market are Mexico, central and southern America and, increasingly, the Caribbean basin.

QUESTION *The dilemma for the Dutch growers is should they use their limited resources to continue to build their presence in Western Europe, or should they try to develop a presence in the US market and, if so, how should they go about it?*

SOURCE: PROFESSOR STEVE CARTER, LEEDS METROPOLITAN UNIVERSITY

the company has a superior product or an entirely new concept to offer the market.

2 **Latent markets.** In this type of market there are recognised potentialcustomers but no company has yet offered a product to fulfil the latent need. As there is no direct competition, market entry would be easier than in existing markets as long as the company could convey the benefits of its product to the market. Coca-Cola and Pepsi Cola dominate the global market. Qibla Cola, however, has tapped into a latent market by targeting consumers who do not want to buy a US brand. They have launched their cola not on its product benefits but as an alternative for consumers around the globe who oppose US policies in the Middle East and who wish to support ethical causes – and Qibla gives 10 per cent of all profits made to good causes (see Dilemma 4.2).

3 **Incipient markets.** Incipient markets are ones that do not exist at present but conditions and trends can be identified that indicate the future emergence of needs that, under present circumstances, would be unfulfilled. It may be, of course, that existing companies in the market are positioning themselves to take advantage of emerging markets but at present there is no direct competition.

The nature of competition can be analysed in a broadly similar way, with three distinct product types: competitive products, improved products and breakthrough products. A competitive product is one that has no significant advantages over those already on offer. An improved product is one that, whilst not unique, represents an improvement upon those currently available. A breakthrough product, by way of contrast, represents an innovation and as such, is likely to have a significant competitive advantage.

The level and nature of competition that a firm will encounter can therefore be analysed by relating the three types of demand to the three types of product. This is illustrated in Figure 4.1 and can be used as a basis for determining first, whether market entry is likely to succeed, and second, whether the company possesses any degree of competitive advantage. This, in turn, provides an insight into the nature of the marketing task needed. In saying this, however, it needs to be emphasised that this sort of insight provides an initial framework for analysis and nothing more. What is then needed is a far more detailed assessment of the degree of competitive advantage that the company possesses.

Obviously the greatest opportunities, together with the greatest risk and potential for profit, are in the identification of incipient markets. The problem is that because markets do not yet exist there is no market data. Researchers therefore use analytical techniques to make sure they identify and recognise conditions in incipient markets, thus enabling their companies to develop strategies by which to be first into the market.

In the research techniques used, the basic principle is to compare, contrast or correlate various factors in the market under study with some external variant to

DILEMMA 4.2

Optcan assess Saudi Arabia

A Canadian company, Optcan, is in the business of Free Space Optics (FSOs), an emerging technology that transports data via laser technology. They are considering entering the Saudi Arabian market and so wish to carry out a feasibility study to help them decide whether they should set up a

presence in the market. However, there is no actual market data as there is no company, as yet, operating directly in the market.

QUESTION *How should Optcan evaluate whether Saudi Arabia is potentially viable and how should they assess the level of potential risks involved?*

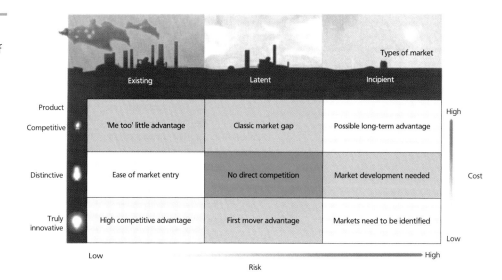

identify similarities within the market or with other markets, thus assessing
whether the right conditions exist for a market to emerge.

Some of the key techniques used are now discussed.

Demand pattern analysis

In this technique, it is assumed that countries at different levels of economic
development have differing patterns of demand and consumption. By comparing
the pattern of demand in the country under study with the pattern of demand in
an established market when the product was first introduced, a broad estimate of
an incipient market can be achieved.

Multiple factor indices

This assumes that the demand for a product correlates to demand for other products. By measuring demand for the correlated product, estimates of potential
demand can be made. For example, a manufacturer of frozen foods may make an
assessment by measuring the number of houses with freezers.

Analogy estimation

Analogy estimation is used where there is a lack of market data in a particular
country. Analogies are made with existing markets – perhaps the US – comparing
and contrasting certain ratios to test for market potential. This technique arouses
mixed levels of enthusiasm, since experiences with it have been variable. In addition, it is an expensive technique to implement and doubts have been expressed
about the accuracy of its forecasts. Those who have used it typically adopt one of
two approaches:

- A cross-section approach, where the product market size for one country
  is related to some appropriate gross economic indicator in order to establish
  a ratio. This ratio is then applied to the specific country under analysis
  to estimate the potential for the product market in that country.

- A time-series approach based on the belief that product usage moves through
  a cycle. Thus one assumes that the country under analysis will follow the

same pattern of consumption as a more advanced economy, albeit with a predetermined time lag.

Regression analysis

This technique is typically used to complement an analogy approach. Regression analysis is particularly useful in enhancing the likely accuracy and eventual confidence that can be placed on cross-sectional studies.

Macrosurvey technique

This method is essentially anthropological in approach and can help companies to establish themselves early in emerging countries with obvious long-term marketing benefits. The technique is based on the notion that as a community grows and develops, more specialised institutions come into being. Thus, one can construct a scale of successively more differentiated institutions against which any particular country can be evaluated to assess its level of development and hence its market potential.

These techniques highlight the importance of comparative research and regular market screening if incipient demand is to be identified at an early stage. However, the value of several of the techniques does rest upon the assumption that all countries and their consumption patterns will develop along broadly common lines. If firms are to make effective use of many of these techniques, the assumption of common economic development patterns must stand. Increasingly, however, evidence is emerging to suggest that global commonality does not exist to this degree and there are strong arguments for companies grouping country markets for the purposes of this sort of comparative analysis.

Risk evaluation

As previously stated, incipient markets offer the greatest opportunity for profit potential, but with profit comes risk.

The risk factor in opportunity analysis cannot be over-estimated. Sometimes political risk itself can be the most important determining factor to the success or failure of an international marketing campaign. In the markets where opportunities have been identified, researchers need to make an assessment first as to the type of risk apparent in that market (political, commercial, industrial or financial), and second as to the degree of that risk. Matrices such as the one identified in Figure 4.2 can be useful in carrying out such assessments.

FIGURE 4.2
The four-risk matrix

Country						
Risk level	A	B	C	D	E	F
Risk type	Low	Moderate	Some	Risky	Very risky	Dangerous
Political						
Commercial						
Industrial						
Financial						

Over recent years marketers have developed various indices to help assess the risk factor in the evaluation of potential market opportunities. Two such indices are the Business Environment Risk Index (BERI) and the Goodnow and Hansz temperature gradient.

BERI

BERI provides country risk forecasts for 50 countries throughout the world and is updated three times a year. This index assesses 15 environment factors, including political stability, balance of payments volatility, inflation, labour productivity, local management skills, bureaucratic delays, etc. Each factor is rated on a scale of 0–4 ranging from unacceptable conditions (0) to superior conditions (4). The key factors are individually weighted to take account of their importance. For example, political stability is weighted by a factor of 2.5. The final score is out of 100 and scores of over 80 indicate a favourable environment for investors and an advanced economy. Scores of less than 40 indicate very high risk for companies committing capital.

The Goodnow and Hansz temperature gradient

This classification system rates a country's environmental factors on a temperature gradient, whereby environmental factors are defined as being on a scale from hot to moderate to cold. The system examines such factors as political stability, economic development and performance, cultural unity, legal barriers and geocultural barriers. Relative positive values on the gradient give degrees of hotness. Relative negative values indicate degrees of coldness. Thus, an advanced economy such as the USA would achieve a hot score, whereas a less developed economy such as India would be given a cold score.

The main value of subscribing to such indices is to give companies an appreciation of the risk involved in opportunities identified. There are a number of organisations around the globe who publish country risk ratings – Standard and Poor, the OECD, *The Economist*, and Moodys – so information on risk evaluation is readily available to the Internet researcher.

Major global corporations such as IBM, Honeywell and ICI have specialist political risk analysts, monitoring environmental trends to alert senior managers to changes and developments which may affect their markets.

INTERNATIONAL MARKETING SEGMENTATION

At the scanning stage, the manager researching international markets is identifying and then analysing opportunities to evaluate which markets to prioritise for further research and development. Some framework is then needed to evaluate those opportunities and try to reduce the plethora of countries to a more manageable number. To do this, managers need to divide markets into groups so they can decide which markets to prioritise or even to target.

Market segmentation is the strategy by which a firm partitions a market into submarkets or segments likely to manifest similar responses to marketing inputs. The aim is to identify the markets on which a company can concentrate its resources and efforts so that they can achieve maximum penetration of that market, rather than going for a market-spreading strategy where they aim to achieve a presence, however small, in as many markets as possible.

The Pareto law usually applies to international marketing strategies with its full vigour. The most broad-based and well-established international firms find that 20 per cent of the countries they serve generate at least 80 per cent of the results. Obviously these countries must receive greater managerial attention and allocation of resources. The two main bases for segmenting international markets are by geographical criteria (i.e. countries) and transnational criteria (i.e. individual decision makers).

Geographical criteria

The traditional practice is to use a country-based classification system as a basis for categorising international markets. The business portfolio matrix (Figure 4.3) is indicative of the approach taken by many companies. In this, markets are classified in three categories.

The business portfolio matrix

PRIMARY OPPORTUNITY

These markets indicate the best opportunities for long-term strategic development. Companies may want to establish a permanent presence and so embark on a thorough research programme.

SECONDARY OPPORTUNITY

These are the markets where opportunities are identified but political or economic risk is perceived as being too high to make long-term irrevocable commitments. These markets would be handled in a more pragmatic way due to

FIGURE 4.3
Business portfolio matrix

SOURCE: HARRELL AND KEIFER (1993)

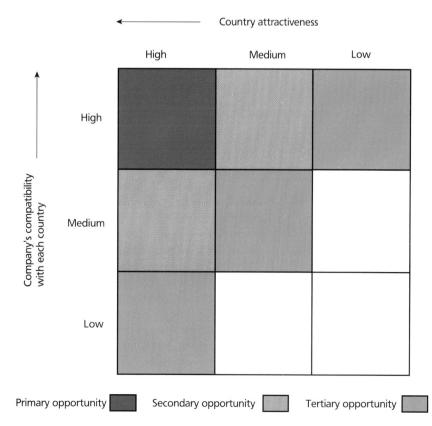

Primary opportunity ▮ Secondary opportunity ▮ Tertiary opportunity ▮

the potential risks identified. A comprehensive marketing information system would be needed.

TERTIARY OPPORTUNITY

These are the catch-what-you-can markets. They will be perceived as high risk and so the allocation of resources will be minimal. Objectives in such countries would be short term and opportunistic, companies would give no real commitment. No significant research would be carried out.

Figure 4.3 illustrates the business portfolio matrix. The horizontal axis evaluates the attractiveness of each country on objective and measurable criteria (e.g. size, stability and wealth). The vertical axis evaluates the firm's compatibility with each country on a more subjective and judgemental basis. Primary markets would score high on both axes.

This is a particularly useful device for companies operating in a portfolio of markets to prioritise market opportunity. Ford Tractor carried out such an analysis of key markets. In assessing market attractiveness they explored four basic elements: market size, market growth rate, government regulations and economic and political stability. Competitive strength and compatibility were defined in the international context and such factors as market share, market representation, contribution margin and market support were examined. Using this analysis they identified Kenya, Pakistan and Venezuela as primary markets.

Equally, a company may use the BERI index, Hofstede's cultural dimensions or the Goodnow and Hansz country temperature gradient as a basis for classifying countries. Whatever measurement base is used, once the primary markets have been identified, companies then normally use standard methods to segment the markets within countries using such variables as demographic/ economic factors, lifestyles, consumer motivations, geography, buyer behaviour, psychographics, etc.

Thus the primary segmentation base is geographic (by country) and the secondary bases are within countries. The problem here is that depending on the information base, it may be difficult to fully formulate secondary segmentation bases. Furthermore, such an approach can run the risk of leading to a differentiated marketing approach which may leave the company with a very fragmented international strategy.

Infrastructure/marketing institution matrix

Sheth and Arma (2005) suggest international markets be categorised by the country's infrastructure and marketing institutional development. A country's infrastructure development refers to roads, telecommunication, legislative bodies and open and free justice systems etc. Infrastructure development is usually associated with economic development. The availability of media efficiency of the distribution channels are used as indicators for marketing institutional development as it is associated with competitive marketing offerings, i.e. competitive, efficient and effective marketing institutions, are available to marketers in country with highly developed marketing institutions, which generally includes efficient and effective distribution channels.

Using these dimensions countries can be classified as *Developed infrastructure and developed marketing institutions*, e.g. the US, UK and Scandinavia. *Developed infrastructure but restricted marketing development*, e.g Japan and Germany. Examples of marketing development restrictions are countries that have time restrictions on when the store can be open (e.g. Germany) or restrictions on the size of stores (e.g. Japan). *Low levels of infrastructure development but have developed marketing institutions* such as retailers and media, e.g. India and Mexico. The last category is both low *infrastructure development and low marketing institutional development.* Typically these are countries that have not developed efficient and effective distribution systems due to geography (e.g. Indonesia) or legal restrictions (e.g. Vietnam).

A major drawback with the country-based approach is that countries do not buy products, consumers do. Global markets therefore need to be understood in terms of groups of buyers who share the need and desire for a product and the ability to pay for it, not just those who share a national border (as is the case in Illustration 4.1). If companies are to establish brand positions across a number of international markets, an increasingly common strategic goal, then they need to use a segmentation strategy that enables them to build a consistent brand position across those markets. If a company is to try to achieve a consistent and controlled marketing strategy across all its international markets, it needs a transnational approach to its segmentation strategy. If the basis for global market segmentation is one that cuts across national boundaries, then marketing strategies can be developed that will work for similar segments around the globe.

Transnational segmentation

Buyers in any particular segment seek similar benefits from and exhibit similar behaviour in buying a product. According to Hassan and Stephen (2005), although these consumers may live in different areas of the world and come from very different backgrounds and value systems, they have commonalities in

ILLUSTRATION 4.1

Dr Martens goes ethnographic

SOURCE: ADAPTED FROM 'BIG BRANDS TURNING TO BIG BROTHER', THE *DAILY TELEGRAPH* 29 MARCH, 2007

To make sure their products succeed across national boundaries global brands are turning to ethnographic market research. As the costs of launching new products rises exponentially companies have to minimise the risk of failure, and ethnographical research can help them develop deep insights into their global market segments to help them develop innovative marketing platforms.

While retailers mine data from microchipped loyalty cards to segment markets and target special offers, this kind of number-crunching misses the bigger picture of how products are chosen and how they could be improved.

PHOTO CREDIT: MICHAEL JENNER/ALAMY

One ethnographic research company, EverydayLives, researches fast-moving consumer brands for companies such as Unilever, Proctor and Gamble, Pedigree and GlaxoSmithKline. It has conducted research for new products launched in Russia, Poland, Latin America and Africa.

For Dr Martens, the EverydayLives team questioned youth buying patterns. The client brief was: how are young people using fashion brands in their everyday lives? Why, for example, have Nike trainers, baseball caps and hoodies become so embedded in youth culture across the globe?

Young researchers fanned out to the east and west coasts of America, Japan, Europe and beyond. They found individuals who conformed to Dr Martens' target market and followed paid volunteers for several days, shooting hours and hours of their daily routine with a hand-held digital camera.

At the end of it hundreds of hours of film were edited down to just one hour of highlights with an analysis and commentary. It emerged from the analysis that teenagers preferred fashions that allowed them to customise the item of clothing and take ownership of it, such as wearing a cap the wrong way round or pulling the tongue of a pair of trainers out from behind the laces. The researchers concluded iconic products had something distinctive – a label or a style – that made wearers stand out as part of a tribe. As a result of this research, teenagers around the world could soon be sporting a new range of Doc Martens trainers with coloured laces and a long tongue that pulls out of the shoe.

association with a given global brand. To achieve a transnational approach to segmentation therefore, a country as a unit of analysis is too large to be of operational use. An alternative approach is to examine the individual decision-maker (Hassan and Stephen 2005). Key bases for segmentation would include such variables as value systems, demographic, psychographic and behavioural criteria.

Demographic variables have obvious potential as cross-national segmentation criteria. The most commonly used variables include sex, age, income level, social class and educational achievement. Frequently use is made of a battery of demographic variables when delineating transnational market segments.

Psychographic segmentation involves using lifestyle factors in the segmentation process. Appropriate criteria are usually of an inferred nature and concern consumer interests and perceptions of 'way of living' in regard to work and leisure habits. Critical dimensions of lifestyle thus include activities, interests and opinions. Objective criteria, normally of a demographic nature, may also be helpful when defining lifestyle segments. Research International, when researching the transnational segments of young adults globally, divided them into four broad categories. 'Enthusiastic materialists' are optimistic and aspirational and to be found in developing countries and emerging markets like India and Latin America. 'Swimmers against the tide', on the other hand, demonstrate a degree of underlying pessimism, tend to live for the moment and are likely to be found in southern Europe. In northern Europe, the US and Australasia are the 'new realists', looking for a balance between work and leisure with some underlying pessimism in outlook and, finally, the 'complacent materialists' are defined as passively optimistic and located in Japan.

Behavioural variables also have a lot of potential as a basis for global market segmentation. In particular, attention to patterns of consumption and loyalty in respect of product category and brand can be useful, along with a focus on the context for usage. Variables such as the benefit sought or the buying motivations may be used. Behaviourally defined segments may be identified in terms of a specific aspect of behaviour which is not broad enough to be defined as a lifestyle. Goodyear have effectively used behavioural characteristics to develop a global segmentation strategy (see Illustration 4.2).

EuroMosaic

One of the trends enabling segmentation using individualistic characteristics to become a feasible strategy for many companies is the development of geodemographic databases. One such database is the CCN EuroMosaic. This claims to be the first pan-European segmentation system allowing the classification of 500 million consumers across the European Union on the basis of the types of neighbourhood in which they live. Ten EuroMosaic types have been identified:

1 Elite suburbs
2 Average areas
3 Luxury flats
4 Low-income inner city
5 High-rise social housing
6 Industrial communities
7 Dynamic families
8 Low-income families
9 Rural agricultural
10 Vacation retirement.

ILLUSTRATION 4.2

Goodyear global segmentation research

Goodyear Tyre and Rubber Company investigated the feasibility of developing a segmentation strategy that could be applied globally to their world markets. The requirement was that the strategy would provide a practical base for an international marketing strategy and prove to be consistent and durable.

This is an important part of their objective to gain 1 per cent market share globally and a further 2 per cent of the US market by 2005.

After considerable research they identified three decision orientations which could constitute primary attitude segments when buying tyres: brand, outlet and price.

From consumer research they then developed six consumer segments:

1 The *Prestige Buyer* makes the brand decision first and the outlet decision second. This segment is male-dominated, very 'upscale', brand and retailer loyal, does very little information-gathering prior to making a purchase and is predisposed to major brands.

2 The *Comfortable Conservative* looks for the outlet first and the brand second. This segment has the same characteristics of the first group but includes more women who are dependent on the retailer for expert advice. These shoppers tend to develop a lasting relationship with a retailer.

PHOTO CREDIT: IMAGES COURTESY OF GOODYEAR

3 The *Value Shopper* considers brand first and price second. This segment is seen as Mr Average. Its members are predisposed to major brands, have a very low retailer loyalty and search for information extensively to educate themselves prior to making the purchase.

4 The *Pretender* wants a major brand but the price ultimately determines the choice. The first decision is price, the second is brand. This group has two subsegments – the aspiring young and emulating old – but all these shoppers exhibit very little loyalty to retailers or brands and do a lot of information searching.

5 The *Trusting Patron* chooses the outlet first and the price second. This group is somewhat 'downscale', heavily female and extremely retailer loyal. The brand is totally unimportant and little searching for information is undertaken.

6 The *Bargain Hunter* shops for price first, outlet second but price is really the only consideration. This group primarily consists of young, 'downscale' people who have low retailer and brand loyalty and who delay the tyre purchase as long as possible.

QUESTION *Do you think these segments are valid across all global markets?*

SOURCE: ADAPTED FROM MARKETING NEWS (1996) AND RUBBER AND PLASTIC NEWS (2003)

The distribution of these typologies can be mapped by country and across Europe. Given the addresses of a company's customers, the system gives the researcher the ability to identify the type of people using certain products and services and to identify at a local level where the similar geodemographic types are, thus acting as an aid to the segmentation of markets and the identification of primary and secondary markets. EuroMosaic will also be of use in identifying the sample in a research survey and for building lists in a direct marketing exercise.

Despite the attractiveness of using individualistic characteristics, it is apparent there is strong potential for significant differences in the patterns of consumer behaviour within global segments derived using this method. Also, international similarities in lifestyle and behaviour do tend to be specific, and relevant primarily to specialist products and niche markets.

Hierarchical country – consumer segmentation

To overcome some of the above problems, a compromise approach would be to implement a procedure for global segmentation which integrated features of both processes.

Hassan and Stephen (2005) propose a hierarchical approach to global market segmentation that takes into account country factors but also incorporates individual behaviourist characteristics into a segmentmentation strategy that helps companies develop cross-national segments to allow for a global positioning strategy.

On this basis the marketing strategy would build on the premise that world markets consist of both similarities and differences and that the most effective strategies reflect a full recognition of similarities and differences *across* rather than *within* markets. Thus companies competing internationally should segment markets on the basis of consumers, not countries. Segmentation by purely geographical factors leads to national stereotyping. It ignores the differences between customers within a nation and ignores similarities across boundaries. Colgate and Palmolive reached such a conclusion when carrying out an analytical review of their own segmentation strategies, and now use the hierarchical approach.

Any global segmentation strategy needs to be carried out in stages:

1 Identify those countries that have the infrastructure to support the product and are accessible to the company.

2 Screen those countries to arrive at a shorter list of countries with the characteristics that make the market attractive, e.g. a frozen dessert manufacturer may say that for a market to be attractive there need to be at least five million refrigerators per market.

3 Develop mini-segments within these countries based on factors such as:
   ■ information search behaviour
   ■ product characteristics required.

   The outcome of this process would be a series of mini-segments within qualified countries.

4 The development of transnational segments begins by looking for similarities across segments. Factor analysis of the behavioural patterns of these segments would enable managers to understand the characteristics of the demand of each segment as regards marketing mix issues. Each mini-segment would therefore be rated on several strategic factors in terms of potential response.

5 Cluster analysis is then used to identify meaningful cross-national segments, each of which, it is thought, would evoke a similar response to any marketing mix strategy.

It is argued that this approach would enable marketers to design strategies for cross-national segments and so take a more consumer-orientated approach to international marketing. In prioritising markets, companies would use consumers as their primary base. Some writers argue that companies still need a secondary segmentation stage to identify the key countries where these transnational segments can be found.

THE INTERNATIONAL MARKETING INFORMATION SYSTEM

Building the information base

Having completed the scanning stage, the researcher will have reduced the number of potential countries to a feasible list requiring further research. The company needs a systematic method for evaluating the markets identified, and this is primarily the role of the marketing information system (MIS).

In building any MIS, the objective of the company is to develop a cost-effective communication channel between the environment in which the company operates and the decision makers. One of the great difficulties in international marketing planning is the long communication lines between headquarters and subsidiaries: it often causes inadequate data flow which results in misunderstandings and in wrong decisions being made.

An effective MIS can contribute to solving these problems and provide a solid base for strategic decisions to be made. Using the 12C environmental analysis model in Table 4.1, we can identify some of the major inputs that an international marketing information system should contain.

The information input into the MIS is used to draw up a market profile analysis, as shown in Figure 4.4.

The objective of a market profile analysis is to enable the company to use the environmental information built up in the system to identify opportunities and problems in the potential marketing strategies. For example, the fact that television advertising is prohibited in a country will have major implications for a promotional strategy.

It is this type of detailed assessment that helps companies determine the degree of competitive advantage they may possess and the most appropriate method of market entry. Using consistent frameworks also enables the researcher to make cross-country comparisons much more easily.

Sources of information

In building an MIS, companies would utilise a variety of information services and sources. The starting point for most international researchers in the UK is UK Trade and Investment (see the UKTI case study at the end of Chapter 2). This government department helps businesses export and grow overseas and provides a variety of support services to such organisations. The majority of Western nations have similar government-sponsored organisations helping exporters to develop information on international markets.

Some reports have been critical of the deficiencies in the provision of market intelligence by government departments and of firms' abilities to use this information. The main criticisms are:

- information is non-specific to particular industries
- firms experience problems with the bureaucratic nature of some government services

■ data is often in a form which is unsuitable for the company's needs, or too general to be of use

■ services have been available only in the capital city

■ inadequate publicity about the information and services available.

TABLE 4.1 The 12C framework for analysing international markets

Country
- general country information
- basic SLEPT data
- impact of environmental dimensions

Concentration
- structure of the market segments
- geographical spread

Culture/consumer behaviour
- characteristics of the country
- diversity of cultural groupings
- nature of decision-making
- major influences of purchasing behaviour

Choices
- analysis of supply
- international and external competition
- characteristics of competitors
- import analysis
- competitive strengths and weaknesses

Consumption
- demand and end use analysis of economic sectors that use the product
- market share by demand sector
- growth patterns of sectors
- evaluation of the threat of substitute products

Contractual obligations
- business practices
- insurance
- legal obligations

Commitment
- access to market
- trade incentives and barriers
- custom tariffs

Channels
- purchasing behaviour
- capabilities of intermediaries
- coverage of distribution costs
- physical distribution
- infrastructure
- size and grade of products purchased

Communication
- promotion
- media infrastructure and availability
- which marketing approaches are effective
- cost of promotion
- common selling practices
- media information

Capacity to pay
- pricing
- extrapolation of pricing to examine trends
- culture of pricing
- conditions of payment
- insurance terms

Currency
- stability
- restrictions
- exchange controls

Caveats
- factors to beware of

FIGURE 4.4
Market profile analysis

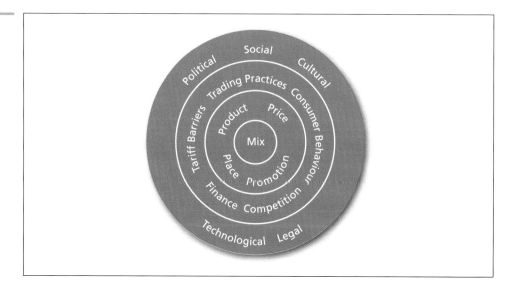

Other institutions that offer advice and information to companies researching international markets include:

- business libraries
- university libraries
- international chambers of commerce
- UK Trade and Investment: national and regional international marketing intelligence centres
- local business links
- embassies
- banks
- trade associations
- export councils
- overseas distributors
- overseas sales subsidiaries
- foreign brokerage houses
- foreign trade organisations such as the Japanese Export Trade and Research Organisation (JETRO).

Online databases

As previously stated, one of the main developments in the availability of secondary information for international markets over the past five years has been the emergence of a plethora of Internet information sites, online databases, company customer response management (CRM) databases and online research services. Nokia's analysis of its own CRM database allowed it to identify that their customers viewed phones as fashion accessories – which enabled Nokia to reposition themselves and steal global market share from Ericsson.

Online databases are systems which hold computerised information which can be accessed through the Internet, making a wide range of information available from an online database to a manager in a matter of seconds. Information can be transmitted from anywhere in the world instantaneously, bringing obvious benefits.

There are numerous advantages in using online databases. They are regularly updated – two or three times per day – and are therefore much more current than traditional printed sources. Retrieving information online is much more cost-effective than manual searching and is considerably faster. Many online databases can be accessed 24 hours a day, seven days a week. You also retrieve – and consequently pay for – only the information you want.

Online data sources can also be a solution for carrying out cross-cultural marketing research when primary data collection is prohibitive due to its cost. Marketing information globally is now becoming much more consolidated as global organisations develop databases that are excellent for cross-country comparisons and for global market information. Table 4.2 gives examples of some of the globally based online databases that managers wishing to carry out comparative studies or globally based marketing research may find useful.

Organisations in developing countries are increasingly using online computerised databases for their market research work as they become better equipped with telecommunication facilities. The type and volume of trade information available through online databases has expanded dramatically over recent years, with new databases of interest to business and trade organisations continuously being introduced to the market.

The use of the Internet for marketing intelligence, therefore, is one of the most important ways in which connectivity can improve a firm's ability to develop international markets. Buying or commissioning market research reports can be a prohibitively expensive business. For a fraction of the cost and in many cases free of charge, much of the same information can be gathered electronically. Given the time and expense associated with the collection of primary data, the use of Internet-based secondary data in international marketing research will continue to expand.

However, researchers do need to be wary using such databases and ensure they fully evaluate the credibility and worthiness of the data they obtain from such sources to ensure the accuracy and validity. The volume of relevant international marketing information available on the Internet is too extensive to describe in detail in this chapter but includes numerous online newspapers and journals, an extensive list of individual country and industry market research reports, trade lists of suppliers, agents, distributors and government contacts in a large number of countries, details on host country legislation covering imports, agency agreements, joint ventures, etc.

TABLE 4.2 Online databases

Company Information

Duns European Marketing Database:	1.8 million companies in 16 countries
European Kompass:	320,000 companies
Datastream:	Financial data on companies worldwide
Extel:	Worldwide company information
McCarthys:	Articles on companies/industries
Predicast:	Worldwide business and industry information

Trade Data

Textline:	Reuters
Comtrade:	UN Foreign trade database
Tradstrat:	Import/export on 22 countries
Croners:	Wide range of data on EC/USA/JAPAN
Eurostar– context:	EU statistical data
IMF/World Bank/UN:	World trade statistics

Market Information

Business International:	Market forecasts worldwide
Euro Monitor:	Covers market reports on 100 consumer markets, www.euromonitor.com/World_Consumer_ Lifestyles_covers comparable country lifestyle_ data across 71 countries.
Profound/MAID:	Full text market research reports
Informat:	Abstracts from 500 newspapers and trade journals
PTS Prompt:	Abstracts/articles from 1500 trade journals
Mintel:	Market reports

Some of the best sites for undertaking general country screening and international marketing research include:

- Brand data: www.brandchannel.com; www.gbrands.com; www.globalstrategies.com
- *Business Week*: www.businessweek.com
- *The Economist*: www.economist.com
- European Union: www.europa.eu.int
- UK Trade and Investment: www.uktradeinvest.gov.uk
- UK Chambers of Commerce: www.britishchambers.org.uk
- United Nations: www.un.org
- World Bank: www.worldbank.org
- World Fact Book: www.cia.gov/cia/publications/**factbook**
- World Trade Organisation: www.wto.org.

These are just a few examples of the large number of websites which provide access to sources of international trade and marketing data as well as other useful services.

Problems in using secondary data

In carrying out marketing research internationally, problems arise by virtue of the very nature of the number and complexities of the markets being investigated. Whilst the use of secondary data is essential in international marketing research, the reader needs to be aware of its limitations and some of the problems that occur in using secondary data.

Perhaps the most frequently discussed issue is the availability and accessibility of quality secondary information in international markets. The collection of secondary data concerning the economy and the business infrastructure in some countries varies in quality and consistency and evaluation of secondary data is critical for international marketing research. Different countries, even for internationally based statistics, may report different values for a given statistic, such as GDP, because of differences in the way the unit is defined. Measurement units may not be equivalent across countries and the accuracy of secondary data may also vary from country to country. Business and income statistics are affected by the taxation structures and the extent of tax evasion. Population censuses may vary in frequency and year in which the data are collected.

One of the reasons for the distortion of data in some countries is the political considerations of governments. The International Labour Organisation found the actual unemployment rate in Russia was 10 per cent rather than the officially reported 2 per cent. The Indian government estimates that India's middle class numbers 250 million but, according to a recent survey of consumer patterns conducted by the National Council of Applied Economic Research in Delhi, the Indian middle-class probably totals 100 million at best and there is much stratification amongst them. This problem might be solved by obtaining authentic data from international organisations such as the OECD, EU, World Bank, etc.

The inconsistencies which can be found in the classification of various types of data in various countries are also a problem when carrying out any comparative analysis across markets. Sarathy *et al.* (2006) say that the most important problem associated with the secondary data, especially in developing countries, is its scarcity. A futher problem which can be quite misleading is the timeliness of the collected secondary data: it might have been collected several years earlier and never updated and is therefore outdated and of little value for future planning.

Many countries attempt to attract foreign investment by overstating certain factors that make the economic picture look better. On the other hand, some countries understate certain factors, making the economic situation appear worse in order to attract foreign aid (see Illustration 4.3).

The Asia-Pacific market is an important market and so obtaining reliable information in this region is of crucial importance for many companies. In a recent survey by INSEAD of one thousand managers of European companies operating in the Asia-Pacific region, it was found that only in Japan and Singapore were companies able to easily access data that was viewed as being of a reliable quality. In China, Taiwan and Vietnam data was not trusted by researchers. Even though Japanese data was relatively accessible, there were still difficulties due to the fact that the information was over-abundant and so it was difficult to select and interpret the relevant data or to give it any practical application.

None of the limitations discussed above should devalue the importance of secondary data in international marketing research. For many smaller companies lacking the resources to carry out primary research in markets which are geographically distant, it may be the only information to which there is relative ease of access.

ILLUSTRATION 4.3

Statistics in Siberia

Amidst a growing concern for the environment and the introduction of both domestic and international legislation for the permissible levels of pollutants and emissions, Eastern European states found themselves desperately trying to find new international markets for their surplus production now they were free to do so. Nowhere more so than in western Siberia, where the old Soviet practice of grouping together key

industries into geographic zones created a large number of mono-industry towns, primarily dependent upon coal mining and chemical production.

Conscious of the need to remove any possible barriers to international trade and in response to Western pressure, chemical plants were tasked with reducing pollutant emissions. Acceptable levels were agreed and companies were instructed to monitor regularly and report emission levels. Fines were imposed for any transgression.

The local administration (government) had responsibility for monitoring, control and checking, and so recorded and reported the local companies' compliance with the agreements made. This information was made publicly available.

As the twenty-first century progressed, official data on emissions revealed that rates were improving, but the levels were still 10 per cent above agreed figures. However, the official figures ignored a number of important points. First, few companies had monitoring equipment that worked, and so estimated their emission levels. Second, the administration had no monitoring equipment at all and so accepted the returns without question. Finally, no fines were ever imposed as no one could afford to pay them anyway.

Whilst official data painted a picture of progress, the real picture was far different.

QUESTION *Evaluate the problem of using secondary data such as this in international markets.*

PRIMARY RESEARCH IN INTERNATIONAL MARKETS

We have discussed scanning international markets to identify potential market opportunities and the building of market information systems from which the market profile analysis is formulated. So far we have only discussed obtaining information from secondary sources. It is unlikely that a researcher will be able to obtain the information for input into a marketing information system from secondary sources alone. Having exhausted these sources the researcher will need to embark on the collection of primary data to obtain the information required.

In the following sections we will discuss the issues facing the researcher which should be considered when endeavouring to carry out primary research studies. To do this we use the seven-step framework (Malhotra *et al.* 2006) depicted in Figure 4.5.

Problem definition and establishing objectives

The precise definition of the marketing research problem is more difficult and more important in international marketing research than in domestic marketing research. Unfamiliarity with the cultures and environmental factors of the countries where the research is being conducted can greatly increase the difficulty of obtaining accurate findings.

On a practical level, the differences in climate and infrastructure create problems. A survey on floor-cleaning products across Europe would have to take account of the fact that Scandinavians have wooden floors, there are lots of tiled and stone floors in the Mediterranean and in the UK many houses have carpets.

Many international marketing efforts fail not because research was not conducted but because the issue of comparability was not adequately addressed in defining the marketing research problem. This is why, as we saw in Chapter 3, it is so important to isolate the impact of self-reference criteria (SRC) and the unconscious reference to our own cultural values when defining the problem we are attempting to research in international markets.

DILEMMA 4.3

How to research the Canadian market

The account manager of a small food manufacturer in Groningen, in the Netherlands, was keen to expand the business in Canada. The company had 50 employees and manufactured a traditional Dutch ready-meal dish. The account manager was convinced from her knowledge of the marketplace that there were huge opportunities in Canada. Canada and the Netherlands had a strong relationship with a larger number of Dutch expatriates residing in Canada; English and French were the key 'second languages' for the account manager and her fellow employees. She had also read in a European Food Association newsletter that a UK manufacturer of a UK traditional dish, 'bangers and mash', had entered the Canadian market and used it as a springboard into the US.

As a small company the board of directors were reluctant to invest in overseas markets without the possibility of substantial return; the home market had declined and resources to invest were precious. Having persuaded the board to consider exporting, another member of the board felt that testing a market with closer proximity to the Netherlands such as Germany would be cheaper and easier.

The account manager had four weeks to provide a business case for Canada.

QUESTION *Without visiting the marketplace and no budget to purchase market information, how could the account manager identify sufficient evidence in such a short period of time to substantiate her proposal to invest in Canada?*

Developing an innovative approach

It is important in international marketing research to maintain flexibility in the approach you may have in the initial stages of the research. In the first stage of primary research, companies often use informal means to gather preliminary information and extensive use is made of the network of contacts available to the company both at home and abroad. It is unlikely that a full understanding of the foreign market will be obtained without visiting that market to gain information first hand. The first steps in doing this would be by networking and obtaining information through relatively informal means such as networking consortia or multi-client studies. The company in Dilemma 4.3 was seeking for such an innovative approach.

Networking

The use of contact networks to build information is vitally important because of the sometimes prohibitive cost of carrying out detailed market research studies

FIGURE 4.5

The international marketing research process

SOURCE: ADAPTED FROM MALHOTRA *ET AL.* (2006)

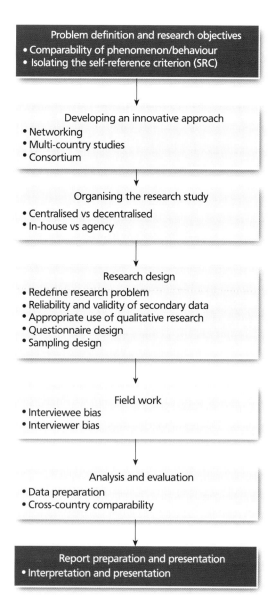

overseas. Before any detailed studies are undertaken, trade contacts need to be fully explored.

In order to find solutions to the many international marketing research problems, improvisation in international research is essential.

Most companies will make extensive use of their existing networks to build the market profiles and develop information bases. These could be agents, distributors, licensees, joint venture partners or other companies operating in the country under investigation.

Consortia

Marketing research consortia enable the comparison of data across different cultures and aid international marketing research efforts. Consortia are used by companies as a way of overcoming the difficulties involved in gathering data and establishing contacts in foreign markets. Essentially a group of companies will come together to research a particular market area in which they have a common interest. The advantages are:

- the consortium is more visible in the foreign market
- it is more likely to enjoy the support of the home export promotion organisation
- it achieves economies through the joint use of export facilities both at home and in foreign markets
- it increases the resources available to support the research operation.

However, if a company is to join a consortium, then it has to be prepared to have its autonomy reduced; this fact alone is the major reason most consortia fail. There also has to be a strong reason to join together for the relationship to develop. Nevertheless, by the pooling of resources, consortia are very useful in giving companies the resources needed to acquire knowledge on markets. Often agencies will offer multi-client studies which have much the same benefits (see Illustration 4.4).

Due to the problems and considerations we have discussed above, it may be that detailed research studies will only be carried out in markets where the market viability is seen to be positive and when detailed consumer/market information is required to develop marketing strategy. The cost of primary field research can be high and so it will only be carried out after all other sources have been investigated.

A survey carried out by INSEAD of European companies operating in the Asia-Pacific region showed that companies perceived the most significant sources of information as being personal contacts of the companies themselves, whether these were customers, other business relationships or their own market surveys.

A second tier of usefulness was then identified as consisting of other direct sources such as government contacts and contacts with competitors or trade associations. Finally, there was a third tier comprising publicly available information such as newspapers and magazines. This information may be widely read but relatively little weight seems to be given to its strategic value. The importance of directly collected information seems to confirm the view that business in Asia depends more heavily on the creation of a network of relationships than on analysis of hard data collected through surveys or other published information.

The collection of primary data

The cost and effort of collecting primary data in new markets is far higher than that of collecting such data in the domestic market. This is particularly the case in developing countries where no marketing research infrastructure or experience is available. Primary research in these circumstances would entail substantial investment costs in developing basic information relating, for example, to sampling frames or trained qualified interviewers. This, of course, reinforces the importance of secondary data for research purposes and the need for a systematic planning process when embarking on a primary research project.

Organising the research study

There are two major organisational questions which the international marketing manager will need to address:

- Should the research be carried out by foreign local subsidiaries or should all marketing research be centralised at headquarters?
- Should the fieldwork be carried out in-house or by an agency?

Centralisation vs decentralisation

If a centralised approach is adopted, then decisions have to be made regarding the specific responsibilities of the operating unit and what managerial arrangements should exist between the unit and headquarters staff. Further to this, decisions have to be taken as to what relationship is to exist between the local research staff who are ultimately responsible to headquarters and the local line management.

ILLUSTRATION 4.4

Use of multi-client studies

Multi-client studies have the advantage of enabling the client to participate in large surveys with focused questions at much less expense than would be the case otherwise. A significant growth in this type of field research has been seen in the past few years, particularly as more companies have become operational on international markets. Multi-client studies have become particularly prevalent across Europe since the formation of the Euro zone and the inclusion of Eastern European countries into the EU. It enables companies to gather primary market intelligence across a large number of countries at a fraction of the cost of carrying out their own study. These studies target specific audiences in specified countries and offer fast analysis. An example follows.

The East European Omnibus

Guaranteed: to run twice each month in the Czech Republic, Slovakia, Slovenia Hungary and Bulgaria: 1000 face-to-face interviews per country in respondents' homes.

Genuinely comparable: no subcontracting, using only qualified field force means absolutely identical methods, procedures and quality controls every time in every country.

High quality: all interviewer training, supervision, back-checking and other procedures are to the same high standards. True random preselected sample.

Fast: results two weeks after field work.

Other services include: online surveys, focus groups, local telephone surveys, hall tests and B2B research.

QUESTION *Identify a number of examples where multi-client studies would be effective in international marketing research.*

If a decentralised approach is chosen, then arrangements have to be made for research findings to be transferred from one operating unit to another. There is also the question of who has the overall responsibility for administering and overseeing the market research budget to ensure that resources are not wasted by a possible duplication of research effort.

Such issues are complex and are also related to overall organisational issues, which are examined in some depth in Chapter 5. In this chapter we will concentrate our discussion on the decision as to whether the company should carry out international research itself, or involve independent research agencies.

In-house or agency

Whether the company chooses to do all the research in-house or to use an agency will largely be determined by factors such as company resources, market expertise and product complexity.

If a company operates in a specialist B2B market with highly technological and complex products and has significant experience in the market, it may have no choice but to carry out research itself as it may be difficult to find an agency with the necessary competence.

However, if the company is operating in the consumer markets then a different scenario applies. Consumer research may require an established field force and the size of the markets may mean that a research company with field work resources is needed. A priority could well be to obtain an independent objective assessment of a foreign country; this could require specialist interviewing skills which a company alone might not be able to resource and thus would require the services of an agency. If the company is carrying out a multi-country study and needs a consistent research approach across all markets, then an international agency with resources across markets may be much more able to handle the research programme. Often, however, research in foreign markets may require a local firm that can do the field work, gather data and provide some analysis and interpretation. The selection and use of a foreign firm may be extremely important to the success of the whole project.

In choosing an agency, a company has six basic options:

- a local agency in the market under investigation
- a domestic agency with overseas offices
- a domestic agency with overseas associate companies
- a domestic agency which subcontracts field work to an agency in the market under investigation
- a domestic agency with competent foreign staff
- a global agency with offices around the world.

Which solution is best for the researcher will depend on a number of factors: the ease of briefing the agency, supervising and coordinating the project, the probability of language problems arising, the requirements of specialist market knowledge, the standard of competence required and the budget available.

Thus no single option is universally the best to select. It is primarily dependent on the budget available, the requirements of the research, the expertise within the company and, of course, the market under investigation. In a research study in Saudi Arabia the UK agency wished to maintain control and coordination of the project. However, Western interviewers would have had little success in eliciting meaningful information from Saudi businessmen. Therefore it was decided to employ a Cypriot field work agency to translate the questionnaire into Arabic and carry out the interviews etc. This led to certain control and communication problems, but it was the only realistic methodology to obtain the required information.

It may often be the case that in a multi-country study a combination of agencies are used. A typical multi-country study will go through the following steps:

1 The project is discussed at length with the client.
2 The field work agencies in each country are selected.
3 The questionnaire is designed centrally.
4 The questionnaire is translated locally and the translation is checked centrally.
5 The questionnaire is piloted locally.
6 The questionnaire is finalised centrally.
7 The inteviewers are briefed locally by an executive of the central company.
8 The field work is carried out locally.
9 The coding and editing plan is provided for the local agencies.
10 The edited and coded questionnaires are returned to head office.
11 A coding and editing check is carried out centrally.
12 Computing and analysis are carried out centrally.

Research design

In formulating a research design, considerable effort is needed to ensure that the methods used will ensure comparability of data. In order to handle problems such as cultural bias in research design and interpretation of data etc., perspectives of researchers from different countries and cultures could be incorporated in the process so that the bias is minimal. However, this method will only work if there are no major problems of communication between researchers from different environments. If this is not the case, there is a possibility that some other kind of unknown bias might be introduced into the research process which could be even more harmful. A study of the cultural and social values and the method of conducting research in the host country could play an important role in facilitating the process of international marketing research.

One of the first factors to consider in developing a research design is the reliability and validity of the secondary data used. As we have previously discussed, the accuracy of secondary data varies enormously across countries. This means that the database being used to develop primary research may be inaccurate or highly biased or lack the capability to make multi-country comparisons.

Further to this, the research design needs to incorporate methods which will be feasible in the foreign country markets, as well as allowing the international researcher to obtain meaningful and relevant findings.

For example, in India, illiteracy affects 64 per cent of the population outside the main areas, there are hundreds of languages and there can be very real fears that the interviewer is a government inspector in disguise. In such a scenario, a researcher would have problems throughout the research process in establishing the basic sample, designing the questionnaire and applying analytical techniques. However, India also has an affluent and educated middle class that in absolute terms is larger in size than the total population of any Western European country.

Social and cultural factors are one of the most important issues which affect the process of international marketing research. In collecting primary data, the researcher needs to consider the issues facing them in evaluating the possible methods under consideration.

In this context, qualitative research, survey methods, questionnaire design and sampling considerations are particularly important.

Qualitative research

Because the researcher is often unfamiliar with the foreign market to be examined, qualitative research is crucial in international marketing research. In the initial stages, qualitative research can provide insights into the problem and help in developing an approach by generating relevant research questions and hypotheses, models and characteristics which influence the research design. Thus, qualitative research may reveal the differences between foreign and domestic markets. It may also help to reduce the psychological distance between the researcher and the respondent. In some cases, the researcher must rely on qualitative research because secondary data may not be available. Some problems associated with qualitative techniques in developing countries are such things as accessibility (different concept of time), sampling (extended demographic factors such as religion and tribal membership), shorter span of attention and less familiarity with abstract thinking.

Focus groups can be used in many settings, particularly in newly emerging markets where there is scant data and companies are trying to establish the cultural sensitivities in the market to their products and services. In some cultures, such as in the Middle or Far East, people are hesitant to discuss their feelings in a group setting. In these cases, in-depth interviews can be used.

The use of projective techniques is sometimes appropriate. Association techniques (word association), completion techniques (sentence completion, story completion) and expressive techniques (role playing, third-person technique) involve the use of verbal cues and so are all good cross-cultural research techniques. An interesting example of qualitative research in international markets is given in Illustration 4.5.

ILLUSTRATION 4.5

The use of qualitative research to overhaul global brand image

Unilever, using a range of qualitative research techniques, such as focus groups, psychological testing and in-depth interviewing, have spent several years investigating the attitude to dirt of their consumers in a number of different cultures.

PHOTO CREDIT: ROBERT BROOK/ALAMY

As a result of their research they have recently re-launched their leading soap powder on the premise that 'dirt is good' – completely contrary to the line soap powders advertisements usually take – that 'dirt is bad'. The advertisements promote the image of children playing on the beach in the sand and ask consumers to think differently about how children get their clothes dirty. They suggest playing isn't about creating dirty clothes but about kids being creative and so the clothes that need washing as a result of their playing should be a cause of celebration for their mums, not despair.

The Unilever brand in most countries is known as Omo. In the US it is called Wisk, in France, Skip and in the UK, Persil. Unilever plan to launch the campaign across its global markets, starting in Europe, in a bid to reposition the concept of their brand in the eyes of their consumers. If they succeed they may well throw down the gauntlet to their arch rivals Procter and Gamble.

QUESTION *Identify the main benefits of using qualitative research when deciding to enter a new international market.*

SOURCE: ADAPTED FROM *MARKETING*, MAY 2003

Survey methods

There are several issues to consider in evaluating the various interviewing methods available.

Online surveys. As the Internet achieves greater penetration even in less developed markets, greater use is being made of online surveys. In the US and Europe online surveys are now becoming predominant in the marketplace. Speed of execution, the obtaining of timely responses, ease of interview and speed of analysis are all major benefits to international marketing researchers. Globally access to the Internet is still scarce in some countries and in others subject to government controls. This could mean potential bias in both the sampling and in the answers given by respondents.

Telephone interviewing. In the US, Canada and Europe, the telephone has achieved almost total penetration of households. In most developing nations, however, mobile phones are more prevalent than land lines and it could be that only a few households have telephones (e.g. many African countries, India, Brazil). Even in countries like Saudi Arabia, where telephone ownership is extensive, telephone directories tend to be incomplete and out of date.

Therefore, telephone interviews are most useful when employed with relatively upscale consumers who are accustomed to business transactions by phone, be it mobile or land line, or consumers who can be reached by phone and can express themselves easily. With the setting up of global call centres, Internet telephony and the collapse in the price of international telephone calls, multi-country studies are now often conducted from a single global location and are much cheaper and easier to control than previously.

Mail interviewing. Because of the rise of the online survey the use of mail interviews internationally has declined. However, in countries where literacy is high and the postal system is well developed but there are still problems in terms of access to the Internet they still continue to be used. In Africa, Asia and South America, however, the use of mail surveys and mail panels is low because of illiteracy and the large proportion of population living in rural areas.

No questionnaire administration method is superior in all situations. Table 4.3 presents a comparative evaluation of the major modes of collecting primary data in the context of international marketing research.

Questionnaire design

The questionnaire or research instrument should be adapted to the specific cultural environment and should not be biased in terms of any one culture. This requires careful attention to each step of the questionnaire design process. It is important to take into account any differences in underlying consumer behaviour, decision-making processes, psychographics, lifestyles and demographic variables.

The use of unstructured or open-ended questions may be desirable if the researcher lacks knowledge of the possible responses in other cultures. Unstructured questions also reduce cultural bias because they do not impose any response alternatives. However, unstructured questions are more affected by differences in educational levels than structured questions. They should be used with caution in countries with high illiteracy rates.

The questions may have to be translated for administration in different cultures. A set of guidelines has been proposed by Brislin (2001) for writing questionnaires in English so that they can be easily translated. These include:

■ use short and simple sentences

■ repeat nouns rather than using pronouns

- avoid metaphors
- avoid adverbs and prepositions related to place and time
- avoid possessive forms
- use specific rather than general terms
- avoid vague words
- avoid sentences with two different verbs if the verbs suggest different actions.

The problems of language and translation were discussed in Chapter 3 and equally apply in marketing research. A translation of a questionnaire might be grammatically correct but this does not necessarily mean that it is conveying the appropriate message. For example: value for money is not a common phrase in Spain; the equivalent phrase is 'price for product'. In the Middle East 'payment' is a transactional word; it refers to repaying a debt and so would be inappropriate in the context of purchasing a product.

Another problem is that countries sometimes have more than one official language: a decision has then to be made as to what the most appropriate language is. In Malaysia and Singapore, for instance, consumer surveys regularly employ three languages (English, Malay and Chinese). An interviewer may need a command of several languages or dialects to undertake field work. In Pakistan, the official language is Urdu, but most of the official work in government departments is done in English. However, most local nationals who understand English also usually understand Urdu. There is also a particular segment of social class in the country which prefers English to Urdu in their daily routines. Should the researcher use English or Urdu?

The literal translation of a questionnaire can pose problems. A different language is not just a matter of different spellings but of different linguistic concepts. This is why translation agencies recommend back translation into the

TABLE 4.3 A comparative evaluation of survey methods for use in international marketing research

Criteria	Online	Telephone	Personal	Mail
High sample control	+	+	+	−
Difficulty in locating respondents at home	+	+	−	+
Inaccessibility of homes	+	+	−	+
Unavailability of a large pool of trained interviewers	+	+	−	+
Large population in rural areas	+	−	+	−
Unavailability of current telephone directory	+	−	+	−
Unavailability of mailing lists	+	+	+	−
Low penetration of telephones	−	−	+	+
Lack of an efficient postal system	+	+	+	−
Low level of literacy	+	−	+	−
Face-to-face communication culture	−	−	+	−

NOTE: + DENOTES AN ADVANTAGE; − DENOTES A DISADVANTAGE
SOURCE: MALHOTRA ET AL. (1997)

original language This identifies and corrects many of the problems faced in simple translation. The technique of 'decentring' in translation, where the material is translated and retranslated each time by a different translator, also minimises mistakes being made.

Sample frame

The problems of obtaining valid sampling frames tend to be more complicated in researching international markets. It might be difficult or even impossible to obtain a reliable sampling frame. Due to problems associated with the validity and reliability of secondary data in some countries, experience and judgement need to play an important part in constructing the sample where there is no reliable database. It may mean that accepted techniques of marketing research in developed countries cannot always be directly transferred, even to other developed countries where data might have to be collected through less formalised methods. This applies especially in countries lacking a marketing infrastructure where, unless sufficient care is taken in selecting the sampling frame, the sample chosen will invariably be distorted.

Field work

INTERVIEWEE BIAS

The major problems in field work are errors caused through bias in the interviewing stage of the process which can mean that reliable multi-country studies where results can be compared and contrasted across different countries are sometimes difficult to achieve.

Different cultures will produce a varied response to interviews or questionnaires. For example, purchase intentions for new products frequently peak in Italy because Italians have a propensity to over-claim their likelihood to buy, whereas German results are much closer to reality. If Germans say they will buy a product they probably will.

Another problem is that in some countries it is not possible for the female members of a household to respond personally to a survey. In such countries, mail questionnaires for researching the female market might obtain a much better rate of response.

In some countries the rate of response of a particular segment of society might be quite low due to tax evasion problems, with respondents unwilling to provide any information which gives an idea of their economic status (Sarathy *et al.* 2006). Even within the same country, different social classes of customers could have differing responses to marketing research techniques. In some cultures the respondent may cause bias by attempting to please the interviewer and give the answers they think they want to hear. This happened to BSN in Japan. The French conglomerate carried out a study in Japan to find out people's attitudes to yogurt. The results indicated that the Japanese were becoming much more Westernised in their food and eating habits and that there was a potential market for yogurts. BSN launched their products, set up distribution and invested heavily in promotion. However, the sales were disappointing. Follow-up research showed that the questions used in the original research were too simplistic to elicit accurate responses. The Japanese were far too polite to reply NO to a question. Therefore the responses to yes/no questions were highly misleading. Likewise, they did not wish to offend Westerners by criticising the usage of a spoon as an eating implement.

INTERVIEWER BIAS

Interviewer biases are often due to communication problems between the interviewer and respondents. Several biases have been identified in multicultural research, including rudeness bias, 'I can answer any question' bias, courtesy bias, sucker bias, hidden premises bias, reticence–loquaciousness bias, social desirability, status difference bias, racial difference bias and individual group opinion bias (Malhotra and Peterson, 2001).

Extensive training and close supervision of the interviewers and other field staff may be required to minimise these biases.

The selection, training, supervision and evaluation of field workers are critical in multi-country research. Local field work agencies are unavailable in many countries. It may be necessary therefore to recruit and train local field workers or import trained foreign workers. The use of local field workers is desirable as they are familiar with the local language and culture. They can thus create an appropriate climate for the interview and be sensitive to the concerns of the respondents

DATA ANALYSIS

A number of issues need to be considered at the data analysis stage. First, in preparing data for analysis in multi-country or cross-cultural studies, how do you deal with 'outliers'? These are countries where the data is quite obviously different from the bulk of the data. It may not be a problem at all but, likewise, it could be due to some cultural bias, a problem in the sampling or a problem of translation in the questionnaire.

Second, the issue of how to ensure comparability of data across cultures. Some researchers prefer to standardise data to ensure comparability. In contrast, others prefer statistics based on unstandardised data on the basis that this allows a truer comparative analysis.

Report preparation and presentation

In any research study there is the chance of cultural bias in the research findings. International research often involves researchers from one cultural environment conducting research in another cultural environment or communicating with researchers from another cultural environment. In international research situations, effective communication between the respondents and the researcher is essential to avoid problems of misinterpretation of the data. The phenomenon of cultural self-reference criteria is cited as a possible cause of the misinterpretation of data and can lead to a systematic bias in the findings. The reader is referred to the discussion in Chapter 3 and the discussion on the steps that can be taken to remedy self-reference criteria.

Some agencies follow the practice of always ensuring foreign market studies are written in the local language and include interpretation as well as analysis. The nuance can then be discussed with the translator.

Face-to-face debriefings with agencies and researchers are also a good way to synthesise the results from multi-country surveys and form coherent conclusions through open discussions with representatives who have participated in the research across a range of countries.

CONTINUOUS RESEARCH

In this chapter, in order to discuss the relevant issues in a logical manner, we have used the six-step research design framework. It is perhaps important to stress, however, that international market research, whilst expensive, is by no means a 'one-off' activity. In today's dynamic environment where changes occur almost on a daily basis in some rapidly growing markets (e.g. China), it is important that research be on a continuous basis to ensure a company keeps ahead of its competition.

SUMMARY

■ In this chapter we have examined the three main roles of the international marketing researcher: scanning international markets, building up market profiles and carrying out primary research across global markets. The rise of the Internet has impacted critically on the role of international market research and led to the development of better decision tools and the development of globally based research supplier networks and global databases.

■ International research is, in many cases, a complex, expensive and time-consuming task and evidence suggests that for these reasons many international firms fail to research markets to the extent that is really necessary. The consequences of this are significant in terms of both missed opportunities and the failure to meet existing and developing market demand.

■ The issues relevant to the identifying and analysing of opportunities across the globe were discussed and the problems involved in categorising and segmenting international markets identified. Several models used in the segmentation process of international markets were presented.

■ Within this chapter, we illustrated the strategic importance of opportunity analysis and the contribution that the information system and market research can make to the decision-making process.

■ In examining the international marketing research process the six-step research design framework was used. It was suggested that many international marketing efforts fail not because research was not conducted but because the issue of comparability was not adequately addressed in defining the marketing research problem. The importance of self-reference criteria (SRC) was discussed and at each of the six stages the relevant issues for the international marketer highlighted.

KEYWORDS

Comparative research	Market profile analysis	Online databases
Cross-cultural research	Marketing information	Pareto law
Differentiated marketing	system	Primary data
Existing markets	Market research	Qualitative research
Global segments	Market segmentation	Research process
Incipient markets	Multi-client studies	Secondary data
Latent markets	Multi-country study	Transnational segmentation

CASE STUDY

Segmenting the global mobile phone gaming market

In 2003 Rob Anderson, CEO of Cometa Wireless Gaming Systems, came up with the idea of transferring the 'feel of the casino/slot machine' to the mobile phone. His own experience and information in the industry press suggested that interest in the traditional fruit machine sector was waning. The market for playing slots and gambling games was still there, but the expectations of consumers as to the delivery modes of games was changing. Given the level of mobile phone ownership and penetration of mobile phones as a key medium for 'entertainment' – i.e. ringtones, music delivery, etc. – mobile phones seemed to be an ideal platform to deliver casino style games.

Initial secondary research using the Internet and industry press showed there were few companies delivering fruit machine-style games on mobile phones. Closer inspection of their games revealed the games were basic and designed from the perspective of a games designer rather than a fruit machine designer. Juniper research (a leading provider of mobile entertainment reports) also estimated that the mobile gambling market was set to rise rapidly through to 2011 to $23bn (Source: Juniper Research Gambling on Mobile III, 2006). The market for mobile gambling games was showing some real potential. Cometa would be able to deliver superior quality games compared with its competitors, bringing the feel of playing on the Las Vegas slots to the mobile phone. Games could be played any time, anywhere; on the way to work on the bus/train, waiting in the bus queue etc. Competitors however had a few years foothold in the market, they had acquired key partners and had begun to establish a mobile casino brand. In addition one main competitor floated on the Alternative Investment Market (AIM) in 2006.

The mobile gambling market was split into a number of sectors providing different style games; the lottery and bingo style games, more traditional fruit machine/casino games including roulette and blackjack, skills-based games such as quiz games, points for prizes games and non-gambling games such as just for fun slot machines where players paid just for the download to their phone. It also included more functional gambling services such as placing bets for horse racing, football and other sporting activities. Cometa decided to focus on delivering games which encompassed its core expertise, i.e. the fruit machine/casino style gambling games. Its initial portfolio of games included a range of slot machine style games such as 'Adders and Ladders', 'Cop the Cash', casino style games such as roulette, blackjack and poker as well as bingo, virtual horse racing and a World Cup shoot out.

Global market potential looked promising. Cometa were confident in their ability to design high-quality games based on superior software design. The platform on which the mobile casino operated, Arcadia™, was patent protected and Cometa had a team of highly qualified software designers led by a technical director with experience in the fruit machine industry. Cometa would need to sell their mobile casino package to industry intermediaries around the globe who could reach the 'mobile gambler'. Therefore as a business to business operation, Cometa needed to consider how to segment the global markets to identify companies with the largest penetration of potential mobile phone gamblers. Cometa needed to understand (a) the profile of the mobile phone gambling game player around the world and (b) which companies could best reach those players globally.

Cometa planned to sell mobile casino via a website where players downloaded games directly to their mobile phones. Cometa had to identify which companies would want to operate their own mobile casino. In principal anybody could set up their own mobile casino, however, given that Cometa's revenue streams would be based on a percentage of gambling revenues, their target customers needed to have access to a large database of potential mobile gambling games players. Which companies would have access to such a large database of potential players, how do they identify them and how do they reach them? Would it be online casinos looking for a mobile arm to their operations, or is it any entrepreneur with sufficient revenues to manage a mobile casino? The latter would need a heavily supported promotional campaign to build a large enough database to capture a percentage of mobile phone gamblers.

Given the 'virtual' nature of the product and its user, i.e. the online mobile casino and the mobile gambler, Cometa had a difficult decision to make in trying to segment the global market. In its simplest terms the mobile phone gambler could be anyone in the world with a mobile phone with the capacity to download games, but segmenting the world market on that basis would be costly and ineffective. In terms of the mobile gambling game player, was their profile the same as the fruit machine player, i.e. the 18 to 35 male? Was it same as the mobile phone games player? Research also showed an increase in the number of women playing mobile gambling games. Did they play the same games as men? Did they fall in the same income, age brackets or lifestage segments? It was more likely that the mobile phone gambler was a niche customer located in different countries across the world.

Geography was only an issue in terms of gambling legislation. Players could be global but legislation was not. Culture and legal issues played a big role in the gambling sector. Many gambling-style companies were basing operations offshore, or had to acquire expensive gambling licences. Legislation was continually changing. The US recently outlawed gambling over a telephone wire, although 'games of chance' were not. As far as Cometa understood, the situation in the UK was different again, in that the 1968 Gaming Act was based around where a bet is taken, e.g. if it is taken in a bookmakers then that bookmakers must have a licence to take bets, if that bookmaker is overseas, in the case of Internet gambling, then it is 'out of the jurisdiction' of the British government. The latest amendments in the 2005 Gambling Act meant that in order to advertise gambling in the UK, a company must be in a jurisdiction that is on the British government's 'white list' by September 2007. France and Germany were reported to be in breach of European

PHOTO CREDIT: KEITH LEIGHTON/ALAMY

law for outlawing online gambling whilst allowing state-run online Lottos. Spain allowed Internet gambling from European destinations. Italy's attempted ban recently back-fired and online gambling has been allowed. Legislation and the lack of conformity across regions meant Cometa would have to segment the global market carefully.

Cometa knew it had the right combination of expertise in games and software design and experience in the fruit machine sector. It only needed to find the best way to reach the mobile gambling game player around the globe and identify the best route to the market ensuring it did not breach gambling legislation.

QUESTIONS

1 Critically evaluate the arguments for and against the use of country by country versus global market segment descriptors as bases for the segmentation of global mobile phone gambling market.

2 How can Cometa develop a global segmentation strategy that could be used as the basis for a global marketing plan?

3 Advise Cometa on how they should research the global opportunities to better understand the market for mobile gambling.

DISCUSSION QUESTIONS

1 What are the problems in carrying out multi-country studies? As a international market resarcher, how would you avoid these dangers?

2 Many companies are looking to emerging markets in their internationalisation programmes. What are the problems in researching these markets? How, if at all, may they be overcome?

3 Identify the principal methods that companies might use in assessing and reviewing opportunities across international markets. Suggest the alternative means by which firms can prioritise and segment international markets.

4 As firms become more global so does their requirement to gather global information. Outline the key categories of a global information system and explain their relevance.

5 Citing specific examples, show how the spread of the Internet has impacted on international market research. What are the problems and limitations of using web-based research?

References

Brislin, R.W. (2001) *Understanding cultures' influence on behaviour*, 2nd edn. Harcourt.
Czinkota, M.E. and Ronkainen, I.A. (2006) *International marketing*, 8th edn. Thomson Learning.
Douglas, C. (1999) *International marketing research*, 2nd edn. Prentice Hall.
Gorton, K. and Doole, I. (1989) *Low cost marketing research*. John Wiley.
Hamill, J. and Stevenson, J. (2002) 'Internet forum', *International Marketing Review*, 19 (5) 545.
Harrell, G.D. and Keifer, R.D. (1993) 'Multinational market portfolio in global strategy development', *International Marketing Review*, 10 (1).
Hassan, S.S. and Stephen, H.C.T. (2005) 'Linking global market segmentation decisions with strategic positioning options', *Journal of Consumer Marketing*, 22 (2) 81–9.
Malhotra, N.K., Agrawal, J. and Peterson, M. (1997) 'Methodological issues in cross cultural marketing research', *International Marketing Review*, 13 (6) 7–43.
Malhotra, N.K. and Peterson, M. (2001) 'Marketing research in the new millennium: emerging issues and trends', *Marketing Intelligence and Planning*, 19 (4) 216–32.
Malhotra, N.K., Peterson, M. and Uslay, C. (2006) 'Helping marketing research earn a seat at the table for decision-making. An assessment and prescription for the future', *European Business Review* 18 (4) 294–306.
Sarathy, R. Terpstra, V. and Russow, L.C. (2006) *International marketing*, 9th edn. Dryden Press.
Sheth, J. and Ama, A. (2005) 'International e-marketing: opportunities and issues', *International Marketing Review* 22 (6) 611–22.
Walters, P.G.P. (1997) 'Global market segmentation: methodologies and challenges', *Journal of Marketing Management*, 13, 165–77.

INTEGRATIVE LEARNING ACTIVITIES

An Introduction

Successful international marketing is about taking a planned approach to analysis, strategy development and implementation. The chapters of this book focus upon providing the underpinning knowledge to support the process of planning an international marketing strategy. The purpose of the three integrated learning activities at the end of each of the three parts of the book is to integrate the four chapters that make up each of the parts. More importantly, however, is that as a whole, the three activities provide a framework for planning an international marketing strategy and give the opportunity for readers to consider the practical issues involved in developing, planning and implementing an outline international marketing strategy.

Learning objectives

On completing the three integrated learning activities the reader should be able to:

- Analyse the international marketing environment of a given company situation critically
- Apply relevant concepts and models to each of the development stages of an international marketing strategy
- Make clear links between analysis and the chosen response. The issues identified in the analysis should lead directly to the development and implementation of a strategy
- Develop a realistic and cohesive international marketing strategy

The aims of the integrated learning activities (ILAs) therefore are much wider in scope than the short case studies found at the end of each chapter. The objective is to provide a vehicle through which the reader is able to develop practical skills in research, analysis, evaluation and strategy development. In completing these activities you will need to synthesise the various strands and themes explored throughout the book and apply them to a practical situation. To complete each of the activities the reader must move well beyond the boundaries of the textbook,

researching new material and exploring the interplay of the concepts discussed in the text and possible solutions to the practical problems identified in each activity.

Each ILA depicts very different scenarios.

Part 1: Li Ning is a Chinese entrepreneur in the highly competitive sports goods market that is dominated by famous global brands, such as Nike and Adidas. How does the small Chinese business identify a global niche through which it could compete against the global players?

Part 2: We identify a number of companies from emerging markets that are developing as global brands competing against entrenched Western global players. How do such companies compete effectively against existing global competitors, and how can they ensure they build a sustainable competitive advantage?

Part 3: Microsoft provides the Windows software that is used for operating many of the world's computers. Due to changes in the market environment, customer expectations and competition, it must focus on implementation of its international marketing strategies to maintain its growth.

In each of the activities a series of questions is posed, together with suggestions on how to get started, a framework depicting the key factors to consider in completing the task and suggested websites you may find useful.

Additional observations are also made that will assist you in addressing the key issues and how you could develop the activity further.

In all the activities we have provided only outline information on the scenarios. A key skill in international marketing is *finding* information about international markets, analysing it, deciding what is most important and preparing a structured, logical rationale for the decisions that must ultimately be made. In each activity, therefore, you will need to seek information outside of the case to complete the task. Much of the information you can use is available online. You should not have to approach staff in the organisations depicted for further information to complete the task.

INTEGRATIVE LEARNING ACTIVITY 1

INTERNATIONAL MARKETING PLANNING: ANALYSIS

Introduction

In this activity we explore the issues facing a Chinese company that is trying to develop a global marketing strategy which will then explore the international marketing opportunities they have identified.

As a medium-sized enterprise, Li Ning faces issues as to how he should internationalise and how quickly. Perhaps most importantly at this stage he needs to develop a thorough understanding of the complexities of the international marketing environment in which he is competing and decide how to segment the global market, which segment he should target, and how to develop a positioning strategy to achieve competitive leverage. Increasing global competition in this market necessitates greater innovation not just in products and services, but in all aspects of the operation of the firm. To understand such issues we need to build the skills to research, analyse and evaluate how such factors impact international strategy development. We hope the reader will develop these skills in this activity.

Learning objectives

On completing this activity the reader should be able to:

- Identify and analyse international market opportunities

- Use appropriate conceptual frameworks to develop a transnational segmentation methodology on which to base a global marketing strategy

- Identify sources of information, methods of information collection and methods of information analysis suitable for international marketing operations

- Understand the complexities of researching international markets and be able to identify possible solutions

The scenario: Li Ning

China's best known gymnast, Li Ning, won three gold medals at the 1984 Olympics but he rather regretted the fact that he was not able to wear Chinese labelled sportswear because the sector was dominated by foreign-owned sports goods. His solution was to set up his own sports goods company, Li Ning Sports Goods Company. The company has now grown to become the largest sports goods company in China with a turnover of 3,180 million Chinese yuan (RMB) (US$411 million) and now dominates the Chinese sportswear market, with a bigger share than companies such as Nike and Reebok. The group has established an extensive distribution and retail network throughout China and has 4,297 stores. In 2005 Li Ning formed a joint venture with AIGLE whereby they now have the exclusive right to manufacture, market and distribute AIGLE sports products in China for the next 50 years.

The Chinese market environment

Since China joined the World Trade Organisation many Chinese tariff and other trade barriers have reduced, allowing sports goods companies from the West, such as Nike and Adidas, to compete more strongly in China, but Li Ning has fought back by building its own brand and promoting its products.

The firm is also very aware of Chinese customer attitudes to sport. Only 15 per cent of people aged 15–35 from the Chinese mainland play sport regularly compared to 50 per cent in the US. However, this is now starting to change. With greater leisure time and spending power than ever before, Chinese people have developed a national obsession with sports and leisure activities. This in turn has led to a boom in the number

SOURCES: ADAPTED FROM VARIOUS SOURCES, INCLUDING: WWW.ENGLISH.LI-NING.COM ADVERTISING AGE, 13 JANUARY 2003, AND THE ECONOMIST, 2 AUGUST 2003

of fitness centres and sports clubs being established in cities across the country.

Company expertise and marketing capability

Li Ning started expanding internationally in the late 1990s by exporting into the European market in countries such as Spain, France and Greece. Having taken its first tentative steps in international markets, Li Ning is now starting to build a more sophisticated product offering for the home market to provide a launch pad for a global assault. For example, Li Ning is improving product design by using European and South Korean designers and launching more innovative products.

Part of Li Ning's competitive advantage has traditionally been maintaining prices that are low by international standards. By Chinese standards, however, the prices of Li Ning sports equipment are quite high – sports shoes cost 198–388 yuan and T-shirts 90–200 yuan. However, the firm believes that through brand-building activity it will be possible to double the prices of their most expensive products over the next few years. This in turn will help Li Ning to generate the revenue at home to enable them to compete more effectively in export markets. The question, of course, is whether the market will accept higher prices.

To support its brand building both at home and abroad the firm has begun to promote its products more heavily. Li Ning launched an advertising campaign on Chinese television with an expenditure eight times its previous level, using the mottos 'Goodbye' (to the hard lives of the past) and 'Anything is possible' (the future is filled with unlimited opportunities), echoing Nike's 'Just do it' campaign. It also began sponsorship deals for teams in France and Russia, even though the firm did not do any international advertising.

The firm is building capability throughout the business. For example, with his business partner, Singapore Internet entrepreneur Danny Toe, Li Ning has set up two businesses supported by Internet websites, Etosports, a sports portal, and Etochannel, a technology platform for sports e-business. These businesses support the sportswear business and will be essential for international development.

Future growth prospects

Li Ning has to compete with the likes of Nike, Reebok and Adidas in the international market, not only to generate growth, but also to avoid becoming vulnerable in the Chinese market. The company needs to monitor the international market environment for sports goods, specifically identify a global customer segment that it can serve and understand the purchasing behaviour of those customers.

The 2008 Beijing Olympics offer Li Ning an exceptional, well-timed opportunity. The global television audience for the Olympic Games offers the firm a unique opportunity to gain visibility amongst a worldwide audience. Li Ning is one of 33 companies that have signed agreements to use the five rings logo. The Olympics will raise further interest in sport in China, too, and expand Li Ning's local market. To maximise this opportunity Li Ning signed a cooperation agreement with CCTV National Sports TV Channel. Li Ning will provide Li Ning brand or AIGLE brand apparel, footwear and accessories to all the hosts and reporters of all the programmes and tournaments shown on CCTV National Sports TV Channel for two years. The scope of cooperation includes the exclusive sponsorship of apparel for the hosts and reporters of all the programmes broadcast on the 'Olympic Channel', aired during the 2008 Beijing Olympics.

In building their international profile Li Ning have concentrated on creating awareness through sponsorship deals of teams and individuals. They agreed sponsorship deals with the Argentina national basketball teams, who will wear Li Ning apparel at major international sports events, the 2008 Beijing Olympics and the 2012 London Olympics. Li Ning are the official sponsor of the Swedish Olympic delegation, providing them with a range of sports apparel in a four-year deal to cover the London and Beijing Olympics. They have also signed up two US sports superstars to endorse their brand. A two-year contract has been signed with the US national basketball star, Cleveland Cavaliers' guard Damon Jones, and with Miami Heat's all-star centre Shaquille O'Neal. The latter has been rumoured to have cost Li Ning at least 10 million yuan (US$1.25 million), making it the most expensive deal in the company's history. In Spain they have signed up the Spanish national men's basketball team, which features Pau Gasol of the Memphis Grizzlies.

Interestingly, the Olympics may have another beneficial effect by tackling another environmental factor over which Li Ning has little control. The International Olympic Committee relies on sponsorship for most of its income and Beijing hopes to pay for most, if not all, of the cost of the stadia from sponsorship. Since joining the WTO, China has been working to reduce the extent of piracy in the country. This is important to them in attracting international sponsors for the Olympics, and these efforts are as beneficial to Li Ning as they are to Nike and Adidas.

Li Ning is probably too old to be the sporting hero of the new generation of Chinese, but his company's sports goods could be on the way to becoming the 'cool' brand favourite of a worldwide market segment of sporting youngsters.

The task

1 Analyse and evaluate the major environmental influences that will impact on the Li Ning Company becoming a global player in the sportswear goods market.

2 Propose and justify an effective segmentation strategy of the global market that will form the basis on which Li Ning can build a global marketing strategy.

3 Choose either the USA or the European Union . Using the results of your analysis from question 2 and with reference to Li Ning draw up a market profile analysis for the region you have chosen. This should form the basis on which Li Ning can enter and develop the global segment you have specified.

4 Make recommendations to Li Ning on how he should develop the segment identified. In doing so you will need to fully apprise him of the challenges and problems he will face and how you think he should solve these.

Useful websites

www.lining.com
www.1chinastar.com

www.china.org
www.wto.org
www.globalexchange.org
www.ita.doc.gov/tradestats
www.worldbank.com
www.foreign-trade.com
www.chinaci.net
www.manufacturers.com.tw/sports/sportswear-manufacturers.html
www.made-in-china.com

Getting started

For a company to operate in its own domestic market there are considerable difficulties in understanding and in forecasting the future facing the company. In international markets it is exceedingly difficult to obtain a comprehensive understanding of the relevant market environment. In tackling task 1 it is useful to categorise the elements of the environment into social and cultural, legal, economic, political and technological forces (SLEPT).

In the increasingly global marketplace, companies are trying to identify methodologies for segmenting

TABLE I
Li Ning: Key factors to consider

The element of the plan	Some concepts, models and issues to be addressed
Environment	• The global SLEPT factors, including political and economic issues and socio/cultural factors affecting the opportunities for the firm • The changing global trends in competition and customer expectations that impact on Li Ning's business • The international challenges to be met
Home and possible international markets	• The level of market development and competitive structures • Prioritisation of markets using country attractiveness and latent assessment of markets • Commercial, home, host country stakeholder expectations and ethical issues
Company capability	• SWOT, competitive advantage • Products: international product life cycle, knowledge and capability
Segmentation	• Basis of segmentation/criteria for global segmentation/global niche possibilities • Hierarchy of segmentation
Market Information	• Market profile analysis and the information systems, data collection and management to support it • Market and environmental risk and potential commercial opportunity using the 12C framework
Strategic options	• Potential strategic alternatives for Li Ning • The challenges faced and potential responses to the issues identified in the analysis • The resource constraints of Li Ning

and evaluating international markets that transcend national and cultural boundaries. In task 2 you are asked to develop a segmentation strategy. It is important here to remember that simply segmenting the market on a geographical basis will be too simplistic and not form a basis on which Li Ning can build a global niche strategy. You will need a hierarchical approach where your segmentation strategy has several steps and can incorporate the multidimensional aspects of a global niche segment.

In task 3 we focus on the role of international market analysis. It is important for Li Ning to develop a systematic method for building a market information system on the international markets the company has prioritised. The 12C framework is a useful tool when developing profiles of international markets. Finally, in task 4 we need to think through the implications of our research and consider the issues the analysis has highlighted that Li Ning has to consider if he is to succeed in his ambitions. Of particular importance is to consider these issues in the light of possible resources/cultural/management constraints that may face Li Ning.

In summary, therefore, the framework shown in Table 1 provides a guide to the key factors that need to be considered in tackling the task identified.

The way forward

After reading Part 2 of the textbook you may wish to return to plan the next stage of Li Ning's strategy. The most important issue is deciding how quickly the firm should develop internationally and how – country by country, concentrating on a particular segment or seeking global distribution. You should define a strategy that builds upon the firm's competitive advantage, identifying a positioning strategy that meets the needs of the target segment you have chosen. Then you should identify the criteria that will determine the choice of market entry.

After reading Part 3 you will be in a position to define the implementation plan and make decisions on the marketing mix elements, relationship building and supply chain management. You can identify how management and technology systems might support the international expansion. Finally, you will be able to identify the monitoring and control systems that will be used.

PART 2 STRATEGY DEVELOPMENT

Having identified and analysed the opportunities that exist within international markets in the first section of the book, we now turn our attention to the ways in which firms can use international marketing to develop their international business in order to exploit these opportunities profitably. The focus in Part 2 is on developing an international marketing strategy that is appropriate for the firm, given the environment and market context in which it is working, the firm's capability, and the ambition of its management. Throughout the section are a number of themes, including the need for the management of the firm to plan their international marketing and take decisive action to deal with the challenges that are posed.

The first chapter in Part 2, Chapter 5, concentrates on the international marketing strategies of small and medium-sized enterprises. The discussion ranges from firms taking their first steps in international markets or marketing to international customers from their home base to those dynamic small firms that have the ambition and capability to grow quickly to become the major global players of the future.

When we think of globalisation it is the very largest firms in the world that come to mind. Chapter 6 is concerned with the global strategies of the firms that operate within a global context and build brands that are instantly recognisable. Their global strategies aim to appeal to customers worldwide and ensure that as many customers as possible choose their products and services.

For any firm moving into a new international market the key step is to decide which market entry method should be chosen in order to achieve the best outcome from the investment that is made. In Chapter 7 we discuss the factors that firms must consider in selecting an appropriate market entry method.

In Chapter 8 we consider the product and service management strategy and focus upon the need to have a portfolio of products and services that meet the current and future needs of global customers.

CHAPTER 5

INTERNATIONAL NICHE MARKETING STRATEGIES FOR SMALL AND MEDIUM-SIZED ENTERPRISES

INTRODUCTION

Small and medium-sized enterprises (SMEs) have always been significant creators of wealth and employment in domestic economies, but are a less powerful force outside their home territory, usually because of their limited resources. Indeed many SMEs, despite what may be obvious business capability, never move into international markets at all. However, for reasons which will be explored in this chapter, SMEs have growth potential both in fast-growing business sectors that involve applying new technology and in market niches, where innovation in mature industry sectors can lead to new opportunities. In less developed markets entrepreneurs can play a vital role in countering poverty by creating new businesses to employ local people. The impact of these SMEs in regenerating the economy can increase considerably if they can gain access to international markets.

In this chapter we discuss the factors which influence the patterns of international development of small and medium-sized firms, including the strategic options available to them, and the particular problems they face in implementing their strategy.

The traditional model of SME internationalisation is exporting, in which goods are manufactured in one country and transferred to buyers in other countries, but many SMEs are involved in a broader range of international marketing activity and it is for this reason we prefer the term niche marketing. Small service providers generate revenue from customers in foreign markets either by providing services from the home country which customers can access wherever they are situated (for example, information and advice supplied via the Internet) or by providing services in the firm's home country, and requiring the customers to visit (for example, tourism, training and education residential courses).

Increasingly, large firms are finding that operating on a global scale often makes them inflexible and unresponsive to fast-changing markets, with the result that smaller, more entrepreneurial firms can compete with them in their chosen niche market. To be successful, however, all these international market approaches require an understanding of the various dimensions of international marketing and also the capability to manage in different situations.

LEARNING OBJECTIVES

After reading this chapter you should be able to:

■ Appreciate the nature and types of international marketing undertaken in the SME sector

■ Compare the different strategic approaches to international marketing adopted by SMEs

■ Understand the factors affecting SME international strategic management

■ Identify the characteristics of the different stages of international development of SMEs

■ Be able to evaluate the factors for success and failure in SME international marketing

THE SME SECTOR AND ITS ROLE WITHIN THE GLOBAL ECONOMY

A number of definitions of the small and medium-sized firm sector exist, but the most commonly used terms relate to the number of employees in the company. The European Union, for example, defines SMEs as those firms employing less than 250 staff. This characterisation, however, effectively includes 99 per cent of all firms in Europe and accounts for roughly 50 per cent of employment and, because it includes sole operators as well as quite sophisticated businesses, is not particularly useful for segmenting the smaller firms sector.

In this chapter, therefore, the review of smaller firm international strategies is not restricted to firms with a specific number of employees but instead focuses on those issues that apply to businesses in general which think and act like small and medium-sized enterprises. The reason for adopting this stance is that a garment-making firm with 250 employees has a very restricted capacity to internationalise, whereas a 250-employee financial services or computer software company could be a significant international player. Many quite large companies take business decisions within a small group of major shareholders or senior managers in much the same way that the family owners of small firms take decisions. Many of the fastest-growing international firms grow rapidly through the 250 employee ceiling without making significant changes to their international strategic approach or management style. Our discussion therefore relates to issues affecting firms which could not be described as large multinational enterprises (MNEs) with the global power to dominate their sector.

SMEs can be vulnerable and there are high failure rates. Because of globalisation, the liberalisation of trade policies and removal of protectionism and most trade barriers, virtually all firms now realise that choosing not to participate in global markets may no longer be an option. In practice, however, many SMEs do remain focused on the domestic market and this may be one reason why many firms fail to grow. Only a small percentage of SMEs, perhaps less than 5 per cent, grow significantly.

Despite this the SME sector is increasingly recognised as a creator of wealth and employment because over the last 20 years many large firms have periodically downsized by reducing their workforce, rationalising their operations and outsourcing their activities, often to smaller firms. Public sector organisations have also increased their outsourcing and in many countries this has left the small and medium-sized firms sector as the only significant growing source of wealth and employment.

The role of SME Internationalisation in Economic Regeneration

Encouraging entrepreneurship is seen by many as the route to future prosperity for emerging markets. It can be argued that growing the private business sector helps put money in people's pockets, increases domestic demand, generates tax revenues and reduces dependency on international aid. Indeed there is considerable debate about the proportion of international aid that should be used for alleviating hunger, addressing basic health care and education, and improving a country's infrastructure, as opposed to supporting and promoting business creation and development.

In practice, however, it can be argued that it is those SMEs that trade internationally that are most important. SMEs that market their products and services in the domestic economy often grow at the expense of other domestic SMEs because of the relatively limited home market, whereas export markets offer seemingly unlimited scope for SMEs to grow, have the effect of importing jobs and foreign currency, and so create wealth in the domestic economy. As we shall see in Chapter 7, the first 'level' of international market entry strategies include domestic purchasing in which the international customer purchases products from the emerging market SME in its home country, so the SME has little or no influence or control over how its products are marketed. Examples would include a supermarket sourcing fruit or coffee shop chains sourcing coffee beans from African farmers who have little power in negotiating with international customers. In Chapter 7 we discuss this in more detail and Illustration 7.1 provides an example of domesting purchasing from China.

The challenges for SMEs from less developed countries

Small organizations from emerging markets are often severely disadvantaged in international marketing. For example, small farmers from poor countries are frequently exploited by aggressive multinational retailers who ruthlessly use the global competition amongst small organisations, the poor negotiating position of the farmers and the perceived demand from consumers to force down prices of products to below the poverty line for the farmers and their workers. Although the multinational retailers sign up to ethical social corporate responsibility principles many fail to behave ethically in their everyday transactions and there are many stories of unacceptable behaviour.

FAIRTRADE AND THE PROTECTION OF THE INTERESTS OF FARMERS

Nicholls and Opal (2005) discuss the Fairtrade organisation (www.fairtrade.org) which was developed to promote ethical consumption. It is an independent consumer label which appears on products as an independent guarantee that disadvantaged producers in the developing world are getting a better deal.

For a product to display the Fairtrade mark it must meet international Fairtrade standards. These standards are set by the international certification body Fairtrade Labelling Oraganisations International (FLO), which inspects and certifies them. They receive a minimum price that covers the cost of sustainable production and an extra premium that is invested in social or economic development projects. Fairtrade principles include:

- Direct purchasing from producers;
- Transparent and long-term trading partnerships;
- Cooperation not competition;
- Agreed minimum prices to cover the costs of production, usually set higher than market minimums;
- Focus on development and technical assistance via the payment to suppliers of an agreed social premium (often 10 per cent or more of the cost price of goods);
- Provision of market information; and
- Sustainable and environmentally responsible production.

By 2007 Fairtrade claimed to have certified 422 producer groups in 49 countries, who were selling to hundreds of Fairtrade registered importers, licensees and retailers in 19 countries. Fairtrade turnover had reached in excess of £1 billion.

There are arguments for and against the Fairtrade principles. The major argument against Fairtrade is that it acts as a kind of subsidy and creates artificially high prices which can then encourage the creation of surpluses. In practice the key step is connecting the farmers better with their distant markets, helping them to develop their market knowledge, build their export or processing capability, or to diversify to meet newly identified demand. Fairtrade provides examples including coffee growers developing citrus or macadamia nuts, banana farmers moving into other premium tropical produce, or investment in alternative income-generation projects such as ecotourism, as well as support for community health and education programmes.

INFRASTRUCTURE WEAKNESSES

The challenges for international marketers from emerging markets are huge. Many of the emerging countries have difficult geography and terrain with remote areas and an inhospitable climate. Many have a poorly developed infrastructure and suffer unreliable and often poor quality supplies of utilities, such as energy, water and power. Fixed line telecommunications and transport are slow and unreliable. Usually there is an overly bureaucratic and inefficient financial and business support infrastructure.

The informal economy is huge in less developed countries (LDCs) and, in addition, bribery and corruption are rife at all levels. War and terrorism can have a devastating long-term effect on trade.

However, organisations from emerging markets can and do succeed in building their businesses despite these challenges if they can connect with their market and thus build the knowledge and capabilities to compete. For example, simply knowing what the actual international market price is for their products, rather than relying for price information on a buyer or a third party, is crucial and can have a huge impact on the viability of a small organisation. By enabling a real time connection with international market information that bypasses incomplete, unreliable and out-of-date infrastructure, the mobile phone could bring about the next 'industrial revolution'. It is also important for these SMEs to understand the value contributions of the supply chain, identifying changing customer demands and expectations, market trends, understanding what quality standards are required and knowing how to meet them, and appreciating the power of branding to raise the perception of the products.

In countries that have a small, unsophisticated domestic market these issues may not be so significant, but in international markets the goods and services must compete with those from other countries, even though they may be cheaper or unique. This poses the problem of the customer's perceptions of the quality of their goods and service. What is acceptable in a local emerging market may not be acceptable to consumers in a developed country.

Whilst the obvious route to the international market is by becoming a contract manufacturer or grower, the Internet offers further potential. To address the imbalance in power between the supplier and major international customers, improved networking of small growers and manufacturer can help. Illustration 5.1 shows how the Fairtrade principles have underpinned just such an arrangement.

ILLUSTRATION 5.1

Fairtrade networking to supply the supermarkets

Juliana-Jaramillo is a group of about 70 farmers in the Dominican Republic who sell 100 per cent of their crop of bananas to Fairtrade. The farmers live near the border with Haiti, the poorest country in Latin America. The level of education in rural areas throughout the Dominican Republic is low: 35 per cent cannot read or write.

In the 1950s, the giant Granada Food Company was farming bananas in the area, but when it moved out in 1962, the government divided about 15 per cent of the land among the workers, giving each worker about 2 hectares each.

With help from a Dutch development aid agency 39 local farmers started supplying to the Dutch Fairtrade market in 1996. Whereas the farmers around them were mainly supplying to the domestic market in the Dominican Republic and were at the mercy of market prices rising and falling, the Fairtrade farmers were assured a steady demand for their crop throughout the year and a guaranteed minimum price.

Now the farmers sell to Sainsbury's supermarkets through a UK-based company called Mack Multiples. An excellent relationship has been built up between Mack Multiples and the farmers, who work together to improve the quality of their fruit to the standards demanded by the export market, which are much higher than those for the domestic market. At an annual meeting, the farmers decide how to use the Fairtrade 'premium', a bonus on sales that can be spent on joint community projects.

QUESTION *What steps should commercial organisations take to encourage fair trade?*

Government support

We have explained the potential contribution of entrepreneurs and SMEs to the regeneration of national economies in terms of jobs and wealth creation through internationalisation and the challenges they face. It is hardly surprising, therefore, that governments in developed and developing countries encourage SMEs to internationalise by running export promotion programmes providing support and advice. An example of this is provided in the Chapter 2 case study.

Governments often provide support in the form of resources and advice but at significantly different levels, ranging from help with documentation, comprehensive country market information, export credit guarantees, trade missions and, in some cases, target country representative offices. Crick and Czinkota (1995) emphasise the need for policy makers to be more concerned with determining what assistance might be useful in helping firms to become more marketing oriented and focused on satisfying customer needs by improving quality, service and specifications to meet international standards and becoming more effective in conducting business overseas. Whilst help with language training is usually available, it is cultural training in both the social and business culture that is often more important. In South Africa, Proudly South African (www.proudlysouthafrican.co.za) is an initiative of the National Economic Development and Labour Council (Nedlac) and is supported by organised business, organised labour, government and the community to encourage firms to achieve the high standards necessary to compete against international competition and in foreign markets. Other public and private sector organisations, such as Chambers of Commerce, local authorities, local business support agencies, banks and accountants also provide SMEs with a range of services to support their international marketing activity.

Dilemma 5.1 is concerned with the role of marketing in stimulating business in some of the poorest countries but also prompts the broader question about how to get the best value from public money provided by governments to small firms.

SMEs play different roles in the global economy, have different ambitions and exploit different types of opportunity and it is this diversity that leads to SMEs adopting different approaches to international development. There is insufficient understanding of these different approaches and Balabanis, Theodosiou and Katsikea (2004) observe that it would be interesting to see more research into the factors that contribute to the success of exporters from emerging markets, noting that China was already the fourth largest exporter. Such insights would be useful not only to firms from emerging markets but also to firms from developed

---

DILEMMA 5.1

International marketing helping social enterprises

For the most part in this book we discuss international marketing as it applies to private sector organisations and occasionally we refer to the larger global charities, such as Oxfam and Save the Children.

In practice the for-profit and not-for-profit sectors converge in the area of social entrepreneurship. There has been unprecedented interest from public, private and charitable organisations and companies in addressing the problems of

Africa, for example through UN initiatives, interventions by companies and campaigns, such as Make Poverty History.

The Skoll World Forum on Social Entrepreneurship founded by Jeff Skoll, the first president of eBay, suggests that such initiatives do not work and that the people in the country can succeed in business provided a longer-term view of investment is taken.

The principles of international marketing are fundamental to and can be applied to all aspects of the work of campaigning, interventions and generating success for small firms in the poorest parts of the world. The dilemma is how marketing can be best used to help.

countries that might use an emerging market such as China as a base for exporting to the wider Asian region.

Very often SMEs are forced to take a passive role in exporting, but if circumstances change as shown in Illustration 5.2 there can be scope for greater innovation.

THE NATURE OF SME INTERNATIONAL MARKETING STRATEGIES

In exploiting these opportunities to generate revenue from international markets SMEs have a number of alternative strategies which provide a useful method of categorisation of SME internationalisation.

- *Exporting* is primarily concerned with selling domestically developed and produced goods and services abroad.
- *International niche marketing* is concerned with marketing a differentiated product or service overseas, usually to a single customer segment, using the full range of market entry and marketing mix options available.
- *Domestically delivered or developed niche services* can be marketed or delivered internationally to potential visitors.
- *Direct marketing including electronic commerce* allows firms to market products and services globally from a domestic location.
- *Participation in the international supply chain* of an MNE can lead to SMEs piggybacking on the MNE's international development. This may involve either domestic production or establishing a facility close to where the MNE's new locations are established in other countries.

ILLUSTRATION 5.2

Tariff reduction prompts innovation

Australia's macadamia growers used to send their exports to the United States as raw nuts, but when the Australia-United States Free Trade Agreement (AUSFTA) came into force in January 2005, value-added tariffs on processed nuts began reducing. By 2008 the rate will have reached zero. Suncoast Gold Macadamias (Aust) Limited is a cooperative of 150 macadamia nut growers in Gympie, Queensland. The cooperative's CEO, Jim Twentyman, said 'The United States is the largest market for macadamias in the world. They consume half the world's production – so the drop in tariff through the AUSFTA has made a very significant difference to our exports.'

With the reduction in costs Suncoast Gold has the opportunity to be more innovative in the ways nuts are packaged and processed. Suncoast Gold offers plain roasted, chilli, smoked, BBQ, honey roast and chocolate coated among the more traditional tastes, and has also developed macadamias flavoured with abalone, lobster, seaweed and wasabi for Asian consumers.

In addition to AUSFTA, Australia has implemented Free Trade Agreements with Thailand (TAFTA) and Singapore.

QUESTION *What should governments do to help small businesses become more effective exporters?*

SOURCE: WWW.AUSTRADE.GOV.AU

EXPORTING

The emergence of global competition and the opening up of international markets has stimulated many firms to embark on the the internationalisation process: for many of them, exporting is the first significant stage. Leonidou *et al.* (2002) suggests that exporting has been the most popular approach adopted by firms to enter and penetrate foreign markets as it requires less commitment of resources, has little effect on the firm's existing opperations and involves low investment and financial risks. However, exporting, when defined as the marketing of goods and/or services across national and political boundaries, is not solely the preserve of small and medium-sized businesses, nor is it a temporary stage in the process of internationalisation for many firms. Many companies, both large and small, do not progress beyond the stage of relatively limited involvement in international markets.

MOTIVATION

Balabanis *et al.* (2004) refer to a large volume of literature covering exporting including export stimuli, export and promotion programmes. Despite the wide variation in the contexts in which the research was carried out some broad conclusions can be reached.

The research draws the important distinction between whether the **motivations** to export are principally reactive stimuli or proactive stimuli. Two examples of reactive strategies are: if a product has reached maturity or is in decline in the home market, the company may find new foreign markets where the product has not reached the same life cycle stage and which, therefore, offer potential for further growth. Companies may seek new markets abroad to utilise their production facilities to their full capacity. In these circumstances companies may well embark on marginal pricing and sell at lower prices on the export markets, seeking only a contribution to their overall cost for their home base market.

The following are reactive stimuli:

- adverse domestic market conditions
- an opportunity to reduce inventories
- the availability of production capacity
- favourable currency movements
- the opportunity to increase the number of country markets and reduce the market-related risk
- unsolicited orders from overseas customers.

Proactive stimuli for exporting include market diversification. If a company sees only limited growth opportunities in the home market for a proven product it may well see market diversification as a means of expansion. This could lead to the identification of new market segments within a domestic market but it may well lead to geographic expansion in foreign markets. Thus companies try to spread risks and reduce their dependence on any one market. Equally the firm may identify market gaps. The proactive company with a well-managed marketing information system may identify foreign market opportunities through its research system. This could, of course, be by undertaking formal structured research or by identifying opportunities through a network of contacts scanning international markets for potential opportunities.

The following are proactive stimuli:

- attractive profit and growth opportunities
- the ability to easily modify products for export markets
- public policy programmes for export promotion

- foreign country regulations
- the possession of unique products
- economies resulting from additional orders.

And certain managerial elements including:

- the presence of an export-minded manager
- the opportunity to better utilise management talent and skills
- management beliefs about the value of exporting.

Illustration 5.3 is a good example of how the changes in the market environment forced Landcatch to redefine its business.

Barriers to internationalisation

Many companies with export potential never become involved in international marketing, and a series of export studies have found that it is often a great deal easier to encourage existing exporters to increase their involvement in international markets than to encourage those who are not exporting to begin the process. The reasons given by companies for not exporting are numerous. The biggest barrier to entry into export markets for these companies is the fear that their products are not marketable overseas: consequently they become preoccupied with the domestic market. Other SMEs believe that because of the particular nature of their business sector, their domestic market continues to offer the best potential

SOURCE: ADAPTED FROM A. BOLGER, 'SALMON ADDS TO HIGHLANDS PROSPERITY', THE FINANCIAL TIMES 21 AUGUST, 2006

ILLUSTRATION 5.3

Salmon or eggs: which comes first?

SMEs often have to redefine their market and reformulate their business when changes occur in the competitive environment. Landcatch was set up on the Ormsary estate in Argyll, Scotland, by Sir William Lithgow, proprietor of Scott Lithgow shipyard on the Clyde, in 1980 as demand for farmed salmon increased. The farm used the natural resources of the estate – hydro-electric

PHOTO CREDIT: LEWIS HOUGHTON/ALAMY

power – and helped to provide jobs in an area of high unemployment.

However, as new firms entered the market, supply began to exceed demand and, with little opportunity to differentiate the product, salmon became a commodity with fish farmers competing mainly on price. Ten years later the company stopped producing salmon for consumption. It now focuses on producing eggs and young fish for other farmers to grow to maturity.

Landcatch took control from its Dutch partner of its Chilean joint venture. It invested £17 million in its breeding programme over ten years and now has a fully traceable bank of records of salmon families.

The company now has a 14 per cent share of the world market for Atlantic salmon eggs. Since its launch landcatch has reinvented itself from a fish farming company to a knowledge-based organisation focusing on higher added value activity. Of its 56 permanent staff, 40 per cent have degrees. The company expects current sales of £10 m to double over the next four years.

QUESTIONS *How would you define a niche marketing strategy? What is the basis of Landcatch's competitive advantage that will sustain the business in a competitive market?*

for market growth or market share growth and is not so vulnerable to international competition, so a domestically focused strategy makes the best use of their resources.

Some of the most important areas which non-exporters identify as barriers to exporting include:

- too much red tape
- trade barriers
- transportation difficulties
- lack of trained personnel
- lack of export incentives
- lack of coordinated assistance
- unfavourable conditions overseas
- slow payment by buyers
- lack of competitive products
- payment defaults
- language barriers
- limited information from which to locate and analyse foreign markets.

Experienced exporters tend not to highlight issues such as the bureaucracy associated with international markets and trade barriers, which suggests that they have overcome the problems through managerial proactivity, for example, by training staff and seeking expert assistance, so that these potential problem areas can be dealt with.

NICHE MARKETING

Having identified the motivations and barriers to exporting it is tempting to conclude that many exporters are characterised by being product-oriented – selling abroad the products and services that are successful in the domestic market. Moreover, exporters often seem to throw away their successful domestic marketing strategies in international markets, preferring instead to delegate their marketing to agents and distributors. In doing this they seem to overlook the alternative market entry and marketing mix strategies that are available to them, opting instead for a strategy of least involvement. In many cases this approach may meet the exporting firm's immediate objectives, especially if, for example, they are simply seeking to offload excess production capacity, but it does not provide them with a sound basis for substantially increasing their international market presence.

By contrast, international niche marketing occurs where firms become a strong force in a narrow specialised market of one or two segments across a number of country markets. Parrish, Cassill and Oxenham (2006) explain how niche marketing can be used in a mature sector – for example global textiles – to increase competitiveness, despite the presence of strong rivals.

Brown and McDonald (1994) explain that the segments must be too small or specialised to attract large competitors: true niche marketing does not include small brands or companies that are minor players in a mass market offering undifferentiated products. For the international niche to be successful the product or service must be distinctive (highly differentiated), be recognised by consumers and other participants in the international supply chain and have clear positioning.

To sustain and develop the niche the firm must:

- have good information about the segment needs;
- have a clear understanding of the important segmentation criteria;

- understand the value of the product niche to the targeted segment(s);
- provide high levels of service;
- carry out small scale innovations;
- seek cost efficiency in the supply chain;
- maintain a separate focus, perhaps, by being content to remain relatively small;
- concentrate on profit rather than market share; and
- evaluate and apply appropriate market entry and marketing mix strategies to build market share in each country in which they wish to become involved.

Beatson Clark is an example of a niche marketer (Illustration 5.4) operating in a highly competitive commodity market.

There are, therefore, significant differences between the traditional view of exporting and international niche marketing and these are summarised in Table 5.1.

Niche marketing of domestically delivered services

In the past this category of international marketing has largely been dominated by the travel industry with domestic firms such as hotels, tour operators and leisure attractions generating foreign earnings for the country by attracting visitors. International destination marketing of cities, regions and countries, such as Prague, the wildlife reserves of Botswana and Vietnam is increasingly important for economic success in certain areas. The international marketing of destinations is

TABLE 5.1 The difference between exporting and international niche marketing

	Exporting	International Marketing
Marketing Strategy	Selling production capacity	Meeting customer needs
Financial Objective	To amortise overheads	To add value
Segmentation	Usually by country and consumer characteristics	By identifying common international customer benefit
Pricing	Cost based	Market or customer based
Management focus	Efficiency in operations	Meeting market requirements
Distribution	Using existing agents or distributor	Managing the supply chain
Market information	Relying on agent or distributor feedback	Analysing the market situation and customer needs
Customer relationship	Working through intermediaries	Building multiple level relationships

usually undertaken by relatively small organisations such as tourist boards that represent a huge network of dependent providers of accomodation, catering, leisure activities and experiences. Their role is becoming increasingly important as the economies of the destinations become ever more dependent on tourism, and competition between destinations and the number of potential visitors increases.

With increased international travel and improved access to worldwide communications a much wider range of services is being offered to visiting customers. Examples include the provision of education, specialised training, medical

ILLUSTRATION 5.4

Beatson Clark: defining a niche in a commodity market

Beatson Clark are manufacturers of glass containers for the pharmaceutical, food and drinks industry. They export to over 100 countries worldwide. The global glass container market is highly competitive and virtually all countries have their large indigenous producers who sell the containers as commodity products. This makes it difficult to compete given the high costs involved in physically distributing large glass containers to overseas markets.

Beatson Clark have developed a very effective niche market strategy by focusing on low volume small items which are not of great interest to the large producers. Their competitive advantage has been developed internationally by building a highly effective customer service operation for their customers throughout the world.

The company offer a design service for the small items, something that is too much hassle for their major competitors. In each market the company builds up close relationships with a number of trusted distributors who operate in the packaging market and have a good customer base. The company keeps in regular touch with all their international partners, sometimes contacting to them 10–15 times a day.

They have, then, built an effective customer service operation to service all customers wherever they are. This is based on three fundamental principles. First, there is an explicit commitment to quality which is shared throughout the company. All prospective customers throughout the world are sent a signed letter from the MD setting out the commitment to quality procedures and there is an explicit process for translating the company's quality policy into departmental goals.

Second, the company has a team who are dedicated to the effective movement of goods throughout the world and take full responsibility for ensuring safe delivery of all orders to their international destinations, which is no easy task in the glass business!

Third, the company place great emphasis on establishing effective monitoring procedures to measure their performance in customer service as well as their financial performance by customer, order, country etc. to ensure that at all times they have full control in their international operations.

This has meant the company has been able to build an international strategy which operates on good margins, is relatively low risk and has achieved a steady rate of growth whilst enabling the company to achieve an element of control in the marketplace.

QUESTION *How did the firm reduce its vulnerability to international competition in a commodity market?*

treatment, sports, cultural and leisure events and specialist retailing, such as luxury goods. For example, in 2007 330 000 foreign students studied at 168 higher education institutions in the UK, almost a third of the student population of 1.07 million (Higher Education Statistics Agency 2007). The British Council supports the international marketing efforts of what are largely independent institutions.

Clearly these activities lead to wealth and jobs being generated in the local economy in much the same way as with exporting and niche marketing. The international marketing strategy processes and programmes are similar too, in that the products and services must meet the requirements of and be promoted to international customers. Consequently, issues of standardisation and adaptation of the marketing mix elements are equally important. The additional challenge is that the benefits obtained from the service provided must be unique and superior, and thus outweigh the benefits to the consumer of their locally available services as well as the cost of travel that the customers will incur in the purchasing and consumption process.

In addition to the services designed to be offered to individuals in both consumer or business-to-business markets, a whole range of additional services which fall into this category of being domestically delivered are concerned with developing solutions for opportunities or problems identified abroad. These might include technology developments, such as research into new drugs, trial and testing facilities, software development and product and packaging design services.

There are many examples of research and development companies that licence their new technologies to customers around the world. One is shown in Illustration 5.5.

Importing and reciprocal trading

Importing is clearly the opposite process to international marketing and as such might be seen by governments as 'exporting' jobs and potential wealth. However, the purpose of raising this issue here is to highlight the nature of international

ILLUSTRATION 5.5

Creating a mobile music software niche

In 2007 Apple launched its i-Phone, which combined a music facility and a mobile phone. This put pressure on the mobile network operators to develop their own versions of a mobile

PHOTO CREDIT: MARIO TAMA/GETTY IMAGES

music product. Whilst mobile music has long been expected to be a revenue generator, none of the existing service providers had succeeded, so the Apple was expected to be successful. However, the i-Phone was a 'sideloaded' product, requiring a computer connection to load music on to a phone. This would not generate data transfer revenues for the service provider. Omniphone, founded by Rob Lewis – an entrepreneur who previously ran a technology news website – had developed software to power a subscription service to download music and in 2007 was reported to be in discussion with over twenty service providers. The system managed memory intelligently and deleted rarely used songs to free up room for more downloads. The big advantage claimed by Omniphone was that its software worked on three-quarters of existing handsets and even on slower networks too, so overcoming the problem that many mobile applications are incompatible with the huge variety of handsets operating systems and networks.

QUESTION *What are the challenges for a niche international B2B marketer in a market dominated by industry giants?*

SOURCE: ADAPTED FROM 'NEW SERVICE THREATENS I-PHONE', SUNDAY TIMES, 11 FEBRUARY, 2007

trade as it is today. Rarely do supply chains for products and services involve solely domestic production and delivery. There has been a substantial increase in outsourcing, not only by large firms but by SMEs too. Exporting and importing have become inextricably linked so that the challenge is one of adding value to imported components and services, no matter where they are sourced, so that they can then be re-exported in order to meet the international customers' needs effectively and profitably.

Importing activity can also considerably enhance a company's potential to network, leading ultimately, perhaps, to reciprocal trading in which, as a result, the supplier might take other products or services in return from the customer.

FOREIGN DIRECT INVESTMENT

It might be concluded from this that raising the level of value-adding supply chain activity in a particular country is the ultimate aim of governments. Most governments take this further by encouraging foreign direct investment (FDI) by multinationals in the belief that as well as aiding the economy through increasing employment and tax revenues, the MNEs, operations will benefit the indigenous SME supply sector by:

- providing additional B2B sales opportunities for the SME suppliers to provide components, subcontracted fabrication work and non-core services as part of the MNE's supply chain; and

- setting and establishing higher international quality standards amongst the suppliers, which will then enable them to compete better in international markets.

The danger with FDI is that MNEs will only maintain their operations in a particular country while it is financially advantageous. When the MNE finds a lower labour cost country location for its operations it will move on. Many countries have found that low-cost assembly-type manufacturing or call centre operations can be easily relocated with the associated loss of jobs and tax revenues. Whilst the government can take action to encourage continuing high levels of FDI through ensuring a well-educated and flexible workforce, an efficient, responsive and flexible SME supply chain will also be a significant factor in MNE location decisions.

Direct marketing and electronic commerce

A rapidly growing area of international trading is direct marketing and, in particular, electronic commerce. Direct marketing offers the benefits of cutting out other distribution channel members such as importers, agents, distributors, wholesalers and retailers, by using a variety of communications media, including post, telephone, television and networked computers in the form of the Internet. All these allow borders to be crossed relatively easily with limited investment and risk, and without the SME having to face many of the barriers already highlighted in this chapter.

Direct marketing also has a number of disadvantages. Despite the range of media available, communicating can still be problematic as personalisation of the communication is essential for direct marketing success. In cross-border direct marketing there is always the danger of cultural insensitivity and language mistakes in the communications. Many of the following comments apply to both traditional direct marketing, using physical media and electronic commerce, but we have focused on online trading as it is this method that has had the most impact on SME internationalisation.

If customers speak different languages then it may be necessary for online retailers to have multilingual websites. This can add cost in setting up and servicing the website. The continued growth of online retailers may depend on selling to international customers who do not speak the home country language. Moreover, because of the need to manage large numbers of customers it is necessary to use databases which must be up to date, accurate and be capable of dealing with foreign languages. Even an incorrectly spelt name can be insulting to the recipient.

The Internet provides smaller firms with a shop window and also the means of obtaining payment, organising and tracking shipment and delivery. For some products and services it can provide the means by which market information can be accumulated and new ideas collected, developed and modified by customers and other stakeholders.

Electronic commerce has led firms to redefine their business and it can also be a business in its own right. For example, many electronic commerce services take the form of information transfer and this forms the basis of the product or service itself, for example specialist advice on personal finance, travel and hobbies.

As well as being a route to market in its own right in the form of direct commerce, the Internet as an interactive marketing information provider has an increasingly important role in each of the above international niche marketing strategies.

The Internet offers the benefits to SMEs of real time communications across distances and the levelling of the corporate playing field, leading to more rapid internationalisation as well as achieving competitive advantage by:

- creating new opportunities;
- erecting barriers to entry;
- making cost savings from online communications;
- providing online support for inter-firm collaboration, especially in research and development, as an information search and retrieval tool;
- the establishment of company websites for marketing and sales promotion; and
- the transmission of any type of data including manuscripts, financial information and CAD/CAM (computer-aided design, computer-aided manufacture) files.

There are some disadvantages, especially the relative ease with which it is possible to become flooded with electronic messages (spam) and orders. Whilst this may be manageable for certain products and services where production volumes can easily be increased or decreased, sales feasts and famines can cause havoc where production capacity is less flexible.

As advanced search engines become more sophisticated it is essential (and expensive) to make sure that the firm's offer is listed on the first page of search results for key words. The implications of this are that instead of marketing being essentially passive in electronic commerce, the marketing input required in designing websites needs to become increasingly sophisticated in promoting the products, providing interactive product design development and safe payment arrangements. Technical and customer service support and initial customer segmentation and targeting are becoming increasingly important to the delivery of an effective, focused business. Thus, whilst many SMEs see the Internet as a low-cost distribution channel, the greater competition and more sophisticated versions of electronic commerce make it more difficult for SMEs to compete. SMEs frequently face the dilemma of how to cope with powerful competitors.

The advent of e-business and the Internet appears to offer the benefits to SMEs of being able to ignore borders and make more direct interaction possible between international SMES and their customers. However, Servais, Madsen and Rasmussen (2007) explain that even 'born global' SMEs use the Internet only to a limited extent to sell their products and as a tool to support existing relationships.

THE NATURE OF INTERNATIONAL DEVELOPMENT

The internationalisation process differs enormously depending on whether the company first serves the domestic market and later develops into foreign markets (adaptive exporter), or is expressly established from its inception to enter foreign markets (born global). Adaptive and born global exporters differ in a variety of ways, including their respective market assessment processes, reasons for international market involvement, managerial attitudes and the propensity to take risks. Successful born globals are seen to surmount their distinctive challenges with flexible managerial attitudes and practices. This managerial attitude and behaviour of innate exporters is seen by writers as being more conducive to eventual success than those of adaptive exporters. On the other hand, adaptive exporters that are willing to adapt to change have generally proved to be highly successful in international markets and usually develop enormously in management and company expertise.

Many exporting firms, especially in high-technology or industrial markets, internationalise through their network of relationships. Firms in any market establish and develop relationships through interactions with other individuals and firms, leading the parties to build mutual trust, respect and knowledge. Internationalisation of the firm therefore becomes a consequence of the interaction between the firms in the network they have formed. The network of business relationships comprises a number of different stakeholders – customers, customers' customers, competitors, supplementary suppliers, suppliers, distributors, agents and consultants – as well as regulatory and other public agencies. In any specific country, different networks can be distinguished. Any or all of these relationships may become the conduit for the internationalisation of a company. In these cases the internationalisation process of a company is more aptly visualised as a series of multilateral cycles rather than a linear process (see Figure 5.1).

Thus the internationalisation process manifests itself by the development of business relationships in other countries:

- through the establishment of relationships in country networks that are new to the firm, i.e. international extension;
- through the development of relationships in those networks, i.e. penetration;
- through connecting networks in different countries, i.e. international integration.

FIGURE 5.1
The multilateral aspects of the internationalisation process

SOURCE: JOHANNSON AND VAHINE (1992)

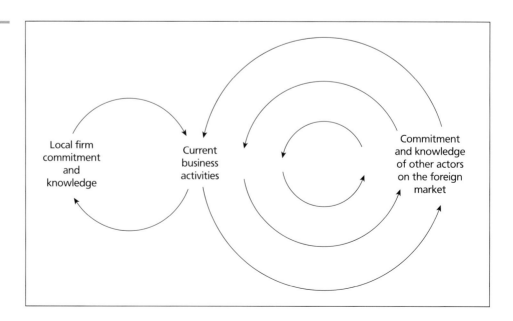

Relationship and network building are especially important in the fast changing, global environment, but particularly in high technology industries. Studies of the internationalisation process of small hi-tech firms indicates that some of these companies follow the traditional internationalisation patterns, whilst others behave differently. They go directly to more distant markets and rapidly set up their own subsidiaries. One reason seems to be that the entrepreneurs behind those companies have networks of colleagues dealing with the new technology. Internationalisation, in these cases, is an exploitation of the advantage created by networking.

Crick and Spence (2005) found that internationalisation strategy formation for high performing SMEs is not always systematic and capable of being described by one single theory. Some firms take a much more opportunistic approach towards their internationalising strategy and it is necessary to take a more holistic view of the organisation and its context to explain its decisions.

Balabanis and Katsikea (2003) explain the further dimensions and add that there is some evidence to suggest that an entrepreneurial approach, which involves risk-taking, being proactive and innovative in developing strategies, is useful in international marketing development.

Geographic development of SMEs

For SMEs, country market selection and development of market share within each country are particularly important for growth. Given their limited resources and narrow margin for failure it is vital that their method of country market development is effective. The various patterns of SME international development are shown in Figure 5.2.

FIGURE 5.2
Geographic development of SMEs

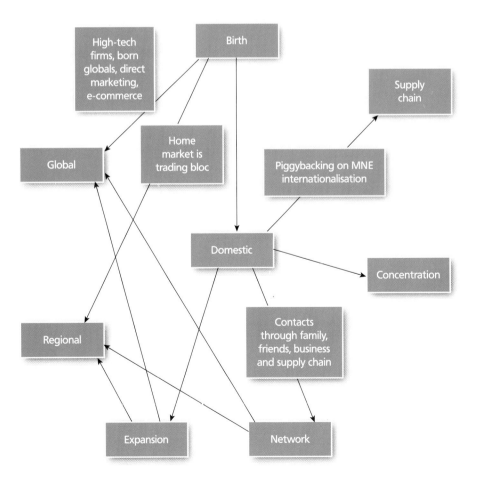

The conventional approach is for new companies to test the viability of their products in the domestic market before spreading internationally, but we have already indicated that a number of firms become international players almost immediately after they have been formed, either because they are born global or they operate within a common regional market. Figure 5.3 represents the internationalisation strategies in terms of the key dimensions of the number of country markets and market share.

The different patterns of international spreading are now discussed.

Market expansion and concentration

The conventional view of country selection is that from a sound domestic base SMEs develop either by choosing between expanding into many markets, gaining a superficial presence and accepting a low overall market share, or concentrating their marketing activities in a small number of markets in which a significant market share can be built. The research in this area is inconclusive about the precise reasons why firms adopt one strategy or another.

Katsikeas and Leonidou (1996) found that market concentrators tend, in general, to be smaller firms, because of their greater interest in export profitability and lesser concern with export sales objectives. Typically they make regular visits overseas and this appears to play a key role in their strategy for penetrating the market. Concentrators experience more problems associated with product adaptation to the needs of their customers but pricing and their marketing organisation needs present less of a problem.

Market expanders tend to be larger firms who are more concerned with export sales objectives, do more export marketing research, and have greater overall market share expectations. They place less emphasis on profitability, personal visits are less important and they perceive fewer product adaptation-related problems. E-commerce businesses are typical market expanders.

Where the domestic market is redefined

The lowering or removal of barriers between countries and the move, for example, in the EU to the harmonisation of standards, the removal of tariff barriers, reduction of non-tariff barriers and the introduction of a common currency within a regional trading bloc mean that SMEs are more likely to be active in more than one country market because the regional market is considered to be

FIGURE 5.3
Growth for niche marketers

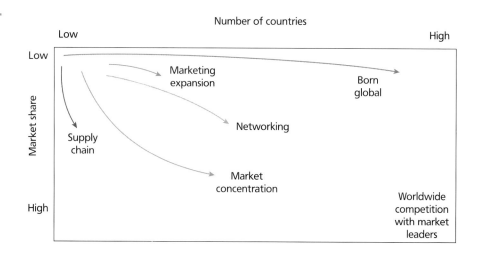

a domestic market. This is particularly the case, for example, in mainland Europe where there are no additional costs in travelling to a neighbouring country and, often, a common language may be used.

Where the SME international development is the result of networking

Many SMEs adopt what appears to be a rather unsystematic approach to country market selection. Their patterns of development tend to be the result of a network approach where the selection of the market is not merely made on the relative attractiveness of the markets and their match with the company capability, but rather on the reduction of the risk of entering unknown markets by working with individuals or companies they know. International development through using existing networks of contacts is more typical of Asian firms than SMEs from Western countries.

Internationalising through networking using a small business management model still provides entrepreneurs with the means of achieving security, often because it allows fast adaptation in a rapidly changing world. Through a global network many small units can come up with a variety of solutions at an acceptable level of risk. Hardman, Messinger and Bergson (2005) have taken this further and suggest that to compete effectively with the largest competitors, with their scale advantages, small organisations will have to achieve virtual scale by working in alliances to achieve the necessary leverage. The Internet can facilitate this and the success of social networking will lead to greater online business networking.

Family networks

Nueno (2000) explains that the Chinese can be very effective entrepreneurs. Whilst 1 per cent of the population of the Philippines is ethnic Chinese they control 40 per cent of the economy, half the economies of Indonesia and Thailand are controlled by 4 per cent and 10 per cent ethnic Chinese respectively and in Malaysia two-thirds of the economy is controlled by ethnic Chinese.

They operate effectively within a family network and, because the Chinese are spread throughout the world, they can lay the foundations for stronger links amongst businesses across borders as a network of entrepreneurial relationships. As we indicated earlier, in practice most SMEs operate within a network of personal contacts, but this is much more formalised in some cultures, such as the Chinese, because it is based on *guanxi* and the obligation to return favours. The Confucian tradition of hard work, thrift and respect for one's social network provides continuity, and the small network-based enterprises bound by strong cultural links is well suited to fast-changing markets. Illustration 5.6 explains the impact of family groups on international trade.

Networking and relationship marketing are now emphasised as key components of most SME internationalisation strategies.

Where the SME is born global

Some SMEs market their products and services globally from birth because the customer segment or competition is global (especially in high technology) or because the distribution method is global, for example, direct marketing and telecommunications-based international marketing (e.g. Internet).

Knight and Cavusgil (1996) believe that in born global firms the management views the world as its marketplace from the outset and, unlike traditional companies, does not see foreign markets as simple adjuncts to the domestic market. They begin international trade within two years of establishing the firm and of course e-commerce is an important element of the born global operation. The majority of born globals are formed by active entrepreneurs and tend to emerge as a result of a significant breakthrough in some process or technology. They may apply cutting-edge technology to developing a unique product idea or to a new way of doing business. The products and services that born globals sell directly involve substantial value added and the majority of such products may be intended for industrial use.

Several trends have given rise to the emergence of born global firms:

- The increasing role of niche markets, especially in the developed world. As markets mature products increasingly become commodities, and SMEs respond by identifying subsegments of customers that require a more specialised or customised product or service.

- To compete with large, powerful MNEs smaller firms must specialise. However, whilst the demand from a domestic niche market may be very

ILLUSTRATION 5.6

Family networking

Success in Asia still runs on power, prestige, influence, favours given and received, family fortune and connections. Without these even the simplest deal can come unstuck for no obvious reasons. For example, the Chinese, Japanese, Koreans and Indians have their own special connections and their business styles come down to trust and credibility – who vouches for whom.

There are six big economic groups in Asia that are growing fast as a result of networking as:

- Japanese *keiretsu* company connections;
- Koreans with *chaebol* conglomerates;
- mainland Chinese with party and military links;

PHOTO CREDIT: VARIO IMAGES GMBH & CO.KG/ALAMY

- ethnic or overseas Chinese with their stored wealth, extended family, dialect and guild connections;

- the emerging *pribumi* and *bumiputera* (indigenous) business leaders of Indonesia and Malaysia with their political connections;

- the Indians with their family dynasties.

It is networking on a grand scale that provides the basis of the international operations as there are an estimated 57 million Chinese and 18 million Indians that are living abroad. A Singaporean Chinese trader may have family connections in Taiwan, Hong Kong, Guandong, Fujian or Vietnam that can provide legal, banking and support services when moving across borders.

A small group of families also control the Indian economy and are successfully developing their global businesses. However, it is internal family disagreements that are their major concern, whereas the traditional power of the mainland Chinese dynasties was disrupted during the communist era and new dynasties will be created.

In the West many of the old, great family business dynasties have declined in importance and given way to the new entrepreneurs who have exploited new technologies, such as Rupert Mudoch of News International, which includes Sky. Perhaps such organisations are creating new family dynasties.

QUESTION *To what extent do you expect the old family groups to be the future successes and to what extent do you expect the new groups that have created their wealth through new technologies succeed them?*

SOURCE: ADAPTED FROM C. CHANDLER, 'DEALING WITH DYNASTIES', FORTUNE INTERNATIONAL 31 OCTOBER, 2005, ACCESSED AT WWW.KELLOGG.NORTHWESTERN.EDU AND G. HISCOCK, 'MEET ASIA'S NEW SUPER RICH', SUNDAY TIMES, 8 JUNE, 1997

small, the global demand can sustain an SME that is prepared to supply the niche on a worldwide basis.

- Recent advances in process technology mean low-scale batch production can be economical and new technologies mean that SMEs can compete with large firms to produce sophisticated products.

- Communications technologies allow SMEs to manage across borders and information is more readily accessible to everyone. It is now much less expensive to go international than it was just 20 years ago.

- Quicker response time, flexibility and adaptability to foreign tastes and specific customer requirements give these firms an immediate competitive edge.

- SMEs can gain access to funding and support, benefit from joint research programmes and technology transfer and employ cross-border educated managers more easily than ever before.

- Increasingly international business is facilitated through partnership with foreign businesses – distributors, trading companies, subcontractors and alliances – allowing new specialist firms to participate in global networks more easily than before.

A number of studies of born global firms have been made in different country contexts. Mort and Weerawardena (2006) explain that the new concept of international entrepreneurship has followed research into born global firms and highlighted the importance of relationships and networking in enabling the identification and exploitation of market opportunities and facilitating the development of knowledge-intensive products. Harris and Wheeler (2005) focus on the role of the entrepreneur's interpersonal relationships in the internationalisation process and explain that strong, deep relationships are developed in wide social/personal and business situations that do not just provide information and access to networks but, more importantly, can be influential in directing strategy and can lead to the transformation of the firm.

Supply chain internationalisation

The pattern of internationalisation of firms that are part of the supply chain of an MNE is usually determined by the international strategy adopted by the MNE. The downsizing that occurred in many large Western firms as a cost-cutting response to the recession in the 1990s and the low-priced competitive challenges of the 2000s led firms to think about what was their core competence and answer the question 'what business are we in?' The response to this question led a number of MNEs to identify those components and services that were part of the overall product offer but which they regarded as being peripheral to their business. As a result of this many decided to outsource more of their supplies, either from MNE specialist component makers and service providers, or from SMEs that have exploited these new opportunities to grow.

The reasons for MNEs to outsource can be summarised as follows:

- It reduces the capital requirements of the business (the supplier rather than the MNE invests in new processes and facilities).

- It overcomes the difficulty of developing quickly and maintaining in-house knowledge in many different specialist knowledge areas.

- It improves flexibility, as some firms are better equipped and can carry out small production runs, special designs and development tasks more quickly.

- The MNE can take risks in more peripheral activities where their expertise is weak, stopping the firm from falling behind in the effectiveness of its non-core operations.

- The economies of scale of suppliers may make components much cheaper through outsourcing rather than from in-house supplies.

- The expertise of business support service providers, for example in transport and delivery systems, cannot be matched.

- Downsizing without outsourcing can lead to management resources becoming too stretched and unfocused.

The disadvantages of outsourcing are:

- *Loss of know-how* – Western businesses in many sectors have outsourced manufacturing to Asian firms who have subsequently opened up as competitors.

- *The costs of managing the outsourced supplies* – managing outsourced components and services does require time and technical expertise and, particularly in the case of IT, there have been some difficulties of integrating the service with the firm's primary strategic objectives.

Both large and smaller firms have been the beneficiaries of this increased outsourcing but for smaller firms there are particular challenges. These include:

- The need to become closely linked with one or two major customers, upon which the SME is almost entirely dependent for survival and success.

- Internationalisation is driven by the demands of the MNE. Failure to follow their product or market development demands may result in the loss of all the business as they seek alternative suppliers.

- They are under continual pressure to make operational efficiencies and design improvements in order to offer even better value for money.

- Concentration on developing the relationship with the MNE may lead to the firm becoming relatively weaker in external marketing, putting the firm at a disadvantage if it needs to find new customers when difficulties occur.

The advantages for SMEs are:

- The opportunities to learn from working with the MNE. This is likely to improve the smaller firms' strategic and operational management systems, communications and purchasing efficiency.

- They get greater business security through reliable and predictable ordering whilst the customer is successful.

- The opportunity to focus on production and technical issues rather than being diverted by the need to analyse changes to the market, customer and competition to the same degree.

Developing relationships

The key to success in working within the supply chain of an MNE is developing an effective relationship which can build upon the advantages and minimise the disadvantages of cooperative working between firms which may have some business objectives in common, but also may have a number of differences. As more SMEs become involved in international supply chains, the ways in which relationships between smaller suppliers and the MNE differ between Western and Asian styles of management become particularly significant.

The Western way of arranging sourcing is a much more competition-based approach and has the advantage of a much sharper focus on cost reduction and profit and individual creativity. The Asian approach is much more cooperative-based and includes ensuring that more than one strong supplier is available, expertise is shared and built upon and the competitive focus is always on the much larger market opportunity.

Over the past few years the number of cooperative arrangements between Western and Asian styles within one supply chain has increased and, as a result, arrangements which could be described as a combination of the two have been developed in which longer-term contracts have been agreed in order to maximise the cooperation between the MNE and supplier, but without the insistence on sharing information with the losing contractor, which was often a feature of the Asian approach.

INTERNATIONAL STRATEGIC MARKETING MANAGEMENT IN SMEs

Having considered the various categories of SME internationalisation and the nature of SME international development, we now turn to the factors which influence the international marketing management of SMEs. The McKinsey 7S framework, shown in Figure 5.4, is useful for discussing the elements.

The McKinsey 7S framework

The first three elements – strategy, structure and systems – are considered to be the hardware of successful management and as such can be implemented across international markets without the need for significant adaptation. The other four – management style, staff, skills and shared values – are the software, and are affected by cultural differences. Often it is the management of these aspects of the business that highlights good management in the best firms and relatively unimpressive management in poorer performing firms. It is quite obvious too that it is these elements of the framework which can vary considerably from country to country and provide the most significant challenges for SMEs developing from their home base into an organisation with involvement in a number of different countries.

The characteristics of these four software elements are:

1 *Style*: In organisations such as McDonald's, it is the consistency across the world of the management and their operational style that is one of the

FIGURE 5.4
McKinsey 7S framework

SOURCE: MCKINSEY AND CO.

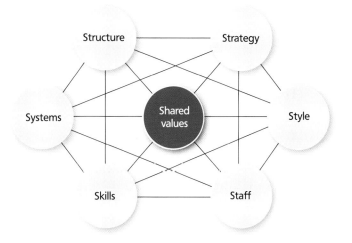

distinguishing features of the companies. For SMEs the management and operational style often reflects the personality, standards and values of the owner, and is often maintained as the firm matures, as is the case with Richard Branson of Virgin, Steve Jobs of Apple and Azim Premji of Wipro, discussed in Illustration 5.7.

2 *Skills*: The sorts of skills that are needed to carry out the strategy vary considerably between countries and also over time as the firm grows rapidly and new strategies and systems are introduced. Because the levels and quality of education of staff may vary considerably too, an effective human resource development strategy can be important to identify and build the necessary skills.

3 *Staff*: The people that are recruited around the world need to be capable, well trained, and given the jobs that will best allow them to make use of their talents. Recognition of the contributions of the staff, the criteria for advancement, acceptance of appraisal and disciplinary processes vary considerably between countries.

4 *Shared values*: Despite the fact that staff come from different cultural backgrounds there is a need for employees to understand what the organisation stands for, where it is going and to share the same organisational values.

The first part of this next section on international strategic management focuses broadly upon the 'hardware' and the second part on the 'software' of the McKinsey 7S framework.

ILLUSTRATION 5.7

Azim Premji – from cooking oil to IT billionaire

In 1966 Azim Premji was 21 and studying at Stanford University when his father Hasham died suddenly. Hasham Premji had set up Western India Vegetable Products Ltd (WIPRO) in 1945. Azim rushed back to India and attended the first annual general meeting of the company. A vociferous and articulate

PHOTO CREDIT: DIBY ANGSHU SARICAR/GETTY IMAGES

shareholder told him to sell his shareholding and give it to more mature management, as there was no way a person of his age and experience could lead the company! He was rated the richest person in the country from 1999 to 2005 by Forbes and is now worth US$17.1 billion.

When Premji took over, the firm's main product was edible oils, but in the 1970s the company moved into computer and printer hardware, and in the 1980s it moved into software. Wipro's software is used in many mobile phones, such as Nokia and NEC. Wipro also spotted the opportunity to help Indian firms with complex IT problems before multi-nationals, such as IBM and EDS, became established in India.

Wipro's growth in the 1990s and through into the new millennium was based on a further activity – offering outsourcing possibilities to large international firms. At the end of the 1980s firms were looking for low-cost manufacturing centres: now IT is enabling firms to outsource business processing services. Wipro has a turnover in excess of US$2.5 billion.

The firm manages a range of services, including call centres, financial administration, accounting, credit card renewal and marketing for clients as diverse as Boeing, Prudential and Sony.

QUESTION *What lessons can be learned from Azim Premji's outstanding success?*

SOURCE: ADAPTED FROM N. HOPKINS, 'THE INDIAN BILLIONAIRE ON THE END OF THE LINE', *TIMES*, 14 FEBRUARY, 2003 AND 'DEFINING MOMENTS: AZIM PREMJI', BBC NEWS ONLINE, 14 JULY 2003

The generic marketing strategies for SME internationalisation

Whilst there are an infinite number of individual implementation strategies that an SME might adopt, the generic marketing strategies provide a useful starting point.

SEGMENTATION, TARGETING AND POSITIONING

The principal approach to marketing strategy development follows three stages, normally referred to as segmentation, targeting and positioning (STP marketing):

1 Identification of the various segments that exist within the sector, using the various segmentation methods which we discussed in Chapter 4. It is important for the SME to define cross-border segments with clearly identifiable requirements that it is able to serve.

2 The firm must then target the segments which appear to be most attractive in terms of their size, growth potential, the ease with which they can be reached and their likely purchasing power.

3 In seeking to defend and develop its business the firm needs to position its products or services in a way that will distinguish them from those of its local and international competitors and build up barriers which will prevent those competitors taking its business.

COMPETITIVE STRATEGIES

In order to create the competitive advantage necessary to achieve growth, Porter (1990) suggests that firms should adopt one of the following three generic competitive strategies. However, each poses particular challenges for SMEs in international markets:

1 *Cost leadership* requires the firm to establish a lower cost base than its local or international competitors. This strategy has typically been adopted by companies that are located in countries with lower labour costs and who develop business usually as a component or service provider. Because of their limited financial resources, however, SMEs that adopt a low-cost strategy spend little on marketing activity and are vulnerable to either local firms or larger multi-nationals temporarily cutting prices to force the firm out of the market. Alternatively changes in currency exchange rates or other instability in the economic climate can result in newer, lower priced competitors emerging.

2 *Focus*, in which the firm concentrates on one or more narrow segments and thus builds up a specialist knowledge of each segment. Such segments in the international marketplace are transnational in nature and companies work to dominate one particular segment across a number of country markets. Typically this strategy necessitates the SME providing high levels of customer and technical service support, which can be resource intensive. Moreover, unless the SME has created a highly specialised niche, it may be difficult to defend against local and international competition.

3 *Differentiation* is achieved through emphasising particular benefits in the product, service, or marketing mix, which customers think are important and a significant improvement over competitive offers. Differentiation typically requires systematic incremental innovation to continually add customer value. Whilst SMEs are capable of the flexibility, adaptability and responsiveness to customer needs necessary with this strategy, the cost of maintaining high levels of differentiation over competitors in a number of international markets can be demanding of management time and financial resources.

Many SMEs base their international strategy on the generic strategy which has given them competitive advantage in domestic markets and then attempt to apply this same successful strategy in international markets. Of fundamental importance to the development of an effective international strategy for some SMEs is having a very strong position in the home country. US firms have benefited from having a huge domestic market. Chinese firms will also have the opportunity to become strong through exploiting the huge home market before venturing into international markets. By contrast, SMEs from emerging markets and from countries with smaller domestic markets often have to export merely to find enough customers to enable them to survive.

GROWTH STRATEGIES

SMEs also face a further strategic option. SMEs typically have limited resources and so need to make difficult decisions about how to use their limited resources to grow the business. Ansoff (1957) identified four growth strategies – product penetration, market development, product development and diversification – and these are shown in Figure 5.5. Following a product penetration strategy is appropriate if a company has an existing portfolio of products and a presence in its target markets, which offer considerable potential expansion of sales. The resources available to the company under these circumstances can be best used in concentrating on doing more of what is already being done well.

Diversification, on the other hand, is a strategy used in international markets in situations where demand for the company's existing products is falling rapidly (for example, in recent years in the defence industry), where resources are available but would not generate an acceptable return if used on existing activities or in the case of firms run by entrepreneurs, the owner often becomes bored with the firm's current activities and seeks out new challenges, by developing a new product for a new market.

For most companies the most obvious strategic development opportunities are in increasing geographical coverage (market development), which is discussed in Chapter 7, and product development, which is discussed in Chapter 8. However, these options compete for resources and firms have to choose which approach will generate a greater return on investment.

The factors which affect the choice of an SME's international marketing strategy

Figure 5.6 indicates a number of the factors which influence the choice and development of an SME's international strategy. Particular issues include

FIGURE 5.5
Ansoff growth matrix

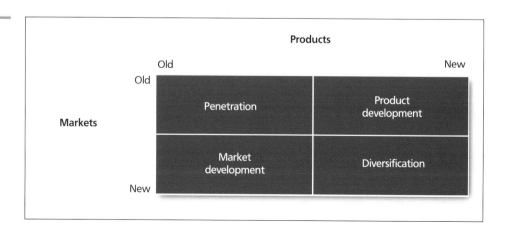

environmental trends, the market and industry structure, the customer requirements from different countries, the nature and intensity of local and international competition and the degree to which the SME can defend its niche. In SMEs, however, specific company factors are particularly important in the decision. These include the resources available, the products and services that have been developed and the firm's attitudes to international development and management of risk. These will result in the firm adopting a specific approach to individual country selection as the strategy develops.

Market factors

The most significant factor inherent in SMEs is their relatively small size and lack of power in most international markets in which they wish to be active. This puts them at a disadvantage to local competitors and MNEs, as they often lack the management resources to spend researching new markets, the contacts necessary to quickly develop effective distribution of their products and sufficient financial resources to enable them to compete with the promotional spend of their competitors and thus be strong enough to withstand a 'price war'.

At the same time smaller size means that SMEs can offer customers the benefits of a more personal service from the firm's owners or senior managers, faster decision making and, usually, a greater willingness to listen but, of course, the SME must work out how to profit from international market developments by building on these potential strengths.

FIGURE 5.6
Factors affecting SME internationalisation

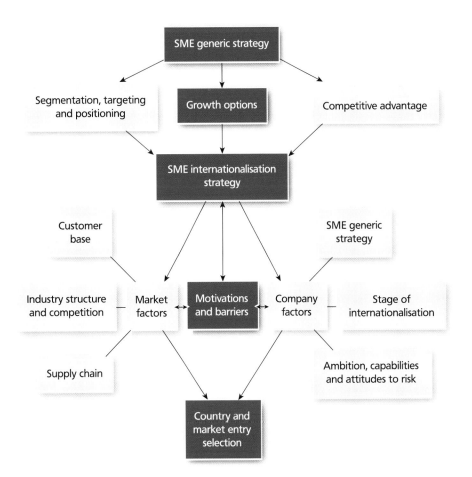

In addressing these issues, the SMEs' challenge is to communicate some unique selling propositions to their customers and create other competitive advantage dimensions, thus building barriers to entry around the niche that they have identified in order to stop attacks by competitors. There are a number of ways that this can be done. First, underpinning any product/service offer must be a significant improvement in customer added value – there is little point in SMEs trying to market 'me-too' products internationally. This is dealt with in more detail at the end of this chapter.

Second, if the product is a technical or design breakthrough it should be protected wherever possible by patent or copyright. It is worth saying, however, that if the patent is challenged, the costs of fighting a court case, particularly in a foreign country, can be prohibitive for an SME with limited resources.

Third, the firm must exploit any creative way of shortcutting the route to market, for example by convincing experts or influential participants in the supply chain of the value of the product offer so they might recommend it, or by gaining exposure for the product at important events or in highly visible places. Some SMEs are using e-commerce to achieve some of these objectives: as a direct route to their international customers, to improve their efficiency in an international supply chain and to achieve greater effectiveness through collaboration with other SMEs.

Fourth, instead of using the traditional exporting routes to market such as agents and distributors, alternative methods of market entry, for example using licensing, franchising or joint ventures, can be considered. They are relatively rarely used by the vast majority of SMEs and yet these methods are likely to increase the diffusion of the product or service into the market more cost-effectively. Finally, in some situations an alternative way of improving the firm's competitive position is to cooperate with another firm – a customer, competitor or a firm engaged in a complementary activity.

Company factors

Given the statistics, it is obvious that only a minute proportion of the world's SMEs can be characterised as fast growth organisations likely to become the multinational enterprises of the future. Therefore, it is important to realise at the outset that the majority of SMEs are developing strategies which will deliver modest growth principally in order to maintain the company's security and viability. The objective of many businesses, such as the corner shop, the market trader and the car mechanic is to look for sufficient business to provide enough income to survive, and they look no further than their domestic market.

The very nature of SMEs means that their smaller size and their entrepreneurial approach offer the advantages of flexibility and adaptability to new demands placed on them, speed of response to new opportunities and, usually, very focused management. They suffer from certain disadvantages too, for example lack of adequate planning skills and being unwilling or unable to devote sufficient time and finances to the research and development of new business opportunities, which can result in wasted effort and some expensive failures.

Against this background must be set the obvious risk to SMEs of trading in other countries about which they have insufficient knowledge of the culture, market structure and business practices. The response of SMEs to international marketing is affected by their perceptions of this risk. At one extreme the SME will be deterred from becoming involved at all. At the other extreme the risk-taking SME will experiment with international marketing, perhaps with very little preparation, believing that the firm will be able to respond quickly enough to deal with any difficulties that emerge. More cautious SMEs will attempt to assess and manage the risks involved by evaluating the market opportunity and planning their use of management operations and financial resources to enable a cost-effective internationalisation approach to be developed.

Underlying the diversity in the range of a firm's attitudes to risk are the owners' ambition for the firm and how this fits with the firm's capabilities. To be successful the firm needs a vision of its international future which can be delivered using capabilities and resources that already exist but also include those that can be acquired over a realistic timescale. It is often the case that successful SMEs are those that are able to clearly recognise the threats and opportunities in each marketplace, correct their weaknesses and build upon their strengths. SMEs that are unsuccessful in internationalising are those that do not understand how their market is changing and what new resources and skills are needed, or are unwilling or unable to acquire them.

It is worth saying that many SMEs are so dominated by their owner that they become almost the personification of the owner, whose opinions, knowledge and attitudes determine the strategies adopted and decisions made. Usually decision making is well thought-through with the owner being aware, understanding and managing the risks of working in an unfamiliar market, but sometimes owners lacking international expertise make decisions that can be irrational and even foolhardy.

Country selection

In the past international trade has been dominated by developed countries, such as the US and Japan, and this has often been the main determinant of the choice of country for entry for SMEs. More recently, however, high levels of existing competition in developed countries have made market entry challenging. At the same time the new emerging markets have experienced high growth, thus offering sales opportunites for SMEs of their specialised niche products and services. For Chinese entrepreneurs, neighbouring countries such as Vietnam and Cambodia offer advantages in country selection not just because of low labour cost but also because they may have family connections.

Whilst the fast-growing markets of Asia appear to offer the most attractive opportunities, it can be argued that these should now be regarded as established markets with high levels of competition. Increasing amounts of investment are now focused on the remaining emerging markets in the world, principally in Africa and South America. The most adventurous SMEs recognise the need to be an early market entrant: thus, for some, the most promising markets for their specialised products and services are in Africa and South America but, at the same time, they are also the most risky.

SYSTEMS AND SUPPORT NETWORKS

Typically SMEs tend not to have sophisticated systems and support networks for managing their international operations as is the case for large firms. Of course, advances in technology and the lower cost of IT systems, discussed in Chapter 12, are enabling SMEs to develop more advanced systems than they have had in the past. However, SMEs tend to rely on more informal, 'soft' systems and support networks that are based on personal contacts with family, friends, other business managers and officials for support, advice, information and knowledge.

Organisation structure

As an SME increases its involvement in international markets, so it needs to set up an **organisation structure** that will enable the leadership and management to support, direct and control its often widespread and growing organisation effectively.

Sarathy, *et al.* (2006) have identified some of the variables which might influence the decision:

- size of the business
- number of markets in which it operates
- level and nature of involvement in the markets
- company objectives
- company international experience
- nature of the products
- width and diversity of the product range, and
- nature of the marketing task.

For a firm starting out in export markets, the decision is relatively simple. Either its international business is integrated within the domestic business or separated as a specialist activity. Setting up a separate activity, such as concentrating the international marketing skills and expertise in one department, avoids a situation where the international business is low priority, and allows the department greater independence to look specifically at international marketing opportunities.

There are, however, some disadvantages too, as it may be seen as less important by senior managers and could, as a result, create possible conflicts between domestic and international market demands. There is also the possibility of duplication and ineffective use of company resources. As the company develops further, it is faced with deciding how its international operations should be organised, for example by area, by product and by function. Figures 5.7 and 5.8 show typical organisational structures along geographic and product lines. Organisation by function is only really appropriate for smaller companies with relatively simple product ranges.

As the firm grows it may decide to establish control in different ways – for example it may wish to control branding and corporate identity issues centrally through the use of international product managers – but at the same time it might

FIGURE 5.7
Product structure

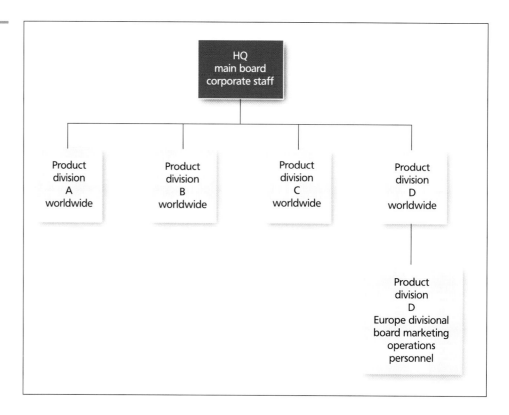

wish to control the profitability of the business by having a chief executive in each individual country. In this way, the firm operates as a matrix structure within which individual managers might be responsible to different senior managers for different activities.

SKILLS, CAPABILITY AND THE STAGES OF INTERNATIONALISATION

Having discussed the alternative categories of international marketing and the strategies which SMEs adopt, we now turn to the process of SME internationalisation and the factors which lead to success and failure. In looking at a cross-section of firms involved in international trade it is possible to find some firms that are taking the major step from being a solely domestic company to generating their first revenue from foreign country sales, others that are moving from the early **stages of internationalisation** to a point where international marketing is totally integrated as part of the firm's activities, and a limited number of firms which are still small but have become confident world-class marketing companies.

THE FIRST STEP

Firms typically approach involvement in international marketing rather cautiously, as the first step towards what may appear to them to be a rather unpredictable future. For small and medium-sized firms in particular, exporting remains the more promising alternative to a full-blooded international marketing effort, since it appears to offer a degree of control over risk, cost and resource commitment.

The further internationalisation of the firm is the process in which the enterprise gradually increases its international involvement. This evolves in an interplay between the development of knowledge about foreign markets and operations on one hand and an increasing commitment of resources to foreign markets on the other. Market knowledge and market commitment are assumed to affect decisions regarding the commitment of resources to foreign markets and the way current activities are performed. Market knowledge and market commitment are, in turn, affected by current activities and operational decisions.

Thus firms start internationalisation by going to those markets that they can most easily understand. There they will see opportunities, perceive low market uncertainty and gain experience – as they go through the internationalisation process they will enter new more challenging markets where there is greater

FIGURE 5.8
Geographic structure

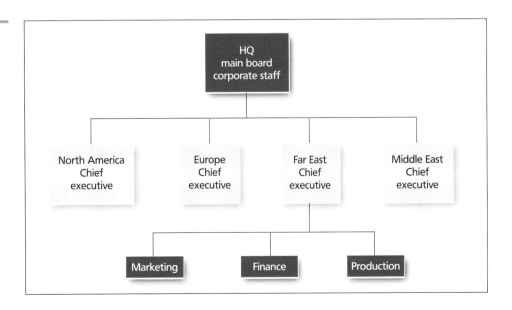

psychic distance. Psychic distance is defined in terms of factors such as differences in language, culture, political systems, etc., which disturb the flow of information between the firm and the market. This means that as the companies' market knowledge grows so does their commitment, which in turn affects the type of strategy they use.

MORE ADVANCED STAGES OF INTERNATIONALISATION

As companies increase their international involvement so improvements occur in the organisation, management and attitudes of those companies. Longer-term resources are committed and international business becomes part of the strategy rather than a tactical opportunity. Greater involvement in export marketing leads to better training and development, higher research and development expenditures, improvements in quality control, lower perceptions of risk and reduced costs of doing business, all of which leads to increased performance.

Figure 5.9 provides a stage approach to conceptualising the internationalisation process based on a composite of various writers' ideas. Firms can be characterised as being at one of the stages shown.

Lowe and Doole (1997) suggest that the internationalisation process of companies is not a gradual incremental process but a series of step changes. There may be a number of factors which might initiate a step change, for example, an unexpected product or market success, the recruitment of a new chief executive, serious failure leading to a reassessment of the business, loss of markets, the changing expectations of stakeholders, owners impatient for a more substantial return on their investment or business or family connections keen to share in the SME's success.

Grimes, Doole and Kitchen (2007) developed profiles of the internationalising firms and it is possible to use this to characterise firms at each stage of internationalisation.

THE PASSIVE EXPORTER

The passive exporter tends to lack any international focus, and perceives export markets as having a high hassle factor. Many passive exporters are relatively new to the export business, often reacting to unsolicited orders, and tend to see their market as essentially home based.

Such firms do not carry out research or invest in export promotion campaigns and have little direct contact with foreign companies. Firms at this stage perceive little real need to export and have no plans to do so in the future.

FIGURE 5.9
Levels of internationalisation

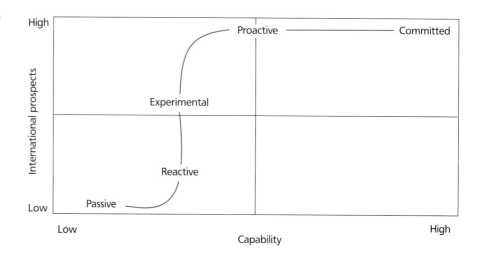

THE REACTIVE EXPORTER

The reactive exporter sees export markets as secondary to the domestic markets but will put effort into dealing with key export accounts. Although they do not invest heavily in attracting export orders, once they have done business with a foreign customer they will follow up for repeat orders.

Such firms may have started to promote their export capacity and be starting to visit overseas clients. However, they have only a basic knowledge of their markets and are still undecided about their future role as an exporter.

THE EXPERIMENTAL EXPORTER

The experimental exporter is beginning to develop a commitment to exporting and starting to structure the organisation around international activities. They are in regular contact with key accounts and are beginning to develop alliances with export partners to build better products and services by using information from their successful markets.

Although they would prefer not to, such firms are prepared to make product adaptations to suit overseas customer needs and may have appointed dedicated export staff to look after this part of the business.

THE PROACTIVE EXPORTER

The proactive exporter is focused on key export markets, and devotes substantial amounts of time and resources to entering and developing new markets. Regular market assessment in the form of desk research and using partners' information is carried out, and promotional materials are produced in a number of foreign languages.

Senior management regularly visit key accounts to maintain healthy relationships with clients and exporting may account for up to 50 per cent of turnover. Exporting opportunities are welcomed and seen as crucial to the business.

THE WELL-ESTABLISHED EXPORTER

The committed exporter knows that exporting is integral to the business and sees the domestic market as just another market. The majority of the turnover is generated through international trade and significant amounts of time are spent on this activity, with senior and middle managers frequently visiting customers.

FIGURE 5.10

Characteristics of successful international business-to-business marketers

SOURCE: DOOLE (2000)

Successful international business-to-business marketers:

1 Have a clear competitive focus in international marketplaces and a specific directional policy as to where the top management intend taking the firm.

2 Have high levels of repeat business and operate tight financial controls in export markets.

3 Have the tenacity and the resilience to face challenges and drive through change.

4 Have a perception that risk indicates a problem to be solved, not an insurmountable barrier.

5 View themselves as international niche marketers, not necessarily as good exporters.

6 Fully invest in ensuring they have thorough knowledge of the international markets in which they operate.

7 Are able to exploit distinctive product advantages in international markets.

8 Are strongly committed to supplying quality products and services to all their customers wherever they are in the world.

9 Build close relationships throughout the supply chain and invest in maintaining regular communications with their overseas partners.

10 Have a well-defined communications strategy and invest in good quality promotional materials.

Investment in training is substantial as skills are needed in-house and thinking on export markets is both short-term tactical and longer-term strategic, with regular reviews of the overall mission and plan of action. Networks abroad provide excellent information and quality assured partners deliver on time, every time.

The firm's movement from one stage to the next, for example from reactive to experimental, experimental to proactive and proactive to world class, therefore, is not gradual. Each of these step changes requires a coordinated strategy to improve the performance of the firm. Doole, Grimes and Demack (2006) explored the management practices and processes most closely associated with high levels of export capability: from this ten benchmarks of international marketing practice are identified (Figure 5.10) which indicate the most critical areas of the firms' management skills. Closer examination of the nature of these benchmarks reinforces the idea that successful international marketing is a predictor of fast growth. Further analysis suggests three key areas that SME international marketers needed to focus on to ensure success:

1 developing the characteristics of a learning organisation

2 developing effective relationships, and

3 having a clear international competitive focus.

LEARNING ORGANISATION

A culture of innovation and learning throughout the firm is a common feature of successful firms that compete internationally. There is clear commitment from the top with senior management demonstrating detailed knowledge of key indicators, and time and resources are invested in learning at all levels.

Investment in skills development enables the firms to be flexible in overcoming barriers and to be persistent in the face of difficulties. High levels of emotional energy are invested in the firm and staff are innovative and willing to learn. A shared vision and a sharing of experiences amongst internal partners are also key elements of the successful organisations' commitment to learning. Tight financial measurement and performance are seen as crucial.

EFFECTIVE RELATIONSHIPS

Firms who compete successfully in international markets build close relationships, not only with customers but with others throughout the supply chain. Effective relationships are crucial and sometimes the focus of successful organisations' competitive advantage may not be the product itself but the added value given to the product and the ability to exploit opportunities by the close, meaningful and regular communication with customers, increasingly through e-commerce.

A commitment to quality procedures, a quality mission and the use of quality-assured intermediaries are seen as vital. Service reliability is key to the firm's relationships and underpins its contribution to the supply chain.

CLEAR COMPETITIVE FOCUS

Firms establish a clear and truly international focus, demonstrating a strong competitive position in a precisely identified market. Many successful firms adopt niche marketing strategies based on a clear mission statement and a planned development strategy.

Other features usually include clearly differentiated products, strong brand positioning and high levels of flexibility in adapting products to suit particular markets.

A thorough knowledge of markets is built up through innovative and informal means of collecting information and through focused research capability, concentrating resources where they are of most use. Most successful companies have primary markets which account for at least 30 per cent of their export turnover.

INTERNATIONAL ENTREPRENEURSHIP AND FAST GROWTH

Earlier in this chapter it was suggested that the vast majority of SMEs grow modestly in a risk-averse series of incremental steps with a conservative management style. We have also emphasised that long-standing family networks, especially in Asia, have created some very large and successful businesses. Other manufacturing firms in low labour cost countries have also expanded fast. However, there are a small number of firms which achieve hypergrowth through commercially exploiting a revolutionary idea, innovative business method or adopting a marketing strategy which simply leaves all the competitors behind. It is important to make the point that whilst some of these firms succeed as a result of a new technical or scientific invention, more important is the entrepreneurial flair needed to exploit the idea commercially. Some of the greatest successes are, therefore, associated with individual entrepreneurs who have the vision, determination, ability and ambition to succeed.

The secret of high growth

For many firms high growth in revenue and profits is the ultimate goal, but this challenge is set against a global background of ever-greater competition and the increasing expectations of customers. Even through a hostile business environment at times of recession or entry by new and more intense competition some firms still manage to grow at a spectacular rate. It is by studying these firms that the drivers of fast growth in SMEs can be identified.

Kim and Mauborgne (2005) explain that it is necessary to find market areas that are uncontentested. Slower growth firms typically focus upon the competition by benchmarking and seeking to meet the customers' (slightly) increased expectations. Their goal is to outperform their rivals, usually by offering a little more value for a little less cost. The competitive response from the rivals is to do the same and, inevitably, this leads to a cycle of small-scale leapfrogging.

Becoming embroiled within this competitive scenario initiates a pattern of strategic behaviour which is, in fact, opposite of that which is associated with growth. Firms become reactive, drawing in resources to respond to the short-term competitive actions, and have no time or resources to think about the sorts of products and services that are needed for the future on a worldwide basis. Without this creativity the firms fall back on imitating competitors, believing the competitors' actions to be right for the market, rather than really exploiting the changes taking place in their customers' needs and wants.

By contrast, high growth firms leave the competitors to fight amongst themselves and, instead, seek to offer customers a quantum leap in value. The question that they need to pose is not what is needed to beat the competition but rather what is needed to win over the mass of customers. The implications of this are that it is necessary to challenge the conventional wisdom and assumptions of the industry about the basis on which firms compete and what customers value. An additional bonus from challenging the way the industry does things is that if the firm thinks on an international scale it can also lead to large cost savings as unnecessary operations are cut out. If the benefits really lead to a step change in value they will be perceived as such by customers all round the world.

Cirque du Soleil was a small organisation that challenged the ideas that circuses were for children and should have animals, which were expensive to keep. For many it was also unethical to keep animals. Instead they created a spectacular show for adults which focused on a combination of performance, art and music and quickly became a world-wide phenomenon.

In starting to change the way the firm thinks about its competitive strategy, it should address the following questions:

■ What factors that your industry takes for granted should be eliminated?

■ What factors that your industry competes on should be reduced well below the standard?

■ What factors that your industry competes on should be raised well above the standard?

■ What factors should be created that your industry has never offered?

By finding answers to these questions the firm can create new markets and new expectations for customers in existing markets. The Apple i-Pod, low-cost airlines (South West Airlines, easyJet and Ryanair) online communities (YouTube and MySpace), and mobile phones (Nokia) show how providing a quantum leap in value to customers can reward the innovators. Typically it is smaller firms that are not weighed down by the industry traditions and standards that challenge conventional wisdom. If the ideas are sufficiently innovative and appealing they will create new international niche opportunities. Dyson (Dilemma 5.2) was a fast growth start-up business that succeeded internationally but had to make a difficult decision on the way.

SHARED VALUES

The core advantages of SMEs and main factors for success are their innovative capability, responsiveness, adaptability and flexibility, which enable them to avoid direct competition from larger competitors. These values, which must come from senior management, must be shared and encouraged throughout the organisation. They must also be underpinned by good strategic planning and management.

Because of the small scale of operations of SMEs, staff around the world often relate closely to and communicate regularly with the owner or senior manager of the SME, so it is often the personal values of the owner and their view of how the products and services should be marketed that become the shared values of the organisation.

DILEMMA 5.2

Dyson – still cleaning up?

In 1993 James Dyson introduced his high-suction vacuum cleaner onto the UK market. It revolutionised the vacuum cleaner market by dispensing with the need for a bag. The cleaners were also a change from convention. They were brightly coloured, had a highly functional chunky design and the dirt that had been collected was clearly visible. They were priced much higher than the competition, typically around £200.

The Dyson company grew rapidly during the 1990s. However, the competitors, such as Electrolux of Sweden and

Glen Dimplex (the Morphy Richards brand) began fighting back and low-priced competitors, such as LG and Samsung of South Korea, offered products for less than £100. In response to this Dyson moved production to Malaysia in order to save 25 per cent on production costs whilst maintaining the R and D base in the UK. Some critics suggested that the move, which resulted in 600 manufacturing job losses, would affect sales in the UK. In practice, however, Dyson continued to achieve rapid growth, building the business in Asia and becoming the leading vacuum cleaner in the US. The dilemma for companies that started small is the extent to which they should stay loyal to their home country.

THE REASONS FOR FAILURE

Many SMEs fail to reach their full potential because they do not manage effectively the international marketing and operational activities that are critical for international success. They often also stop being entrepreneurial and innovative. A number of these and other areas of weakness can seriously impede their progress in international markets and in some cases lead to bankruptcy. These factors include:

- failure to scan the international environment effectively
- overdependence on one product
- the ease with which larger, more powerful competitors or a number of smaller local competitors can copy the idea
- failure to respond to worldwide changes in customer needs
- failure to plan financial resources
- failure to plan for fluctuation in currency values
- failure to manage and resource both market and operations expansion
- the prohibitive cost of enforcing patents and trademarks in foreign courts which may favour local firms.

One of the possible consequences of niche marketing is that success in one international market segment may lead to complacency and overdependence on that market, or the erroneous belief that the firm has built up barriers to entry which will prevent the entry of potential competitors. Against powerful global competitors the barriers are often an illusion. The product may be superseded by an even better idea from a competitor or, alternatively, larger competitors can often gain business with an inferior product simply because of their greater promotional power or their control over the distribution channels.

Because of the often ad hoc, unplanned way that SMEs develop internationally they underestimate the level of resourcing that is needed in both time and money, the difficulties and delays that may arise and consequently the length of time it takes to reach profitability in new foreign markets. The investment that is needed is often greater than the firms expect and they often fail to negotiate a suitable arrangement with their bank or other funders before difficulties emerge.

The main danger associated with international niche marketing is that the income stream is often dependent upon one single product or service idea or a very limited product portfolio. Given the capacity of competitors to copy product ideas, the firm must be absolutely sure that it has built in some unique competitive advantage such as a strong brand, unique technology or reliable business contacts to sustain it against the competition.

Small manufacturing firms may face particular difficulties in internationalising further, because they may need to make substantial investments in equipment and facilities if they need to significantly expand their manufacturing capacity to cope with the demand from newly created markets. For some firms it may be possible to increase capacity gradually, for example by running equipment on overtime or contracting out certain parts of the assembly process, but for others it may be necessary to make large step changes in the facility, for example buying an expensive new piece of machinery or equipping a new factory, just at the time when the firm is incurring the additional costs of entry to a new country. In this situation many firms make the decision not to go ahead with their international expansion and simply continue in their present markets. More creative SMEs find alternative ways to strengthen their international position, perhaps by finding a different way of expanding, for example by forming a joint venture or alliance with another firm, contracting out production to a firm with spare capacity, licensing the product or process or even agreeing to be taken over.

THE FUTURE OF SME INTERNATIONALISATION

There are, therefore, many pitfalls for an SME that is active in international markets. For some SMEs the greatest risk is internationalising at all, particularly if they have no definable source of competitive advantage and little understanding of international marketing but, with increasing globalisation, firms such as these are no longer able to hide their inefficiency or lack of creativity in the domestic market as they will come under attack from international competitors.

Almost as risky is operating as a traditional exporter – selling excess capacity into markets about which the SME has little or no information and with which its managers have little cultural empathy. Manufacturing SME exporters from developed countries struggle to compete with companies from emerging markets because of their lower labour costs. However, small low-cost manufacturers in emerging markets are coming under pressure from manufacturers from less developed countries that can undercut their prices. For SMEs that are innovative and ambitious, are prepared to embrace new technology, use new routes to market and find new ways of doing business there are opportunities for success on a scale never before envisaged, provided they are willing to learn, have a clear competitive focus and a strong network of connections.

SUMMARY

- SMEs have always been involved in international marketing but now have greater opportunities to develop internationally and create wealth and employment for their domestic economy. New technology allows smaller firms to access information and communicate internationally in a way that was not possible before.

- Successful SME international marketers are those that build relationships with individuals and organisations that can help them understand the nature and value of the competitive advantage that they possess, and learn from their own experiences and those of others.

- The principles of international marketing can be applied to all categories of SME international activity, ranging from exporting manufactured goods, through e-commerce to marketing domestic attractions to tourists. However, SMEs use different ways of internationalising and selecting countries for market entry from an incremental selection of countries, based on market potential or a network of contacts, through to high technology businesses that are 'born global'. This depends upon the context in which the firm is internationalising.

- The chosen SME internationalisation strategies are underpinned by generic marketing strategies but are often also affected by the management's perception of the barriers in the environment, the support that is provided in the domestic country and the specific market factors that affect their business sector.

- The stage of international development that the SME has reached reflects the company's capability, the confidence and attitude of the senior management to internationalisation. It usually shows how the SMEs have utilised their inherent strengths of flexibility, adaptability, innovative capability and speed of response in developing their markets.

- There are a number of factors that lead to success and failure for SME international development, but the most significant factor is the ability of SMEs to offer customers a quantum leap in value by innovating throughout the marketing process.

KEYWORDS

7S framework	International niche	Organisation structure
Barrier to entry	marketing	Outsource
Born global	Internationalisation	Reciprocal trading
Domestically delivered or	Market concentrators	Small and medium-sized
developed niche services	Market expanders	enterprises
Electronic commerce	Motivations	Stages of internationalisation
Generic marketing strategies	Network	Supply chain

CASE STUDY

Ebac – dipping their toes further into the water

When entrepreneur John Elliott, launched Ebac over 30 years ago he had to create the market for dehumidifiers in the UK. Dehumidifiers are used in the home to suck moisture out of the air, condense it over refrigerator coils and collect it for disposal. During cold wet weather, when walls become damp and windows drip with water, the compact units help to prevent mould and mildew growth and damage to decorations and woodwork.

Initially in the early 1980s Elliot had to use direct marketing and door-to door selling because stores refused to sell the product. However, he managed to prove that there was a demand and sales soon grew to 100 000 units per year. Now Elliot's daughter Pamela, who has taken over as managing director, faces new challenges. The highly specified Ebac dehumidifiers are being undercut in price by Asian imports, which are sold for as little as £50, a quarter of the price of the best selling Ebac product. In the big electrical retailers in the UK, such as Currys, Comet and Argos, there is pressure to

force down prices and many customers are unwilling to pay such a premium, even for a higher specified product. Ebac claim that their product uses technology that enables it to be designed to be particularly effective in the UK. They claim that it is much more energy efficient than imported products when used in the UK situation.

Despite this competitive challenge Ebac has resisted the temptation to move its manufacturing to lower cost Asian markets, preferring to maintain its manufacturing base in the north east of England, where the Elliott family has always lived.

By 2004 Ebac's UK market share had fallen to 25 per cent (40 000 units) and the dehumidifier division was making a small loss on £6 million sales. In response Ebac decided to return to its direct marketing roots and sell online, investing in a range of product designs, a call centre, television and magazine advertising and promising next day delivery. Following this change of direction sales have grown 60 per cent in 12 months in 2006. Ebac has offices in the US, Germany, France, Belgium, Greece, Singapore, Israel and Saudi Arabia.

As the company has grown it has also diversified. For example, since 1994 it has made water coolers for commercial customers, such as Nestlé PowWow, which rents them out, delivers water and services the equipment. Ebac have developed a patented technology which prevents bacteria entering the pipes when water bottles are changed. Following a major investment in research and development the company has now developed a 'bottom loading' water cooler that avoids customers having to lift heavy water bottles into position in the 'top-loaded' coolers. Making both water coolers and dehumidifiers makes sense because sales of water coolers increase in the summer, a slow time for sales of dehumidifiers.

The company is now looking to exploit its core capabilities in refrigeration technology, innovation and customer service and apply them to new markets. They have recently launched a rental and delivery venture in Germany and Spain. In markets such as India and Russia there are further opportunities for water coolers.

The company has further diversified, launching Waterfall Spa in 2005, a boutique ladies only one-day spa in the centre of the city of Leeds. The start-up cost for this venture was the main reason for the £2.3m loss against total group sales of £30 million in 2006, but the company is confident that this venture will succeed and is planning ten more outlets.

When asked to comment on Ebac's current situation and suggest a way forward three experts came up with different views:

Expert 1: Ebac is endangering its opportunities in bottled water coolers and spas, which will require further financial investment to exploit their potential internationally, by insisting on manufacturing in the UK. Humidifier prices would always have to be much higher and so would require considerable investment in advertising, brand development and innovation.

Expert 2: Given the intense competition in dehumidifiers, the diversification is sensible, providing the opportunity to develop a new customer base. Moreover online marketing should reduce the risk. However, there are the additional operational risks of entering new country markets, with currency, insurance, recruitment and defending the patented technology adding new problems. Ebac must also decide whether to internationalise using distributors or set up their own offices.

They should therefore not expand too far or too fast in new country markets.

Expert 3: Ebac must now develop its brand to justify higher prices to image conscious customers with higher incomes and explain to them the benefits of the well-made, higher specification product, which on the face of it appears to be the same product. The US and Australia are new country markets where this appeal would work. Diversification of the business works when selling existing core skills and products into new markets, or developing new products for existing markets. The Waterfall Spa is a completely new business, is highly risky and should essentially be regarded as a start-up.

QUESTIONS

1 Carry out a full analysis of Ebac's current environment, market and company situation.

2 Identify three strategic options for Ebac's further international development and explain, with justification, which strategy you would recommend.

SOURCE: ADAPTED FROM C. WHEATLEY, WATER COOLER COMPANY FEELS THE CHILL, *SUNDAY TIMES* 13 FEBRUARY, 2007.

DISCUSSION QUESTIONS

1 How can the smaller business compensate for its lack of resources and expertise in international marketing when trying to enter new markets?

2 Why is international niche marketing likely to be a superior approach to export selling?

3 What would you consider to be the international marketing factors that would ensure success for a long-term supplier of giftware from an emerging market, such as Vietnam or Nigeria?

4 Why are some firms 'born global'? What specific risks do they face in international markets?

5 Small international marketing firms do not have the resources to carry out market research systematically. What advice would you give to a firm that wishes to enter a new emerging market?

References

Ansoff, I. (1957) 'Strategies for diversification', *Harvard Business Review*, 35 (5): 113–24.

Balabanis, G., Theodosiou, M. and Katsikea, E.S. (2004) 'Export marketing: developments and a research agenda', *International Marketing Review*, 21 (4/5): 353–77.

Balabanis, G. and Katsikea, E.S. (2003) 'The relationship between environment, export strategy development approaches and export performance', *Proceedings of the Annual Conference of the Academy of Marketing Science*, Washington DC, 26, 17–18.

Brown, L. and McDonald, M.H.B. (1994) *Competitive marketing strategy for Europe*, Macmillan.

Crick, D. and Czinkota, M.R. (1995) 'Export assistance. Another look at whether we are supporting the best programmes', *International Marketing Review*, 12 (3): 61–72.

Crick, D. and Spence, M. (2005) 'The internationalisation of "high performing" UK high tech SMEs: a study of planned and unplanned strategies', *IMR*, 14 (2): 167–85.

Doole, I., Grimes, A. and Demack, S. (2006) 'An exploration of the management practices and processes most closely associated with high levels of export capability in SMEs', *Marketing Intelligence and Planning*, 24 (6).

Grimes, A., Doole, I. and Kitchen, P.J. (2007) 'Profiling the capabilities of SMEs to compete internationally', *Journal of Small Business and Enterprise Development*, 14 (1): 64–80.

Hardman, D., Messinger, D.and Bergson, S. (2005) *Virtual scale: alliances for leverage, resilience report*, Booz, Allen, Hamilton, 14 July. Accessed at www.strategy+business.com.

Harris, S. and Wheeler, C. (2005) 'Entrepreneurs' relationships for internationalisation: functions, origins and strategies', *International Business Review*, 14 (2): 187–207.

Higher Education Statistics Agency (2007) 'HESA students in Higher Education institutions 2005/06', press release PR 108, 26 March, accessed at www.hesa.ac.uk/ on 18 April 2007.

Katsikeas, C.S. and Leonidou, L.C. (1996) 'Export marketing expansion strategy: differences between market concentration and market spreading', *Journal of Marketing Management*, 12.

Kim, W.C. and Mauborgne, R. (2005) *Blue ocean strategy: how to create uncontested market space and make competition irrelevant*, Harvard Business Press.

Knight, G.A. and Cavusgil, S.T. (1996) 'The born global firm: a challenge to traditional internationalisation theory', *Advances in International Marketing*, 8.

Leonidou, L.C., Katsikeas, C.S. and Samiee, S. (2002) 'Marketing strategy determination of export performance: a meta analysis', *Journal of Business Research*, 55, 51–67.

Lowe, R. and Doole, I. (1997) 'The characteristics of exporting firms at different stages of internationalisation', *International Marketing Strategy Contemporary Readings*, International Thomson Business Press.

Mort, G.S. and Weerawardena, J. (2006) 'Networking capability and international entrepreneurship', *International Marketing Review*, 23 (5): 549–72.

Nicholls, A. and Opal, C. (2005) *Fairtrade: market-driven ethical consumption*, Sage.

Nueno, P. (2000) 'The dragon breathes enterprising fire', In S. Bailey. and F. Muzyka, *Mastering entrepreneurship*, FT Prentice Hall.

Parrish, E., Cassill, N. and Oxenham, W. (2006) 'Niche marketing strategy for a mature market place', *Marketing Intelligence and Planning*, 24 (7): 694–707.

Porter, M.E. (1990) *Competitive advantage of nations*, Free Press.

Quelch, J.A. and Klein, L.R. (1996) 'The Internet and international marketing', *Sloan Management Review*, Spring.

Storey, D.J. (1994) *Understanding the small business sector*, Routledge.

Sarathy, R. Terpstra, V. and Russow, (2006) *International marketing*, 9th edn. Dryden Press.

Servais, P., Madsen, T.K. and Rasmussen, E.S. (2007) 'Small manufacturing firms involvement in international e-business activities', *Advances in International Marketing*, 17: 297–317.

CHAPTER 6

GLOBAL STRATEGIES

INTRODUCTION

Having discussed the nature of international development in smaller firms we now consider the global marketing strategies of the largest firms that compete on a worldwide basis. For the largest firms **globalisation** should be the route to maximising performance by introducing, where possible, standardised marketing programmes and processes, but at the same time, adapting certain operational activities to local needs in order to maximise short-term revenue generation. The problem that such firms face is exactly which aspects of their international activity to standardise and which to adapt because the decisions are often context specific and are affected by the particular factors which drive change within their particular industry. This leads to firms adopting a variety of global strategies, from those that are very similar from country to country to those that are substantially different in each country in which the firm operates. In the past the global organisations have originated from developed countries, but an increasing number of firms from emerging markets are taking significant steps to become the next global players.

In this chapter we start by reviewing the dimensions of the concept and drivers of globalisation before considering the alternative strategic approaches and the factors that drive strategic choice. This discussion is then followed by an examination of the strategy implementation issues that MNEs might face in managing their global business and building their global presence, with particular emphasis on global branding. We end the chapter with a discussion of the issues that must be addressed in order to manage global marketing effectively.

LEARNING OBJECTIVES

After reading this chapter you should be able to:

■ Appreciate the various aspects of globalisation and be able to compare and contrast the alternative global strategies

■ Evaluate the factors that determine a firm's choice of global strategy

■ Identify the challenges that firms face in developing a global presence

■ Appreciate the role of branding in globalisation

■ Understand the factors affecting global marketing management

THE ALTERNATIVE VIEWS OF GLOBALISATION

Over the past two decades the term globalisation seems to have led to a polarisation of views. For some, globalisation is associated with opportunity, the removal of barriers to prosperity for all countries of the world and greater exposure to and understanding of different cultures. Others see globalisation, capitalism and MNE activity as the same thing, believing global companies dominate international business, ruthlessly exploit the countries' resources and adversely influence the economy and culture of every country, moving their operations from country to country according to which offers the lowest wage rates, with no thought either for those who lose their jobs or the well-being of those who are paid extremely low wages.

In practice globalisation is about progress towards an, as yet, undefined end and few companies, even those with the most familiar brand names, are truly global, as Table 6.1 shows. Most firms are strongly dependent on a few key markets. Unctad (2006) provide a measure of the transnationality of multinationals by analysing their total foreign assets that result from foreign direct investment (FDI): their foreign sales, foreign employment and number of foreign affiliates.

Table 6.1 shows the top 15 transnational companies (TNC) by foreign assets in 2006. Taking the index of transnationality an average of the measures of transnationality (foreign to total assets, sales and employment) perhaps provides a better picture of the most transnational companies (Table 6.2). The reason that this list is different from 6.1 is that firms from the US have a huge domestic market in which to grow before embarking upon international, then global activity (note the positions of the five US firms). By contrast, firms from smaller countries have always had to internationalise simply to grow.

The most dominant TNCs still come from developed economies and are typically from the motor, pharmaceuticals and telecommunications sectors. However, the TNCs from developed countries (top 12 in Table 6.3) are now gaining a significant presence. In the top 100 they typically come from the electrical, electronic and computer sectors. Five TNCs from emerging countries are now in the top 100 in the world. Unctad also identies the geographic spread of TNCs, which is indicated by the number of foreign afiliates. On average TNCs from developed countries have 40 foreign affiliates, whilst TNCs from emerging countries have just six, showing perhaps the importance of developing a strong home or regional base before competing throughout global markets.

There is no doubt, however, that the world's largest firms are seeking a worldwide presence. Driving this acceleration of global MNE activity appears to be increased competition which Sjobolom (1998) suggests is being brought about by four forces: changes in consumer expectations; technological change; deregulation; and regional forces. Firms must find a basis upon which they can compete and Illustration 6.1 shows the contrasting strategies of IBM and Lenovo.

In seeking to compete successfully in increasingly globalised markets multinational enterprises realise that a precondition of long-term growth is a worldwide presence. Over the past two decades a number of writers such as Levitt and Kotler have debated whether or not this will result in globally standardised products and services.

So far, the only examples of product and service offers which have been completely standardised across the world are probably those sold over the Internet in the business-to-business sector. Some of the most widely available

TABLE 6.1 The top 15 transnational companies by foreign assets 2005

Foreign assets position	Transnationality index position	Company	Home economy	Industry	Foreign assets (US$bn)
1	68	General Electric	US	Electronic	449
2	4	Vodafone Group	UK	Telecoms	248
3	67	Ford	US	Automotive	180
4	90	General Motors	US	Automotive	174
5	10	BP	UK	Petroleum expl/ref/dist	155
6	38	Exxon Mobil Corporation	US	Petroleum expl/ref/dist	135
7	25	Royal Dutch/ Shell Group	UK/Netherlands	Petroleum expl/ref/dist	130
8	62	Toyota Motor Corporation	Japan	Automotive	123
9	20	Total	France	Petroleum expl/ref/dist	99
10	66	France Telecom	France	Telecommunications	86
11	49	Volkswagen Group	Germany	Automotive	84
12	16	Sanofi-Aventis	France	Pharmaceuticals	83
13	61	Deutche Telecom	Germany	Telecommunications	80
14	60	RWE Group	Germany	Electricity, Gas, water	79
15	19	Suez	France	Electricity, Gas, water	74

SOURCE: UNCTAD

products which might be considered to be standardised in fact are substantially adapted. You can taste the Coca-Cola variants from around the world at the museum in Atlanta and try the different McDonald's menus as you travel. Computer companies use different language options in their service manuals. The concept of globalisation, therefore, is often characterised by contradictions, such as the need to standardise some elements of the marketing mix whilst, at the same time, accepting the need to respond to local needs and tastes by adapting the product or service. Some believe that the true nature of globalisation is encapsulated in the phrase 'think global, act local', in which there is an acknowledgement of the need to balance standardisation and adaptation according to the particular situation. Even this concept is challenged because it implies that the starting point for the strategy is based on a standardised marketing mix. For many MNEs the alternative – 'think local, act global' – may be more appropriate given that it implies focusing on local needs, but taking the opportunity, whenever feasible and appropriate, to standardise elements of the marketing mix and globalise support services.

Against this background the word globalisation is associated in a very imprecise way with many different aspects of the international marketing strategy process.

TABLE 6.2 Top 10 companies: index of transnationality* 2005

	Company	Home economy	Industry	Index*
1	Thomson Corporation	Canada	Media	97.3
2	CRH Plc	Ireland	Lumber, building materials	94.5
3	Nestlé	Switzerland	Food	93.5
4	Vodafone group	UK	Telecoms	87.1
5	Alcan	Canada	Metal, metal products	85.6
6	Royal Ahold	Netherlands	Retail	85.6
7	Philips Electrical	Netherlands	Electrical	84.0
8	Nortel Networks	Canada	Telecommunications	83.2
9	Unilever	UK	Diversified	82.8
10	BP	UK	Petroleum expl/ ref/dist	81.5
27	Coca-Cola**	US	Beverages	72.7
35	McDonald's**	US	Retail	61.8
54	IBM**	US	IT	55.5
67	Ford Motor Company**	US	Automotive	30.1
97	Wal-Mart Stores	US	Retail	24.1

*THE AVERAGE OF FOREIGN TO TOTAL ASSETS, FOREIGN TO TOTAL SALES, AND FOREIGN TO TOTAL EMPLOYMENT ** IT IS WORTH THE POSITIONS OF COCA-COLA, MCDONALDS, IBM, AND FORD. THEY ARE VIEWED AS HUGE TRANSNATIONAL FIRMS BUT NONE ARE IN THE TOP 10 BASED ON THE CRITERIA USED TO ASSESS TRANSNATIONALITY.

The drivers of globalisation

Although globalisation may be difficult to define satisfactorily, there are a number of drivers of globalisation that can be used to explain its impact and discuss its implications.

- market access
- market opportunities
- industry standards
- sourcing
- products and services
- technology
- customer requirements
- competition
- cooperation
- distribution
- communication
- the company's strategy, business programmes and processes.

TABLE 6.3 Top 12 companies from developing economies: index of transnationality 2005 ranked by foreign assets

Rank	Company	Home economy	Industry	Foreign assets (US$bn)	TNI
1	Hutchinson Whampoa	Hong Kong/China	Diversified	67.6	70.9
2	Petronas – Petroliiam Nasional BHd	Malaysia	Petroleum expl/ref/dist	22.6	25.7
3	Singtel Ltd	Singapore	Telecommunications	18.6	67.1
4	Samsung Electronics Co Ltd	Republic of Korea	Electrical and electronics	14.6	44.7
5	CITIC Group	China	Diversified	14.5	20.4
6	Cemex S A	Mexico	Construction	13.3	69.2
7	LG Electronics Inc	Republic of Korea	Electrical and electronics	10.4	84.5
8	China Ocean Shipping Group Co	China	Shipping	9.0	36.3
9	Petroleos De Venezuela	Venezuela	Petroleum expl/ref/dist	8.7	28.7
10	Jardine Matheson Holdings	Hong Kong, China	Diversified	7.1	61.7
11	Formosa Plastics Group	Taiwan	Industrial chemicals	7.0	35.1
12	Petroleo Brasileiro S A Petrobras	Brazil	Petroleum expl/ref/dist	6.2	14.3

Globalisation of market access has increased as the number of inaccessible markets has reduced following the political changes that have opened up markets, for example in Central and Eastern Europe and China, to much greater MNE involvement. Whilst these 'new' markets have become more accessible, firms entering them usually face more difficult problems in viably establishing their global products there because of the differences in social and business culture and the lack of an infrastructure, legal framework and standards of business practice. Whilst these markets offer attractive growth prospects, many Western global firms have shown themselves to be ill-equipped to exploit these opportunities. Initially they were unwilling or unable to 'go it alone' in these markets, which were unsophisticated by developed country standards, and found it necessary to form partnerships with local firms, with mixed results.

In the short period since these markets have opened up many local companies have experienced phenomenal domestic growth which has enabled them to build a platform from which they themselves can become global players.

Market access is also being improved by the increasing regionalisation, resulting from the growth of trading blocs. Firms are reinforcing this effect by helping to reduce inter-country barriers and thus improve market access by operating more standardised pan-regional marketing programmes and processes such as product development and advertising.

Globalisation of market opportunities has increased with the continued deregulation of certain sectors, such as financial services where the traditional

ILLUSTRATION 6.1

A new direction for IBM and Lenovo

Periodically an organisation must review its strategy and decide if it is still pursuing a direction that will continue to generate value for its stakeholders. In 1981 IBM introduced the first personal computer to the market and was essentially responsible for turning computing into a mass market. However, very quickly competitors started to sell 'IBM compatible' copies and over time IBM has been unable to stop the PC hardware becoming a commodity. It is now a highly competitive market in which only very focused, specialist companies are able to compete.

Perhaps the biggest mistake that IBM made, however, was failing to realise that the profits from the industry would be

made from the software. Unfortunately it allowed Microsoft, at that stage a fledgling business, to provide the software that would control its PC.

Eventually IBM had little competitive advantage and realised that it could no longer operate on the slender profit margins in the PC industry against competitors such as Dell. In 2004 IBM sold its PC hardware division to the Chinese firm Lenovo (formerly known as Legend) for US$1.25 billion. 10 000 IBM staff transferred to the new company, which moved its HQ from Beijing to upstate New York. IBM's new direction meant it could concentrate on large systems and providing consultancy and business solutions for organisations that wished to outsource their IT management.

Lenovo believed that this deal would help it create a global brand. In the first quarter of 2006 – and to the surprise of many business analysts – the strategy seemed to be working in this highly competitive market as their global market share increased and Lenovo's profits exceeded forecasts. Shipments of notebooks initially leapt 23 per cent. By 2007, however, Lenovo announced 1400 job losses, 5 per cent of the total workforce, in an effort to reduce costs, streamline sales and marketing operations and build closer links in its supply chain. It was a response to the price war in personal computers. Commentators also criticised some marketing mistakes and a failure to overhaul the IBM operation more quickly.

QUESTION *Why would Lenovo believe that it could succeed where IBM had failed?*

SOURCE: ROBIN LOWE FROM VARIOUS PUBLIC SOURCES

barriers between the various parts of an industry, such as banking, insurance, pensions, specialist savings, mortgage and loan suppliers, are being broken down. This has enabled supermarket groups to enter many market sectors, including financial services and pharmacy product retailing.

Removal of sector barriers has resulted in mergers of specialist firms to form larger and more powerful groups which can offer a complete range of products or services to their customers in the sector. For such MNEs, the power base may be a large domestic or regional market, as was the case for Citigroup when two companies from the US merged. As will be discussed later, MNEs from different countries, for example Mercedes Benz (Germany) and Chrysler (USA), merged in 1998 to create a more comprehensive product range in their industry sector but as Illustration 7.7 shows, by 2007 the merger was being reversed, as the struggling Chrysler was about to be sold off.

The privatisation of government-owned utilities such as electricity, gas and telephone is leading to industry restructuring where previously there were monopolies with tight operating restrictions. This is allowing firms to compete in geographic areas and industry sectors from which they have previously been excluded.

The privatisation of the Pakistan government's Oil and Gas Development Company by listing on the London Stock Exchange was part of a sale of the state assets. Whilst US$6bn had already been raised by selling stakes in 160 state owned companies since 1991, this placing was the largest and expected to raise about US$1bn. With a rapidly growing economy and further privatisations planned the country appeared attractive to foreign investors, although concerns remained regarding the threat posed by Islamic fundamentalism and the political and economic stability of the country.

Globalisation of industry standards is increasing as technical operating standards, professional rules and guidelines are being adopted more widely primarily due to the harmonisation of regulations within trading blocs, but more generally around the world as a result of the increased mobility of experts and advisers, and the wider use of quality standards, such as ISO 9000. Despite this there is a long way to go. For example, many adapters are needed to enable a portable computer to be plugged in locally throughout Europe. It is a precondition of supplying major customers that firms operate to certain product and service standards that can be recognised regionally and globally. In addition, the largest MNEs are expected to work to ethical standards which cover such diverse areas as employment, environmental protection and unfair competition. As a result, MNEs demand that their staff work to exacting company standards. Professional staff are usually also regulated by national bodies and so greater regional harmonisation is affecting standards of behaviour and performance.

Globalisation of sourcing has increased as companies search the world for the best and cheapest materials, components and services rather than rely on local suppliers. The benefits of global sourcing include:

- *Cheaper labour rates*. Fashion and clothing marketers obtain supplies from low labour rate countries such as China, Indonesia, Costa Rica, Vietnam and Latin America. There can, however, be problems of product quality and criticism of unethical behaviour as these firms resort to 'island hopping' to the new lower labour rate areas that result from changes in local country economic development, or their contractors may employ child labour.

- *Better or more uniform quality*. Certain countries and companies have competitive advantage over others as suppliers because of the local availability of materials and skills.

- *Access to the best technology, innovation and ideas*. Firms search the world to identify a particular research or design centre which might offer the specialist expertise they require. For example, Nissan set up design facilities in California and Microsoft have established research facilities close to Cambridge University in the UK.

- *Access to local markets.* Developing stronger links with a country through sourcing can help to generate new business in that country. For example, the aircraft maker Boeing has opened up the market in China following its decision to purchase components there.

- *Economies of scale advantages.* Where the location of a manufacturing or distribution operation is convenient to supply a whole region it can lead to significant cost advantages.

- *Lower taxes and duties.* Certain countries may offer tax advantages to manufacturers and low rates of duty when shipping goods to the customer. The relocation of some of higher added value activities can help by spreading currency risk.

- *Potentially lower logistics costs.* Global transport and warehousing companies use IT more effectively to control product movement and inventory.

- *More consistent supply.* Some foods would be restricted because of seasonality if steps had not been taken to arrange supplies from countries with different growing seasons.

The major risks in global sourcing are in dealing with countries where there might be political, economic and exchange rate risks. There are also specific risks associated with an individual supplier that might use the knowledge gained and power which results from a strong position in the supply chain to become a competitor. Quality and service provided by the supplier can be critical and if not managed can begin to affect the reputation of the customer. An example of this is shown in Dilemma 6.1. What is crucial is that the MNE must retain its competitive advantage and not outsource its supplies to the point where it gives away all its technical and commercial secrets, power in the market or risks supply problems. This potential danger needs to be managed by purchasers improving their supplier–purchaser relationships or, perhaps, even forming longer-term strategic

DILEMMA 6.1

Toyota – growing too fast?

In the first few years of the new millennium the future prospects of the leading car makers changed. The US carmakers lost out as high fuel costs hit demand hard for 4-wheel drive Sports Utility Vehicles and other large cars. They were crippled by very high healthcare costs. Already the number two leading carmaker, Toyota, had General Motors in its sights. The Japanese car makers had focused on being profitable and responding quickly to market changes and had developed a policy of manufacturing where they sell. By contrast, the US carmakers were basing their strategies on manufacturing in partnership with other firms in lower-cost markets and seemed to be transforming themselves into marketing businesses that import, export and market products rather than manufacture. However, by the summer of 2006 Toyota's apparently perfect image

was starting to become a little tarnished, surprisingly, because of quality problems. In the US, Toyota's largest market, it recalled 2.2 million vehicles and in Japan 1.9 million to correct faults, including potential power steering failure in its hybrid car, tyres bulging and possibly bursting in their small pick-up and the possibility that air bags would not inflate in a crash.

Toyota's competitive advantage has always been built around quality and reliability but of course as the development and manufacture of products has increasingly been outsourced, it is more difficult to maintain high quality standards. Fast growth places considerable strain on the supply chain especially where, as in Toyota's case, it constitutes such a high proportion of the car's value.

QUESTION *What must a leading brand do to maintain control of its reputation and brand image?*

SOURCE: ADAPTED FROM M. MAYNARD AND M. FACKLER A RISE IN DEFECTS AT TOYOTA PUTS ITS REPUTATION AT STAKE; *NEW YORK TIMES*, 5 AUGUST, 2006

alliances. The additional benefit of better supplier–purchaser relationships can be improved communications and the avoidance of some unnecessary supply chain costs resulting from inadequate specifications, misunderstandings about quality and generally poor management.

Globalisation of core products and services. More and more products are reaching the mature phase of their product life cycle and this is leading to greater commoditisation of products and services. Consumers see very little difference between the offerings of many competing suppliers and the increased speed at which new innovations can be copied by other competitors means that core benefits can no longer be a point of differentiation between competitors. MNEs are responding to this and gaining competitive advantage over local competition by differentiating their products through such things as the brand image, higher levels of service, or better technical support.

Globalisation of technology. Technology is converging within and between industries, with similar processes and ideas being used, for example, in telecommunications, information technology hardware and software and entertainment and consumer electronics, so that new multifunctional products and services cross the traditional boundaries between the industry sectors. New technologies are adopted around the world at ever greater speeds. In many industries this is being driven by a small number of global players that have the market power to change the ways of working and generate sufficient demand from customers to make the wider application of the ideas more cost-effective. In this way the globalisation of technology is contributing very significantly to the competitive advantage of the MNEs, who are able to market products in a number of industry sectors because they have developed effective distribution channels and international promotion.

Globalisation of customer requirements is resulting from the identification of worldwide customer segments, such as teenagers with similar worldwide tastes in music, fashion and 'junk' food, and the very rich, who buy the most expensive fashion brands, fly first class or hire their own plane, stay at the same luxury hotels and own super performance cars. No matter where they originate they consume the same products and services. With industries becoming more globalised, the demands placed on the business support services, such as advertising agencies, accountants, law firms and consultants, are converging too. Customers in both the consumer and business-to-business markets are demanding and getting what they perceive to be added value global products and services which better meet their changing needs than those they have been used to receiving from national companies.

Globalisation of competition between industry giants tends to result in the same fight being replicated in each corner of the world, with MNEs using largely similar competing product or service offers. Traditional national firms have been outmanoeuvred by aggressive fast-growing international competitors who are far better at exploiting technical changes and other globalisation effects. They are also able to cross-subsidise their activities in different countries, so helping to make the markets more interdependent.

Mature industries, as well as new technology sectors, are being affected by global competition. For example, whilst the majority of the top ten chemical companies are European, there is increasing competition particularly from Asian companies, which have different cost structures and systems of industry regulation. Success in these component and raw material industries has traditionally been dependent upon the product portfolio, the relationship with customers and the levels of technical service and support provided, but increasingly the fact that these are components in the supply chain of branded consumer products means that successful suppliers must carry out more effective marketing to members of the supply chain that are closer to the customer.

Globalisation of cooperation. To compete in all the major world markets it is necessary to make available huge financial resources, often outside the scope of individual firms. This is leading to the formation of alliances between major MNEs, members of a supply chain, or between firms with complementary activities. The Japanese *keiretsu* go further in that they are formal organisations between banks, manufacturers and trading companies with cross-share ownership, and have the huge resources necessary to build businesses in the major world markets. This has enabled them to make investments over a number of years to establish a dominant long-term market position in a particular industry.

Globalisation of distribution is occurring, first, as the supply chain becomes increasingly concentrated on fewer, more powerful channel distributors, retailers and logistics companies; second, as e-business technology dominates the exchange and transfer of data and the whole process of product and service transactions, including methods of product and service selling, ordering, customising, progress chasing, payment arrangement and delivery confirmation; and third, as logistics become a source of competitive advantage, for example in retailing, having contributed to the international success of Walmart, Ikea and Tesco. For many organisations it can be argued that a global approach to distribution means organising according to factors such as proximity to the population and transport infrastructure, rather than country borders.

Globalisation of distribution is particularly important for companies such as Amazon that use e-commerce as they must be able to make transaction and logistics arrangements to enable them to provide high levels of service and efficiency to customers, wherever they are located.

Globalisation of communication. Major changes in telecommunications and information technology have had two effects. First, global communications such as satellite and cable TV have made it essential that MNEs develop a consistent worldwide corporate identity and brand image. As consumers travel physically or virtually by way of the media or World Wide Web, they are exposed to communications and advertising originating from MNEs from many parts of the world. Consistency of the communication is vital for reinforcing brand familiarity, quality and values.

Second, digital technology is driving the localisation and individuality of communications, for example through the proliferation of local TV channels, on-demand video and television and the development of the Internet, which allows greater exposure for individual communications. These developments go further than simply improving the accessibility of the traditional one-way communications with customers by adding a two-way, interactive dimension to the firms' relationships with their global customers.

Globalisation of the company's strategy, business programmes and processes. The result of these globalisation effects is to pose challenges to firms to achieve both improved global operational efficiency and greater global market effectiveness. The global firm's response to managing the complexity of international marketing must include developing an all-embracing global strategy supported by effective marketing programmes and processes that will integrate the various disparate activities of the firm's far-flung strategic business units.

In considering each of these areas of globalisation in turn it is possible to identify business sector examples in which the globalisation trend is relatively advanced and others in which it is in its early stages. For example, until the late 1990s retailing could be regarded as a largely national or, at most, subregional activity with few examples of retailers active in more than five or six countries. The challenge for global companies is to lead the development towards globalisation in industry sectors where there is the greatest potential for growth. However, there is no guarantee that by simply being globally active in an industry sector a firm will benefit. Firms must be able to manage the environmental threats and exploit their market opportunities by building global competitive advantage. Illustration 6.2 shows how Gillette is responding to global factors.

ALTERNATIVE STRATEGIC RESPONSES

It is against the background of the trend towards globalisation and the need to build a worldwide presence that firms must develop strategic responses which are appropriate to their situation and are feasible to implement. For MNEs, the question may be how to rationalise their activities to gain greater focus and effectiveness. For firms that have progressed through the early stages of expansion into new country markets, as we discussed in the previous chapter, the next stage is to decide whether or not to progress further and, if so, what strategy they might adopt to enable them to manage their involvement in many countries. Underpinning the growth strategy in either case must be some fundamental decisions about the product portfolio and expansion into new country markets.

The international competitive posture

The level of geographic development and product strength determine the strategic options available to a company. Gogel and Larreche (1989) argue that the threats

---

ILLUSTRATION 6.2

Gillette planning a close shave

In the late 1970s and 1980s the change to disposable razors by many consumers in the US and Europe meant that shaving products appeared to be turning into a commodity market. For Gillette, which had a 65 per cent share of this market, this was extremely serious. Gillette in the US cut advertising by a quarter and appeared to have almost given up on razors.

In Europe, however, Gillette started to spend on a pan-European campaign featuring the slogan 'Gillette – the best a man can get' to promote the top-of-the-range Contour Plus brand, and this led to a gain in market share and an increase in margins.

Gillette's mission statement over the past 25 years has been 'There is a better way to shave and we will find it', and Sensor,

launched in 1989, spearheaded Gillette's fightback. Sensor was shown to be significantly better than anything else on the market and user tests showed that 80 per cent of men who tried it kept on using it. Gillette decided to centralise its marketing by combining the European and US sections into one group, headed by the previous European head, to ensure an effective launch of Sensor. Previously, marketing had been carried out by brand managers in each local country.

Sensor helped Gillette to a 70 per cent share of the world razor market, but by 1997 the sales growth was flattening, signifying the need for a new product. The successor, Mach 3, cost well over US$1bn to develop but sold at a premium of 25–35 per cent over the price of Sensor, which Gillette retained as it does not withdraw older products.

By 2006 the competition was beginning to fight back: Schick, recently taken over by Energiser, with its four-blade Quattro and a South Korean company, Dorco, which developed a Mach 3 competitor with prices 30 per cent cheaper than Gillette. Men and women do not shave more often, so the only way to increase sales and profits is to increase prices in developed countries, persuade customers to buy more products and win new customers in emerging markets. Fusion was introduced at a premium of 30 per cent over Mach 3. This time a five-blade battery-powered product was also introduced as well as a range of branded toiletry products.

QUESTIONS *How should Gillette keep its technological lead? Will technology be the only factor in its future success in the global shaving market?*

of global competition place higher pressures on the effective use of resources. The two main axes for allocating strategic resources are the development of product strength and geographic coverage. These two axes have to be managed in a balanced way. Focusing too much attention on product investments at the expense of geographic coverage may result in missed international opportunities. On the other hand, focusing on geographic expansion may result in underinvestment in products, weakening the competitive position of the firm.

Gogel and Larreche identify four types of competitors along the two dimensions of product range and geographic coverage, as shown in Figure 6.1. The position of a company on the international competitive posture matrix will determine the strategic options.

Kings. Because these firms have a wide geographic coverage and strong product portfolio they are in a strong competitive position. They have been able to expand geographically and have not dispersed their resources into weak products. They are in the best position to have an effective global strategy.

Barons. These companies have strong products in a limited number of countries. This makes geographic expansion attractive to them. It also makes them attractive to companies wishing to supplement their own product strength and therefore they may be takeover targets.

Adventurers. These have been driven to expand geographically, but they lack a strong portfolio. They are vulnerable to an increasing level of global competition. Their challenge is to consolidate their product position by focusing on internal product development, acquisition, or by eliminating products to concentrate on a narrower portfolio.

Commoners. Commoners have a product portfolio with relatively weak international potential and narrow geographic coverage. They may have benefited from legal barriers protecting them from intense competition in their existing markets. They are likely acquisition targets, and before any geographical expansion they need to build their product portfolio. A likely international strategy could be one of supplying own-brand products to retailers.

The key issue for firms is that increasing geographic coverage and product strength compete for resources and each quadrant of the matrix reflects the trade-offs that may become necessary. Whilst the position of a firm on the matrix reflects how it has been able to balance its resources between consolidation and expansion of geographic coverage and product strength, the decision it has made will have also

FIGURE 6.1

The international competitive posture matrix

SOURCE: ADAPTED FROM GOGEL AND LARRECHE (1989)

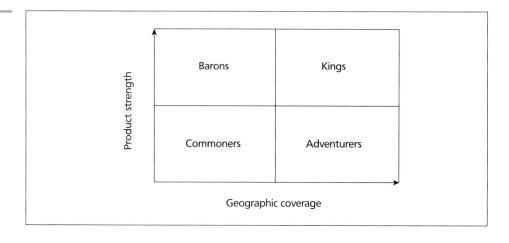

been based on its chosen attitude and commitment to achieving a global strategy. Technology companies such as Microsoft could be best described as adventurers in their early days. They marketed their operating system widely before building up their product range to become the 'kings' they are today. As we saw earlier, transnational companies from Asian markets are typical 'barons', developing a strong product range and building their home or close regional markets before developing internationally.

Global strategy

The options for global strategic development are shown in Figure 6.2. However, before considering the alternative strategic approaches, it is useful to discuss the issue of whether to globally standardise the marketing activity or adapt it to address local differences and expectations.

The standardisation/adaptation discussion leads, at one extreme, to the concept of a multidomestic approach in which the firm has a completely different strategy for every single market and, at the other extreme, a global approach in which everything in the marketing activity is standardised in all countries. In practice firms adopt a combination of standardisation and adaptation of the various elements of the marketing management programmes and processes by globalising some elements and localising others. In broad terms it is possible to categorise a firm's strategic development as multidomestic, global or regional, a third strategy in which separate, but largely standardised marketing strategies are implemented across a region of the world.

The largest, most complex companies in the world use a combination of all these strategies. A transnational approach is one in which the firm has a standardised identity and corporate values throughout the firm but delivers its strategic objectives through composite strategies which contain elements of multidomestic, regional and global strategies. The global marketing strategy is influenced significantly by the supply chain decisions relating to location of operations and outsourcing arrangements.

Zou and Cavusgil (2002) identify three perspectives of global marketing strategy: the standardisation perspective, the configuration perspective and the

FIGURE 6.2
Alternative worldwide strategies

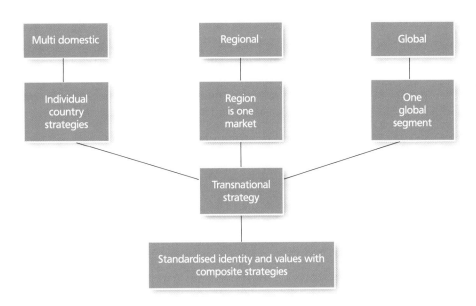

integration perspective. The global firm locates its supply chain activities in those countries where they can be carried out most efficiently. Components are then transferred to another country for assembly, before the highly standardised finished goods are exported to the countries in which they will be sold, supported by largely standardised marketing. Global firms then integrate their activities and competitive moves to enable them to become major players in all major markets. Increased outsourcing makes these tasks more challenging as success depends on customer requirements being met on time.

Standardising the various elements of the marketing process has the aim of scale economies and experience curve effects in operations, research and development and marketing and concentrating value chain activity in a few country locations to exploit comparitive advantage and so improve efficiency. The experience curve effect or learning curve relates to the relationship between experience and efficiency. In the 1960s research by Boston Consulting Group found that, provided that there was a desire to achieve results efficiency improved as the cumulative (lifetime) experience of carrying out the same tasks increased.

Standardisation and adaptation

The challenge facing firms with aspirations to become truly effective global players appears to be turning widespread international presence into global competitive advantage. The critical success factor in achieving this is to offer added value for global customers by providing them with benefits that are significantly better than those provided by the competitors, particularly local competitors. The benefits can be tangible, for example a global product, such as Intel processors, that are broadly the same worldwide, or intangible, for example a brand such as Rolex that is recognised worldwide. At the same time they must aggressively seek cost efficiencies that will enable the firm to offer better value for money than their competitors.

In practice, firms manage these apparently incompatible requirements by using strategies that are appropriate to their own situation, and striking a balance between the different degrees of standardisation or adaptation of the various elements of international marketing process.

In general:

- Marketing objectives and strategies are more readily standardised than operational marketing decisions.

- Within the marketing mix, products are most easily standardised, promotion less so and distribution and pricing only with difficulty.

- The more operational the decision the more likely it is to be differentiated.

Consequently the elements of marketing management should be seen as being at different points of a continuum of standardisation, where the product and service image is generally easier to standardise than individual country pricing.

Pricing   ↑ Adaptation
Distribution
Sales force
Sales promotion
Product
Image
Objective
Strategy   ↓ Standardisation

Globally standardised strategy

A company adopting a global strategic orientation makes no distinction between domestic and foreign market opportunities, seeking to serve an essentially identical market appearing in many countries around the world and developing global strategies to compete with other global firms. Global marketing can be defined as the focusing of an organisation's resources on the selection and exploitation of global market opportunities consistent with and supportive of its short-term strategic objectives and goals.

Global marketing is the realisation that a firm's foreign marketing activities, in whatever form they take, need to be supportive of some higher objective than just the immediate exploitation of a foreign market opportunity. Global marketing can, therefore, involve the selection of a country for its potential contribution to globalisation benefits, even entering an unattractive market which has global strategic significance – for example, the home market of a competitor. Thus an organisation with such a global focus formulates a long-term strategy for the company as a whole and then coordinates the strategies of local subsidiaries to support this.

Many writers have offered views on this issue. For example Levitt (1983) suggested that in order to be competitive in the world market, firms should shift their emphasis from local customised products to globally standardised products that are advanced, functional, reliable and low priced. Buzzell (1968) argued that product standardisation has the benefits of (a) economies of scale, (b) faster accumulation of learning through experience that can aid efficiency and effectiveness and (c) reduced costs of design modification.

In summarising the forces at work in the standardisation debate Meffet and Bolz (1993) describe the globalisation push and pull factors, shown in Figure 6.3, which are driving marketing standardisation, in terms of both the marketing programmes, such as the product portfolio development plan, the new product launch and the advertising programme, and the marketing processes, for example how the marketing information system and the marketing planning processes can be integrated around the world.

FIGURE 6.3
Globalisation push and pull factors

SOURCE: MEFFET AND BOLZ (1993) IN HALLIBURTON AND HUNERBERG (EDS) EUROPEAN MARKETING READINGS AND CASES, ADDISON-WESLEY

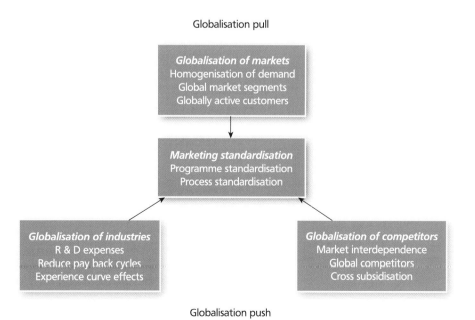

In considering this model, it is important to recognise that the global business environment has changed considerably, with many barriers to standardisation being removed or reduced, as discussed earlier in this chapter. Some of the globalisation effects such as economies of scale, the experience effect (or learning curve) explained on page 200 and the high costs of innovation have become more significant drivers of standardisation.

At the same time market fragmentation has also increased and, in practice, global firms have to strike an appropriate balance between the relative advantages of standardisation and adaptation to local tastes. There is little point in standardising programmes for marketing products and services if consumers reject them and only buy the products and services that meet their specific needs.

McDonald's, for example, is not only adapting its traditional products to the tastes of different cultures but is also recognising the need for greater variety on its menu. Coca-Cola uses different recipes around the world, varying sweetness according to local tastes.

MULTIDOMESTIC STRATEGIES

The multidomestic or multi-national market concept focuses on maximising the company's effectiveness and efficiency in exploiting economies of scale, experience and skill in marketing, production and logistics. A company adopting such an orientation assumes that foreign market opportunities are as important as home market opportunities. However, the company takes the view that the differences between its international markets are so acute that widespread adaptation is necessary to meet market needs and to retain competitive leverage in local markets. Thus the company essentially follows a differentiated marketing strategy with individual marketing mix strategies in many of their world markets.

There has been considerable debate amongst writers about the pros and cons of multidomestic strategies to achieve a worldwide competitive advantage as opposed to the pursuance of a global strategy through the standardisation of marketing activities. However, it is quite clear that for many major businesses there are few benefits to be obtained from widespread standardisation of their activities. Consequently a well-organised and managed multidomestic strategy is an effective method for many companies for developing a global business.

An example of an organisation which can be accurately characterised as having a multidomestic strategy is Asea Brown Boveri (ABB), discussed in Illustration 6.3. The firm used a multidomestic strategy to gain competitive advantage in its target country markets. A key factor in the strategy is encouraging senior managers to be entrepreneurial in responding to local customer needs, industry standards and different stages of economic development.

Thus whilst there are many forces driving companies towards achieving a global strategy through standardising as many marketing activities as possible, there are also very important prevailing arguments persuading companies that they can also achieve an effective worldwide strategy through a multidomestic approach. These forces are as follows.

INDUSTRY STANDARDS REMAIN DIVERSE

For many traditional industries such as those based upon engineering and particularly those that involve large investment in plant and equipment, the cost of harmonisation of standards is high and the progress to harmonisation is slow. The markets for these industries often involve a country's infrastructure, transport and utilities and, consequently, depend on often protracted government spending decisions. Usually in making decisions such as these governments will give consideration not simply to market factors, but also to the impact on the economy, environment and the electorate's expectations.

CUSTOMERS CONTINUE TO DEMAND LOCALLY DIFFERENTIATED PRODUCTS

Cultural heritage and traditions still play a strong role in areas such as food, drink and shopping. Whilst there are increasing moves to accept cross-border products, there is still resistance in many cultures.

BEING AN INSIDER REMAINS CRITICALLY IMPORTANT

The perceived country of origin effect of goods still has a bearing on take-up of products and local manufacturing of goods is frequently necessary to overcome this scepticism. In business-to-business marketing, there is a definite bias in favour of products sourced from particular areas, such as Silicon Valley in the US, and so IT/electronic firms often decide to set up local manufacture there.

ILLUSTRATION 6.3

ABB: a new model of global entrepreneurialism – good while it lasted?

In 1988 Sweden's ASEA and the Swiss company Brown Boveri merged to form ABB. It had customers in the process industries, manufacturing and consumer industries, and in utilities (oil, gas and petrochemicals). As chief executive Percy Barnevik was faced with merging two companies with different business cultures and operations. He decided to create a fundamentally different model of how a large MNE could be organised and managed. He created the new head office in Zurich to make the merger less like a takeover by the Swedes, and started dispersing the two head offices of 6000 staff amongst a number of front-line units.

He created a head office with 135 staff managing 1300 companies with 5000 profit centres. He cut 90 per cent of

CREDIT LINE: © CORBIS SYGMA

headquarters staff by moving 30 per cent into the small business units (SBUs), 30 per cent into free-standing service centres concerned with value-adding activities and eliminating 30 per cent of the jobs. Similar huge cuts in management were made in the headquarters of the subsidiaries.

The management within the SBUs, which usually had fewer than 200 employees, were given a substantially enhanced role in managing their business. ABB was one of the most admired firms of the 1990s. Ghoshall and Bartlett (2001) said that Barnevik's achievement was combining the contradictions of big and small, local and global, economies of scale and intimate market knowledge to create a truly global organisation.

ABB employed 160 000 staff in 100 countries and a large part of their manufacturing was moved away from the developed countries to the developing countries, including Eastern Europe. By employing people in developing countries ABB was in a position to sell further expertise and services as they helped build the countries' infrastructure.

Barnevik was succeeded by Jorgen Centremann in October 2000, but he lasted less than two years as the company's share price halved. ABB missed its profit targets, it nearly ran out of cash as its debts mounted, and in 2002 it made its first loss of US$787 million. The problems were compounded by the threat that a US unit would go bankrupt because of the potential liabilities (capped at US$1.3 billion by a US court) resulting from a number of massive lawsuits involving asbestos. Whilst this was still under negotiation ABB could not divest its oil and gas division, which it needed to do to reduce debt.

QUESTION *Could the model be blamed for ABB's problems?*

GLOBAL ORGANISATIONS ARE DIFFICULT TO MANAGE

In finding ways to coordinate far-flung operations, firms have to decentralise and replace home country loyalties with a system of corporate values and loyalties that is acceptable to the firm's staff around the world. For some companies this proves to be problematic and, in some cases, the head office values and culture can be significantly different from those of the workforce. Their desire to impose standardised products with little or no consultation on their country operations is very often seen as arrogant by local staff.

MANAGEMENT MYOPIA

Products and product categories are sometimes suitable candidates for global marketing but managers fail to seize the opportunity. Equally, other products that work well in the managers' home market are believed erroneously to be acceptable to customers worldwide. Self-reference criterion often makes it difficult for managers to take other than a narrow, national view of international marketing. Managers must exploit the potential for changing the competitive nature of the industry in their favour by triggering a shift from multidomestic to a global strategy. Because there are no guarantees that a business can succeed, the firm must be willing to risk the heavy investment that a global strategy requires. For some, the resources required and the risks involved are simply too great.

Regional strategy

One of the most significant developments in global marketing strategy is how firms respond to the rise of the regional trading blocs. Even in globalised industries, company strategies are becoming more of a composite of regionally focused strategies and programmes. For many companies, regionalisation represents a more manageable compromise between the extremes of global standardisation and multidomestic strategies. For example, there are some obvious differences in the challenges of marketing to North America, Africa and South East Asia and different strategies are required.

Regional trading blocs tend to favour their own MNEs, and for those companies located outside the region there can be significant tariff and non-tariff barriers. For example, the indigenous regional manufacturers usually get early warning of imminent regional legislation as they tend to be part of the consultation and decision-making process. Public–private sector committees decide on standards, such as car emissions, safety standards and security. By shifting operations and decision making inside the region an MNE can gain the benefits of insider advantage.

The key to developing effective regional strategies must be in deciding what makes the region distinctive and in what ways the marketing strategy for one region should be differentiated from the others. It is also about observing trends that pose threats or provide opportunities. For example, for many automobile firms sales to developed regions are showing only small growth or even decline. By contrast, car sales in China in 2006 increased 37 per cent to 5.2 million units. GM reported an increase on the previous year of 32 per cent, Ford 87 per cent and Rolls Royce 60 per cent. Now the number two market in the world, China is expected to overtake the US as the leading car market by 2015 (BBC News online 2007). Therefore it may be vital for a global company to respond quickly to a specific regional, rather than global trend.

However, whilst regional strategies are built around the common elements within a region and the distinctivess of the region, perhaps encapsulated in the buzzword 'glocalisation', in practice the differences within the region are still huge. Cagni (2006) explains how with the enlargement of the EU there is an increasing management challenge, posed by conflict between the single market concentration and multimarket fragmentation, exacerbated by the mix of cultures, histories, economics and trends of the 'New Europe'. Big differences in the country environments and markets are highlighted requiring the traditional centralised multinational management to be replaced by more modern approaches. Companies are taking the opportunity from the formation of regional trading blocs to include regional objectives and plans as a significant part of their worldwide strategy and build on existing, or form new, cooperative trading relationships.

The prime motivation in the formation of the regional trading blocs is to enable indigenous companies to build the critical mass of activity within the home region necessary to enable them to compete effectively in global markets. The European Union, for example, has strived to create collaborative working between participants in a common supply chain, or those offering complementary or competitive products. Where the companies come from different countries political differences do still arise, particularly if national governments are concerned about the retention of jobs in sensitive industries, such as the defence and airline industries. Airbus is one such consortium in the manufacture of aeroplanes in Europe that has at different times benefited and suffered from political interference, as Illustration 6.4 shows.

ILLUSTRATION 6.4

SOURCE: ADAPTED FROM A. EVANS-PRITCHARD, 'AIRBUS IS EDGING CLOSER TO THE BRINK', *DAILY TELEGRAPH* 20 FEBRUARY, 2007.

Airbus

Airbus, the European plane maker, is number two only to Boeing. It was owned by firms originating from France, Germany and Spain and had partners in other European countries. In 2006 it suffered from a number of problems, particularly in delays to its new A380 plane. To put the organisation back on course, CEO Louis Gallois announced a plan to reduce the company's annual costs by US$2bn by 2010: however, because of intervention by European politicians the management was prevented from taking the necessary action. The German government was not prepared to bear the burden of the majority of the 10 000 job losses and threatened retaliation if any German production plants were closed and Germany did not get a fair share of the work. The retaliation would have taken the form of reconsidering weapons orders placed with the parent company, EADS.

QUESTION *What are the advantages and disadvantages of cross-border ownership of companies that are high profile in the region?*

TRANSNATIONAL STRATEGIES

If a firm has sufficient power and resources to exploit all the available opportunities on a worldwide basis, with little need to adapt strategies or involve partners to any great extent, then a simple strategy can be developed. However, many multi-nationals have a wide range of products and services, some of which might be suited to global and others to multidomestic development. The successful exploitation of these opportunities might require a much more flexible approach to strategic development and involve a number of partners in licensing, joint ventures and strategic alliances as well as wholly owned operations.

Transnational companies integrate diverse assets, resources and people into operating units around the world. Through flexible management processes and networks, transnational companies aim to build three strategic capabilities:

- Global scale efficiency and competitiveness.
- National level responsiveness and flexibility.
- Cross-market capacity to leverage learning on a worldwide basis.

In such organisations the ownership of the operations becomes less clear in terms of where any particular product was made, what the domestic nationality of the manufacturing or service provider was, or which firms manufacture and market the product and services.

Bartlett and Ghoshal (2001) argue that the aim of transnational companies is to further the firm's global scale efficiency and competitiveness in its totality. This task means the firm needs the ability to recognise market opportunities and risks across national borders. The overall goal is to achieve global competitiveness through a fully integrated strategy and operations. Thus a transnational approach is not a particular strategy, but a strategic perspective that evolves as firms and the markets in which they operate increase in complexity. Hewlett Packard is a transnational organisation because certain of its marketing operations and research and development are centralised and standardised, whereas other units operate with a substantial degree of independence. It has a strong corporate identity and some of its promotional themes, for example around e-business, are common throughout the firm. It has also formed strategic alliances with partners in order to carry out certain research and development activities where it is likely to benefit from the participation of partners. In such organisations the implications for strategic development are significant. Any strategy that is to achieve global competitive advantage needs to accommodate some, or all of the following:

- Simple and complex individual product and market policies, which may be independent or interdependent.
- Customer segments that are specific and unique to a cross-national niche market so the resultant segments are transnational and valid across borders.
- Working closely with firms that are customers, suppliers, competitors and partners at the same time, but simultaneously ensuring that the values of the company are maintained and demonstrated to the external stakeholders through establishing clear and unambiguous positioning in all markets.
- Maintaining and building meaningful and added value relationships in the supply chain.

INTERNATIONAL MARKETING MANAGEMENT FOR GLOBAL FIRMS

So far in this chapter we have identified the changing trends in the business environment that are leading to increasing globalisation and the factors that affect the firms' response to this, particularly in the way they standardise or adapt their marketing programmes and processes. We have shown distinct differences in the way global strategies can be developed to meet individual firms' situations. Implementing these global strategies, however, poses considerable problems and it is to these that we now turn.

As in the previous chapter, it is useful for the discussion to be based loosely upon the McKinsey 7S framework, which includes the hardware elements of strategy, structure and systems and the software elements of management style, staff, skills and shared values. Again we start with the hardware elements of strategy, systems and organisation structure.

Global strategy implementation

Global firms have the objective of developing effective business operations in all the major markets in the world in order to maximise their performance. In the past they may well have prioritised the developed economies in North America, Europe and Asia, principally Japan. More recently these firms have developed a significant presence in many more emerging markets in China, India, other countries in Asia, central and Eastern Europe, particularly Russia, South America and Brazil, that will offer much higher growth in the future.

Building a global presence is hugely expensive, and many firms see no value in expanding globally if their home country or region offers sufficient growth prospects without marketing their products and services in what they might perceive to be higher risk areas. US companies have a large domestic market and, despite the rapid growth prospects of other regions of the world, their unfamiliarity often makes them unattractive. However, with growth rates four times as high in Asia as in the rest of the world, almost all the Fortune 500 and leading European companies invested heavily in this area.

Asian firms have usually taken a longer-term view in the way they have developed new markets because they often rely on private capital rather than on shareholders who seek short-term gains. This has resulted in a more conservative, cost-conscious and risk-averse approach and this has favoured regional development. However, their highly profitable fast growth has provided the financial resources to drive them to pursue opportunities in developed countries too.

For firms wishing to build a truly global presence, there are a number of challenges, including:

- Responding to the changing basis of competitive advantage.
- Increasing global appeal by building the global brand.
- Creating a global presence by achieving global reach.
- Managing diverse and complex activities across a range of often similar but often disparate markets and cultures.

Global appeal and the changing basis of competitive advantage

In the past, companies differentiated their products and services by 'new to the world' innovation that generated new core benefits to customers, but now genuinely new products are getting harder to find. All major firms today are capable of offering good-quality products and service that offer value for customers so this is no longer a source of differentiation and competitive advantage as competitors quickly offer reasonable and usually lower cost alternatives.

The rapid growth of the Japanese car industry was largely based on value for money criteria, with quality, reliability and performance at a reasonable cost being the basis of the appeal. However, many of their competitors from the emerging economies are now able to offer cheaper and even better value for money cars. Carmakers from the developed countries have substantially improved their quality and reliability and are able to offer designs and brand imagery with better consumer appeal. The focus seems to have moved away from the cheap reliable global car to cars made from global components but with designs and styling which meet the requirements of regional customer segments. Japanese manufacturer Toyota has succeeded in combining aspects of styling and image, performance economy and reliability with a very efficient, local supply chain. The car market is highly competitive and characterised by over-capacity, and it is becoming harder for major global players to be consistently profitable.

It is possible to observe similar changes in the information technology industry as consumers increasingly expect computer suppliers to offer improved perform-ance, functionality, quality, security and greater reliability as well as becoming more 'user-friendly' – all at considerably reduced prices. The long-established firms must now offer more intangible benefits, including better styling, higher levels of service support and advice, and more interesting and appealing software and online services. The spectacular performance of Apple in the early 2000s was the appeal of the i-Mac and i-Pod to a design-conscious segment. Consumers are becoming more confident with technology, and are willing to experiment by downloading software and content from a variety of suppliers.

With the availability of lower-cost sources of production in some industry sectors, value to customers means low cost. The cost of basic clothing and shoes sold through supermarkets has fallen dramatically in recent years, making it difficult for retailers to operate in the middle ground between high fashion and low cost.

While low cost is attractive globally to customers, the implications of basing appeal on the less tangible aspects of service are that these are exactly the ele-ments of the total product offer where there are the greatest cultural differences and the greatest need for adaptations. What constitutes an enjoyable fast-food menu, an attractive car design or interesting website is clearly affected by local consumer tastes, values and attitudes. In business-to-business situations, whilst the core benefits of the product and service offer may be standardised it will have to be tailored to satisfy specific business requirements. There is no such thing as a standard power station, advertising agency service or mainframe computer.

Increasing global appeal by building the global brand

Branding is usually considered within the marketing strategy as part of the product and service policy, and we have addressed the use of brands in international marketing there. Global brands, however, are inextricably tied up with achieving global appeal and building a global presence, so we have included a broader-based discussion of global branding at this point.

Global brand management

Holt, Quelch and Taylor (2004) noted that two decades ago Levitt was arguing that organisations should offer standardised products globally, but now consumers find it difficult to relate to generic standardised products, so firms have adopted 'glocal' strategies in which they have customised product features, selling and marketing to local tastes and instead build their efficiencies on a global scale around 'back office' activities of which customers are unaware.

Holt *et al.* found that most transnational firms are perceived differently from other firms because of their power, and have suffered from this because they have been major targets for anti-globalisation protests. However, most people choose one global brand over another based on three dimensions: quality, indicated by the firms' global stature, the cultural myths and stories created by the firms, and the firms' efforts in corporate social responsibility. In the past for some brands the country of origin of the brand was important as it was often part of the cultural myth, but Holt *et al.* believe that this is no longer important. Indeed the trend for a number of global brands has been to dissociate themselves from their country of origin, for example, British Airways has renamed itself BA, British Petroleum has become BP and Kentucky Fried Chicken has become KFC.

Recent recessions sparked off the first real challenges to the power of the biggest global brands. Before then, apart from a few exceptions, they had seemed to simply increase their dominant position steadily and consistently over decades. Against the threat of unemployment or reduced incomes, however, many consumers sought to restrict their household spending by becoming more cost conscious. In a number of cases they found that the second or minor brands, and especially supermarket own brands, were often indistinguishable from the premium priced brands in perceived quality and so consumers simply traded down.

Khashani (1995) draws attention to changes in a number of factors which affect the performance of the brands.

- Customers are better educated, better informed, more sceptical, more willing to experiment, less brand loyal, much more media aware and have higher expectations of the total package.
- Competition is more aggressive, with more rapid launches of higher quality 'me-too' products.
- Retailers have installed better electronic point of sale technology and, as a result, have greater awareness of brand performance. In response to better consumer information, they have introduced better quality private labels.

These changes in the brand market environment have been compounded by weaknesses in brand management, including:

- low investment;
- inadequate product development;
- poor consumer communication;
- an emphasis on quick paybacks rather than long-term brand building;
- too little innovation; and
- an emphasis upon small modifications.

For global brand success it is essential to listen to the market and get closer to global customers. It is necessary to be bold, think creatively, set new market and performance standards and take risks. The aim must be to think globally, launch products and services sequentially and rapidly across markets and build world brands. There are many 'almost great' brands but only a few are truly great. Illustration 6.5 shows how the management of LG are making bold decisions in order to develop a global brand.

Whilst the progress of global brands seems to be unstoppable, they do not always succeed. Wal-Mart withdrew from South Korea and Germany in 2006 because financial losses could no longer be tolerated. Despite promising for years that performance could be improved, it never managed a turnaround. In both countries Wal-Mart failed to compete with dominant local companies that were better at catering for local tastes. Moreover, Barbaro (2006) notes that in Germany in the late 1990s Wal-Mart changed the name of its stores from a well known reliable local brand to Wal-Mart, a name that was unfamiliar to local shoppers.

Business-to-business branding So far the discussion has focused on global consumer branding, but branding is important in business-to-business marketing too. The reason for this is that purchasers and users value the commitment of suppliers to the product and service and benefit from the added value from dealing with a firm. For example, buyers talk about suppliers such as Cisco or Vodafone as brands, which lends a sense of authority to the purchasing decision, or users might detail a specific product or service that must be purchased, e.g. Hewlett Packard printers. In some situations there may be benefits which can be gained from co-branding or association with globally recognised branded components (e.g. Intel microprocessors in computers and Lycra in garments). This trend is becoming increasingly important as consumers become more influential in the choice of components and services in the supply chain and demand products that contain branded components.

In international business-to-business branding firms use different naming strategies, with some firms concentrating less on corporate brand endorsement and more on the individual brand in the same way as Procter and Gamble and Unilever do in consumer markets. For example, the pharmaceutical product brands Zantac and Tagamet are promoted by GlaxoSmithKline without any obvious association with the manufacturer in the brand name.

Ultimately, the rationale for the existence of brands in business-to-business marketing is the same as in consumer goods marketing – to avoid the commoditisation of products, which leads to decisions being based only on price. As an example, purchasers of capital equipment would expect to pay price premiums

ILLUSTRATION 6.5

LG innovating to the top

LG is Korea's biggest and now the third-largest household appliance maker in the world after Whirlpool (US) and Electrolux (Sweden). LG's profit percentage in the first half

of 2006 was 9.8 per cent compared with Whirlpool's 5.6 per cent and contrasted sharply with Korea's other appliance business – Samsung – which made an operating loss during the same period. LG is also easily the leader in annual growth rate for several years. It is the leader in home air conditioners, canister vacuum cleaners and microwave ovens and hopes to become number one in system air conditioners, front-loading washing machines and side by side refrigerators.

LG's white goods business was once losing money, but when Kim Ssang-su took over as chairman in 2003 he instituted a broad-based innovation programme throughout the company and even the fast rising prices of raw materials and strong Korean currency have not held back progress. Innovation has helped LG to attack the global high end market. Its refrigerators for the US include the Space Dios which, with a selection of ten colours, has swept away the belief that refrigerators should be white, and another refrigerator which incorporates a four inch crystal display panel that provides a five-day weather forecast based on satellite information

QUESTION *What lessons can be drawn from LG's success?*

SOURCE: ADAPTED FROM TEE-GYU K'LG LOOKS TO DOUBLE WORLD'S BEST PRODUCTS BY 20110Y, KOREAN TIMES, SEPTEMBER 12 2006

for a number of perceived benefits from globally recognised suppliers:

- interchangeability of parts
- short delivery time
- working with prestigious suppliers
- full range of spare parts available
- lower operating costs
- lower installation costs
- higher quality materials.

Brands are also important in the not-for-profit areas. For example, although the charity sector is fragmented into many thousands of organisations it is the global charities with well marketed brands, such as Red Crescent/Red Cross, Oxfam and Save the Children, that are the most successful in terms of scale of activities. When major disasters occur it is these organisations that have the resources to cope.

Creating a global presence by achieving global reach

The aim of many MNEs is to dominate their market sector by building a presence in every worthwhile market. However, few firms have the resources to build a strong presence in all the countries in the world and so rely on third parties to enable them to reach into similar markets. Many firms cannot afford to wait until they have built the products, services, image and resources through organic growth within the firm. Instead, they use a wide range of growth, market entry and marketing mix strategies to achieve global reach and these are discussed in later chapters. Acquisition and mergers are discussed here because they are being used by MNEs to extend global reach much more quickly and achieve effective marketing worldwide, as the Chapter 6 case study shows.

Mergers and acquisitions The rationale for acquisitions and mergers has been that a well-managed company should take over a weaker rival marketer of competing or complementary products in order to achieve higher growth and savings in operating, management and marketing costs. As market entry methods, acquisition or mergers are used to facilitate access to particular markets. In some business sectors, however, there appears to be a view that it is only by operating on a very large scale on a worldwide basis that customers can receive the level and quality of service that they need. This seems logical in the case of aircraft manufacture where industry consolidation has left only two main players, Boeing and Airbus. Scale economies in accountancy may not be so obvious and, of course, there are still many small accountancy practices but the global sector is dominated by four companies, Deloitte, KPMG, Ernst and Young and Pricewaterhouse Coopers, whereas there were eight major players in 1989.

In some sectors, therefore, there have been a number of mergers of equals in which firms of similar market power agree to combine, believing that their future success depends upon achieving comprehensive global reach; for example, Citigroup and Travelers Group in financial services and Glaxo Wellcome and Smith Kline Beecham in pharmaceuticals.

Cross-border mergers and acquisitions are becoming increasingly common too, for example in telecommunications Vodafone (UK) with Mannesmann (Germany), and in automobiles Daimler-Benz (Germany) and Chrysler (US). One of the implications of mergers, particularly mergers of equals, is the impact upon branding decisions and whether the merged firm will retain two separate brand identities or whether they will merge them. The decision is taken often against a background of whether the senior management believes the brand is important for their particular company or industry sector. Smith (1998) reports research by McKinsey which suggests that there are three routes to brand consolidation:

■ Phasing out brands over time, when the strategy is to retain loyal customers who will buy as long as the brand is available.

■ Quickly changing some of the branding, which only works well if the firm has control over distribution, advertising and promotion.

■ Co-branding to manage the transition, which is the most common approach, used, for example, when Whirlpool bought Philips domestic appliances.

The pitfalls of mergers and acquisitions There are serious pitfalls associated with mergers and acquisitions, particularly where they involve cross-border ownership and cooperation. Finkelstein (1998) refers to a study of 89 US companies acquired by foreign buyers during the period 1977–90 and found the performance of most of them had not improved within one year.

As well as the obvious organisational challenges that follow from a merger, such as who will be in charge, whose products and services will be offered (or dropped) and where costs savings should be made, particularly if the merger or acquisition was not entirely harmonious, there are the cross-cultural challenges, such as the different ways of doing business in Europe, the US and Asia, different corporate governance, the status and power of different employee and management groups, job security guarantees, government regulations and customer expectations.

Finkelstein (1998) recommends that the integration process should focus on value creation by ensuring employees actually achieve the synergy that is promised before the deal is done, planning in detail how the various cross-border problems will be overcome and developing a clear communication plan to cope with the whole process.

Managing diverse and complex activities across a range of often similar but often disparate markets and cultures

The implications of pursuing a global strategy are that organisations must continually expand into what are likely to be less stable markets, perhaps tertiary opportunities from Figure 4.3 on page 111 or incipient markets in Figure 4.1 on page 107. Typically these will be in some way less attractive (at least at the present time) because of the associated political and economic risks of entering less developed markets, more difficult trading conditions and barriers to 'free' trade. By comparison with the firms' existing markets, these emerging markets may demand disproportionately high investment in management time and financial resources as well as involving the firm in considerable additional financial and reputation risk if things go wrong.

The risks associated with specific emerging country market involvement can be substantial, however, and include some or all of the following:

■ financial loss associated with inappropriate investment, such as buying unusable assets, being unable to achieve acceptable levels of performance from the purchased assets, losing the assets by misappropriation to the host country government or to partners;

■ damage to the firm's reputation through association with the country, its government and intermediaries, especially where they are seen to be corrupt, engage in unacceptable social or business practices, or have close relationships with other countries or organisations which are considered to be corrupt;

- litigation arising from offering an unacceptable product and/or service to the country, or becoming involved in questionable business practices;

- prompting an unexpected international competitor response by attacking a market which it considers to be its home territory;

- initially making arrangements with joint venture partners, distributors, agents or government agencies to secure entry but which become inappropriate in the medium to long term;

- damage to the firm's reputation through insensitivity in its operations in the country, when it might be accused of exploiting local labour, the country's resources or causing environmental damage to the country.

The problem for international strategic management in less developed countries is that the 'rule book' that managers rely on in developed countries does not always apply, because business infrastructure and processes are not well established.

Opportunities in emerging markets for global firms

Most multinational enterprises, particularly from developed countries, focus on the customers that are wealthy enough now or in the future to purchase their premium goods and services.

In response to the rapid development of emerging markets over the last few years, many global organisations have realised that most of their future growth will come from the growing middle class in emerging markets. For example, McDonald's expects to open at least 100 restaurants per year in China, so overtaking the 1200-strong UK chain by 2010. The informal out-of-home eating market in China is estimated to be worth US$260bn. In contrast in the UK it closed 25 restaurants because of competition from firms such as Starbucks and Costa Coffee, and growth is being limited because of continuing adverse publicity over health concerns (Kleinman 2006).

For many multinationals the very poorest parts of the world appear to be largely economically inactive and offer little opportunity for profitable growth. A small number of MNEs have traded with these countries for many years, often buying and selling raw materials or selling processing machinery, and have developed a presence by selling basic products to the consumer and B2B market. Prahalad and Hart (2002) have suggested that there is a pyramid of wealth, shown in Table 6.4, and emphasise that those with the lowest incomes still have the potential to create a significant demand for goods and services if they meet the specific needs of poor consumers and products and services are marketed to them in a sensitive way. Whilst it might be expected that consumers from emerging markets simply

SOURCE: ADAPTED FROM C.K. PRAHALAD AND S.L. HART (2002). THE FORTUNE AT THE BOTTOM OF THE PYRAMID', *STRATEGY AND BUSINESS*, 26 (54): 67

TABLE 6.4 The global pyramid of wealth

	Global population (m)	Purchasing power (US$)
The wealthy	800	15 000
The emerging middle class	1500	1500–15 000
Low income markets	4000	<1500

want unsophisticated products, it may well prove a mistake to try to market to emerging markets those products that have reached the end of their life cycle and been replaced in developing countries. The particular situation in an emerging market may require a specific, innovative solution and this may miss out a particular technology development stage. An example of this is in Illustration 12.2. Cars designed for emerging markets are also discussed in Illustration 6.6.

Hart and London (2005) have identified examples of innovative solutions that not only satisfy customer demand but also create new routes to market that are more efficient in these emerging markets. This often requires the MNE to work with partners through less formal channels and networks than they are used to.

The instability of emerging markets, crime and corruption are some of the main problems that MNEs have to deal with directly to ensure they protect their staff and reputation; however, their unfamiliarity with these markets makes this difficult, and here too local partners can prove invaluable.

The emergence of MNEs from emerging markets

In past decades it has been the high growth in the EU, US and Japanese markets that has driven the growth of MNEs originating from developed countries. Now however there is a suggestion by Bracken (2007) that it will be multinationals from emerging markets that could achieve the greatest growth in the future. Developing countries have traditionally depended upon foreign companies to supply job training and know-how and, in exchange, multinationals, usually from Western countries, could force concessions from national governments enabling them to build sales in new markets. Globalisation and the requirements of a market economy therefore reduced the power of national governments. Now the governments of the strongest emerging countries are no longer willing to surrender their home market to foreign companies which exert undue influence in the industry sector and which might delay technology transfer into the developing country.

ILLUSTRATION 6.6

Cars designed for emerging markets

There have been a number of attempts by major car manufacturers to produce a car suitable for the Third World. In the past the production lines of obsolete models were typically transferred to labour-intensive factories in developing countries. However, over the last few years the move towards developing a low-cost car has increased. General Motor's Daewoo boss believes that as people in developing countries move up from bicycles, mopeds and rickshaws up to 35 per cent of the market could be represented by low-cost cars.

Perhaps the first successful attempt to design a car specially was the Fiat Palio, which was launched in Brazil in 1996 and has been made and sold successfully in developing countries worldwide since. The problem is that car manufacturers in the past have offered cars that they thought were wanted in developing countries without finding out exactly what was wanted. Chrysler developed a plastic-bodied US$6000 car but the Chinese hated it, wanting a 'proper' car instead.

In 2004 Renault took a radically different approach with the €5000 (£3125) Logan, a four-door saloon built in Romania but with plans to build it also in Russia, Morocco, Iran, Colombia and China. Although modern components are used, most of the assembly is by hand rather than by robots. Tata planned to launch a 600cc car in India for 100 000 rupees (£1167).

It is important that carmakers do not confuse the different concepts – the low-cost car, the lightweight car, the economical car and the small car – because they are all different things. Moreover, the most innovative step would be to design and develop a car that leapfrogged fossil fuel technology and was based on new environmental technology and created jobs, wealth and mobility for the world's poorest nations.

QUESTION *What do you consider to be the critical success factors for a car designed for emerging markets?*

SOURCE: ADAPTED FROM A ENGLISH THE THIRD WORLD CAR WAR, *DAILY TELEGRAPH* 31 MARCH 2007

In some sectors this could delay the economic development of the country. The size of the home markets in India and China provides domestic companies with a large base to build the potential multinational companies of the future. China for example has decided to develop its own car industry and India, following the removal of central planning and bureaucracy in the 1990s, has created some strong IT outsourcing businesses, such as Wipro, Tata and Infosys.

Multinationals from developed markets will now have to work harder to access these fast-growing emerging markets as it will prove to be much harder to go it alone and more difficult to exert control over local partners who now see the possibility of developing their own global businesses.

Multinationals from the last generation of emerging markets have already become global players with dominant market shares in Western markets. Toyota, from Japan, now close to becoming the leading US carmaker, was virtually unknown in the west until 1965, and Samsung from South Korea was unknown ten years ago.

Changes are reshaping the competitive game in Asia and Williamson (2005) found that new strategies were called for. These new strategies should include a new productivity drive, greater focus on brand building and service quality, cross-border synergies, driving industry consolidation and relocating innovation activities into Asia.

Organisation structure for transnational firms

Having discussed the simple organisation structures that are appropriate for managing the international strategies of SMEs in the previous chapter, we now turn to the organisation structure concepts that large firms might use.

Transnational strategies, by their very nature, are complex and specific to the firms' context. As a result, organisation structures differ from firm to firm, but it is possible to make some general comments.

Strategic business units and the three management levels

In Figure 6.4 the conceptual framework of a company shows the three management levels – strategic, management and operational. The broad functional areas of the three levels are illustrated in Figure 6.5.

FIGURE 6.4
The conceptual framework
of a firm

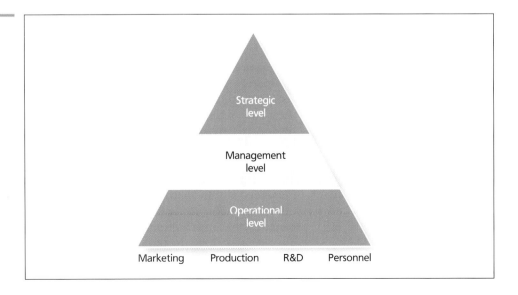

FIGURE 6.5
Functions of different
management levels

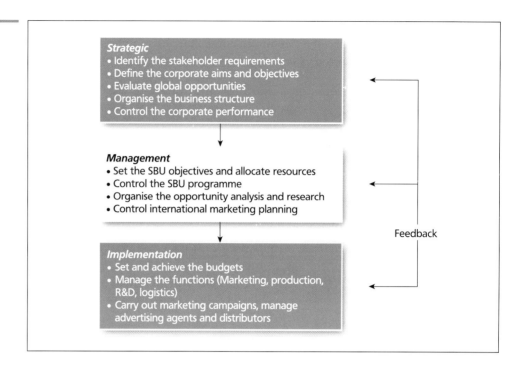

In most companies the strategic level of the firm is typically responsible for formulating the broad aims of the company, setting corporate objectives, identifying resources that can be utilised and selecting broad strategies. These aims, objectives and resources are then broken down into the constituent parts and allocated between the individual subsidiaries or operating units, which are referred to as strategic business units (SBUs).

The management level then breaks down these allocations into departmental objectives, budgets and tasks for which the functional managers (for example, in R & D or marketing) at the operational level are responsible.

The performance of the company in implementing the plans is monitored and controlled by operating the process in reverse. The operational-level managers are responsible for achieving the objectives set by the management level and the management level is expected to achieve the objectives set by the strategic level.

At an early stage in the company's development, the distinctions between levels are unclear as decisions are made in a largely unplanned, reactive way. As the company develops, the separation of management levels and functions becomes clearer and is reinforced by formalised procedures (reports and meetings) to plan and control the business. Whilst we have indicated three broad levels of management, the number of links in the chain between the chief executive and the customer can vary considerably. The recent trend in many companies has been to remove layers of management in order to have a flatter structure to give individual managers far greater responsibility and authority for their part of the company and so replicate the greater flexibility, adaptability and responsiveness of smaller, more entrepreneurial businesses. This has resulted in less distinction between the management activities, with managers at all levels being required to think strategically as well as operationally.

Large firms typically operate matrix management structures, with individual members of staff that have international as well as domestic company responsibilities typically having to report to both country and product or brand managers. Majaro (1991) has identified three basic structures in international organisations: the macropyramid, the umbrella and the interglomerate structures (see Figure 6.6), based on the three levels of management within the organisation identified previously – strategic, management and operational.

The macropyramid

The macropyramid is found in multi-national organisations which have a strong nerve centre or headquarters. The organisation is usually highly centralised and the foreign SBUs operate at the management or operational levels of the organisation. Examples of this type of company are McDonald's, IBM, Marks and Spencer and Sony. The individual SBUs have relatively little autonomy and their strategies and tactics are largely determined by the strategic level at the centre. The implications of this structure for marketing are that:

- marketing plans are produced centrally;
- all major decisions regarding the marketing mix are taken centrally and so can be slow and unresponsive to local needs;
- marketing is standardised as much as possible;
- world markets for their products and services are regarded as largely the same;
- local creativity is inhibited;

FIGURE 6.6
Development of strategy

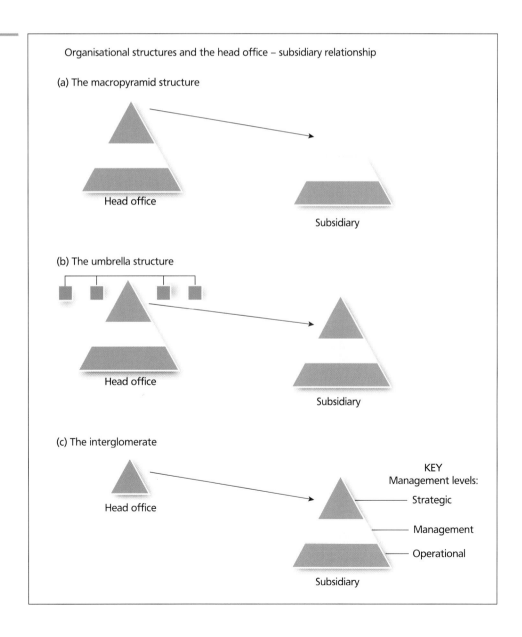

■ communication problems occur as a result of difficulty in interpreting instructions from the centre; and

■ the lack of local autonomy is a disincentive to good managers who must move to the centre for career advancement.

The umbrella structure

Organisations with the umbrella structure take the opposite view to those with the macropyramid. They have fully decentralised planning and control, and give full independence at all levels of management to the foreign subsidiaries. Procter & Gamble and Unilever have in the past operated such a structure. The centre sets only broad corporate objectives and will provide advice and support, but essentially, each SBU will develop a plan for their area of responsibility.

The implications for the marketing mix of an umbrella structure are:

■ the SBUs can adopt an appropriate marketing mix strategy for the local market;

■ an effective local marketing function can develop local marketing plans;

■ market planning can respond to local environmental developments and changes;

■ different strategies will be followed for each market and there are implications for usually centralised functions, such as R & D, personnel and finance;

■ there is little chance of a global strategy; and

■ there can be considerable duplication as different SBUs work on similar strategies and tactics.

This structure, quite obviously, is complex and it is interesting to note the change of strategy by Unilever (Dilemma 6.2) in the redevelopment of its portfolio and in the reorganisation of its structure.

The interglomerate

The interglomerate embraces multimarkets, multiproducts and multitechnologies. No attempt is made by the centre to develop strategies for the individual SBUs which are likely to be international businesses in their own right. Because of the diversity of the firm's activities the centre takes no significant, active management role, and is concerned purely with financial planning and control.

The implications for international marketing are that:

■ interglomerates are finance driven;

■ the marketing function will not be represented at the strategic level; and

■ corporate and marketing strategies are the sole responsibility of the SBU.

Many Western interglomerates of the 1990s, such as Hanson and BTR, have broken up their organisations by demerger and selling off non-core or unprofitable activities. ABB is another example of a company that is under pressure to reconstruct the business. This model remains more common in Asian-owned businesses such as Hutchinson Whampoa, Tata and Guandong Investments, which have significantly different patterns of development.

There is a suggestion that some of the Asian conglomerates are reaching the limits of their founding families to manage them and need to respond to new competitive pressures. It is possible that in the long term, business methods in Asia will resemble those in the West.

Systems, processes and control

Given the complexity of international strategic marketing in global firms it is essential that the organisation operates effective processes for the management of its complex operations, processes and systems to enable managers to be able to share information effectively.

Control

Control is the cornerstone of management. Control provides the means to direct, regulate and manage business operations. A significant amount of interaction is required between the individual areas of marketing (such as market development, advertising and selling) and the other functional areas (such as human resources, finance, production, research and development).

DILEMMA 6.2

Unilever: redefining product policy for a global future

Unilever illustrates many of the problems faced in developing and managing a global strategy.

When Patrick Cescau took over as CEO of Unilever in 2005 the company was still suffering from the shock of its first ever profits warning. The previous CEO, Niall Fitzgerald, had developed a five-year 'Path to Growth' plan which involved reducing the company's portfolio of brands from 1600 to 400 in the belief that focusing resources and effort would deliver the target 5–6 per cent growth per annum. However, the sales of a number of high-profile brands, such as Surf and Slim-fast, significantly underperformed expectations.

By 2007 the performance of Unilever was back on course with sales growth of 3.8 per cent and profits up 7 per cent. The turnaround was achieved by focusing resources on those specific products with the most potential for growth, for example its care brands such as Dove and Lifebuoy, its 'vitality' brands that encourage healthy living, such as Knorr Vie, Flora and Blue Band Idea, as well as emerging market opportunities.

Cescau also changed Unilever's organisation. He slimmed down the executive board from 20 members to only 7. There is one Dutchman, two Indians, two Americans and two British. Before Cescau there used to be two joint executive chairmen, one representing the British side of the business and one the Dutch, a tradition started in 1930 when Lever Brothers merged with its rival Van Den Bergh.

Previously it operated as a federation of national businesses. The chairmen of country operations were responsible for managing everything from the local supply chain to advertising and human resources and they wanted to be self-sufficient. This led to complexity and fragmentation. The executive in charge of marketing deodorants across Europe recalls that the firm's Swiss marketing director argued that a different size of roller ball was needed on the deodorant dispenser because Swiss armpits were of a different size! It took some persuasion before the standard sized product was accepted.

Whilst the old structure encouraged entrepreneurship in the national businesses it inhibited exploitation of innovation – any local innovation would have only a 50 per cent chance of being adopted in one more country and innovations in food often stayed local. For example, despite the success in Europe of Pro Activ, the range of cholesterol-lowering margarines, yoghurt and drinks, it had not been adopted in the US despite the obesity and coronary disease problems there. Cescau believed the reason was the 'not invented here' syndrome – but the brand was eventually launched in the US in 2007.

Cescau explained that the country operations had to 'take the baton and pass it on, not look at the colour of the baton'. They had the single responsibility of 'getting things done' and their crucial role was to manage relationships with the big customers – the retailers, instead of consumers. Indeed Cescau took on personal responsibility for the biggest retailers – Wal-Mart and Tesco. HR was outsourced and supply chains were organised regionally. Specialist global teams were set up 'to go to market'.

This meant considerable rationalisation. For example, there were 64 variants of tomato soup in Europe. The 64 pieces of advertising for the Pond's range of beauty products in Asia was reduced to four. Two or three adverts were created for Axe (Lynx in the UK) where previously there were 30 or 40. However, cultural difference still needed to be respected, particularly in advertising. For example, in the Dove ads women in Brazil hug one another, but that is not acceptable in the US where they stand slightly apart.

The dilemma is which organisation structure – centralised or decentralised – is best?

SOURCE: ADAPTED FROM D. REECE 'VITALITY TREATMENT FROM MAN OF ACTION', DAILY TELEGRAPH, 9 FEBRUARY, 2007 AND B. LAWRENCE 'UNILEVER GETS IT'S GLOBAL ACT TOGETHER', SUNDAY TIMES 18 MARCH, 2007

However, for many firms, control means a separate activity through which senior managers are able to keep a check periodically (weekly, monthly or quarterly) on more junior levels of management, who often see this in terms of being called upon to justify their actions. Feedback and control systems should be regarded as an integrated part of the whole planning process, and they are essential in ensuring that the marketing plans are not only being implemented worldwide but are still appropriate for the changing environment in each country.

There are a number of benefits of an effective strategic control system. It encourages higher standards of performance, forces greater clarity and realism and permits corporate management to intervene when necessary. Moreover, it ensures that the financial objectives do not overwhelm the strategic objectives, encourages clearer definition of responsibilities making decentralisation work more effectively, and so provides more motivation for managers.

There are three essential elements of the control process:

1 *Setting standards*: the standards that are set need to be relevant to the corporate goals such as growth and profits reported by financial measures, such as return on capital employed and on sales, and non-financial indicators, such as market share. Intermediate goals and individual targets can be set by breaking the plan down into measurable parts which, when successfully completed, will lead to the overall objectives being achieved. The standards must be understandable, achievable and relevant to each local country situation.

2 *Measuring performance against standards*: to obtain measurements and ensure rapid feedback of information, firms use a variety of techniques, including reports, meetings and special measurements of specific parts of the marketing programme, such as cost–benefit analysis of customers, product lines and territories or marketing audits for a thorough examination of every aspect of marketing in a particular country. They also use benchmarking which allows comparisons of various aspects of the business, such as efficiency of distribution, customer response times, service levels and complaints, with other companies that are not necessarily from the same business sector.

3 *Correcting deviations from the plan*: perhaps the most difficult decisions that must be made are to determine when performance has deviated sufficiently from the plan to require corrective action to be taken, either by changing the plan or the management team charged with the responsibility of carrying out the plan. Evaluation of the performance of a particular management team is particularly difficult in international marketing as the performance of a particular SBU can only be compared with its own plan, a plan determined by the headquarters or with the performance of a 'similar' SBU. There are obvious weaknesses in making any of these comparisons, resulting in considerable difference of opinion between the head office and subsidiary.

A key element in the control process is the input from people, both the directly employed staff of the company but also the staff of the other members of the supply chain. Various quality management models, such as Total Quality Management, Continuous Quality Improvement and Business Excellence, supported by international standards such as ISO 9000, are used by firms to underpin the control process. Consistency across the firm's global operations can be increased and general improvements made using a variety of techniques.

- Benchmarking against other SBUs within the firm, other firms within the business sector and the 'best in the class' in a particular activity, such as just in time operations control, service centre response rates or delivery performance.

- Identifying good practice wherever in the world it occurs and applying the lessons either in individual SBUs or across the firm.
- Encouraging performance improvement through self-assessment (individuals completing questionnaires and improvement plans alone), peer review (evaluation by staff at the same level) and appraisals completed by more senior managers.

Setting standards to achieve consistency and establishing continuous performance improvement projects throughout the global company can, however, be problematic because of cultural barriers, differences in language and ethical standards causing different levels of motivation, communications problems and misinterpretation of instructions and advice. In addition, different measuring techniques, standards and imprecise reporting procedures and processes can create difficulties in achieving a meaningful control process.

Return on marketing investment

One of the problems for marketing is the concern that marketing and promotion expenditure is simply seen as a cost to the business with no benefits linked to it. As a key control tool, therefore, measuring the return on marketing investment is essential for any business-to-business or consumer marketing manager looking to improve their ability to produce real results in revenue growth. In much of the traditional marketing activity it is difficult to define the specific benefits that can be attributed to one individual activity. With online marketing, as we shall see later, it is easier to link the marketing investment with its impact. In practice, firms need to measure the effect of an integrated marketing programme, in order to learn good and bad practice.

Planning systems and processes

The increasingly turbulent environment resulting from more rapid changes in technology, competition, consumer taste and fashion means that the traditional systems and processes for preparing the analysis, strategy development and action plans take too long. Balabanis *et al.* (2004) emphasised that global information systems are needed to enable HQ and subsidiary managers to keep track of environmental changes (opportunities and threats), facilitate the coordination and control of operations in different locations and assist in sharing of new ideas and knowledge.

Timescales must be reduced to make sure that the plan is still relevant when it is being implemented. Consequently it is necessary to avoid planning that is too general and unfocused and to improve the quality of implementation and the relevance and responsiveness of the process.

As a result of this, increasing emphasis is being placed by MNEs on scenario and contingency planning to take account of things going wrong because of unexpected changes in the environment. Moreover, greater reliance is being placed on expert systems for understanding market changes, carrying out forecasting, resource planning and gap analysis. The plans prepared tend to be based on the understanding that they will be emergent, and will evolve during the timescale of the plan rather than be decided before the time period of the plan begins. The plans may be designed to be incremental, with the start of each new phase being prompted by a change in the environment or by the successful completion of a previous implementation phase.

Building skills in transnational organisations

Whilst the structures outlined provide some general understanding of the alternative methods of organising the management, they are for most companies an over-simplification. Bartlett and Ghoshal (2001) explain that 'the very act of going international multiplies the firm's organisational complexity'. The domestic organisational variables of product and function are extended by adding the geographic dimension. In a study of nine firms, including ITT, Phillips and Procter and Gamble, they found that the challenge of breaking down biases and building a truly multidimensional organisation has proved difficult because there are inbuilt assumptions within the firm about the roles of the organisational units and the way that they should be managed. The traditional view is that relationships between SBUs should be clear and unambiguous and that the decision-making mechanisms should be clearly understood, but in fact the most successful firms have challenged these assumptions and replaced them with new standards. Cagni (2006) explains that old-fashioned, centralised, multinational management is no longer appropriate as it creates a single process overseen from head office. Whilst this creates scale advantages, improved efficiency and the capability to share knowledge, local staff see a loss of autonomy, the creation of an ivory tower for the elite and the disempowerment of local managers, leaving them with less interesting jobs. The structure needs be developed in a way that avoids rigidity as flexibility is needed to respond to the changes in environment and market, something that Unilever (Dilemma 6.2) needs to consider.

This has implications for the roles of the international marketing manager, as Bartlett and Ghoshal (2003) have concluded. The management of transnational businesses requires highly specialised, closely linked groups of global business managers, country or regional managers, and functional managers who work in networks. They explain the implications for managers in such transnational organisations. Global business or product division managers have the responsibility to further the company's global-scale efficiency and competitiveness. They must combine the strategist skills of recognising opportunities and risks across national and functional boundaries, be the architect for worldwide resource and asset utilisation, and the coordinator of activities and capabilities.

The country manager must play a pivotal role by sensing local customer needs, but also satisfying the host government's requirements and defending the company's market position. The country manager is likely to have objectives that conflict with the business manager and so must be prepared to negotiate to overcome the differences. The functional manager's role is the business environment scanner, cross-pollinator of ideas and champion of specific aspects of the business which are essential for success. The global manager may be required to play a number of roles. The complexity of global operations means that no one person can fulfil the required tasks alone. This manager, therefore, must provide leadership, whilst acting as the talent scout and the developer of the other levels of management.

As a result, patterns of activity in a transnational company will vary considerably in each new situation. Innovations, for example, should be generated at several locations and in several ways throughout the world, so that the company is not restricted to making centralised decisions. For the past 10 to 20 years, firms such as Shell, Phillips and Unilever have used an integrated network approach, with resources and capabilities concentrated in various locations and accessed through the free flow of knowledge, technology, components, products, resources and people. By developing matrix structures, firms can achieve efficiency, responsiveness and the ability to develop and exploit their knowledge and capability for competitive advantage.

As the international operations of firms increase in diversity and tangible ties between the activities become strained, so the nature of the formal systems and organisational structures must change too. Training programmes, career path planning, job rotation, company-wide accounting, evaluation and data-processing systems become more important as part of the shared value system of the firm.

Staff and the problems of international management

Of the potential sources of problems of planning in international marketing, it is the relationship between headquarters and local subsidiary staff that is likely to be the largest single factor. Headquarters staff, as guardians of the overall company strategies, claim to have a far broader perspective of the company's activities and might expect that subsidiary staff should simply be concerned with implementation of the details of the plan. Subsidiary staff claim that, by being closer to the individual markets, they are in a better position to identify opportunities and should therefore play a large part in developing objectives and strategies. This situation must be resolved if the planning process is to be effective, so that all staff have a clear idea of their own role in setting, developing and implementing policy, and understanding how their individual contributions might be integrated into the corporate objectives and strategies.

The difficulties of planning in international markets are further developed by Brandt *et al.* (1980), in a framework of international planning problems, and Weichmann and Pringle (1979), who identified the key problems experienced by large US and European multi-nationals. Figure 6.7 is a list of problems at head office and in the subsidiary which are the main sources of conflict between headquarters and overseas staff.

Many companies recognise that for strategies to be successful, the managers of all parts of the company must share ownership of them through playing an active part

FIGURE 6.7
International planning problems

Headquarters	Overseas subsidiary
Management	**Management**
Unclear allocation of responsibilities and authority	Resistance to planning
Lack of multinational orientation	Lack of qualified personnel
Unrealistic expectations	Inadequate abilities
Lack of awareness of foreign markets	Misinterpretation of information
Unclear guidelines	Misunderstanding requirements and objectives
Insensitivity to local decisions	Resentment of HQ involvement
Insufficient provision of useful information	Lack of strategic thinking
	Lack of marketing expertise
Processes	**Processes**
Lack of standardized bases for evaluation	Lack of control by HQ
Poor IT systems and support	Incomplete or outdated internal and market information
Poor feedback and control systems	Poorly developed procedures
Excessive bureaucratic control procedures	Too little communication with HQ
Excessive marketing and financial constraints	Inaccurate data returns
Insufficient participation of subsidiaries in process	Insufficient use of multinational marketing expertise
	Excessive financial and marketing constraints

in the development and implementation stages of the process itself. With greater emphasis on staff at all levels in the organisation providing increased levels of service to customers, it is important to involve all staff in the marketing planning process. This is becoming more difficult as MNEs have ever greater numbers of their workers employed outside the head office country. As the company grows, therefore, a company-wide planning culture should be developed, with the following objectives:

- planning becomes part of the continuous process of management rather than an annual 'event';
- strategic thinking becomes the responsibility of every manager rather than being restricted to a separate strategic planning department;
- the planning process becomes standardised, with a format that allows contributions from all parts of the company;
- the plan becomes the working document, updated periodically for all aspects of the company, so allowing performance evaluation to be carried out regularly; and
- the planning process is itself regularly reviewed and refined through the use of new tools and techniques in order to improve its relevance and effectiveness.

Brett, Behfar and Kern (2006) identify the advantages of multicultural teams in international firms, including deep knowledge of different product markets and culturally sensitive customer service, but also note the problems caused when cultural differences affect team effectiveness, direct versus indirect communication, trouble with accents and fluency, differing attitudes to hierarchy and authority and conflicting norms for decision making. The authors emphasise the need to pinpoint the root cause of the problems, intervene early and see the challenges as stemming from culture rather than personalities.

What makes a good international manager

For many of the most powerful businesses increasing globalisation is the future scenario, and the most successful will be managed by people who can best embrace and thrive on the ambiguity and complexity of transnational operations. Despite the rapid internationalisation of businesses, there are still few really international managers – but the creation of cross-cultural managers with genuinely transferable management skills is the goal for the global companies.

A number of researchers have emphasised the need for managers to be able to handle national differences in business, including cultural divergence on hierarchy, humour, assertiveness and working hours. In France, Germany, Italy and a large part of Asia, for example, performance-related pay is seen negatively as revealing the shortcomings of some members of the work group. Feedback sessions are seen positively in the US but German managers see them as 'enforced admissions of failure'.

The international manager, therefore, must be more culturally aware and show greater sensitivity, but it can be difficult to adapt to the culture and values of a foreign country whilst upholding the culture and values of a parent company. The only way is to give managers experience overseas but the cost of sending people abroad is typically two-and-a-half times that for a local manager, so firms look for alternatives, such as short-term secondments, exchanges and participation in multicultural project teams.

Wills and Barham (1994) believe that international managers require four sets of attributes. They must:

1 Be able to cope with cognitive complexity and be able to understand issues from a variety of complicated perspectives.

2 Have cultural empathy, a sense of humility and the power of active listening. Because of their unfamiliarity with different cultural settings international managers cannot be as competent or confident in a foreign environment.

3 Have emotional energy and be capable of adding depth and quality to interactions through their emotional self-awareness, emotional resilience, ability to accept risk. They must be able to rely on the support of the family.

4 Demonstrate psychological maturity by having the curiosity to learn, an awareness of time constraints and a fundamental personal morality that will enable them to cope with the diversity of demands made on them.

Management culture

There has been considerable discussion about the difference between the Asian and Western models of management and the reasons for the differences, such as the elements of a deeply embedded culture and more recent history, for example, the effects on management of working within a centrally planned economy. Deshpande *et al.* (2004) however also note the differences between Asian management cultures and suggest that Chinese and Vietnamese firms, emerging from centrally planned economies to some form of market socialism, tend to be bureaucratic. Indian firms tend to be entrepreneurial. Japanese culture is the most consensual and the least entrepreneurial. Hong Kong tends to be about average in that it reflects the mixed Chinese and Western influences on its management culture.

They conclude that there are in fact four organisational culture types:

1 Competitive or market culture which is characterised by an emphasis on competitive advantage and market superiority.

2 Entrepreneurial or adhocracy culture which emphasises innovation and risk-taking.

3 Bureaucratic or hierarchy culture in which regulations and formal structures are important. And

4 Consensual or clan culture which emphasises loyalty, tradition and internal maintenance.

They found that in each country more competitive and entrepreneurial firms perform better and consensual and bureaucratic firms perform worse than their national peers. They also noted that market orientation has a greater effect on performance in Asia and innovativeness has a greater effect in the more industrialised nations. Illustration 6.7 shows an example of different management styles in Mittal Steel.

Research by PricewaterhouseCoopers and Cranfield School of Management (2007) suggests that firms should plan the return of expatriate executives that have carried out assignments abroad. They show that 40 per cent of executives that return home from overseas postings resign after being frustrated at being sidelined after successfully completing their assignment. Firms often offer generous financial packages to help the overseas transition but fail to meet the expatriate's expectations of an increase in salary and status on their return. The cost of an overseas posting averages US$311 000 for a typical 29-month assignment. The executives are usually given high levels of support from personnel managers and only 4 per cent return prematurely. However, when they returned their measured performance did not match that when abroad and only 24 per cent managed to move up the promotion ladder in the first year back, despite the fact that these executives were typically among the best in the company.

Management style and shared values

The different contexts and stages of global development of firms mean that there is no proven right and wrong management style and shared values for the firm. Indeed the shared values, as we have seen earlier, may be the only common aspect of the company that binds the various parts together and may be based upon a long tradition in the firm, built up over many years. This is particularly the case in companies dominated by extended family ownership, such as in many Asian businesses, or where the principles of the founding family of a business are maintained.

What is important to recognise is that although global businesses are complex and diverse, the chief executive can have a major effect on the business. The personality of entrepreneurs such as Steve Jobs, Michael Dell and Richard Branson shapes the management style and shared values of the businesses they create from their early days. Influential managers that turn around an ailing business or drive the business in a new direction, such as Lakshmi Mittal, discussed in Illustration 6.7 have a similar impact.

ILLUSTRATION 6.7

Mittal: ready to iron out a possible culture clash?

Arcelor Mittal was formed as a result of the $34.3bn takeover of Arcelor Steel of Luxembourg by Mittal Steel in 2006. The combined company had annual sales of US$70bn, produced 120m tonnes of steel (10 per cent of the world total) and had a workforce of 320 000. The company had a higher market share than that of the next three competitors (Nippon Steel and JFE of Japan, and Posco of South Korea) combined.

Lakshmi Mittal was the founder of Mittal Steel and, with a fortune of US$23.5bn, was ranked by *Forbes* magazine as the world's fifth richest man. For many years financial returns from the steel sector lagged behind other similar sectors, such as chemicals and telecommunications, and it had long been the aim of Mittal to improve performance through consolidation in the industry.

The takeover was opposed by the Arcelor chairman and CEO who believed that there was a different culture in Mittal, which had been built largely through 25 years of buying low-value steel assets in countries such as Poland, Mexico and Kazakhstan, whereas Arcelor's operations were concentrated in Western Europe, making higher-value steel for more technologically advanced customers. It was opposed by European politicians, particularly in France and Luxembourg, who were concerned that the merger would destroy a world-beating European-based firm.

Mittal set up a six person management group (three each from Mittal Steel and Arcelor) to run the combined business and agreed to take on the non-executive chairmanship of the combined company in 2007. Industry experts, however, were sceptical that Mittal was about to take a back seat. Bankers and fund managers alike saw Mittal as being a good operator with a great track record and recognised that he was the one decision maker in the company. Mittal's son Aditya, although only 30, was chief financial officer for the firm and was expected by some to be a future chief executive.

Arcelor's management style was often seen as bureaucratic and bumbling, with slow decision-making amongst the many divisional managers. By contrast Mittal's style was very entrepreneurial, with most of their top managers tasked to collect information and feed it upwards so that Mittal could make decisions. Clearly it could be difficult to merge these two management styles.

PHOTO CREDIT: © CHRISTOPHE KARABA/EPA/CORBIS

QUESTION *What must Mittal do for the company to become a truly global player?*

SOURCE: ADAPTED FROM P. MARSH 'A FEEL FOR STEEL: WHY MITTAL WILL PRESS HOME THE BENEFITS OF SIZE', FINANCIAL TIMES, 26 SEPTEMBER, 2006

SUMMARY

- The increase in global business activity has resulted from a number of drivers in the environment, particulary through technological developments. Clearly it is communications and information technology that have had the greatest effect on creating a global marketplace. Firms have also accelerated the move towards greater globalisation by developing a worldwide presence and strategy, and offering similar products and services.

- To exploit global markets firms have developed appropriate strategies for their particular situation. These range from multidomestic strategies, in which each market is seen as separate and individual, through to globally standardised strategies in which the firm has identified one global segment with similar needs. In practice, the largest firms are too complex for one simple strategy to be appropriate and so they use a combination of different strategies to build global efficiency, local effectiveness and knowledge assets.

- In the past global trade has been dominated by MNEs from developed countries, but now companies from emerging markets that have built their capability and resources in the domestic market, are becoming global players investing in developed countries too. The competitive advantage that they have built in their home market must then be tested in the global marketplace.

- To succeed globally firms must build global appeal through globally recognised brands, but also innovate as the basis of competitive advantage in many industries changes continually.

- An increasingly common feature of transnational strategies is the greater level of cooperation between firms that would otherwise be competitors, customers or suppliers.

- To enable managers to set and control the operations of the business an appropriate organisation structure is needed. International managers must also be able to recruit and develop the right staff that will have the skills necessary to deal with the complexity, diversity and conflicting challenges of global business development.

KEYWORDS

Competitive advantage	Global reach	Organisation structure
Control	Global sourcing	Standardisation/ adaptation
Global appeal	Globalisation	
Global brand	International manager	Transnationality
Global presence	Market access	World Wide Web
	Mergers of equals	

CASE STUDY

Conglomerate breaks out from India

Over the last two decades multinationals from developed countries have focused on their core activities where there appeared to be the most attractive global market opportunities. For many firms this has meant withdrawing from sectors by selling off unwanted parts of the business. The conglomerate model, in which hundreds of often disparate businesses are held in an organisation that perhaps resembles a private equity fund, is not so common in developed countries but is still favoured in emerging markets, and there are a number of examples in India and China. The activities that have bound these businesses together in the conglomerate model in the past have often been manufacturing or international trading. Western multinationals, however, seem to have focused on global branding and marketing, and outsourcing manufacturing wherever possible.

What will be interesting to observe over the next few years is how these conglomerates from emerging markets globalise their activities, whether they focus on marketing and global branding as, for example, LG and Samsung from South Korea have done, adopt a Western-style multinational approach or develop their own model.

Tata is an example of an Indian conglomerate that is now investing in foreign markets. India's growth has been around 8 per cent for four successive years and this has enabled Indian companies to develop strong balance sheets so that they have been able to borrow huge amounts of money abroad to fuel their international expansion and takeovers.

Ratan Tata became chairman of Tata Sons, a disorganised family business in 1991. He is a shy and unassuming figure who shuns the trappings of wealth, despite being one of India's richest men. He took over at a time when the Indian government began removing the bureaucratic controls that had previously curtailed the development of Indian firms. He set about rationalising the group's hundreds of businesses with the aim of making them more efficient. The organisation is still diverse, with interests in steel, cars, hotels, mobile telephony, chemicals and tea, and it is India's largest software firm.

A feature of most fast-growing companies from emerging markets is that they have lower costs than their competitors from developed countries. However, Tata's competitive advantage comes not just from the supply of low-cost, well-educated labour necessary for the technology-based activities. It has also built expertise in developing and operating automated, capital-intensive production, typical of steel making. Moreover during India's 1991 reforms Tata learned how to thrive in a highly competitive market place that still had a highly regulated environment and a poor infrastructure, and this serves them well as they pursue a strategy of mergers and acquisitions in different world markets.

Ratan Tata has single-handedly made the company into respected MNE. In 2007 Tata completed a £6.7 billion takeover of Corus, the British–Dutch steel maker, in the process beating a Brazilian steel-making company CSN. A few years ago few experts would have thought that Tata could have progressed to the point where it would be in position to take over Corus but Tata had strengthened its position with the acquisition of Singapore's Natsteel in 2004 and Thailand's Millennium Steel in 2005. It also mines all the coal and iron ore it needs. It aims to produce steel close to its iron ore deposits and ship semi-finished steel to be finished close to its markets, so adding value in the various countries in which it is operating. In 2000 Tata took over Tetley Tea, a British business with a global brand, with the intention of linking India tea production with the overseas tea markets. Tata decided that Tata Motors would make its own car, turning away from the possibility of a joint venture with a more established manufacturer to produce an existing model. By 2007 the company was India's second biggest car manufacturer and had plans for a vehicle to sell for under US$3000.

Investment does not only take the form of acquisitions. Tata made Bangladesh's single largest foreign investment of £1.1bn when it agreed to build a power plant, steel unit and fertiliser factory after the government guaranteed a supply of gas for 20 years from its proven reserves. This deal was part of Bangladesh's aims of becoming more self-reliant and reducing its dependence on foreign aid.

Although he has made Tata's businesses more competitive and more global in outlook, the company has a tradition of being public spirited and Ratan Tata has said in interviews that he would prefer his legacy to be having caused no damage to others. The company has a reputation for refusing to accept bribes and treating its workers well. Two-thirds of Tata Sons is owned by charitable trusts that do good works in India. Although the company is competitive, some foreign investors wonder if this approach is right for running the global business.

PHOTO CREDIT: DAVID PEARSON/ALAMY

QUESTION

1   What are the key issues that Tata faces as it progresses to becoming a global company?

2   What international strategic marketing options does it have and what recommendations would you make to the company to enable it to become a global company?

SOURCES: ADAPTED FROM 'CIRCLE THE WAGONS', THE ECONOMIST, 12 OCTOBER, 2006; 'STEELY LOGIC', THE ECONOMIST, 28 OCTOBER, 2006; 'THE SHY ARCHITECT', THE ECONOMIST, 11 JANUARY, 2007 AND 'BANGLADESH WINS $2BN INDIA DEAL' BBC NEWS ONLINE, 19 AUGUST, 2004

DISCUSSION QUESTIONS

1 What do you consider to be the definition of globalisation? Using examples, explain how globalisation affects the international marketing strategy of a MNE.

2 Identify the reasons why global strategies sometimes fail in their objective to achieve a global marketing advantage.

3 What is the rationale behind mega mergers and major acquisitions? How will they lead to global competitive advantage and what problems might result?

4 What are the critical success factors in developing a global brand? What additional factors would you consider to be necessary in developing a successful global e-business brand?

5 What are the main challenges that are faced by international managers in managing and controlling a global marketing strategy? What advice would you give to a manager with this responsibility?

References

Balabanis, G., Theodosiou, M. and Katsikea, E.S. (2004) 'Export marketing: developments and a research agenda', *International Marketing Review*, 21 (4/5): 353–77.

Bartlett, C.A. and Ghoshal, S. (2001) *Managing across borders. The transnational solution*. HBS Press.

Bartlett, C.A. and Ghoshal, S. (2003) 'What is a global manager?', *Harvard Business Review*, 81 (8): 101–8.

Bracken, P. (2007) Revenge of the domestic tigers, accessed at www.strategy-business.com on 10 April 2007.

BBC News online (2007) 'Chinese Car market is world No 2', 11 January 2007.

Brandt, W., Hulbert, J. and Richers, R. (1980) 'Pitfalls in planning for multinational operations', *Long Range Planning*, December.

Brett, J., Behfar, K. and Kern, M.C. (2006) 'Managing multicultural teams,'*Harvard Business Review*, 84 (11): 84–91.

Barbaro, M. (2006) 'Wal-Mart profits falls 26%, its first drop in 10 years', *New York Times*, 16 August.

Buzzell, R.D. (1968) 'Can you standardise multinational marketing?', *Harvard Business Review*, 46 (6): 101–14.

Cagni, P. (2006) 'Think global, act European', available at www.strategy-business.com

Cranfield School of Management (2007) International Assignments accessed at www.som.cranfield.ac.uk/som/news

Deshpandé, R., Farley, J.U. and Bowman D. (2004) 'Tigers, dragons and others: profiling high performance in Asian firms', *Journal of International Marketing*, 12 (3): 5–29.

Finkelstein, S. (1998) 'Safe ways to cross the merger minefield', *Mastering Global Business Part 4, Financial Times*, 20 February.

Gogel, R. and Larreche, J.C. (1989) 'The battlefield for 1992: product strength and geograhical coverage', *European Journal of Management*, 17, 289.

Hart, S.L. and London, T. (2005) Developing native capability: why multinational corporations can learn from the base of the pyramid, *Stanford Social Innovation Review*, Summer, accessed at www.ssireview.org/.

Holt, D.B., Quelch, J.A. and Taylor, E.L. (2004) 'How global brands compete', *Harvard Business Review* 82 (9): 68–75.

Khashani, K. (1995) 'A new future for brands', *Financial Times*, 10 November.

Kleinman, M. (2006) 'McDonald's Chinese soar away', *Daily Telegraph*, 8 November 2006.

Levitt, T. (1983) 'The globalisation of markets', *Harvard Business Review*, May/June.

Majaro, S. (1991) *International Marketing*. Routledge.

Meffet, H. and Bolz, J. (1993) 'Standardization of marketing in Europe needs effort', in C. Haliburton and R. Hunerberg (eds) *European Marketing Readings*, Addison-Wesley.

Prahalad, C.K. and Hart, S.L. (2002) 'The fortune at the bottom of the pyramid', *Strategy and Business*, 26 (54): 67.

Sjobolom, L. (1998) 'Success lies one step ahead of the consumer', *Mastering Global Management, Financial Times*, 6 February.

Smith, A. (1998) 'The conundrum of maintaining image', *Financial Times*, 8 May.

UNCTAD (2006) *World investment report 2006*, UN conference on Trade and Development, available at http://www.unctad.org.

Weichmann, U.E. and Pringle, L.G. (1979) 'Problems that plague multinational marketers', *Harvard Business Review*, July/August.

Williamson, P. (2005) 'Strategies for Asia's new competitive game', *Journal of Business Strategy*, 26 (2): 37–43.

Wills, S. and Barham, K. (1994) 'Being an international manager', *European Management Journal*, 12 (1).

Zou, S. and Cavusgil, S.T. (2002) 'The GMS: a broad conceptualisation of global marketing strategy and its effect on firm performance', *Journal of Marketing*, 66: 40–56.

CHAPTER 7

MARKET ENTRY STRATEGIES

INTRODUCTION

For the majority of companies, the most significant international marketing decision they are likely to take is how they should enter new markets, as the commitments that they make will affect every aspect of their business for many years ahead. Having identified potential country, regional and world markets in previous chapters and discussed the development of international marketing strategies in both smaller and global firms, in this chapter we examine the different market entry options open to firms to enable them to select the most appropriate method for their given situation. For most small and medium-sized businesses this represents a critical first step, but for established companies, the problem is how to exploit opportunities more effectively within the context of their existing network of international operations and, particularly, how to enter new emerging markets.

There are advantages and disadvantages with each market entry method: critical in the decision-making process are the firm's assessment of the cost and risk associated with each method and the level of involvement the company is allowed by the government, or wishes to have in the market. These factors determine the degree of control it can exert over the total product and service offer and the method of distribution.

There is, however, no ideal market entry strategy and different market entry methods might be adopted by different firms entering the same market and/or by the same firm in different markets.

LEARNING OBJECTIVES

After reading this chapter you should be able to:

- Identify the alternative market entry options available to firms seeking to develop new country markets

- Compare the different levels of involvement, risk and marketing control of these market entry methods

- Understand the criteria for selecting between the market entry options

- Appreciate the advantages and disadvantages of the different market entry methods

- Understand the motivations and challenges of market entry partnership strategies, such as alliances and joint ventures

THE ALTERNATIVE MARKET ENTRY METHODS

The various alternative market entry methods are shown in Figure 7.1, and cover a span of international involvement from almost zero, when the firm merely makes the products available for others to export but effectively does nothing itself to market its products internationally, to total involvement where the firm might operate wholly-owned subsidiaries in all its key markets. These are approximate relative positions and vary according the specific situation. E-commerce might be placed in a range of positions depending upon the particular business model adopted.

The market entry decision is taken within the firm and is determined to a large extent by the firm's objectives and attitudes to international marketing and the confidence in the capability of its managers to operate in foreign countries. In order to select an appropriate and potentially successful market entry method, it is necessary to consider a number of criteria including:

- the company objectives and expectations relating to the size and value of anticipated business

- the size and financial resources of the company

- its existing foreign market involvement

- the skill, abilities and attitudes of the company management towards international marketing

FIGURE 7.1

Market entry methods and the levels of involvement in international markets

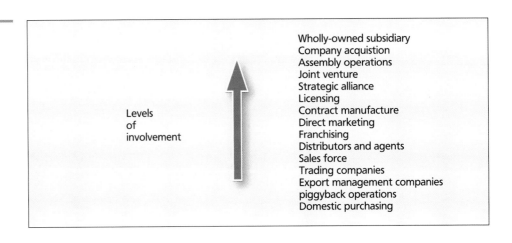

Levels of involvement

Wholly-owned subsidiary
Company acquistion
Assembly operations
Joint venture
Strategic alliance
Licensing
Contract manufacture
Direct marketing
Franchising
Distributors and agents
Sales force
Trading companies
Export management companies
piggyback operations
Domestic purchasing

- the nature and power of the competition within the market
- the nature of existing and anticipated tariff and non-tariff barriers
- the nature of the product itself, particularly any areas of competitive advantage, such as trademark or patent protection, and
- the timing of the move in relation to the market and competitive situation.

This list is not exhaustive, as the entry method might be influenced by other factors which are specific to the firm's particular situation. For example, the laws of a host country might prevent a firm from owning 100 per cent of an operation in that country. Trade embargos put in place by the United Nations may prevent a firm entering the country, during times of war or terrorism the country of origin of the product or service may make market entry inadvisable. In 2007 Rolls Royce bowed to pressure from humanitarian groups to stop supplying engines and pumps for oil and gas to Sudan.

Timing is another particularly important factor in considering entry. For example, emerging markets typically have bursts of optimism and growth often followed by setbacks caused by political or economic factors, or changing customer expectations. The Asian approach of allocating time and resources in the expectation of improved trading conditions in the future has paid off in many emerging markets. Chinese companies are investing heavily in the infrastructure in Africa in exchange for valuable resources and assets and in the expectation that the economies of African countries will improve in the near future. This approach contrasts with that of many Western companies who seem to invest only when a particular country is about to 'take off', but it may be already too late if their Asian rivals are already well entrenched.

Risk and control in market entry

We referred earlier to the fact that one of the most important characteristics of the different market entry methods is the level of involvement of the firm in international operations. This has significant implications in terms of levels of **risk and control** and is shown diagramatically in Figure 7.2. Figure 7.2 also shows

FIGURE 7.2
Risk and control in market entry

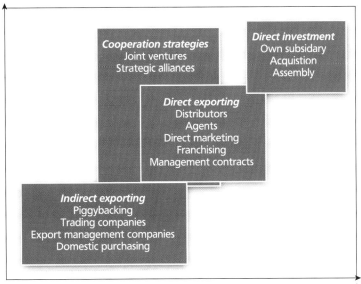

the four categories of market entry methods: indirect and direct market entry, cooperation and direct investment.

The cost of resourcing the alternative methods usually equates closely to levels of involvement and risk. The diagram does suggest, however, that higher levels of involvement bring greater potential for control over its foreign country marketing activities and also higher potential risk, usually due to the high cost of investment. In practice this is an oversimplification, because firms whose products are marketed internationally through domestic purchasing are at risk of losing all their income from international markets without knowing why, because of their total reliance on their customer's strategy for success.

Partnerships, in the form of joint ventures and strategic alliances, have become increasingly common over the past few years because they are thought to offer the advantage of achieving higher levels of control in market entry at lower levels of risk and cost, provided that there is a high degree of cooperation between companies and that the individual objectives of the partner companies are not incompatible.

In making a decision on market entry, therefore, the most fundamental questions that the firm must answer are:

- What level of control over our international business activities do we require?
- What level of risk are we willing to take?
- What cost can we afford to bear?

In answering these questions it is important to consider not just the level of control, risk and cost, but also the relative importance that the firm might place upon the different elements of its marketing activity. For example, lack of control over certain aspects of the marketing process, such as after-sales servicing which is often undertaken by third party contractors, may affect the reputation and image of a company or brand because consumers frequently blame the manufacturer rather than a distributor or retailer for the poor quality of after-sales service that they have received.

INDIRECT EXPORTING

For firms that have little inclination or few resources for international marketing, the simplest and lowest cost method of market entry is for them to have their products sold overseas by others. The objective of firms which use this method of entry may be to benefit from opportunities that arise without incurring any expense or simply to sell off excess capacity into foreign markets with the least possible inconvenience. Firms such as these often withdraw from this activity as soon as their sales into the home market improve. Whilst indirect exporting has the advantage of the least cost and risk of any entry method, it allows the firm little control over how, when, where and by whom the products are sold. In some cases the domestic company may even be unaware that its products are being exported.

There are four main methods of indirect exporting and these are by using:

1 domestic purchasing
2 an export management company (EMC) or export house (EH)
3 piggyback operations, and
4 trading companies.

Domestic purchasing

Some firms or individuals do not realise that their products or services have potential export value until they are approached by the buyer from a foreign organisation, who might make the initial contact, purchase the product at the factory gate and take on the task of exporting, marketing and distributing the product in one or more overseas market. Anita Roddick used this approach to source naturally occurring ingredients for Body Shop's ranges of toiletries and cosmetics and made domestic purchasing from deprived regions of the world a feature of Body Shop's marketing activity. Taking a moral stance and demonstrating environmental concern, however, can make the firm a target for detractors. Ben and Jerry's took this route, in sourcing ingredients for their ice cream from community-based suppliers, but when fashions changed and certain ingredients were no longer popular, they were criticised for stopping supply arrangements with community groups.

Local subcontractors to original equipment manufacturers (OEMs) fall into this category, as their international market potential is derived entirely from being a member of the OEM's supply chain. Whilst for the manufacturer or supplier domestic purchasing could hardly be called an entry strategy, it does provide the firm with access to and limited knowledge of international markets. However, the supplying organisation is able to exert little control over the choice of markets and the strategies adopted in marketing its products. Small firms find that this is the easiest method of obtaining foreign sales but, being totally dependent on the purchaser, they are unlikely to be aware of a change in consumer behaviour and competitor activity or of the purchasing firm's intention to terminate the arrangement. Illustration 7.1 shows how Chinese manufacturers are gaining sales in developed countries.

ILLUSTRATION 7.1

SOURCE: ADAPTED FROM M. SHERIDAN, THE CROWN JEWELS OF THE CHINA TRADER, *SUNDAY TIMES*, 18 FEBRUARY, 2007

In search of the 99p bargain

One of the fastest-growing markets is the world is the single price item. Supermarkets around the world want to sell items for 99p, 99 cents, 100 yen or one euro and some shops are set up just to sell these items. Consumers want to buy cheap 'things' – things that when you get them home you realise you should not have bought – but console yourself that they were cheap. Low income groups see the items as necessary, high income groups see them as amusing.

The source of the 'things' is China and the hundreds of thousands of factories that are listed on Alibaba.com and MadeInChina.com that make toys, trivia and accessories, usually from plastic. Buyers from importers, distributors and agencies scour the factories or go to the 'biggest wholesale market in the world' at Yiwu, where 100 000 businesses are represented, doing deals at high speed and expecting the vast orders to be shipped within 30 days. The calculation works in sterling as follows. Of the 99p, 17.3p will go in VAT and the supermarket will keep 81.7 pence. To make their profit margin the supermarket will want to buy the product at 45p from the importer, who will want to buy the products landed in the UK at 31.5p. When shipping, customs duties, insurance and unloading are taken off, the products must be bought 'free on board' for 22p from the supplier. Typically raw materials would cost around 15.5p leaving the factors 6.5p to cover wages, overheads and wafer-thin profits, meaning of course that very low wages are paid and even big percentage increases in wages will not make very much difference to the costs.

There are many stories of buyers making huge sums of money through 'kickbacks' (bribes from the supplier), frauds when a supplier has taken money for orders and disappeared and goods that are short, defective, broken or dangerous.

QUESTION *What advice would you give to the factories to enable them to improve their performance and growth prospects?*

If a company is intent upon seeking longer-term viability for its export business it must adapt a more proactive approach, which will inevitably involve obtaining a greater understanding of the markets in which their products are sold. This can happen if prompted by a change of management or ownership.

Export management companies or export houses

Export houses or export marketing companies (EMCs) are specialist companies set up to act as the export department for a range of companies. They can help small and medium-sized companies to initiate, develop and maintain their international sales. As well as taking orders from foreign buyers, they provide indirect access to international market information and contacts. By offering ranges of products from various companies they provide a more attractive overall sales package to foreign buyers, and by carrying a large range they can spread selling and administration costs over more products and companies, and reduce transport costs because of the economies of making larger shipments of goods from a number of companies.

EMCs deal with the necessary documentation and their knowledge of local purchasing practices and government regulations is particularly useful in markets that might prove difficult to penetrate. The use of EMCs, therefore, allows individual companies to gain far wider exposure of their products in foreign markets at much lower overall costs than they could achieve on their own, but there are a number of disadvantages too. The export house may specialise by geographical area, product or customer type (retail, industrial or institutional) and this may not coincide with the suppliers' objectives. As a result of this, the selection of markets may be made on the basis of what is best for the EMC rather than the manufacturer. As EMCs are paid by commission, they might be tempted to concentrate upon products with immediate sales potential rather than those that might require greater customer education and sustained marketing effort to achieve success in the longer term. EMCs may also be tempted to carry too many product ranges and as a result the manufacturer's products may not be given the necessary attention from sales people. The EMC may also carry competitive products which they promote preferentially, again to the disadvantage of a particular firm.

Manufacturers should, therefore, take care in selecting a suitable EMC and be prepared to devote resources to managing the relationship and monitoring their performance. The firm must also take the time to learn more about the markets in which their products are being sold in order to ensure that opportunities to sell products into new markets are not being missed by the EMC.

As sales increase, the manufacturer may feel that they could benefit from increased involvement in international markets by exporting directly themselves. However, the transition may not be very easy. First, the firm is likely to have become very dependent on the export house and unless steps have been taken to build contacts with foreign customers and increase their knowledge of the markets, moving away from using EMCs could prove difficult. Second, the firm could find it difficult to withdraw from its contractual commitments to the export house. This often happens when firms are first setting up the arrangement because they are unable to predict the kind of relationship they would like to have with the EMC some time in the future. Many agreements, therefore, are based only on the current and short-term situation. Third, the EMC may be able to substitute products from an alternative manufacturer and so use their customer contacts as a basis for introducing new competition against the original manufacturer.

E-business was expected to have a very significant adverse effect on EMCs and even threaten their survival. However, in assessing the impact of e-business Varinder (2005) found that by linking e-business with their market-based assests, EMCs could still play an efficient and effective role.

Piggybacking

In **piggybacking**, an established international distribution network of one manufacturer might be used to carry the products of a second manufacturer. The second manufacturer is able to ride on the back of the existing reputation, contacts and administration of the carrier with little direct investment themselves. Terpstra and Yu (1990) explain that this makes a particularly effective way for firms from developing countries to break into markets in developed countries.

The carrier is either paid by commission and so acts as an agent, or alternatively, buys the product outright and so acts as an independent distributor. There are also advantages in piggybacking for the carrier as they are able first, to carry a wider product range and so present a more attractive sales package to potential buyers and second, to benefit from economies of scale by increasing their revenue without incurring additional costs of marketing, selling administration and distribution.

There can, however, be problems as the terms and conditions of the marketing arrangements are often poorly thought out because piggybacking often starts on a 'try it and see' basis. Either company might become locked into an arrangement that proves unsatisfactory for them, particularly as a firm's strategic objectives change over a period of time. Decisions about such marketing mix issues as branding might not suit both companies, and arrangements for providing technical support and service for products often prove to be a source of disagreement and difficulty.

For smaller firms, piggybacking can work when two products are interdependent, or if the second product provides a service for the first. Larger companies, too, have found it successful, particularly when the rider has experienced some kind of barrier to entering particular markets, or the use of an existing distribution network can provide faster market development.

A form of piggybacking occurs when an MNE moves into an emerging market. This provides the opportunity for their key suppliers, such as advertising, market research and consultancy companies, to set up local offices there.

Trading companies

Trading companies are part of the historical legacy from the colonial days and although different in nature now, they are still important trading forces in Africa and Asia. The United Africa Company, part of Unilever, for example, was once claimed to be the largest trader in Africa and the *Sogo shosha* have traditionally played an important role in Japanese international business although, as Illustration 7.2 shows, different patterns of business activity could result in them becoming less significant in some sectors.

The success of trading companies is the result of building long-term relationships over many years. This is the experience in the US where export trading companies have been permitted only since 1982 and were slow to get off the ground.

One of the major benefits of using trading houses is that their extensive operations and contacts allow them to operate in more difficult trading areas. One important aspect of their operations is to manage countertrade activities, in which sales into one market are paid for by taking other products from that market in exchange. The essential role of the trading company is to quickly find a buyer for the products that have been taken in exchange.

Indirect exporting is often a small company's first experience of international marketing: it has the advantages of being a simple and low-cost method of gaining exposure of products in foreign markets without the company first having to gain the necessary expertise in the various aspects of international trading. However, the company has little control over its international marketing activities and is restricted to simply reacting to new situations and opportunities as they arise. It is extremely difficult to build up international marketing knowledge and expertise by marketing at arm's length, or to develop any significant long-term product and promotional strategies. Moreover, because of the lack of direct contact between the firm and the market, indirect entry approaches are usually perceived as lacking long-term commitment. As a result, customers and other members of the distribution channels are likely to withhold their full commitment to the firm and its products until the firm becomes more involved in the market, by adopting a more direct approach.

ILLUSTRATION 7.2

The future of *Sogo shosha*

In Japan after the Second World War, the dominant industrial powers that emerged tended to be the *keiretsu* (industrial groups), which grew out of the pre-war conglomerates, and the *zaibatsu* (financial cliques) such as Mitsui, Mitsubishi, Sumimoto and Yasuda. These had evolved from family business empires and government favour and were a key part of the government's expansion abroad. Each *zaibatsu/keiretsu* has its own *Sogo shosha* (trading company) which in the seventeenth century were simple import–export businesses. Their influence was enormous because their employees, 'shosha-men', spent years overseas developing their expertise. For example, it was suggested that during the Gulf War the Japanese foreign ministry relied on these contacts rather than its own diplomatic sources. The *Sogo shosha* played a major role, for example, in facilitating the relocation of Japanese production facilities by developing industrial parks in Thailand, Indonesia, Philippines, Myanmar and Vietnam with distribution centres for suppliers and finished goods.

PHOTO CREDIT: TORU YAMANAKA/GETTY IMAGES

At the height of their power the *Sogo shosha* wielded great power: for example, in 1991 they accounted for 43 per cent of Japan's exports and 79 per cent of imports. Now things are changing. The top five, Mitsubishi, Mitsui, Sumimoto, Itochu and Marabeni, are still major players but are having to restructure and embark on joint ventures to maintain their position. Under great pressure from the government and banks they are having to get rid of non-performing assets, to partner with other firms and to cut costs. Because they are trading companies their gross turnover is huge but their profits are very thin. Some estimates suggest that up to 30 per cent of a *Sogo shosha*'s subsidiaries and ventures could be loss-making at any one time. They suffered in the 1990s due to the long recession in the Japanese economy, where they conduct 50 per cent of their transactions. The need for Japanese companies to adopt global standards in management and more transparent accounting procedures led to harder decisions being taken on loss-making subsidiaries. The problem was that Japanese employers were reluctant to sack workers in large numbers, especially when this might lead to sacking staff in other firms with which they were closely tied.

The pressure was greater for the smaller *Sogo shosha*. The sixth and eighth largest, Nissho Iwai and Nichimen, merged with the loss of 4000 jobs. This was a big shock for the *shosha*-men: until a few years ago, like lawyers and doctors, being a *shosha*-man was a very honourable lifetime career for a university graduate.

The *Sogo shosha* have a history of reinventing themselves when it has become necessary. However, the main problem they are facing is caused by the change in business practice. For example, Nippon Steel bought from all the *Sogo shosha* to maintain good relations, but have now cut suppliers and buy in greater volumes at lower prices. Moreover, e-commerce has the potential to cut out the intermediary's role altogether.

QUESTION *What must they do to survive?*

SOURCE: ADAPTED FROM S. KAWAKAMI 'GOODBYE TO THE GLORY DAYS', FEBRUARY 2003, WWW.JAPANINC.NET

DIRECT EXPORTING

If a company wishes to secure a more permanent long-term place in international markets, it must become more proactive through becoming directly involved in the process of exporting. Indeed exporting is the most popular approach for firms as it requires less resources, has little effect on existng operation and involves low investment and financial risks (Leonidou, Katsikeas and Samiee (2002)). However, this requires definite commitment from the company and takes the form of investment in the international operation through allocating time and resources to a number of supporting activities. The key components of the export marketing mix are summarised in Figure 7.3.

The benefits of direct over indirect exporting are that the proactive approach makes it easier to exert more influence over international activities, resulting in a number of specific advantages for the exporter such as greater control over the selection of markets, greater control over the elements of the marketing mix, improved feedback about the performance of individual products, changing situations in individual markets and competitor activity and the opportunity to build up expertise in international marketing.

The disadvantages of direct exporting are that the direct investment necessary is considerable because the whole of the marketing, distribution and administration costs will now be borne by the company. In taking this decision, the company must be quite sure that the costs can be justified in the light of the market opportunities identified.

Illustration 7.3 shows how an exporter from an emerging market has eliminated competition in a global market.

For those firms wishing to change from indirect to direct exporting or to significantly increase their marketing efforts the timing can be critical, as the extra costs involved can often place a huge financial burden on the company. The solution to this is, wherever possible, to make the transition gradually and in a well-planned way, starting with a beachhead or initial landing in the foreign market.

Factors for success in exporting

A considerable amount of research has been carried out into the barriers and motivations for new exporters and the stages of internationalisation, and we discussed this in Chapter 5.

Katsikeas, Leonidou and Morgan (2000) concluded that the way exporting performance is assessed is important. The simplest measure is whether firms do or do not export. Measurement of the financial performance, of the firm in terms of export sales volume, growth and profitability, and the ratio of export to total sales is useful to measure longitudinal firm performance, but is less useful for

FIGURE 7.3
The components of the export marketing mix

Product:	selection, development and sourcing
Pricing:	policy, strategies, discount structures and trading terms
Promotion:	corporate promotions and local selling, trade shows and literature
Distribution:	sales force management, agents, distributors and logistics
Services:	market research, training and sales servicing
Finance and administration:	budgets, order processing, insurance and credit control
Technical:	specifications, testing and product quality

comparing firm performance between industry sectors because the industry sectors may be structured quite differently. Subjective measurements of the performance of the management of the firm are often helpful but pose a problem, too, in their comparability between firms and sectors.

Katsikeas *et al.* did, however, conclude that a number of factors were important in contributing to successful exporting:

- commitment of the firms' management
- an exporting approach in the firm which emphasised the importance of augmenting and maintaining skills
- a good marketing information and communication system
- sufficient production capacity and capability, product superiority and competitive pricing
- effective market research to reduce the psychic distance between the home country and target country market given that it is knowledge that generates business opportunities and drives the international process
- an effective national export policy which provides support at an individual firm level, and emphasises the need for knowledge-based programmes which prioritise market information about foreign market opportunities.

ILLUSTRATION 7.3

High-flying Brazilian exporter

Asked to name the product made by Brazil's top value private sector exporter for three years up to 2001, some readers might suggest soccer players and others brazil nuts! (In fact your Brazil nuts are more likely to originate from Bolivia.) The answer is aircraft from Embraer. This is surprising, especially as North American and European manufacturers, such as Boeing and Airbus, dominate the global market for aircraft. Embraer has demolished its opposition to become the fourth-largest commercial airline manufacturer.

The origins of the Brazilian aircraft industry, however, go back a long way. Whilst the Wright brothers' flight in 1903 was not witnessed and recorded by the authorities, the powered

flight three years later by the Brazilian Alberto Santos Dumont in the Bois de Boulogne near Paris was. (Consequently many Brazilians believe that they really invented powered flight.)

Inspired by Santos Dumont, the country has become a leader in small, 30 to 50 seat regional jets that are necessary in a country larger in size than the US. The firm was set up in 1969 as a state industry with a mix of domestic and foreign investment. Despite the scepticism – even from Brazilians – the firm has thrived. There used to be nine manufacturers in the market but now only Bombardier Aerospace of Canada is a competitor. A number of well-known producers of small planes have gone out of production including Fairchild Dornier (US–Germany), British Aerospace (UK), Fokker (Netherlands), Saab (Sweden) and Shorts (UK). At the same time Embraer has developed exports worldwide and even sold products to its Canadian rival.

How did Embraer succeed? The company had vision and a degree of luck and ignored turbo-propeller planes, which effectively died in the 1990s. Instead it went straight to producing jets, which were ideal for the growing air travel market in the US, especially since it was deregulated. It employs 19 000 people and its production facilities are midway between Rio and São Paulo and probably just as sophisticated as Boeing and Airbus. As part of its growth plans Embraer has launched a 70-seater plane which can compete with the smaller aircraft in the Airbus range.

QUESTION *What makes an exporter from an emerging market successful against worldwide competition?*

SOURCE: ADAPTED FROM J. WALTERS 'BRAZIL'S WINGED VICTORY', *OBSERVER*, 8 DECEMBER, 2002

They found that the cost of export planning incurred by the firm did not correlate with export performance, and suggested that this might be explained by the fact that a major source of strength in exporting is flexibility and adaptability to export opportunities and the ability to make an immediate strategic response. Moreover, firm size and the managers' experience were not critical factors in export success, but they did recognise that these factors may be the source of the export stimuli in the first place, and could be major determinants of the firm's commitment to exporting and its ability to solve problems.

It is generally accepted, therefore, that in small business, attitudes and commitment to international expansion are crucial for success, whereas in larger companies other factors can have a bearing on performance. The size of a company can either hinder or encourage international development because of the variations in the capability of the staff for planning, the lack of consistency of information and the degree to which adaptation of the mix is necessary. A number of other factors, such as the types of strategies that are pursued, segmentation, product and pricing can also affect export success.

International marketing of services is more fully explored in Chapter 8, but early stage exporting of services is different from exporting of products. Styles, Patterson and La (2005) found there is limited research into the unique success factors in the sector but report some key success factors, emphasising appropriate use of the tangible and intangible assets and personnel-related factors where there is high face-to-face contact.

Selection of exporting method

The choice of the specific individual markets for exporting was discussed in the first section of this book, but it is important to re-emphasise that the more subjective factors, such as a senior executive's existing formal or informal links, particular knowledge of culture or language and perceived attractiveness of markets, may well influence an individual firm's decision.

Once individual markets have been selected and the responsibilities for exporting have been allocated, the decision needs to be taken about precisely how the firm should be represented in the new market. Clearly the nature, size and structure of the market will be significant in determining the method adopted. In a large market, particularly if a high level of market knowledge and customer contact is needed, it may be necessary to have a member of the firm's staff resident in or close to the market. This cannot be justified if the market is small or levels of customer contact need not be so high. Alternatively a home-based sales force may be used to make periodic sales trips in conjunction with follow-up communications by telephone, fax and email.

Many other factors will affect the cost–benefit analysis of maintaining the company's own staff in foreign markets, such as whether the market is likely to be attractive in the long term as well as the short term and whether the high cost of installing a member of the firm's own staff will be offset by the improvements in the quality of contacts, market expertise and communications. The alternative, and usually the first stage in exporting, is to appoint an agent or distributor.

Agents

Agents provide the most common form of low-cost direct involvement in foreign markets and are independent individuals or firms who are contracted to act on behalf of exporters to obtain orders on a commission basis. They typically represent a number of manufacturers and will handle non-competitive ranges.

As part of their contract they would be expected to agree sales targets and contribute substantially to the preparation of forecasts, development of strategies and tactics using their knowledge of the local market. Agents do not take ownership of the goods but work instead on commission, sometimes as low as 2–3 per cent on large volume and orders.

The selection of suitable agents or **distributors** can be a problematic process. The selection criteria might include:

- The financial strength of the agents.
- Their contacts with potential customers.
- The nature and extent of their responsibilities to other organisations.
- Their premises, equipment and resources, including sales representatives.

Clearly, the nature of the agreement between the firm and its agent is crucial in ensuring the success of the arrangement, particularly in terms of clarifying what is expected of each party, setting out the basis for the relationships that will be built up and ensuring that adequate feedback on the market and product development is provided.

There are various sources for finding a suitable agent at low cost to the exporter:

- Asking potential customers to suggest a suitable agent.
- Obtaining recommendations from institutions such as trade associations, chambers of commerce and government trade departments.
- Using commercial agencies.
- Using agents for non-competing products.
- Poaching a competitor's agent.
- Advertising in suitable trade papers.

Achieving a satisfactory manufacturer–agent relationship

To achieve success the exporter–agent relationship needs to be managed by:

- Allocating time and resources to finding a suitably qualified agent.
- Ensuring that both the manufacturer and agent understand what each expects of the other.
- Ensuring that the agent is motivated to improve performance.
- Providing adequate support on a continuing basis including training, joint promotion and developing contacts.
- Ensuring that there is sufficient advice and information transfer in both directions.

Distributors

Distributors buy the product from the manufacturer, organise selling and distribution and so take the market risk on unsold products as well as the profit. For this reason, they usually expect to take a higher percentage to cover their costs and risk.

Distributors usually seek exclusive rights for a specific sales territory and generally represent the manufacturer in all aspects of sales and servicing in that area. The exclusivity, therefore, is in return for the substantial capital investment that may be required in handling and selling the products. The capital investment can be particularly high if the product requires special handling equipment or transport and storage equipment in the case of perishable goods, chemicals, materials or components.

The issue of agreeing territories is becoming increasingly important as in many markets, distributors are becoming fewer in number, larger in size and sometimes more specialised in their activity. The trend to regionalisation is leading distributors increasingly to extend their territories through organic growth, mergers and acquisitions. Also, within regional trading blocs competition laws are used to avoid exclusive distribution being set up for individual territories. However, the car industry in the EU was allowed to retain exclusive distribution until block exemption was removed in 2002. By this time Mercedes decided to take over its dealerships in order to retain control.

Other direct exporting methods

There are three other modes of exporting which are considered to be direct: management contracts, franchising and direct marketing.

MANAGEMENT CONTRACTS

Management contracts emphasise the growing importance of services, business skills and management expertise as saleable commodities in international trade. Normally the contracts undertaken are concerned with installing management operating and control systems, and training local staff to take over when the contract is completed. Many construction projects, such as the rebuilding of Afghanistan and Iraq, were undertaken in this way.

Other examples of management contracts may be as part of a deal to sell a processing plant as a turnkey operation, in which the capital plant and a management team are provided by the firm to set up and run the plant for the first few months of operation, and then train the local team to take over. With increased privatisation and outsourcing of facilities management by public and private sector organisations there is a substantial growth in management contracts and in firms providing these services.

FRANCHISING

Franchising is a means of marketing goods and services in which the franchiser grants the legal right to use branding, trademarks and products, and the method of operation is transferred to a third party – the franchisee – in return for a franchise fee. The franchiser provides assistance, training and help with sourcing components, and exercises significant control over the franchisee's method of operation. It is considered to be a relatively less risky business start-up for the franchisee but still harnesses the motivation, time and energy of the people who are investing their own capital in the business. For the franchiser it has a number of advantages, including the opportunity to build greater market coverage and obtain a steady, predictable stream of income without requiring excessive investment.

Chan (1994) identifies two types of franchise. With product/trade franchises, for example car dealerships, petrol service stations and soft drinks bottlers, the franchisees are granted the right to distribute a manufacturer's product in a specified territory. Business format franchise is the growing sector and includes many types of businesses, including restaurants, convenience stores and hotels. This type of franchise includes the licensing of a trademark and the system for operating the business, and the appearance of the location.

Franchising can take the form of single-unit franchising in which the arrangement is made with a single franchisee, or multi-unit in which the franchisee, operates more than one unit. The multi-unit franchisee may be given the responsibility for developing a territory and opening a specified number of units alone or, as is common in international markets, operating a master franchise, in which the master franchisee can subfranchise to others. In this case the master franchisee is responsible for collecting the fees, enforcing the agreement and providing the necessary services, such as training and advice.

Franchising grew rapidly during the 1990s (Welch 1992) due to the strong interest in a variety of franchise formats. Trading companies have frequently been appointed as master franchisees and, whilst this has helped to accelerate the growth of franchising, it has also influenced the franchiser's internationalisation process. Because of the global power of these trading companies they are able to challenge the franchiser's decisions in the franchise process and have a considerable say in the strategic development of the business. As competition has increased in franchising so more franchisers, such as Pizza Hut in Australia, have resorted to acquisition of existing chains of similar businesses for conversion to the new franchise.

Welch comments that there is increasing evidence that franchisees, either individually or collectively, are prepared to resort to legal action to control the franchisers' activities when they are considered harmful to their own interests, because they realise that it is not usually in the franchisers' interests to go to court, given the likely adverse publicity. The Arby restaurant chain in the US, Burger King, Benetton, the Italian clothing group and Body Shop, the UK toiletries retailer, have all experienced problems with franchisees.

There are also differences in the way local culture affects franchise operations, and one of the main problems for franchisers is deciding to what extent the franchise format should be modified to take account of local demands and expectations; for example, McDonald's have added spaghetti to the menu to compete more effectively with Jollibee in the Philippines, Pizza Hut find that corn and not pepperoni sells well in Japan and KFC find that gravy, peas and pumpkin are popular in Australia.

For hotel franchises brand management is a key part of the operation and *The Economist* (2006) notes that 40 years after Conrad Hilton sold off the Hilton International Division from the US operation, the two companies merged again their 2800 hotels in 80 countries (they had merged their reward and reservation systems in 1997). Most US hotels are part of branded groups but considerable scope exists in China and India, where hotels remain independent. The group sells off hotels to investment companies but offers franchises and management contracts to ensure a steady flow of bookings.

DIRECT MARKETING

Direct marketing is concerned with marketing and selling activities which do not depend for success on direct face-to-face contact, this includes mail order, telephone marketing, television marketing, media marketing, direct mail and electronic commerce using the Internet. We discuss e-commerce developments more fully in Chapter 12. There is considerable growth in all these areas, largely encouraged by increased availability of information and processes for analysing it, the development of information and communication technology, the changing lifestyles and purchasing behaviour of consumers and the increasing cost of more traditional methods of entering new markets. The critical success factors for direct marketing are in the standardisation of the product coupled with the personalisation of the communication. Whilst technical data about the product might be available in one language, often English, the recipients of the direct marketing in international markets expect to receive accurate communications in their domestic language. International direct marketing, therefore, poses considerable challenges, such as the need to build and maintain up-to-date databases, use sophisticated multilingual data processing and personalisation software programs, develop reliable credit control and secure payment systems.

However, it also offers advantages. Whereas American firms have had trouble breaking into the Japanese market, catalogue firms have been highly successful because they are positioned as good value for money for well-known clothing brands, compared to Japanese catalogues which are priced higher for similar quality items.

Direct marketing techniques can also be used to support traditional methods of marketing by providing sales leads, maintaining contact or simply providing improved customer service through international call centres. Where multiple direct channels are used for market entry, it is the integration of channels through effective customer relationship management systems that is essential to ensure customer satisfaction.

FOREIGN MANUFACTURING STRATEGIES WITHOUT DIRECT INVESTMENT

Having so far considered market entry strategies that have been based upon the development, manufacture and supply of products and services from the firms' domestic operations, we now turn our attention to strategies which involve production and service supply from overseas plants. Before discussing the alternatives available for ownership and control of overseas operations, it is necessary to consider the factors which may lead a firm to start having its products and services produced in one or more of its international markets.

Reasons for setting up overseas manufacture and service operations

The benefits of overseas manufacturing and service operations are:

Product. Avoiding problems due to the nature of the product, such as perishability.

Services that are dependent for success on local intellectual property, knowledge and sensitivity to the local market.

Transporting and warehousing. The cost of transporting heavy, bulky components and finished products over long distances is reduced.

Tariff barriers/quotas. Barriers to trade, which make the market inaccessible, are reduced.

Government regulations. Entry to some markets, such as central and Eastern Europe, are difficult unless accompanied by investment in local operations.

Market. Local manufacture and service operations may be viewed more favourably by customers.

Government contacts. Firms are likely to be viewed more favourably if they contribute more to the local economy.

Information. A strong local presence improves the quality of market feedback.

International culture. Local presence encourages a more international outlook and ensures greater commitment by the firm to international markets.

Delivery. Local manufacture and service operations can facilitate faster response and just-in-time delivery.

Labour costs. Production, distribution and service centres can be moved to lower labour cost markets provided there are appropriate skills and adequate information technology infrastructure to maintain satisfactory quality.

For most companies, the cost of setting up an overseas operation is initially much higher than expanding the domestic facility by an equivalent amount, as we indicated earlier in this chapter. Whilst the equipment costs are likely to be similar, and other costs such as labour, land purchase and building may even be cheaper, it is the cost involved in transferring technology, skills and knowledge that normally proves to be expensive and often underestimated.

For many firms, transferring operations from a domestic to an overseas plant also immediately reduces the demand on the home plant, which might have traditionally supplied all the firm's overseas markets. In response to this reduced demand on the domestic plant, the firm must plan either to reduce the capacity of the domestic plant quickly or find new business to replace the production that has been transferred, otherwise the viability of the domestic plant might be put at risk. Whereas the expansion of existing plants can often be achieved in an incremental way, setting up new plants overseas involves large cash outflows and can put a significant strain on the firms' finances. Poor planning, underestimation of costs or unforeseen problems associated with setting up a plant overseas have frequently caused businesses to fail or be vulnerable to takeover. Moreover, if the overseas plant ultimately fails and the firm finds it necessary to reduce its commitment in the market, it may find that its reputation has been severely damaged.

Whilst the most common reason in the past has related to the nature of the product and been particularly concerned with locating the manufacturing plant close to the market, increasingly it is the costs of manufacture (including labour, raw materials and government support) as well as the costs of transport and being 'close to the market' that are likely to influence the decision about which country location to choose. For many firms, setting up foreign country operations for market entry reasons has prompted them to review their business and frequently resulted in them closing down their domestic operation and transferring labour-intensive activity to lower labour-cost countries.

Regionalisation is also having a significant effect on plant location; for example, in the car industry location decisions are being based on a variety of factors, such as the participation of the country in monetary union, the different levels of productivity and the need to be closer to the most attractive potential markets. Mexico has expanded its car manufacturing business within NAFTA. Hutton (2006) observed that Eastern Europe has become the new Detroit: General Motors, Volkswagen, Audi, Renault Daewoo, Suzuki, Toyota, Peugeot, Hyundai, Skoda and Kia all have factories there. Interestingly South Korean firms are looking to 'make where they sell' to avoid paying tariffs and high transport costs, but Kia noted that wage rates in Slovenia were one-fifth of those in South Korea.

Having emphasised that a move into overseas manufacturing and service operations involves high cost and risk, firms can choose between different levels of financial commitment. They can, for example, embark upon foreign manufacturing strategies which do not involve direct investment, such as contract manufacture and licensing agreements, or strategies which do involve direct investment albeit at different levels of cost and risk, for example, assembly operations, wholly-owned subsidiary, company acquisition, joint venture and strategic alliances.

Contract manufacture

A firm which markets and sells products into international markets might arrange for a local manufacturer to produce the product for them under contract. Examples include Nike and Gap, both of whom use contract clothing and shoe manufacturers in lower labour-cost countries. The advantage of arranging contract manufacture is that it allows the firm to concentrate upon its sales and marketing activities and, because investment is kept to a minimum, it makes withdrawal relatively easy and less costly if the product proves to be unsuccessful.

Contract manufacture might be necessary in order to overcome trade barriers and sometimes it is the only way to gain entry to a country in which the government attempts to secure local employment by insisting on local production. If political instability makes foreign investment unwise, this may be the best way of achieving a marketing presence without having the risk of a large investment in manufacturing. The disadvantage of contract manufacture as an entry method is that it does not allow the buyer control over the manufacturer's activities. In the brewing industry there are a variety of arrangements where brewers contract the manufacture of beer brands but other market entry methods are used by the beer brand owners to increase market share, as Dilemma 7.1 shows.

Outsourcing from contract manufacturers allows firms such as Sara Lee to be very flexible by supplying differentiated food products for different regional markets and adjusting costs more quickly when necessary. It also has the financial benefit of lower capital employed, but the risks are that the local contractor may not achieve the desired quality levels or may gain the necessary knowledge to market the product themselves and compete directly with the international marketer. The marketing firm has less control over the conditions in the factory (intentionally or unintentionally). Some years ago Nike and Gap had bad publicity with the sweatshop conditions in plants it has used in Asia. As a result they had to sever contracts with plants which refused to comply with company standards for wage levels, working conditions and the use of child labour.

Two Scottish companies, Young's and Dawnfresh, provide further examples of contract manufacture. They are processors and marketers of shellfish caught in Scottish waters. However, both companies announced in 2006 that they were closing their processing plants in Scotland with the resulting loss of 190 jobs. Young's decided to ship 120 000 tonnes of scampi 12 000 miles to Thailand for

DILEMMA 7.1

Global marketing or local heritage

SOURCE: ADAPTED FROM 'SEEKING NEW BEER DRINKERS IN THE HIGH ANDES', THE ECONOMIST, 20 JULY, 2005

Faced with slowing or even stagnant growth of beer sales in developed countries a number of the largest brewers in the world have increased their involvement in developing markets, using a variety of market entry arrangements. China's beer market is the largest and growing at 6–8 per cent per year and Anheuser Busch, the world's third largest brewer, best known for its top-selling Budweiser, bought China's fourth largest brewer, outbidding rival SABMiller, in 2005, having already moved to increase its stake in Tsingtao to 27 per cent.

Anheuser also owns over 50 per cent of Grupo Modelo of Mexico, best known for its Corona brand, which is exported to 150 countries. South America and Russia are also fast-growing beer markets. SABMiller moved into second place when it bought Bavaria, a Colombian firm with strong sales in South America, behind InBev, which was created when Belgium's Interbrew bought Brazil's Ambev. Inbev had recently bought Russia's Tinkoff. In the early 1990s the world's top five brewers accounted for 15 per cent of world beer sales, but they were expected to reach 50 per cent by 2010.

The problem is that there is no 'Coca-Cola' of the beer industry and drinkers often remain loyal to their local brands, particularly in emerging markets. It is the younger generations that start to drink more premium international brands, and only as the countries become more prosperous.

The dilemma is whether to invest in local beer brands or build the premium international brands.

peeling before they make the return journey. Dawnfresh shipped its scampi to China for peeling.

Licensing

Licensing also requires relatively low levels of investment. Organisations involved in the film, television and sports industries, as diverse as Disney, the Olympic Games Committee and Manchester United Football Club, have been particularly successful in licensing the use of brands, characters and themes, generating huge sales of licensed products (an example appears in Illustration 7.4). It is a form of management contract in which the licenser confers to the licensee the right to use one or more of the following: patent rights, trademark rights, copyrights and/or product or process know-how. In some situations, the licensor may continue to sell essential components or services to the licensee as part of the agreement.

There are a number of reasons why licensing is a useful entry method. Financial and management commitments can be kept low, the high cost of setting up a manufacturing, retailing or marketing subsidiary can be reduced and tariff and non-tariff barriers can be avoided. Licensing is particularly useful, therefore, to deal with difficult markets where direct involvement would not be possible, and where the market segments to be targeted may not be sufficiently large for full involvement.

Licensing usually has a number of benefits for the licenser. The licensee pays for the licence normally as a percentage of sales and thus, as the sales grow, so does the revenue to the licenser. Considerable control exists as the licensee uses the rights or know-how in an agreed way for an agreed quantity of product, and the licensee markets and purchases products for an agreed fee.

For the licensee, there are a number of advantages. For a relatively low outlay, it is possible to capitalise on established know-how with little risk and avoid the

ILLUSTRATION 7.4

Mr Men: a licence to storm the US market

To succeed in the US$2 billion global children's television market it is necessary to succeed in the US, the single largest territory.

PHOTO CREDIT: THE PHOTOLIBRARY WALES/ALAMY

After that Japan, France, and Germany are big markets too. British programme makers are fortunate having a common language with the US, but the most successful formats transcend language barriers. *Teletubbies* achieved sales of US$1 billion, making more money for the BBC than any other programme. A key part of marketing is to generate license fees from associated merchandise. More than 90 per cent of the income from *Bob the Builder*, owned by Hit, came from spin-off toys, clothes, DVDs and CDs.

Chlorian are spending £5 million creating and marketing a new *Mr Men* series in the US. Roger Hargreaves created 73 Mr Men and Little Miss characters to explain particular emotions to his children. There are some changes, with Mr Grumpy having his hat and nose tweaked, Mr Strong getting Arnold Swarzenegger pecs and, of course, all the characters getting American accents. This may not go down too well with British viewers, who will also be able to see the new series.

QUESTION *What are the most appropriate situations for licensing?*

SOURCE: ADAPTED FROM M. GOODMAN 'MR MEN TAKE ON AMERICAN TELEVISION', *SUNDAY TIMES*, 15 APRIL, 2007

high research and development cost associated with launching a new product in many markets. This is particularly important in the industrial market, for example, where licensing of proven technology enables companies to enter markets with products which would be prohibitively expensive to develop.

Problems can occur in licensing if the licenser does not respond to changes in the market or technology, or does not help to develop the market for the licensee. A very capable licensee may have learned so much about the market and product that the contribution from the licenser is no longer required. The licensee too may either be unwilling or unable to develop the market in the way that the licenser would wish. These sources of conflict often arise as a result of the environment, competitors and market demand changing over the licensing period.

Sarathy *et al.* (2006) identify a number of techniques that can be adopted in order to minimise the potential problems of licensing:

- develop a clear policy and plan
- allocate licensing responsibility to a senior manager
- select licensees carefully
- draft the agreement carefully to include duration, royalties, trade secrets, quality control and performance measures
- supply the critical ingredients
- obtain equity in the licensee
- limit the product and territorial coverage
- retain patents, trademarks, copyrights
- be an important part of the licensee's business.

FOREIGN MANUFACTURING STRATEGIES WITH DIRECT INVESTMENT

At some point in its international development, a stage is reached when the pressure increases upon a firm to make a much more substantial commitment to an individual market or region. The reasons for investment in local operations are:

- *To gain new business*. Local production demonstrates strong commitment and is the best way to persuade customers to change suppliers, particularly in industrial markets where service and reliability are often the main factors when making purchasing decisions.
- *To defend existing business*. Car imports to a number of countries are subject to restrictions and as their sales increase, so they become more vulnerable to locally produced competitive products.
- *To move with an established customer*. Component suppliers or service providers often set up their own local subsidiaries in order to retain their existing business, compete with local component makers and benefit from increased sales.
- *To save costs*. By locating production facilities overseas, costs can be saved in a variety of areas such as labour, raw materials and transport.
- *To avoid government restrictions* which might be in force to restrict imports of certain goods.

For most multi-nationals operating a global or multidomestic strategy, there is a strong requirement to demonstrate that they have a permanent presence in all their major markets. The actual form of their operations in each market is likely to vary considerably from country to country, with the largest multi-national companies operating many variants.

Increasingly multi-nationals are seeking to reduce their own manufacturing and operations costs and investments through making the supply chain more cost-effective. This takes a number of different forms. Some firms, for example, in the shoe and footwear industries obtain component or finished product supplies from the lowest labour cost areas; Ford locates its component suppliers on a manufacturing campus close to its assembly plants.

Assembly

A foreign owned operation might be set up simply to assemble components which have been manufactured in the domestic market. It has the advantage of reducing the effect of tariff barriers, which are normally lower on components than on finished goods. It is also advantageous if the product is large and transport costs are high, for example in the case of cars. There are other benefits for the firm too, as retaining component manufacture in the domestic plant allows development and production skills and investment to be concentrated, thus maintaining the benefit from economies of scale. By contrast, the assembly plant can be made a relatively simple activity requiring low levels of local management, engineering skills and development support.

There is an argument that assembly plants do not contribute significantly to the local economy in the long term. In initially attracting Nissan, Honda and Toyota assembly plants, the UK government claimed that many jobs would be created at relatively low cost but critics claimed that the number of jobs created in the assembly plants was not very significant and, unless the components were made locally, little transfer of technology would be achieved and the assembly plants could relatively easily be moved to a new location. In practice as other car manufacturers withdrew from the UK market these Japanese manufacturers became the only major established firms. Both to counter threats such as this and also to generate further employment, countries can take steps to develop the component supply business either by interrupting the component supply chain through imposition of import or foreign exchange rate restrictions or, as in the case of CzechInvest, the inward investment arm of the Czech Republic, by supporting local component manufacturers who can supply 'just in time'. For the international firm, of course, using the assembly option presents an opportunity to move plant from country to country in order to take advantage of lower wage costs and government incentives.

Tait (1997) suggests that one of the considerations of local assembly plants is that costings can be subject to rapid change and global companies investing in them may need to think how quickly they can pull out. Companies typically select a number of regional manufacturing bases which are viewed as longer-term investments useful for testing product innovation, and supplement them with lower skilled assembly plants which can be easily moved between markets. For example, Whirlpool have two microwave plants, one acquired when it took control of Philips European domestic appliance businesses in Sweden, which drives product development, and the other added later in China, which manufactures competitively for Asian customers and is used for exporting into developed markets.

Wholly-owned subsidiary

As we indicated in Figure 7.2 at the start of the chapter, for any firm the most expensive method of market entry is likely to be the development of its own foreign subsidiary, as this requires the greatest commitment in terms of management time and resources. It can only be undertaken when demand for the market appears to be assured.

This market entry method indicates that the firm is taking a long-term view, especially if full manufacturing facilities are developed rather than simply setting up an assembly plant. Even greater commitment is shown when the R & D facilities are established in local countries too. If the company believes its products have long-term market potential in a relatively politically stable country then only full ownership will provide the level of control necessary to fully meet the firm's strategic marketing objectives. There are considerable risks too, as subsequent withdrawal from the market can be extremely costly, not simply in terms of financial outlay, but also in terms of the firm's reputation in the international and domestic market, particularly with shareholders, customers and staff.

Japanese companies have used this strategy in the past to build a powerful presence in international markets over a long period of time. Their patience has been rewarded with high market shares and substantial profits, but this has not been achieved overnight. They have sometimes spent more than five years gaining an understanding of markets, customers and competition, as well as selecting locations for manufacturing, before making a significant move.

Company acquisitions and mergers

In the previous chapters we discussed the role of acquisitions and mergers in achieving globalisation. For many Western companies, particularly those from the UK and US, the considerable pressure to produce short-term profits means that speed of market entry is essential and this can be achieved by acquiring an existing company in the market. Amongst other advantages, acquisition gives immediate access to a trained labour force, existing customer and supplier contacts, recognised brands, an established distribution network and an immediate source of revenue. Sometimes organisations do not understand the market sufficiently and do not apply appropriate controls over their acquired business, as Illustration 7.5 shows.

In certain situations acquisition is the only route into a market. This is the case with previously state owned utilities. Many utilities and infrastructure companies in the UK are foreign owned, for example water companies are owned by Australian investment fund Macquarie, Suez, Vivendi and Bouygues (France),

ILLUSTRATION 7.5

SOURCE: P. ALDRICK 'HSBC "TO AXE LOAN ARM CHIEFS", ' DAILY TELEGRAPH, 9 FEBRUARY, 2007

HSBC buying problems in the US

If expansion is too rapid it can cause problems. In February 2007 HSBC announced its first profits warning for 142 years. The unexpected profit underperformance was attributed to

PHOTO CREDIT: FERRUCCIO/ALAMY

Household (renamed HFC) its US subsidiary which was bought for £9 bn in 2003. HSBC had to increase its bad debt provision by £900 million when US borrowers failed to make their mortgage repayments.

HSBC's profits came from the regions of the world as follows.

	Profit to 30 June 2006 US$bn
UK	2.35
Rest of Europe	1.26
Hong Kong	2.65
Rest of Asia	1.65
HFC	2.50
Rest of North America	1.77
South America	0.34

Perhaps most surprisingly, given that HFC was the leading profit generator in the six months to June 2006, was that there was no American representative on HSBC's main board.

QUESTION How can an organisation reduce the risk of new market entry?

Union Fenosa (Spain) and YTL (Malaysia), the British Airports Authority by Ferrovial of Spain and electricity companies by EDF of France.

Sometimes the reasons for international business acquisition are, perhaps, not driven by business logic. There have been a number of takeovers of British premiership football clubs, starting with Roman Abramovitch's purchase of Chelsea – it is questionable whether any will make money. By 2007 Americans George Gillett and Tom Hicks owned Liverpool, the Glazer family owned Manchester United and Randy Lerner owned Aston Villa, the Frenchman Alexandre Gaydamak owned Portsmouth, an Egyptian Mohammed Al Fayed owned Fulham and Icelandic Eggert Magnusson owned West Ham.

An acquisition strategy is based upon the assumption that companies for potential acquisition will be available, but if the choice of companies is limited, the decision may be taken on the basis of expediency rather than suitability. The belief that acquisitions will be a time-saving alternative to waiting for organic growth to take effect may not prove to be true in practice. It can take a considerable amount of time to search and evaluate possible acquisition targets, engage in protracted negotiations and then integrate the acquired company into the existing organisation structure.

Another disadvantage of acquisition is that the acquiring company might take over a demotivated labour force, a poor image and reputation, and out of date products and processes. All of these problems can prove costly and time-consuming to overcome.

Takeover of companies which are regarded as part of a country's heritage can raise considerable national resentment if it seems that they are being taken over by foreign firms. This is often a problem at the time of privatisation, as Illustration 7.6 shows. A country looking to develop its own technology and manufacturing is likely to believe that acquisition of a domestic company by a MNE is not as desirable as the

ILLUSTRATION 7.6

Absolut privatisation in Sweden

A change of government in Sweden, when the Social Democrats lost out to the Alliance for Sweden party, led to a huge privatisation of previously state-owned assets. It was expected that around 50 nationally owned organisations would raise almost US$50 billion. Goldman Sachs, Deutsche Bank and

PHOTO CREDIT: JOHN PHOTOGRAPHER/ALAMY

Morgan Stanley all opened up new offices in Stockholm in anticipation of new fees for banking, legal services and consultancy. Nordea Bank, telecom group TeliaSonera, mortgage lender SBAB and property company Vasakronan will be some of the first candidates. Other future organisations to be privatised include SAS airlines, Svenska Spel (the gambling network) and the pharmacy monopoly Apotoket.

One of the most interesting immediate privatisations is Vin and Sprit, owners of Absolut Vodka, a world-beating brand and world number three in spirits sales. The company was nationalised in 1917 to stop rampant drunkenness and under a string of politician bosses with MPs on the board has performed extremely well, showing real international marketing flair. Absolut's brand was created around an old medical flask spotted in the window of a Stockholm antique shop, and US artist Andy Warhol was persuaded to paint a picture of the bottle with the caption 'Absolut Warhol'.

Of course, privatisation is not welcomed by all Swedes, and some think it a disgrace to let Russian, Chinese or French companies get control of the country's infrastructure and prize assets.

QUESTION *How might the type of ownership of a MNE affect its international marketing performance?*

SOURCE: ROBIN LOWE FROM VARIOUS PUBLIC SOURCES

MNE setting up a local subsidiary. Moreover, acquisition by a large international firm is often associated with job losses and transfer of production facilities overseas. In the past few years there has been considerable debate about acquisition and mergers as a method of achieving rapid expansion. The rationale that is used for acquisition is that an ineffective company can be purchased by a more effective company which will be able, first, to reduce costs, second, improve performance through applying better management skills and techniques and third, build upon the synergy between the two companies and so achieve better results. During the late 1980s many takeovers in the UK and US were financed by huge bank loans justified on the basis that an improvement in future profits would be used to pay the high interest charges. In practice few companies were able to realise the true benefits of synergy. The recession of the new millennium reduced demand, and mergers such as AOL–Time Warner and Daimler-Chrysler (Illustration 7.7) underperformed. Other firms focused on their core business and sold off peripheral activities.

COOPERATIVE STRATEGIES

There are a number of situations in which two or more firms might work together to exploit a new opportunity. The methods that are adopted are joint ventures, strategic alliances and reciprocal ownership, in which two firms hold a stake in each other's business.

Joint ventures

Joint ventures occur when a company decides that shared ownership of a specially set up new company for marketing and/or manufacturing is the most appropriate method of exploiting a business opportunity. It is usually based on the premise that two or more companies can contribute complementary expertise or resources to the joint company, which, as a result, will have a unique competitive advantage

ILLUSTRATION 7.7

Chrysler: dissolving a merger

Mergers and acquisitions often fail to deliver their anticipated potential. Daimler, the German automotive group that own

PHOTO CREDIT: JEFF HAYNES/GETTY IMAGES

Mercedes Benz, bought US group Chrysler in 1998 in one of the most ambitious transatlantic acquisitions ever. Apart from one or two years Daimler failed to turn Chrysler around. As it was about to report another big loss in 2007 the company announced 13 000 job losses, a 15 per cent cut in dealerships and a one in five cut in the product range.

For three decades the big three US automobile manufacturers have failed to compete against low-cost Asian competition and GM was thought to be interested in buying Chrysler in order to remove excess production capacity from the American market. However, the huge pension deficit and mounting healthcare costs for its workers was a significant barrier for any purchaser. The many parties interested in the acquisition included private equity firms but also Hyundai, the South Korean industrial giant.

QUESTION *What might be the reasons for the failure of mergers and what should a new buyer do to try to improve the prospects of success?*

SOURCE: L. ARMITSTEAD AND D. O'CONNELL 'HYUNDAI REVS UP IN RACE FOR CHRYSLER DEAL' SUNDAY TIMES, 18 FEBRUARY, 2007

to exploit. It has typically been used for market entry as Illustration 7.7 shows. Table 7.1 shows the contributions of partners from developed and developing countries.

Whilst two companies contributing complementary expertise might be a significant feature of other entry methods, such as licensing, the difference with joint ventures is that each company takes an equity stake in the newly formed firm. The stake taken by one company might be as low as 10 per cent but this still gives them a voice in the management of the joint venture.

There are a number of reasons given for setting up joint ventures. These include:

- some countries, such as the Philippines, try to restrict foreign ownership

- many firms find that partners in the host country can increase the speed of market entry when good business and government contacts are essential for success

- complementary technology or management skills provided by the partners can lead to new opportunities in existing sectors, such as in multimedia

- global operations in R & D and production are prohibitively expensive, but necessary to achieve competitive advantage.

The main advantages to companies entering joint ventures to achieve market entry in emerging markets are that, first, they have more direct participation in the local market, and thus gain a better understanding of how it works, second, they should be better able to finance and profit from their activities and third, they are able to exert greater control over the operation of the joint venture.

TABLE 7.1 Who provides what in partnerships between firms from developed and developing countries

Developed	Developing
Marketing systems	Customer insights
Brands and communication	Land
Financial management	Buildings and equipment
Forecasting	Distribution networks
Planning	Skills
Technology	Low costs
Information systems	Beneficial wage rates
Capital	
Supply chain management	Tax relief
Know-how	Political connections
Human resources	Neighbouring markets
Financial incentives	

SOURCE: SCHIFFMAN, L. G. AND KANUK, L. L. (2000) *CONSUMER BEHAVIOUR*, PRENTICE HALL

ECONOMIST, 16 NOVEMBER 2006 AND D. LITTERICK 'IBM JOINS CITIGROUP IN CHINA BID', *DAILY TELEGRAPH* 14 NOVEMBER 2006

There are, however, some significant disadvantages of joint ventures as a market entry method. As joint venture companies involve joint ownership, there are often differences in the aims and objectives of the participating companies which can cause disagreements over the strategies adopted by the particular companies. If ownership is evenly divided between the participant firms, these disagreements can often lead to delays and failure to develop clear policies. In some joint ventures the greater motivation of one partner rather than another, particularly if they have a greater equity stake, can lead to them becoming dominant and the other partner becoming resentful.

The other disadvantages of this form of market entry compared to, for example, licensing or the use of agents is that a substantial commitment of investment of capital and management resources must be made in order to ensure success. Many companies would argue that the demands on management time might be even greater for a joint venture than for a directly owned subsidiary because of the need to educate, negotiate and agree with the partner many of the operational details of the joint venture.

Some experts recommend that a joint venture should be used by companies to extend their capabilities rather than merely exploit existing advantages, and is not recommended if there are potential conflicts of interest between partners. The role of the government in joint ventures can be particularly influential, as it may control access to the domestic market. Moreover, a government may be persuaded to adapt its policy if a firm is bringing in advanced technology or is willing to make a major investment. Most of the major multi-nationals have increased their involvement in joint ventures, but the implications of this are that it leads to increasingly decentralised management and operations, more closely aligned to transnational operation than to global standardisation, in which more centralised control is necessary. Illustration 7.8 shows how IBM is trying to gain access to lucrative potential opportunities but there may be significant challenges that need to be overcome before the venture adds real value.

It was anticipated that in central and Eastern Europe following the collapse of communist regimes joint ventures would play a significant part in achieving economic regeneration, but this has not, so far, proved to be the case. The reasons for this include the lack of an adequate legal framework to facilitate joint ventures and the lack of suitably qualified people to operate the joint venture, particularly in financial control. There is also the possibility of a conflict of objectives which can occur between the international company, which wishes to develop a new market, and the local company which wishes to develop its own foreign markets or withdraw profits from the joint venture to finance other projects.

ILLUSTRATION 7.8

Buying into a joint venture to win work in the future

IBM bought 5 per cent alongside Citigroup's 20 per cent share in a joint US$3bn bid for Guangdong Development Bank of China. The 25 per cent share was the limit imposed by the China government. IBM's objective in the move was to help it gain contracts from the bank when it upgrades its computer systems. Mainland China banks needed to upgrade their IT systems to improve risk management, tighten control over their branches and improve efficiency as they face global competition. This move was intended to provide a stable platform to demonstrate its understanding of the local Chinese environment and enable it to win future work of this sensitive nature in China. Guangdong Development Bank has 13 million customers and 500 branches and this is the first time foreigners have been allowed to control a national, Chinese bank but commentators suggest that the main reason for this is that Guangdong is in trouble with loans at risk of non repayment at an alarming 22 per cent of its portfolio.

QUESTION *How valuable do you think this type of joint venture will be?*

Finally, companies from developed countries are unable to take out profits if there is a lack of hard currency and are unwilling to wait the 10 to 15 years that it is anticipated that these markets will take to develop.

In analysing the results of joint ventures in China, Vankonacker (1997) observes that joint ventures are hard to sustain in unstable environments and concludes that more direct investment in China will be wholly-owned, offering Johnson and Johnson's oral care, baby and feminine hygiene products business as a success story. Moreover, as Dilemma 7.2 shows, there can be a danger of creating a new competitor.

Strategic alliances

Whilst all market entry methods essentially involve alliances of some kind, during the 1980s the term strategic alliance started to be used, without being precisely defined, to cover a variety of contractual arrangements which are intended to be strategically beneficial to both parties but cannot be defined as clearly as licensing or joint ventures. Bronder and Pritzl (1992) have defined strategic alliances in terms of at least two companies combining value chain activities for the purpose of competitive advantage.

Some examples of the bases of alliances are:

- technology swaps
- R & D exchanges
- distribution relationships
- marketing relationships
- manufacturer–supplier relationships
- cross-licensing.

Perhaps one of the most significant aspects of strategic alliances has been that many have involved cooperation between partners that might also be competitors. This can pose problems for the participants, who must be careful about sharing information with their alliance partner but avoid information leakage where the organisation may be competing.

There are a number of driving forces for the formation and operation of strategic alliances.

DILEMMA 7.2

Airbus: creating a new competitor?

A major risk of joint ventures is that they can lead to the creation of a new competitor. Airbus, the European plane-maker, formed a joint venture with China's TJFTZ consortium to build its best-selling A320 jet in Tianjin. The deal helped it gain an order for 150 jets and 20 bigger A350s. Whilst the main sections of the planes would still be built in Europe it was expected that the Chinese would quickly begin to make the more sophisticated parts too. Airbus already used six Chinese companies to supply parts, including components, emergency doors and tools.

Knowledge leakage from the A320 to the Chinese technicians was inevitable, but Airbus considered the A320 to be an old model with little risk of leakage of leading edge technology and thought this a price worth paying to gain a foothold in the Chinese market. Boeing dominated the China market, which was expected to require 2900 passenger jets over the next 20 years as the new middle classes take to the air.

The Chinese state already had a joint venture with Embraer to build a turbo fan plane. It also had a US$3bn five-year project to develop an entirely Chinese designed short haul, 175-seat commuter aircraft intended to compete directly with Airbus and Boeing.

The dilemma is whether to cooperate to gain larger immediate orders and accept the risk of creating a competitor, or go it alone and try to win orders on merit.

SOURCE: A. EVANS-PRITCHARD, TAKEOFF FOR CHINA AS AIRBUS BUILDER 27 OCTOBER, 2006, DAILY TELEGRAPH

Insufficient resources: the central argument is that no organisation alone has sufficient resources to realise the full global potential of its existing and particularly its new products. Equally if it fails to satisfy all the markets which demand these products, competitors will exploit the opportunities which arise and become stronger. In order to remain competitive, powerful and independent companies need to cooperate.

Pace of innovation and market diffusion: the rate of change of technology and consequent shorter product life cycles mean that new products must be exploited quickly by effective diffusion out into the market. This requires not only effective promotion and efficient physical distribution but also needs good channel management, especially when other members of the channel are powerful, and so, for example, the strength of alliances within the recorded music industry including artists, recording labels and retailers, has a powerful effect on the success of individual hardware products such as the MP3 players.

High research and development costs: as technology becomes more complex and genuinely new products become rarer, so the costs of R & D become higher.

Concentration of firms in mature industries: many industries have used alliances to manage the problem of excess production capacity in mature markets. There have been a number of alliances in the car and airline business, such as One World and the Star Alliance. Some of these have led ultimately to full joint ventures or takeovers.

Government cooperation: as the trend towards regionalisation continues, so governments are more prepared to cooperate on high-cost projects rather than try to go it alone. There have been a number of alliances in Europe – for example, the European airbus has been developed to challenge Boeing, and the Eurofighter aircraft project has been developed by Britain, Germany, Italy and Spain.

Self-protection: a number of alliances have been formed in the belief that they might afford protection against competition in the form of individual companies or newly formed alliances. This is particularly the case in the emerging global high technology sectors such as information technology, telecommunications, media and entertainment.

Market access: strategic alliances have been used by companies to gain access to difficult markets; for instance, Caterpillar used an alliance with Mitsubishi to enter the Japanese market.

As with all entry strategies, success with strategic alliances depends on effective management, good planning, adequate research, accountability and monitoring. It is also important to recognise the limitations of this as an entry method. Companies need to be aware of the dangers of becoming drawn into activities for which they are not designed.

Voss Johnson, Cullen, Sakano and Takenouchi (2006) emphasise the importance of cultural sensitivity in cross-border alliances and the implications for trust and quality information exchange.

Reciprocal share holdings

In this chapter we have considered many different methods of cooperation between partners. Over the years many firms have taken an equity stake in another firm for a variety of reasons. It might provide the opportunity to influence the strategy of that firm, create a basis upon which to share expertise between the firms or establish a platform that might lead to a more formal business relationship, such as a merger, as well as generating an immediate return on the investment. Renault took a stake in Nissan to save the company from bankruptcy and succeeded in turning the company around by helping it to launch a more attractive and competitive range of cars. Renault then became the recipients of Nissan's expertise in improving quality and production efficiency.

What is quite clear is that global firms are adopting a range of market entry partnership arrangements to maximise their global performance and presence. The businesses are becoming increasingly complex as they embark on joint ventures, with the associated formal responsibilities, strategic alliances, short-term contractual obligations and shareholdings which might be the basis for closer future cooperation.

Inevitably the challenge for management is to manage the various stakeholder expectations and maximise the opportunities that come from synergy and the complementary activity of the partners. To do this it is necessary to select partners that are willing and able to contribute at least some of:

- complementary products and services
- knowledge and expertise in building customer relationships
- capability in technology and research
- capacity in manufacturing and logistics
- power in distribution channels, and
- money and management time.

The management must also deal with the added complexity and potential for conflicts between two quite different partners that arise because of differences in:

- objectives and strategies
- approach to repatriation of profits and investment in the business
- social, business and organisation cultures, and
- commitment to partnership and understanding of management responsibilities.

Whilst cooperative strategies promise synergy, the potential for cost saving and faster market entry, it requires considerable management effort to overcome the inherent difficulties and dedication to see the partnerships through to success.

SUMMARY

- For a firm at the start of internationalisation, market entry can be regarded as a critical first step which is vital not only for financial reasons, but also because it will set a pattern of future international involvement. It determines not just the opportunities for sales but also a valuable source of market information.

- Market entry methods can be seen as a series of alternatives available to international firms, and a global strategy might utilise a number of different approaches. A firm can make individual decisions based on the factors affecting one specific country or the whole region and choose the most appropriate method for the particular set of circumstances.

- The choice of market entry method should be based on an assessment of the firm's desired involvement in the market and the level of control of its marketing mix in the country, set against the financial and marketing risks.

- For large established companies that already have extensive involvement in international markets, the market entry decision is taken against the background of the competitive nature of the market, a global strategy and an existing and substantial network of operations.

■ The company's competitive strategy is likely to require simultaneous decisions affecting its arrangements in a number of markets in order to improve its competitive position by entering untapped or emerging markets, or expanding its activities in existing markets.

■ In order to achieve these objectives within a very short timescale, rather than relying on organic growth the companies have used a variety of market entry strategies, including joint ventures and alliances, often with competitors. This is leading to increasingly complex operations being created in which companies strive to balance the opposing forces of competitiveness and cooperation, and quite frequently such arrangements fail to deliver the expected benefits.

KEYWORDS

Acquisitions	Franchising	Piggybacking
Contract manufacture	Indirect exporting	Risk and control
Direct marketing	Joint ventures	*Sogo shosha*
Distributors	Licensing	Strategic alliance
Domestic purchasing	Management contracts	Trading companies
Export houses	Market involvement	Wholly-owned
Exporting	Market entry	subsidiary

CASE STUDY

When joint ventures go wrong

Ten or even five years ago the arguments for strategic alliances and joint ventures as international market entry strategies for companies from developed countries entering a developing country seemed clear and compelling. They seemed particularly appropriate for China and in some cases appeared the only way. The theory was that the Chinese company provided access to cheap labour, local regulatory knowledge and access

PHOTO CREDIT: WENDY CONNETT/ALAMY

to what ten years ago appeared to be a relatively small, high-risk domestic market. The foreign partner provided capital knowledge, access to international markets and the promise of jobs in China. The attraction was that the market was promising, although at the same time it was geographically vast with very complex, contradictory and often invisible rules. Many of the largest companies in the world pursued collaborations of this type with what were then local Chinese companies in the belief that the arrangement would reduce risk but still allow high levels of control over the marketing strategy in China.

Danone, a French Food multinational, acquired a 51 per cent stake in the Chinese firm Wahaha Beverage in 1996 and believed they had struck an excellent deal. HSBC acquired a 19.9 per cent stake in Bank of Communications, the smallest of the Chinese national banks and were pleased because this was the only bank by law allowed the possibility of a full takeover.

In practice like many other joint ventures and alliances they have failed to deliver the original promise. The list of joint venture failures involves companies from just about every industry sector, including Peugeot (cars), Remy Martin (spirits), Foster's (beer), media (News Corporation) and many telecoms firms.

Chinese companies originally were keen to receive money, technology and business 'know-how', but they now have global ambitions of their own and do not want to be constrained by a global multinational partner who may want to curtail these ambitions. The joint venture partners frequently argued about the allocations of profits and decisions on investments.

China itself has also changed: having become a member of the World Trade Organisation it had to agree to be more open legally. As the domestic economy grew more rapidly than any-one expected domestic capital was freely available, with the result that there was little need for money from foreign investors. As the Chinese market became one of the most attractive in the world and sentiment in China became more nationalistic and self-reliant the balance of power shifted between the Chinese and foreign partners, and providing access to China for foreign partners was of much less interest.

Whilst Wahaha originally knew little about business and welcomed a partner, it now is aware of all the attractive poss-ibilities and it objects to the fact that it must clear plans with its foreign majority owner before going ahead, especially as Danone is pursuing alternative strategies in China through its joint ventures with other Chinese companies. Even worse, Danone wants full ownership of the firm. Things came to a head when Danone eventually realised that Wahaha was operating a parallel firm, marketing similar products. The com-panies are involved in an acrimonious public dispute.

HSBC's problems are the result of success. Bank of Communication's assets have grown so much that it has now been included in the Chinese government's list of powerful banks that it will not allow to be taken over. HSBC has responded by pursuing local incorporation, something only recently allowed, and made investments in the Bank of Shanghai and Ping An, an insurance firm, but these are far less attractive options.

A smaller number of firms that had a better understanding of the situation were able to legally end their joint ventures without too much pain. Unilever shut down more than a dozen joint ventures and Coca-Cola and Starbucks bought out their Chinese partners.

The moral of this experience confirms conventional wisdom about forming joint ventures – to ensure the joint ventures will be successful the most careful planning should focus on how to end them.

QUESTIONS

1 What are the factors that a multinational firm should consider when deciding to use a joint venture as a market entry strategy for a developing country? What are the potential benefits and risks in taking this course of action?

2 Develop an outline international marketing strategy for a joint venture between Danone, a French multinational food company, and a food producer from a developing country. Explain which companies would be responsible for providing the leadership and decision-making for the various activities detailed.

DISCUSSION QUESTIONS

1 Outline the market entry methods and the levels of involvement associated with the development of a company's globalisation process from initial exporting through to becoming a global corporation. Specify what you consider to be the important criteria in deciding the appropriate entry method.

2 Selecting the market entry strategy is the key decision many companies have to take in expanding into overseas markets because it involves both risk and levels of control. Using examples to illustrate your answer, explain how risk and control are affected by different entry methods.

3 International marketing of intellectual property, such as technological inventions, creative works, the performing arts and consultancy pose particular challenges for market entry. Using examples to illustrate your answer, explain what the particular challenges might be and what criteria might be used for selecting an appropriate strategy.

4 Why is acquisition often the preferred way to establish wholly-owned operations abroad, and what are its limitations as an entry method?

5 Projects that involve large amounts of development money are sometimes undertaken through a strategic alliance. Explain the rationale behind this form of global partnering and outline the major advantages and disadvantages of the arrangement.

References

Bronder, C. and Pritzl, R. (1992) 'Developing strategic alliances: a conceptual framework for successful co-operation', *European Management Journal*, 10 (4).

Chan, P.S. (1994) 'Franchising: key to global expansion', *Journal of International Marketing*, 2 (3).

Economist, The (2006) 'Hilton Hotels together again', *The Economist*, 5 January.

Hutton, R. (2006) 'Eastern Europe the new Detroit', *Sunday Times*, 15 October.

Katsikeas, C.S., Leonidou, L.C. and Morgan, N.A. (2000) 'Firm-level performance assessment: review, evaluation and development', *Journal of Academy of Marketing Science*, 28 (4): 493–511.

Leonidou, L.C., Katsikeas, C.S. and Samiee, S. (2002) 'Marketing strategy determination of export performance: a meta analysis', *Journal of Business Research*, 55, 51–67.

Sarathy, R., Terpstra, V. and Russow. (2006) *International marketing*, 9th edn. Dryden Press.

Styles, C., Patterson, P.G. and La, V.Q. (2005) 'Executive insights: exporting services to South East Asia: lessons from Australian knowledge-based service exporters', *Journal of International Marketing*, 13 (4): 104–28.

Tait, N. (1997) *Financial Times*, 15 October.

Terpstra, V. and Sarathy, R. (1999) *International Marketing*, 8th edn, Dryden Press.

Terpstra, V. and Yu, C.J. (1990) 'Piggybacking: a quick road to internationalisation', *International Marketing Review*, 7 (4).

Vankonacker, W. (1997) 'Entering China: an unconventional approach', *Harvard Business Review*, March–April.

Varinder, S. (2005) 'Export management companies and e-business: impact on export services, product portfolio and global market coverage', *Journal of Marketing Theory and Practice*, 13 (4): 61–71.

Voss, K. E., Johnson, J.L., Cullen, J.B., Sakano, T. and Takenouchi, H. (2006) 'Relational exchange in US-Japanese marketing strategic alliances', *International Marketing Review*, 23 (6): 610–35

Welch, L.S. (1992) 'Developments in international franchising', *Journal of Global Marketing*, 6 (1/2).

CHAPTER 8

INTERNATIONAL PRODUCT AND SERVICE MANAGEMENT

INTRODUCTION

Success in international marketing depends to a large extent upon satisfying the demands of the market and ultimately, on whether the product or service offered is suitable and acceptable for its purpose. More markets are reaching maturity and fewer and fewer products can be differentiated by their core benefits and so are becoming commodities. In defining the term 'product', therefore, we include additional elements such as packaging, warranties, after-sales service and branding that make up the total product and a complete package of tangible and intangible benefits for the customer. Services are taking an increasing share of international trade, but managing services internationally poses particular challenges. This is because the delivery of services is so dependent on the context, which is usually influenced by the varying cultural perceptions of what is acceptable service. In both product and service markets increasing customer expectations and competition mean that it is essential for firms to continually add better value through innovation and new product development. Much of this innovation is related to technological developments.

In this chapter we focus upon some of the key aspects and recent trends of international product policy by considering the changes in the nature of the products and services offered individually and within the portfolio, their relationship with the market and how new products and services can be developed. Particularly important is the need to provide customers around the world with a satisfactory experience when using the product or service. To achieve this requires a clear understanding of when to meet the similar needs and wants of transnational customer segments and when to adapt to local tastes and requirements.

LEARNING OBJECTIVES

After reading this chapter you should be able to:

■ Understand the nature of international product and service marketing and appreciate the elements that make up the product and service offer

■ Evaluate the factors affecting international product and service strategy development both external and internal to the firm

■ Explain the issues that affect international product and service management across borders

■ Identify the implications of the image, branding and positioning of products and services in international markets

■ Understand how new product development contributes to the international product and service strategy

THE NATURE OF PRODUCTS AND SERVICES

The reason that the majority of companies initially develop international markets is to generate new market opportunities, increase sales of an existing product or service or to offload excess capacity. However, the product must be seen as a bundle of satisfactions, providing people not just with products but with satisfying experiences in terms of the benefits they provide rather than the functions the products perform. These concepts are particularly important in international marketing, because, for example, the growth of such global consumer products as McDonald's and Coca-Cola cannot be attributable solely to a distinctive taste. Much of their success might be attributed to the aspirations of their international customers to be part of the American way of life, the 'Coca-Cola Culture', by deriving satisfaction from a close association with the product and the brand.

In understanding how products can provide satisfying experiences and benefits for people, it is necessary to clearly identify and understand the motivations of the target consumer and not make assumptions about them. A typical response to Nike sports shoes, reported in *Sky* magazine was: 'It's kind of like, Nike don't give a * * * * what you do, they don't care where you come from, and they don't want to hear you talk about it. They just want to see what you can do.'

International product and service marketing

The term 'product' is used in marketing to refer both to physical goods, such as a can of baked beans or a refrigerator, and services such as insurance or a holiday. In fact few products can be described as pure product with no service element – salt is often suggested as approaching a pure product. Teaching is probably the closest to a pure service. All offers are a combination of product and service components, as shown in Figure 8.1. Before considering the total product 'offer' in more detail, it is important to consider the specific nature of services and the challenges they pose in international marketing.

Services are characterised by their:

■ **Intangibility**: air transportation, insurance and education cannot be touched, smelled or seen. Tangible elements of the service, such as food, drink and personal video on airline flights; a written policy and a free gift in insurance and a certificate and a photograph of graduation for success in education, are used as part of the service in order to confirm the benefit provided and enhance its perceived value. However, the physical evidence of the service that is offered may be valued very differently from country to country.

■ **Perishability**: services cannot be stored – for example, the revenues from unfilled airline seats are lost once the aircraft takes off. This characteristic causes considerable problems in planning and promotion in order to match supply and demand at busy and quiet times of the day. Predicting unfamiliar patterns of demand and managing capacity in distant and varied locations is particularly difficult.

■ **Heterogeneity**: services are rarely the same, because they involve interactions between people. For fast food companies this can cause problems in maintaining consistent quality, particularly in international markets where there are quite different attitudes towards and expectations of customer service.

■ **Inseparability**: the service is created at the point of sale. This means that economies of scale and the experience curve benefits can be difficult to achieve and supplying the service in scattered markets can be expensive, particularly in the initial setting up phase. Where the service involves some special expertise, such as pop music, the number of consumers is limited by the size and number of venues that can be visited by the performer. If the fans are in a market which is remote, they are unlikely to see the artist and need other tangible forms of communication, such as videos, website and books, in order not to feel too separated from the performer.

THE THREE ADDITIONAL MARKETING MIX ELEMENTS

These differences between product and service offers have certain implications for the international marketing mix and, in addition to the usual four Ps for products – product, price, place and promotion – another three Ps for services are added. Because of the importance and nature of service delivery, special emphasis must be placed upon:

■ *People*. Consumers must be educated in order for their expectations of the service to be managed, and employees must be motivated and well trained in order to ensure that high standards of service are maintained. However, because of cultural differences the staff and customers in various countries often respond differently not only to training and education but also in their attitudes to the speed of service, punctuality willingness to queue and so on. Firms such as consultancies, advertising

FIGURE 8.1
The product–service continuum

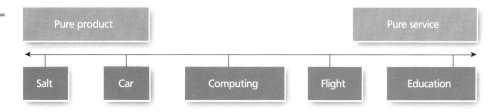

agencies or IT management supplying services around the world to an MNE customer, will be expected to maintain the same standards at every country location, but staff and customers, may have different attitudes to service in each.

■ *Process*. As the success of the service is dependent on the total customer experience, a well-designed delivery process is essential. Customer expectations of process standards vary with different cultures and standardisation is difficult in many varied contexts. Frequently the service process is affected by elements for which the service deliverer may be blamed by frustrated customers but over which they have little control. Sports fans might travel to an event at great expense only to experience delays at an airport, excessive policing or bad weather. Although their team may perform well the fans may be reluctant to travel to future matches because of their unsatisfactory overall experience. At its most basic the process of customer management should make it easy for the customer to deal with the firm no matter where they are in the world.

■ *Physical aspects*. Many physical reminders, including the appearance of the delivery location and the elements provided to make the service more tangible, can enhance the overall customer experience. Apart from using appropriate artefacts to generate the right atmosphere, constant reminders of the firm's corporate identity help to build customer awareness and loyalty. For example, the familiar logos of Vodafone, CNN and Cathay Pacific airline may give the reassurance necessary for a consumer to use a service in a foreign market and not question the source.

Illustration 8.1 shows how low-cost airlines, such as Ryanair and easyJet, have put pressure on the national flag carriers by changing each element of the marketing mix. There are some specific problems in marketing services internationally. There are particular difficulties in achieving uniformity of standards of the three additional Ps in remote locations where exerting control can be particularly difficult. Pricing, too, can be extremely problematic, because fixed costs can be a very significant part of the total service costs but may vary between locations, for example, in the case of mobile telephony. As a result the consumer's ability to buy and their perceptions of the service may vary considerably between markets, resulting in significantly different prices being set and profits generated. Increasingly important in service marketing is the need to provide largely standardised services customised to individual requirements. This clearly poses considerable challenges to international service providers. For example, a MNE might employ an international law firm to protect its interests but the scope for offering a standardised service is limited by the fact that every country has its own different legal system.

There are a number of generalisations that can be made about international marketing of services. Foreign markets present greater opportunities for gaining market share and long-term profits, partly because local firms are often less experienced and less competitive on quality. Information technology and communications in service delivery and the development of expert knowledge networks are the sources of competitive advantage for international service marketers. Due to the high initial cost of financing overseas operations, joint ventures and franchising are rapidly growing entry methods, and frequently the market entry strategy is based on forming alliances or piggybacking as existing clients move into new markets. Whilst government regulations and attitudes to the protection of local suppliers vary considerably from country to country, more new markets are opening up. Most importantly, however, because of the significance of interpersonal relationships in service marketing, it is often cultural empathy in the way services are developed and delivered that is critical for success.

Whilst it might seem appropriate to categorise physical goods as tangible and services as intangible, marketing increasingly appears to be concerned with blurring this distinction. For example, a product such as perfume is not promoted as a complex chemical solution, but instead, as one perfume house executive put it, 'dreams in a bottle'. Many services appear to compete over tangible 'add-ons' as we discussed earlier in this chapter.

The international marketing of service

One of the achievements of the Uruguay Round of negotiations on the General Agreement on Trade in Services (GATS) was to identify four modes of delivery or ways in which services may be exported. This is useful in detailing the nature of international services:

1 Cross-border trade, where the trade takes place from one country to another, without the movement of persons. Only the service itself, for example, market research or training, crosses the border electronically (email), by telecommunications (telephone, radio) or by infrastructure (air, rail).

ILLUSTRATION 8.1

SOURCE: ROBIN LOWE FROM VARIOUS PUBLIC SOURCES INCLUDING BBC NEWS ONLINE AND R. GREEN, ROUND THE WORLD FOR £500, SUNDAY TIMES, 15 APRIL, 2007

Flying low cost with frills or no frills

Over the last decade there has been a huge growth in low cost airlines around the world. The Irish airline Ryanair has been particularly successful. The no frills airlines followed a model pioneered in the US by South West Airlines. To do this the company cuts the service to the bone. Food on board has to be paid for, there is no seat allocation and around 90 per cent of seat bookings are made on the Internet. The compensation for 'no frills' is low prices. The pricing model is based on yield management software that is designed to maximise the revenue achieved on each flight, by rewarding early customers with low prices and charging high prices to latecomers. This model contrasts with the full service airlines which have traditionally tried to maintain high ticket prices, even when running the plane half-full, and have focused on alliances with

PHOTO CREDIT: STEVEN MAY/ALAMY

other airlines to ensure that long-haul passengers have a seamless service.

The chief executive of Ryanair, Michael O'Leary, is outspoken and combative and has attacked any moves by stakeholders to add costs to the business model, restrict the airline's activities or criticise its activities – governments putting green taxes on flights, airport authorities increasing landing charges and pressure groups criticising the contribution to carbon emissions. In a rare climbdown O'Leary had to acknowledge that its fuel use has increased eightfold between 1998 and 2006, leading to a similar increase in carbon emissions, a retreat from his earlier position that carbon dioxide emissions had been halved. Although the basic price of a flight might be very low, the cost to the customer can be much higher when taxes are taken into account. Moreover Ryanair adds other charges, for example, for payment by credit card and for carrying luggage over a certain weight.

Along with easyJet, Ryanair transformed air travel in Europe where distances are short. There is some scepticism about whether the model would work for long haul but O'Leary announced his intentions of launching a UK-US flight.

However, the distinction needs to be made between low cost and no frills. Oasis Airlines offered one way flights from the UK to Hong Kong and Hong Kong to California for £150, and Zoom Airlines from the US to UK for a similar price, making it possible to go round the world for around £500, compared to BA's price of £1400. Oasis and Zoom included free meals, in-flight entertainment and reasonable leg room between seats.

QUESTION *What are the challenges of running low-cost airlines and what will be the critical success factors be?*

2 Consumption abroad, where the customer travels to the country where the service is supplied (tourism, education or training, legal services).

3 Commercial presence, where the supplier establishes a commercial presence abroad (banks, construction project offices or warehousing and logistics).

4 Movement of natural persons, where the provider of the services crosses the border (arts and culture, recreation and sports).

Any of the four modes constitute trade so long as the local firm is being paid by the foreign firm, no matter where the service is provided.

'Invisible', services contribute to all aspects of economic activity. For example infrastructure services (transport, communications and financial services) provide support to any type of business. Education, health and recreational services influence the quality of labour available, professional services provide the specialised expertise to increase firms' competitiveness, Services make up an increasing proportion of value added, even in products, through market research, accounting, advertising, administration and distribution. Services are expanding fast and, for example, in 2007 ranged from 39 per cent of GDP in Nigeria to 89 per cent of GDP in Hong Kong.

THE COMPONENTS OF THE INTERNATIONAL PRODUCT OFFER

In creating a suitable and acceptable product offer for international markets, it is necessary to examine first, what contributes to the 'total' product, and second, decide what might make the product acceptable to the international market. Kotler (2002) suggests three essential aspects of the product offer, which should be considered by marketers in order to meet consumer needs and wants:

1 *Product benefits*: the elements that consumers perceive as meeting their needs and providing satisfaction through performance and image.

2 *Product attributes*: the elements most closely associated with the core product, such as features, specifications, styling, branding and packaging.

3 *The marketing support services*: the additional elements to the core product which contribute to providing satisfaction, and include delivery, after-sales service and guarantees.

These elements form the augmented product, an extended version of which is shown in Figure 8.2. Moving down and to the right of the diagram shows the elements that are relatively more difficult to standardise in different country markets.

Having introduced the concept of the total product offer, it is essential to evaluate each aspect of the product in terms of what benefits the consumer might expect to gain and how the value of the offer will be perceived by consumers. This can be done by answering the following six questions for each market:

1 For what purpose has the product been developed and how would the product be used in that country?

2 What distinctive properties does the product have?

3 What benefits is the consumer expected to gain?

4 How is the product positioned and what image do consumers perceive it to have?

5 Which consumer segments of the total market are expected to buy it, on what occasions and for what purposes?

6 How does the product fit into the total market?

The main issue for a company about to commence marketing internationally is to assess the suitability of the existing products for international markets. As a minimum, a purchaser in an overseas market expects to have a clear explanation of how a product should be used, so the instructions on the domestic packaging usually have to be translated for international markets. Interestingly, one cosmetics marketer found that in some countries customers objected if their language was not printed first on multilingual packs.

The question is, however, to what extent the components of the total product offer can and should be adapted for international markets. In the case of a product where only the packaging needs to be changed, the effect on the overall cost is likely to be minimal, but if more fundamental changes to the product itself are required, because of differences in use or safety regulations, the higher cost might prove prohibitive for a small company. Such problems can be circumvented by taking an alternative market entry approach such as licensing or franchising, but in making strategic decisions of this type, the company must decide exactly what product or aspect of the augmented product will be most valued by customers in the target market.

Whilst the core benefit might remain constant, the point of differentiation of one product from another can change as, for example, Samsung has recognised. Samsung originally focused on efficient production of high-quality technologically advanced products at affordable prices, but increasingly recognises the need for a well-known brand and effective promotion. Providing three or even five-year warranties is also providing a point of differentiation for some companies.

FIGURE 8.2
The three elements of the product or service

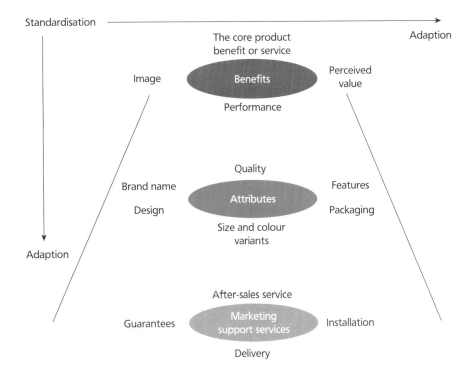

Products, services and value propositions

The distinction between products and services is becoming increasingly blurred. In practice there are few 'pure' products and services and most offerings from firms are a combination of the two, as Figure 8.1 suggests. In Illustration 6.1 we discussed IBM's change of focus from being a computer and business machines (product) company to a software and hardware supplier and a solutions provider (product and service). They have changed to an IT and business processing outsourcing firm, which could be regarded as having a service emphasis. This is now a common trend which recognises the need to focus on making value propositions to combine product and service solutions that will satisfy customer expectations. Most companies are seeking to provide benefits and add customer value and differentiate their offering from that of competitors.

At this point it is worth noting that customer expectations are increasing. Simply claiming to offer a good quality product or service no longer satisfies customers. Customers will be dissatisfied if they do not receive good quality products and service, but they will only be satisfied if they are delighted with the product or service because of some extra benefits. Of course, what will delight customers around the world varies considerably.

FACTORS AFFECTING INTERNATIONAL PRODUCT AND SERVICE MANAGEMENT

There are a number of factors that affect the international management of products and services including:

- the balance between standardisation and adaptation owing to:
  - cultural factors
  - usage factors
  - legal factors
- product accessibility and ethical issues
- green environmental issues
- shortening product life cycles
- the effect of different market entry methods
- changes in marketing management.

Towards standardisation

The discussion in Chapter 6 on globalisation leads to the conclusion that for the largest companies in the world the benefits of marketing standardised products are very significant indeed, but whilst firms may be prepared to invest heavily to achieve standardisation, in practice virtually all products must be adapted to some degree. The issue then becomes to what degree their industrial or consumer product or service should be standardised or adapted to the needs of the local market. Even the most obviously global companies achieve only partial standardisation of products. For example, whilst Coca-Cola adopt a global standardised branding strategy, they modify the product for particular customer segments by offering Diet and Caffeine-Free Coca-Cola and altering the sweetness for different national tastes. McDonald's, too, alters its menu in different countries to cater for local tastes.

All firms must identify the benefit or satisfaction that the consumer recognises and will purchase. This benefit must provide the basis upon which the company differentiates its products from those of its competitors. For a product such as the mobile phone, when it was first introduced, the competitive advantage was a technical breakthrough, the first portable long distance mobile voice communication, and so standardisation of the core benefit was possible. As products were copied and developed so new sources of competitive advantage were sought for the mobile phone and this led to standardisation of non-core elements of the augmented product, for example, additional functions such as texting, camera facilities, music and video downloading and so on. Fragmentation then occurs as manufacturers choose to differentiate their product in different ways, such as design, greater functionality, a more robust product for rough use or producing a very basic phone that will appeal to specific segments. Also different business models such as 'Pay and Go' accelerated usage. Sometimes, however, the differention does not appeal. Vodafone withdrew a very basic phone soon after its introduction because of lack of demand. Illustration 8.2 discusses the convergence between mobile phone and mobile music developments.

The decision for most companies to standardise or adapt is based on a cost–benefit analysis of what they believe the implications of adaptation and standardisation might be for revenue, profitability and market share. In normal circumstances, the cost of adaptation would be expected to be greater than the cost of successful standardisation. Only if the needs and tastes identified in the target market segment are significantly different and substantial additional business generated, can the extra cost involved in making and delivering adapted products be justified.

ILLUSTRATION 8.2

SOURCE: ADAPTED FROM P. DURMAN 'PHONE RIVALS THREATEN TO SPOIL IPOD'S PARTY' SUNDAY TIMES, 15 APRIL, 2007

Apple's lead challenged

Between 2001 and 2007 Apple's annual sales increased from US$5 billion to US$25 million. More than half the increase came from the sales of iPods and iTunes. In 2007 Apple sold its 100 millionth iPod, the fastest selling music player in history. However, the future of the personal entertainment industry revolved around Internet delivery of music, movies and other content to portable devices. The question was whether iPod would dominate the next generation of devices, as the mobile phone industry targeted the same customers. With improved storage capacity, software and design developments mobile phone companies were already ahead of the game. For some years millions of phones had been sold with integrated MP3 players, albeit with severe usage limitations. Sony Ericsson changed this with sales of its Walkman phones achieving 20 million in 18 months – a faster initial take off than the iPod. The phone also included a two megapixel camera. However, even this was dwarfed by Nokia who sold 70 million music-capable phones in 2006. Their research suggested that 60 per cent of customers used the music playing capability, a huge change brought about by the increased storage capacity of the phone.

Nokia has always emphasised ease of use with its phones and its US$60 million acquisition of Loudeye helped it launch its own digital music store. One of the key advantages of the mobile industry has been that network operators had always subsidised the cost of phones, selling them at a fraction of their value and making them look better value than a stand-alone product like an iPod.

The question was who would win in the convergence of mobile telephony, photography and digital media?

QUESTION *To what degree is it technological advances, design or marketing capability that leads to success in global markets?*

PART 2 STRATEGY DEVELOPMENT

Whilst some companies are tempted to adopt a policy of adaptation in order to satisfy immediate demand, others believe that continual exposure to the standardised products will redefine customer needs and ultimately change their tastes, leading to greater market share in the longer term. It is interesting to contrast the strategies of firms of different nations. American companies have traditionally been very unwilling to adapt products because of the dominance of the home market, whereas Japanese companies, being increasingly dependent on exports, have been prepared to adapt products much more readily. Indeed, product differentiation has become a central part of the strategy of Japanese companies and has led to significant manufacturing process advances, such as production operations being geared to producing small batch sizes and minimum stockholding.

Summarising the advantages of product standardisation, the company benefits from more rapid recovery of investment, easier organisation and control of product management, the possibility to reduce costs through economies of scale and the experience effect throughout most of the firm's operations, such as production, advertising and distribution.

Product standardisation is both encouraging and being encouraged by the globalisation trends in markets, which are emerging because of three factors:

1 markets are becoming more homogeneous

2 there are more identifiable transnational consumer segments, and

3 there is an increase in the number of firms moving towards globalisation, so forcing greater standardisation throughout industry sectors.

There are some disadvantages of product standardisation too; for example, market opportunities might be lost when it is impossible to match very specific local requirements. Some managers of local subsidiaries who are only expected to implement global or regional product policies can become demotivated and miss market opportunities if they are not given the opportunity to innovate.

Greater standardisation of products makes it easier for competitors to copy at ever-lower prices, but this leads inevitably to standardisation within a product category so that consumers are unable to differentiate between competing products, with the result that a 'commodity market' is created. To counter this, competition is focusing increasingly upon the augmented product elements. In the family car market, for example, there is very little to choose between the performance, reliability and economy of the main competitors, including Ford, General Motors, Renault, Toyota, Peugeot and Nissan. Against this background, the promotion of individual cars focuses upon design, image, warranties and financing arrangements and rather less on individual performance comparisons. The industry is also continually developing products for subsegments, examples being the Smart car, Toyota Prius hybrid energy source car and sports utility vehicles.

Reasons for adaptation of the product

In some instances, product standardisation may not be possible due to environmental constraints either through mandatory legislation, because of such reasons as differences in electrical systems, legal standards, safety requirements or product liability, or because the firm believes that the product appeal can be increased in a particular market by addressing cultural and usage factors.

CULTURAL FACTORS

Certain products and services, such as computers and airline flights, are not culturally sensitive as the benefits they offer are valued internationally. Here the adaptation is peripheral, for example, translation of instructions into different languages. Other products and services are more culturally sensitive and might need to be adapted more substantially. For example, food is a particularly difficult area for standardisation, as the preparation and eating of food are often embedded in the history, religion and/or culture of the country. This presents specific problems for fast food firms, for example, where the main ingredients of McDonald's and Burger King, beef and pork, prove unacceptable to many potential customers, and the necessary ingredients for fast food, such as the specific type of wheat for pizza bases, suitable chicken and mozzarella cheese are unavailable or are of variable quality in certain countries. Indian consumers prefer a variety of foods, so Pizza Hut and KFC are located under one roof in New Delhi.

One example of service development is Islamic banking, which for many years was regarded as a small niche activity. However, the growing sense of religious identity in the Muslim world following the 11 September attacks in 2001 together with the significant increase in construction in the Middle East has led to rapid growth in the sector, which by 2006 was estimated to be worth US$1000 bn and forecast to treble in the following five years (Ringshaw 2006).

However, a large potential market does not guarantee success. Kellogg's invested US$65 million to launch cornflakes in India which has a population of 1 billion people but, after initial success, the sales plummeted. Usually Indians eat a bowl of hot vegetables for breakfast rather than cold cereal. Kellogg's has since introduced other cereals and claims 55 per cent of the cereal market, but they have a long way to go before 1 billion people are converted.

Whilst the music tastes of older people from different cultures can be distinctly different, music is becoming increasingly standardised amongst young people, who have much more in common with the same age group around the world than with older people in their own country. There are limitations with this and sometimes a regional strategy is more effective. The Japanese entertainment industry, having failed to establish itself in the West, has turned to other South East Asian markets which are believed to be some years behind in developing popular music talent. Whilst older generations in South East Asia remember being forced to learn Japanese during the Second World War, younger generations see Tokyo in the same way as Western youth sees New York.

Changes are taking place in product acceptance however. For example, fashion is becoming increasingly globalised and the traditional domination of the fashion industry by Western designers is gradually being broken down. Denim jeans have now infiltrated countries like India which had hitherto only accepted traditional dress. Some people believe that the erosion of the country's traditional heritage and culture, particularly by the media and MNE advertising, is unethical and should be resisted. Others suggest that larger countries such as India and China simply take those international products which serve a particular need and ignore other global products.

USAGE FACTORS

The same product might be used in quite different ways in different markets, partly due to the culture of the country, but also due to the geographical factors of climate and terrain. Unilever and Procter & Gamble have a large variety of products adapted and branded for different markets because of the different ways products are used. For example, French people wash clothes in scalding hot water, whilst the Australians tend to use cold water. Most Europeans use front-loading washing machines, whereas the French use top-loaders. Equipment supplied to armies fighting in unfamiliar and inhospitable climates has often proved ineffective.

Honda found that when they first introduced motorcycles into the US they were unreliable and frequently broke down. Whereas Japanese riders were only able to travel short distances, American riders were used to riding the bikes over longer distances and much rougher terrain. Honda quickly realised, however, that Americans were fascinated by their 50cc bikes and promoted them instead. Honda quickly became established and were able to introduce better perfoming larger bikes too.

LEGAL STANDARDS

The standardisation of products and services can be significantly affected by legislation. Legal standards are often very country-specific – sometimes because obscure laws have been left unchanged for decades. There have been considerable problems for the European Union in attempting to harmonise standards during the creation of the single market and it has taken a number of years to achieve agreement on relatively simple products, such as confectionery, jam and sausage.

Lack of precise, reliable, understandable and universally accepted scientific information, for example in food safety (beef, lamb and chicken), serves only to make it more difficult to achieve a satisfactory industry standard. Pharmaceutical companies experience problems in introducing products into different markets, because individual governments have differing standards of public health and approaches to healthcare. Many countries insist that they carry out their own supervised clinical testing on all drugs prior to the products being available on the market and, for example, the instructions and contraindications might need to be changed and agreed with health authorities locally.

PRODUCT LIABILITY

In the US, over the past few years there has been a considerable increase in litigation, with lawyers seeking clients on a no win–no fee basis. For marketers, particularly those selling potentially life-threatening products such as pharmaceuticals and cars, this demands much greater caution when introducing standard products based on the home country specification into these markets. In extreme circumstances litigation can lead to huge financial settlements, for example in cases related to the tobacco and asbestos industries.

By way of contrast, unscrupulous companies have exploited the different legal controls and lower risks of litigation by sending unchecked lower specification or even hazardous products, such as chemical waste, to less developed countries with lower standards. However, this practice is being increasingly challenged by international pressure groups and is backed up in the US courts, which have the power to control the actions of US subsidiaries abroad.

Product acceptability and ethical considerations

Consumers generally are becoming much more discerning and have greater expectations of all the elements of the augmented product. The manufacturer must take responsibility for controlling the pre- and post-purchase servicing and warranties provided by independent distributors and retailers. The packaging, branding and trademark decisions are becoming increasingly important because the global village no longer allows mistakes and failures to go unpublicised.

Consumers, too, have different perceptions of the value and satisfaction of products and their view of what is acceptable will vary considerably from country to country. The product usage and production process may not fit with the culture and environment of the country and the product or service may not be acceptable for its intended use, as was the case with Nestlé powdered milk which was sold in less developed countries (LDCs) despite its high cost and the lack of clean water to make up the milk, resulting in the malnutrition of babies.

Green environmental issues

Concern for environmental issues is becoming greater in many countries and has considerable implications for product policies, but the nature, patterns and strength of interest vary considerably from country to country.

Howard (1998) highlights a number of things that are making it necessary for firms to pay more attention to global green environmental concerns. These are:

- greater public awareness following the publicity given to environmental disasters, such as floods, fires in Indonesia, Thailand and Mexico, deforestation of the rain forest, water pollution, and reduction in biodiversity

- greater national and local regulation of actions which are likely to affect the environment

- greater stakeholder awareness of MNE activity through better global communications

- greater expectations that MNEs will be more responsive because of their need to preserve a good image of corporate citizenship

- increasing cross-border concerns being shown, with the effect that more powerful countries can exert pressure and influence on MNE activities wherever they are.

Against this background MNEs must respond in an appropriate way to the global and local concerns by taking a more comprehensive approach to dealing with environmental issues by anticipating and, where appropriate, initiating changes. They must also evaluate and manage proactively all the effects on the environment of their operations.

Malagasy is a gourmet food company that sells high-quality products to supermarkets. It has partners in Madagascar that produce and package the chocolate, nuts, spices and honey it uses. It is a social enterprise that balances its commercial aims with social and economic objectives. The company realised that with many firms 95 per cent of the final value of a chocolate bar is created outside the country from which the chocolate ingredients originate. However, more value can be retained in the country where the ingredients originated if the finished product is made and packaged in that country – and that is what Malagasy do (Stone 2006).

A number of companies have set corporate strategies which address these issues. Sony for example incorporate environmental considerations into the planning of every product, and Ford has adopted the environmental standard, ISO4001 worldwide.

The goal is to achieve environmental excellence with firms such as The Body Shop, 3M, British Telecom, Johnson Matthey, Merck, Norsk Hydro and Rank Xerox taking a strategic approach rather than making ad hoc decisions. There are many problems in building environmental considerations into corporate strategy, including the uncertainties of the science, for example different views on global warming, and the difficulty of deciding on appropriate action because replacement processes or chemicals often give rise to new problems. The problems of adjusting to the scale of the issue have been underestimated as the concerns are increasingly global and cross-border. The precise cause of environmental problems, the effect they have and the best solution are often the source of discussion and controversy. For example, there were significant differences in the scientific evidence offered by Shell and Greenpeace for the disposal either at sea or on land of the Brent Spar North Sea drilling rig. Consumers are much more concerned about the conditions under which products are produced but their concern can be misplaced and ultimately lead to unfortunate consequences, as Dilemma 8.1 shows.

'Other trends'

Shortening product life cycles: the merging of markets through increasing globalisation is leading to greater concentration of powerful suppliers who have the resources to rapidly copy a competitor's product or develop their own products to exploit a new market opportunity. The increasing pace of technology means that a technical lead in a product is not likely to be held for very long, as competitors catch up quickly. This means that product life cycles are becoming shorter and improvements are introduced more frequently. To this must be added the much higher cost of research, development and commercialisation of new products, which places much greater pressures on the firm to distribute the new product throughout world markets as quickly and widely as possible in order to achieve a high return on research and development investment before new products are introduced.

Franchising, joint ventures and alliances: the pressure to exploit new technology and products as quickly and widely as possible has encouraged the rapid expansion of more creative and cost-effective ways of achieving cooperation in research, development and distribution, such as franchising, joint ventures and strategic alliances. As discussed in the previous chapter, whilst these market entry methods allow less control than total ownership, they do enable firms to develop a wider sphere of activity than they could do alone. Of course, the challenge is to find partners with truly complementary expertise, knowledge and capability.

Marketing management: these trends have led to significant changes in the way that marketing management operates, allowing a more creative approach to be adopted in developing product policy. Firstly, there are a wider range of options available in international marketing management, particularly by using the marketing mix elements which will be discussed later in this book. Secondly, there have been significant improvements in the tools available for marketing research, performance measurement and planning. Thirdly, there are more accurate and widely available sources of information which allow greater power for global brand management. It must be pointed out that success in using them depends upon managers being more flexible in redefining niche segments and creative in innovating in all areas of the marketing mix. Fourthly, with improved

DILEMMA 8.1

The football stitching game

A poster in the Chamber of Commerce building in Sialkot, a village in Pakistan, reads 'A child employed is a future destroyed'. Sialkot was a major centre for producing footballs and it received bad publicity when a journalist exposed local manufacturers who were employing child labour to stitch the balls. In 1997, the Atlanta Agreement was signed and 66 local manufacturers volunteered to stop child labour and allow monitors to check on their production. Now Save the Children believe that there is almost zero child labour in that area.

Before the agreement, most of the cutting and laminate printing was done in factories whereas stitching was outsourced to families around the villages. Now stitching is done by full-time adults in centres. This has had a number of beneficial effects. Saga Sports, which makes 4–5 million balls a year for Nike and other brands, now has better control systems, shorter delivery times and lower inventory.

However, the balls are now costly to make and consumers are not willing to pay extra for adult-only certified products. Chinese machine-stitched balls are cheaper and their machine stitching is now suitable for more expensive balls. Indeed, Saga are setting up a factory there. Pakistan's share of the football market dropped from 65 to 45 per cent between 1996 and 1998, some smaller producers went out of business and family incomes fell by about 20 per cent.

Save the Children supports the Atlanta Agreement but makes a distinction between child labour and child work, which they believe can give children income, skills and self-confidence without damaging schooling. Before the agreement 80–90 per cent of children who were stitching footballs at home already went to school. Of greater concern are child workers in industries, such as brick and surgical instrument-making, which are less publicised and controlled.

The dilemma is: how can the ethical concerns of consumers buying products be balanced with the needs of local communities producing them?

SOURCE: ROBIN LOWE

internal and external networking, new product development can become much more integrated within the firm's strategies and be capable of more satisfactorily meeting customer needs through the management of supply chain relationships. The Internet plays a significant role here too.

PRODUCT POLICY

Having considered the factors which underpin the development of an **international product portfolio**, the next steps are to look first at the suitability of the existing products before embarking on the development of new or modified products. The decision about which products should be included in the range to be marketed internationally is determined by several factors:

- the company's overall objectives in terms of growth and profits
- the experience, philosophies and attitude of the company to international development, and which of the company's financial and managerial resources will be allocated to international marketing
- the characteristics of the markets, such as the economic development and the barriers to trade of the firm's domestic and host countries
- the requirements, expectations and attitudes of the consumers in the market, for example as in Dilemma 8.2
- the products and services themselves, their attributes, appeal and perceived values (their positioning), the stage that they are at in the life cycle and economies of scale
- the ease of distributing and selling them
- the support the products require from other elements of the marketing mix and after-sales services
- environmental constraints (such as legal or political factors) which must be overcome
- the level of risk that the company is prepared to take.

Dilemma 8.2 shows that threats can be posed to products that seem to have the most secure future.

DILEMMA 8.2

Trying to ensure that diamonds are forever

SOURCE: ROBIN LOWE FROM VARIOUS PUBLIC SOURCES INCLUDING BBCNEWS ONLINE

Consumers are concerned about the source of products, the conditions under which they are produced and any adverse implications of production for host countries. De Beers, the South African diamond cartel, was accused by non-governmental organisations (NGOs) of buying diamonds from war zones, thus allegedly providing rebels with the cash to buy arms. As a result, De Beers wound down its business in Angola, withdrew its buyers from Congo and Guinea and promised to refuse supplies from Sierra Leone. De Beers but says that only 4 per cent of diamonds come from war zones and that other less scrupulous diamond traders will step in to trade in these countries. Moreover, it argues that the damage that could be done to the industry's image could be similar to that done by animal rights protesters in the fur trade. Loss of sales of diamonds could put at risk the livelihoods of miners in more peaceful countries, such as Botswana, Namibia and India. The company has also responded to South Africa's black economic empowerment laws by selling off a 26 per cent stake in its mining operations to company employees and pensioners.

The market for diamonds is increasing with the growing wealth in China and India and De Beers expects to exploit this through its marketing arm, the Diamond Trading Organisation. However, De Beers also faces a further threat. The quality of sythetic diamonds has improved considerably and many people cannot tell the difference

The dilemma for the legitimate diamond company is: how can it protect and build its image and reputation, and yet compete effectively in the industry?

Product strategies

Against the background of so many variables, it is inevitable that companies adopt a very wide range of product strategies in international markets. In formulating product policies, Mesdag (1985) postulated that a company has three basic choices:

SWYG   Sell What You have Got.

SWAB   Sell What people Actually Buy.

GLOB   Sell the same thing GLOBally disregarding national frontiers.

All three strategies have been used for a long time. Heinz, Mars, Heineken and Johnnie Walker have been international brands for decades using global product and brand strategies to enable them to clearly position their products as global brands. The Danes have long dominated the UK bacon market by following a SWAB strategy as have the French in their marketing of Cheddar cheese in the UK. The disadvantage of the SWAB strategy is that it is only possible to penetrate one market at a time. It may be also difficult to compete with local firms on their own terms. Furthermore, it is sometimes difficult for a foreign company to establish credibility as a supplier of products which have a strong domestic demand; for example, Suntory of Japan made good whisky but could not market it in the UK so it acquired Morrison Boxmore Distillers, which produces distinctively Scottish single malt whisky brands.

The SWAB approach is the classic differentiated approach, but whilst it is responsive to market needs it does make considerable demands on the firm's development, manufacturing, logistics and financial resources and is often impractical for these reasons.

SWYG are the most common form of export strategies, but they are also the most common reason for failure. The key objective for most firms following such strategies is to fill production lines at home rather than meet a market need, but by concentrating only on a few markets, many companies do successfully implement this kind of strategy. Mesdag argues also that some of the most successful global products started off as domestic products with a SWYG strategy, for example pizza, hamburgers and yoghurt. Success has been the result of the company's ability to meet new international emerging demand for the convenience of fast foods. The products may not necessarily be formulated identically across markets but they appeal to a pan-regional or global need and can therefore be positioned as cross-frontier brands. The success of the strategy has been based on identifying and meeting the needs of transnational customer segments. Heineken, the Dutch brewing firm, took over Egypt's only brewery, Al Harham Beverages, in 2002 and in so doing acquired Fayrouz, a fruit flavoured non-alcoholic malt drink popular in Egypt and certified halal by Al Azhar, a leading Sunni Islam religious institution. Heineken then had the opportunity to market Fayrouz in the Indian subcontinent and to Muslims in the UK, Germany, Netherlands and France.

Keegan (1989) has highlighted the key aspects of international marketing strategy as a combination of standardisation or adaptation of product and promotion elements of the mix, and offers five alternative and more specific approaches to product policy.

ONE PRODUCT, ONE MESSAGE WORLDWIDE

Since the 1920s, Coca-Cola have adopted a global approach, which has allowed them to make enormous cost savings and benefit from continual reinforcement of the same message. Whilst a number of writers have argued that this will be the strategy adopted for many products in the future, in practice only a handful of products might claim to have achieved this already. A number of firms have tried this and failed.

PRODUCT EXTENSION, PROMOTION ADAPTATION

Whilst the product stays the same, this strategy allows for the adaptation of the promotional effort to target either new customer segments or appeal to the particular tastes of individual countries; for example, Yoplait yoghurt attempts to capture the mood of the country in its various television adverts.

PRODUCT ADAPTATION, PROMOTION EXTENSION

This strategy is used if a promotional campaign has achieved international appeal, but the product needs to be adapted because of the local needs. Many suppliers of capital goods, IT management and consultancy promote the idea of providing technical solutions rather than selling industrial plants or computer hardware; and IBM have used 'Solutions for a small planet'.

DUAL ADAPTATION

By adapting both products and promotion for each market, the firm is adopting a totally differentiated approach. This strategy is often adopted by firms when one of the previous three strategies has failed, but particularly if the firm is not in a leadership position and, instead, must react to the market or follow the competitors. This is closest to a multidomestic strategy.

PRODUCT INVENTION

Product invention is adopted by firms, usually from advanced nations, who are supplying products to less well-developed countries. Products are specifically developed to meet the needs of the individual markets. After watching a programme on TV about AIDS in Africa at his home on Eel Pie Island in the middle of the Thames in London, Trevor Bayliss invented the clockwork radio to help the news to be spread to areas which did not have electricity and could not afford batteries. Despite rejections by major MNEs, Bayliss persevered and 50 000 radios per month were made by disabled staff by BayGen in South Africa.

MANAGING PRODUCTS ACROSS BORDERS

The product life cycle

In the domestic market models such as the product life cycle and Boston Consulting Group's portfolio matrix are used to manage a portfolio of products. The concepts can be applied in international markets to the management of a product, brand or product range across a portfolio of countries.

The life cycle concept is used as a model for considering the implications for marketing management of a product passing through the stages of introduction, growth, maturity and decline, and can be applied to international marketing. The British popular music industry was outstandingly successful as a major exporter during the 1960s, 1970s and early 1980s, all starting, perhaps, with the era of the Beatles and the Rolling Stones, when British artists rapidly gained global recognition. The UK market share of the industry declined during the early 1990s from 23 per cent to 18 per cent of the world market, and this share resulted largely from re-releases and new offerings from ageing rock stars such as Eric Clapton, Elton John and Sting. The mid-1990s saw the emergence of new groups such as the Spice Girls, Take That and Oasis, but shortening product life cycles appear to affect this industry too, with new stars staying at the top for much shorter periods.

Stars such as Kylie Minogue that have maintained their success over a long time have periodically repositioned themselves to 'rejuvenate' their product life cycle and brand.

The **international product life cycle** suggests that products in international markets can have consecutive 'lives' in different countries; this is illustrated in Figure 8.3. Soon after the product was launched in its domestic market it was introduced into another developed country, A. Later it was introduced to other developed and newly industrialised countries, B and C, and only recently to a less developed country, D. In the domestic market and country A, a replacement product is required, whilst considerable growth is still possible in the other countries. This illustrates the dilemma that firms often face: they must decide how to allocate scarce resources between product and market development.

In the past the length of the total product life cycle from birth to death has been unpredictable, but in some high technology markets it is now possible to accurately predict when new technology will force a new product's introduction. As a result it is now necessary for the product to be project managed for a limited and specific lifetime to ensure that by the end of its life the product has been profitable and recouped the initial investment.

The most significant change for both life cycle models is that the international communication revolution has led to more frequent simultaneous product introductions, particularly of consumer products, by global companies into different world markets backed by global branding and promotion, and so the sequential approach to marketing and manufacturing that is encapsulated in the original model applies less frequently. However, as we established earlier, not all companies operating internationally are global corporations, and it is therefore important not to ignore the model altogether. The concept of phases in the life cycle is still useful for a company that is not in a fast-changing market, perhaps simply exporting specialist engineering components and tools from an advanced economy.

FIGURE 8.3

The international product life cycle

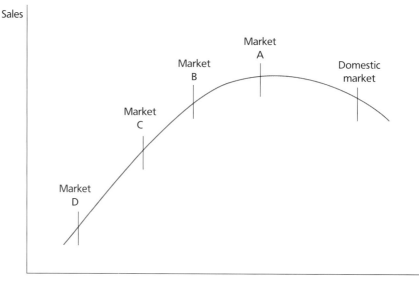

On balance, therefore, although the validity of the product life cycle has at various times been attacked by a variety of writers, it does have a role to play for certain types of company insofar as it is a model that provides a framework for thinking in detail about product policy, new product development, product introduction and product elimination. Because life cycles generally are shortening, there is an increased need for a well-developed policy of new product development or repositioning for new markets in order to replace or extend the life cycle, as Tiger Balm has done (Illustration 8.3).

Product portfolio analysis

The use of portfolio approaches in international product management centres around the Boston Consulting Group's (BCG) Growth–Share Matrix, the General Electric/McKinsey Screen, and the Arthur D. Little Business Profile Matrix. They are designed primarily to clarify the current strategic position of a company, its products and those of its competitors, and to help identify any future strategic options.

The dimensions of the analysis increase considerably when applied to the firm's international portfolio as the competitive positions occupied by a product are likely to differ significantly from one market to another, as indeed will the nature and intensity of competition. Comparing the strength of a portfolio across a variety of markets becomes difficult as the analytical base constantly changes. For these reasons, the BCG matrix, for example, might be based on one product range or on one brand with the circles in the matrices representing country sales instead of different product sales, as shown in Figure 8.4. This then provides a basis for analysing the current international product portfolio, assessing competitors' product/market strengths and forecasting the likely development of future portfolios both for itself and its competitors.

ILLUSTRATION 8.3

Tiger Balm: relieving the pains of warlords and sports stars

Tiger Balm is a herbal ointment remedy that was developed to relieve the aches and pains of the warlords and emperors in the imperial courts of China. The patriarch of the Aw family,

PHOTO CREDIT: IMAGE COURTESY OF HAW PAR HEALTHCARE LTD

Aw Chu Kin, passed his knowledge of Chinese medicine to his sons Boon Par (meaning gentle leopard) and Boon Haw (meaning gentle tiger), who was the marketing pioneer. The company name Haw Par comes from the names of both brothers.

Control of Haw Par has passed from the family to a large corporate group based in Singapore and now has sales in excess of US$150 million. The product sells into over 100 countries on the basis of its strong Asian heritage. The packaging is unique, with its springing tiger logo. It still retains the old reproduction photographs of the brothers with their names in Chinese and English and has an imitation official-looking seal as the cover round the small hexagonal jars and round cans. The original recipe has been enhanced with Chinese and Western additives to increase its effectiveness. It is now used by young and old and endorsement by sports stars has increased its appeal.

QUESTION *What strategies could be used to further grow the brand?*

Introduction and elimination activities

Whilst the major focus of product policy is upon new product development, the increased pace of the activity has a number of consequences for product management at both ends of the product life cycle. The factors that need to be taken into account in managing the product portfolio are:

- the firm's objectives
- the profitability of the company's existing range of products and degree of overlap in the positioning of products in the range
- the stage in the life cycle that the products have reached
- the manufacturing capacity available
- the likely receptiveness of the market to the new product, and
- the competitive structure of the market.

These factors have a number of implications for the product policy. Too many product introductions can risk overburdening the firm's marketing system. There is a constant need for a regular review of the range and for elimination decisions to be made where a product is either in its decline stage or simply failing to generate sufficient profit. The international perspective, however, means that decision-making is more difficult, since a product may be manufactured principally in a plant in one country, be a 'cash cow' in one market and a 'dog' in another. Careful analysis is therefore needed before the product elimination decision is taken. The identification of overlaps in the product range or poor performance of specific products may necessitate elimination of products if they are in the declining stage of the product life cycle, have been duplicated or have been replaced by a newer product.

The complexity of managing a wide portfolio of products is shown in Illustration 8.4, and it raises some fundamental issues about the product strategy alternatives.

FIGURE 8.4

The portfolio approach to strategic analysis (BCG matrix)

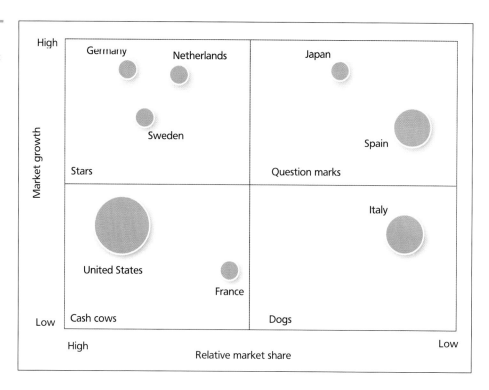

IMAGE, BRANDING AND POSITIONING

Of all the elements of the product or service offer, it is the image of the brand which is the most visible and it is the perceived value which consumers attach to this that is the central factor in positioning the products in the various markets.

The image of products, companies and countries can confer different values to consumers in different countries. Research by a number of writers has shown that products from particular countries have a stereotyped national image for such attributes as quality, price and reliability. Individual corporate brands either benefit from positive country of origin perceptions or must overcome negative perceptions to succeed in international markets.

Country of origin effects

Buyers evaluate the products that they may wish to purchase based on their assessment of intrinsic – taste, design, performance and quality – and extrinsic cues – brand names, packaging and country of origin.

Where the buyers' knowledge about the product is limited, for example because they do not understand the technology, country of origin perceptions influence their buying decisions. The consumers' perceptions of companies are usually based on national stereotypes, for example Japanese products tend to be regarded as high quality, reliable and 'miniaturised' whereas US products are big and 'brash'.

ILLUSTRATION 8.4

Core competence and centralisation in consumer products

The consumer packaged goods (CPG) business, which includes businesses such as Gillette, Proctor & Gamble (P & G) and, Colgate has shown very modest growth over the last few years, with revenues increasing by only 3–5 per cent annually (which would be expected from the natural gains from population growth and inflation), and profits up 8–12 per cent (largely achieved by cost cutting). Despite the introduction of successful new products, such as the M3 Power, Gillette's annual rate of sales shrank from a ten year average of 6 per cent from 1993–2003 to 1 per cent for the three years 2000–2003. Lauster and Neely (2005) note that by contrast Wrigley (makers of chewing gum) have achieved revenue growth of 8 per cent for the past ten years and increased operating income by 9 per cent a year. They note that the poorly performing companies have suffered because they have:

- Become a complicated mix of unrelated businesses, with different competitors, customer bases, infrastructure and success factors. Despite its rationalisation Unilever still has 400 brands.

- Before the 1990s retailers were weak distribution channel members, but now Wal-Mart and Tesco are dominant customers of CPG companies and, because of their power,

able to dictate negotiations. For example, whilst Wal-Mart accounts for 18 per cent of P & G sales, no single supplier has more than 5 per cent of Wal-Mart's sales.

- Retailers have been able to control not just the channel but the loyalty of the end user.

- In their desire to increase sales with these customers CPG companies have been willing to give up control in setting prices to the retailers, and been persuaded to limit advertising to enable retailers to charge low prices.

- Some retailers have wanted to limit the product ranges on shelves innovation has suffered.

- Been willing to customise according to the retailers' demands.

The successful CPG companies, such as Wrigley, beat their competition and outflank the powerful channel partners (the retailers) by promoting a distinctive brand-linked value proposition. They use this competitive advantage to customise their offering depending on the shopping occasion, channel and customer, building profit on the customer and consumer offering. At the same time they have organised for efficiency and helped retailers to make money.

QUESTION *What product policy should the MNE's adopt?*

SOURCE: ADAPTED FROM S.M. LAUSTER AND J. NEELY (2005) 'THE CORE'S COMPETENCE', ACCESSED FROM WWW.STRATEGY+BUSINESS.COM, ISSUE 38, FIRST QUARTER

By contrast, products from developing countries are often seen by Western consumers as low quality, unreliable, inexpensive and usually copies of products from developed countries. This was the perception of Japanese products some decades ago, and shows that it is possible to change consumer attitudes.

There are significant differences between countries in the willingness of consumers to buy locally produced products. Usually this appears to be related to the feeling of nationalism that exists in the country at the particular time the assessment is made. In developing countries, such as China, Ho (1997) found that nationally produced goods are often seen to be inferior to foreign goods but that this often changes with further economic development.

The country of origin effect does extend further. For example, the stereotyping relates just as much to developed countries. For example, there are strong associations between countries and the products that they are known for: Italy and pizza and Germany and machine tools. Overcoming these stereotypes is often the first challenge for international marketers who must prove that their product does not reinforce negative stereotypes. This is particularly important as customers become more knowledgeable. For example, many new car buyers know where their car has been designed and manufacturered as well as the country of origin of the brand. Increasingly, of course, the MNE's headquarters, the brand's perceived 'home', the location of product design and places of manufacture may all be in different countries. Many MNEs such as Nike are marketing, not manufacturing companies and source products from many countries. Their brand becomes the 'badge of quality' that overlays the country of origin effect.

Historical associations can be very important in some industries, as Illustration 8.5 shows.

Product image: As we have already emphasised, product image is one of the most powerful points of differentiation for consumers. The aspirational and achiever groups of purchasers wish to belong to particular worldwide customer segments and are keen to purchase products associated with that group. An interesting example of this is that the sales of luxury goods

ILLUSTRATION 8.5

Cooperation after a century of fighting

Two beer firms, Anheuser Busch (US) and Budejovicky Budvar (owned by the Czech government) have been fighting for

PHOTO CREDIT: EYE UBIQUITOUS/ALAMY

a century over ownership of the Budweiser brand. Anheuser Busch is the largest US brewer and its two beers, Bud Light and Budweiser, are the country's two best sellers. It claimed the right to the brand as it started brewing Budweiser in 1876, 19 years before Budejovicky Budvar was founded. However, Budejovicky Budvar claims Budweiser is simply named after its hometown Ceske Budejovice, called Budweis in German, where beer has been brewed since 1265.

At last the two companies have moved past discussions between lawyers and have come up with a practical solution. They have formed an alliance: Anheuser Busch will now distribute the Czech firm's rival Budweiser beer in the US under the Czechvar name. It will mean that the Czech company will gain access to the Anheuser Busch network of 600 independent distributors.

QUESTION *What are the key factors in developing an international beer brand?*

SOURCE: 'RIVAL BUDWEISER'S FORM AN ALLIANCE', BBCNEWS ONLINE, 8 JANUARY 2007

remained buoyant during recent recessions due to increased sales to emerging countries as the 'new' rich sought to buy similar products and services to the 'old' rich.

Company image is becoming increasingly important in creating a central theme running through diverse product ranges. It reinforces the vision and the values of the company, which can be recognised by employees and customers alike. For this reason many companies have spent considerable effort and resources on controlling and enhancing the corporate identity through consistent style and communications, discussed in more detail in Chapter 9.

Image can be equally important at the other end of the product spectrum to luxury goods. Aldi (Germany), Netto (Denmark) and Lidl (Sweden) use a no-frills approach to retailing by reinforcing their message of low prices with simple decor, warehouse-type displays and single colour understated packaging.

The image of a company also plays a vital role in business-to-business marketing, for example, when quoting for international capital projects. Decisions are likely to be made on the grounds of the perceived reputation of the company as, without a strong international presence, it can be quite difficult to break into a small elite circle of international companies, even if very low prices are quoted.

Connections too can be important. Reconstruction projects following wars are extremely lucrative and are usually awarded to global companies, such as the Halliburton group which has strong political connections in the US – it was once led by Vice President Dick Cheney.

International branding

Closely linked with the image of the product is the issue of branding. The role of branding, important as it is in domestic markets, takes on an additional dimension in international markets as it is the most visible of the firm's activities particularly for global companies, as we discussed in Chapter 6. Brands allow customers to identify products or services which will 'guarantee' satisfaction by providing specific benefits, such as performance, price, quality or image. For the firm, brands provide a point of differentiation from their competitors' products and are a way of adding value to the product. Brands have the potential to add value to the organisation by providing the following benefits:

Price premium: They should allow higher prices to be charged than for products that have an equivalent specification but no brand.

Higher volumes: Alternatively branded products can generate higher volumes than non-branded products if they are priced at market rates, rather than at a premium.

Lower costs: Higher volumes should lead to cost reduction from the economies of scale and the experience effect, so improving competitiveness.

Better utilisation of assets: The predictably high level of sales should lead brand managers to make effective use of assets such as equipment, the supply chain and distribution channels.

The constituents of the brand can include both tangible benefits, such as quality and reliability, and intangible benefits which may bring out a whole range of feelings, such as status, being fashionable or possessing good judgement by purchasing a particular brand. Very young children are now fully aware of which fashion label is 'cool' at the moment and advertisers are well aware of the effects of 'pester power' on all the family purchasing decisions.

Brand categories

Three brands categories are identified (Doyle 2000):

1 *Attribute brands* are created around the functional product or service attributes, such as quality, specification and performance, to build confidence amongst customers in situations where it is difficult for them to evaluate the difference between competitive products. The brand provides a 'guarantee'. Examples include Volvo for safety, Asda and Wal-Mart for everyday low prices and Intel for computer processing.

2 *Aspirational brands* create images in the minds of customers about the type of people who purchase the brand and convey the standards and values that the brand is associated with. Such brands do not simply deliver the customer's functional requirements of the products and services, such as high specification and quality, but also recognise the customer's status, recognition and esteem that can be associated with the brand. Examples include Ferrari, Rolex and high fashion.

3 *Experience brands* focus on a shared philosophy between the customer and brand and on shared associations and emotions, but not necessarily on claims of superiority. Examples include Nike, Virgin and easyJet.

The appeal of these different types of brand varies according to the context of the purchasing decision. In luxury product markets aspirational brands are likely to be most successful, whereas in consumer markets, where there is little to distinguish between the attributes and performance of products, experience branding is more appropriate. Attribute branding would be more appropriate in business-to-business markets where the purchasing process should be more rational, objective and based on specifications.

In global markets, too, because of different culture, customer expectations and market sophistication, the appeal of a particular branding approach might be more relevant for a similar product. For example, in some cultures the attributes, functionality and specification may be more important, whereas in others aspirational branding might be more appealing.

The brand value equation (Figure 8.5) draws attention to the offer to consumers of the intangible benefits that the brand adds over and above the tangible, functional benefits of a commoditised product or service. The challenge for international branding, of course, is to what extent the intangible benefits from branded products and services vary between countries, cultures and individuals.

The iPod was the 'must have' for the teenage and young adult generation of the early part of the millenium, not just because of its functionality and design but also because of peer pressure.

FIGURE 8.5
The brand value equation

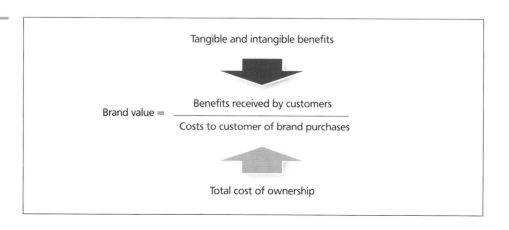

Rappa and Hirsh (2007) found that superb service was the indispensable ingredient of successful high-end brands and identified four principles to deliver customer satisfaction:

- Create a customer-centred culture.
- Use a rigorous staff selection process.
- Constantly retrain employees.
- Systematically measure and reward customer-centric behaviour.

Tangible and intangible benefits must also be valued against the background of the total cost of ownership of the branded product by the customer. The total cost of ownership and the tangible and intangible benefits are accrued over the lifetime of the product. For example, car ownership offers different benefits and costs in different markets, especially when considering the longer-term implications of, for example, warranty and servicing costs, car resale value and changing car fashions. Brand strength for cars is, to some extent, determined by the second-hand car values, with car marques such as BMW and Mercedes holding their value exceptionally well and some cars, such as Ferrari, even increasing in value.

Brand value

It has been suggested that the strongest brands convey a core value to all their customers by the associations that are made with their name. By adding '-ness' to the brand names consumers instantly associate values which are globally recognised – 'Pradaness', from 'Gucciness', and 'Appleness' from 'Sonyness'. The great brands (Table 8.1) have achieved their global status through high levels of investment and consistent management across their country markets of the dimensions used to value the brand over a long period of time. Usually the investment includes a large commitment to advertising but other factors, such as understanding their customers' needs and wants, totally consistent quality, reliability and continuous innovation are just as important to achieve widespread customer loyalty and recommendations.

Brand valuation is inevitably subjective to some degree, but the dimensions indicated in Figure 8.6 show that building the brand requires dedicated management of the complete marketing mix across the various markets, and there is evidence of this in all the successful brands. Brands can, of course, also decline in value from time to time due, for example, to a failure to understand customer expectations (Marks and Spencer), to inappropriate brand stretching (a number of the top fashion brands), to a failure to reposition in response to market decline (manufacturers of tractors and other agricultural machinery) or failure to respond to new competition (formerly state-owned airlines and telecoms businesses and many of the European and American car manufacturers at some point in their recent history).

Branding strategies

BRANDING STRATEGIES AND THE BRAND PORTFOLIO

The first decision is to choose between the alternative branding strategies that can be applied to the brand portfolio. The alternatives are:

- *Umbrella brands* occurs when one brand supports several products, as is the case with Philips electrical products.

■ *Product brands* occur, for example, Unilever, Procter & Gamble and pharmaceutical firms give each product a unique and distinctive brand.

■ *Line brands* occur where a company has a number of complementary products sharing the same brand concept. L'Oréal sells haircare products under the Studio Line of products.

■ *Range brands* are similar to Line brands but include a broader range of products. Heinz uses Weightwatchers and Nestlé uses Findus for frozen foods.

■ *Endorsing brands* is a weaker association of a corporate name with a product brand name and is often used after acquisition. Over time, Nestlé has

TABLE 8.1　The best global brands 2006

Rank	Brand	Country of origin	Sector	2006 Brand Value (US$m)	Change in brand Value per cent
1	Coco-cola	US	Beverages	67 000	-1
2	Microsoft	US	Computer Software	56 927	-5
3	IBM	US	Computer Services	56 201	5
4	GE	US	Diversified	48 907	4
5	Intel	US	Computer Hardware	32 319	-9
6	Nokia	Finland	Telecoms Equipment	30 131	14
7	Toyota	Japan	Automotive	27 941	13
8	Disney	US	Media	27 848	5
9	McDonald's	US	Restaurants	27 501	6
10	Mercedes	Germany	Automotive	21 795	9
11	citi	US	Financial Services	21 458	8
12	Marlboro	US	Tobacco	21 350	1
13	Hewlett-Packard	US	Computer Hardware	20 458	8
14	American Express	US	Financial Services	19 641	6
15	BMW	Germany	Automotive	19 617	15
16	Gillette	US	Personal Care	19 579	12
17	Louis Vuitton	France	Luxury	17 606	10
18	Cisco	US	Computer Services	17 532	6
19	Honda	Japan	Automotive	17 049	8
20	Samsung	Republic of Korea	Consumer Electronics	16 169	8
21	Merrill Lynch	US	Financial Services	13 001	8
22	Pepsi	US	Beverages	12 690	2
23	Nescafe	Switzerland	Beverages	12 507	2
24	Google	US	Internet Services	12 376	46
25	Dell	US	Computer Hardware	12 256	-7
26	Sony	Japan	Consumer Electronics	11 695	9
27	Budweiser	US	Alcohol	11 663	-2
28	HSBC	UK	Financial Services	11 622	11
29	Oracle	US	Computer Software	11 459	5
30	Ford	US	Automotive	11 056	-16
31	Nike	US	Sporting Goods	10 897	8
32	UPS	US	Transportation	10 712	8
33	J.P. Morgan	US	Financial Services	10 205	8
34	SAP	Germany	Computer Software	10 007	11
35	Cannon	Japan	Computer Hardware	9968	10

SOURCE: ADAPTED FROM 'THE 100 TOP BRANDS' AT HTTP://BWNT.BUSINESSWEEK.COM/BRAND/2006

gradually increased the size of 'Nestlé' on the packaging of its acquired brands, such as Kit-Kat. This may be one step towards umbrella branding.

■ *Source brands* occur where products are double branded with a corporate or range name and a product name, for example, Ford Mondeo.

Essentially the decision about which strategy to use is determined by whether the benefits of a shared identity outweigh the importance of differentiation between the individual product brands.

A further branding strategy, private branding, is the practice of supplying products to a third party for sale under their brand name. The two South Korean companies, Samsung and LG, achieved success initially largely by being original equipment manufacturers (OEM), but have rapidly developed internationally to the point where they now have high shares of certain product categories by building their own brands.

Private branding is used widely in retailing and as the major retailers have become more powerful, so the private brand share of the market has increased significantly, especially during times of recession. This is because the consumers perceive private brands as providing value for money, and this has been encouraged as retailers have continually improved the quality of their own label products.

Brand piracy

One of the most difficult challenges for brand management is dealing with brand piracy. Research suggests that the problem of forgery of famous brand names is increasing, and many but by no means all of the fake products have been found to originate in developing countries and in Asia. It is important to recognise the differences between the ways in which forgery takes place. Kaitiki (1981) identifies:

■ Outright piracy in which a product is in the same form and uses the same trademark as the original but is false.

■ Reverse engineering in which the original product is stripped down, copied and then undersold to the original manufacturer, particularly in the electronics industry.

■ Counterfeiting in which the product quality has been altered but the same trademark appears on the label. Benetton, Levi Strauss and LaCoste have all been victims.

■ Passing off involves modifying the product but retaining a trademark which is similar in appearance, phonetic quality or meaning – for example Coalgate for Colgate and Del Mundo for Del Monte.

■ Wholesale infringement is the questionable registration of the names of famous brands overseas rather than the introduction of fake products.

FIGURE 8.6
Brand valuation

The most basic criteria for brand evaluation include:

• title to the brand has to be clear and separately disposable from the rest of the business
• the value has to be substantial and long term, based on separately identifiable earnings that have to be in excess of those achieved by unbranded products

This might be considered brand piracy but it is entirely within the law. This has been very prevalent in e-business with the registration of dotcom sites by individuals hoping to sell the site later, at substantial profit, to the famous name.

There is a vast trade in pirated brands and copied products. It has been estimated that 90 per cent of the software used in India and China is counterfeit. However, some cultures do not accept that individuals should gain from ideas which should benefit everyone – there are substantial differences in the perception of the importance of counterfeiting. Others believe that the development of many underdeveloped economies would have been set back considerably if they had paid market rates for software, which raises the ethical question of whether oligopolistic companies such as Microsoft should be allowed to make fortunes for certain individuals by charging very high prices, whilst effectively excluding customers in underdeveloped countries who cannot afford to pay.

The issue of brand piracy clearly is costing MNEs vast revenues, and the US has led the way in insisting that governments crack down on the companies undertaking the counterfeiting. However, such firms have sophisticated networking operations, with much of their revenue coming from sales to consumers in developed countries. Trying to reduce or eliminate their activities is costly and time-consuming and unlikely to be a priority for governments in less developed countries. Moreover, pursuing legal action in foreign markets can be expensive, particularly for small companies, and can result in adverse publicity for larger firms.

The music industry has particularly suffered from illegal practices. A report published by the International Federation of the Phonographic Industry (IFPI) (2003) showed that the illegal music market was worth US$4.6bn (£2.8bn) globally. The myth of music piracy was of a victimless crime, but the IFPI reported that the money was going to support criminal gangs as well as sucking out money from the legitimate music industry.

Two out of five CDs were illegal and the top ten countries for piracy were Brazil, China, Mexico, Paraguay, Poland, Russia, Spain, Taiwan, Thailand and Ukraine. Forty per cent came from factories that produced professional-looking products but did not pay royalties. There was a growing problem of CD-burning software which allowed mass production cheaply and discreetly. Sanctions were applied by the US against Ukraine, but the illegal trade had simply moved across the border into Russia.

Illustration 8.6 shows that it is not only small products but cars too that are faked in China.

Positioning

Closely related to brand strategy and at the heart of its implementation is positioning. Positioning is largely concerned with how a product or service might be differentiated from the competition. However, it is important to stress that it is the customers' perceptions of the product or service offer that will indirectly confirm the positioning and so determine its success. Firms can only seek to establish and confirm the positioning in the consumers' minds through their management of the marketing mix. In countries at different stages of economic development the customer segments that are likely to be able to purchase the product and the occasions on which it is bought may be significantly different. For example, whilst KFC and McDonald's restaurants aim at everyday eating for the mass market in the developed countries, in less developed countries they are perceived as places for special occasion eating, and out of reach of the poorest segments of the population. A Mercedes car may be perceived as a luxury car in many countries but as an everyday taxi in Germany.

Unilever has a different approach. It introduced a new logo for its ice cream so that whilst the familiar names stay the same, for example Wall's in the UK and Ola in the Netherlands, the background design and font are being standardised around the world.

The perceptions of the product positioning are likely to vary in some dimensions. However, there appears to be an increasing demand for standardised products, particularly in the developed countries, amongst market segments that are mobile and susceptible to influence by the media and through travel, and clearly there is a strongly emerging demand for the same products amongst consumers in the less developed countries. Achieving unique positioning for a product or service must come from the creative dimensions of positioning rather than resorting to simple price positioning.

In confirming the positioning of a product or service in a specific market or region, it is necessary, therefore, to establish in the consumers' perception exactly what the product stands for and how it differs from existing and potential competition by designing an identity which will clarify the value of the product. In doing this it is necessary to emphasise the basis of the positioning strategy, which might focus upon one or more elements of the total product offer. The differentiation might be based upon price and quality, one or more product or service attributes, a specific application, a target consumer or direct comparison with one competitor.

ILLUSTRATION 8.6

The sincerest form of flattery

There is a saying goes in Shanghai that 'we can copy everything except your mother'. Soy sauce is mixed with fizzy water and passed off as Pepsi, fake Rolex watches, top fashions and even fake blood plasma can be found. A surprising area for fakes is cars given that they involve complex production processes in highly efficient factories using expensive equipment managed by highly trained engineers. There are an increasing number of fakes of western car models.

PHOTO CREDIT: ULANA SWITUCHA/ALAMY

At the 2006 Beijing motor show, Great Wall showed its Coolbear, Gwperi and Florid cars, clones of the Nissan Cube, Fiat Panda and Toyota Yaris. Chana, a company that builds the Ford Focus, Volvo S40 and Mazda 3 for the Chinese market had clearly learnt from its Western partners and launched its coupe-convertible, the BYD F8, which appeared to be a Mercedes CLK at the front and Astra TwinTop at the back. The Hover appeared to be very like a Honda CR-V stretch limo.

In the past Volkswagen copies have appeared as well as 'Hongda' motorcycles. Shuanghuan copied Audi's logo and Honda's CR-V, calling it the SR-V and then started exporting a BMW X5 look-alike to Romania and Italy. SG Automotive, a truck and bus manufacturer, has produced copies of the Chevrolet Colorado and Toyota Tacoma trucks.

None of the legal action brought by foreign firms has been successful as they have become embroiled in slow court proceedings, thrown out on technical grounds, or have failed because the designs have not been properly registered in China. The major car makers are also reluctant to cause too much trouble, given the potential size of the market.

QUESTION *What should the international car makers do to protect their business and reputation?*

FORM OF FLATTERY', *THE ECONOMIST* 4 APRIL 2007 AND SHANGHAI AUTO SHOW: HUANGHAI PIRATES TOYOTA, CHEVY PICKUPS APRIL 25TH, 2007 ACCESSED AT WWW.NEWS.WINDINGROAD.COM

NEW PRODUCT DEVELOPMENT

A recurring theme of discussions of international marketing issues is the increasing need for companies to have a dynamic and proactive policy for developing new products in order to satisfy the apparently insatiable demand of consumers for new experiences and to reinforce and, where necessary, renew their source of competitive advantage. Some companies have new product development as a corporate objective. Johnson and Johnson generates 35 per cent of its sales from products that are less than five years old compared to 30 per cent in 1980. Lim, Sharkey and Heinrichs (2006) argue that faster **new product development** capability is essential for firms striving for a higher degree of export involvement.

The nature of new product development

It is important to recognise at the outset, however, that few new products are actually revolutionary products. Figure 8.7 shows the various categories of new products in terms of their newness to the market and company. The implications of this are that firms need to innovate in every aspect of their business through a process of continual improvement rather than wait for the next breakthrough invention.

Many of the products are largely intended to refresh and reinforce the product range by complementing the existing company and brand image, rather than causing a change of direction. In the infamous New Coke fiasco, the new recipe, preferred in taste tests and intended to improve the product, was resisted in the US in favour of retaining a traditional image because it was seen to pose a threat to American culture.

Major invention breakthroughs still occur, although significantly less frequently than before, but there are exceptions. Usually, developing new technologies is hugely expensive. For example, it is estimated that the cost of developing a new drug is now in excess of US$300 million and takes over 15 years. In order to recover the research and development costs it is necessary to market new ideas simultaneously in all developed countries, as the time taken by competitors to copy or improve products and circumvent patents is shortening. Moreover, when pharmaceutical products come out of the patent period, they can legitimately be

FIGURE 8.7
New product categories

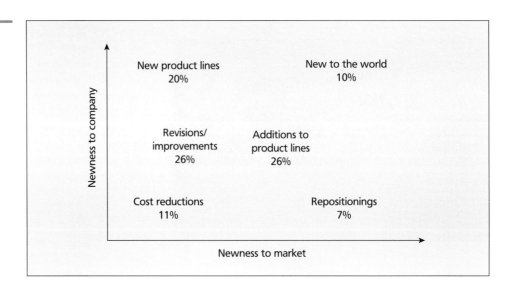

copied as generic drugs – companies such as Ranbaxy in India have grown fast and built a strong global business doing this. Increasingly, as Illustration 8.7 shows, research and development, supported by patents, is being undertaken by firms from emerging markets.

Even the largest companies do not have sufficient resources on their own to achieve rapid distribution of a new product into all world markets, so the diffusion of new products into world markets is at least as important a part of the process as the initial idea. This leads to the use of different market entry methods, such as licensing, franchising and strategic alliances, to secure cost-effective diffusion.

The new product development process

In its simplest form, developing products follows a similar process for international markets to that in domestic situations:

- idea generation
- initial screening
- business analysis
- development
- market testing
- commercialisation and launch.

Where the process does differ in international markets, however, is in the level of analysis, coordination and communication that becomes necessary when assessing the new product's suitability for a variety of markets. Particular emphasis must be placed upon the quality of the information system, as it is essential that the product or service meets the needs of the customers and is positioned accurately in each market from the outset. With this in mind, the international development process should incorporate the following elements.

Idea generation must ensure that ideas worldwide are accessed so that duplication is avoided and synergy is optimised by effectively using all available internal and external resources to generate new ideas, including employees, R & D departments, competitors, sales people, customers, distributors and external experts.

Initial screening involves establishing rigorous international criteria, including both production and marketing factors, to test the ideas for suitability in all world regions so that opportunities and limitations are not overlooked. Ideas that may,

---

ILLUSTRATION 8.7

China promoting IP rights

In response to major criticism in recent years that there was widespread patent infringement in China and following its acceptance in the WTO, the country made Intellectual Property Rights (IPR) a top priority. It set up a national system, the State Intellectual property Office (SIPO) for accepting patent applications for IPR protection and handling complaints about IPR infringements. SIPO noted that 1076 cases were prosecuted in the first half of 2006. Against the background of a stronger government policy, American companies increased their patent applications in China by over 20 per cent per year. However, by 2006 only IBM was in the top ten foreign firms in terms of patent applications. Five of the others were Japanese and three were South Korean. China was listed in the top ten countries for patent applications for the first time.

QUESTION *What are the advantages and disadvantages for multinational firms in legally protecting their intellectual property rights in this way?*

for example, be inappropriate for Western Europe might be appropriate for South America. In doing this an assessment should be made of the degree of adaptation that will be necessary for individual markets.

Business analysis must involve establishing criteria for potential success or failure of the product and linking the criteria with regions and/or markets. It must make provision for contingencies such as environmental and competitive situations and unexpected events which might adversely affect the business case.

Product development must include ensuring that all relevant functions such as production, design and packaging become involved in the process. The most appropriate R & D centres for the development process should be selected, with particular attention being paid to such factors as access to technological expertise and location near prime target and lead markets.

Market testing must involve ensuring the test area is representative of the prime target markets, an adequate infrastructure in terms of the necessary services such as advertising and market research agencies, and an appropriate distribution network. It should also take account of potential competitor response both in the test market and globally.

The launch must be planned either to be sequential, with an initial concentration upon prime markets or lead markets, or to be a simultaneous launch. Allowance must be made for aggressive competitive responses, as few competitors will give up market share without a fight.

To protect the firm's competitive advantage the company needs to pay particular attention to the ability of competitors to copy a new product and launch it in a separate market. There are a number of actions that companies might take to protect their intellectual property, such as taking strong patent protection, or entering into licensing arrangements to ensure fast, widespread penetration of the world or regional markets.

Timing is perhaps the most critical element of the process, not only in terms of exploiting an opportunity or competitive weakness at the right moment but also minimising the time to market – how long it takes from when the idea was first generated to making it available commercially and the time it takes to achieve the desired level of diffusion.

Approaches to technology transfer and the benefits for marketing

The traditional, sequential and largely internal approach to new product development has considerable disadvantages because of a number of factors, including:

- shortening of product life cycles
- risk and cost of internal development
- time, cost and expertise required for testing, and
- need to have 'non-core' activities such as product and packaging design and process development as part of the in-house development process.

In an attempt to resolve these problems, many firms are adopting a more inter-active approach in which new product developments are carried out jointly between the manufacturer, component maker, designer and technology supplier. A variety of specialist organisations including design companies, R & D companies and universities might be used by the manufacturer to increase the speed and quality of the development. The main benefits of an interactive approach to new product development for the company are the concentration of skills and expertise on core activities, the ability to condense timescales and access to the best knowledge available on a particular topic.

This is of course problematic if managers in many countries need to be consulted at each stage of the NPD process, as this leads to delays. Eppinger and Chitkara (2006) note that companies in many industries have engineering teams located in different parts of the world to collaborate in new product development, but that without frameworks to help managers find it difficult to achieve the necessary cohesion in the operation to drive efficient growth and innovation. The authors highlight Hyundai, Hewlett Packard and Alcatel as firms that have achieved this.

To further speed up the NPD process the stages can be regarded as simultaneous rather than linear, for example testing the concept on customers around the world, carrying out the detailed analysis for the business case and designing the product packaging, could go ahead at the same time.

Research and development strategies

No matter which approach is adopted, major international companies must still decide upon the aims of their own R & D, the exact nature of the activities undertaken and where they should be located. They must take decisions on:

- the location of their own internal R & D facilities
- the extent to which they contract out certain parts of their research and development programme
- whether or not they might acquire a company which can provide either the required new technology or a new product
- licensing the technology and process from another company, or
- funding joint ventures or strategic alliances with companies that have complementary technology.

Smaller companies, with low-key international operations which amount to little more than ad hoc exporting, are rarely involved in genuine considerations of international new product development and concentrate their R & D activities in the domestic country, but as they grow, pressures emerge to establish R & D facilities in other locations and it becomes necessary to balance the arguments for and against centralisation. As the operations of transnational companies and the diversity of sources of supply become increasingly complex, different patterns of involvement in R & D investments emerge, such as:

- units to transfer technology from the parent company to foreign subsidiaries
- local technology units to specifically develop new and improved products in the local markets
- global technology units, not necessarily based at the head office, to develop and launch products simultaneously into the major world markets, and
- corporate technology units, which concentrate upon the generation of new technology of a long-term/exploratory nature.

In general, the R & D activities of international companies tend to follow an evolutionary path, but for many the major question is whether or not they should move away from the dominance of their domestic country R & D location and if so, where should their R & D facilities be located.

Many companies still concentrate a large proportion of R & D activity in their country of origin, but as they move increasingly towards transnational operations so the concept of the home country becomes increasingly meaningless. It is, however, useful to consider the arguments for and against the centralisation of R & D activities, and these are shown in Figure 8.8.

Success and failure in new product development

One of the most difficult aspects of NPD is to reduce the high levels of risk (and therefore the cost) of new product failure. The classic studies of success and failure of new products in developed countries, particularly the US and UK, emphasise that for success it is necessary to place greater emphasis upon marketing rather than technical factors. The key to success is an effective NPD strategy which includes the development of the central and supporting processes, in order to generate a flow of new products that might vary in market impact, but will include some high revenue or high-margin generators. This approach is preferable to trying to spot one blockbuster new product some time in the future.

In order to do this, Griffin (2003) suggests three fundamental requirements of the process;

- Uncover unmet needs and problems.
- Develop a product with competitive advantage.
- Shepherd the products through the firm.

The reasons for the failure of new product developments in international markets include:

- tariff barriers and non-tariff barriers
- local competitor subsidies
- cultural insensitivity
- poor planning
- poor timing
- lack of a unique selling proposition in the international market
- product deficiencies in the market, and
- misguided enthusiasm of top management.

Tzokas, Hart and Saren (2003) suggest that market information is central to achieving success in NPD, and summarise the research studies that have high-lighted its role within the strategic success factors:

- Ensuring product performance improvements over what is already available.

FIGURE 8.8
The arguments for and against centralisation of R and D

Arguments for centralisation	Arguments against centralisation
• economies of scale	• pressure from subsidiaries
• easier and faster communication	• pressure from governments
• better coordination	• benefits of public relations
• greater control over outflow of information with implications for secrecy	• use of wider range of skills and abilities
• greater synergy	• benefits from comparative advantage
• avoiding duplication	• greater sensitivity to local tastes
• overcoming problems of ownership	• better monitoring of local competitive activity
	• closeness to possible acquisitions
	• access new technology wherever it is located

■ Achieving synergy with existing firm technologies and manufacturing capability and learning new capabilities quickly.

■ Achieving marketing synergies, such as channels and promotion, often because of the need to target a new segment.

■ Integrating the contributions of marketing and R & D.

■ Identifying attractive markets with growth potential.

■ Effectively carrying out the NPD process, including pre-development activities, such as idea generation, screening, concept and business case investigation.

■ Obtaining support from top management.

■ Speed in development.

Key to success in technology sectors is generating a continual flow of new product introductions, but success is by no means guaranteed. Even for technologically leading edge companies such as Motorola (see Illustration 8.8) not every idea will make it to the market and be a commercial success, so risk-taking and tolerating failure must be accepted by the firm's management, otherwise staff will simply not suggest ideas in case they are blamed for a failure.

ILLUSTRATION 8.8

Restarting the innovation culture at Motorola

Ed Zander was appointed CEO of Motorola in 2004. One of his first tasks was to tell staff to forget about Iridium, an ambitious satellite communication project, launched in 1998, which had gone bankrupt within months. The failure had a significant effect on the firm's confidence and risk-taking with new innovations. Zander encouraged staff throughout the company to start taking risks, believing that good execution of a company strategy requires many staff to take risks. Teams from across functions, such as design, engineering, marketing and finance, got together to sort out the complexities of new product

development and launch. Cooperation improved as members of the teams were much more prepared to try difficult things to help others rather than worrying about being blamed for something failing.

Initially the new strategy worked. Motorola's fortunes changed. Sales of its RAZR phone had exceeded 50 million by 2006. However it was not just the technology that made the difference. Through its innovative design it was probably the first phone to have achieved a similar iconic status to the iPod or Blackberry. Motorola introduced a stream of follow-on products including the SLVR (silver), KRZR, Q (an email smart phone that was slimmer than the Blackberry or Palm Treo) and SCPL, a low-cost slimline phone for developing markets. Motorola lost its market leader position to Nokia in 1998 and by 2004 Nokia handset revenues were double those of Motorola, whereas by 2006 Motorola revenues were just 30 per cent behind.

However, by 2007 Motorola appeared to be taking even bigger risks as it pursued the route of 'seamless mobility', as more communications technologies moved from fixed line to wireless technology. It invested in IPTV television services supplied through broadband links and WiMax, an emerging wireless standard that links mobile devices to the Internet at broadband speed. One influential investor was concerned and critical of the directors as the company's share price fell to its lowest level for some time.

QUESTION *What are the key factors necessary for an effective new product development policy?*

SOURCE: ADAPTED FROM 'THE CUTTING EDGE', ED ZANDER, *THE ECONOMIST*, 5 OCTOBER 2006, AND MOTOROLA'S RAZR THICK PROFILES, WWW.BUSINESSWEEK.COM, 18 OCTOBER 2005

SUMMARY

■ In many business sectors product and service strategies are being affected by the increased globalisation of consumer tastes, communications, technological advances and the concentration of business activity. At the same time, however, given the level of competition and choice available, there is an increasing expectation amongst customers that their individual needs will be met.

■ Product managers are balancing the efficiency benefits of standardisation in terms of economies of scale and the experience effect with the need and cost of adapting products and services to meet the needs of local customers, regulations and usage conditions.

■ The growth of international services is a feature of international marketing and it is being driven by low labour costs and increasing demand in developing countries and the increased possibilities for transferring information through information technology and communications.

■ As more products are reaching the mature phase of the life cycle they are becoming commodities, and there is a need to use additional services to differentiate them from competitor offerings. However, services are often difficult to standardise globally because they are affected significantly by the different expectations of service delivery that exist in different cultures.

■ The product or service strategy is usually at the centre of international marketing operations. Branding is a key part of product and service management, particularly in international markets, but it is difficult to establish truly global brands that are truly distinctive and have images that appeal to cross-cultural customer segments.

■ New product and service development and innovation throughout the marketing process are essential for growth and the renewal of the international portfolio and, particularly for culturally sensitive products and services, it is vital to obtain input from the different stakeholders around the world in order to ensure that they will be successful.

KEYWORDS

Adaptation	Inseparability	New product
Brand piracy	Intangibility	development
Branding strategies	International branding	Perishability
Country of origin	International product life cycle	Product strategies
effect	International product offer	Services
Heterogeneity	International product portfolio	Standardisation

CASE STUDY

Lego

Lego is one of the world's best known toy brands, yet things have not been going well. For 70 years Lego, the leading European toymaker, has prospered, promoting learning and development through play by explaining that play is 'nutrition for the soul'. Lego sells its colourful bricks in 130 countries, claiming that on average everyone on earth has 52 bricks.

However, in 1998 it made its first loss and in 2004, following six years of declining sales and profits it made a huge loss of US$240 million, and rumours circulated that it would be taken over by Mattel, America's biggest toy maker. Lego was still owned by the family of Ole Kirk Christiansen, the Danish carpenter who founded the company in 1932. The family decided to stand by the company, injected their own money and appointed Jorgen Vig Knudstorp, a former management consultant for McKinsey, as the new CEO.

SOURCE: ADAPTED FROM 'PICKING UP THE PIECES', *THE ECONOMIST*, 28 OCTOBER, 2006 AND OTHER PUBLIC SOURCES

Lego had years of unbroken sales growth and for 50 years the plastic bricks faced little competition. Today children are growing up more quickly. Although Lego recognised this, some commentators felt they had lost their way in trying to address the problem. After the company posted its first losses in 1998 it negotiated lucrative tie-ins with Disney, the Harry Potter and Star Wars movies. More than one million Hogwarts Castle lego sets were sold when the first two Harry Potter films came out, helping the firm back into profits in 2001 and 2002, but the company became too dependent on these licensing agreements and sales slumped again when no blockbuster Harry Potter films were released.

Other brand extension strategies failed to deliver the desired growth, when products such as Galidor, a cartoon-related series of Lego figures, was criticised because it lacked the open-ended imaginative play that the Lego brand was known for, and Lego music builder, aimed at pre-school children, under performed. Lego phased out the Duplo brand, established in 1969, and replaced it with Lego Explore but parents thought Lego no longer made larger sized bricks for children aged 18 months to 5 years and Lego's revenues in the pre-school market halved. Poor forecasting in the US of what its best sellers in its popular Bionicle range would be resulted in being overstocked in some products and out of stock in some successful products, and there were worldwide complaints that colours did not match.

With the aim of becoming a lifestyle brand, Lego had diversified into clothes, watches and video games. Lego had also tried to attract more girls. However it had neglected its core customer segment of boys aged 5–9. Knudstorp believed that Lego had become arrogant and had stopped listening, so he went around to talk to the retailers. They told him that Lego should not change the core brand and the company should stick to what it had always been good at.

The traditional toy market was slimming down due to low-cost copies, hi-tech competitors and falling birth rates in developed countries. The turnaround plan, begun in March 2004, was painful as 3500 of the firm's 8000 workers lost their jobs. Half the 2400 jobs in Billund, the home of Lego, were due to be phased out. Factories in Switzerland and the US were closed and production moved to Eastern Europe and Mexico. Major stakes in the four Legoland theme parks and other assets in America, South Korea and Australia were sold off.

The management structure was simplified and a more commercial culture was fostered through a performance-based pay scheme and frank discussions about the financial position of the company took place between the management and employees, who had never before been used to talking about money. By 2006, having placed greater emphasis on the core business, the company had returned to profit and was increasing sales.

Although much of its diversification was stopped some parts were paying off well. Its Bionicle range, based on Polynesian mythology, was expanded and further new toys based on tie-ins with films such as Star Wars and Harry Potter were developed under licence. The Lego Star Wars video game in which Lego figures enact Star Wars was a best seller.

QUESTIONS

1 Critically evaluate the branding strategy that Lego pursued in its effort to re-establish itself in the global market since 1998, identifying its future options.

2 Develop an outline international marketing strategy for Lego based on your preferred strategic option.

DISCUSSION QUESTIONS

1 Identify the major macro environmental trends in world trade. Using examples from one product and one service sector explain how these trends have affected product and service portfolio management across international markets.

2 In an ideal world companies would like to manufacture a standardised product. What are the factors that support the case for a standardised product and what are the circumstances that are likely to prevent its implementation?

3 Examine the ways in which a major company operating in many countries around the world can use new product development and commercialisation to enhance its ambitions to become a global company.

4 What challenges would you expect to face in marketing products and/or services from:

(a) A developing country to a developed country?

(b) A developed to a less developed country?

How might these challenges be overcome? Illustrate your answer by focusing on a product or service of your choice.

5 International services marketing is a major growth area. Using one service sector as an example, explain what the main barriers to success are and what strategies might be used to overcome them.

References

Doyle, P. (2000) *Value based marketing strategies for corporate growth and shareholder value*. Wiley.

Eppinger, S.D. and Chitkara, A.R. (2006) 'The new practice of global product development', *MIT Sloan Management Review* 47 (4): 22–30.

Griffin, A. (2003) 'Marketing's role in new product development and product decisions', in *Marketing best practice*. Thomson South-Western.

Ho, S. (1997) 'The emergence of consumer power in China', *Business Horizons*, September–October.

Howard, E. (1998) 'Keeping ahead of the green regulators', *Mastering Global Management*, Part 10, *Financial Times*.

IFPI (2003) *Commercial piracy report*, July, London, available at www.ifpi.org.

Kaitiki, S. (1981) 'How multinationals cope with the international trade mark forgery', *Journal of International Marketing*, 1, (2): 69–80.

Keegan, W.J. (1989) *Multinational marketing management*, Prentice Hall.

Kotler, P. (2002) *Marketing management: analysis, planning, implementation and control*, Prentice Hall.

Lim. J., Sharkey, T.W. and Heinrichs, J.H. (2006) 'Strategic impact of new product development on export involvement', *European Journal of Marketing*, 40, 44–60.

Mesdag, M. van (1985) 'The frontiers of choice', *Marketing*, 10 October.

Rappa, R. and Hirsh, E. (2007) 'The luxury touch', accessed at www-strategy-business.com, 3 April.

Ringshaw, G. (2006) 'Bankers face Mecca', *Sunday Times*, 15 October.

Stone, A. (2006) 'Profits save the world', *Sunday Times*, 10 December.

Tzokas, N., Hart, S. and Saren, M. (2003) 'New product development, a marketing agenda for change' in S. Hart, *Marketing changes*. Thomson.

INTEGRATIVE LEARNING ACTIVITY 2

INTERNATIONAL MARKETING PLANNING: STRATEGY DEVELOPMENT

Introduction

In the Li Ning activity, against the background of information on the market structure and customer needs, a segmentation approach was developed. In this activity we focus on possible strategic alternatives and the development of a global marketing strategy by companies from emerging markets who are becoming global players in the industries within which they operate.

Arguably the most significant change in international marketing over recent years has been the changing competitive landscape globally, as major players who were previously national champions in their own countries in emerging economies, ranging from China and Taiwan to Korea and Brazil, have developed as potential global players.

These companies have not really developed their global strategies through the traditional multi-national route, but are becoming global by developing global brands, either organically or by buying Western companies to aid their global growth. Interesting, however, as they develop is their transnational approach to strategic development. In this activity we consider a number of companies from emerging markets who are highly competitive and who are aiming to become truly global. You are able to make a choice of which one to investigate, but essentially the activity is about analysing the basis of the competitive advantage of the firms involved and thinking through how this has to develop and shift if they are to build and sustain a global competitive advantage. This gives you the opportunity to consider how an altering global competitive landscape changes the competitive behaviour of companies in their struggle for a global competitive advantage. It is these issues and how the company

you choose should resolve them that are explored in this activity.

Learning objectives

After completing this unit the reader should be able to:

- Critically appraise the global marketing strategy that a company is following and evaluate the potential for their success or failure.

- Understand the role and value of global marketing planning and its implications for the organisation structure.

- Understand the concept of globalisation and how it affects the strategies of organisations.

The scenario: the future global players from emerging markets

Boston Consulting Group (BCG) have identified 100 newcomers (called the RDE 100) from developing economies, such as China, India, Brazil, Mexico and Russia – firms who are cash rich and hungry for global growth. Their operating profits are about £100 billion following several years in which they grew at an average rate of 24 per cent annually.

Shareholders of these new firms have reaped a reward of 150 per cent in dividends and share price gains in the past five years, compared with a negative return in the Standard and Poor's 500 list.

Previously newcomers from emerging markets have focused on building their competitive advantage through marketing low-value manufacturing and service activities. These firms, however, are building the capability to compete with the established firms by the use of much more sophisticated marketing approaches: for example by using their success in meeting customer needs in their huge and rapidly growing domestic markets as a platform for global expansion. The question for all of these companies is whether they can compete on a more sustainable basis in the global marketing environment.

The following ten firms are typical of the 100 identified by BCG

Firm	Country of origin	Sector
Embraer	Brazil	Aerospace
Natura	Brazil	Cosmetics
Haier	China	Home appliances
China Mobile Communications	China	Telecommunications services
Tsingtao Brewery	China	Food and beverages
Lenovo	China	Computers and IT equipment
Wipro	India	IT services/business process outsourcing
Grope Modelo	Mexico	Food and beverages
Indofood Sukses Marmur	Indonesia	Food and beverages
Vestel Group	Turkey	Consumer electronics

The companies identified cover a range of industries and have adopted a variety of strategies in their fight to develop a global brand. China's computer-maker Lenovo paid US$1.5 billion to buy IBM's ailing PC business, partly because it wanted to gain control of the ThinkPad brand. Others gained the strength to pull off big deals after securing access to cheap funding through growing a strong domestic position. Tsingtao is one of the few Chinese drinks brands known globally. Over the past several years it has made a number of acquisitions and mergers to fulfil its global strategic goals. Another brewer in the list, Grupo Modelo from Mexico, exports to 150 countries worldwide. Its international business has sprung from a very strong domestic position in Mexico where it has 70 per cent of the total beer market. Its best-selling global brand is Corona Extra which is fourth in the list of the world's best-selling brands.

PT Indofood Sukses Makmur (Indofood) is one of the world's largest makers of instant noodles, commonly referred to as ramen. The Indonesian company also manufactures a range of food products for the retail and food service sectors. The company's instant noodles are exported to more than 50 countries in Asia, Europe, the Americas, Australia and Africa.

Natura from Brazil is the only cosmetics company to feature on the list. It is one of the highest valued brands in Brazil and internationally has operations in Argentina, Chile, Peru, Mexico, Venezuela and France. Natura have a strong commitment to environmental protection and have used this as a distinctive competence in building their brand. They have committed themselves to being an eco-friendly company, aiding the fight against global warming. This platform is central to their international development.

Another Brazilian Company listed is Embraer (the Empresa Brasileira de Aeronáutica S.A.), a Brazilian aircraft manufacturer. They produce commercial, military, and corporate aircraft and are one of the three top exporters in Brazil. It has a workforce of 20 000, and a firm order book totalling US$14.8 billion. This means that globally Embraer has the third-largest yearly delivery of commercial aircraft (behind Boeing and Airbus) and the fourth-largest workforce (behind Boeing, Airbus and Bombardier).

China Mobile is the world's largest mobile telephone operator ranked by number of subscribers, but still operates predominantly in its home market. In turnover it is second only to Vodafone, who have a share of the company. In China less than 30 per cent of the population have a mobile telephone so there is clearly a lot more scope for local market growth.

Wipro (India) is in the ICT market offering IT services and business process outsourcing services. They have revenues of US$38 billion and a growth rate of 20 per cent per annum. Whilst their major strength is in the Asian markets, they are developing a large number of strategic alliances around the globe which are helping to build their global presence.

The Turkish group Vestel operates in the consumer electronics market, producing a wide range of products from television and satellite receivers to cooking appliances and telephones. Vestel has a number of operations around the world and 11 research and development centres strategically located in different parts of the globe. Although they started life as a contract manufacturer, they have grown to be a substantial presence under their own brand across a number of international markets, particularly in the European Union. The Haier group, on the other hand, is perhaps one of the largest. They have a global turnover of US$12.8 billion and have over 240 subsidiaries worldwide. The company produces 96 product lines and its products are sold in over 100 countries.

The task: Developing a strategy for a global challenger from an emerging market

You are required to select one of the companies listed, all of whom come from emerging markets and are embarking on global expansion. Your brief is to develop an outline global marketing strategy to enable it to challenge the existing competitors in the market.

You should prepare a report of approximately 3500 words.

Tasks

1 Critically and briefly evaluate the trends in the international market sector in which the company operates.

2 Against the background of your answer to question 1, comment on how well your chosen firm is placed to develop globally.

SOURCE: ADAPTED FROM VARIOUS SOURCES INCLUDING :'THE RISE OF NEWCOMERS FROM EMERGING MARKETS' WWW.TELEGRAPH.CO.UK/MONEY, 6 JUNE 2006, G RINGSHAW 'THE INCREDIBLE EMERGING HULKS', SUNDAY TIMES, FEB.11 2007

3 Advise the company on how to develop a sustainable long-term global marketing strategy.

The report should include the following sections:

Section 1

- Trends in the environment and market for the sector.

- The market structure for the sector, including the geographic spread of products, customer segmentation, competitive positioning of key global players.

Section 2

- Summary of product and market focus, including reasons for the company's domestic, regional and international success to date.

- Basis of current competitive advantage.

- The strategic marketing challenges it is likely to face as it aims to improve its international competitive position.

Section 3

- Recommendations on how to build sustainable competitive advantage in the future.

- Implementation actions that will be critical in building competitive advantage.

Useful websites

www.businessweek.com
www.telegraph.co.uk
www.oecd.org/statistics
www.ft.com/markets/emerging
ifcblog.ifc.org/emergingmarketsifc
www.businessmonitor.com/risk
etf.seekingalpha.com

Getting started

In this section the case study focuses on the companies from emerging markets that are developing global competitive positions. You should use the information outlined above to obtain an understanding of who the companies are, where they come from and why they may be interesting to examine, as well as for general background information. It is important of course to use the information to decide which company you are going to use as a basis for this learning activity. To complete the learning activity, however, you will need to access a range of research material from libraries and Web-based sources as well as perhaps external sources of information.

In task 1 we build on the skills developed in ILA 1. However, in this task it is important to pay particular attention to the key trends affecting the development of the company you have chosen, their competitive positioning and how the trends in the market are impacting on the way the global market is structured.

In considering task 2 you will need to carry out some research to understand the company background, its activities and progress to date and you will also need to gain an understanding of the competition and the market environment.

Given that your company may be relatively unknown, you should not expect to obtain very detailed information on the company and you should not try to carry out a critical evaluation of its strategy.

You are, however, required to demonstrate your understanding of the global challenges (threats and opportunities) that a firm from an emerging market faces and you are encouraged to be creative in your response to the questions asked.

The starting point for task 3 is articulating an overall vision and setting appropriate corporate objectives for the firm in terms of developing globally. The global marketing strategy that is developed should be based on a relevant response to the analysis you have developed in answering questions 1 and 2. Against the background of the firm's capabilities, existing and potential future competition, the firm should consider the strategic options it has and develop a positioning statement that will ensure the firm can build a global competitive position in which its products and services are clearly differentiated from the competition.

Key decisions in the strategy development will relate to the degree to which the firm wishes, and is able, to standardise its product and service offerings or needs to adapt them to the requirements of the local markets. Market entry methods need to be selected if it is to enter new markets and the products and services that will be the portfolio need to be chosen. You also need to consider how the recommendations made contribute to the development of a long-term global competitive advantage across the region and the implications your recommendations have for resource allocation and portfolio management for the specified company. In summary, in completing the task you need to ensure you consider the key factors listed in the table below.

Key pointers for the integrated learning activity 2

	Key pointers
Task 1	- the key international trends impacting on the development of the market
	- an evaluation of how the global market is structured/segmented
	- the competitive positioning of the key global players

- the ability to analyse and synthesise material from a variety of sources
- relevance and coherence of analysis

Task 2
- assessment of current competitiveness of the specified company
- identification of the key strategic marketing issues the company need to address to compete effectively in the global market

Task 3
- clearly stated recommendations
- ability to contextualise
- clear and logical link between analysis and response
- innovation and creativity in your response
- coherence and justification of your recommendations
- appreciation of the contribution to a long-term global competitive advantage

The way forward

The task in this activity shows how the diversity encountered in developing a global marketing strategy is a difficult activity to carry out satisfactorily. After studying Part 3 of the text you may wish to revisit the solutions you have recommended in this activity, and consider how your recommendations could be successfully implemented.

In doing so you may wish to consider such aspects as: what is an appropriate organisation management structure for delivering your strategy? How can you ensure a systematic planning system throughout the globe that will enable the company to satisfactorily implement the strategy, organise the diverse operations and ensure the managers around the globe respond to the challenges you have identified? All of this is hard to achieve in a global marketing strategy. For senior managers, the problem is how to maintain cohesion between all staff in order to ensure uniform standards, a coherent worldwide strategy, retain a unique vision and purpose and yet at the same time create an operation which has empathy with consumers in each host country.

For most firms the international planning process is concerned with managing a number of tensions and ambiguities. It is how you would resolve such tensions that you may wish to consider on completion of Part 3. There is a need to adopt a regular, thorough and systematic sequence, but at the same time provide the flexibility which allows more junior managers to realise opportunities and address problems when and where they occur. Whilst detailed analysis is necessary to fully appreciate the complexities of a situation at the host country level, there is also a need for a clear uncluttered vision, shared by all staff, of where the company intends to go.

PART 3 IMPLEMENTATION

Having defined the international marketing strategy and determined the market entry method and product policy in Part 2, we now turn to implementation. The aim of this, Part 3 of *International Marketing Strategy*, is to examine the implementation issues and determine the activities that will ensure that the strategies, products and services are effective in meeting the needs of the customers. Whilst we address the elements of the marketing mix in turn, throughout the section we emphasise the need to integrate the various elements of marketing activity, as they are mutually reinforcing. Where possible, many firms seek to standardise their marketing activities but recognise too that they need to be adapted to the needs of the specific markets in which they are operating. In this respect market entry and product and service management are also considerations in both strategic development and implementation.

The first chapter in Part 3, Chapter 9, is a broad examination of the importance of integrating communications. International communications is not only concerned with the promotion of products and services and differentiating them from those of competitors: it is also about achieving effective communications internally, establishing a corporate identity that is understood worldwide and building long-term relationships with customers.

In Chapter 10, we turn to the more operational aspects of the marketing mix, involving the distribution of goods and services that make up a significant proportion of costs and contribute to customer satisfaction. This includes the different retailing infrastructures around the globe and the challenges of physically distributing products.

For most firms pricing is a complex area, especially so when pricing across international markets. Firms face currency risks, transaction risks and the risks of not being paid at all. In Chapter 11 we examine the problems companies face when pricing across foreign markets and look at some of the tools and techniques used by companies to combat these problems.

Finally, in Chapter 12 we explore the increasing role technology plays in providing a source of growth and enabling managers to implement their international marketing strategy efficiently and effectively. Whilst technology has enabled managers to overcome problems, such as the speed of market entry, it has also set new challenges, because it has further emphasised the truly global nature of business.

CHAPTER 9

INTERNATIONAL COMMUNICATIONS

INTRODUCTION

The geographical and cultural separation of the company from its marketplaces causes great difficulty in communicating effectively with its stakeholders. In this chapter we take a broad view of communications and include not just the traditional promotional mix of personal selling, advertising, sponsorship, sales and public relations but also other methods of communications which have the objective of developing better and more personalised relationships with global customers, often using online media. In our discussions we acknowledge the fact that the target audience extends beyond existing and potential customers and includes other stakeholder groups that have a potential impact on the global development of firms and their international reputation.

In doing this, the development of internal relationships between staff from different strategic business units within the global organisation and with close business partners is vital in influencing overall performance. Some remote strategic business units often appear to have a closer relationship with their customers and competition than they have with the parent organisation, and ensuring good communications seems to be particularly important as firms embark on joint ventures and strategic alliances.

Building a convincing value proposition for stakeholders and achieving cost-effectiveness requires the integration of marketing communications and the distribution channel. Success in this depends upon building good relationships with all of these interested parties.

LEARNING OBJECTIVES

After reading this chapter you will:

■ Appreciate the nature and role of communications in implementing international marketing strategies

■ Understand the challenges faced in the successful management and effective integration of international marketing communications

■ Be able to explain the use of the elements of an international communications strategy, including corporate identity, products and services promotion and the development of relationships with customers

■ Identify the use and the limitations of the communications tools in international marketing

■ Recognise the value of integrating the communications to meet the requirements of different audiences, where possible by standardising programmes and processes, but also by adapting to local needs, where necessary

THE ROLE OF MARKETING COMMUNICATIONS

Marketing communications are concerned with presenting and exchanging information with various individuals and organisations to achieve specific results. This means not only that the information must be understood accurately but that, often, elements of persuasion are also required. In a domestic environment this process is difficult enough, but the management of international marketing communications is made particularly challenging by a number of factors including the complexity of different market conditions, differences in media availability, languages, cultural sensitivities, regulations controlling advertising and sales promotions and the challenge of providing adequate resourcing levels.

A variety of approaches have been taken to define and describe the marketing mix area, which is concerned with persuasive communications. Some writers refer to the 'communications mix', others to the 'promotional mix' and others, for example Kotler (2002), use the two terms interchangeably to mean the same thing. Communications, embracing as it does the ideas of conveying information, is the most helpful term and implies the need for a two-way process in international marketing. It also includes internal communications between the organisation's staff, especially as organisations become larger, more diverse and complex. In addition, the boundaries between what should be considered as internal and external are becoming less distinct as organisations seek to add customer value through their participation in alliances and supply chains.

Figure 9.1 shows the external and internal marketing communication flows and emphasises the need to consider three dimensions: external, internal and interactive or relationship marketing.

Internal marketing

For a large diverse multi-national firm it is a key task to ensure that all staff employed in its business units around the world are aware of the strategies, tactics, priorities and procedures to achieve the firm's mission and objectives. As partnerships between supply chain members become closer it is necessary to include external firms within the internal communications network.

Staff in remote locations are often overlooked in communications or receive messages that become unclear as they cross cultural and language boundaries, in the same way that external audiences may misunderstand the firm's external communications. As a result staff in remote locations can become closer to the staff of local customers and even competitors, making it vital that they regularly receive helpful information about the strategy as well as being reminded of the organisation's standards and values.

Increasingly organisations form closer collaborations with supply chain and distribution channel members, work with joint venture and strategic alliance partners and participate in marketing networks. Organisations are dependent on staff in the extended organisation working to a common set of objectives and they need to be informed about the appropriate marketing strategies.

Interactive marketing

Because many customers of MNEs are MNEs themselves it is essential for staff around the world to deliver consistent service. This includes call centre operators, service engineers and salespersons in each location. Staff are trained in how to communicate with stakeholders in a consistent way, take appropriate decisions that fit with the strategy and deliver a standardised service. The consequences of poor coordination and lack of consistency in communications are discussed later in this chapter.

External marketing

The traditional role of international marketing communications is largely concerned with providing a mechanism by which the features and benefits of the product or service can be promoted as cost effectively as possible to existing and potential customers in different countries, using the promotion mix – personal selling, advertising, sales promotion and public relations – with the ultimate purpose of persuading customers to buy specific products and services. International marketing communications, however, have now become much more important

FIGURE 9.1
External, internal and interactive marketing

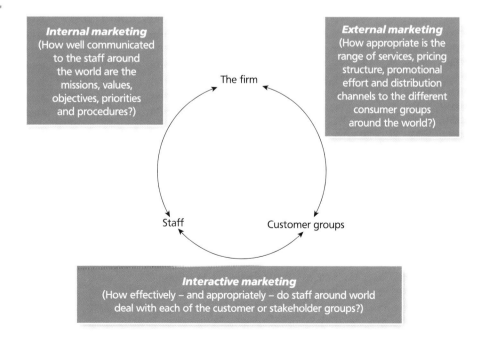

Internal marketing
(How well communicated to the staff around the world are the missions, values, objectives, priorities and procedures?)

External marketing
(How appropriate is the range of services, pricing structure, promotional effort and distribution channels to the different consumer groups around the world?)

The firm

Staff   Customer groups

Interactive marketing
(How effectively – and appropriately – do staff around world deal with each of the customer or stakeholder groups?)

within the marketing mix and the purposes for which marketing communications might be used externally in international markets are now more diverse. They include the need to communicate with a more diverse range of stakeholders and build higher levels of customer service through interactive or relationship marketing. International marketing communications could now be considered to include the three distinct strategic elements shown in Figure 9.2.

Communicating product and service differentiation

As we have discussed in Chapters 6 and 8, increased competition and the maturation of markets have led to many firms offering largely similar core product and service specifications, with the result that in addition to its traditional role of promoting products and services, international marketing communications is increasingly used to provide the firm with an important source of differentiation, for example by providing customers with an easily recognisable and distinctive brand image, or by explaining the unique positioning of the product.

Online and mobile communications have contributed to the vast increase in the range and volume of communications to which consumers are exposed as they go about their normal work and leisure, and making one product or service distinctive becomes an increasing challenge. There are a wide variety of promotional tools that might be used to persuade customers to buy the firm's products and services, and the newer information and communications technologies are increasing this choice all the time. The challenge for the firm is to use these tools as cost-effectively as possible to reach out to consumers – wherever they are in the world.

Communicating the corporate identity to international stakeholders

As stakeholders in general have become more aware of how they are affected by international organisations – both good and bad – companies have found it necessary to justify their international activities by constantly and more widely communicating their core values and standards to their internal and external

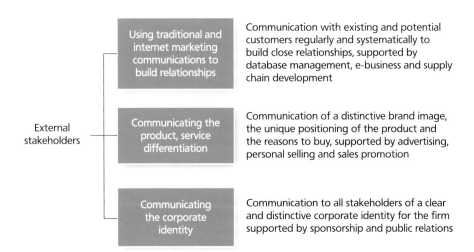

FIGURE 9.2
The dimensions of external marketing communications

External stakeholders

Using traditional and internet marketing communications to build relationships — Communication with existing and potential customers regularly and systematically to build close relationships, supported by database management, e-business and supply chain development

Communicating the product, service differentiation — Communication of a distinctive brand image, the unique positioning of the product and the reasons to buy, supported by advertising, personal selling and sales promotion

Communicating the corporate identity — Communication to all stakeholders of a clear and distinctive corporate identity for the firm supported by sponsorship and public relations audience. This is essential in order to demonstrate their responsibility to share-holders, trustworthiness to customers and care and concern for the local community, environment and local employees. The corporate image or logo is the most visible part of the identity and, in some firms, is the only standardised element of the marketing mix, because it constantly reminds stakeholders of the organisation's reputation. The corporate identity of the firm should be deeper and more pervasive and reflected in a clear and distinctive message supported by appropriate and proactive public relations activity. Illustration 9.1 shows the importance of a corporate identity and sponsorship in the international marketing of the host city for the Olympic Games.

Using communications to build relationships

More intense global competition has provided consumers with greater choice of products and services which they perceive to be capable of satisfying their needs and providing new experiences. Customers also feel that there is less risk of dissatisfaction in switching to alternative products and services, and so are becoming less likely to stay loyal to one supplier or brand.

With the increasing cost of marketing communications and the need to reach an ever wider international audience, organisations are becoming much more

ILLUSTRATION 9.1

Corporate identity and the Olympic Games

It is arguable that the most expensive and prestigious sponsorship event in the world is the Olympic Games. It reaches a huge audience in just about every corner of the world. Some would suggest that the five rings of the Olympic committee is the most recognised symbol (as opposed to a company name) in the world. The elite group of tier 1 sponsors of the London Olympics in 2012 were expected to have to pay £80m for the privilege of sponsoring the Games. The Organising Committees for the Olympic and Paralympic Games have an obligation to the International Olympic Committee (IOC), its sponsors and government partners to protect the Olympic and Paralympic

brands and provide protection against any unauthorised business association with the Games, known as 'ambush marketing'. This poses challenges for the organising committees for the games in London.

A key part of the international marketing of the Games is to maximise sponsorship by creating a corporate identity but also to enhance the reputation and image of the city so that it lives on after the Games.

To the host city, the management of the Games and the effectiveness of their international marketing, too, is vital. Montreal's 1976 Games and the Athens 2004 Games left their cities in debt and the Atlanta 1996 Games will be remembered, at least in part, for some poor organisation and questionable commercial activities. By contrast, Los Angeles in 1984 was deemed a complete success. In 1992 Barcelona used the event to rebrand and transform the city by emphasising both its elegance and excitement. Sydney 2000 was heralded as the most successful Games ever. Beijing 2008 presents the opportunity to showcase China's development and part of the justification for London's 2012 bid was the regeneration of East London. The biggest challenge in international marketing is to recoup the enormous cost of the games. By 2007, five years before the Games, the estimate of the cost of the London games had risen from £2.4bn at the time of the bid to £9.35bn.

QUESTION *Can a logo be effective in communicating the complex messages that might come from an event such as the Games internationally?*

aware of the high costs of winning new customers and the relatively lower costs of retaining existing customers. Attention has been drawn to how much a single customer of one product might purchase over his or her lifetime. Readers might like to calculate how much they buy from a food retailer, car manufacturer or a travel company if they stay loyal to that supplier for five, ten or twenty years. Food retailers offer incentives for customer loyalty, such as bonus cards and money-off vouchers for other products and services they offer, such as petrol and insurance services. They routinely communicate with consumers using direct mail to inform them of new product offers.

The concept of relationship marketing has taken on greater significance as customer relationship management (CRM) systems enable firms to communicate in a much more intelligent way by basing their messages on a better knowledge of the characteristics and responses of their existing and potential customers and a better understanding of what they might wish to hear. In this way firms are able to develop better relationships with their customers and other influential stakeholders, irrespective of their location in the world.

THE FUNDAMENTAL CHALLENGES FOR INTERNATIONAL MARKETING COMMUNICATIONS

All forms of international marketing communication have a fundamental purpose, which is to ensure that the intended messages (those which are part of the firm's international marketing strategy) are conveyed accurately between the sender and the receiver, and that the impact of unintentional messages (those which are likely to have an adverse effect on the firm's market performance and reputation) are kept to a minimum. The communications process should be two-way and the sender should always make provision for feedback to ensure that the receiver has understood the message as it was intended and has responded positively to it.

In practice this apparently simple process poses considerable challenges for firms trying to manage their international marketing communications. This is often discussed in the business press, which contains many serious but frequently amusing anecdotes about the failed attempts of major firms to communicate in international markets. Cadbury caused offence in India and Pakistan with an advertisement to promote Temptations chocolates. It showed Kashmir with the strapline 'Too good to share'. Mistakes in the use of language, particularly using messages which do not translate or are mistranslated are a particular problem: more serious is a lack of sensitivity to different cultures amongst international communicators.

Many of the failures of communications are unintentional, of course. Following negotiations with the Council on America–Islamic Relations, Nike had to scrap almost 40 000 pairs of sports shoes because the flame design which was used bore a resemblance to the Arabic for Allah. Two years earlier Nike was forced to withdraw a billboard showing a basketball player above the caption 'They Called him Allah' when it caused an outcry amongst Muslims.

Besides the often highly visible failures which make firms appear to be incompetent and insensitive there are many examples of wasted effort and resources which are not so widely publicised. There are a number of reasons for international marketing communications failure, including:

■ inconsistency in the messages conveyed to customers by staff at different levels and from different countries and cultures

- different styles of presentation of corporate identity, brand and product image from different departments and country business units which can leave customers confused

- a lack of coordination of messages, such as press releases, advertising campaigns and changes in product specification or pricing across the various country markets

- failure to appreciate the differences in the fields of perception (the way the message is understood) of the sender and receiver. The field of perception tends to be affected significantly by the self-reference criteria of both parties. This is, perhaps, where the greatest problems arise because, as we have already discussed, avoiding this requires knowledge of different market environments, cultural empathy and the willingness to adapt the communications programmes and processes to local requirements.

Illustration 9.2 shows the importance of appreciating the subtlety of language and tone in communications.

Whilst this last area is influenced by knowledge, attitudes and empathy, the other three areas of potential communications failure are concerned with the effectiveness of the firm's strategy and planning and the degree to which the staff within the organisation understand and are involved in the communications planning process. It is almost inevitable that some communication failures occur from time to time and it is vital that firms learn from their mistakes. To ensure success in these areas it is important to have an effective control process in place.

Whilst it can be argued that the majority of these failures are ultimately within the control of the company, a number of situations arise where the firm's communications can be affected by factors which are outside the firm's control or are extremely difficult to control. Examples of these are situations where:

- *counterfeiting or other infringements* of patents or copyright as discussed in Chapter 8 take place. Not only does the firm lose revenue, but it may also suffer damage to its image if consumers believe the low-quality goods supplied by the counterfeiter are genuine. Even if the customer knows the product is counterfeit the brand name might still be subconsciously associated with a poorly performing product;

ILLUSTRATION 9.2

Negativity in advertising

SOURCE: ADAPTED FROM MARKETING BUSINESS, 2000

Global firms see the cost benefits and brand-building benefits of standardisation of creative work. However, to understand the reason why advertisements might or might not cross borders requires more subtlety, particularly in Asian markets.

There are many reasons. One is the issue of negativity. If a person in some western countries is asked, 'How are you?', the answer might be 'Good' or 'Fine'. It also might be 'Not bad', which really also means good. For many on the Indian subcontinent, 'Not bad' is more precise and often means neutrality – neither this nor that. They place great significance on negative expressions, such as nonviolence, non-greed and non-hatred, which are embedded in the culture and convey important personal values. In Western advertising, the appeal might be based on an unacceptable or annoying situation that can occur if a particular product is not bought. A Western advertisement for a TV set might emphasise the picture is 'free from distortion', whereas in Asian markets a TV that has a clear picture might communicate a more precise message.

In Western advertising there is little distinction between praise and flattery, whereas in Sinhala and Tamil languages, spoken in Sri Lanka, flattery is regarded as deceitful and false. In this case, care needs to be taken with overpositive expressions in advertising.

In the West, emphasis is placed on logic and rationality in advertising, whereas the Asian view is that the truth will emerge.

QUESTION *How can managers responsible for cross-border campaigns ensure that they will convey the message effectively?*

■ *parallel importing*, which is discussed in greater detail in Chapter 11, communicates contradictory messages that do not reflect the image of the brand and thus confuse consumers. This can be particularly problematic if the parallel importer seriously undercuts the prices charged by the official channel, leading customers to feel they have been 'ripped off';

■ *competitors, governments or pressure groups* attack the standards and values of the MNE by alleging, fairly or unfairly, bad business practice. Perhaps surprisingly, despite their huge resources, some of the largest firms are not very effective in responding to allegations from relatively less powerful stakeholders. Companies such as Shell, Exxon and McDonald's have suffered following criticism of their lack of concern for the environment. The lack of standards and controls on the Internet has made the problem worse, for example, anti Coca-Cola Websites post negative communications without the need to substantiate the messages.

International marketing communications, standardisation and adaptation

The most obvious tactic for reducing instances of international communications failure might appear to be to adopt a strict policy of standardisation in the implementation of communications plans. Firms adopt this principle, for example, in their use of corporate identity and global advertising campaigns. However, given the need to also demonstrate cultural sensitivity and empathy with a wide range of international customers *and* to avoid the type of mistakes referred to earlier, it is necessary to adapt the international communications to local market needs with sensitivity. In this section, therefore, we address the factors both in and outside of the control of the firm that affect the degree to which international marketing communications can be standardised or should be adapted.

Towards standardisation

The drivers for standardisation of international marketing communications come first, from the organisation's desire to improve efficiency. Cost-saving activity in marketing communications includes benefits from economies of scale, for example, in advertising creative work, media buying, making better use of staff time and from the experience effect, by achieving efficiencies through replicating successful marketing communications programmes and processes in different countries.

Second, standardisation of communications provides customers with perceived added value, particularly in the intangible elements of the product/service offer. Customers believe that they gain additional benefit and value from a consistent and widely recognised brand image that reflects their own self-image; for example, teenagers (as well as rather more elderly sports enthusiasts too) gain peer recognition, credibility and prestige from wearing branded sports wear which has strong associations with sports stars. A company may use a top international business consultancy or advertising agency with a prestigious image just as much because the association is perceived positively by the company's suppliers and customers as for the cost-effectiveness of the work that is carried out.

Consistency in the corporate identity and branding, reinforces awareness in stakeholders' minds and provides the familiarity with the company which leads to a feeling of confidence, trust and loyalty. For example, it may be reassuring for a visitor to see the familiar logo and appearance of a fast food outlet, hotel chain or bank in a foreign country that they are visiting.

Over the years changes in the political and economic environment have led to greater prosperity and thus greater buying power – at least for some people – and a greater acceptance of imported products. Consumers and business-to-business customers often prefer internationally available products with which they have become familiar through increased travel, radio and television communications and the written media. This familiarity has increased further because of the greater impact of telecommunications and the Internet. Satellite and cable television, for example, have assisted considerably in creating worldwide customer segments for many more globally standardised products and services.

The Internet, too, allows customers to access products from organisations from very distant locations. It allows specialist suppliers to make their standard products and services globally available to customers, and enables smaller companies to compete essentially on equal terms with their much larger competitors, so 'punching above their weight'. Of course, companies that only communicate using the Internet are limiting their customer base to those customer segments that can access the Internet.

At an operational level, advertising standardisation can be used when a number of conditions apply:

- visual messages form the main content of the advertisement
- well-known international film stars, popular celebrities and sports personalities are featured
- music is an important part of the communication
- well-known symbols and trademarks are featured. For example, the Grand Canyon in the US can be used to symbolise certain types of outdoor American values.

Even then the real impact of the promotion may be restricted to a particular region. Advertisements do not travel well to other countries:

- when the use of spoken and written language forms an important part of the communication
- if humour is used – humour is often *very* specific to certain cultures
- if personalities are used who are well-known in one country but are not known internationally
- if campaigns are used that rely on specific knowledge of previous advertising.

TOWARDS ADAPTATION

The principal drivers of international marketing communications adaptation are the cultural differences that must be managed when communicating with customers in different countries. As we have already seen in this book, there are some fundamental differences in the ways that consumers from different cultures respond to different communication approaches. More specifically, however, in a comparison between the US and Chinese responses to advertising Zhang and Neelankavil (1997) observe that, overall, US subjects preferred the individualistic appeal (self-orientation, self-sufficiency and control, the pursuit of individual gains) whereas Chinese subjects favoured the collective appeal (subordination of personal interests to the goals of the group, with emphasis on sharing, cooperation and harmony, and a concern for the group's welfare). It is these differences which must be recognised, but there is also likely to be continuing convergence across cultures and moves toward standardisation.

Neelankavil *et al.* (1996) studied the contents of advertisements for language, customs and values in local language magazines in Hong Kong, Japan, Korea and Taiwan, countries which they considered to be steeped in ancient Asian culture but that were also major forces in the global marketplace. They found that the use of Western language and models was affected by the product type, customer countries, countries of origin and countries of manufacture. They observe that with greater liberalisation there is likely to be a convergence of ideas, cultures, values and even language in advertising, but they add that not enough is known about the effects of the benefits of such standardisation.

Advertisers believe that advertising is most effective when it is relevant to the target audience – one area where there are significant differences is in the portrayal of women in advertising.

Siu and Au (1997) report that research studies of advertising suggest that:

- over 80 per cent of voiceovers are male
- women are depicted as housewives, mothers and/or sex objects
- females are shown as product users whereas males are shown in the roles of authority.

However, the role of women is changing rapidly as many more women are entering the workforce. In research carried out by Siu and Au in China and Singapore, they found that sex-role stereotyping was more apparent in China – women were depicted as product users and men as having product authority – whereas in Singapore women generally appeared as the spokesperson for the product, to have product authority and be the providers of help and advice.

Other environmental factors also make it necessary for the communications strategy to be adapted for local situations. There are political and legal constraints: for example, Wentz (1997) argues that rather than pricing itself out of the world markets the EU has regulated itself out, restricting promotional activity, and cites instances such as the French ban on alcohol advertising and a Danish attack on loyalty programmes. Certain countries, too, prohibit comparative advertising, advertising alcohol, tobacco and products for children.

There are many local reasons why firms may need to adapt their communications strategy. Many companies have to change their brand names because of different meanings they have when they move to new markets. The New Zealand Dairy Board, a large exporter of dairy foods, uses the brand name Fern for its butter in Malaysia, although Anchor is the flagship brand well known in Western Europe. In Malaysia Anchor is a widely advertised local beer, and Malaysian housewives are unlikely to buy dairy products for their children which they would subconsciously associate with alcohol.

When Johnson and Johnson entered the Hong Kong market they used the name *zhuang-cheng* which means 'an official or lord during feudal times'. This upper-class association was seen as inappropriate for China, and the more upbeat modern tone of '*qiang-sheng*', meaning 'active life', was used instead, to better reflect the drive for modernisation.

The differences in appeal between Western and Asian communications are more fundamental than simply changing brand names. Chan and Huang (1997) suggest that brands can be enhanced if names and/or symbols of favourite animals and flowers and lucky numbers are used. In Asia written figures may be perceived as potent symbols; thus, as Schmitt and Pan (1994) point out, in Asian countries the emphasis may be heavier on the distinctive writing and logo of the brand than on the jingles that Western marketing communications favour.

Firms use a variety of ways of becoming more sensitive to cultural differences. Unilever has set up innovation centres in Asia in order to bring together research, production and marketing staff to speed up development of international brands which have a local appeal. In Bangkok there are innovation centres responsible for ice cream, laundry detergents and hair care. Asian Delight is a regional brand of ice cream – between the Magnum brand and local brands – and uses English and Thai on its packaging in Thailand, but English only in Malaysia, Singapore and Indonesia. It is sold from Wall's mobile units and cabinets in convenience stores and supermarkets. The flavours have a local appeal and include coconut-milk based ice cream mixed with fruits and vegetables traditionally used in desserts or chewy strings of green flour, black beans and sago.

Illustration 9.3 shows how Pepsi is taking some lessons from international marketing to develop multicultural marketing in the US. What is significant here is that the segmentation approach driving the promotion strategy is moving beyond borders, traditional language and culture to tribalism based on popular culture. It is reinforcing this further by developing packaging material in line with the popular interests and 'tribal' culture.

Adaptation taken to its limits means customisation, one-to-one marketing and interactivity, and this is dealt with more fully in Chapter 12.

INTERNATIONAL MARKETING COMMUNICATIONS STRATEGY

So far in this chapter we have highlighted the need to consider the nature and role of international marketing communications more broadly than was the case in the past, by focusing upon both internal and external communications and a wider range of communications tools. In thinking about developing strategy there are two significant issues to address. First, the need to state clear and

ILLUSTRATION 9.3

Pepsi – promoting to tribes

Pepsi did its first African-American ad in 1948. Many firms use ethnic segmentation for advertising to underpin the advertising strategy but Pepsi realises that this is over-simplistic, particularly for its young ethnic consumers. Pepsi believe that race and whether you are African-American or Latino is not the unifier, but interests, such as music, are. In the US Pepsi see their market as 20 per cent Latino, 15 per cent African-American and 6 per cent Asian-American. Forty per cent of Pepsi's market is in major urban centres, such as New York, Los Angeles and Miami, where the youth minorities can be the majorities. For them popular culture is at the heart of their lives.

Pepsi aims to be multicultural throughout. It targets specialist local media to carry targeted campaigns. A typical music ad, therefore, has two versions, one sung in Spanish and one in English. Pepsi can combine promotion of its cola with Doritos, its tortilla snack, but promotes it in different ways for Latins, who love a fiesta, and for Afro-Americans who are mellow and cool – and love barbecue flavour! Products have been specifically developed and promoted to other ethnic groups too.

Pepsi realises that much of its youth market, such as bicultural Hispanics, read more English media than Spanish, so language is not the key to unlock the market. What is important is culture, but more importantly *popular* culture and appealing to the popular culture 'tribes'.

In 2007 the company launched a global restyling of its cans based on 35 new design themes, such as music, sport and fashion, which will be rolled out every few weeks. A website with video clips was intended to further entice the youth audience. The cans retained the same globe logo and lettering, but not the red white and blue colours. The aim was to communicate to people of all ages the 'fun, optimistic and youthful' spirit of Pepsi to its global audience.

QUESTION *How might the marketers of consumer packaged goods use the different dimensions of culture to communicate their brand message?*

PHOTO CREDIT: KEES METSELAAR/ALAMY

SOURCE: ADAPTED FROM L. WENTZ 'PEPSI'S NEW MULTICULTURAL CAMPAIGNS GO TRIBAL', ADAGE.COM, 7 JULY, 2003, AND 'TROUBLE BREWING', THE ECONOMIST, 1 MARCH, 2007

precise objectives for the international marketing communications strategy and, second, how the various communications activities might be coordinated to maximise their cost effectiveness.

The promotional objectives (Wilson and Gilligan 2003) can be categorised as sales-related and brand/product communications-related, which might be stated in terms of increasing sales by:

- increasing market share at the expense of local and/or international competitors
- identifying new potential customers
- obtaining a specific number of responses to a promotional campaign
- reducing the impact of competitors in the market

and brand/product communications related by:

- increasing the value of the corporate brand and product image
- helping to establish the position or to reposition the product or brand
- increasing awareness levels especially in new country markets
- changing consumers' perceptions of products, brands or the firm.

The options that are available for a generic marketing communications strategy centre around the extent to which a push or pull strategy could and should be adopted (Figure 9.3). A push strategy means promoting the product or service to retailers and wholesalers in order to force the product or service down the distribution channel by using promotional methods, such as personal selling, discounts and special deals. A pull strategy means communicating with the final consumer to attract them to the retailer or distributor to purchase the product. In this case mass advertising, sales promotions and point of sales promotions are the most obvious promotional methods. In domestic markets firms realise the need to have a combination of push and pull strategies, including both encouraging the intermediaries to stock the products and attracting end users to buy.

In domestic markets the nature of the market structure that already exists may well affect the degree to which push and pull strategies are used; for example, how well the distribution channel is established, how powerful the retailers or distributors are, how well established the competitors are and whether the firm marketing its products or services wishes to, or has the power to, challenge the existing 'route to market' by setting up a new channel.

FIGURE 9.3
Push and pull strategies

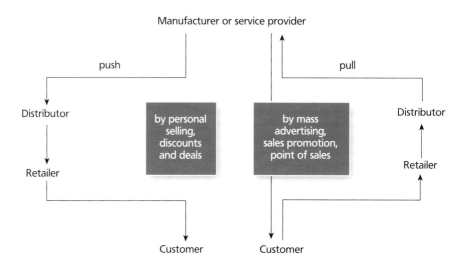

Frequently, the international marketing communications strategy of a firm has to be adapted because of the variation in the market structures and distribution channels from country to country (for example, some are highly fragmented, whilst others are very concentrated). More often than not, however, it is the weakness of the marketing firm in the target country markets that limits its strategic choice. It may well not have sufficient resources to implement a successful domestic strategy in the new market and yet there may be a need for quick success. As a result the firm may be forced into making use of and relying heavily upon established intermediaries to do the promotion through existing channels. For this reason it is possible to find organisations that have a pull strategy in their domestic or other established markets and a push strategy in their newer markets. Because of this the firm's promotional and communications mix may be significantly different in different markets.

Having determined the objectives and decided upon the degree to which a push and pull strategy might be used, the dimensions of the international marketing communications implementation strategy can be defined. These are:

- the message to be communicated
- the target audience to which the message will be directed
- the media that will be used to carry the message
- the ways in which the impact of the communications will be measured.

As we said at the start of this chapter, continually evaluating the impact of the communications is vital, not only in improving the effectiveness of the communication but also in assessing the degree to which each of these dimensions can be standardised across international markets.

Communicating with existing and potential customers

Given that the primary objective of international marketing communications is to persuade customers to buy products and services which will meet their requirements, it is appropriate to consider how international marketing communications are used strategically to influence each of the stages of the buying process and to help customers to complete their purchase.

A number of writers have developed models of buying behaviour which tend to vary according to the context of the study, but all acknowledge that there are a number of stages in the buying process. A simplified version of these stages (AIDA) includes:

- Awareness of the firm, its products and services, and their reputation.
- Interest in the products and services, because they may be suited to the consumers' needs and worthy of consideration for potential purchase.
- Desire to buy the product or service, in preference to that of the competitor, after consumers have become better informed about its performance.
- Action by the customer in overcoming any remaining reservations or barriers and purchasing the product or service.

Different messages must be prepared and the most appropriate promotional tool selected for each part of the buying process in order to persuade customers to move to the next stage. At each stage in this process the marketing firm faces particular problems in international markets. For example, in fast-moving consumer goods marketing, advertising can be used to raise awareness, create interest and encourage consumers to purchase, but only if the messages are sensitive and appealing and the customers have access to the media used for advertising. Other tools such as point of sale promotion can be used to support the strategy, provided it is possible for the firm to maintain some level of control over the displays used by local retailers. At the final stage and having been entirely convinced about the firm's offer, customers may still have reservations about buying from a foreign supplier.

There are significant differences between consumer markets, business-to-business and institutional market purchasing. Selling capital equipment usually depends more on personal selling and providing technical service to a buying committee. This would typically be supported by awareness-raising in the trade press, using PR and corporate advertising. Here the need for monitoring the consistency of approach and ensuring good communications with the manufacturing operation must be balanced against the need for sensitivity to the way that business is done in that particular country. Institutional purchasing is often undertaken through competitive tenders which often, directly or indirectly, favour local suppliers.

THE INTEGRATION OF COMMUNICATIONS

Stakeholders receive messages, both intended and unintended, from every part of the organisation's activities, from the clothes that customer-facing staff wear, the packaging design, the delays in answering the telephone at the call centre to stories in the newspaper about the inappropriate remarks of the chief executive. As the number of communications have increased dramatically and customers have become more critical and sceptical, the importance of integrated marketing communications has been emphasised in order to avoid conflicting messages and instead communicate consistent and mutually supporting messages. Fill (2006) points out that traditional mass-communication strategies have given way to more personalised, customer-oriented and technology-driven approaches. To be successful the firm requires a completely different approach, focusing on the individual customer and Kotler (2003) says that 'companies need to orchestrate a consistent set of impressions from its personnel, facilities and actions that deliver the company's brand meaning and promise to its various audiences'.

Davidson (2002) explains that an organisation communicates in eight ways:

1 Actions – what it does.
2 Behaviour, how things are done.
3 Face-to-face by management: through talks, visits and meetings it shows what the management thinks is important.
4 Signals, from the organisations' actions, facilities and objects, including executive bonuses, dress, buildings.
5 Product and services, and particularly their quality.
6 Intended communications, such as advertising, which is not always received as the organisation expects.
7 Word of mouth and word of Web (including email), and
8 Comment by other organisations, such as pressure groups, competitors and the media.

Shimp (2006) provides a definition of integrated marketing communications which focuses on five features:

1 Start with the customer or prospect.
2 Use any form of relevant contact.
3 Achieve synergy through consistency across the communication elements.

4 Build relationships.

5 Affect behaviour.

The emphasis of this is on marketing promotion whereas, in practice, communications should be a two-way process and interactivity between the organisation and its customer should be part of integration too.

THE BENEFITS OF INTEGRATION

Given the fact that individual messages have little overall impact on customers on their own, it follows that the effect of communications will be significantly greater if the many messages are consistent, uniform and mutually supporting in the way that they build the image of the brand, product and service and reinforce the standards and values of the organisation around the world.

It is easier both to justify the cost and control communications activities if they are integrated and the cumulative effect, rather than individual effect, is assessed. Measurement of individual actions is difficult, given the 'noise' in the environment, and so it is more sensible to measure the effects of the combined actions.

INTEGRATION WITH THE GLOBAL STRATEGY

Although usually considered to be a part of the marketing mix, in many organisations communications takes on a much more important role. It is essential in disseminating the organisation's corporate, business unit and marketing strategies to stakeholders, including shareholders. As organisations become more global so the consistency of internal and external communications across borders becomes essential.

Business unit integration At business unit level, managers in charge of communications must work closely with colleagues responsible for development, operations, key account management, sales and customer service centre management to develop a highly integrated global approach that offers a seamless service to customers.

Marketing mix integration Customers continually receive communications from the organisation that are the result of marketing mix actions. Every element of the marketing mix communicates with customers and the intended messages should be integrated.

It is important to remember that non-verbal communication in many markets has a greater impact than verbal communications or written words, especially given the amount of time that a customer might give to one communication. For example, the colours and styles used in creative packaging or signage work communicate non-verbally with the customers, reinforcing the images and customer perceptions. Customers can pick up small errors in colour matching and design, so discipline in the use of the corporate identity is essential. In different cultures the significance of colours, symbols and numbers is so great that they alone could deter customers from buying a product.

Coordination and planning of the international marketing communications strategy

To achieve its objectives, the communications strategy will almost certainly include a variety of promotional tools. The key to success is integrating the various promotion elements in a cost-efficient way and adding value through choosing the communications methods that will have the most impact on the customers. The actual mix chosen will depend upon a number of issues surrounding the context of the purchasing situation, including:

■ the market area and industry sector

■ whether it is consumer, institutional or business-to-business marketing

■ the customer segment to be targeted

■ the participants in the purchasing process, their requirements and expectations and the best methods to reach and influence them

■ the country or region, the culture, the communications infrastructure and the preferred methods of communicating

■ the resources made available by the organisation and the implications for the level of involvement and control it wishes to exert over the communications process.

The value of different promotional methods varies according to the context in which the marketing communications are being used and the degree to which they are integrated within a marketing communications strategy, as shown in Figure 9.4.

The critical issue is the extent to which they must be adapted so that they can be effective in international markets. Dilemma 9.1 shows how difficult it is for managers to make decisions that require them to go against their instincts and self-reference criteria.

FIGURE 9.4.

Internal and external international communications programmes

Marketing programmes influencing communications	International communication aims
Internally focused programmes	
Corporate identity	Consistency in all aspects of company logo, signs and image
Internal marketing communications	Reinforce motivation through telling staff what is happening
Sales force, dealer and distributor training and development	Training through conferences, manuals and brochures
Retailing merchandising	Point of sale persuasion through displays and shelf facings
First contact customer service	Welcoming first contact through telephonist and receptionist training
After-sales service	Customer retention and satisfaction through staff training and brochures
Quality management	Assuring a continuous quality approach in all programmes
Brand management	Achieving common brand standards and values
Externally focused programmes (marketing mix)	
Product attributes	Offering innovative, high-quality products
Distribution channel	Ensuring easy access to products and frequent customer encounters with the products
Price	Messages about quality and status
Product/service promotion	Managing customer expectations through the integration of the marketing mix communications
People	Using staff–customer interactions to reinforce the aims, standards and values of the firm
Customer service process	Providing a satisfactory total experience through the service offer
Physical evidence for the service delivery	All contacts with the facilities reinforce the firm's messages

THE MARKETING COMMUNICATIONS TOOLS

There are a number of offline and online marketing communications tools for the external market and it is to these that we now turn. For convenience we have grouped these tools within broad categories. In practice there is some flexibility in the way the tools are used within a coordinated strategy but the tools are listed as follows:

> Communicating product and service differentiation. This group includes personal selling and word of mouth communications, exhibitions and trade fairs, trade missions, advertising and the use of agencies, sales promotion and direct marketing.

> Communicating with a wider range of stakeholders. This includes the corporate identity, sponsorship and public relations.

Online communications are used in all areas of communications, either complementing or as an alternative to offline communications, and they are discussed later in this chapter.

Personal selling and word of mouth

For many companies the first proactive use of the communications mix to promote exports is personal selling. Selling is often used to gain the first few orders in a new market and as the main component of a push strategy to persuade distribution channel members, such as agents, distributors or retailers to stock the product. It is expensive, however.

The use of personal selling tends to be limited to situations in which benefits can be derived from two-way information flows and ones in which the revenue

---

DILEMMA 9.1

Self-reference criteria in advertising decisions

Advertising managers who are involved in cross-border campaigns face the problem of self-reference criteria. A European brand manager for Heinz, based in the UK, was responsible for approving advertising campaigns that had been developed by local agencies for the local country subsidiary as part of a pan-European campaign. In Germany the local agency produced a television advertising campaign. The European brand manager, his boss and his boss's boss, all English, turned down the agency's creative work.

The advertisement was meant to be humorous but they did not find it at all funny, and they were concerned that it would devalue the brand and the campaign. The agency insisted that they had tested the ad on consumers and the humour would work in Germany. After various delays the manager had to make the decision whether or not the ad should go ahead on the following Monday. However, it was the weekend and he could not reach his bosses for help with the decision. The campaign would cost £1 million which

would be lost if it did not go ahead. If the campaign adversely affected the product it would be a greater disaster – his job could be on the line! Against his better judgement, and overcoming his self-reference criteria, he decided the advert should be broadcast. The campaign was a great success!

Western firms also realise that it is important to appreciate the levels of intelligence and sophistication of emerging markets. When Heinz first launched tomato ketchup in Russia they used an existing TV ad from the UK with minor modifications. Now it would be unacceptable as the Russian audience is more sophisticated. Russian actors would be needed on the advertisement. Heinz is particularly sensitive to the need to adapt to local markets and this is part of their strategy.

Consumers are very knowledgeable and well aware when some big brands are behaving in an arrogant manner and telling them what to buy. They can become annoyed when firms insult their intelligence. A number of firms have seen their reputation and share price suffer because of insensitive promotion and PR. The dilemma for firms is when should they insist on standardisation and consistency, and when should they trust partners with local knowledge?

SOURCE: ROBIN LCWE

from the sale is sufficiently high to justify the costs. This is typically the case with business-to-business marketing and in consumer markets where the purchase price justifies the high cost of personal selling, for example for cars, holidays, homes and for consumer durable products. Even here the need for personal selling is being challenged as direct marketing, particularly using the Internet, is now being used routinely to purchase these products.

In countries where labour costs are very low, personal selling is used to a greater extent than in high cost countries. This ranges from street and market trading to quite sophisticated multilevel distribution chains for business-to-business products. In high labour-cost countries personal selling of low unit cost products is used rarely, except for illegal trading, for example of drugs. It is of course a successful method of selling niche products, such as Avon cosmetics, Tupperware and Amway household products. The basis of the appeal of these products is to make shopping a more social event, by selling to friends or family, and introducing a 'party' atmosphere into the selling process.

Effective selling in international business-to-business and consumer markets involves a wide range of tasks and skills, including product and market knowledge, listening and questioning skills. However, it is in the core selling activities of negotiation and persuasion discussed in Chapter 3 that higher-order expertise is required. It is likely that local people will be more effective than home-based representatives in understanding the subtleties of the negotiation process as they apply within the local business culture. They will have fluent language skills and an intimate knowledge of the culture of the country. However, where the negotiations relate to high-value contracts they may well require high levels of specialist technical knowledge, an understanding of the processes and systems and strict adherence to the firm's standards and values. For these reasons the company may well prefer to use staff from its head office to ensure that the sales people are well informed about the firm's capabilities and that their activities can be controlled.

This is particularly the case if the opportunities to make a sale are very infrequent (e.g. with capital goods) when high levels of technical skill and an understanding of the company's systems are needed but not easily learnt by new people. For example, Rolls-Royce use a complete team of UK-based engineers, accountants, and sales people to sell aero engines to customers in foreign markets. Some of the team will make frequent visits, others will be based in close online and offline contact with the customer for a period of many months. The sheer complexity of the contracts means that only Rolls-Royce employees could understand the detail sufficiently to handle the negotiations. The high contract price provides sufficient revenue to pay for the costs of the UK-based sales team.

An alternative compromise arrangement to the two extremes of employing local or head office sales staff (both have their advantages and disadvantages) is to employ expatriates, staff from the domestic country to work for extended periods in the host country in order to bridge the culture and company standards gap.

In practice the expatriate is likely to experience a culture shock caused by living in a foreign culture where the familiar symbols, cues and everyday reassurances are missing, often causing feelings of frustration, stress and anxiety. The expatriate can respond to the situation in one of three ways. At one extreme, adjustment is made to the expatriate culture only. In effect the expatriate only adjusts to the way of life of a ready-made cultural island within the host country and makes little attempt to adjust to the host culture. At the other extreme the expatriate's reaction is to completely embrace the host culture and actively minimise contact with the expatriate community – and the firm too. Ideally the expatriate adjusts to both the local culture and the expatriate culture. In this way the expatriate retains the home country's and firm's system of values and beliefs, but is considerate and respectful towards the people of his or her host country and to their culture. It is this last option that is usually most beneficial for the firm's sales effort.

Whichever approach to selling is adopted, it is through relevant training that firms aim to manage their sales staff's involvement with the firm and the market, and maintain their enthusiasm for selling. Honeycutt (2005) explains that global firms have a training culture, employ a more formal training curriculum and focus on 'soft' competencies, whereas local Singaporean firms used more on the job training and did not appear to understand how sales training could be used for competitive advantage. As the cost of personal selling is increasing, so firms are seeking ways of improving their cost-effectiveness by using more systematic ways of analysing customer requirements and carrying out the sales role, rather than relying on a good firm handshake for closing the deal.

Exhibitions and trade fairs

Exhibitions and trade fairs are an effective way of meeting many existing and potential customers from different countries. The cost of exhibiting at international trade fairs is very high when the cost of the stand, space rental, sales staff time and travelling expenses are taken into account. It is for this reason that the selection of the most appropriate fairs for the industry is critical. Also important are the creative work for the stand, preparation of sales literature and selection of suitable personnel for the stand, bearing in mind the need for cultural and language empathy.

To obtain the maximum benefit from an exhibition it is essential to publicise the firm's attendance at the event to encourage potential customers to visit and also to ensure that all leads are followed up. Shimp (2006) explains that the real cost of exhibitions can be two or three times higher than the cost of the event itself.

An additional benefit of exhibitions is that they can provide experiential marketing, also called customer experience marketing, in which customers obtain an engaging, entertaining and interactive brand experience. There are of course other communications tools for providing experiential marketing. For example, Apple operates stores in which customers can try out their products and Harley Davidson provides opportunities for visitors to ride its bikes.

Given the importance of context in many markets, such as Asia, experiential marketing, involving life experiences at events for external communications to customers and internal communications, were shown to be valuable (Whiteling 2007).

Trade missions

Trade missions are organised visits to a country or region by a group of senior business managers from a number of firms, perhaps from the same geographic region or the same industry. They are often subsidised by national or local government. Discussions with potential customers are arranged in advance in the host country.

Trade missions are usually associated with exporting, and may be used to carry out introductory talks with prospective clients or to negotiate a contract. As with trade fairs, good preparation work before the visit is essential to ensure that meetings are arranged with appropriate customers where there is a genuine possibility of business being generated. Usually the home country's local embassy staff will provide support for trade missions and often, too, depending on the importance of the mission, there will be discussions with the host government, civil servants and politicians about how trade between the two countries can be developed.

Advertising

Online and offline advertising are usually the most visible forms of communication and are often considered the most important part of the whole strategy for consumer products in countries with a well-developed media industry. Traditionally offline advertising has disadvantages because it is essentially a one-way method of communication and in international marketing it can be difficult to control in terms of its reach (the geographic area in which consumers are exposed to the messages). The objective is to obtain the maximum exposure of the product or brand to the largest possible target audience. Clearly the opportunities for precise targeting are limited in some advertising media, especially television, and this presents problems in international marketing in terms of targeting specific user segments or even specific countries.

In most business-to-business markets advertising tends to be used as a supporting activity, for example to increase awareness or interest in the company as a whole or in a new concept. In business-to-business markets the number of important customers is often comparatively small and it is essential that advertising is precisely targeted, using appropriate specialist trade media.

Together with the increased harmonisation of consumer demands for some products and the benefits of standardised products and services to firms, there is a strong move to pan-regional advertising campaigns. Advertising agency Young and Rubicam say that pan-European campaigns make up 40 per cent of their business, twice the amount of five years ago. Reckitt and Benckiser, the household goods and pharmaceutical products group, find that 90 per cent of media spending is on regional campaigns. Consumers increasingly share common values and characteristics but there are differences: for example, consumers in developing markets are still developing their habits as consumers. There are few differences in purchasing between European countries for home and personal-care products, such as deodorants and disinfectants.

There are considerable differences in the availability and usefulness of other advertising media such as radio, cinema, outdoor and transport posters. These differences make it essential to obtain data about media effectiveness in order to make informed decisions about international media schedules. For instance, in remote regions exposure to certain media is prevented because of the poor transmission output quality from radio stations, lack of electricity to power TVs or computers, the target audience having insufficient disposable income to afford television or radio and low adult literacy levels preventing significant numbers of adults from reading printed advertising. In contrast, the South Korean electronic manufacturer LG has installed a huge LED screen in Piccadilly Circus in London to increase awareness in the UK. It will keep the screen for seven years.

The opportunity to use mass-communications media to reach the target market is therefore severely limited in some countries. Even in developed countries it may not be possible to reach the majority of the market because of the increasingly fragmented nature of the national press and television. Many households have access to multiple channels where audience share is increasing whilst the traditional channels have lost audiences, particularly in the 16–24 age group. Vollmer, Frelinghuysen and Rothenberg (2007) explain the changes taking place in the balance between offline and online advertising.

In these situations it may be necessary to develop a campaign based upon a multitude of individual media activities, but this does mean that the measurement of the cost-effectiveness of the campaign is extremely difficult, given that individual components of the campaign may produce different effects.

Advertising does work in emerging countries. Increased spending has led to Coca-Cola becoming the best-selling soft drink in China and overtaking Pepsi in a number of central and Eastern European republics. There is also an apparent trend towards advertising amongst conglomerates from emerging countries that appears to recognise the value of moving from product orientation to marketing orientation. Companies such as Daewoo, LG and Samsung have built substantial brands through global advertising.

In emerging markets the appeal of advertising is greater. For example, in China the appeal of advertising is driven by young people who are optimistic rather than cynical – they expect to be better off than their parents and so wish to be part of the move to greater consumerism. Despite this modernism, Chinese traditions still prevail and family values have a powerful selling appeal, even with the young. The Chinese know that foreign brands may be better at the moment but do not like to have this overemphasised. Advertising of local brands is as sophisticated and pervasive as that of global brands.

Table 9.1 shows the top ten advertising spenders in 2005 worldwide and in the US, Asia and Europe. It also compares their spending in the three major trading regions. The information is collected from 84 countries.

Television advertising

The main influence on television advertising expenditure is the size of the economy in gross domestic product per capita, but the regulatory environment also affects spending, particularly television which tends to be more closely regulated than other media.

Cable and satellite television have contributed to a proliferation of television channels so that viewers can receive a rapidly increasing number of programmes.

SOURCE: REPRINTED WITH PERMISSION FROM 20 NOVEMBER 2006 ISSUE OF *ADVERTISING AGE*, © CRAIN COMMUNICATIONS INC 2006

TABLE 9.1 Top 10 global advertisers

Rank			Spending by US$million			
2005	2004	Advertiser	Worldwide	US	Asia	Europe
1	1	Proctor & Gamble	8.19	3.41	1.74	2.55
2	3	Unilever	4.27	0.76	1.05	2.10
3	2	General Motors	4.17	3.00	0.14	0.80
4	6	Toyota	2.80	1.08	1.10	0.51
5	5	L'Oréal	2.77	0.79	0.24	1.63
6	4	Ford	2.64	1.58	0.10	0.80
7	7	Time Warner	2.49	2.06	0.09	0.27
8	8	DaimlerChrysler	2.10	1.59	0.05	0.38
9	11	Nestlé	2.03	0.56	0.27	1.05
10	10	Johnson and Johnson	1.97	1.38	0.19	0.32

This means that there is a greater capacity for television advertising but, of course, there is greater competition for prime television advertising spots (and much higher costs) if there is likely to be a large audience. Both satellite and cable television have the potential to cross country borders and attract large audiences for programmes of common international interest, for example major sporting events.

It is not only overt television advertising in large amounts that sells. The prominent placing of products on television shows or sponsorship of programmes that are likely to be transmitted in other countries can also become an important part of the advertising campaign, particularly as placements and sponsorship cannot be removed by viewers 'zapping' between channels.

An interesting development is shown in illustration 9.4. With a more sceptical and knowledgeable audience, advertisers are adopting different, more inclusive approaches to win over customers

ILLUSTRATION 9.4

Dove uses consumer-created ads

The academy awards ceremony is the second most watched TV programme in the US after the Superbowl. In 2007 Unilever took a very expensive 30 second spot for its new product, Dove Cream Oil Body Wash. The featured advertisement was the winning entry in a contest in which consumers created their own advertisement. It was a reflection of the combination of new and old media, and a move to engaging consumers through user-generated content, rather than simply pushing the product. It followed on Dove's award-winning global campaign that featured ordinary-looking women and departed from conventional ideas of beauty. The Evolution ad won a Grand Prix best commercial ad at Cannes in 2007.

The creators of the Dove campaign were Ogilvy and Mather, owned by WPP, a British advertising company that along with three others, America's Omnicom and Interpublic and France's Publicis, dominates global advertising. Chief Executive of Ogilvy, Shelly Lazarus, explains that whereas in the past advertising a brand simply meant coming up with a good idea for a few television and print ads and intruding into the lives of its viewers, campaigns must now be an invitation to them, using the most appropriate media and communication tools available.

The Dove campaign was an illustration of this new approach and was designed to banish stereotypes and prompt a debate about beauty by involving consumers in 'Real Beauty' online workshops through the combination of traditional make up, digital enhancement and altering of the resulting images to prompt a debate over the Internet.

Dove's 'Campaign for Real Beauty' was launched in 2004 and as part of it, and reflecting the research that found only 2 per cent of women in the world think they are beautiful, Unilever were persuaded by Ogilvy to launch a worldwide 'self-esteem fund' to persuade girls and young women to embrace more positive images of themselves.

To manage worldwide integrated campaigns such as Dove's it was necessary for Ogilvy to change its way of working. It brought together previously separate creative departments so Internet 'types' would sit together with television, print, outdoor advertising, direct marketing and public relations specialists to develop an integrated 'idea' that would appeal to the boss of the client company, who are much more aware of the importance of reputation, image and being a good corporate citizen.

let's face it, firming the thighs of a size 8 supermodel is no challenge.

There's not much point in testing a new firming lotion on size-eight supermodel thighs, is there? That's why Dove's Firming range was tested on ordinary women with real lives to live – and real, curvy thighs to firm. After using Dove's nourishing and effective combination of moisturisers and seaweed extracts, we asked if they'd go in front of the camera. What better way to show the unretouched, unairbrushed results?

new Dove Firming Range

PHOTO CREDIT: IMAGE COURTESY OF THE ADVERTISING ARCHIVE

QUESTION *What factors will have most impact on traditional advertising?*

SOURCE: ADAPTED FROM 'QUEEN OF MADISON AVENUE', THE ECONOMIST 22 FEBRUARY 2007 AND G HAYCOCK, 'UNILEVER'S DOVE AD FLIES HOME WITH TOP PRIZE', REUTERS, 23 JUNE 2007 ACCESSED AT HTTP://UK.NEWS.YAHOO.COM AND FROM HTTP://WWW.UNILEVER.COM/OURBRANDS/PERSONALCARE/DOVE.ASP.

Press advertising

Media availability and effectiveness are particularly important in deciding the nature of campaigns, because they can vary from country to country. High levels of readership of the press in a country are still unusual. The general situation is that the press is available but with only token readership outside certain usually urban regions.

In some countries in Africa and Asia, adult literacy levels might restrict newspaper and magazine sales opportunities but the lack of mass-circulation national titles might cause distribution difficulties too, as it is easier to distribute quickly in small compact countries than in much larger ones such as France or Spain. Vast countries like the USA have a regional press. Newer publishing and printing technology has allowed many more local newspapers and specialist magazines to be introduced to both consumer and business-to-business markets. By their very nature they tend to be highly targeted at specific market segments and can be useful to niche marketers. However, for mass marketers the resulting fragmentation of readership that comes from very localised media titles means that national campaigns are more difficult to coordinate.

The use of agencies and consultancies

Most companies in which marketing communications are an important part of the marketing mix will use agencies and consultancies. The reasons why this is so can be explained by financial considerations, specialist knowledge, creative input and external perspective.

Financial. Advertising agents that are recognised by the media are eligible for a commission based on booked advertising space. The agency can therefore perform the advertising services of creation, media planning and booking more economically than the client.

Agencies and consultancies can use specialist people and resources, such as a database for media planning, with a number of clients. This helps spread costs for both the agency and client.

Specialist knowledge. By concentrating on one particular area, agencies and consultancies can become experts in specialised techniques, for example international database marketing or training sales people. Client companies might have an infrequent need for these services and so find it more cost-effective to subcontract the work.

Creative input. Creativity is very important in marketing communications. The organisation culture of client companies is unlikely to encourage true creativity in external communications. The challenge of new and different projects for different clients contributes to the creativity of agencies.

External perspective. The external view of agencies reduces some of the myopia of the client company. This might be particularly valuable at times of major transition, for example in moving from international marketing towards global marketing.

The selection of agencies and consultants is an important business decision. If the agency is going to be involved over a long period and be trusted with large expenditures of time and money the decision process will be significant. A dilemma for global marketers is whether they should select one central agency or many local agencies, both of which approaches have advantages and disadvantages.

Sales promotions

Sales promotions can be used in a variety of ways to add value to the sale and are particularly effective if they are part of an integrated communications strategy.

They can be used within the promotions mix for fast-moving consumer goods and business-to-business markets. Consumer goods sales promotions might include coupons or money-off vouchers, special offer price reductions and competitions. As well as these, business-to-business sales promotions might also include database and direct marketing, exhibitions and trade fairs, bundled sales deals in which extra product features might be added, such as trade-ins on old products, extra warranty and service cover and operative training.

Sales promotions are usually used close to the purchase decision and have the objective of offering better value to the customer at the most influential moment in the purchase process. In some markets there may be no meaningful differences between a number of companies or brands, except for the degree of attractiveness of the sales promotion offer. The customers' perception of the relative value of the alternative promotions depends to a great extent on their cultural values and differences, which lead to certain types of sales promotion being very successful in one country but failing in another.

Legal restrictions also affect the opportunity for firms to standardise sales promotion across country borders. There are limitations on the amount of cash discounts and special sales promotions in some countries in Europe. Different legal definitions of the rules for lotteries, too, prevent some competition-based promotions being operated across borders.

Direct marketing

In the past, direct marketing has usually taken the form of direct mail or telephone selling, but in markets with high computer ownership the Internet has taken the lead. The key elements of direct marketing are an accurate up-to-date database, the ability to purge the database of incorrect data and to merge the database with a firm's promotional message. Usually it is important to offer a telephone (toll-free) number and, of course, the customers need to have a telephone if telephone marketing is to be used! Usually firms subcontract direct marketing to specialist agencies which provide the various services, such as list brokering, purging and merging.

Communicating with the wider range of stakeholders

At the outset we said that the principal objective of the international marketing communications strategy was to sell products and services. However, before messages are communicated with the specific purpose of encouraging consumers to buy it is necessary to make them more broadly aware of the company and its products. In the early stages of the buying process it is the reputation which the international firm has in the wider community that is important. Quite simply customers in a host country are unlikely to even contemplate buying from a foreign firm that is perceived to be exploiting its local workers, bribing government officials, showing little regard to environmental protection issues, offering poor or variable product quality or is likely to pull out from the country at any moment and thus be unable to fulfil its guarantees and obligations. By contrast a foreign firm can build increased loyalty amongst its customers at the expense of local firms if it is perceived to offer better quality and value for money, to be a more reliable supplier, more caring about the local community and, in some cases, through association, to be respected by world personalities.

These objectives can be achieved through the effective use of a number of communications elements under the following general headings:

- Corporate identity.
- Sponsorship.
- Public relations and lobbying.

Corporate identity

Corporate identity is concerned with consistently communicating not just what business the firm is in and what image it wishes to project in the market, but also how it does its business. It must reflect the standards and values it aims to uphold in its dealings with all its stakeholders. For this reason there are two distinct elements. For many MNEs the focus is upon the image it wishes to create, which is reinforced by consistency in the way the company name and logo is presented and applied to the vast range of physical outputs and assets of the company including signs, staff uniforms, letterheads, visiting cards, gifts, annual reports, packaging specification and promotional literature.

In principle, whilst these can all be controlled by the firm, there are many challenges in applying them consistently in all the countries where the firm operates, especially where it develops alliances with partners who might also wish to maintain their corporate identity in joint communications.

Arguably of more importance is the underlying identity of the firm and its beliefs, standards and values, which will show through in everything it does. These may pose more difficulties in the firm's attempts to achieve consistency and a favourable impact throughout the world because of the different cultural values of its staff and stakeholders in different countries.

Sponsorship and celebrity endorsement

Sponsorship involves a firm (the sponsor) providing finance, resources or other support for an event, activity, firm, person, product or service. In return the sponsor would expect to gain some advantage, such as the exposure of its brand, logo or advertising message. Sponsorship of music, performing arts and sporting events provides opportunities for:

- brand exposure and publicity
- opportunities to entertain customers and employees
- association between brands and events, with the events often reinforcing the brand positioning, for example Dunhill's golf sponsorship and BMW's sponsorship of classical music concerts
- improving community relations by supporting community-based projects
- creating the opportunity to promote the brands at the event, either through providing free products or gifts such as T-shirts carrying the brand logo.

Expenditure on global sponsorship has expanded rapidly over the past two decades, and it is being used much more for the following reasons:

- restrictive government policies on tobacco and alcohol advertising make sponsorship the most effective way of communicating the brand imagery to a mass market, for example in Formula 1 car racing
- the escalating costs of media advertising
- increased leisure activities and sporting events

- the proven record of sponsorship
- greater media coverage of sponsored events
- the reduced efficiencies of traditional media advertising because of clutter and zapping between television programmes, especially during advertising breaks.

Masterson (2005) explains the need to achieve a fit between the sponsor and the activity being sponsored, introduces the concept of integrated product relevance and explains the ways in which this can be used to affect the consumers' reponses to the sponsor's products, by focusing on function and image similarity.

There has been an increase in the amount of broadcast sponsorship in film, television and radio programmes. This can result in the benefit of the event sponsorship being reduced. For example, Heinz sponsored a Rugby World Cup only to find that Sony sponsored the national commercial television coverage in the UK, resulting in most viewers thinking that Sony had sponsored the whole event.

Product placement

Because many television viewers record programmes and are able to fast-forward through advertising, product placement within the programmes is becoming more attractive. Those films that will gain a global TV audience, such as James Bond, as shown in Illustration 9.5 offer the most potential from product placement for global firms.

ILLUSTRATION 9.5

James Bond – licensed to sell

In the 2006 film *Casino Royale*, James Bond ditched his Dom Perignon champagne for Bollinger, Finlandia vodka for Smirnoff and Rolex watch for Omega. The 26 brands which sponsored the previous film to the tune of £45 million were cut to six main brands for Casino Royale: Sony Ericsson phones, Sony Electronics, Omega watches, Smirnoff,

PHOTO CREDIT: © DENIS BALIBOUSE/REUTERS/CORBIS

Heineken beer and Ford, which included the Aston Martin brand.

There were a small number of other associated brands, including Bollinger, Turnbull and Asser for pyjamas and Virgin. Interestingly Richard Branson had a walk-on part in the film, but when the film was shown on the plane journeys of his arch rival British Airways he was cut out of the film.

No-one knows how much of the £60 million costs of *Casino Royale* were generated by sponsorship, but Ford alone were rumoured to have spent £15 million. Eon Productions, owned by the family of the original producer, 'Cubby' Broccoli, control the James Bond franchise. Eon decided to reduce the number of sponsors and get more focused partners because they feared the damage 'over-sponsorship' might do.

The benefits for sponsors are clear. Casino Royale is expected to take close to £500 million at the box office. This adds up to £2.6 billion worldwide box office takings from the 21 Bond films before DVD sales and licenses are taken into account, making it the most valuable film franchise, beating even *Star Wars*.

QUESTION *What are the critical success factors for sponsorship, for the sponsor and the organisation or product being sponsored?*

SOURCE: ADAPTED FROM '007 LICENSED TO SELL', *DAILY TELEGRAPH*, 18 NOVEMBER, 2006 AND 'JAMES BOND: LICENSED TO SELL' FROM WWW.FORBES.COM, 16 NOVEMBER 2006.

Celebrity endorsement

Sponsorship of individuals such as sports stars and the use of celebrities to endorse brands are very beneficial because of the perceived shared values and image association between the celebrity and the brand. The problem is that individuals can be unpredictable and this can lead to unfortunate and undesirable associations.

Global brands ambassadors need to be leaders in their field and recognisable by global consumers. As David Beckham came towards the end of his footballing career, he was replaced as the face of Gillette by Tiger Woods, Thierry Henry and Roger Federer. Usually brand ambassadors are associated with B2C brands but B2B brands also see the benefit. Lenovo signed up footballer Ronaldinho for a new product launch.

Public relations

Public relations is concerned with communicating news stories about the firm, its people, standards and values – particularly its attitude to social responsibility – products and services through the media without charge for their use in order to develop relationships, goodwill and mutual understanding between the firm and its stakeholders. The press is always hungry for stories in order to fill their ever-expanding programmes and newspapers, and are grateful for interesting and newsworthy stories that are inexpensive to obtain.

The purposes of PR are as follows:

- helping to foster the prestige and reputation of the firm through its public image
- raising awareness and creating interest in the firm's products
- dealing with social and environmental issues and opportunities
- improving goodwill with customers through presenting useful information and dealing effectively with complaints
- promoting the sense of identification of employees with the firm through newsletters, social activities and recognition
- discovering and eliminating rumours and other sources of misunderstanding and misconceptions
- building a reputation as a good customer and reliable supplier
- influencing the opinions of public officials and politicians, especially in explaining the responsible operation of the business and the importance of its activities to the community
- dealing promptly, accurately and effectively with unfavourable negative publicity, especially where it is perceived to be a crisis which might damage the firm's reputation
- attracting and keeping good employees.

An important aspect of PR is explaining the corporate social responsibility policy of organisations and dealing with the cynicism of pressure groups and individuals communicating online and using traditional media.

Public relations is concerned with a wide variety of activities in order to deliver these objectives, including:

- dealing with press relations
- arranging facility visits
- publishing house journals and newsletters

- preparing videos, audiovisual presentations, printed reports and publications describing the firm's activities
- training courses
- arranging community projects
- lobbying governments.

From a communications perspective the effect of public relations-generated stories in the media is different from advertising. The viewer, listener or reader will perceive the information differently. Editorial material in the media is perceived by consumers to be factual and comparatively neutral whereas advertising material is expected to be persuasive and present a positive statement for the advertisers' products. Whereas the firm controls every aspect of advertising, a press release covering a firm's news story will be interpreted by the journalist who writes the story for the press or edits the videotape for television.

Stakeholders

MNEs have a larger number of stakeholders than those firms limited to domestic markets. These stakeholders or target groups have varying degrees of connection with such organisations. Some will be part of the value system of a firm and some will be part of the environment surrounding the firm, both domestically and internationally. Some may be supportive, others may have a controlling role, such as government departments, and yet others may have the intention of being destructive, for example, some pressure groups. Even though the firm may want to achieve the same objectives in different country markets its patterns of engagement with stakeholders can be quite different, as Illustration 9.6 shows.

One of the main roles of international public relations is to try to manage the often substantially different and conflicting expectations of stakeholders. Frequently the problem is one of when to disclose information that could prove damaging to the company's image and reputation.

In international marketing one of the most important responsibilities of public relations is to manage unexpected crises (an example is given in Illustration 9.7) which occur from time to time. Over the past few years there have been a number of examples of good and bad practice in managing information when dealing with a crisis within the company. Crises of this type have included environmental pollution, unethical promotion, exploitation of labour and health scares caused by food contamination. The golden rule is that the firm should be seen to act, before the media or government forces it to do so, in order to show that it is sorry that an incident has occurred. However, it should neither accept responsibility nor apportion blame until the evidence is investigated and the real cause of the problem identified.

Many MNEs consider government lobbying an essential part of international marketing, with the aim of influencing foreign governments both directly and indirectly through asking the home country government to help. Recent examples of lobbying have been US firms seeking to reduce Chinese piracy of products and services and greater access to Japanese markets over the past two decades, and the main objectives of the strategy have been to convince both governments that allowing market access is in both their interests.

As government lobbying becomes increasingly important it raises issues for the company about how high profile it should be in pressing its case and how much effort should be expended on persuading the home country government to put pressure on the host country government. Some firms go one stage further by making donations to political parties. This, of course, can have the effect of alienating other stakeholders. There is little doubt that firms are increasingly making lobbying a major responsibility of senior management, given the pivotal role of governments in making decisions which might affect the MNE.

Online communications

In Chapter 12 we discuss the use of technology in shaping the international marketing strategy of firms at greater length and, clearly, facilitating communications is at the heart. Here however we discuss the tactical use of online integrated marketing communications.

The nature of online communications

A useful starting point is to consider the key, distinctive characteristics of the internet (Table 9.2) that provide the basis upon which online communications add value to the organisation and its stakeholders.

ILLUSTRATION 9.6

Charity begins in the neighbourhood

When National Westminster Bank (now the Royal Bank of Scotland) expanded into New England, US they found it necessary to adapt their approach to corporate charitable giving. The logic of this may not at first be apparent. Being East Coast, English speaking and attuned culturally to giving (sometimes more than 1 per cent of profit), Natwest America, in a similar way to its parent organisation, appreciated the need to demonstrate corporate citizenship and cement relationships with its customers, employees, the media and shareholders by giving. Furthermore, patterns of donation were alike, with roughly 60 per cent going to social and community affairs and the balance split fairly equally between the arts and sport. The whole approach practised by the community relations managers converged and on both sides of the Atlantic a blend of altruism and high-impact giving, matched closely to

SOURCE: ROD RADFORD, SHEFFIELD HALLAM UNIVERSITY

corporate identity, prevailed. What then was the difference requiring alternative working practices?

Divergence originated not in cultural differences, though Natwest America probably looked a little harder for value and donated alongside a more established network of personal philanthropy. It derived largely from structural environmental barriers associated with geography and the legal/political make-up of the US banking industry. At the time the US banking system was highly fragmented by legislation, which inhibited the development of multi-state banks. In addition, conditions of New York State banking licences involved a quota system requiring prescribed levels of business within narrow 'blue lined' geographic communities. Natwest UK faced no such restrictions and, although they gave locally, they were able to maintain a much more regional and narrow focus.

Corporate benevolence in the US banking sector was much more highly localised and even individual, for example support for students from the Hispanic community. The US was also simply so large that the key stakeholders associated little with corporate activity outside their own state. Because their media, such as the *New York Times*, was regional, they were unlikely to hear about 'good works' elsewhere, rendering such giving unattractive to an organisation altogether. In contrast, the UK is small and has a particularly developed national media network. The corporate quotas for Natwest America meant it had to maintain and build relationships and attract new business from various groups within the local community, and this drove the different charitable profile from the UK approach. Corporate communications were divided by more than just a common language!

QUESTION *What should drive the strategy for corporate giving?*

A number of online tools are used to create brand awareness and product and service associations and drive users to their websites, where customers might obtain further information, purchase an item from an online store or direct the customer to a traditional store.

ILLUSTRATION 9.7

Corruption concerns at BAE

A key role of PR is to manage a variety of stakeholders and sometimes this can become problematic. Major defense

contracts are usually worth billions of dollars and provide thousands of well paid, skilled jobs. This makes them politically important and politicians and government officials are usually closely involved in the negotiations. Such contracts are often associated with allegations of bribery. In 2006 BAE systems the aerospace company was under investigation by the UK's Serious Fraud Office (SFO) regarding its contracts in South Africa, Tanzania, Romania, Chile and the Czech Republic. The SFO's investigation into the £40 bn Al-Yamamah contract with Suadi Arabia was dropped when the UK government said it was concerned the Saudis would stop co-operating on the war on terror. The Saudis had suspended negotiations on a £10 bn extension to the Al-Yamamah contract when the SFO tried to gain access to the Saudi royal family's Swiss bank accounts. BAE Syatems denied allegations that it had set up a £20 million account to provide perks to Saudi royal family members to hold on to the contract.

QUESTION *What do you consider to be the role of PR in a contract of this sort?*

SOURCE: ADAPTED FROM K. GRIFFITHS 'BAE FLIES UNSCATHED THROUGH THE FLAK', *DAILY TELEGRAPH*, 22 FEBRUARY 2007

TABLE 9.2   The characteristics of the Internet – the Six 'I's

	Characteristics
Interactivity	Customer initiates contact Marketer has 100 per cent customer attention and can store responses
Intelligence	Ability to collect and analyse information continuously and make individually focused offers
Individualisation	Tailored communication using stored data to achieve mass customisation
Integration	Achieve integration of communication and manage customer switching channels during purchasing
Industry restructuring	Distintermediation involved removal of traditional intermediaries Reintermediation to gain presence on websites
Independence of location	Reach extended to countries where a physical support presence would not be viable.

SOURCE: ADAPTED FROM J.DEIGHTON (1996) THE FUTURE OF INTERACTIVE MARKETING; *HARVARD BUSINESS REVIEW*, NOVEMBER–DECEMBER 151–42

Advertising is placed on partner sites that charge a 'click-through' fee in return for providing the sales lead and link. Search engines and comparative pricing sites provide sales leads by listing websites based on brand searches or brand associations with key words. Being listed on the first page of a key word search is valuable and firms can pay heavily to ensure this happens.

Websites Some websites are clearly defined as marketplaces either owned by one specific organisation or where links to commercial sites should be expected, for example, financial services supermarkets, online travel agents or insurance brokers. Dilemma 12.2 (page 435) discusses advertisements placed on social networking sites where content is dictated by users.

Email Organisations use email to convey their marketing messages directly to their customers. However, many customers have been irritated by the large volume of spam they receive. Godin (2002) found that customers were bombarded by up to 500 marketing messages per day from traditional communication sources but today customers can expect to see up to 3000 messages, because of the rise in online communications. This means that the effect of individual messages is diluted amongst this volume of what he refers to as interruption marketing (spam). He has introduced the term 'permission marketing' to suggest that the communications will be more effective if customers agree to receive more communications from the firm. This opt-in approach is preferable to an opt-out, in which the customer would have to take the initiative in asking a firm not to send messages.

Viral marketing has extended the effectiveness by encouraging recipients of email messages to pass them onto the others to create a 'buzz' in the marketplace.

Mobile communications For some time it has been predicted that mobile communications would be valuable, but in practice users may be unwilling to have their mobile phone inbox overloaded with largely irrelevant marketing messages that get in the way of their desired phone and text messages.

One significant advantage of online communications is that it is easier to measure the actions of customers and their response. However, Dilemma 9.2 considers how decisions can be taken on using online and offline media and whether investment should be made in those elements that can be most easily measured.

DILEMMA 9.2

Measuring online and offline promotion effectiveness

While most organisations believe that an integrated approach to marketing communications involving online and offline media is most effective, deciding on a balance between spend on the two types poses a dilemma. Both types of media raise awareness and drive brand association, but the difference is that direct measurement of the effectiveness of communications in affecting online behaviour is possible, making it easier to justify campaign spend, whereas the measurement of the effectiveness of promotion in influencing offline behaviour tends to be indirect and therefore not as clear.

For example, by combining the expertise of three companies, Hitwise, an online competitive intelligence service with 1200 global clients, i-level, which claims to be Europe's largest online media buyer and Yahoo! Search Marketing it is possible to track the effectiveness of campaigns, such as creating buzz in appropriate online communities, PR and banner advertising, on share of brand and website searches, and their effectiveness in driving customers to websites. Where substantial business is transacted through the website, for example in the purchase of car insurance, there is a directly attributable outcome. Although offline media impact on online behaviour can be measured quite precisely too, if the customer purchases offline, decisions might also depend on other influences.

Given that the influence of online media extends across country boundaries, the dilemma for international marketing firms is how to decide on online and offline promotional spend and to what degree choice of media to use should be driven by those elements that are most easily measured.

Privacy There is a conflict between the interests of the firm and customer in developing databases. In order to offer more individually targeted, personalised and relevant communications, the firm requires ever more detailed and potentially sensitive information from the customer. However, the customer is reluctant to give firms personal information. They appreciate that certain firms such as insurance companies might need the information in order to process a transaction, can be trusted and will respect local country privacy laws, such as the 1998 Data Protection Act in the UK. They have more concern over the possibility of the firms passing on the sensitive information – deliberately or accidentally – to other firms that will not be so scrupulous in its use. It is very easy to pass information electronically to other companies or countries.

One aspect of online communications and PR is the adverse comments that are posted uncensored on many websites. Even the charity the Bill and Melinda Gates Foundation was accused in the *Los Angeles Times* of profiting from investments in companies whose activities in deprived areas of the world contributed to the problems the foundation was trying to solve. Online communications are difficult to deal with because they are often vicious, and critical comments by individual bloggers who do not belong to a well organised group. *The Economist* (2006) notes that leaders of better organised pressure groups can often help firms to correct their mistakes and prevent misinformed comment.

DEVELOPING PROFITABLE, LONG-TERM MARKETING RELATIONSHIPS

So far in this chapter we have focused upon the communications strategies that might be used to ensure that the firm's broad base of stakeholders around the world are aware of the company's standards and values, the distinctiveness and quality of its brands, products, and services and that customers are exposed to the messages that will encourage them to buy the firm's products and services rather than the competitor's and receive delivery of the products and services, where appropriate, through intermediaries and partners. Once customers have been won over, usually at a considerable cost, firms increasingly realise that it is less costly if they can persuade them to stay loyal to the firm rather than lose them to a competitor and so face the cost of winning them over again. The potential cost of failing to satisfy customers can be high.

Customer retention is particularly important for B2B marketing, where the number of opportunities to win over new customers may be very limited and the loss of a major customer could have a disastrous effect on the firm. The lifetime value of the customer is considerable, but the cost to the customer of changing to a new supplier can be considerable too. Both supplier and customer have something to gain from the relationship marketing (RM) concept, which is concerned with developing and maintaining mutually advantageous relationships between two or more firms in a supply chain and using their combined capability and resources to deliver the maximum added value for the ultimate customer. It involves a more holistic approach to understanding the market dynamics and developing implementation strategies to respond to the changes in the market needs that have been identified.

The concept of relationship marketing

There are significant differences between adopting a traditional marketing approach based on individual transactions, in which the emphasis is placed on the 4Ps of the product marketing mix (particularly the product P) and an approach based upon building relationships by emphasising the three extra Ps of the service mix (particularly the people P). At the core of relationship marketing is the idea that rather than simply trying to add customer service onto a predetermined product offer, based on a rigid marketing mix, the firm should provide customer satisfaction by offering a flexible marketing mix offer to meet the customer's evolving needs.

Horovitz (2000) suggests that in relationship marketing the 4Ps of the traditional marketing mix are changed altogether and replaced by the 4Cs of relationship marketing: customer needs and wants; costs; convenience and communication. Clearly this makes sense for high-involvement B2B purchases but less so for low-involvement purchases of consumer packaged goods.

Throughout the firm the objectives of relationship marketing are to:

- Maintain and build existing customers by offering more tailored and cost-effective business solutions.
- Use existing relationships to obtain referral to business units and other supply chain members that are perhaps in different parts of the world and not currently customers.
- Increase the revenue from customers by offering solutions that are a combination of products and services.
- Reduce the operational and communications cost of servicing the customers, including the work prior to a trading relationship.

Relationships must be built with those that might influence the final purchase decision, and includes internal staff as individuals and groups, experts, celebrities and other influential individuals that have the power to connect the organisation with the market.

The power and influence of the organisation's stakeholders in these markets will vary considerably around the world and their relative importance depends upon the specific context of the firm's activity. In the technology sector, for example, key influencers and high profile, lead customers may be located in a particular country market but their decisions might influence purchasing decisions across the world.

Database development

The starting point is to build an information technology system that will integrate the RM activity. Central to the system is a database that will identify those customers with which it is worthwhile developing a relationship. The database can best be built from the company records of its interactions with customers and then supplemented with purchased lists of possible customers. Chaffey *et al.* (2003) explain that the details about the customer should include:

- Personal and profile data, including contact details.
- Transaction data including purchase quantities, channels, timing and locations.
- Communications data, including response to campaigns.

Shimp (2006) explains how recency, frequency and monetary value of purchases can be used to identify the priority customers, which in relationship marketing terms are likely to be the most valuable to the firm.

Wasserman, Khermouch and Green (2000) explained that data mining is used to 'discover hidden facts contained in databases'. Identifying relationships between data contained in databases provides a basis for targeting prospective customers cost-effectively, developing cooperative relationships with other companies and better understanding the patterns of customer purchasing behaviour.

Chaffey *et al.* (2003) explain that the key objectives are: customer retention, customer extension (increasing the depth and range of customers) and customer selection (segmenting and targeting).

Customer relationship management

International consumer markets are characterised by their sheer size and the relative anonymity of their customers. Even small retailers cannot possibly know their customers' individual behaviour, attitudes, intention to purchase, and experiences (good or bad) in dealing with the firm, whereas an industrial marketer with only a few customers possibly can. As we have discussed in the section on databases, technology has been developed to try to integrate RM activity and manage the vast amounts of supporting information. Customer relationship management (CRM) is effectively computer software coupled with defined management processes and procedures to enable staff throughout organisations to capture and use information about their customers to maintain and build relationships. Companies such as Siebel (US) have built their business around such concepts.

Although CRM should play a decisive role in integrating communications and developing relationships with the customer as the focus, Kotler (2003) points out that in practice many firms have embraced the concept and spent between $5 and 10 million on CRM systems but been less than satisfied with the results. He quotes the CRM Forum research that suggests less than 30 per cent of companies are satisfied with their systems. The problems that companies identify in establishing the systems tend not to be associated with software failure (2 per cent) but rather organisational change (29 per cent), company politics/inertia (22 per cent), lack of CRM understanding (20 per cent) poor planning (12 per cent) lack of CRM skills (6 per cent) budget problems (4 per cent) bad advice (1 per cent) and other (4 per cent).

The problems arise when firms see CRM systems as a quick fix to try to manage vast amounts of data. They make broad generalisations about customer segments and are often too insensitive to different consumer cultures and concerns. Too often CRM is not adopted on an organisation-wide basis and instead is adopted by individual departments for very specific reasons. It also gets modified because of the need to interface it with existing legacy systems and so becomes fragmented and, rather than reducing cost, actually increases it. The introduction of CRM leads to raised expectations of service levels amongst customers and staff and if this is not delivered CRM can have a detrimental effect on the business.

The opportunities for relationship marketing to offer benefits are increasing because of improvements in communications, IT and increased cross-border purchasing. However it is important to understand that the consumer is not necessarily a willing participant in the relationship mission, and unless this is recognised, relationship marketing will prove to be of limited value. Indeed the question must be asked whether the majority of consumers will derive any benefit from a relationship with a MNE – the benefits will be mainly with the firm.

For relatively low purchase price items there is a danger that the costs to the firm of building customer loyalty might outweigh the costs of a more traditional approach to marketing products and services. It is difficult to measure the relative merits of short-term costs against longer-term revenues and few companies are willing to take a long-term view based upon their assumptions of what might happen in the future.

In practice the methods of relationship marketing in the consumer markets are diverging from relationship marketing in the business sector. In consumer markets relationship marketing will become more concerned with making one-to-one connections with customers through interactivity and promoting and placing products and services in the appropriate media at just the right moment.

SUMMARY

- To be effective in global markets external international marketing communications are driven by the need to have a uniform corporate identity, clearly differentiated product and service offers supported by consistent promotion and strategies in place to build long-term customer relationships.

- Firms also need to focus on internal and interactive communications and ensure that their staff and partners' staff in remote locations deliver consistent and integrated international marketing communications.

- There are benefits to the firm of standardising the promotion processes and programmes to benefit from economies of scale and the learning effect, wherever possible, but communications are extremely sensitive to local culture and conditions and, without attention to detail, they can be the source of problems worldwide for firms.

- The communication tools must be used appropriately to suit the context of the markets being served, different customer needs and the firm's objectives. Media availability, cultural and legislation differences and the nature of the products and services being marketed will influence the communications strategy decisions and choice of tools.

- Customer perceptions can be damaged by poor communications management within the firm and by external factors over which the organisation may have no control. The international firm must concentrate on communicating consistency in its image, standards and values to a diverse range of stakeholders as well as making its direct appeal to existing and potential customers. It must also integrate the traditional communications with online communications to further develop interactive, one-to-one customer relationships.

- Because of the high cost of winning and losing customers firms, particularly in the business-to-business market, must build relationships to retain their most valuable customers in the long term. They must also measure the impact of their marketing communication investment as far as possible to ensure value for money.

KEYWORDS

Communications adaptation
Communications mix
Communications tools
Corporate identity

Customer relationship management
Failures of communications
Product and service differentiation

Promotional mix
Push or pull strategy
Relationship marketing
Standardisation of international marketing communications
Transactions

Google to dominate online ads?

The spectacular growth of the Internet has been driven by people using it to create communities that serve their own particular interests. It has been financed by organisations looking for a more effective route to market and advertise in places where potential customers congregate. These three elements come together in harmony and into potential conflict on social networking sites, such as YouTube and MySpace. These networking websites were set up to facilitate the exchange of videos, photos and stories and enable users to make connections, but their huge popularity brought them to the attention of much bigger players both from old and new media that realised their ability to attract users. Rupert Murdoch's News Corporation paid US$580 million for MySpace in 2005 and Google used US$1.65 billion of its own shares to buy YouTube in 2006.

News Corporation realised that increasingly young consumers were turning away from old to new media attracted by the user-generated content. Sites such as YouTube and MySpace offered a valuable way of reaching these consumers, particularly as they offered the potentially lucrative business opportunity to sell advertising space placed alongside content.

The problem was that the culture on these sites was not conducive to promoting advertising. Users like the fact that the sites 'break the rules' and are not part of the 'establishment' media. Before being taken over, YouTube had refused to insert adverts that could not be skipped over as they thought they might risk annoying or turning off users. Despite only being in business for 19 months YouTube had become one of the world's most visited sites.

Content included not just self-generated material but also video clips that users found and recorded from television, thereby infringing copyright laws in much the same way that a few years previously, sites such as Napster also infringed copyright by facilitating illegal music file sharing between

users. However given the fact that YouTube had not made a profit, television companies had not taken YouTube to court, as there was little prospect of getting a pay-out and every prospect of alienating potential customers.

When Google took over YouTube things were different: suing Google for copyright infringement offered more attractive prospects. After claiming to have had a number of fruitless negotiations with Google, in 2007 Viacom's Nickelodeon, the children's television channel, launched a US$1 billion lawsuit against copyright infringement over Spongebob, a popular cartoon character and other properties. Viacom claimed that YouTube viewers had watched video clips of its shows 1.5 billion times. However, some commentators in the industry suggested that young consumers no longer scanned through television programme schedules, but rather used these sites to find out, and get 'tasters' of programmes, observing that usually the videos posted on the sites were clips rather than complete programmes. Suggestions were that if Nickelodeon material was removed from YouTube the loser would be Viacom. In contrast with Viacom, other media companies such as the BBC and CBS agreed deals with YouTube.

A further problem for potential advertisers was that because of the largely unregulated nature of the content of these sites, they included undesirable and embarrassing content, which advertisers would not wish to be associated with. For some users the illicit material may well provide the main attraction of the sites.

In defence of YouTube, Google claimed that the American copyrighting law covering digital media offered 'safe harbour' protection to online firms that acted quickly to block access to pirated material once they were notified by copyright holders of specific infringements and claimed Google removed material when notified. A senior executive of Microsoft observed that YouTube routinely identified spam and pornography and removed it from the site and it could just as easily do the same with pirated video clips.

As Google faced the lawsuit, News Corporation had taken action with MySpace to avoid the situation. It created its own website in 50/50 partnership with NBC to let viewers watch their material and they agreed to license their content for use on other video sharing sites, including MySpace, Microsoft's MSN, TimeWarner's AOL and Yahoo. Whilst videos were offered free, there would be a charge for premium content and money would be earned through advertising. The content included the Simpsons and other hit NBC shows and an online music shop to rival iTunes.

QUESTIONS

1 *What factors are affecting the growth of online global marketing communications?*

2 *What implications does this have for a*
   a) Google?
   b) a global online advertiser of your choice?

PHOTO CREDIT: RICHARD LEVINE/ALAMY

SOURCE: ADAPTED FROM 'GOOGLE'S YOUNG PARTNER', *THE ECONOMIST*, 10 OCTOBER 2006; D. RUSCHE, 'BIG MEDIA STRIKE BACK AT GOOGLE', *SUNDAY TIMES*, 18 MARCH, 2007 AND D. O'CONNELL, 'BIG MEDIA'S CHALLENGE TO YOUTUBE', *SUNDAY TIMES*, 25 MARCH, 2007

DISCUSSION QUESTIONS

1 Communications are central to effective marketing planning. What are the key issues in planning, executing and controlling an integrated international communications strategy?

2 Critically examine the case for using one advertising agency to create and implement an international advertising campaign.

3 What factors would constrain the use of standardised sales promotion campaigns for a multi-national enterprise in international markets? How might the use of online communications help and hinder the process?

4 Select an economic region. Identify the advantages and disadvantages of pan-regional advertising. How would you manage a pan-regional campaign for a product or service of your choice?

5 Select (1) a business-to-business and (2) a business-to-consumer purchasing situation. Explain the role of relationship marketing in each of these situations and explain the various international marketing communications tools that could be used.

References

Chan, A.K. and Huang, Y. (1997) 'Brand naming in China: a linguistic approach', *Marketing Intelligence and Planning*, 5 (15): 227–34.

Chaffey, D., Meyer, R., Johnston, K. and Ellis-Chadwick, F. (2003) *Internet marketing: strategy, implementation and practice*. FT Prentice Hall.

Davidson, H. (2002) *Committed enterprise: how to make values and visions work. Butterworth-Heinemann*.

Economist, The (2006) 'The blog in the corporate machine', *The Economist*, 2 November 2006.

Fill, C. (2006) *Marketing communications: engagement, strategies and practice*. FT Prentice Hall.

Godin, S. (2002) *Permission marketing: turning strangers into friends and friends into customers*. Free Press.

Honeycutt, E.D. (2005) 'Sales training in a dynamic market: the Singapore service industry', *Services Marketing Quarterly*, 26 (3): 55–70.

Horovitz, J. (2000) 'Using information to bond customers', in D. Marchand (ed.) *Competing with information*. Wiley.

Kotler, P. (2002) *Marketing management*, Prentice Hall.

Kotler, P. (2003) *Marketing insights from A to Z : 80 concepts every manager needs to know*. John Wiley.

Masterson, R. (2005) 'The importance of creative match in television sponsorship', *International Journal of Advertising* 25 (4): 471–88.

Neelankavil, J.P., Mummalaneni, V. and Sessions, D. (1996) 'Use of foreign language and models in print advertisements in East Asian countries: a logit modelling approach', *European Journal of Management*, 29 (4): 24–38.

Schmitt, B.H. and Pan, Y. (1994) 'Managing corporate and brand identities in the Asia Pacific Region', *Californian Business Review*, Summer.

Shimp, T.A. (2006) *Advertising, promotion, and other aspects of integrated marketing communications*. Thomson South-Western.

Siu, W. and Au, A.K. (1997) 'Women in advertising: a comparison of television advertisements in China and Singapore', *Marketing Intelligence and Planning*, 15 (5).

Vollmer, C., Frelinghuysen, J. and Rothenberg, R. (2007) 'The future of advertising is now', accessed at www.strategy-business.com on 17 January 2007.

Wasserman, T., Khermouch, G. and Green, J. (2000) 'Mining everyones' business', *Brandweek*, February.

Wentz, H. (1997) 'A single Europe: reality or mirage', *Advertising Age International*, May.

Whiteling, I. (2007) 'Emerging markets: the China experience', http://eventsreview.com/ accessed 8 February 2007.

Wilson, R. and Gilligan, C. (1997) *Strategic marketing management: planning, implementation and control*. Butterworth-Heinemann.

Zhang, Y. and Neelankavil, J.P. (1997) 'The influence of culture on advertising effectiveness in China and the USA: a cross cultural study', *European Journal of Management*, 31 (2): 134–49.

CHAPTER 10

THE MANAGEMENT OF INTERNATIONAL DISTRIBUTION AND LOGISTICS

INTRODUCTION

In Chapter 7, we examined strategies for international expansion and the options available for firms entering foreign markets. In this chapter we will build on the issues discussed in Chapter 7 but focus on managing the distribution and logistics within foreign markets.

The management of foreign channels of distribution is a key area in a firm's efforts to gain competitive advantage. As products become more standardised across the world, the ability to compete on customer service becomes more vital. In order to be effective in this area, a firm must have a well-managed integrated supply chain within foreign markets and across international boundaries.

In this chapter, we will examine the strategic issues in managing distribution channels and discuss the issues of selecting intermediaries and how to build long-term effective relationships in international markets. We will also examine the developments in retailing and the differences in retailing across markets at different levels of economic development.

Finally, we will examine the logistics of physically moving goods across national boundaries and the importance of efficient distribution management to minimise costs in international markets.

LEARNING OBJECTIVES

After reading this chapter you should be able to:

■ Strategically evaluate potential foreign distribution options for a given situation

■ Discuss the complexities of efficiently managing intermediaries in an international marketing context

■ Appreciate the difference in retailing infrastructures across the globe

■ Advise and recommend potential solutions to developing a logistics strategy in foreign markets

■ Understand the export documentation process

THE CHALLENGES IN MANAGING AN INTERNATIONAL DISTRIBUTION STRATEGY

Distribution channels are the means by which goods are distributed from the manufacturer to the end user. Some companies own their own means of distribution, some only deal directly with the most important customers but many companies rely on other companies to perform distribution services for them. These services include:

■ the purchase of goods

■ the assembly of an attractive assortment of goods

■ holding stocks or inventory

■ promoting the sale of goods to the end customer

■ the physical movement of goods.

In international marketing, companies usually take advantage of a wide number of different organisations to facilitate the distribution of their products. The large number is explained by considerable differences between countries both in their distribution systems and in the expected level of product sales. The physical movement of goods usually includes several modes of transport – for example, by road to a port, by boat to the country of destination and by road to the customer's premises. The selection of the appropriate distribution strategy is a significant decision. Whilst the marketing mix decisions of product and marketing communications are often more glamorous, they are usually dependent upon the chosen distribution channel. The actual distribution channel decision is fundamental as it affects all aspects of the international marketing strategy.

The key objective in building an effective distribution strategy is to build a supply chain to your markets that is, as Kotler and Keller (2005) said, 'a planned and professionally managed vertically integrated marketing system that incorporates both the needs of the manufacturer and the distributors'.

To achieve this across international markets is a daunting task and will mean the international marketing manager has to meet a number of important challenges in order to ensure they develop a distribution strategy which delivers the effective distribution of products and services. The major areas they will need to consider are as follows:

■ *Selection of foreign country intermediaries.* Should the firm use indirect or direct channels? What type of intermediaries will best serve their needs in the marketplace?

■ *How to build a relationship with intermediaries*. The management and motivation of intermediaries in foreign country markets is especially important to firms trying to build a long-term presence, competing on offering quality services.

■ *How to deal with the varying types of retailing infrastructure across international markets*. Achieving a coordinated strategy across markets where retailing is at varying stages of development and the impact of the growth of retailers themselves globalising are important considerations in the distribution strategies of firms competing in consumer goods markets.

■ *How to maximise new and innovative forms of distribution*, particularly opportunities arising through the Internet and electronic forms of distribution.

■ *How to manage the logistics of physically distributing products across foreign markets*. Firms need to evaluate the options available and develop a well-managed logistics system.

In the following sections of the chapter, we will examine the issues in each of these areas of international distribution and logistics.

SELECTING FOREIGN COUNTRY MARKET INTERMEDIARIES

A distribution decision is a long-term decision, as once established it can be difficult to extract a company from existing agreements. This means that channels chosen have to be appropriate for today and flexible enough to adapt to long-term market developments.

In some instances, difficulties may arise because of legal contracts, as in the case of the termination of an agency; in other situations they result from relationships that need to be initiated and then nurtured. For example, the development of sales through wholesalers and distributors might be substantially influenced by the past trading pattern and the expectation of future profitable sales. Therefore a long-term relationship needs to be developed before a firm is willing to invest significantly in an intermediary.

The long-term nature of distribution decisions forces a careful analysis of future developments. If new forms of distribution are emerging, for example, TV and mobile phone shopping, interactive media and e-retailing, this has to be considered early in the planning stage of the distribution channels for your market.

Another important challenge is the comparative inexperience of managers in the channel selection process in international markets. In domestic marketing, most marketing managers develop marketing plans which will usually be implemented within the existing arrangement of the company's distribution channels. This is quite a different proposition to the pioneering process of establishing a distribution channel in the first place and then achieving a well-supported availability through channel members in different country markets.

Furthermore, if foreign market channels are being managed from the home market, there may be preconceived notions and preferences that home market systems can operate elsewhere. Because they are unfamiliar with the market, managers may underestimate the barriers to entry erected by local competitors and even government regulations. For instance, in both France and Japan there are restrictive laws which inhibit the growth of large retailers. In Japan no one can open a store larger than 5382 square feet without permission from the community store owners: thus it can take eight to ten years for a store to win approval.

Indirect and direct channels

One of the first decisions to make in selecting intermediaries for international markets is, should the product be distributed indirectly? In other words, using outside sales agents and distributors in the country or should the product be distributed directly, using the company's sales force, company-owned distribution channel or other intermediaries in a foreign country? The former option is an independent channel which is non-integrated and provides very little or no control over its international distribution and affords virtually no links with the end users. On the other hand, direct distribution, which is an integrated channel, generally affords the supplier more control and, at the same time, brings responsibility, commitment and attendant risks. As we have discussed, distribution decisions are difficult to change and so it is important for firms to consider the alternatives available and the differing degrees of commitment and risk, evaluate the alternatives and select the most appropriate type of distribution.

Integrated (direct) channels of distribution are seen to be beneficial when a firm's marketing strategy requires a high level of service before or after the sale. Integrated channels will be more helpful than independent channels in ensuring that high levels of customer service will be achieved.

Indirect channels on the other hand require less investment in terms of both money and management time. Indirect channels also are seen to be beneficial in overcoming freight rate, negotiating disadvantages, lowering the cost of exporting and allowing higher margins and profits for the manufacturer. An independent channel, therefore, allows the international firm to tap the benefits of a distribution specialist within a foreign market, such as economies of scale and pooling the demand for the distribution services of several manufacturers.

The advantages and disadvantages of indirect exporting were discussed in Chapter 7. In this section we will focus on issues facing firms who have made the decision to involve themselves with intermediaries in foreign country markets, either through the use of agents or distributors or using their own company-owned sales force. These intermediaries offer a wide range of services.

- *Export distributors* – usually perform a variety of functions including: stock inventories, handling promotion, extending customer credit, processing orders, arranging shipping, product maintenance and repair.
- *Export agents* – responsibilities often include: buyer/seller introductions, host market information, trade fair exhibitions, general promotional activities.
- *Cooperative organisations* – carry on exporting activities on behalf of several producers and are partly under their administrative control (often used by producers of primary products – e.g. bananas, coffee, sugar).

A company-owned sales force may be one of three types:

1 *Travelling export sales representatives*. The company can begin by sending home-based sales people abroad to gather important information, to make the necessary customer contacts and to conduct the negotiating and selling process.

2 *Domestic-based export department or division*. An export sales manager carries on the actual selling and draws on market assistance as needed. It might evolve into a self-contained export department performing all the activities in export and operating as a profit centre.

3 *Foreign-based sales branch or subsidiary*. A foreign-based sales branch allows the company to achieve greater presence and programme control in the foreign market. The sales branch handles sales and distribution and may also handle warehousing and promotion. It often serves as a display centre and customer service centre as well.

The choices available to a firm may well be determined by whether they are operating in the business-to-business (B2B) or business to consumer (B2C) sector. Figure 10.1 illustrates the choices for a supplier in the business to business market internationally.

The main channels in the B2B market, therefore, tend to be agents, distributors and companies' wholly-owned sales force. The main distribution channels in the B2C market are shown in Figure 10.2.

Over the past few years there have been considerable developments in retailing across national boundaries. In a later section in this chapter, we will examine these trends and other new forms of retailing. First, however, we will look at the factors to consider in selecting channels of distribution and then building effective relationships with intermediaries.

FIGURE 10.1

Distribution channels for business goods

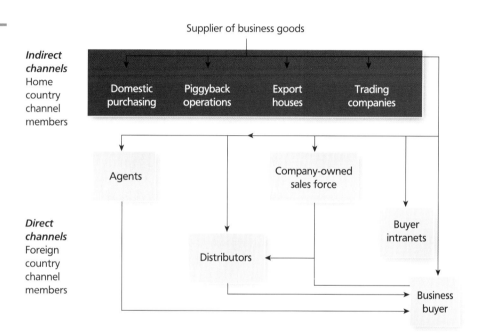

FIGURE 10.2

Distribution channels for consumer goods

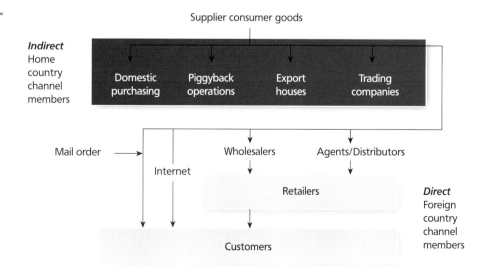

Channel selection

In selecting appropriate channel intermediaries, a firm has to consider many factors. Czinkota and Ronkainen (2006) suggested the 11C model to explain the factors a firm should consider in their selection process. The eleven elements to consider are:

1 Customer characteristics
2 Culture
3 Competition
4 Company objectives
5 Character of the market
6 Cost
7 Capital required
8 Coverage needed
9 Control issues
10 Continuity provided
11 Communication effectiveness.

Customer characteristics and culture

Channels of distribution have usually developed through the cultural traditions of the country and so there are great disparities across nations, making the development of any standardised approach difficult.

The distribution system of a country can vary enormously. In Finland, there are four centralised wholesalers covering the whole market for most product categories. In Japan there are over 300 000 wholesalers and over 1.6 million retailers. The entire distribution system is based on networks with lots of wholesalers selling to other wholesalers. Because the price of land is so high in Japan, many wholesalers cannot carry stock in the traditional sense, so may order on a daily basis. This means that there are many layers between the foreign company and the final consumer.

The Japanese system centres on distributor linkages to *dainyo* manufacturers, where the distributor accepts a subservient social status in return for economic security. From this interaction emerges the *ryatsu*-keiretsu, a political hierarchy in which units are arrayed in hierarchical layers and power resides at the 'commanding heights' of large *keiretsu.*

Keiretsu refers to a uniquely Japanese form of corporate organisation. A *keiretsu* is a grouping or family of affiliated companies that form a tight-knit alliance to work toward each other's mutual success. It can best be understood as the intricate web of relationships that links banks, manufacturers, suppliers and distributors with the Japanese government.

Distributors at 'lower' layers in the structure are tied to the *keiretsu* system by bonds of loyalty, mutual obligation, trust and power that extend throughout existing distribution structures. Whilst this arrangement guarantees members some degree of security, it also deprives them of economic freedom. Distributors that choose to deal with firms outside of the established group risk severing their ties with the group.

Whilst distributors lack the freedom to transact with whomever they wish, they are also relieved of many costs associated with being independent – for example, smaller distributors in the system need not shoulder the risk of carrying inventories of products that will not sell and can depend on reliable delivery and financial help where necessary.

In the past decade the power of the *keiretsu* has started to diminish. Many faced debts through bad loan portfolios and were forced to merge or go out of business. Furthermore companies from outside the *keiretsu* system, such as Sony and new international retailers entering Japan such as Toys R Us and McDonalds, have managed to grow by circumventing the system and outperforming their counterparts within the *keiretsu* networks. E-retailing has also had a major impact on the power of the *keiretsu* as can be seen in Illustration 10.1.

Sometimes non-Japanese businesses are described as *keiretsu*. The Virgin Group (UK) and Tata Group (India) and airline alliances such as Oneworld and the Star Alliance (USA) are seen to have similar characteristics to those of the Japanese *keiretsu*.

Thus the characteristics of the customer and the cultural traditions of the country have a major impact on the choices available to a firm. A Belgian shopper may buy groceries from huge hypermarkets, concentrating on purchases which have long shelf lives and are easy to store in their spacious apartments and houses. The Japanese customers on the other hand can be characterised by their logistical imperatives, as confined living space makes storage of goods very difficult. Therefore, customers make frequent visits to shops and rely on stores to keep their inventories. Moreover, Japan's narrow roads and lack of parking space (except for suburbs) predispose most of its population to do its shopping on foot.

Company objectives and competitive activity

The channel choice will also be determined by the company's objectives and what the firm's competitors are doing in a particular market. The distribution

ILLUSTRATION 10.1

Internet retailing helps Western countries penetrate Japan

The impact of Internet retailing is proving to be powerful in the more restricted economies of Japan and Europe. This is because

by increasing price transparency and competition the Internet is having its greatest impact on those economies that have built-in structural inefficiencies.

Japan, with high distribution margins, is starting to see considerable price erosion and big gains in efficiency. By exposing firms to more intense global competition in order to compete effectively, businesses are having to rethink old inefficient habits and seek new ways to eliminate market rigidities that have previously protected them from international predators.

In Japan the Internet strikes at the heart of the archaic and expensive *keiretsu* distribution system that holds prices artificially high. Suppliers and retailers tend to be tied to manufacturers. This allows manufacturers to control prices by restricting distribution to their own retailers. The Internet, by giving more power to the consumer through price transparency, is allowing Western companies to bypass the many layers of middlemen that have in the past proved to be such a formidable barrier to them. Foreign companies that have failed to penetrate the market previously are finally being able to reach potential consumers in the Japanese market.

QUESTION *What are the other benefits of using Internet marketing in countries with high operational barriers?*

policy is part of a firm's international direction. Therefore, the distribution system developed will depend on the company's objective, i.e. whether their strategic objective is long term or short term and how quickly they need to realise their investment.

Most firms operating in international markets will endeavour to maintain a cost-effective balance between direct and indirect channels of distribution. Firms will use **direct channels**, perhaps their own sales force, in foreign country markets where their company's objective is to deliver high-value solutions to buying problems in order to maximise customer satisfaction. Thus the firm is practising 'interaction' marketing as opposed to 'transaction' marketing. A firm whose objective is to build long-term, stable relationships with its foreign customers will have quite different objectives in the building of relationships throughout the supply chain than a firm with relatively short-term objectives in foreign country markets who purely wishes to complete the transaction before moving on to the next customer.

Character of the market

The characteristics of the market will also determine the choice available. Products often are introduced later into international markets than to the home domestic market; the company's image and awareness is normally lower, in many cases much lower, than in the domestic market and the market share attainable in the market is lower, at least initially. This makes it a much less profitable business proposition for distribution channel intermediaries. Furthermore, distribution channels are already being used by other companies who will have built up relationships with the intermediaries. This provides less space and opportunity for firms newly entering the market.

Developing countries are characterised by distribution systems consisting of a myriad of intermediaries and retail outlets. Such fragmentation results in cost inefficiencies as large volumes of product cannot be centralised and moved quickly from manufacturers to wholesalers to retailers.

Fragmented and circuitous channels also diminish possible competitive advantage by reducing the abilities of firms to get their products and services quickly and efficiently to masses of buyers. This is particularly the case for time-sensitive products. For example, overnight package couriers in some markets have failed in some cases to live up to delivery promises due to flight cancellations, poor road conditions and insufficient phone lines.

Often in emerging markets, the problems of fragmented distribution are compounded by legal restrictions as to which channels of distribution can be used by foreign importers.

The World Trade Organisation is working towards the opening up of participation in distribution systems by foreign firms in a number of countries. Indonesia eased restrictions recently, making it much easier for international companies to develop their own distribution systems. Previously foreign companies had not been allowed to set up their own distribution networks. Thailand has welcomed foreign investment but now Tesco (UK) are facing severe restrictions as they attempt to grow and develop the market (see Illustration 10.2).

Capital required and costings

In assessing the financial implications of channel selection, a firm needs to assess the relative cost of each channel, the consequences on cash flow and the capital required.

The relative costs of each channel. It is generally considered that it may be cheaper to use agents than set up a firm's own sales force in international markets. However, the firm has little control and may have little commitment from the agent. Also, if the company has long-term objectives in the market, then as sales develop the use of agents may be more expensive than employing the company's own sales force. A break-even analysis is necessary to evaluate the relative cost of each channel alternative over time.

Consequences on cashflow. If a firm uses wholesalers or distributors then traditionally they take ownership of the goods and the risks. This has a positive impact on cash flow. If the firm wishes to circumvent such channels and deal direct with the retailer or even the consumer, it means they have to be prepared to take on some of the traditional wholesaler services e.g. offering of credit, breaking bulk, small orders. This means the firm will have capital and resources tied up in managing the distribution chain rather than developing the market.

Capital required. Direct distribution systems need capital injected to establish them. Non-recurring capital costs, as well as the recurring running costs when evaluating expected return in the long term, have to be taken into account.

A company also needs to evaluate whether it can raise the finance locally or whether borrowing restrictions are placed on foreign companies, what grants are available and what the regulations on earnings capital repatriation will be.

The coverage needed

Required coverage will also be a determining factor. In some markets, to get 100 per cent coverage of a market, the costs of using the company's own sales force may be too high making indirect channels are more appropriate, especially

ILLUSTRATION 10.2

Thai military leaders restrict the expansion of Tesco

Thailand's ruling military council restricted the expansion plans of Tesco and other major retailers by freezing the opening of new stores. Tesco is the largest international retailer in Thailand

PHOTO CREDIT: DAN VINCENT/ALAMY

ahead of Casino and Carrefour. The supermarket has expanded rapidly in the country since opening its first store ten years ago.

Tesco has a joint venture with Lotus and is the country's largest food retailer, operating 54 supermarkets, 15 discount stores, 15 Lotus markets and 189 Express convenience stores. Its stores have a combined selling space of nearly seven million square feet and are located across the country, ranging from Chiang Mai in the north to Hat Yai in the south.

Thailand is Tesco's third largest market in the world, after Korea and the UK. The 200-strong chain generates almost £1 bn of sales a year. The retailer intends to double its size in Thailand by opening 170 new stores.

The Thai authorities used the expansion freeze to draw up new rules and regulations to protect small shopkeepers who feared the expansion of the global retailing giants will put them out of business. Needless to say Tesco viewed the new regulations as unreasonably onerous but had to agree to them if they were to continue expanding in the market.

QUESTION *Discuss the possible means by which retailers can deal with such uncertainties in international markets.*

SOURCE: ADAPTED FROM BBC NEWS ONLINE 9 SEPTEMBER, 2006 AND R. FLETCHER, DAILY TELEGRAPH 28 SEPTEMBER, 2006

in countries which are characterised by large rural populations. However, firms who rely on sparse retail outlets can maximise the opportunities that fragmented distribution channels afford. Avon has recruited and groomed armies of sales representatives to sell its cosmetics directly to millions in all reaches of Brazil, Mexico, Poland, China and Argentina. Altogether Avon is successfully operating in 26 emerging economies and targeting more (e.g. India, South Africa, Russia and Vietnam).

Control, continuity and communication

If a firm is building an international competitive advantage in providing a quality service throughout the world then channels that enable the firm to achieve rapid response in foreign markets will be important, as will the development of a distribution system which gives them total control in the marketplace and effective direct communication to their customer.

It is the drive to achieve high levels of quality of service that, to some extent, has led to the breakdown of conventional barriers between manufacturers, agents, distributors and retailers, as firms strive to develop effective vertical marketing systems. To achieve this, some manufacturers have bought themselves into retailing and other parts of the supply chain, whilst others, such as Benetton, have pursued similar results by franchising.

Such firms will be selecting intermediaries which will enable them to be solution-oriented service providers operating on high margins across a multitude of international markets.

The selection and contracting process

Having evaluated the criteria discussed above, a firm must select intermediaries capable of helping the firm achieve its goals and objectives. The intermediaries chosen must provide the geographic coverage needed and the services required in the particular international market(s). It is often desirable to select intermediaries that are native to the country where they will be doing business as this will enhance their ability to build and maintain customer relationships.

The selection process for channel members will be based upon an assessment of their sales volume potential, geographic and customer coverage, financial strength (which will be checked through credit rating services and references), managerial capabilities, the size and quality of the sales force, any marketing communications services and the nature and reputation of the business. In some countries, religious or ethnic differences might make an agent suitable for one part of the market coverage but unsuitable in another. This can result in more channel members being required to give an adequate market coverage.

Before final contractual arrangements are made, it is thought wise to make personal visits to the prospective channel member. The long-term commitment involved in distribution channels can become particularly difficult if the contract between the company and the channel member is not carefully drafted. It is normal to prescribe a time limit and a minimum sales level to be achieved in addition to the particular responsibilities for each party. If this is not carried out satisfactorily, the company may be stuck with a weak performer that either cannot be removed or is very costly to buy out from their contract. The difficulties that can arise when contracts in international markets are interpreted differently by the parties concerned are illustrated in the Merry Management case study at the end of the chapter.

BUILDING RELATIONSHIPS IN FOREIGN MARKET CHANNELS

Management of sales activities and business relationships across international boundaries is a particularly complex and often overwhelming task. The combination of diverse languages, dissimilar cultural heritages and remote geographic locations can create strong barriers to building and maintaining effective buyer–seller relationships. Further, in international settings, communications are often complicated by a lack of trust – a critical dimension in any business relationship. Non-verbal cues, product origin biases, sales force nationality issues and differences in intercultural negotiation styles add even more complexity to the international business environment. Added to the traditional responsibilities of a sales manager, these factors make managing international relationships in distribution channels a unique and challenging task. Thus it is crucial for firms and their sales managers both to understand and be able to work within various international markets throughout the world.

Motivating international marketing intermediaries

International marketing intermediaries can pick and choose the products they will promote to their customers. Therefore, they need to be motivated to emphasise the firm's products. As difficult as it is for manufacturers to motivate their domestic distributors or dealers, it is even more difficult in the international arena. The environment, culture and customs affecting seller –intermediary relationships can be complicating factors for the uninitiated.

Motivation, whether in the context of domestic or international channels, is the process through which the manufacturer seeks to gain the support of the marketing intermediary in carrying out the manufacturer's marketing objectives. Three basic elements are involved in this process (Rosenbloom 2002):

1 finding out the needs and problems of marketing intermediaries

2 offering support that is consistent with their needs and problems

3 building continuing relationships.

Firstly, the needs and problems of international marketing intermediaries can be dramatically different from those at home. One of the most common differences is in the size of the intermediary. This is particularly true in some of the emerging economies in Asia, Africa, Latin America and Eastern Europe. However, it also holds even for some highly developed countries such as Japan and Italy. Many of these dealers may be family businesses with little desire to grow larger. Thus, they may not aggressively promote a manufacturer's product.

Secondly, the specific support programme provided by the manufacturer to its international intermediaries should be based on a careful analysis of their needs and problems. Factors to be included are:

- the adequacy of the profit margins available
- the guarantee of exclusive territories
- the adequacy and availability of advertising assistance
- the offer of needed financial assistance.

In light of the cost structures faced by many foreign distributors and dealers, the need to provide them with good margin potentials on the foreign products they handle is even more important. Doing so, however, may force manufacturers to change their ideas of what constitutes a 'fair' or 'reasonable' margin for foreign distributors.

Territorial protection or even the guarantee of exclusive territories sought by many distributors in the domestic market can be even more desirable in foreign markets. Overseas distributors, many of whom have quite limited financial resources, will not want to assume the risk of handling and promoting the manufacturer's product line if other distributors will be competing in the same territory for the same customers.

Advertising assistance for foreign distributors and dealers is another vital form of support. A foreign manufacturer, especially a large one, can have an advantage over indigenous firms in providing advertising support because of its often greater financial resources and experience in the use of advertising. For example, firms such as Johnson Wax (with extensive distribution in Europe) and 3M (in Asia) have used their considerable resources and advertising expertise to support distributors to very good advantage in those markets.

Financial assistance in countries where intermediaries are small and fragmented is essential. Levi-Strauss found in Russia that they needed to give a six month credit period to persuade intermediaries to stock their products. Their usual credit period was 30 to 60 days. Such constraints do not mean that manufacturers selling through international intermediaries cannot build strong relationships with them; it is certainly possible to do so. However, the approach used may have to be quite different from that taken with domestic intermediaries. For example, for thousands of years agents and distributors in the Middle East have been influenced by bazaar trading. Marketing to them means to 'sit on the product' and wait for the customer to come to them. A common attitude amongst merchants is that they do not sell, but people buy. The 'carrot and stick' philosophy of motivating distributors in the US and Europe fails in the Middle East. Financial incentives may not motivate them to push the product aggressively if the process is complex and long.

It is important to keep in regular contact with intermediaries. A consistent flow of all relevant types of communications will stimulate interest and sales performance. The cultural interface between the company and the channel member is the essence of corporate rapport. Business people from low context cultures may be thought to be insensitive and disrespectful by agents in high context culture countries. The problem can be compounded if sales performance is discussed too personally. According to Usunier and Lee (2005), precise measurement of sales people's performance, for example of the agent or the distributors, may be considered as almost evil in some countries. In South East Asia the ethic of non-confrontation clearly clashes with an objective to review performance. Various types of motivation need to be considered. In some cultures, intrinsic and group-related rewards work best. In the US, a country in which individualism and rationalism are the foundations of its society, individual and extrinsic rewards work best.

Controlling intermediaries in international markets

The process of control is difficult. Control problems are substantially reduced if channel members are selected carefully, have appropriately drafted contracts which have been mutually understood and agreed and are motivated in a culturally empathetic way.

Control attempts are often exercised through other companies and sometimes through several layers of distribution intermediaries. Control should be sought through the development of written plans with clearly expressed performance objectives. These performance objectives would include some of the following: sales turnover per year, number of accounts, market share, growth rate, introduction of new products, price charged and marketing communications support. Control should be exercised through a regular report programme and periodic personal meetings.

Evaluation of performance and control against agreed plans has to be interpreted against the changing environment. In some situations, economic recession or fierce competition activity prevent the possibility of objectives being met. However, if poor performance is established, the contract between the company and the channel member will have to be reconsidered and, perhaps, terminated. In an age in which relationship marketing is becoming more important in the Western world, the long-term building of suitable distribution relationships provides something of the Eastern flavour of obligation and working together.

Channel updating

In managing distribution channels, firms need to ensure that as they increase their involvement in global markets they are able to adapt and update their channel strategy accordingly. Thus, the management monitoring and control mechanisms a firm puts in place should give them the ability to develop their presence in the marketplace. In China, Kodak ensured this capability was in place in their early negotiations when setting up their local manufacturing and distribution operations by taking over three loss-making Chinese companies. They also offered a package to all their distributors offering help including marketing assistance of US$2000 or more to corner shops in exchange for becoming a Kodak Express and evicting competing film brands from the stores. Dell built a global brand by focusing on a direct sales model. However they too are adapting their strategy in response to customer needs and introducing a retail presence (see Illustration 10.3).

ILLUSTRATION 10.3

Dell Computers

Dell Computers built their global brand on the principal of keeping things as simple as possible. They focused largely on

the B2B market, based their computers on two important brand alliances – Intel and Microsoft Windows – and built direct selling relationships. As the market has matured, however, there are signs that whilst this model is still globally hugely successful there is a need for adaptation and change as the needs and desires of the consumer changes. Their existing customer is viewed as needing a more concrete relationship with Dell, whilst new potential consumers have the need to see and examine a Dell computer before buying. As Dell move more into the B2C market they have previously paid little attention to, they are setting up retail operations to fully maximise the potential of the global B2C market. The Dell Direct Stores will enable customers to talk to Dell staff, examine computers and discuss design options. However, the stores do not actually sell any merchandise and all orders will still be processed through the company's website.

QUESTION *Fully evaluate the pros and cons of this development in Dell's global channel strategy. What are the risks to Dell in terms of its global competitive position?*

Developing a company-owned international salesforce

Firms with expansion plans and an interest in becoming more involved in global markets will eventually take control of implementing their own marketing strategies and establish and manage their own international sales force. Generally, the firms begin to gradually move from indirect exporting to direct exporting via marketing intermediaries to a company-owned sales force (Kotler and Keller 2005). The company can do this in several ways, including travelling export sales reps, a domestic-based export department or division and a foreign-based sales branch or subsidiary.

The advantages of using a company-owned sales force include:

- it provides far greater control over the sales and marketing effort because the sales force is now directly employed by the company
- it facilitates formation of closer manufacturer – customer relationships
- once established, the company-owned sales force can be helpful in identifying and exploiting new international marketing opportunities.

The disadvantages of developing a company-owned sales force include:

- a relatively larger resource commitment
- somewhat higher exit costs should the firm decide to no longer serve a particular market
- increased exposure to unexpected changes in the political/social environment of the host country.

One common strategy is to begin export operations by establishing a domestic-based export department and/or using home-based travelling salespeople. Then, as sales reach a certain volume in the new market, the decision is made to set up a foreign-based sales branch or subsidiary in the country.

The new unit may be strictly a marketing/sales arm or may also involve a production or warehouse facility. In either event, the firm must make a commitment of resources to develop its own direct sales force to sell the firm's offerings and build relationships with the firm's customers in that market.

It may well be that a firm uses its own sales force for key accounts and agents and distributors for small accounts. Equally, its own sales force may work in conjunction with international intermediaries, building links directly with customers but always with and through the intermediaries. This has the advantage of enabling the firm to build relationships with the customer and the intermediaries whilst not having to make the capital investment required to run a wholly-owned subsidiary.

However, for many multi-nationals, managing international operations is an issue of 'does the company control operations centrally or allow sales subsidiaries around the world a high degree of autonomy?' In some countries they may have little choice, due to the strength of local competition and the loyalty of local distributors to locally made brands. This is the challenge facing Inbev, the Belgian brewer, in China (see Dilemma 10.1).

TRENDS IN RETAILING IN INTERNATIONAL MARKETS

Retailing structures differ across countries, reflecting their different histories, geography and politics. **Retailing** varies across the different levels of economic development and is influenced by cultural variations. The cultural importance attached to food in France provides the opportunity for small specialist food retailers to survive and prosper. In other developed countries, for example the US, the trend is towards very large superstores which incorporate a wide range of speciality foods. The French approach relies on small-scale production by the retail proprietor. The US approach encourages mass production, branding and sophisticated distribution systems to handle inventory and freshness issues.

In this section, our discussion will be concerned with three important issues for international marketers. First, the differences in the patterns of retailing around the world with particular reference to emerging markets and developing countries. Second, the internationalisation of retailers and its impact on distribution channel structures and, third, the emergence of new forms of retailing which are particularly relevant to firms competing on international markets.

The differing patterns of retailing around the world

The concentration of the retailing industry varies significantly between markets. Low concentration ratios of retailer ownership give more power to the manufacturer. A 'no' decision from any one retailer does not make a big impact on total sales. Whilst the low concentration ratios to be found in Japan and Italy and in many lesser developed countries increase the relative power of the manufacturer, there are problems. First, low concentration ratios in retailers might be counterbalanced by powerful wholesalers. Second, the costs of the sales force in calling on a multiplicity of very small retailers and the logistics of delivering products to them can reduce the manufacturer's profitability. If economies are sought by using wholesalers, the power balance might tilt away from the manufacturer to the wholesaler.

The main differences between traditional retailing structures found in lesser developed countries and the advanced retailing structures in more developed economies are illustrated in Table 10.1.

Retailing in developing countries is characterised by low levels of capital investment. The large size, purpose-built retail outlet, full of specialist display shelving

DILEMMA 10.1

Local distributors vs the global operators

A number of Western brewers have entered the Chinese beer market with varying success, despite market growth being estimated at 6 per cent per annum. Anheuser-Busch makes Budweiser in its own brewery in Wuhan, an inland city, and has a stake in Tsingtao, China's largest brewery. SAB Miller, the world's second-largest brewer, has a joint venture with a Chinese firm. However, several Western brewers have failed to break into the market, including Bass and Fosters. Fosters marketed their own global brand name but found it could not compete against the local distribution networks pushing the local brands at low prices, in 2006 they withdrew from the market after being there 13 years without making a profit. Part of the problem is the low consumption of beer. Per capita consumption in China is 22 litres p.a. compared to a figure of

121 litres p.a. consumed by Germans. Carlsberg, however, do not consider this a problem given the huge population. After a very shaky start they invested heaviily in China and now have over 30 breweries.

The big success has been Inbev, the Belgian brewer, who entered the market by buying 70 per cent of K.K. Brewery, the leading beer maker in Zhejiang Province in China's Yangtze delta, as well as the biggest-selling brewery in the Pearl River delta.

Inbev did not want to repeat the mistakes of the other global players and so faced the dilemma as to how they should develop the market without coming under attack from local distribution networks.

QUESTION *What recommendations would you make to them?*

and electronic point of sale equipment, is rarely found in less developed countries (LDCs). The more likely picture is of a very small space with goods sold by the counter service method and technology limited to a cash register or a pocket calculator.

Retail stores are often managed by the owner/proprietor and staffed by the extended family. The lack of capital input is partially offset by large quantities of low-cost labour and the management style is usually based on limiting risks. The retailer will seek to stock goods with a proven demand pattern. In addition, the retailer will try to obtain interest-free credit from the interface channel partners: the wholesaler and the manufacturer.

Distribution channels in developing countries depend on manufacturers and wholesalers for their sales promotion ideas and materials. In developed countries retailers often take the initiative regarding sales promotions and will develop their own schemes. The opportunities for the manufacturer to influence the retailer in advanced countries are becoming fewer and fewer.

Small-scale retailing limits the opportunities to follow own-label strategies. The minimum economies of scale cannot be reached by the small urban and rural retailer in developing countries. The balance of power lies with the manufacturer to innovate and adapt products.

The proliferation of very many small-scale retailers means that the retail market is widely dispersed. The levels of concentration of ownership are much lower than are found in mature economies with relatively structured levels of retailing.

These differences give rise to principally four stages of retailing around the world: traditional, intermediary, structured and advanced (McGoldrick 2002).

TABLE 10.1 Retailers – typical differences between developing and developed countries

Retailing issues	Traditional retailers in developing countries	Advanced retailing structures in mature economies
Concentration of retail power	Low	Often high
Site selection and retail location	Limited to the immediate locality	Very important, often sophisticated techniques to pinpoint the most valuable sites
Size of outlet	Limited	Large and tending to get larger
Retailer initiation of product assortment	Limited to the buy/no buy decision	Wide range of stock possible. Use of own-label and store-specific sales promotions
Retail concepts, images and corporate identity	Rarely used	Very important
Retailer-initiated sales promotion	Rarely used. Reliance on manufacturer and wholesaler-developed sales promotion and point of sale material	Very important
Use of retail technology	Limited	Vital e.g. EDI, EPOS
Service	Mainly counter-service	Mass customisation, sophisticated CRM systems

Traditional retailing

'Traditional retailers' are typically found in Asia, Latin America and Japan. The concentration of operators is weak, segmentation is non-existent and the level of integration of new technology is very low. These are often small-scale family retailing businesses employing few people and with a low turnover. India's organised retail trade has generated a lot of interest amongst domestic and global retailing operators as it is viewed as being on the brink of change and poised for substantial growth. The sector currently has a turnover of US$270 billion but what is classified as the organised sector accounts for only US$12.4 billion and small neighbourhood stores account for 99 per cent of the food and grocery sector. This brings particular challenges to global operators (see Illustration 10.4). However the organised retail sector is rapidly expanding each year and expected to grow by some 42 per cent in 2008 alone (www.theretailbulletin.com). This may bring tremendous change to the whole sector.

Intermediary retailing

Retailing in Italy, Spain and Eastern Europe is in the process of transformation, being both modern and traditional and so examples of intermediary retailing. Most businesses are independent with a turnover lower than the European average. However, there is a marked tendency towards concentration, particularly in the food sector, where the number of food retailing outlets per 1000 people is dropping. The importance of wholesalers and voluntary chains is still very strong, particularly in Italy (192 000 wholesale businesses).

In the major cities of China there have been huge developments in the retail structure of the country, taking retailing in the major cities to a very advanced status. China is encouraging mergers and partnerships between indigenous retailers to reduce costs and improve competitiveness and ensure they have the capacity to compete against such global operators as Wal-Mart and Carrefour, who are fighting for a share of the US$652 billion retail market. China's largest retailer, the Shanghai Bailian group, has now merged with Dalian Dashang, the third largest, to create a retailing group aiming for US$6 billion sales within the next

ILLUSTRATION 10.4

Comparative retailing traditions

In the UK consumers are used to shops being open 7 days a week and in the US 24–7. In Germany, however, it is only recently that shops have been allowed to open on Saturday afternoons: a new federal law allows city centre shops to open until 8 p.m. However, outside the city most still close at 4 p.m. for the weekend and Sunday opening is still highly restricted. This is much the same as New Zealand where stores close at 5.30 p.m. except for one night each week when they are open until 9.00 p.m. Stores are also closed on Sundays and many are closed on Saturday afternoons.

In India opening hours are unrestricted but most retail stores are family owned and are much smaller in size. With the exception of a few (small) super bazaars, consumers are not allowed to walk freely inside the stores, examine and compare labels of different brands before making the selection. Instead, consumers approach shops with a predetermined list of items to purchase, which are then pulled out of the bins by the salesperson.

Retailing in Greece, on the other hand has until recently been small-scale and highly traditional. The majority of stores are family owned and small in size and shopping for pleasure is less popular. Most purchases are made in cash, although credit cards are becoming more popular. However, the entry into the country of some of the big global retailers is starting to change the face of retailing there.

QUESTION *How can a company achieve a global distribution strategy when retailing infrastructures vary so much?*

few years. However, like India, outside the major cities of Shanghai and Bejing, China's retail sector is still dominated by small neighbourhood stores and local markets.

Countries with intermediary retailing structures are obviously attractive locations for retailers expanding internationally as they are seen as latent markets ripe for expansion. The level of economic development and the intermediary structure of retailing has historically meant that these countries are not host to large domestic retailers, making entry into the market relatively easy.

Over the course of the past decade, the entry of foreign operators into regions such as Latin America have altered the retailing landscape. There are now hypermarkets, variety stores and non-food specialists which have stimulated competition and greatly modernised retailing across the continent.

Structured retailing

Retailing in the north of Europe tends to be fairly structured, reflecting the level of economic development. Denmark, Luxembourg, the Netherlands and France have enterprises larger in size, have a higher level of concentration and a greater level of productivity per employee than Southern European retailers.

In these markets, retail competition is fairly well developed and there is a mature relationship between suppliers and retailers.

Retailers also have introduced fairly sophisticated technologies facilitating more elaborate competitive strategies. They are also, themselves, finding growth through opportunities overseas and new retailing formats.

Advanced retailing

The US, Germany and the UK are all examples of countries in which retailing is the most advanced in terms of concentration, segmentation, capitalisation and integration. In Germany and the UK there are about 60 retailing businesses per 10 000 inhabitants, 98 being the European average. Retailer strategies are advanced and are becoming much more marketing focused, and generally incorporate five important dimensions.

Interactive customer marketing. Targeting of customers as individuals, developing strategies to improve retention and increase sales per shop visit.

Mass customisation. Retailers are looking for improved margins through higher volumes, reduced costs and achieving low levels of returns.

Data mining. Retailers are using technology and electronic point of sale (EPOS) information to improve knowledge of customers, ensure the ability to make targeted offers which are timely and clearly differentiated. Data mining is beginning to be used by retailers in emerging and developing markets where previously there has been little reliable data on which to base decisions.

Category management. Retailers are aiming to achieve improved levels of customer satisfaction through reducing costs, reducing mark downs and optimising product assortment.

Effective consumer response. Retailers are establishing permanent links with manufacturers, establishing electronic data interchange (EDI) systems for efficient inventory replenishment and ensuring a continuous just in time delivery of supplies.

In these markets the balance of power in the supply chain, for the present at least, seems to lie firmly with these large retailers, who are increasingly dictating the trends in their home markets and as these reach maturity are seeking growth opportunities by expanding internationally.

The globalisation of retailing

One of the key trends in international distribution over the past few years has been the aggressive strategies pursued by many major retailers as they have pursued global marketing objectives. Tesco, the French hypermarket groups Auchan, Carrefour and Promodes, and the German discount food retailers Aldi, Lidl and Swartz have all expanded globally. The food retailing sector especially is now dominated by huge global retailers. Table 10.2 gives the top ten in the world. However it is not just in food that retailers are going global; the US retailer Wal-Mart and specialists Toys R Us, Home Depot, Staples, Benetton, Body Shop and Hertz are all now global retailers. Hong Kong retailers A S Watson and Dairy Farm entered neighbouring countries with supermarkets and pharmaceutical chains and Japanese department stores Takashimaya and Isetan have established outlets across Asia. More recently this trend has accelerated, with German retailers Metro, Rewe and Tengelmann expanding into the Czech Republic, Hungary and Poland, often using joint ventures with former socialist cooperatives. Three Western European retailers, Tengelmann (Germany), Ahold (Netherlands) and Delhaizae Le Lion (Belgium), now generate more sales and profit from their foreign activities, which include the US, Central Europe and Asia, than they do in their home markets. Tesco, already strong in Ireland, Central Europe and Asia are now expanding into the USA, opening a number of Tesco Express stores on the West Coast. The smaller high-growth economies such as Ireland (see Illustration 10.5) have also been generating the particular interest of the expanding globals.

The expansion of international activity of retailers around the world has given rise to four different types of international retailers: the hypermarket, the power retailers, the niche retailer and the designer flagship stores who target particular global cities for their stores. Examples of these are given in Figure 10.3.

TABLE 10.2 Top ten global food retailers

	Sales (US$bn)	No of stores
Wal-Mart (US)	312	6380
Carrefour (France)	93	12179
Metro (Germany)	70	2458
Tesco (UK)	70	2365
Kroger (US)	61	3726
Ahold (Netherlands)	55	7299
Costco (US)	53	460
Rewe (Germany)	52	11242
Scwartz (Germany)	46	7299
Aldi (Germany)	45	7788

SOURCE: WWW.SUPERMARKETNEWS.COM, ACCESSED APRIL 2007

ILLUSTRATION 10.5

The Irish retailing environment

Ireland is now home to the largest shopping centre in Europe, Dundrum (on the outskirts of Dublin) which, given its geographical size, shows the strength of the growth in its retail sector as the country continues to enjoy buoyant economic growth. There are now over 200 foreign retailers operating in the country including Starbucks, Borders Books, Stradivarius, Quicksilver and Villeroy and Boch. In the past most global retailers going into the market have been American and British but retailers from China, Spain, Switzerland, Australia and Portugal are entering as international retailers see the growth potential in the Irish market.

High investment rates and strong consumer expenditure have seen GDP grow 6 per cent p.a. High levels of employment have also contributed to the increased level of disposable income now available to Irish consumers.

The growth also follows the relaxation of strict planning legislation, obviously attractive to property investors. In the last year, 52 per cent of property investment transactions have involved retail space. Shopping centre floor space increased by 17 per cent, and retail park floor space grew by 25 per cent in the same year.

The changes in legislation are attractive to large stores, such as Ikea and Costco, as they mean retailers are more easily able to drive growth organically through new store openings, rather than through the traditional approach of mergers and acquisitions.

QUESTION *Explore how the impact of the changes in the Irish retailing environment might affect local Irish retailers' wishing to expand internationally.*

PHOTO CREDIT: IMAGESTATE/ALAMY

SOURCE: ADAPTED FROM WWW.EUROMONITOR.COM/RETAIL OCT. 2006 AND WWW.JONESLANGLASALLE.IE

FIGURE 10.3
Global retailer categories

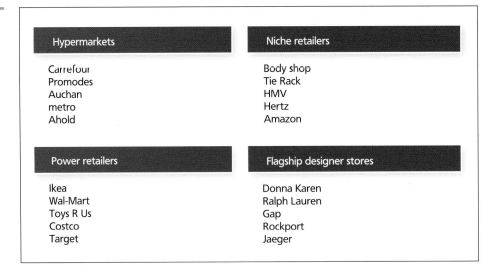

Hypermarkets	Niche retailers
Carrefour	Body shop
Promodes	Tie Rack
Auchan	HMV
metro	Hertz
Ahold	Amazon

Power retailers	Flagship designer stores
Ikea	Donna Karen
Wal-Mart	Ralph Lauren
Toys R Us	Gap
Costco	Rockport
Target	Jaeger

Besides the growing sophistication of the industry and the opening up of new markets around the world, the globalisation of retailers can be attributed to a number of 'pull' and 'push' factors.

The 'push' factors are:

- saturation of the home market or over-competition
- economic recession or limited growth in spending

- a declining or ageing population
- strict planning policies on store development
- high operating costs – labour, rents, taxation
- shareholder pressure to maintain profit growth
- the 'me too' syndrome in retailing.

The 'pull' factors are:

- the underdevelopment of some markets or weak competition
- strong economic growth or rising standards of living
- high population growth or a high concentration of young adults
- a relaxed regulatory framework
- favourable operating costs – labour, rents, taxation
- the geographical spread of trading risks
- the opportunity to innovate under new market conditions.

Marketing implications for development of international distribution strategies

The internationalisation of retailing has meant a new era of distribution is developing. This new competitive landscape in distribution has a number of implications for the development of the distribution strategies of international firms. The most important of these are:

- power shifts in supply chains towards retailers
- intense concentrated competition with significant buyer power across country markets
- rapidly advancing technology facilitating global sourcing and global electronic transactions
- unrelenting performance measures being demanded of suppliers by international retailers
- smart, demanding consumers expecting high levels of customer service.

Thus power in many international markets is moving from the supplier down the supply chain to the consumer. This means effective management is critical to suppliers competing in international markets. It again highlights the importance of ensuring the distribution strategy across international markets is driven by an understanding of the target market segments, both within each foreign country market and across national market boundaries.

This intensive growth in the size and power of retailers in countries with advanced retailing structures and retailers internationalising means there is now tremendous pressure on suppliers to improve the quality of service to them. Retailers are demanding:

- streamlined and flexible supply chains
- suppliers who can guarantee quality and reliability across global markets
- the ability to supply high volumes and close relationships with intermediaries in the supply chain

■ suppliers who can meet the global sourcing requirements of large-scale retailers who wish to buy centrally across the globe.

It could mean, therefore, that the firms who are successful are the firms who develop the capability to compete effectively in the supply chain activities compared to their international competitors. It is for this reason that the distribution strategy of the international company has taken on such an important dimension in recent times.

Internet retailing

Multimedia technology has provided a number of opportunities for **interactive shopping** which offer particular opportunities in international markets. Tele-shopping and the Internet offer suppliers the retailing opportunities for direct contact with consumers throughout the globe. What's more they can achieve this without the problems and expense of having to establish infrastructures in foreign country markets. For example, Amazon.com, the bookshop which sells purely over the Internet, carries no books as they are directly shipped from the publishers' or distributors' warehouses. This means Amazon have few inventory or real estate costs. They offer 2.5 million titles including every English language book in print whereas even the largest bookstore would only stock 170 000. EToys, the Internet competitor to Toys R Us, has no retail outlets but a higher market capitalisation than Toys R Us. EToys proactively trap individual information on consumer purchases and then flash messages back telling consumers of other products bought by consumers making similar purchases, as do Amazon. The diffusion of the Internet is increasingly challenging the traditional channels of distribution. It has the capacity to bring together buyers and sellers around the world through the creation of an online marketplace. However, despite exponential growth in access to the Internet, consumers are still limiting their purchases to relatively few product lines. It is estimated that nearly 40 per cent of all Internet purchases are for travel, another 26 per cent for the purchase of tickets for events and concerts and 25 per cent is spent on books and CDs.

In international marketing the major impact, as we will discuss in Chapter 12, has been the ability of the Internet to enable small and medium-sized companies to access niche markets around the globe that were previously too logistically difficult for them to access. By simply setting up their own sites, a company in effect becomes global and can sell goods and services throughout the world. However, there has also been the development of market sites which have impacted on the way business transactions take place internationally, such as:

■ *Auctions*. Online marketplaces where negotiations of price between independent buyers and sellers is implemented through a standard auction open to all participants (e.g. eBay, Dabs exchange, On Sale).

■ *Single buyer markets*. Where a large buyer establishes an online intranet market for its own suppliers (e.g. GE Trade Web), usually for them to gain access to the site the suppliers will have achieved the status of approved supplier.

■ *Pure exchanges*. Where individual buyers and sellers are matched according to product offers and needs.

The most promising products are often those where existing intermediaries do not perform many of the traditional 'wholesaler' functions for a broad market owing to the high cost of servicing small diverse and geographically or functionally dispersed players. There are several market characteristics in international markets which favour the development of Internet-based distribution:

- *Inefficiencies in traditional distribution channels*, as in Japan where it is difficult for international operators to penetrate the market so sellers cannot gain access to customers.
- *Market fragmentation*. Niche market players where customers are geographically dispersed across the globe and are not concentrated in any one country.
- *Minimum scale barriers*. Smaller exporters have tradtionally been restricted from operating globally because of the costs and difficulties of exporting, and therefore lose out to larger players who reap economies of scale and exploit distribution relationships.
- *Commodity-type products*. Products with well-known technical specifications, or manufacturer brands that can easily be price-compared across countries and do not require substantial after-sales service.
- *Short life-cycle products*. Product-markets with short life cycles create large quantities of obsolete and discontinued items. Customers may experience difficulty finding spare parts or compatible accessories for earlier generations of product.

THE MANAGEMENT OF THE PHYSICAL DISTRIBUTION OF GOODS

Physical distribution management (PDM) is concerned with the planning, implementing and control of physical flows of materials and final goods from points of origin to points of use to meet customer needs at a profit (Kotler and Keller 2005) .

In international physical distribution of goods the total distribution costs will be higher than domestic distribution. The extra activities, increased time taken and the need to adapt to special country requirements will all increase costs. The extra costs centre around three areas:

1 *Increased distance*; this means, in terms of costs, increased transport time, inventory, cash flow and insurance.
2 *New variables to consider*; new modes of transport (air, sea, rail, road), new types of documentation, packaging for long transit times.
3 *Greater market complexity*; language differences requires the translation of documents, the extra costs of bureaucracy and longer lines of communication.

It is important for the firm to take full account of all these extra costs when evaluating alternative distribution strategies. In taking the total distribution cost approach firms will include the costs of transport, warehousing, inventory, order processing, documentation, packaging and the total cost of lost sales if delays occur. Companies find that changes to one element of distribution influence the performance and the costs of other elements, as Cisco found to its advantage in Dilemma 10.2.

The logistics approach to physical distribution

Many writers on physical distribution use logistics and physical distribution as terms meaning the same thing. Kotler and Keller (2005) makes the distinction between physical distribution as a more traditional activity and logistics as being more market-oriented. In this way, physical distribution thinking starts with the finished product at the end of the production line and then attempts to find low-cost solutions to get the product to the customer. Logistics thinking, on the other hand, considers the customer and then works back to the factory. In this section we will use the market-oriented view. We will use the term logistics to mean an integrated view of physical distribution management in which customer demand influences are at least as important as cost-cutting forces. More and more companies are integrating their physical distribution strategies and linking their operations in different countries with more common processes, thus rationalising their manufacturing and distribution infrastructure to make more effective use of business resources and so taking a logistical view of their distribution operations.

In Europe 75 per cent of businesses operating across European markets have a pan-European logistics or distribution strategy in place. McKinsey Consultants estimate the European logistics market to be worth about US$200 billion. The logistics function is having an increasing influence in many parts of the business, especially in inventory planning, information technology, purchasing and manufacturing.

There are a number of factors influencing this change:

- Customers demanding improved levels of customer service.
- Electronic Data Interchange (EDI) becoming the all-pervading technology for firms to build links with customers, suppliers and distribution providers.
- Companies restructuring their physical distribution operations in response to the formation of regional trading blocs.

In the following sections, we will briefly examine the developments in each of the above areas.

Customer service

The main elements of customer service will revolve around:

- order to delivery time
- consistency and reliability of delivery
- inventory availability

DILEMMA 10.2

Cisco Systems

Cisco Systems enforces very high-quality, control standards on all its suppliers. This has always involved the company in lengthy and cumbersome processes of certification which proved very costly. Furthermore, whenever the company put anything out to tender evaluation of those tenders was very time-consuming. In order to maintain their competitive advantage internationally the company prioritised this area as one where significant cost savings could be made.

The dilemma is, how can this be achieved without compromising standards?

■ order size constraints

■ ordering convenience

■ delivery time and flexibility

■ invoicing procedures, documentation and accuracy

■ claims procedure

■ condition of goods

■ salesperson's visits

■ order status information

■ after-sales support.

In developing customer service levels it is essential to use the elements of service that the customer regards as important. Delivery reliability might be more important than a quick order to delivery time that is unreliable in meeting delivery schedules. Understanding the way in which the international customer perceives service is important. There will be considerable differences. Customers who are distant might be more concerned about the guarantees of reliable rapid availability than customers much closer to the production source. The ability and corporate capability to meet widely differing customer requirements in different countries needs to be managed.

In all countries, customers are becoming increasingly demanding. Partnership arrangements are becoming significant in many sectors as supply chains become more integrated. These developments are usually customer-led demands for improved service.

Consumers are demanding ever-quicker delivery and ever more added value from their products that increasingly require just in time distribution. The product cycle from manufacture to payment is becoming shorter, a trend that is likely to accelerate. Moreover, a global manufacturer operates a globally integrated supply chain. If it is to benefit effectively from cheap labour costs at one side of the globe, it will need an efficient global logistics strategy to service the rich consumers at the other side of the globe effectively.

Information technology

Developments in information technology are critical. It is estimated that more than three in four companies actively involved in international markets have introduced multi-national computer systems for logistics processes and international electronic data interchange (EDI).

The 'old Silk Road' has been replaced by the 'new silc road' with optical fibre systems making direct links between Europe, East Asia and Australia. Much of the new SDH-based silc road (syndchronoms digital hierarchy (SOH) which is an enabling technology that increases the speed and volume of traffic using optical fibre networks) has been laid. The network stretches 2500 miles across the former Soviet Union into China through countries such as Uzbekistan, regenerating their economies.

Optic fibre cables have been routed through Japan, South East Asia and through to Australia. Thus there are significant developments in electronic links between companies and distributors and producers around the world.

In regional trading blocs, such as the European Union and NAFTA, there has been the development of common systems for customer order processing, demand forecasting and inventory planning.

Foreign companies are increasingly using the Internet to track the progress of products through the distribution system. The websites which allow customers to track the progress of their packages are attracting 400 000 hits a day. The other major area of IT involvement is in stock control and buying. Despite having 600 stores in 14 countries and using 12 different own labels, C & A is still able to deliver nine times a day to its stores due to its efficient centralised buying operation for men's and childrenswear in Brussels and womenswear in Dusseldorf.

The restructuring of physical distribution operations

In mature trading regions such as the US and Europe, a large number of firms have restructured their distribution networks in response to changes in the trading structures in the region. Cross-border deliveries have increased and the number of factories and warehouses has decreased. The number of distribution centres serving more than one country has increased whereas there has been a decrease in the number of warehouses dedicated to within-country movements.

Lucent Technology dispatches all its products from its factory in Spain to a test and assembly centre in Singapore before final delivery. It might go back to a customer sitting 10 kilometres away from the factory in Spain, but it will still go to Singapore. The company gives a 48-hour delivery guarantee to customers anywhere in the world, posing demanding logistical challenges.

The physical movement of goods is a high-cost activity. Companies often incur 10 to 35 per cent of their expenditure on physical distribution. Because distribution is so expensive, it is now receiving close attention from general management and from marketing management.

The logistics approach is to analyse customer requirements and to review what competitors are providing. Customers are interested in a number of things: deliveries to meet agreed time schedules, zero defect delivery, supplier willingness to meet emergency needs, supplier willingness to replace damaged goods quickly and supplier willingness to engage in just in time (JIT) delivery and inventory holding.

If a company is to achieve a logistically effective system of distribution it will become involved in a highly complex and sophisticated system and will, therefore, need to:

■ clearly define areas of responsibility across foreign country markets
■ have a highly developed planning system
■ have an up to date and comprehensive information support system
■ develop expertise in distribution management
■ have a centralised planning body to coordinate activities and exercise overall control.

Thus, a logistical system helps the company to pay attention to inventory levels and think through market relationships, to minimise costs of stock out and maximise distribution efficiency across a large number of markets.

In developing an efficient logistical system of physical distribution across international markets there are a number of important considerations:

■ how intermediaries such as freight forwarders can enhance our service
■ what modes of transportation should be used
■ how the firm can make effective use of export processing zones
■ what documentation is required
■ what are the packaging requirements for transit and the market
■ how should the export sales contract be organised.

In the following sections, we will briefly discuss some of the important issues in each of these areas.

The use of intermediaries

Traditionally, intermediaries such as forwarders and freight companies simply offered transportation by land, sea and air. There are now many types of intermediaries which offer global logistical services. FedEx, UPS and DPWN (Deutsche Post World Net, which absorbed DHL) have global networks to offer express-delivery services which they also use to offer customised logistics solutions. Broking houses such as Kuehne & Nagel offer their skills in tying together different modes of transport. Other companies offer specialised services, for instance transport and warehouse-management firms which organise the physical movement and storage of goods. Still others are dedicated contract carriers and freight forwarders, who buy capacity on ships and cargo planes, and put together loads from different companies to fill them. Most freight forwarders will offer services such as preparation and processing of international transport documents, coordination of transport services and the provision of warehousing.

However, as we have seen in the above section, recent trends such as just in time delivery, outsourcing of non-core activities, cutting inventories and the trend to build to order (BTO) have meant international firms have had to build a comprehensive but flexible logistical operation to ensure goods reach their customers around the world in the right place at the right time. This is such a challenging task that companies are no longer able to do it all themselves, so more of them are using intermediaries and outsourcing the logistical functions. This has meant the global freight-transport industry itself has had to reshape, as manufacturers seek service suppliers with global reach. Manufacturers want custom-designed delivery systems, using all types of transport – land, sea and air. Many of the larger firms now offer a whole range of options beyond their original specific function. This has meant that distinctions between the various intermediaries, such as freight forwarders, transport companies, express couriers and logistics services, are blurring.

All intermediaries deal with three parallel flows: physical goods, information and finance (leasing, lending, brokerage). What is happening now is that whilst previously intermediaries specialised in one of the flows they are now offering the full range of services. Even global manufacturers are entering the logistics business. Caterpillar, which makes construction equipment, uses the global distribution network it has already developed as a channel for the products of other manufacturers.

There have been two driving forces for this. Firstly, global competition has meant a downward pressure on costs. This has spawned the phenomenon that began in the logistics sector with outsourcing but has extended to the whole range of other services now regarded as legitimate logistics tasks. Indeed, many of the multi-national logistics companies such as DPWN, FedEx, UPS and TNT, the so-called integrators, themselves outsource the functions they take on to small specialist suppliers.

Secondly, the technological advances discussed earlier mean that logistics specialists are able to offer increasingly sophisticated services to exporters that firms cannot provide in-house. For example, a firm's products might once have passed from factory to national warehouse and then on to a foreign regional warehouse, then to a local depot, before delivery to the end consumer: a wasteful process in terms of time and cost. Today, using state-of-the-art systems, a logistics specialist taking responsibility for the warehouse function will deliver to the customer direct from the main warehouse, cutting out three of four links in the chain.

At the more advanced end of the logistics services spectrum, companies are handing control of more and more roles to their logistics partners. This is partly driven by the sheer geographical complexity of many exporters' operations where, for example, head office, factory and customer may be separated by thousands of miles.

As more companies attempt to develop the newly opened emerging markets where they have little knowledge or understanding of the distribution system, the use of third party intermediaries to organise logistics is becoming an essential part of a global marketing strategy.

Transportation

The physical handling and movement of goods over long distances will practically always have to be performed by third parties.

Transportation is the most visible part of the physical distribution strategy. The main options are:

- *Ocean transport*: capacity for large loads of differentiated products, raw materials, semi-finished goods, finished goods. Handling of goods in bulk, in packaged or unitised form, pallets, containers.
- *Inland waterway transport*: heavy and bulk products. Growing container transport. Restrictions because of need for suitable loading/unloading terminals.
- *Air transport*: urgent shipments, perishables, low-density light/high value, relatively small shipments.
- *Road transport*: most flexible door-to-door transport for all kinds of products but mostly finished goods. Container transport.
- *Rail transport*: long distance heavy and bulk products. Container transport.

OCEAN AND INLAND WATERWAYS

Sea and inland waterways provide a very low-cost way to transport bulky, low value or non-perishable products such as coal and oil. Water transport is slow and is subject to difficulties caused by the weather; for example, some ports are iced over for part of the winter. Water transport usually needs to be used with other modes of transport to achieve door-to-door delivery.

One of the policies used to encourage growth in South Korea, a newly industrialised country, has been the stimulation of its shipping and shipbuilding industry.

Ocean shipping can be **open market**, i.e. free ocean where there are very few restrictions, or it can be organised in conferences which are essentially cartels that regulate rates and capacities available on routes.

As in other areas of distribution, the containerisation of ports and the impact of information technology have meant sea transport has become a capital-intensive industry where there is high pressure to achieve full capacity utilisation.

The costs of ocean freight, as a result, have declined over the past decade and so it is still the most cost-effective method of transporting goods to distant markets.

The average cost for a six-metre dry cargo container to be shipped from the UK to Shanghai in China will be £950–£1250 and the approximate transit time would be 20–25 days.

However, a number of hidden costs can arise in overseas shipping:

- overseas warehousing costs due to having to send large inventories in container loads
- inventory losses from handling spoilage, theft, obsolescence and exchange rate charges in manual time
- cost of time in transit
- lost sales from late arrival.

Inland waterways are very important in countries with poor infrastructures. In Vietnam the most popular mode of transportation is by water. A dense network of waterways exists, although even this system will suffer the vagaries of both flood and drought conditions.

AIR

Air freight is considerably more expensive per tonne/kilometre than the other modes of transport. Air freight is particularly appropriate for the movement of high-value low-bulk and perishable items. For example, diamonds, computer software, specialist component parts and cut flowers use air freight. Air freight is extending its market through promoting its advantages. The higher freight charges can often be offset. Packing costs and insurance rates are significantly less by air. Storage en route, overseas warehousing and inventory losses may all be less by air as will the actual cost of the time in transit. In addition, the development of larger and more flexible aeroplanes for air freight has helped reduce costs.

ROAD

Very flexible in route and time. Schedules can deliver direct to customers' premises. Very efficient for short hauls of high-value goods. Restrictions at border controls can be time-consuming, however, and long distances and the need for sea crossings reduce the attractiveness of freight transport by road. In some parts of the world, particularly in LDCs, road surfaces are poor and the distribution infrastructure poor. In Vietnam, an attractive emerging market for many international firms, the majority of the road network is beaten track which, during the wet season (six months of the year), makes transporting anything by road very difficult. The problems of transporting goods across African countries due to poor road infrastructure can be seen in Illustration 10.6.

RAIL

Rail services provide a very good method of transporting bulky goods over long land distances. The increasing use of containers provides a flexible means to use rail and road modes with minimal load transfer times and costs.

In Europe, we are seeing the development of the use of 'Bloc Trains' as a highly efficient means of rail transport. In the US they use 'Double Bloc' trains to transport goods across the vast plains. In a number of markets, rail transport is fraught with difficulties. In China, a shipment from Shanghai to Guangzhou, a distance of approximately 2000 kilometres, can take 25 days. Across the interior it is even slower. Shanghai to Xian, 1500 kilometres, can take 45 days. Much of the rail capacity is antiquated and many of the rail lines are old, leading to frequent derailments.

THE FINAL DECISION ON TRANSPORT

The decision concerning which transport mode to use is discussed by Branch (2005). He identifies four factors as decisive in choosing transport: the terms of the export contract, the commodity specification, freight and overall transit time.

In the terms of the export contract, the customer can specify the mode(s) of transport and can insist on the country's national shipping line or airline being used. In considering different modes of transport, the specification of the commodity will have a strong influence on modal choice. For example, transport of fresh food will have requirements to prevent spoilage and contamination. The cost of transport is of major importance: it creates extra costs above the normal domestic cost. It is important, therefore, that transport options are researched thoroughly so that the best value arrangements can be made for both the buyer and the supplier.

Export processing zones

The principle of **export processing zones** (EPZs) started with the opening of the world's first EPZ at Shannon in the Republic of Ireland. Since then there has been a proliferation in the establishment of EPZs worldwide, with notable examples being Jebel Ali at Dubai in the UAE and Subic Bay in the Philippines. The principle of the EPZ has been embraced as a worldwide instrument for national economic development by the United Nations.

The concept of the EPZ concerns the duty-free and tax-free manufacture or processing of products for export purposes within a customs-controlled ('offshore') environment. Components may be imported into the zone duty free and tax free to be processed or manufactured into the finished product, or stored for onward distribution and then re-exported without any liability of import duties or other taxes. The purpose of the EPZ is to ensure that at least 70 per cent of the zone-produced articles are re-exported. The remaining percentage of items produced within the zone may be imported into domestic territory upon payment of the appropriate import duty and tax for the finished article.

Companies trading from within the export processing zone can be wholly-owned by foreign-based enterprises and, in most cases, all profits may be repatriated to the home country. Foreign direct investment by overseas-based companies is encouraged in zone operations, since normal national rules regarding profits or

ILLUSTRATION 10.6

Nightmare logistics in Cameroon

Douala, Cameroon's major port, is one of Africa's busiest ports, handling 95 per cent of Cameroon's international trade. It also serves Cameroon's neighbours, Chad and the Central African Republic.

Douala was once considered one of the worst ports in the world; however, since borrowing money from the World Bank and investment by the government in the port infrastructure things have improved somewhat. The main problem now is once the goods have landed in the port to transport them safely to their destination. The only viable route is by road and that can be very problematic. Douala suffers from horrendous

PHOTO CREDIT: SYLVIA CORDAIY PHOTO LIBRARY LTD/ALAMY

traffic problems and once outside the city, roads have been built on soft soil with little foundations. Roads are poorly maintained and subject to bad weather, since fewer than 7 per cent of the roadways are tarred. The heat and the rain soon cause wide potholes and huge cracks. Besides the potholes, motorists must dodge the wrecks of cars that have smashed. Under Cameroon law, these cannot be moved until the police have given permission. The many frequent roadblocks often serve little other purpose than to allow police and gendarmes to collect bribes.

Companies like Coca-Cola and Guinness transporting drinks face nightmare problems. On a journey through Cameroon they may lose up to a third of a truckload. The cost of distribution alone can be as much as 15 per cent higher than in a country with decent roads. This is besides the traumas of police controls, local government bureaucracy and the longer length of time it takes for a truck to make a simple journey.

Global operators use specialist logistics companies to deal with such logistical problems. In order to transfer a production unit of the Cameroon Brewery Company from Cameroon to Benin, TBC Logistics organised a special convoy made up of trucks and oversised machines and tanks. They managed to pass through Nigeria and cover a distance of about 5000km. To do this the convoy had to pass through thickly populated towns as well as small isolated villages with tracks rather than roads.

QUESTION *What are the ways in which companies can minimise logistical problems in countries like Cameroon?*

SOURCE: ADAPTED FROM: WWW.ECONOMIST.COM, WWW.TBCLOGISTICS.COM AND WIKIPEDIA.ORG/WIKI/CAMEROON

ownership do not apply. It is also possible for locally based companies to engage in zone operations as long as they are involved in import and export operations.

It is also likely that the workforce used will cost the zone company less than for home-based operations, since the majority of the EPZs are located in developing countries, especially East and South East Asia and Central America.

The advantages for companies in taking advantage of EPZs are:

- All goods entering the EPZ are exempted from customs duties and import permits.
- Firms can use foreign currency to settle transactions.
- EPZs can be used for assembly of products and so help reduce transportation costs.
- EPZs give a company much more flexibility and help avoid the unwanted bureaucracy of customs and excise.

China has developed a number of export processing zones in the coastal regions and special economic zones (SEZs) in the interior of China to help develop export sea trade. Examples of EPZs in China are Hong Kong, Shenzen, Shanghai and Tianjin.

Documentation

A number of different documents are required in cross-border marketing. These include invoices, consignment notes and customs documents. SITRO, the Simpler Trade Procedures Board, has been involved in developing simpler documentation and export procedures with the aim of encouraging international trade. EDI is expanding and now providing a fast integrated system which is reducing documentation preparation time and errors.

The process of documentation has more importance than its rather mechanistic and bureaucratic nature would suggest. Errors made in documents can result in laws being broken, customs regulations being violated or, in financial institutions, refusing to honour demands for payment. Country variations are considerable with regard to export documentation procedures. Different documents are required in different formats. Figure 10.4 shows a typical export order process.

FIGURE 10.4
The export order and physical process

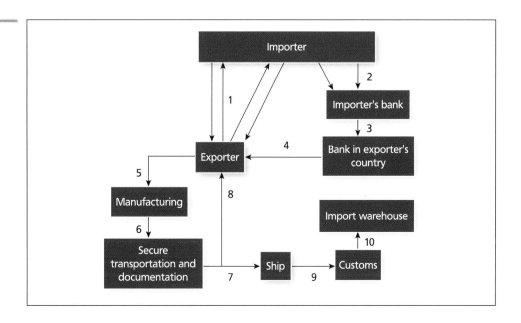

Documentation problems have five main causes: complexity, culture, change, cost and error. Complexity arises from the number of different parties requiring precise documents delivered at the correct time. In addition to the customer, banks, chambers of commerce, consulates, international carriers, domestic carriers, customs, port/terminal/customs clearance areas, insurance companies and the exporting company or freight forwarding company are being used by the exporter.

Different countries require different numbers of copies of documents, sometimes in their own language and sometimes open to official scrutiny that is strongly influenced by the culture of that country. Document clearance can, therefore, be slow and subject to bureaucratic delays.

Errors in documentation can have serious consequences. The definition of an 'error' is open to interpretation. Errors can result in goods being held in customs or in a port. Clearance delays cause failure to meet customer service objectives. In extreme cases, errors result in goods being confiscated or not being paid for.

The development of regional trading blocs is reducing some of the complexity of documentation. Previous to the single European market, a firm transporting goods from Manchester (UK) to Milan (Italy) would require 38 different documents. Now, theoretically, none are required! Some companies seek to minimise their exposure to documentation problems by using freight forwarders to handle freight and documentation. Other companies develop their own expertise and handle documentation in-house.

Packaging

Packaging for international markets needs to reflect climatic, geographical, economic, cultural and distribution channel considerations. In this section we will concentrate on the specific requirements that particularly relate to transport and warehousing.

The main packaging issues of interest for the exporter are: loss, damage and the provision of handling points to cope with the range of transport modes and the levels of handling sophistication and types of equipment used throughout the entire transit.

■ *Loss.* The main concerns of loss of goods relate to misdirection and to theft (pilferage). The use of containers has reduced some of the opportunities for theft. Misdirection can be minimised by the appropriate use of shipping marks and labelling. High-value consignments need to be marked in such a way as to avoid drawing them to the attention of potential thieves. Marking needs to be simple, security-conscious and readily understandable by different people in different countries.

■ *Damage.* The length of transit and variations in climate and physical movement give rise to many opportunities for damage to occur. Goods stowed in large ships might be contaminated by chemical odours or corroding machinery. Goods might be left out in the open air in equatorial or severe winter conditions. Wal-Mart found that local Brazilian suppliers could not meet their standards for packaging and quality control.

A good balance needs to be achieved between the high costs of the substantial export packing required to eliminate all or almost all damage and the price and profit implications that this has for the customer and the exporter.

Over the years, export packaging has been modified from wooden crates and straw, etc., towards fibreboard and cardboard cartons. Different countries have different regulations about what materials are acceptable. In addition, export packaging influences customer satisfaction through its appearance and in its appropriateness to minimise handling costs for the customer.

The export sales contract

The export sales contract covers important terms for the delivery of products in international trade. There are three main areas of uncertainty in international trade contracts which Branch (2005) identifies as:

- uncertainty about which legal system will be used to adjudicate the contract
- difficulties resulting from inadequate and unreliable information
- differences in the interpretation of different trade terms.

The International Chamber of Commerce (ICC) has formulated a set of internationally recognised trade terms called Incoterms. The use of Incoterms will reduce these uncertainties. However, because there are many different ways in which the customer and the supplier could contract for the international delivery of products, the possibility of ambiguity can exist unless care is taken.

At one extreme the customer could buy the product at the factory gate, taking all the responsibility for permits, arrangements and costs of transport and insurance. At the other extreme the supplier can arrange and pay for all costs to the point where the product is delivered to the customer's premises. There are a variety of different steps between manufacture and delivery to the customer. Keegan and Green (2005) identify nine steps:

- obtaining an export permit, if required. For example, for the sale of armaments
- obtaining a currency permit, if required
- packing the goods for export
- transporting the goods to the place of departure. This is usually road transport to a seaport or to an airport. For some countries, for example within continental Europe, transport could be entirely by road
- preparing a bill of lading
- completing necessary customs export papers
- preparing customs or consular invoices as required in the country of destination
- arranging for ocean freight and preparation
- obtaining marine insurance and certificate of the policy.

There are many Incoterms specifying many variations of responsibility for the required steps in the delivery process. The main terms are defined below:

- *Ex-works* (EXW). In this contract the exporter makes goods available at a specified time at the exporter's factory or warehouse. The advantage to the buyer in this arrangement is that of obtaining the goods at the lowest possible price.
- *Free on board (FOB)*. In this contract the exporter is responsible for the costs and risks of moving the goods up to the point of passing them over the ship's rail. The FOB contract will specify the name of the ship and the name of the port. The benefit to the buyer in this arrangement is that the goods can be transported in the national shipping line of the buyer and can be insured using a national insurance company. In this way the amount of foreign currency needed to finance the contract is reduced.
- *Cost, insurance, freight (CIF)*. This contract specifies that the exporter is responsible for all costs and risks to a specified destination port indicated by the buyer. The buyer benefits from receiving the goods in the home country and is, therefore, spared the costs, risks and management of the goods in transit. The exporter can benefit from a higher price for the contract.

Whether the contract is more profitable will depend on the extra total distribution costs associated with the CIF contract. From a national point of view, the use of CIF contracts by a country's exporters is preferred as invisible earnings through extra freight and insurance services are increased when CIF contracts are used rather than FOB contracts.

Governments of all types of political and economic persuasion sometimes develop policies to favour their own national companies, and they can try to influence the availability of transport modes. In addition, the extra incentive to increase foreign currency earnings can change the export sales contract and with it the specification of the Incoterms.

SUMMARY

- The management of international distribution channels and logistics is challenging because it is frequently determined more by the available infrastructure and host country channel structure than by what the firm would like to do.

- The lack of experience in distribution decision-making is exposed further by explicit and implicit cultural differences. It is important to understand and manage cultural differences amongst different members of the variety of distribution channel arrangements in different country markets.

- Cultural differences add to control difficulties. Typically, companies have less control over international channels than they have in their domestic market. The usual pattern is to have a smaller market share and to use longer distribution channels, that is, using more layers of distribution intermediaries. Both of these factors reduce the power of the manufacturer. Less channel power usually results in less control over other channel members.

- The changing nature of retailing patterns influences distribution planning. The long-term commitments that form the basis of successful distribution need to be nurtured. However, change also implies some adapting of distribution channel arrangements. It is a considerable challenge to add new types of distribution intermediaries whilst holding on to long-established accounts.

- Successful management of international distribution channels and logistics represents a significant challenge to the international marketer. The proximity of the company, the distribution intermediaries and the customer make cultural interactions an important influence on success.

- Success in international distribution channel and logistics management has to be based on high-quality strategic decisions and consistent and efficient tactical implementation.

KEYWORDS

Build to order	Export processing zone	Just in time
Buyer–seller relationships	Foreign market channels	Logistics or distribution
Category management	Indirect channels	strategy
Data mining	Globally integrated supply	Mass customisation
Direct channels	chain	Multimedia technology
Distribution channel structures	Integrated supply chain	Open market
Effective consumer response	Interactive customer marketing	Retailing
Electronic data interchange	Interactive shopping	Total distribution cost

CASE STUDY

Merry Management Training

Merry was a training consultancy producing a range of management training courses. Their own staff delivered the courses. They also marketed a range of distance learning management courses which they marketed internationally through agents. A client that successfully completed a training course would receive a Merry certificate.

In the mid-1990s John Razor of Merry investigated the possibility of entering the Middle East. Research had shown that there were potential opportunities for distance learning management programmes, particularly in the Gulf States. By chance he met Yabmob Nig, the managing director of a small management consultancy firm based in Dubai called Ala-Meer Ltd. Ala-Meer was owned by two partners, Yabmob Nig and a silent partner who took no part in the management of the business. The silent partner, a local Dubai businessman, was necessary because Yabmob Nig was an expatriate from India and so could not be sole director of the business.

Yabmob and John had a series of meetings and developed a good rapport. It was not thought necessary to draw up a detailed contract at this stage and so a brief memorandum of understanding (MOU) was signed. The main terms of the MOU were as follows:

1 Ala-Meer had exclusive rights to market and recruit clients throughout the Middle East.

2 Ala-Meer would receive 20 per cent of the fee income.

3 Ala-Meer would charge for other services as agreed.

4 All fees would be made payable to Merry but collected by Ala-Meer.

Ala-Meer were very effective marketers. They very easily got potential clients to sign up for a course but were finding it hard to get clients to make the payments direct to Merry.

Yabmob Nig persuaded John Razor to change the method of payment. The new method of payment allowed clients to pay Ala-Meer in the local currency who would then pass on the payments to Merry. Ala-Meer were then able to market the courses much more easily and were soon recruiting clients from most of the countries in the Middle East. They did this by newspaper advertising, mailshots, Web advertising and subscribing to a number of search engines on the Internet.

Client numbers grew rapidly and everyone was pleased with the market development. Merry was dispatching a large volume of material to the Middle East and Merry staff were conducting seminars in the region on a regular basis. This was the honeymoon period for the business relationship, as both parties had a common objective – to grow sales. A high degree of trust existed between the parties at this stage.

At the end of the first two years of operations Merry undertook a financial audit of the partnership. However, this was quite difficult to do, as there were no proper audited accounts. Under Dubai law, firms do not have to publish audited accounts. Even so, the auditors found evidence to indicate that the business could be a profitable partnership. However, the cash flow was poor. They found that few clients were making payments directly to Merry; most were making payments to Ala-Meer. The audit also showed there was a substantial sum of money that should have been paid to Merry by Ala-Meer which had not been paid.

Yabmob Nig was holding back payment as he and John Razor disagreed on the amount of fees that were outstanding. Ala-Meer were claiming a large amount of expenses that Merry argued had not been agreed in the contract. Ala-Meer saw the 20 per cent margin as pure profit whereas Merry had assumed costs would be defrayed from this percentage. Ala-Meer were also aggrieved that Merry had started marketing their courses in Turkey; they thought they had exclusive rights to the whole of the Middle East, and, to them, that included Turkey.

After long negotiations Merry found it almost impossible to agree the sum that Ala-Meer should pay as a result of the fees they had collected. Ala-Meer were constantly claiming 'additional costs' and reporting lower recruitment figures than Merry had delivered material for. In the end Merry had to send out its own accounting staff to audit Ala-Meer records and agree how much Ala-Meer had to pay to Merry. The relationship between the two parties deteriorated rapidly from this point on and Merry terminated the relationship.

QUESTIONS

1 Why did this promising business relationship go so badly wrong?

2 How could Merry have protected their business in the Middle East more effectively?

3 What lessons can be drawn from this case regarding cross-cultural negotiations?

DISCUSSION QUESTIONS

1 How might companies use the Internet to increse the competitivenss of their international distribution strategy?

2 How might the analysis of the retailer infrastructure and retailer marketing practices in advanced economies influence the development of marketing plans for retailers based in less-developed countries?

3 Discuss what factors contribute to the increasing complexity of global logistics operations. Explain why cooperative relationships are so important in this aspect of international marketing operations.

4 The arrival of the global village has had a major impact on companies' distribution methods. Identify four factors involved and explain how each has influenced distribution.

5 Fully evaluate the statement: 'Distribution and logistics are increasingly becoming the battleground in international markets as companies seek to gain global competitive advantage.'

References

Branch, A.E. (2005) *Export practice and management*, 5th edn. Thomson Learning.

Cateora, P.R. and Graham, J.L. (2006) *International marketing*, 11th edn. Irwin.

Coughlan, A.T., Anderson, E., Stern, L. and El-Ansary, A.I. (2006) *Marketing channels*, 7th edn. Prentice-Hall.

Czinkota, M.E. and Ronkainen, I.A. (2006) *International marketing*, 8th edn. Thomson Learning.

Keegan, W.J. and Green, M.J. (2005) *Global marketing management*. Pearson, Prentice-Hall.

Klein, L.A. and Quelch, J.A. (1997) 'Business to business market making on the Internet', *International Marketing Review*, 14 (5).

Kotler, P. and Keller, K.L. (2005) *Marketing management*, 12th edn. Pearson.

McGoldrick, P.J. (2002) *Retail marketing*. McGraw-Hill.

Rosenbloom, B. (2002) *Marketing channels, a management view*, 7th edn. Dryden Press.

Strandskow, J., Duerr, E. and Albaum, G. (2004) *International marketing and export management*, 5th edn. Addison-Wesley

Usunier, J.C. and Lee, J.A. (2005) *Marketing across cultures*, 4th edn. Prentice Hall.

CHAPTER 11

PRICING FOR INTERNATIONAL MARKETS

INTRODUCTION

Many organisations believe that pricing is the most flexible, independent and controllable element of the marketing mix and that it plays a major role in international marketing management. This is largely based on the fact that pricing changes appear to prompt an immediate response in the market. However, despite the apparent simplicity of using pricing as a major marketing tool, many managers find pricing decisions difficult to make. This is in part due to the fact that whilst most firms recognise the importance of pricing at a tactical level in stimulating short-term demand, far fewer recognise the importance of the strategic role of pricing in international marketing.

In this chapter, we focus upon both the internal and external factors that affect international pricing decisions, the role that pricing plays in developing strategies to meet corporate objectives, and the relationship between pricing and other aspects of the firm's activities. In addition to considering the stages involved in developing a comprehensive international pricing policy, we discuss the specific problems associated with pricing in international marketing which do not affect the domestic business. We then go on to explore the financial issues in managing risk in pricing and of non-payment of debts.

LEARNING OBJECTIVES

After reading this chapter you should be able to:

- Discuss the issues that affect international pricing decisions
- Evaluate different strategic options for pricing across international markets
- Differentiate between the problems facing companies engaged in foreign market pricing and those faced by companies trying to coordinate strategies across a range of global markets
- Find solutions to the problems of pricing in high-risk markets

DOMESTIC VS INTERNATIONAL PRICING

For many companies operating in domestic markets, pricing decisions are based on the relatively straightforward process of allocating the total estimated cost of producing, managing and marketing a product or service between the forecast total volume of sales, and adding an appropriate profit margin. Problems for these firms arise when costs increase, sales do not materialise or competitors undercut the prices. In international markets, however, pricing decisions are much more complex, because they are affected by a number of additional external factors, such as fluctuations in exchange rates, accelerating inflation in certain countries and the use of alternative payment methods such as leasing, barter and countertrade.

In recent years, too, it has become more apparent that customer tastes have become much more sophisticated, and that purchase decisions are made less frequently on the basis of price consideration, but are increasingly influenced by wider expectations of product performance and perceptions of value. This has particular implications for international products, which are often perceived to be of significantly different value – higher or lower – than locally produced products. Pricing strategies are also strongly influenced by the nature and intensity of the competition which exists in the various local markets.

For these reasons, it is important to recognise at the outset that the development and implementation of pricing strategies in international markets should go through the following stages:

1 Analysing the factors which influence international pricing, such as the cost structures, the value of the product, the market structure, competitor pricing levels and a variety of environmental constraints.

2 Confirming what impact the corporate strategies should have on pricing policy.

3 Evaluating the various strategic pricing options and selecting the most appropriate approach.

4 Implementing the strategy through the use of a variety of tactics and procedures to set prices at SBU level.

5 Managing prices and financing international transactions.

THE FACTORS AFFECTING INTERNATIONAL PRICING DECISIONS

A firm exporting speculatively for the first time, with little knowledge of the market environment that it is entering, is likely to set a price based largely on company and product factors. Because of its restricted resources, the firm places particular emphasis on ensuring that sales revenue generated at least covers the costs incurred. However, whilst it is important that firms recognise that the cost structures for production, marketing and distribution of products and services are of vital importance, they should not be regarded as the sole determinants when setting prices. Sarathy, Terpstra and Russow (2006) identify many other factors that firms should take into consideration – environment, market, company and specific product factors – these are summarised below. It is by giving full recognition to the effect of these factors on pricing decisions that the company can develop a strategic rather than a purely tactical approach to pricing.

Factors influencing the pricing strategy

COMPANY AND PRODUCT FACTORS

- corporate and marketing objectives
- firm and product positioning
- product range, life cycle, substitutes, product differentiation and unique selling propositions
- cost structures, manufacturing, experience effect and economies of scale
- marketing, product development
- available resources
- inventory
- shipping costs.

MARKET FACTORS

- consumers' perceptions, expectations and ability to pay
- need for product and promotional adaptation, market servicing, extra packaging requirements
- market structure, distribution channels, discounting pressures
- market growth, demand elasticities
- need for credit
- competition objectives, strategies and strength.

ENVIRONMENTAL FACTORS

- government influences and constraints
- currency fluctuations
- business cycle stage, level of inflation
- use of non-money payment and leasing.

Companies operating internationally must consider all the above factors detailed for each specific country market. However, as with all the other marketing mix factors, the individual country pricing policies need to be integrated and coordinated within a wider regional or global strategy in order to enable corporate objectives to be met.

Whilst it is important that companies consider all the factors listed, some of them, such as corporate objectives, market and product factors, consumer perceptions, competitor responses and cost structures are of particular significance.

Company and product factors

CORPORATE OBJECTIVES

The short-term tactical use of pricing such as discounts, product offers and seasonal reductions is often emphasised by managers, at the expense of its strategic role. Firms will use export markets if they have excess production capacity to dump excess products. This means they use marginal pricing strategies, pricing at really low prices so they cover only the variable costs. Yet pricing over the past few years has played a very significant part in the restructuring of many industries, resulting in the growth of some businesses and the decline of others. A number of authors have explained how Japanese firms, in particular, have approached a new market for a specific product with the intention of building market share over a period of years, through maintaining or even reducing pricing levels, establishing the product, the brand name, and setting up effective distribution and servicing networks. As a result of this strategy, Japanese companies have come to dominate a whole range of industries, from consumer electronics to zip fasteners. This has usually been accomplished at the expense of short-term profits, as Japanese international companies have consistently taken a long-term perspective on profits. The Japanese banks, which are usually part of the same loose groups of companies linked through mutual shareholding, have played a significant part in this process, seeing themselves as being more closely involved with the company rather than simply being external providers of finance. Consequently, they are prepared to wait much longer for returns on investments than some of their Western banking counterparts.

By contrast, US firms have relied in the past more on international corporate strategies with greater emphasis on factors such as advertising and selling, believing that these reduce the need to compete on price. The reason for this is that the cost base of US manufacturing is usually much higher than that of its foreign competitors. However, the rapid growth of China and the Asian economies has led to a change in the priorities of US firms. In a recent survey US firms ranked pricing as more important than any other element of the marketing mix, whereas Asian firms, which have been aggressively reducing their cost base for years, now place greater emphasis upon other factors as they now, as the Japanese before them, seek to build global brands. The move of many Asian manufacturers from being contract manufacturers to marketing their own brands globally has seen them placing much more emphasis on innovation and marketing as they upgrade and develop their products and differentiate themselves by building their own distinctive brands.

The international nature of competition leads to the question of whether firms should aim for a broadly standardised price structure, or whether prices should be adapted in each country.

Product and service factors

Whilst in theory standardisation in pricing might appear easier to manage and therefore be preferable, in practice the different local economic, legal and competitive factors in each market make it rarely achievable. The occasions when price standardisation is achievable are more usually related to the nature of the product and its stage in the life cycle – for example, standardised pricing can be adopted for certain hi-tech products where limited competition exists. Myers, Cavusgil and Diamontopolous (2002), in their examination of export pricing, note that when the technology becomes more freely available, the marketers adopt more market-led pricing. Aircraft makers, for example, because of the relative uniqueness and complexity of the technology, tend to charge the same price regardless of where the customer is based. However, in contrast, shipbuilders, with products in the mature phase of the product life cycle, adapt prices to meet each particular purchase situation.

In developing pricing strategies, a company needs to be aware of the price dynamics of specific products in the various markets. Five characteristics of the product are important in pricing:

- *Frequency of purchase.* Frequently purchased products, for example baby food, petrol, tea and bread, tend to be very price-sensitive in all international markets, whereas occasional purchases are not.

■ *Degree of necessity*. If a product is essential for its users, price changes are unlikely to affect the market size, except in countries where extreme poverty exists and people cannot afford even the most basic necessities.

■ *Unit price*. High-priced products such as holidays and cars are evaluated in greater detail in terms of the consumer's perceptions of value for money, and so, for example, reliability, style and features of cars are extremely important to consumers besides price.

■ *Degree of comparability*. Consumers are less price-conscious about insurance policies than grocery products, because the alternatives are more difficult to compare. Price-setting is particularly difficult in certain services, such as advertising, consultancy and accountancy, which have a different perceived value from country to country.

■ *Degree of fashion or status*. The high prices of luxury goods are seen as establishing their quality and it is usually the goods that have a prestige image, often created in other countries, which are not price-sensitive.

Developing pricing strategies for services across international markets is difficult for several reasons. Services are highly perishable, and human resource constraints often restrict the capacity to grow a service business in foreign country markets, and so companies are restricted by the high costs of expansion and managing short-term capacity issues. Likewise the intangibility of services compared with goods may lead to higher marketing costs because the company has to build the market reputation on the actual service experience of consumers rather than building a brand image in anticipation of the consumer experience. This means positioning optimum prices in foreign country markets can be difficult to judge. In business-to-business marketing, where the growth of international services predominates, managers are often tasked with developing effective global pricing strategies for B2B customers that are characterised by different cultures and differing perceptions as to the value of the different service attributes they are buying. The intensive customer contact, extensive customisation requirements, and the costs of building a service quality reputation in the market make the challenge of formulating international pricing strategies for services across international markets particularly problematic.

Price positioning and value for money

The characteristics of the product or service, particularly the high unit price items, lead international marketers to adopt local pricing strategies which are broadly similar for individual markets, so that the positioning of specific products remains consistent from country to country. Marks and Spencer sell basic foods at higher prices than other food retailers in the UK, by guaranteeing extremely high consistency of quality. This difference is not perceived to be so great in other countries, however, where consumers feel that the general quality is not significantly different to justify a substantially higher price.

Price plays an important role in product differentiation by enhancing the perceived value of the product and helping consumers to distinguish between offers from different competitors in order that their needs can be met. Watch prices, for example, range from very little for a child's watch, to a high premium price for a Rolex. Within this range, individual manufacturers normally confine specific brands within particular pricing bands which are linked to the positioning of the brand and the profile of the watches within the range, and to the characteristics of the target segment.

The key role of price in differentiating products within a category and within a particular market can be used as an offensive strategy. This is demonstrated by the South Korean car manufacturer, Kia, which entered the US car market knowing that its brand name had little credibility there and that the market was already saturated with broadly equivalent products. It targeted its Japanese equivalents, the Honda Civic and Toyota Corolla, by offering a similar car at a 25 per cent lower price.

The influence of cost structures on pricing

There is a close relationship between prices, costs and sales volume of a product, because the price charged affects sales volume by increasing or decreasing the overall demand. As a result of producing or marketing larger volumes the unit cost of an individual product reduces, and so, of all the factors, this often becomes the initial stimulus for firms taking the decision to export.

THE RELATIONSHIP BETWEEN DEMAND AND SALES VOLUME

The way in which price affects demand is influenced by many factors. Some products are characterised by having elastic demand and being extremely price-sensitive, so that sales volumes increase significantly as prices are reduced. In underdeveloped markets, where there is low penetration but considerable desire for Western products such as soft drinks or fast food, sales will increase rapidly if the price is reduced relative to consumers' ability to pay.

By contrast, other products are characterised by inelastic demand. For example, suppliers of power generation equipment cannot significantly stimulate demand in individual markets by reducing the price. For such firms, an increase in business revenue is largely determined by changes in external factors, such as an improvement in the economy. The potential market for the European power generation equipment suppliers National Power and ABB was increased by the political decision in Malaysia to partially privatise state utilities.

THE RELATIONSHIP BETWEEN COST AND SALES VOLUME

A second situation of inelastic demand occurs if a firm finds that it has reached saturation in its home market so that even if prices were reduced, there would not be significant extra sales to offset the loss of profit. The firm might conclude that exporting would provide an alternative method of increasing sales and thereby generate additional profit.

This is especially so when firms can increase sales by entering an export market, make use of existing spare production capacity and so price purely to cover their variable costs. Consider the situation shown in Table 11.1 where all the fixed costs are absorbed by the sales in the domestic market, but in addition, 10 per cent extra sales are obtained in export markets at the same prices. Provided there are no increases in fixed costs, there would be recovery of the fixed costs because of the additional 10 per cent export business. This recovery of fixed costs by the export business would be shown as an additional contribution to the general overheads of the business. The contribution from the export business would all be additional profit.

The fixed production cost of the product includes depreciation of equipment, building rental and business rates. General overheads include advertising, selling, distribution and administration.

The example shows that in practice the additional £100 000 sales have generated an additional £40 000 profit (6.3 per cent on total sales) – far greater than the £30 000 profit generated on the £1 million domestic sales (3 per cent profit on total sales). The firm could therefore afford to reduce its export price considerably and still make a profit, provided that no extra general overhead costs were incurred, as long as there was spare production capacity and no extra investment had to be made.

In export markets, the firm might choose one of the following four alternatives, setting the selling price at:

■ Production cost plus general overhead plus added profit (this would normally be the list price).

■ Production cost, but without general overhead or profit added.

■ Below production cost.

■ Production cost with specific export costs added.

The choice of alternatives will depend on the firm's objectives in entering international markets. The first leads to the safest, albeit least competitive, price and is frequently the approach adopted by new exporters who are unwilling to take any significant risk. The firm might even take the list price, including the domestic gross margin, and add to it all the costs of exporting such as marketing, distribution and administration, resulting in the export price being far greater than the domestic price. In most international markets, however, a list price calculated in this way is unlikely to gain significant market share, and so a lower selling price is required.

The arguments for using the second opinion, to set a lower export selling price, are based on the belief that export costs should not include domestic sales costs such as advertising, marketing research, domestic and administration costs. Whilst this option has some merit, it might well fail to take account of high specific export costs.

The third option is clearly quite risky as it is designed to substantially increase volume. The danger, of course, is that if the increased volume generated does not absorb the fixed and general overhead costs, the product will be unprofitable and losses will result. This approach is often used in overseas markets and is based on marginal costing, whereby unused production capacity or extended production runs can provide extra goods for sale with little or no change in fixed costs, so that the extra production can effectively be produced at a lower cost than the

TABLE 11.1 The effect of additional export sales on contribution

	Domestic sales (100 000 units) £000	+ 10 per cent Export sales	Domestic+ 10 per cent export sales (110 000 units) £000
Sales	1000	100	1100
Fixed production costs	300		300
Variable production costs	500	50	550
Total costs	800	50	850
Contribution to general overheads	200	50	250
General overheads	170	10	180*
Profit	30	40	70

NOTE: *GENERAL OVERHEADS ARE HIGHER DUE TO ADDITIONAL EXPORTING COSTS

original production schedule. Another risk with this strategy is that the firm could be accused of **dumping excess capacity** in foreign markets. This sometimes is exacerbated as a result of government policy, particularly in declining industries, for example, if governments continue to subsidise their own inefficient industries by providing various incentives such as subsidies.

The fourth option begs the question of whether or not export pricing should reflect all the costs specific to export sales, and if so, which costs can be directly attributable to exports. It can be argued that, particularly if a firm intends ultimately to commence manufacture in foreign markets, it is vital to know exactly what are the realistic costs for foreign markets. Allocating costs such as research and development accurately and appropriately, however, can be difficult.

Specific export costs

Whilst export volumes are small in comparison to the domestic market, some experimentation in export pricing is possible, but as exporting becomes a more significant part of the activities of the company, perhaps requiring the allocation of dedicated equipment or staff, it is necessary to reflect all costs that are specific to export sales. These costs include tariffs, special packaging, insurance, tax liabilities, extra transport, warehousing costs and export selling as well as money transmission, hedging and foreign exchange costs.

The most immediate and obvious result of all these costs being passed on is that the price to the consumer in an export market is likely to be much greater than the price to a domestic consumer. An example of this is shown in Table 11.2.

This raises the question of whether foreign consumers will be prepared to pay a higher price for imported rather than locally produced goods. Justifying the cost of the product on the basis of its added value might be possible in the short term,

TABLE 11.2 Escalation of costs through exporting

	Export price (£)	Domestic price (£)
Manufacturer's FOB price	10.00	10.00
Sea freight and insurance	1.20	
Landed cost (CIF)	11.20	
Import tariff: 8 per cent on CIF value	0.90	
CIF plus tariff	12.10	
17.5 per cent VAT	2.12	1.75
Distributor purchase price	14.32	11.75
Distributor mark-up (15 per cent)	2.15	1.75
Retailer purchase price	16.47	13.50
Retail margin 40 per cent	10.98	9.00
Consumer purchase price	27.45	22.50

but is unlikely to provide the international marketer with a basis for long-term viability in each local market. A strategy must be developed to deal with this situation in which the cost to the ultimate consumer is reduced. The main options available to the exporter include:

- aggressively reducing production costs, modifying the product if necessary and sourcing overseas
- shortening the distribution channel, for example, by selling direct to retailers
- selecting a different market entry strategy, such as foreign manufacture, assembly or licensing to avoid the additional costs of exporting.

The implications of changing the market entry and distribution strategy have been dealt with in earlier chapters of this book; here we discuss strategies for reducing cost.

Cost reduction

The rationale behind any firm's decision to enter international markets is usually to increase profitability, and this is based upon a recognition of the fact that the size of the firm's actual market share is a primary determinant of profitability. Thus the argument goes that firms with a larger market share normally have lower unit costs, and they are perceived by customers to market higher-quality products, leading to relatively higher market prices. Both of these factors result in higher profits for the firm.

Most companies in international markets have the potential to benefit from driving down costs through achieving economies of scale, exploiting the benefits of the learning curve and making strategic decisions on the location or relocation of manufacturing plants within the context of worldwide operations.

Economies of scale

Economies of scale are obtained as a result of manufacturing additional products with the same or only slightly higher fixed costs, so that, in practice, for every additional product produced, the unit cost reduces. This is a slight over-simplification of the situation as, for example, installation of new plant might in the short term increase unit costs during the period when the plant is running at below its economic capacity. Whilst in domestic markets the benefits from economies of scale follow directly, in international markets these economies must more than offset savings achieved by having local plants, which result in reduced transport costs and the avoidance of import tariffs.

Learning curve

Some authors have suggested that, although it is less well-known than economies of scale, the learning curve has potentially greater benefit for cost reduction. Its origins lie in the production of aircraft in the Second World War. The observation that the time needed to perform a specific task reduced as the operatives become more familiar with it was made. Since then a series of studies by the Boston Consulting Group have found evidence that the effect was much more widespread than this, and covered all aspects of business, including high and low technology, products and services and consumer and industrial products.

They point out that there is a direct relationship between the cumulative volume of production and the costs incurred in producing the same product benefits. The major sources of savings from the experience gained through the learning curve are:

- greater labour efficiency
- task specialisation and method improvement
- new production processes
- better performance of existing equipment
- changes to the mix of resources
- greater product standardisation
- improved product designs.

Thus the learning curve provides an opportunity for cost reductions, although if managers do not make a concerted effort, costs will rise.

The combined effects of economies of scale and the learning curve were seen in the electronics market, where aggressive firms slashed prices to gain market share, knowing that cost reductions would follow. For example, Sony set the price of its DVD players in the US market at a third of the actual manufacturing cost, on the basis that the volume generated by increased demand would force component and assembly costs down, through a combination of these two effects. A key issue in international marketing is how best these effects can be exploited, particularly as the skills and experience are spread throughout the world. The efficient transfer of these skills and knowledge between different strategic business units then becomes paramount.

Location of production facility

Driven by the continual need to reduce costs, companies have increasingly considered selective location or relocation of production facilities. As firms increasingly market their products globally, so their choice of manufacturing locations is determined by many other considerations than simply being close to particular markets. They might choose to locate a factory in a less developed country in order to take advantage of lower labour costs, but also they may well develop specific skills and areas of specialisation in those locations. For example, a large proportion of televisions, radios, calculators, and jeans are manufactured in China and South East Asia.

India, with 1 billion inhabitants, 100 million of whom are considered to represent a financially aware middle class, presents the attractive opportunity of an emerging market as well as a huge skilled but cheap workforce for multi-nationals seeking low-cost manufacturing bases. Thomson-CSF (France), Coca-Cola, Motorola, IBM and Hewlett Packard have all decided to set up there.

Problems associated with manufacturing in Western countries have helped to accelerate this transfer of manufacturing. Lagging productivity, reluctance to source materials and parts globally, strong unions and high standards of living were the causes of the decline in the US manufacturing base. Many regions and countries are responding to this opportunity for inward investment by marketing a variety of incentives and attractions to companies wishing to relocate.

It is not only in manufacturing that relocation of activities can benefit from lower labour costs. For instance, the introduction of fibreoptic cables allows considerably more information to be transferred quickly and accurately by telecommunications, and so can lead to high labour-content jobs such as data input, order processing and invoicing being carried out in other countries. This has considerable implications for services such as insurance and banking.

Market factors

CONSUMERS' RESPONSE

Perhaps the most critical factor to be considered when developing a pricing strategy in international markets, however, is how the customers and competitors will respond.

There are nine factors which influence the sensitivity of customers to prices and all have implications for the international marketer. Price sensitivity reduces:

- the more distinctive the product is
- the greater the perceived quality
- the less aware consumers are of substitutes in the market
- if it is difficult to make comparisons, for example in the quality of services such as consultancy or accountancy
- if the price of a product represents a small proportion of total expenditure of the customer
- as the perceived benefit increases
- if the product is used in association with a product bought previously so that, for example, components and replacements are usually extremely highly priced
- if costs are shared with other parties
- if the product or service cannot be stored.

The issue with all these factors is that it is customer perceptions and purchasing behaviour which are most important in setting prices. In France, EuroDisney suffered considerably from weaknesses in its financial structure. The fundamental problems were that customer perceptions and demand for EuroDisney were out of step with forecasts. The explanation for the weaknesses in their offer was found to be in the factors affecting price sensitivity. High interest rates and high labour costs were underestimated and the availability of disposable income of potential consumers overestimated. After a five-year major effort EuroDisney became profitable. Customers' perception of credit can also influence purchasing behaviour. In Central Europe and Asia, consumers have been reluctant to borrow money to buy goods. However, as we can see from Illustration 11.1, this is now changing.

COMPETITORS' RESPONSE

As competition increases in virtually every product and market, the likely response of the competitors to a firm's pricing strategy becomes increasingly important. An attempt should be made to forecast how competitors might react to a change in pricing strategy by analysing the market and product factors which affect them, consumer perceptions of their product offers and their internal cost structures. Competitors' pricing strategies will be affected by such issues as their commitment to particular products and markets, and the stance that they might have adopted in the past during periods of fierce competition.

Before implementing pricing strategies and tactics, therefore, it is essential to estimate the likely consumer and competitor response by evaluating similar situations which have arisen in other international markets or countries. The responses of competitors who adopt a global strategic approach are likely to be more easily predicted than a competitor adopting a multidomestic strategy.

It is useful to consider how these factors have affected the competitive responses of a number of companies such as Gillette, Kodak and Philip Morris.

DEVELOPING PRICING STRATEGIES

Having discussed the factors which firms should consider in the pricing process, we now turn to the development of international pricing strategies. The first question to be addressed is to what extent prices should be standardised across the markets. There are three approaches to international pricing strategies.

Standardisation, or ethnocentric pricing, based on setting a price for the product as it leaves the factory, irrespective of its final destination. Whilst each customer pays the same price for the product at the factory gate, they are expected to pay transport and import duties themselves, either directly or indirectly, and this leads to considerable differences in the price to the final consumer.

For the firm, this is a low-risk strategy as a fixed return is guaranteed and the international buyer takes all the exchange rate risk. However, no attempt is made to respond to local conditions in each national market and so no effort

ILLUSTRATION 11.1

Consumer credit fuels consumer purchases

Central and Eastern European countries are seen as high-growth markets, and in recent years many retailers have moved into

the region. However, until recently, retailers have had difficulties in persuading consumers to take on credit and so buy more of their goods. Hampering their efforts was the lack of credit agencies to carry out credit ratings on potential borrowers. Also there were no reliable court procedures through which creditors could recover bad debts. This is now changing; both Poland and the Czech Republic have set up Western-style credit bureaus and whilst court procedures are still slow, lenders have been investing heavily in systems to spot and chase late payments.

Such efforts could reap rich rewards, as it is the view of many that central and Eastern Europeans are fast developing the spending habits of their Western neighbours, and in so doing are starting to accept credit as a necessary cost if they are to realise their aspirations. Lending to households is now growing at 26 per cent per annum. In the Western-owned shops, customers are offered not only groceries and consumer goods but also credit cards and personal loans.

In East Asia it is a similar story. Until recently banks have only been interested in lending to corporate clients but that too is changing. In China banks are actively encouraged to lend to Chinese consumers by the China Central Bank. East Asia is seen by Visa as its fastest-growing market in the world.

However, this growth does come with a risk. The southern province of Guandong is seen as a hotbed of piracy in the production of fake credit cards as pirates shift from designer brands to consumer credit. In one raid alone police seized over 17 000 fake credit cards.

QUESTION *How do you account for the changing attitudes across central Europe and East Asia?*

SOURCE: ADAPTED FROM *THE ECONOMIST*, 27 FEBRUARY, 2003 AND 2 JUNE, 2003

is made to maximise either profits or sales volume. This type of pricing strategy is often used when selling highly specialised manufacturing plant.

Adaptation, or polycentric pricing, allows each local subsidiary or partner to set a price which is considered to be the most appropriate for local conditions, and no attempt is made to coordinate prices from country to country. The only constraints that are applied when using this strategy relate to transfer pricing within the corporate structure.

The weakness with this policy is the lack of control that the headquarters have over the prices set by the subsidiary operations. Significantly different prices must be set in adjacent markets, and this can reflect badly on the image of multi-national firms. It also encourages the creation of grey markets (which are dealt with in greater detail later in this chapter), whereby products can be purchased in one market and sold in another, undercutting the established market prices in the process. Firms marketing on the Internet find it very difficult to pursue such strategies, because of the free flow of information across markets. Gap customers soon discovered they could save up to 40 per cent of the price of a garment by buying online rather than in their local store, leading to a speedy change in their pricing strategy.

Invention, or geocentric pricing, involves neither fixing a single price, nor allowing local subsidiaries total freedom for setting prices either, but attempts to take the best of both approaches. Whilst the need to take account of local factors is recognised, particularly in the short term, the firm still expects local pricing strategies to be integrated into a company-wide long-term strategy. The benefits of this approach are shown in the following example. A firm which intends to establish a manufacturing base within a particular region may need to rapidly increase market share in order to generate the additional sales necessary for a viable production plant. In the short term, the local subsidiary may be required to sell at what for them is an uneconomic price, so that by the time the new plant comes on stream, sufficient sales have built up to make the plant and the individual subsidiaries profitable.

The objectives of pricing

The objectives of the firm's pricing strategy are directly related to the various factors which have been discussed, but it should be emphasised that they will be affected as much by the prevailing company culture and attitudes to international marketing as by market and environmental conditions. The most common pricing objectives for companies are listed below, but it must be recognised that firms also adapt or add other specific objectives according to their own specific and changing circumstances. The alternative approaches are:

- *Rate of return*. Cost-oriented companies set prices to achieve a specific level of return on investment, and may quote the same ex-works price for both domestic and international markets.

- *Market stabilisation*. A firm may choose not to provoke retaliation from the leader, so that market shares are not significantly changed.

- *Demand-led pricing*. Prices are adjusted according to an assessment of demand, so that high prices are charged when demand is buoyant and low prices are charged when demand is weak.

- *Competition-led pricing*. In commodity markets such as coffee and wheat, world market prices are established through continual interaction between buyers and sellers. Selling outside the narrow band of prices that have been mutually agreed will either reduce sales or unnecessarily reduce profits.

- *Pricing to reflect product differentiation*. Individual products are used to emphasise differences between products targeted at various market segments. Carmakers, for example, charge prices for the top of the range models which are far higher than is justified by the cost of the additional features which distinguish them from the basic models, but problems arise in different international markets, as consumers' perceptions vary as to what is considered to be a basic model.

■ *Market skimming*. The objective of market skimming is for the firm to enter the market at a high price and lower the price only gradually, or even abandon the market as competition increases. It is often used by companies in recovering high research and development costs.

■ *Market penetration*. Low prices can be used by a firm to rapidly increase sales by stimulating growth and increasing market share, but at the same time discouraging competition. Japanese companies have used this strategy extensively to gain leadership in a number of markets, such as cars, home entertainment products and electronic components.

■ *Early cash recovery*. Faced with liquidity problems, products in the mature or declining phase of the product life cycle, or products with an uncertain future in the market because of changes in government policy, a firm may aim for early cash recovery, to increase sales and generate cash rapidly. A variety of mechanisms are used, including special offers, discounts for prompt payment and rigorous credit control; all this type of pricing is a form of marginal cost pricing.

■ *Prevent new entry*. Competitors can be discouraged from entering a market by establishing low prices which will indicate to potential competitors the prospect of low returns and price wars. Domestic firms have used this strategy to attempt to prevent entry by international competitors; however, the danger is that the other firm might successfully enter the market with a quite different positioning, such as higher specification or quality, or with improved service levels. The defending firm, due to its low-price strategy, may not have the income to make the necessary investment to compete with the new entrant.

Setting a price

Having determined suitable strategies for pricing in international markets, a company must then consider the options available in setting individual prices. Companies can decide on the basis of their knowledge, objectives and situation to take either a cost, market or competition-oriented approach.

Cost-oriented approaches are intended to either:

■ achieve a specific return on investment; or
■ ensure an early recovery of either cash, or investments made to enter the market.

Market-oriented pricing approaches give the company the opportunity to:

■ stabilise competitive positions within the market
■ skim the most profitable business, or
■ penetrate the market by adopting an aggressive strategy to increase market share.

Competition-oriented approaches are designed to:

■ maintain and improve market position
■ meet and follow competition
■ reflect differences in the perceived value and performance of competitive products, or
■ prevent or discourage new entrants in the market.

No matter which of these broad strategies are adopted, the process for determining export pricing is essentially the same:

- determine export market potential
- estimate the price range and target price
- calculate sales potential at the target price
- evaluate tariff and non-tariff barriers
- select suitable pricing strategy in line with company objectives
- consider likely competitor response
- select pricing tactics, set distributor and end-user prices
- monitor performance and take necessary corrective action.

PROBLEMS OF PRICING AND FINANCING INTERNATIONAL TRANSACTIONS

There are a number of specific problems which arise in setting and managing prices in international markets. Problems arise in four main areas:

1 *Problems in multi-national pricing.* Companies find difficulty in coordinating and controlling prices across their activities sufficiently to enable them to achieve effective financial performance and their desired price positioning:

   - How can prices be coordinated by the company across the various markets?
   - How can a company retain uniform price positioning in different market situations?
   - At what price should a company transfer products or services from a subsidiary in one country to a subsidiary in another?
   - How can a firm deal with importation and sale of its products by an unauthorised dealer?

2 *Problems in managing foreign currency and fluctuating exchange rates.* Considerable problems arise in foreign transactions because of the need to buy and sell products in different currencies:

   - In what currency should a company price its products in international markets?
   - How should the company deal with fluctuating exchange rates?
   - How can a company minimise exchange rate risk over the longer-term transactions?

3 *Problems of obtaining suitable payment in high-risk markets.* Obtaining payment promptly and in a suitable currency from the less developed countries can cause expense and additional difficulties:

   - How might/should a company deal with selling to countries where there is a risk of non-payment?
   - How should a company approach selling to countries which have a shortage of hard currency or high inflation?
   - How can a company obtain payment upfront on long-term transactions?

4 *Administrative problems of cross-border transfer of goods.* Problems of bureaucracy and delays arise as a result of simply moving goods physically across borders:

- At what point should an exporter release control and responsibility for goods?
- What steps can be taken in the export order process to minimise delays?

These four major problem areas will now be dealt with in the following four sections.

PROBLEMS IN MULTI-NATIONAL PRICING

Coordination of prices across markets

The pressure on companies to market truly global products backed by globally standardised advertising campaigns is caused by three major trends: the homogenisation of customer demand, the lowering of trade barriers and the emergence of international competitors. At the same time these largely undifferentiated global products can be sold at very different prices in different countries, based on factors such as purchasing power, exchange rate changes and competition and consumer preferences.

Until recently this has been a perfectly acceptable practice. However, in the past decade it has become increasingly difficult for companies to maintain a differentiated pricing strategy across international markets when they are marketing similar if not standardised products. Readily available information on worldwide prices through modern data transfer and the Internet have greatly increased price transparency. Advances in telecommunications systems have also greatly reduced international transaction costs. Global companies who obviously follow differentiated pricing policies are often threatened, first by an erosion of consumer confidence as customers learn of the more attractive pricing policies in other markets and second by grey marketing which can result in the cannibalisation of sales in countries with relatively high prices and damaging relationships with authorised distributors.

EUROPEAN MONETARY UNION

The issue of achieving price coordination across markets has become particularly pertinent in the European Union (EU) since the establishment of the European Monetary Union (EMU). The EMU, sometimes called the Euro zone or Euro area, is the name given to the union of countries using the Euro as a domestic currency.

National price levels across the EU are far from uniform. Amongst the Euro zone countries, Austria and Finland are viewed as high-priced markets, France, Belgium, Portugal and Germany are seen as average and Spain as having much lower prices. Price levels in Scandinavia can be 40 per cent higher than in southern parts of the Euro zone.

Differences in taxation and excise duties as well as disparities in production costs and wage levels lead to price differentials and difficulties in managing problems in the economy (see Illustration 11.2). Firms in product markets have tended to adapt their prices to the buying power, income levels and consumer preferences of national markets. However, in the service sector and particularly the tourism industry (see Dilemma 11.1) it is not very easy to differentiate prices to reflect the differences in buying power and consumer preferences of the variety of national and international consumers that a company may be targeting.

SOURCE: ADAPTED FROM 'HARD CURRENCY, TIGHT SPOT', *THE ECONOMIST* 26 OCTOBER 2006 AND 'ITALY: THE EURO ZONES

SICKEST PATIENT', *BUSINESS WEEK* 6 JUNE 2005

ILLUSTRATION 11.2

Debt in the Euro zone

A bleak vision is haunting Italy as its industry falters in the face of global competition. In 2005 the Euro zone's third largest economy went officially into recession. That news, coupled with Brussels' upward revision of estimates for Italy's budget deficits in the past two years, has stoked fears that the country is in worse condition than previously thought. Italy's public finances are a bit of a problem. It has a budget deficit of 4.1 per cent of

its GDP and a public debt of 109 per cent of GDP, a growth rate that hovers around 1 per cent and its unit labour costs, relative to Germany's, have risen by more than 20 per cent since 2000. The traditional solution of devaluation is not possible for Italy within a currency union, so does that mean they may be pushed out of the Euro zone? The Centre for European Reform, a London think-tank, puts the probability as high as 40 per cent.

If so, what is to happen to its Euro zone partners with similar problems? Greece has a healthy growth rate but its deficit last year was 5.2 per cent of GDP and its debt, 108 per cent Portugal, which like Italy has a low growth rate, has a deficit of 6 per cent of its GDP and a debt of 63 per cent.

Cheaper borrowing has given governments little incentive to tighten their belts and solve such problems. Before the Euro currency was created, governments strove to cut their deficits to 3 per cent of GDP and to lower their debt towards 60 per cent, the ceiling for new members. Now a stability and growth pact is supposed to keep deficits and debts down. Portugal is trying hard to cut spending, but big countries have done much as they please. Last year four members had deficits in excess of 3 per cent of GDP; another was 2.9 per cent. Seven have debt ratios of more than 60 per cent.

QUESTION *What are the implications for companies outside the Euro zone competing in markets with such high debt ratios and budget deficits?*

DILEMMA 11.1

SOURCE: ANDREW HICKLING

Pricing caravan parks for European customers

Aberdeenshire Council is a rural local authority covering a large geographical area with a varied land mass but a low population of around 250 000. The area covers some of the most beautiful beaches in Scotland and inland encompasses some stunning hills and countryside.

Aberdeenshire Council has nine caravan parks, six of which are located on the coast; two are in established country parks and one in a market town. The local authority lets pitches in two ways; static pitches for the season – March to the end of October – and touring pitches on a per night basis in the same period. Included in the touring category are tents, touring caravans and motor homes. All prices for touring stands are on a per night basis with a concession for customers over 60 years old.

Visitors to the parks traditionally came from the local region as well as from within the UK. However, increasingly touring

customers are now coming from overseas, mainly due to the efforts of VisitScotland promoting the north-east of Scotland. Overseas visitors favour the inland sites, in particular Ballater which is known as Royal Deeside due to the proximity of Balmoral Castle, the summer home of the Queen.

Traditionally the council has priced on a non-profit basis and made no distinction in the pricing between sites with different Tourist Star grades, varying level of usage or between the different market segments from local and overseas markets. Now the caravan parks have to become fully self-financing, so a more business-oriented approach is needed. The dilemma for the authority is, how can they develop a more strategic approach to their pricing which reflects the varying benefits of the sites and the ability to pay of the segments they attract from across Europe as well as their local market?

QUESTION *How would you advise the Council to proceed?*

Prior to the formation of the EMU these differences were largely concealed from the European consumer, despite the formation of the Single European Market. The formation of the EMU and the introduction of the euro has changed all that. Now prices are no longer distorted by fluctuating exchange rates. This means companies competing on the European market need to consider the implications of the price transparency in the Euro zone. The onset of price transparency impacts on firms in different ways. Highly specialised products with few direct rivals are largely immune to the risk of price transparency generating more intense competition. However, companies marketing goods that are supplied direct to the consumer have come under increasing pressure from retailers to reduce margins if retailers themselves have had to cut prices to meet new price points set in euros. Furthermore, more retailers and businesses have moved to a policy of European-wide sourcing and using the Internet to search for the lowest prices for products. It has therefore become virtually impossible for companies to operate on the European market without a sophisticated strategy to effectively coordinate prices across the EU. It is this that has led to so many companies revamping their approach to managing their European marketing strategies.

Firms who have failed to meet this challenge have left themselves open to the threat of grey market goods cannibalising their sales in high-priced national markets.

Single European Payments Area

Economic and Monetary Union and the Euro were introduced to help achieve the goal of a single European market. One particular objective was to create a single market where currency could move as freely and cheaply in the Euro zone as it could within national markets. However, to achieve a truly single market, integration of payment facilities across borders was needed to create a single financial services market across the Euro zone. This is known as the Single European Payments Area (SEPA).

The key problem SEPA resolves for companies marketing across the Euro zone is the differences they face between the way domestic and cross-border payments operate and are priced. With the SEPA in place, companies can execute any payment within the Euro area as easily and at the same cost as they could in their existing domestic markets.

The objective of SEPA introduced in 2008 is to create a single payment area where consumers and businesses can make cross-border payments as easily, safely and efficiently as they can within their own countries and perhaps most importantly, as cheaply. Cross-border Euro payments are treated exactly like domestic payments whatever their amount. It could still take three business days from order to receipt for cross-border payments, as opposed to a single day within a country, and it still means companies face cross-border pricing difficulties with customers outside the SEPA (see Illustration 11.3). In the SEPA there has been a consolidation of the cross-border payment infrastructure which means there are now common rules for clearing and settlement, which means costs are minimised and processes quicker. The harmonised European payments infrastructure, also makes it possible to implement efficient e-solutions. According to GTnews.com, it is expected that by 2011 e-payments will account for 95–99 per cent of the total volume of payments.

What is grey marketing?

As said above, grey marketing has become a particular problem for companies operating across Europe where there are huge price differentials but without

SOURCE: PETER C. MCGREGOR, SHEFFIELD HALLAM UNIVERSITY

ILLUSTRATION 11.3

Dealing with non-SEPA payments

The Single European Payments Area (SEPA) formed 2008 across the countries of the Euro zone, requires banks dealing with funds transfers between Euro zone countries to charge no more for cross-border payments than for domestic payments, which means no charge at all in some countries. Banks outside the Euro area still charge substantial commissions for cross border transfers of funds. Typical costs in the UK are minimum £9 per transaction for small personal payments, and £20 and upwards pro rata for commercial payments. This means that pricing decisions by non-Euro area businesses trading in Europe will have to factor these costs into their prices, possibly affecting their competitiveness in their markets.

QUESTION *What can businesses in the UK who trade with Euro area businesses do to ameliorate this situation?*

trade barriers goods are able to flow freely across borders. Grey marketing is a business phenomenon that has seen unprecedented growth in the past few years as information on prices has flowed across countries and consumers have discovered how varying prices can be when companies try to pursue highly differentiated pricing strategies across markets that can no longer be kept separate.

Grey marketing occurs when trademarked goods are sold through channels of distribution that have not been given authority to sell the goods by the trademark holder. This could occur within a country but more and more it is becoming common across countries. This becomes problematic, especially for global marketers trying to manage a coordinated marketing strategy across different markets. Coca-Cola had to bring forward the European launch of Vanilla Coke after it found the product was already being sold in the UK by a distributor who had imported it directly from Canada, where it had been launched several months previously. Typically, however, grey market goods are international brands with high price differentials and low costs of arbitrage. The costs connected with the arbitrage are transportation, tariffs, taxes and the costs of modifying the product, i.e. changing the language of instructions.

It is perhaps important to point out that there is nothing illegal about grey market goods; it is purely the practice of buying a product in one market and selling it in other markets in order to benefit from the prevailing price differential. Grey markets tend to develop in markets where information on prices for basically the same product in different countries is cheap and easy to obtain (e.g. cars, designer goods, consumer durables). The Anti Grey Marketing Alliance estimates the revenue generated by international grey marketing activities to be about US$20 billion a year. Whilst grey marketing is seen by its critics as a free-riding strategy, it is being increasingly seen as a viable international strategy by smaller firms who, with limited resources, can use it to compete against larger firms in international markets.

There are three types of grey markets (see Figure 11.1):

1 *Parallel importing*, when the product is priced lower in the home market where it is produced than the export market. The grey marketer in the export market will parallel import directly from the home market rather than source from within their own country; for example, there is a strong parallel import trade in Levi jeans between the USA and Europe. Levi Strauss recently took out a lawsuit against the retail chain Tesco for selling Levi jeans they have sourced directly from outside the EU (see Illustration 11.4). Levi are insisting that jeans in Europe should only be sourced from authorised dealers within the EU.

2 *Re-importing*, when the product is priced cheaper in an export market than in the home market where it was produced; re-importation in this case can be profitable to the grey marketer.

3 *Lateral importing.* When there is a price difference between export markets, products are sold from one country to another through unauthorised channels.

A disturbing example of this can be found in the pharmaceutical industry, where it is estimated that US$18 million of reduced-price HIV drugs intended for African markets were diverted back to Europe to be sold at much higher prices on the grey market.

FIGURE 11.1
Three types of grey market

SOURCE: ASSMUS AND WEISSE (1995)

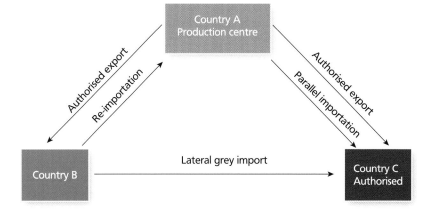

Note: Price in Country B < price in Country C

ILLUSTRATION 11.4

Grey clouds cause black anger

Not so long ago Levi Strauss took the retail chain Tesco to court over its sale of Levi jeans. Tesco had bought the jeans from outside the European Union and the sold them within the EU well below the price that the authorised dealers were charging. The judgment by the court, which shocked consumer rights groups everywhere, was that Tesco should not be allowed to import jeans made by Levi Strauss from outside the

EU and sell them at reduced prices without first getting permission from the jeans maker. The ruling was based on a directive which had been designed to protect EU manufacturers from price dumping, but was used very effectively by the US multi-national to control its brand positioning in a foreign market.

Levi persuaded the court that Tesco was destroying the image and the brand value of Levi: this could ultimately lead to less brand innovation which would have an adverse effect on the consumer. Tesco said such an argument was specious and that they were purely arbitraging the price differential between Levis sold in the US and Europe – something, as a global retailer sourcing around the globe, they should be free to do.

Critics of Levi Strauss suggest it may prove in the long run to be a pyrrhic victory. Tesco was given huge amounts of free sympathetic publicity, whilst Levi's stance was viewed as anti-consumer. Levi has been losing market share in Europe in recent years and is seen by brand experts as no longer strong enough to command premium prices in the market. Its court victory may help it hold on for a while, but in the long run market forces may dictate otherwise.

QUESTIONS *Were Levi Strauss right to take the action against Tesco? What other options could they have considered?*

SOURCE: ADAPTED FROM *THE ECONOMIST*, 24 NOVEMBER, 2001 AND *MARKETING WEEK*, 2C FEBRUARY, 2003

Price coordination strategies

Typically firms try to defend themselves against grey market activities by calling for government intervention or legal protection. As seen in the previous section, companies may resort to imposing restrictions or even threats to retailers. In the US Wal-Mart sourced products through grey markets and suffered the resultant threats from firms such as Adidas and Levi jeans. Other reactive measures have included the refusal to issue warranties in certain markets, or even buying out the grey marketer.

Companies competing in international markets who wish to develop more effective strategies to deal with the problem of price coordination across increasingly interdependent markets and the threat of grey market goods have four options open to them.

1 *Economic measures.* The company can influence the country manager's pricing decision by controlling the input into those decisions. A multi-national can do this through transfer pricing (see the later section in this chapter). By raising the price by which it transfers products to the low-priced country the headquarters essentially imposes a tax on that market. Closely related to transfer pricing is rationing the product quantities allocated to each country or region and so limiting the number of units sold in the diverting country.

2 *Centralisation.* The company can move towards more centralisation in the setting of prices. Traditionally many multi-national companies have given country managers a high degree of decision-making autonomy. Usually they are in the best position to assess consumer response to any given pricing decisions and they are able to react swiftly to competitor activity. A centralised approach, however, could overcome difficulties with grey market goods although it does usually result in dissatisfaction amongst country managers. A compromise approach is to shift the decision-making authority in pricing from a country to a regional level; however, increasingly grey market goods are becoming a global issue.

3 *Formalisation.* The company can standardise the process of planning and implementing pricing decisions. Thus the company influences prices at the local level by prescribing a process that is followed by country managers when establishing pricing policy.

4 *Informal coordination.* A number of companies have moved towards a more informal system of coordination without either a high degree of centralisation or formalisation. This thinking is usual in the transnational company where international subsidiaries make differentiated and innovative contributions to an integrated worldwide operation. Whilst this approach may incorporate a variety of techniques, the essential asset is that there are common shared business values across the subsidiaries that are backed by compatible incentive systems.

In a proactive approach to coordinating its pricing decision across international markets, a company has to select the appropriate strategy which will in effect be determined, first, by the level of local resources available, and then by the level of environmental complexity, as illustrated in Figure 11.2.

Transfer pricing in international markets

Transfer pricing is an area that has created complications for many international marketing firms. It is concerned with the pricing of goods sold within a corporate family, when the transactions involved are from division to division, to a foreign subsidiary, or to a partner in a joint venture agreement. Whilst these transfer prices are internal to the company, they are important externally because goods being transferred from country to country must have a value for cross-border taxation purposes.

The objective of the corporation in this situation is to ensure that the transfer price paid optimises corporate rather than divisional objectives. This can prove difficult when a company internationally is organised into profit centres. For profit centres to work effectively, a price must be set for everything that is transferred, be it working materials, components, finished goods or services. A high transfer price, for example from the domestic division to a foreign subsidiary, is reflected in an apparently poor performance by the foreign subsidiary, whereas a low price would not be acceptable to the domestic division providing the goods. This issue alone can be the cause of much mistrust between subsidiaries – at best leading to fierce arguments, and at worst leading to loss of business through overpricing.

There tend to be three bases for transfer pricing:

1 *Transfer at cost*, in which the transfer price is set at the level of the production cost, and the international division is credited with the entire profit that the firm makes. This means that the production centre is evaluated on efficiency parameters rather than profitability.

2 *Transfer at arm's length*, when the international division is charged the same as any buyer outside the firm. Problems occur if the overseas division is allowed to buy elsewhere when the price is uncompetitive or the product quality is inferior, and further difficulties arise if there are no external buyers, making it difficult to establish a relevant price. This is the strategy most preferred by national governments.

3 *Transfer at cost plus* is the usual compromise, where profits are split between the production and international divisions. The actual formula used for assessing the transfer price can vary, but usually it is this method which has the greatest chance of minimising executive time spent on transfer price disagreements, optimising corporate profits and motivating the home and international divisions. Often a senior executive is appointed to rule on disputes.

However, the real interest of transfer pricing is how it is used strategically by companies either to act as a barrier to entry, or to marshal resources around the world.

FIGURE 11.2
A framework for selecting a coordination method

SOURCE: ASSMUS AND WEISSE (1995)

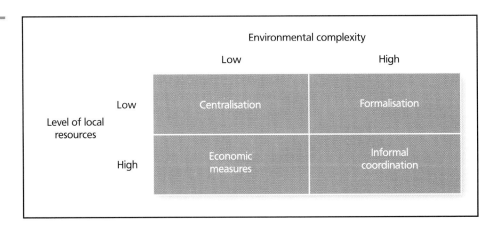

To create barriers to entry

Most oil companies are vertically integrated, from oil exploration right through to selling petrol at the pumps, and use transfer pricing as part of their strategy to maintain barriers to entry. The major cost for oil companies is at the exploration and refining stage and so, by charging high transfer prices for crude oil, profits are generated at the refining stage of the process, rather than in distribution, where it is relatively easy to enter the market. Oil companies therefore attempt, by the use of transfer pricing, to make petrol distribution unattractive to potential competitors. Supermarkets and hypermarkets, with their huge purchasing power, have managed to challenge the dominance of the oil companies by using low-priced petrol as a loss-leader to entice customers to stores.

To avoid domestic tax liabilities

When countries have different levels of taxation on corporate profits, firms try to ensure that profits are accumulated at the most advantageous point. Companies operating in countries with high corporation tax may be tempted to sell at low transfer prices to their subsidiaries in countries with lower corporate taxation.

To avoid foreign tax

Foreign tax authorities wish to maximise the taxable income within their jurisdiction, and there are a number of strategies a company might use to avoid tax – for example, by charging lower transfer prices if there is high customs duty on goods. The impact of such avoidance strategies is diminishing, as customs authorities become more aware of this practice. Recently the US government demanded huge taxes from Sony when it discovered that it generated 60 per cent of its global sales in the USA but very little profit due to Sony's management of transfer pricing. Japan then retaliated by doing the same to Coca-Cola. However, it can be argued that as the general level of import duties is reducing as international trade agreements come into effect, so the need to take avoiding action is declining.

To manage the level of involvement in markets

If a firm has both a wholly owned subsidiary and a joint venture in a particular country, it will wish to sell at a higher price to a company with which it has a joint venture than one that is a wholly-owned subsidiary. Selling at a low price to foreign partnerships or licensees has the effect of sharing more of the profit with the partner.

Transfer pricing is an area where profit objectives, managerial motivations and government regulation interact and so the expertise of many people – accountants, legal counsel, tax advisors and division managers – is needed to achieve an agreement. The international marketing manager's contribution is primarily concerned with two aspects of the problem:

- achieving an effective distribution of goods to world markets
- ensuring that the impact of the transfer price does not affect foreign market opportunities.

PROBLEMS IN MANAGING FOREIGN CURRENCY TRANSACTIONS

Perhaps the most critical issue for managers is how to deal with the various problems involved in managing transactions which involve currency exchange; a second difficulty is what action to take when selling to countries where there is high inflation.

What currency should the price be quoted in?

In any international marketing transaction, the exporter has the option of quoting in either the domestic or the local currency. If the exporter quotes in their own domestic currency, then not only is it administratively much easier, but also the risks associated with changes in the exchange rate are borne by the customer, whereas by quoting prices in the foreign currency the exporter bears the exchange rate risk. However, there are benefits to the exporter in quoting in foreign currency:

- it could provide access to finance abroad at lower interest rates
- good currency management may be a means of gaining additional profits
- quoting in foreign currency could be a condition of the contract
- customers normally prefer to be quoted in their own currency in order to be able to make competitive comparisons and to know exactly what the eventual price will be.

Furthermore, customers in export markets often prefer quotations in their own currency to enable them to more easily compare the tenders of competitors from a range of countries.

Often the choice of currency for the price quotation depends partly on the trade practices in the export market and the industry concerned. Suppliers competing for business in the oil industry, wherever in the world they may be supplying, may well find they are asked to quote in US dollars. In the airline industry things are more complicated. EADS, the European group manufacturing the Airbus plane, has all its costs in Euros, but on the global market, planes are priced in US dollars. This gives the US company Boeing an advantage competing on international markets, because they do not have the same exchange risk as EADS and can forecast their costs and prices with much more certainty than their arch rival Airbus.

UK exporters have recently experienced a period of strong sterling, reducing their competitiveness on international markets and subjecting them to price-cutting pressures from overseas customers, as happened to MDL (see Dilemma 11.2).

Thus as well as the decision as to what currency to quote in, the main worry for both suppliers and customers on international markets is fluctuating exchange rates and how to deal with them.

The introduction of the Euro has effectively eliminated exchange rate risk in the Euro zone countries. Even countries like the UK, who have decided to delay their decision to enter the EMU, increasingly find that companies selling goods into Europe are pressurised to quote prices in the Euro.

Should prices be raised/lowered as exchange rates fluctuate?

One of the most difficult problems that exporters face is caused by fluctuating exchange rates. The major trading nations appear to have differing strategies to deal with exchange rate appreciation – for example, UK, French and Canadian firms all tend to increase their prices by more than the exchange rate appreciation, whereas Japanese firms only passed on about half the appreciation of the yen in the form of a price rise. Japanese exporters have, therefore, preferred to retain market share by absorbing some of the impact of yen appreciation, at the expense of short-term profits.

Sarathy, Terpstra and Russow (2006) identified three types of risk affecting firms, arising from exchange rate fluctuations:

1 *Transaction risk* occurs when the exporter quotes in a foreign currency, which then appreciates, diminishing the financial return to the firm. US hoteliers in Hawaii experienced a noticeable decline in Japanese tourism when the dollar rose in value from ¥90 to ¥120 in just over a year.

2 *Competitive risk* arises because the geographic pattern of a firm's manufacturing and sales puts them at a disadvantage compared to their competition. If, for instance, the firm is manufacturing in a country with an appreciating currency but trying to compete in a marketplace where currencies are depreciating, it could lose out to a local manufacturer. Firms may then try to maximise their expenditure in the market place. This is why Mercedes and BMW are now manufaturing in the USA.

3 *Market portfolio risk* occurs because a company with a narrow market portfolio will be influenced to a much greater extent by changes in exchange rates than a diversified firm that is better able to balance changes in exchange rates through operating in many countries.

Various tactics can be adopted to deal with currency fluctuations. When the domestic currency is weak, the firm should:

- compete on price
- introduce new products with additional features
- source and manufacture in the domestic country

DILEMMA 11.2

Can we avoid the currency risk without losing our customers?

Management Development Ltd (MDL) is a small firm specialising in management training and development. The firm delivers training programmes using a combination of self-study material and study weekends and operates in the UK, Middle East and the Far East.

Ten years ago the firm took a strategic decision to enter the Malaysian market. They appointed an agent in Malaysia to market the courses and recruit students. To encourage students to join training courses payment could be made in stages.

The majority of the firm's costs, developing study material, tutoring etc. were incurred in sterling.

The income from selling in Malaysia would normally be in ringgits. Income in ringgits and costs in sterling meant MDL faced a currency risk. Traditional methods for avoiding currency exposure (hedging) were not considered appropriate due to the small scale of the operation.

Over the last ten years the financial results from the contract had been poor. Prices had been going up by 5 to 10 per cent per year and recruitment had been good but still the firm was failing to make a reasonable return. MDL's accountant said you only need to look at the HM Revenue and Customs exchange rate data base to find the reason (http://www.hmrc.gov.uk/ exrate/malaysia.htm.).

QUESTION *How should MDL resolve their dilemma?*

■ fully exploit export opportunities

■ obtain payment in cash

■ use a full-cost approach for existing markets, but use marginal costs
  for new more competitive markets

■ repatriate foreign-earned income quickly

■ reduce expenditure and buy services (advertising, transport etc.) locally

■ minimise overseas borrowing

■ invoice in domestic currency.

When the domestic currency is strong, the firm should:

■ compete on non-price factors (quality, delivery, service)

■ improve productivity and reduce costs

■ prioritise strong currency countries for exports

■ use countertrade for weak currency countries

■ reduce profit margins and use marginal costs for pricing

■ keep the foreign-earned income in the local country

■ maximise expenditures in local country currency

■ buy services abroad in local currencies

■ borrow money for expansion in local markets

■ invoice foreign customers in their own currency.

PROBLEMS IN MINIMISING THE RISK OF
NON-PAYMENT IN HIGH-RISK COUNTRIES

The international marketing manager increasingly needs to be knowledgeable
about the various complexities of financing international marketing transactions
and sources of finance to support international marketing strategies, especially
when trading with markets seen to be high risk due to adverse economic and
political conditions, high inflation or perhaps lack of hard currency. For a company
exporting goods to such markets there is a considerable risk of non-payment for
a variety of reasons, such as:

■ the buyer failing or refusing to pay for the goods

■ insolvency of the buyer

■ a general moratorium on external debt by the host

■ government political and legal decisions

■ war

■ failure to fulfil the conditions of the contract

■ lack of hard currency

■ high inflation.

Traditionally managers will seek financial support to help reduce the risk of
non-payment due to these factors through home governments, commercial banks
or some kind of cooperation agreement.

GOVERNMENT-SPONSORED FINANCE

Governments are often willing to financially support companies in financing
international trade transactions in the hope that increased exports will generate

economic growth at home and boost employment. National governments approach such support in a variety of ways but in most countries there is an export–import bank or perhaps export bank or, as in the UK, a government department (Trade Partners UK) who fund a variety of support packages to help companies finance export strategies. Governments will also provide low-cost export guarantee insurance to protect their exporters against non-payment by foreign buyers. However, such protection may not be available in particularly high-risk markets.

COMMERCIAL BANKS

Commercial banks compete intensively to offer international trade services to companies operating in international markets. However, they tend only to be willing to support low-risk activities, which sometimes makes it difficult for companies expanding into emerging markets. Commercial banks may also be more interested in short-term financing, and so potentially not such a good source for companies making a long-term investment decision in incipient markets where it may be several years before a full return on investment can be achieved. Many banks who made long-term loans to developing markets have suffered losses when countries not experiencing the growth rates expected have been unable to meet debt repayments. This has led to a number of banks being less willing to expose themselves in long-term high-risk markets.

One of the ways banks can help against the risk of non-payment is by forfaiting.

FORFAITING

This is a way of financing without recourse. It means that companies selling products essentially transfer the transaction risk to a forfaiting house. A bill of exchange, usually requiring a bank guarantee or, as in the US, a back up letter of credit, is drawn up to the value of the contract and the seller transfers the claim resulting from the transaction to the forfaiting house. The seller immediately receives the full amount of the contract minus the discount agreed for the period of the contract. This discount will vary depending on the length of the contract, the level of country risk and whether the invoice is guaranteed by a commercial bank. For the company it provides a source of finance to support medium-term contracts in a market and a means of reducing the risk of non-payment.

COOPERATION AGREEMENTS

These agreements are special kinds of countertrade deals (see below) that extend over long periods of time and may have government involvement. They may be called product purchase transactions, buyback deals or pay as you earn deals. For instance, a company may obtain finance to help set up a factory in a particular country if they then agree to buy back the output of the plant.

Countertrade and leasing

So far in this chapter we have focused upon largely conventional approaches to international pricing; however, over the past two decades there has been a dramatic increase in the use of leasing and countertrade deals, which are used as a response to the lack of hard currency, particularly amongst less developed countries.

Counter trade deals are more prevalent when companies are trying to enter emerging or less developed markets. The reason for this is threefold.

- It is sometimes difficult to obtain finance commercially to enter such markets.

- The markets themselves may have limited access to hard currency which means the finance of joint ventures or strategic alliances has to be sought through less traditional means.

- Emerging markets may see such deals as a way of encouraging job creation in their own countries and so actively encourage such financing deals.

WHAT IS COUNTERTRADE?

Countertrade covers various forms of trading arrangements where part or all of the payment for goods is in the form of other goods or services, and price-setting and financing are dealt with together in one transaction. The original and simple barter system has been developed in order to accommodate modern trading situations. Estimates of countertrade activity range from 20 to 30 per cent of world trade, and it is predicted to grow further due to its ability, first, to overcome market imperfections and, second, to provide opportunities for extraordinary profits to be made.

There are many variants of countertrade, resulting from the need to adapt arrangements to meet the needs of individual transactions. The following are the basic forms:

Barter. This is a single exchange of goods with no direct use of money, and does not require intermediaries. It is the simplest form, but has become unpopular because, first, if the goods are not exchanged simultaneously then one participant is effectively financing the other, and second, one of the parties may well receive unwanted goods as part of the deal.

Compensation trading. This involves an agreement in which payment for goods is accepted in a combination of goods and cash.

Counter-purchase. This involves the negotiation of two contracts. In the first, the international marketer agrees to sell the product at an established price in local currency. In the second, simultaneous, contract the international firm buys goods or services for an equivalent or proportionate cash payment from another local supplier.

Offset. This is similar to counter-purchase, but in this case national governments cooperate to support the deal. Sometimes called a product purchase transaction, it is a way in which the international firm is able to obtain more saleable goods from the country in exchange. For example, Boeing sold AWACS aircraft to the British Ministry of Defence on the basis that the purchase price would be spent on British goods (see Illustration 11.5).

Switch deals involve a third party (usually a merchant house), which specialises in barter trading, disposing of the goods. For example, if an Eastern European company importing Western products can only provide in return heavily discounted relatively low-quality products, which may not be saleable in the West, a third country will need to be found in order that a switch deal can be set up in which these lower-quality goods can be exchanged for other products that are more suitable for the original Western markets.

Cooperation agreements. These can cover buyback deals, pay as you earn deals or a range of other beneficial arrangements made between two parties. It is an arrangement whereby part or all of the cost of purchase of capital equipment might be paid for in the form of production from the equipment supplied, either over time or in the form of some other benefit. Illustration 11.6 gives the example of Ikea who, in one such agreement, leased machinery and equipment to a plant in Poland to upgrade production in exchange for an export contract.

In Japan and South East Asia compensation and offset are the most frequently used forms of countertrade. Barter and counterpurchase tend to be more common in lesser developed countries.

So far, the examples of countertrade have involved deals of products, but many other less tangible elements such as know-how, software and information can be included in agreements. Many of the deals set up are complicated and in some cases have stretched over many years.

Advantages and limitations of countertrade

The advantages of countertrade are as follows:

- New markets can be developed for a country's products, as marketing and quality control skills are often 'imported' with the deal, and it can lead to gaining experience in Western markets.
- Surplus and poorer quality products can be sold through countertrade whereas they could not be sold for cash. Moreover, dumping and heavy discounting can be disguised.
- Countertrade through bilateral and multilateral trade agreement can strengthen political ties.

ILLUSTRATION 11.5

Countertrade deals for GEC

GEC – the Marconi electronics subsidiary – became involved in three offset countertrade deals to entitle them to trade in the Middle East. The contribution to the local economy, in the form of investment in a furniture factory in Abu Dhabi, was made in return for an arms contract. In the deal, local craftsmen assemble furniture and fittings for palaces, hotels etc. in UAE. GEC is in partnership with local sheikhs and a Birmingham company for the venture, who agreed to export at least 50 per cent of the output to Europe and the Far East.

Other offset countertrade projects include the formation of a local company to charter ships for an Emirate group and a joint venture to provide geological and topographical information to help evaluate water, oil and gas and other natural resources.

QUESTION *What are the advantages and disadvantages of such deals?*

■ Countertrade and contract manufacture can be used to enter high-risk areas.

■ Countertrade can provide extraordinary profits as it allows companies to circumvent government restrictions.

However, there are disadvantages and limitations in using countertrade:

■ There is a lack of flexibility, as the transactions are often dependent on product availability, and countertraded products are often of poor quality, overpriced or are available due to a surplus.

■ Products taken in exchange may not fit with the firm's trading objectives, or may be difficult to sell.

■ Dealing with companies and government organisations may be difficult, particularly in locating and organising countertrade products.

■ Negotiations may be difficult, as there are no guide market prices.

■ Countertrade deals are difficult to evaluate in terms of profitability and companies can, through countertrade, create new competition.

It is likely that in the future, countertrading will develop further in the form of longer-term rather than shorter-term partnerships as multi-nationals seek

ILLUSTRATION 11.6

Is Ikea changing its global competitive base?

Ikea's UK profit amounted to £104 million last year, down a third from the previous year. In the UK analysts see the need for the group to upgrade products and prices and improve the retail experience of shoppers – several people were hurt in the crush as thousands flocked to the midnight opening of Ikea's new store in Edmonton, London.

Fortunately for Ikea its international market risk is spread across 28 countries with 130 million people visiting 160 branches, and as such it has been viewed as a highly successful global retailer.

PHOTO CREDIT: KEVIN FOY/ALAMY

Central to its marketing strategy is the standardisation of its core concept of Swedish democratic designs. However, its competitive prices are the mainstay of its competitive edge, and Ikea manages its supply route specifically to ensure it can keep prices down. It sees suppliers in Eastern Europe as playing a key role in its strategy. An essential part of the process is buyback, a form of countertrade in which machinery and equipment for increasing and upgrading production is leased to Eastern European companies in exchange for an export contract. In this way the suppliers are able to meet Ikea's high-quality standards and specifications. The repayment period is between three and five years, and in return, Ikea usually buys three to four times the value of the equipment supplied.

However, Ikea has now gone further by expanding their property development portfolio through a loan of US$100 million from the European Bank for Research and Development. This was to finance the establishment and operation of IKEA MOS, a shopping centre located on a site adjacent to one of IKEA's two existing stores in the Moscow region of Russia. The objective for IKEA was to introduce into Russia a totally new concept of retail and provide local customers with an innovative, customer-oriented retail environment. The centre boasts an IKEA hypermarket as well as 250 other shops, two kilometres of shop fronts, a skating rink and Russia's biggest cinema complex. Those 250 retailers all pay rent to the Swedish furniture giant, Ikea.

QUESTION *Evaluate the pros and cons of such strategies in helping Ikea to sustain its competitive advantage across international markets over the longer term.*

SOURCE: ADAPTED FROM *DAILY MAIL*, 5 FEBRUARY, 2007, AND *EVENING STANDARD*, 10 FEBRUARY, 2005

permanent foreign sources for incorporation in their global sourcing strategy. LDCs offer the benefits of low-cost labour and materials, as well as relatively untapped markets for goods. This has resulted in multi-nationals reversing the traditional countertrade process by first seeking opportunities, and then identifying potential countertrade partners with which to exploit the opportunities.

Leasing

Leasing is used as an alternative to outright purchase in countries where there is a shortage of capital available to purchase high-priced capital and industrial goods. Usually the rental fee will cover servicing and the costs of spares too, and so the problem of poor levels of maintenance, which is often associated with high technology and capital equipment in LDCs, can be overcome. Leasing arrangements can be attractive, too, in countries where investment grants and tax incentives are offered for new plant and machinery, in which case the leaser can take advantage of the tax provisions in a way that the lessee cannot, and share some of the savings. It is estimated that leased aircraft account for about 20 per cent of the world's aircraft fleet.

ADMINISTRATIVE PROBLEMS RESULTING FROM THE CROSS-BORDER TRANSFER OF GOODS

For many companies, particularly those that are infrequent exporters or that have insufficient resources for effective export administration, the process of ensuring that goods reach their ultimate destination is beset with difficulties: goods held in customs warehouses without apparent reason, confusing paperwork, high and apparently arbitrary duties, levies and surcharges, and the need to make exorbitant payments to expedite the release of goods. The UN Conference on Trade and Development (UNCTAD) believe these additional costs to world trade could be as much as 10 per cent of the US$10.5 trillion total world trade. UNCTAD also believes that those costs could be cut by US$250 billion by improved efficiency. It is unlikely, however, that such changes as these will happen quickly, and so companies face a series of decisions about how to manage their own risks and costs, whilst still providing an effective service to their customers.

Deciding at what stage of the export sales process the price should be quoted

Export price quotations are important, because they spell out the legal and cost responsibilities of the buyer and seller. Sellers, as previously mentioned, favour a quote that gives them the least liability and responsibility, such as FOB (free on board), or ex-works, which means the exporter's liability finishes when the goods are loaded on to the buyer's carrier. Buyers, on the other hand, would prefer either franco domicile, where responsibility is borne by the supplier all the way to the customer's warehouse, or CIF port of discharge, which means the buyer's responsibility begins only when the goods are in their own country.

Generally, the more market-oriented pricing policies are based on CIF, which indicates a strong commitment to the market. By pricing ex-works, an exporter is not taking any steps to build relations with the market and so may be indicating only short-term commitment. The major stages at which export prices might be quoted are as follows:

- Ex (point of origin), such as ex-factory, ex-mine, ex-warehouse.
- FOB: free on board.
- FAS: free alongside.
- FAS: vessel (named port of shipment).
- C. and F.: cost and freight.
- CIF: cost, insurance freight.
- DDP: direct to destination point.

The export order process

To further emphasise the complexity of managing international pricing, a major task of the marketer is to choose payment terms that will satisfy importers and at the same time safeguard the interests of the exporter. The transactions process for handling export is illustrated in Figure 11.3.

In the process, the customer agrees to payment. The customer begins the process (1) by sending an enquiry for the goods. The price and terms are confirmed by a pro-forma invoice (2) by the supplier, so that the customer knows for what amount (3) to instruct its bank on the method of payment (4). The method of payment is confirmed and arranged. If this is by letter of credit this will be opened by the issuing bank (5) in the supplier's country.

When the goods are shipped (6) the shipping documents are returned to the supplier (7), so that shipment is confirmed by their presentation (8) together with all stipulated documents and certificates for payment (9). The moneys are automatically transmitted from the customer's account via the issuing bank. The customer may only collect the goods (10) when all the documents have been returned to them.

FIGURE 11.3
The export order process

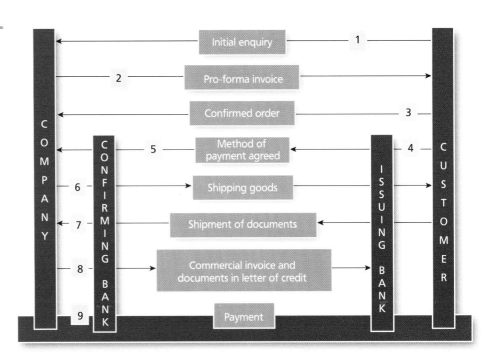

Whilst letters of credit and drafts are the most common payment method, there are also several other methods of payment:

- A *draft* is drawn by the exporter on the importer, who makes it into a trade acceptance by writing on it the word 'accepted'. A *sight draft* is an unconditional order to pay a sum of money on demand or to the order of a specified person. Drafts which are payable at a future date are called *term drafts*.

- A *letter of credit* is similar to a draft, except it is drawn on the bank and becomes a bank acceptance rather than a trade acceptance. There is greater assurance of payment, as an unconditional undertaking is given by the bank that the debts of the buyer will be paid to the seller.

- A *bill of exchange* is an unconditional order in writing which is signed by one person and requires the person to whom it is addressed to pay a certain sum of money on instruction at a specified time.

- A *documentary collection* is when a bill of exchange is presented to the importer via the banking system or alternatively the exporter can present the bill direct. If the importer pays the bill of exchange on presentation, usually by authorising the bank to transfer funds to the exporters bank account, then no further action is required.

- *Open account* is when the sales terms are agreed between buyer and seller, but without documents specifying clearly the importer's payment obligations. There is less paperwork but greater risk of non-payment, so it is only used when a trusting relationship has been developed between the trading parties. In countries where foreign exchange is difficult to obtain, drafts and letters of credit will be given priority in any currency allocation.

- A *consignment note* is when the exporter retains title of the goods until the importer sells them. Exporters own the goods longer in this method than any other, and so the financial burden and risks are at their greatest. In addition, the recovery of either goods or debt could be very difficult, and it is for this reason that consignments tend to be limited to companies trading with their subsidiaries.

The credit terms given are also important in determining the final price to the buyer. When products from international competitors are perceived to be similar, the purchaser may choose the supplier that offers the best credit terms, in order to effect a greater discount. In effect the supplier is offering a source of finance to the buyer, and in some countries – for example Brazil – government support is given to firms to help them gain a competitive advantage through this method. There has been a variety of international agreements to try and stop such practices, but it is still quite prevalent in some countries.

SUMMARY

- In international markets pricing decisions are much more complex, because they are affected by a number of additional external factors, such as fluctuations in exchange rates, accelerating inflation in certain countries and the use of alternative payment methods such as leasing, barter and countertrade.

- Many factors and problems contribute to making effective pricing management one of the most difficult aspects of international marketing to achieve. As well as the market factors associated with pricing decisions in each country it is necessary to deal with the complexities of financing deals based in different currencies and trying to maintain cross-border consistency of pricing.

- Whilst there are cost benefits in standardising products, services and processes, local factors affect the cost base in individual countries and make it difficult to maintain similar prices in different markets.

- In addition to this strategic role, there are a number of issues relating to the detailed operational management of international transactions. These particularly relate to the reduction of risk in carrying out international trade transactions, especially when trading in high-risk countries.

- There are also areas of specific management expertise in pricing that exist in international marketing. These include, for example, the management of transfer pricing between business units within an MNE, grey marketing and countertrade and the administration of cross-border transfers of goods.

- What becomes quite clear in developing international pricing is that there is a need not only to use pricing in a key role in achieving a company's financial objectives, but also as part of an integrated strategy, for example along with other marketing mix elements, to respond positively to the opportunities and threats of the various markets in which it operates.

KEYWORDS

Countertrade	Export administration	Marginal cost pricing
Dumping excess capacity	Fixed production cost	Market-oriented pricing
	Foreign currency	Polycentric
Economies of scale	Geocentric	Price coordination
Elastic demand	Grey marketing	Price standardisation
Ethnocentric	Inelastic demand	Price transparency
Euro zone	Internal cost structures	Production costs
Exchange rate	Learning curve	Transfer pricing
Exchange rate risk	Marginal costing	

CASE STUDY

Beta Automotive

Beta Automotive is an owner-managed firm dealing with the import, export and wholesale of genuine Japanese automotive parts in Singapore.

The managing director, Mr Sing, is a Chinese Singaporean. The firm has eight employees, four of whom have at least eight years of experience in handling Japanese automotive parts. Most of the employees are able to speak and understand Malay as well as Chinese and the managing director also speaks English.

Beta competes by selling genuine automotive parts at a much lower price than the authorised distributor. They also offer technical expertise and ensure all customers are given all the technical information required to make an accurate and informed buying decision. The integrity of the technical information is also personally guaranteed by Beta and all products are sold with a full warranty. Mr Sing believes that even when competing on the grey market a firm must not only be competitive in pricing but should also be able to solve customers' automotive parts problems satisfactorily.

The firm sources the automotive parts from within Singapore and Japan and is able to supply a wide-ranging assortment of genuine automotive parts to car models from a number of manufacturers such as Toyota, Nissan and Isuzu. Besides being a parallel importer, the firm is also the authorised genuine parts dealer of two franchised companies in Singapore.

Sales turnover of the firm is approximately US$3 million. 60 per cent of the sales are generated by exports to South East Asia, principally Malaysia, Indonesia, the Philippines and Pakistan, although since the crisis in Indonesia very little business has been transacted. Beta's export customers can purchase on an (Ident) order basis (delivery time is about 90 to 120 days) or through ex-stock sales (for fast-moving items only). There is a minimum transaction value for any sea shipment and Beta price Free On Board (FOB). The main transaction costs to Beta are local transportation charges, documentation fees, port charges etc. However, to date all the export sales have been indirect export transactions, through agents in Singapore acting on the behalf of buyers in the export market. These agents acted as guarantors and so ensured Beta were paid for the parts and for the services rendered.

Mr Sing is now developing his international marketing strategy and wishes to expand his business further in South East Asia by directly exporting into the markets himself. His main priorities are to spread the firm's existing business and financial risks and to maximise on sales opportunities identified in other South East Asian markets. However, he is concerned that by directly exporting to the country he will need to become involved in many activities previously not undertaken, such as negotiating and liasing with freight forwarders and banks and insurance companies on terms of engagement. This is all besides the complexities of the processing of export documentation to facilitate the transactions. Furthermore, the firm will need to consider how to mitigate its foreign business and financial risks exposures since payment will no longer be guaranteed by an agent.

The main strengths of the firm have been assessed by a consultant as being:

- Access to multiple supply sources which enable Beta to compete effectively on price and give them the flexibility to meet changing parts requirements and demand patterns in both domestic and overseas markets.

- Order fulfilment flexibility. Depending on the nature of the required item, Beta's customers have the options to purchase ex-stock supplies or (Ident) order.

- The range of genuine Japanese automotive parts handled by the firm (e.g. Nissan, Toyota and Isuzu) matches with the major brands of vehicles in circulation in South East Asia.

- Staff at Beta are all highly self-motivated and technically knowledgeable.

- Strong customer-orientation and the commitment and a determination to be successful in overseas markets.

- Little internal bureaucracy compared to authorised distributors.

- Flexible and adaptive staff.

- Short lead-time.

- Language skills.

Their key weaknesses were viewed as being:

- The firm has limited knowledge and exposure to direct export marketing.

- Lack of strategy and marketing planning in the firm.

- No current relationships with direct automotive parts importers or other useful contacts in export markets that can be exploited.

- Limited company resources.

- Inadequate and poor management information.

- The firm does not effectively make use of available external resources to support its foreign market development efforts.

- Contacts with relevant logistical (e.g. freight forwarders) and trade services providers (e.g. banks, insurance companies) are still not well developed.

- Choice of target market segment is limited to those foreign buyers who are able to import more than the minimum transaction value.

QUESTIONS

1 What are the financial risks that Beta will have to face as a direct exporter that they have not had to deal with to date?

2 Fully evaluate the viability of achieving a long-term competitive advantage in international markets as a grey marketer.

3 What advice would you give to Beta?

DISCUSSION QUESTIONS

1 What are the arguments for and against using price and non-price factors when competing in international markets?

2 What pricing problems might a multi-national company face in marketing to less developed countries, and how might they be overcome?

3 Increasingly competing on global markets requires substantial investment, often undertaken by two or more firms in a joint venture or strategic alliance. Consider the implications of such ventures in developing a strategic approach to coordinating pricing strategies across international markets.

4 Why should a domestic supplier invoice export goods in a foreign currency? What are the advantages and disadvantages of foreign currency invoicing?

5 The Internet is increasing price transparency across international markets. Fully evaluate the problems and opportunities this brings to the company trying to build a global competitive advantage.

References

Assmus, G. and Wiesse, C. (1995) 'How to address the gray market threat using price coordination', in I. Doole, and R. Lowe, *International marketing strategy: contemporary readings*, International Thomson Business Press.

Myers, M.B.S., Cavusgil, S.T. and Diamontopolus, A. (2002) 'Antecedents and actions of export pricing strategy: a conceptual framework and research propositions', *Journal of European Marketing*, 36 Iss.1/2.

Sarathy, R., Terpstra, V. and Russow. (2006) *International marketing*, 9th edn. Dryden Press.

CHAPTER 12

INTERNATIONAL MARKETING IMPLEMENTATION THROUGH ENABLING TECHNOLOGIES

INTRODUCTION

Technology is at the forefront of economic development and the increasingly global marketplace. Many of the changes taking place in global marketing, such as global sourcing, social networking and mobile access to the media, have been accelerated because of advances in technology.

As we saw in the first section of the book, technology is a major driver of both the pace and magnitude of change in international marketing. It provides more immediate methods of gathering marketing information from around the world and quicker and more effective methods of analysis and prediction of future customer needs and wants.

It also provides the enabling mechanism by which effective and integrated responses can be made to change and is therefore an essential element in the development of the international marketing strategy. Technology both influences and underpins the choice of implementation strategies of the marketing mix, facilitates the process of learning and sharing best practice and enables the more effective control of a firm's diverse international activities.

High labour costs in developed countries compared to those in emerging markets limit the capability of many organisations to add value through manufacturing and services and they must instead focus on technological, business process and marketing innovations to achieve competitive advantage in global markets.

In this chapter, therefore, we focus upon the ways in which technological, business and marketing innovation have facilitated further development of international marketing, in providing solutions to international marketing problems and the mechanisms to exploit opportunities. The technology tools that are available to develop appropriate strategic responses will be identified and, as we shall see, this often involves integrating separate elements of international marketing into a cohesive approach, for example through supply chain and customer relationship management. Finally, we focus on the challenges and opportunities faced in international markets in the future and consider the role enabling technologies will play in them.

LEARNING OBJECTIVES

After reading this chapter you should be able to:

- Understand how technology has presented opportunities and posed challenges for international marketing strategy development

- Appreciate the role of the enabling technologies in the international marketing strategy process

- Identify the technology enabling tools and their use in the international marketing strategy

- Understand the integration of solutions to international marketing strategy problems through the use of enabling technologies

- Identify the challenges posed by the use of enabling technologies now and in the future

THE ENABLING TECHNOLOGIES

Down the centuries, advances in technology, business and marketing innovations have provided solutions for business problems, such as in design, manufacturing, operations, internal and external communications, inventory control, managing finances and so on. Technological advances have enabled innovative firms to make product and service developments that provide distinctive benefits to customers. The technology is either industry sector specific or generic in nature. Of course, a specific industry technology may sometimes start off being used in one sector and over time be transferred to others. For example, the Internet was initially developed for use in the defence industry. Marketing innovations have often built on and enhanced technological advances, for example, in the mobile phone sector.

However, it is the IT and communications technologies of the past three decades that have been all-pervasive, grown at a phenomenal rate and had a major impact on the way business is done. In particular, the Internet has had the effect of 'shrinking the world' and has facilitated the worldwide integration of the different technologies, systems and processes that are being used locally by different parts of the organisation and its partners. It enables experts around the world to be accessed virtually and instantly. When some advanced GE medical equipment being used to treat a child broke down in the middle of the night in the US the customer was not able to get hold of a local engineer. However, it was normal working hours for the call-centre in France. The problem could be diagnosed online and expert help provided from France to solve the problem.

We refer here to enabling technologies, because there is no single technology that supports international marketing. The major steps forward in recent years have been associated with the integration of many technologies, such as those that support e-commerce, information management, mobile telecommunications, computer-aided design, process, inventory and logistics management. So, enabling technologies in international marketing provide the solutions to old problems, such as how can customers in remote locations around the world contribute to the design of a new global product as much as the customer next door, how can a ten-person business market its products or services to its potential customers in 40 or 50 countries and how can an organisation use the advocates for its products to share their good experiences with potential customers around the world? Managing market entry in so many countries through agents and distributors would probably be beyond the resources of most small businesses.

Technology does not change the elements, challenges and dilemmas associated with the international marketing process, such as the impact of culture on international marketing, the need to make products and services available to customers worldwide with minimum investment and the need to achieve a balance between the standardisation and adaptation of the international marketing process and programmes, but it does have a major impact on the nature of the international marketing strategy that is used and improves the effectiveness of the possible solutions.

Technological innovation

In considering the application of technology it useful to focus specifically upon how technology innovation both creates new marketing opportunities for firms (see Illustration 12.1) and also helps firms and their managers to address the international marketing challenges. Technology often both drives change and provides a means of responding to change. The development of new and existing technology allows things to be done better and faster than before. At the outset, however, it is important to emphasise that technology is of no value until it has a practical application. As illustrated in Figure 12.1, those firms that are first to embrace a new technology and find a practical application, for example in creating a new product or service or a new route to market, will gain a new source of competitive advantage. However, this might well set new standards for the industry sector that will mean that competitors will also have to achieve those standards if they wish to compete in the future. Global communications make customers worldwide aware of the latest products and create a demand, so all competitors

---

ILLUSTRATION 12.1

A new challenge for the energy sector

Climate change presents both threats and opportunities for international marketing. Clearly the energy sector influences most human activities to some degree and therefore it affects and is affected by all the macro and micro-environmental forces. The public are concerned about their own personal future existence and prosperity, politicians see climate change as a way of gaining the support of voters but also recognise that they might be blamed for having to change people's lifestyles through legislation and taxation. For firms there are huge potential new costs that are incurred by having to adapt to higher energy costs and possible damage to their reputation if they are seen as wasteful of resources.

Various specific global business opportunities are emerging, for example, energy and environmental management, consultancy and training, identifying and developing new sources and types of energy, and the management of carbon trading. Whilst these are global opportunities they vary according to the local situation and the entrepreneurial capability of the firms exploiting them. Richard Branson made a widely publicised decision to invest US$3 billion, the equivalent of the projected profits from his firm Virgin Atlantic, in renewable energy technologies.

For international marketing, climate change offers challenges – opportunities and threats – throughout the international marketing process and, not least, the need to adopt an ethical marketing stance.

QUESTION *Choosing one industry sector or company, identify where technology is being used to address specific challenges. What role does and should international marketing play in implementing the technological change?*

SOURCE: ROBIN LOWE

in the sector have to catch up by embracing the new technology if they wish to survive. Moreover, the innovative firm has to find a new technological advance that allows them to get ahead again.

Communications technology helps people around the world to become more aware of changes in the market environment and to the response of companies to those changes in the form of products and services. Customers have changing lifestyles, are more easily bored with their existing products and services and are always looking for innovative new products and services that will regain their interest. They are less brand-loyal, so if one firm does not meet the needs of international customers then a competitor will. Customers find out about the global development of new products, have new ways of assessing their suitability and use new quicker and more cost-effective ways of accessing products. Customers want it and they want it now!

Businesses must respond to the changes in order to retain and develop their customers. With technology changing so quickly it is necessary to make choices about where to focus the business activity. Timing too is critical. In the telecoms sector firms paid huge fees for third-generation mobile phone licenses years before customer demand and applications were sufficient to make them worthwhile.

The rate of growth of the Internet has outstripped the rate of growth in the early years of other communications technologies such as telephone, radio and television. However, it is important to recognise that many people in emerging economies do not even have access to these old technologies, let alone the latest information and telecommunications technology, and so the division between rich and poor nations will further increase.

There are interesting examples of innovation that are appropriate to the specific situation, such as the development by Trevor Bayliss of the wind-up radio for remote areas of Africa.

Often the innovative application of technology enables some countries to leapfrog existing technology, as shown in Illustration 12.2, and miss out an entire stage of development. For example, the cost of a fixed line telecommunications structure would be prohibitively expensive in some largely rural countries of Africa, but mobile telephony and satellite systems are more cost-effective and bypass the poor quality or non-existent infrastructure. Many isolated communities are not linked to electricity supply systems, but local solar energy systems are used to power communications equipment, and recharge mobile phone batteries.

FIGURE 12.1
The vicious circle of technology and competitive advantage

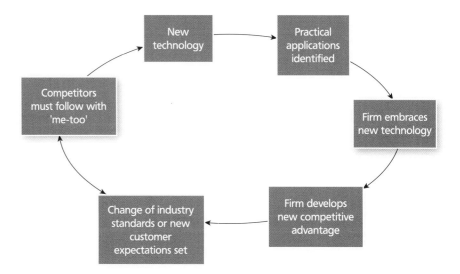

The challenge, of course, is to find a way of reducing the cost of these advanced technical solutions in emerging economies.

An advanced infrastructure is needed to support e-business, but care must be taken in developing it. The UK Department for International Development in research in Bangladesh, Kenya and South Africa claimed that a number of software sellers sold expensive software in emerging economies which was inappropriate. Except in a few cases business has not accelerated for firms from

ILLUSTRATION 12.2

Mobile phones aid African development

Many of the things that readers in developed and developing countries take for granted, such as good roads, democracy, energy and water on tap, are just not available in Africa. It is for these reasons, as well as war and corruption, that Africa missed out on the last industrial revolution that fuelled the phenomenal growth of Asia. It is technology and particularly access to global communications through the Internet that

threatens to bypass Africa again. The continued corruption and war means that significant amounts of international aid will continue to be misused or misappropriated and the essential infrastructure to support internal and international trade will still not be built. If African countries are to develop then they have to skip this stage in economic and social development.

One in three adults now carry a mobile phone in Kenya and the economic and social impact has been huge. Coverage is about 80 per cent meaning that even in remote Masai villages in the Rift Valley families can keep in touch. The vital infrastructure, an efficient, country-wide network, was built in four years by the two providers Celtel and Safaricom, part-owned by Vodafone. This contrasts with the decades of work done and not completed on the roads and railways. The main road between Nairobi and Mombassa, the principal East African port, is belatedly being completed by Chinese engineers in exchange for oil.

The matatu (minibus) owners everyday face the challenges of keeping their vehicles on the road, obtaining spare parts and keeping contact with their manic drivers, who are frequently arrested for a variety of offences. The mobile speeds up their business. The farmer in a remote area can get a text message informing him of the prices that he can obtain for his produce in the capital Nairobi, compared to his local market and they could be two or three times higher. He has never been able to do this before.

Credit cards and bank accounts are not common in Kenya, so the launch in 2007 of a service allowing money to be sent by mobile phone could revolutionise local trade, creating a much more liquid economy. Even the shanty towns that have been subjected in the past to brutal destruction by the authorities have a network that enables them to receive early warning of trouble.

Of course teenagers use mobile phones for leisure as they do worldwide, but perhaps the surprising things is that it is poor kids as well as rich kids that are part of the revolution. The obvious question is how can customers recharge their mobile phone batteries in a country where electricity is frequently unavailable? The answer again is an example of skipping a technology step – they use solar panels.

QUESTION *How can technological change and international marketing combine to help developing countries?*

SOURCE: ADAPTED FROM P. MASON 'FROM MATATA TO THE MASAI VIA MOBILE', BBC NEWS ONLINE, 8 JANUARY, 2007

poor countries that have gone online. The reason given is that buyers from developed countries, such as the US, need to build a personal relationship with suppliers from emerging economies before they are prepared to take the risk of doing business online. There also needs to be a supportive business infrastructure, including appropriate banking facilities.

Disruptive technologies

From time to time technological advances make existing products and services redundant and sometimes challenge the existence of businesses if they fail to react. For example, the conventional worldwide photography sector was virtually destroyed by digital camera technology, severely damaging companies such as Kodak. Traditional fixed line telephony was the cornerstone of the former state-owned telecommunications firms for over a century, but the introduction of voice-over-Internet-protocol (VoIP) using software such as Skpe has completely changed the economics of the sector.

Convergent technology

An important trend is the integration of technologies and technology gadgets for consumer markets so, for example, the mobile phone became a mobile communications device that embraces not just voice, text and games but also downloaded music, video, television and Internet access. In the same way traditional home television and recording devices are merging with personal computers. Integration goes further because revenues can be generated by products (such as the hardware – the mobile phone or DVD player), services (e.g. broadband Internet access) and content (e.g. music, podcasts, videos, games).

As Dilemma 12.1 shows, whilst integration is inevitable the dilemma for firms in the sector is whether to try to provide the complete solution under one brand or to use a cooperative strategy.

DILEMMA 12.1

Technology convergence: one brand or pick and mix?

The integration of technologies, supported by communications technologies, leads to fully mobile computing that allows 'computing' to control multiple functions, for example, it can control many activities within the home – not just leisure, but also security and energy efficiency. There are a handful of extremely powerful global players that are driving the consumer integration innovation, such as Sony, Apple and Microsoft, but their strategies are based upon persuading consumers to purchase their own complete solution of hardware and software products. In the recent past companies have moved away from competitive strategies of this nature and, perhaps mainly driven by the open access nature of the

Internet, towards a 'pick and mix' strategy, which allowed consumers to freely choose products, services and content from different providers because they were usually compatible.

There would not be room for more than a small number of very dominant global brands, supported by their supply chain partners to offer complete integrated solutions. Independent firms that supply associated products (and customers) have to decide whether or not they wish to align themselves with one major supplier. If a rival solution proves to be most popular and successful, it could be an expensive mistake for the 'losing' global brand, their supply chain and customers.

QUESTION *What are the arguments for and against aligning a firm's marketing strategy alongside one powerful brand in the consumer electronics market?*

The prevelance of information and communication technology in developing countries

Internet World Stats (2007) estimate that there are 1.1 billion Internet users worldwide, representing 16.9 per cent of the world's population. This included 400 million in Asia (10.7 per cent of the population), 315 million in Europe (38.9 per cent) 233 million in the US (69.7 per cent) and just 33 million in Africa. This compares with an estimate of 655 million in 2003, one-tenth of the world's population.

In its Information Economy Report Unctad (2006) emphasised that it was the use of broadband for Internet connections by business that was most significant in facilitating more sophisticated e-business processes, thus maximising the benefits of information and communications technology by increasing competitiveness and productivity. In rich countries, particularly in Europe, business broadband users were increasing rapidly, whereas in poor countries where there was any Internet connection at all, it was still dial-up. Unctad concluded this was a major reason why business in developing countries would still be constrained. Moreover, it meant that other activities including e-government, e-learning and remote working were almost non-existent in developing countries.

By contrast Unctad estimated that mobile phone users in developing countries (1.2 billion) exceeded users in developed countries (800 million). However, penetration levels were very different at over 100 per cent in some developed countries compared to less than 10 per cent in many developing countries. The high growth in developing countries has been the result of low price, pre-paid payment schemes.

The other interesting developments in information and communications technology (ICT) were that in a ten-year period exports of computer and information services grew six times faster than total export services and the share of developing countries in the computer and information sector exports increased from 4 per cent to 20 per cent.

Clearly, to benefit from ICT sector development either as a supplier or to use it to support business and international marketing, governments must facilitate provision of the supporting infrastructure and international firms must see the potential benefit from their investments.

THE INTERNET AND E-BUSINESS

The Internet, from its origins in 1969, has developed into an unstructured network of computers linking private and business users around the world, allowing them to communicate and transfer data instantly and relatively inexpensively. The computer networks are linked by telephone lines, fibre optic cables, microwave relays and satellite. Individual users gain access to the Internet from their computer through portals that provide powerful search engines (such as Google and Yahoo!) to find the information and services they need.

The main Internet services are email (individual electronic messaging), the World Wide Web (the collection of electronic files that provide the information content that is read using a Web browser, such as Microsoft Internet Explorer) and Usenet (the network of discussion newsgroups). The Internet also supports extranets, which are private networks that make connections between organisations, and intranets, which are the networks that make connections within organisations.

The Internet has had a profound effect on the way that individuals and organisations from developed countries now communicate around the world. Words, both stationary and video images, sound and complex data can be transferred instantly to the most remote parts of the world. The effect has been dramatic on the way that firms carry out their international trade. No longer is international marketing limited by the physical boundaries of the media footprint or the salesperson's or distribution company's territory. Moreover, new developments in Wireless Application Protocol (WAP) allow Web pages to be viewed on hand-held devices, such as mobile phones and organisers, whilst travelling.

The provision of this virtual infrastructure for electronic communication has created huge business opportunities for firms supplying information technology hardware and software, consultancy, business support services and telecommunications businesses, such as IBM, Cisco, Deloitte Consulting and Vodafone. For e-businesses the role of the Internet is to provide a global marketplace that is open to everyone, and particularly:

- a method of collecting, searching for and exchanging marketing and business information
- an alternative route to market to traditional distribution channels
- a means of building customer relationships
- a device for the digital delivery of certain information services
- a networked system for managing the supply chain, and
- a virtual marketplace, trading floor and auction house.

The Internet also provides a mechanism for social networking through dedicated websites. The relevance of social networking for international marketing, which will be discussed in more detail later, is that it provides the opportunity for individuals and groups to discuss new products and services, problems encountered in dealing with organisations and dissatisfaction with the behaviour of organisations.

The purpose of websites

Websites are created by individuals and organisations as a shop window for activities. Whilst they are used for many purposes, their relevance for international marketing falls into four main categories:

- Organisation sites
- Service online
- Information online
- Business transactions online.

Organisation sites

Many organisations use their website to provide information to their stakeholders about the organisation, ranging from its origins, business mission and areas of activity, standards and values, brands, financial performance, job opportunities and contact points through to quite specific information about products and their applications. Firms appealing to global customers must consider the degree to which their website should build much closer relationships with customers by providing a site in the local language. Wenyu, Boonghee and Ma (2003) explain the increasing use in global communications of ethnic portals for those whose first language is not English.

There are, of course, dangers too in just translating web content without addressing the need for it to be sensitive to cultural needs.

As well as providing information about products, some sites take customers through the purchasing process. For example, BMW help customers to design their new car from a range of options, such as whether to have cruise control, petrol or diesel, metallic paint and alloy wheels, but when the customer has designed the car they are then referred to their local dealer to complete the purchase.

Service online

Online banking puts customers more in control of their accounts, enabling them to obtain information from anywhere in the world and make transactions any time of the day or night. The saving to the bank is being able to reduce the resourcing of bank branches and service centres and cut the cost of individual banking transactions.

Firms delivering packages, such as Federal Express, have been able to make huge savings on staff employed to answer queries from customers about where their package is, by providing an online tracking service around the world. The system involves applying a barcode to the package, which is then scanned each time it progresses past a key point on its journey. This information can then be transferred to the website and accessed by customers worldwide. Another example is real-time in-flight information that can be accessed online by those that are going to meet a flight, letting them know if the plane is going to be late.

Information online

Organisations in the business of providing information, such as the *Financial Times*, provide websites that enable customers to access current and archived past files of news, data and images. Often, such sites provide one level of access free, but may charge a subscription for heavier users or may require payment for more valuable information. As this information is in digital form it can be accessed and delivered online anywhere in the world.

Sites of media organisations are used to maintain and build the relationship with their consumers considerably beyond the scheduled content. The BBC site is one of the most popular and best-presented sites in the UK and provides background and supporting material for programmes, a searchable database of their own stories, news for a broad range of international consumers and the ability to access programmes online around the world. Programmes and videos can be downloaded. Information is increasingly available from many sources and big competitors provide comprehensive services.

Business transactions online

In the above types of sites, business is not transacted online but information is provided and exchanged that allows the traditional business transaction to be conducted more effectively. Increasingly, however, it is vital that customers are able to make purchases on impulse online.

INTERNATIONAL E-MARKETS AND E-MARKETING

There are a number of e-marketing business models and e-marketplaces that originally started as digital extensions of physical marketing models. These business models are consumer marketing, usually referred to as **business to consumer** (B2C), and industrial marketing, referred to as **business to business** (B2B), but others exist too.

Business to consumer

In the B2C sector, the Internet has allowed individuals or businesses of any size to set up a website as a virtual shop – an online showcase for their products and services. The best websites offer potential customers the choice of which language they wish to communicate in and are sensitive to the local culture and legal frameworks. Existing and potential customers are able to browse through the information that is available about the products and services they are seeking to buy and, at their leisure, compare an online product 'offer' with other offers from competitive websites or from the local shop. Having selected the product they wish to buy customers can purchase and pay for the product online, using credit cards to make payment. In practice, many more customers are prepared to use the Internet to carry out their information search on companies, products and services but are still unwilling to pay online because of fears about the security of online payment and the potential for fraud, or unable, because of the lack of a suitable payment method such as a credit card. Firms that have both virtual and physical stores allow customers to find out information and then choose whether to buy online or go to the store. For example, Argos (UK) allow customers to buy online or check if a product is in a physical store, in which case the customer can reserve the product and collect it later.

In principle, buyers that have access to a computer almost anywhere in the world can purchase any product or service but, in practice, certain products and services lend themselves to online retailing more than others. Products that are sold on the basis of their design or quality of manufacture may not be seen to their best effect without allowing customers to feel them and touch them.

Some services can be supplied as digital services online over the Internet. For example, information, software, financial advice, ticketless travel and music can be downloaded direct to the customer's computer.

For physical products, however, the supplier still needs a suitable distribution method to deliver the goods to the consumer. Fulfilment of the order depends on more traditional distribution, with its associated limitations of the existing infrastructure and the availability of appropriate logistics in each customer's country. Small items such as CDs and books can be posted but delivering valuable goods, very bulky goods such as furniture or goods that require special storage conditions, such as food, directly to the door also requires arrangements to be made for the customer to receive them.

Using the Internet to transact business in this way grossly underutilises its potential, however. The rather basic form of **e-commerce** improves the speed and flexibility of the purchasing process and increases the geographical reach of communications compared to the physical media. Just having a website, however, does little to build competitive advantage, or improve the overall effectiveness of the operation in winning global customers and developing their loyalty.

Moreover, without building competitive advantage and unique selling propositions, firms using the Internet to sell their products are vulnerable to lower priced offers from other global competitors, because sophisticated search engines identify the cheapest offers of comparable products or services supplied from anywhere in the world. Many companies believe they can survive and grow by offering the lowest priced products direct to customers but inevitably new entrants will always offer lower prices, even if they are not sustainable in the longer term.

E-business operations are expensive to establish and maintain, given the large outlay for information technology, systems, management and website development. Moreover, e-commerce firms require sophisticated systems and need to innovate constantly to fulfil orders promptly and accurately to retain customer interest and loyalty. The challenge for a business is therefore to maximise income. Chaffy *et al.* (2006) identify a number of opportunities for generating income from a website, for example, by charging for sponsorship, advertising and 'click-through' fees, for sales generated by a second firm that has a direct link to its own site.

Business to business (B2B)

Whereas B2C is primarily based on pre-priced products made to a standard specification, albeit with some exceptions, the interactions in B2B are much more complex because of the one-off nature of many transactions. Interactions involve the exchange of significant amounts of information between the seller and customer before, during and after any transaction. The information includes such things as specifications, designs and drawings, purchase contracts, manufacturing and delivery schedules, inventory control, negotiation of price and delivery. The information comes from different departments within the firms and is exchanged between the firms.

For many years firms have been using information technology to improve the efficiency and effectiveness of the internal firm processes, for example demand forecasting, inventory control, computer-aided design and manufacturing: the Internet enables this to be linked with external organisations and customers. The Internet has enabled a far wider range of data to be exchanged without restriction on the number of participant organisations. The mechanisms by which the exchanges take place and business can be transacted are Web portals. These are 'hubs' where all the interested participants congregate. Typically there are two types of hubs:

- **industry-specific hubs**, such as automobile or aerospace manufacturing; and
- **function-specific hubs**, such as advertising or human resource management.

Using e-hubs, firms improve the efficiency of the processes of transactions and thereby lower costs. The hubs can reduce the transaction cost by bringing together all the purchasing requirements of many hundreds of customers world-wide (Kaplan and Sawhney 2000). E-hubs attract many buyers who are able to negotiate bulk discounts on behalf of a range of smaller, individual buyers.

If the products are commodities with no need to negotiate specifications then dynamic pricing enables buyers and sellers to negotiate prices and volumes in real time. In sectors such as energy purchasing the peaks and troughs of supply and demand can be smoothed.

The US originally dominated B2B and much of the innovation in B2B came from the US, but firms around the world recognise that the potential savings can be quite significant with the increasing internationalisation of sourcing and supply chain management. A culture change in the attitude of firms is needed as companies that may normally be competing can cooperate for the mutual benefit of reducing costs.

The benefits of e-procurement, such as convenience and cost saving through group purchasing, appeal to governments for public sector and private–public sector purchasing but often progress is much slower than in private business.

Timmers (1999) has identified other internet business models involving exchange between supplier and customer. These include the following.

Consumer to consumer (C2C)

Consumers sell to each other through an online auction. eBay is the most successful site for trading between individuals who buy and sell antiques, collectable items and memorabilia by virtual bidding. This type of buying and selling tends to become almost a hobby in itself for customers. eBay takes a fee to insert the advertisement and a fee based on the final value. In the UK by 2007 it was estimated that over 65 000 people generated a substantial part or all of their income through trading on eBay. eBay has been very successful internationally but has had problems competing in certain markets. It pulled out of Japan and failed to compete with Alibaba, as Illustration 12.3 shows, partly because it did not really understand the Chinese culture.

ILLUSTRATION 12.3

Jack Ma creating Chinese entrepreneurs

To thousands of Chinese, Jack Ma has achieved rock star status to the point where he needs bodyguards to hold back the adoring fans. He has achieved this status by enabling them to become their own boss – a dream ingrained in the Chinese culture. Ma set up Alibaba which is now the world's largest B2B market place and, through the acquisition of Yahoo! China, the twelfth most popular website in the world, making it a challenger to US global online giants, Google, eBay, Yahoo! and Amazon. Alibaba has become a leader in its own right though its own innovations that deliver value to users.

Alibaba has two B2B websites at its heart, alibaba.com, a marketplace for firms across the world to trade in English, and china.alibaba.com, a domestic Chinese service. Whilst the aim of rival western sites, such as Ariba and Commerce One, was to cut the procurement costs for multinationals, Alibaba's was to build markets for many Chinese SMEs, which make a vast

PHOTO CREDIT: PETER PARKS/GETTY IMAGES

array of manufactured goods available to western traders, who might resell on eBay.

Ma has led the Chinese development of online communities and social networking with a consumer auction site, Taobao, that has an innovation that reflects a cultural difference. Whereas eBay transactions are between largely anonymous buyers and sellers, Taobao facilitates instant messaging, voicemail and allows personal photographs and details to be posted, creating a community of 'friends' in a country where there is still a lack of trust.

Ma has also addressed the problem of settlement risks in online payments in China, where there are no credit cards, by introducing AliPay, which holds cash until the goods are delivered. AliPay is effectively an online bank that is able to maintain many thousands of supplier and customer credit histories. AliPay was so successful that by 2007 there were 300 000 non-users of Alibaba and Taobao who used AliPay, so the company decided to start charging them commission.

Alibaba International claims to be the world's largest B2B marketplace for global trade with 500 000 people visiting the site every day and Alibaba China is the largest site for domestic China trade with 16 million registered users. Taoboa has 30 million registered users and is the largest e-commerce website in Asia.

The interesting aspect of Ma is that he is a business entrepreneur rather than a computer geek like the founders of Yahoo! and Google. He believes that 'someone as dumb as me should be able to use technology'. He will not accept a new feature unless he can understand it and use it.

Ma is keen to grow the business believing that forecast expansion could create another 1 million jobs in China by 2010.

QUESTION *What are the critical success factors in creating a successful B2B and C2C electronic market place?*

SOURCE: ADAPTED FROM 'JACK MA IS ATTRACTING A FOLLOWING AMONG ENTREPRENEURS IN CHINA AND INTERNET COMPANIES WORLDWIDE' *THE ECONOMIST* 21 SEPTEMBER 2006, 'TAOBAO'S ALIPAY WILL CHARGE FEES' 16 MARCH, 2007 *HTTP://WWW.CHINATECHNEWS.COM* AND 'ALIBABA IPO WOULD TOUCH US$1 BILLION' 1 JUNE 2007 ACCESSED AT *HTTP://WWW.CHINAECONOMICREVIEW.COM/IT/CATEGORY/SERVICES/*

Consumer to business (C2B)

This works in reverse to the normal type of auction as consumers join together to reduce the prices they pay through bulk buying. A final date is set and the price falls as more customers join the buying group. Whilst this is an established model in the business-to-business sector, it is less well established in C2B. Sites such as www.letsbuyit.com facilitate the process. Priceline.com is similar but provides a mechanism for consumers to say what they are prepared to pay for a product or service, such as an airline flight. Suppliers decide whether they are prepared to accept the offer.

It is increasingly recognised that whilst online retailing has many benefits as a route to market for international development, a combination of virtual and physical routes to market might deliver the best results for many businesses. Amazon.com formed an alliance with Toys R Us and increased its own warehousing capacity to increase the speed and quality of its service. Barnes and Noble has 1000 bookstores in the US and has joined with Bertelsmann (Germany) to provide online retailing. Amazon has also provided the technology on which other alliance partners have built e-business platforms.

THE IMPACT OF E-BUSINESS ON INTERNATIONAL MARKETING

Disintermediation and reintermediation

The Internet offers the possibility for an organisation to efficiently handle many more transactions than was possible previously. An evaluation of the contribution of the channel might lead to a reassessment of the value of the intermediary and a decision to remove the intermediary. The benefits to the organisation are the removal of channel infrastructure costs and intermediary margins and the opportunity to develop a direct relationship with the final customer. 'Cutting out the middleman' is described as disintermediation. Chaffey *et al.* (2006) observes that at the start of the e-business boom it was expected that there would be widespread disintermediation. In some sectors there has been disintermediation, but in others the results have been disappointing with the marketing organisation incurring substantial additional IT, order management and logistics costs, offsetting the forecast savings. Other sectors have continued without significant restructuring. In practice it seems that in many sectors customers still need additional help from an intermediary in selecting products and services.

The counter change to disintermediation is re-intermediation and the creation of new firms to provide the purchasing advice in a different form. Whilst many financial services products and offers from utilities lend themselves to online selling, it is a laborious task to compare the many offerings from competing companies. Consequently many brokers have set up websites such as Uswitch and moneyextra to allow customers to compare many different financial product offerings.

In many sectors now there are intermediary websites that enable potential customers to compare products for the home, holidays and travel. Of course this means that the Internet marketer must ensure that they are represented on key sites where there are high volumes of potential customers and ensure that they are offering competitive prices.

Alternatively the marketer might set up his own intermediary to compete with the existing intermediaries: this is referred to as countermediation. A group of airlines set up www.Opodo.com as an alternative to www.expedia.com to offer airline tickets and Thomson Travel Group set up www.latedeals.com to compete with www.lastminute.com for late holiday bookings.

Social networking

Social networking has always been a feature of the Internet and, for example, people recorded web logs before the term 'blogs', which focus on what is happening in a person's life and on the web, was coined. Websites with automated publishing systems such as blogger.com accelerated the process. As early as 1995 Amazon allowed users to write reviews and consumer guides. Collaborative learning and collaborative working have been encouraged by, for example, Lotus Notes and Lotus Domino.

The phrase Web 2.0 was coined to indicate a second generation of Web services including social networking websites and online communications tools and emphasises collaboration using the web as a platform, users owning and exercising control over the data rather than hierarchical control being exercised.

Weblogs, chat rooms and community websites, such as CraigsList, MySpace and Bebo provide a platform for millions of consumers to air their views. It was estimated that in 2007 there were 20 million blogs worldwide with 75 000 started every day. Blogs are updated thousands of times an hour. Many of the comments relate to product, services and opinions about companies and it is essential for organisations to know what is being said about them. This requires intelligent search engines, such as Attentio, that can dig deeper than general searches and aggregate the data to provide a fuller picture of the trends and conversations that are taking place.

INTERNATIONAL MARKETING SOLUTION INTEGRATION

The most significant international marketing strategy development that is facilitated by technology is business solution integration. As competition increases, so firms must seek to find new sources of competitive advantage, secure ever-lower costs, increase their speed of action and offer new innovative products and services perceived by customers to be valuable. They must also develop better relationships with their customers and business partners in order to retain their business. The strategy to achieve these outcomes is based on the effective integration of the elements of the marketing and business processes.

Knowledge management

The move to an increasingly global market served by e-business has prompted firms to redefine their sources of competitive advantage. In a global market the traditional sources of competitive advantage can be easily challenged. A company that operates in a small number of countries or within a restricted business sector may believe that its competitive advantage comes from low-cost manufacturing, design capability, sales expertise and distribution efficiency. However, when exposed to global competition it may find that its own competitive advantage cannot be transported to new countries and discover, instead, that regional or global competitors have even greater competitive advantage in their own domestic market as well as in the target country market.

By contrast, knowledge, expertise and experience have the potential to be transferable if they can be effectively collected, stored, accessed and communicated around the world (hence the term knowledge management). Below we discuss the processes for managing knowledge to support the customer–client interface, but knowledge management is essential to maximise added value throughout the supply chain. There is a danger in building competitive advantage through knowledge management, of course, because the knowledge assets of a firm are locked into their staff and their records, typically contained in their computers. Staff are becoming increasingly mobile, computer systems are still notoriously insecure and the potential loss of knowledge to a competitor is an ever greater problem for firms.

Supply chain management

Technology-enabled supply chain management has helped firms to grow through exploiting market development opportunities, reducing investment by buying rather than manufacturing components, and enabling small firms to have similar costs to large firms through e-procurement. It is vital that each part of the supply chain of the product maximises the added value and this is made possible by integrating the activities. A supply chain for a complex product might typically involve such distinctly different activities as design, manufacture of raw materials, component assembly, advertising, logistics and local servicing. It is highly unlikely that one company could be the leader in each of these areas of activity, particularly when the most efficient members of the supply chain will increasingly be located around the world.

The implications, of course, are that through using e-commerce for procurement, partnerships can be set up and dissolved instantly. Of course, suppliers need to have huge flexibility and excellent systems to manage the rapid changes that are necessary to survive in this type of market. Suppliers are in completely open competition with other firms around the world.

Cost savings can be made in all areas of the supply chain, such as inventory reduction and just in time sourcing. Amazon is able to offer millions of books and music titles and other items by quickly obtaining stocks held anywhere in the world, whereas an average traditional bookstore might physically hold only 170 000 titles. Savings can be made in evaluating suppliers, specifications and delivery times and arranging scheduling. Marketing costs can be reduced because it is easier, quicker and cheaper to make alterations to Web content than incur the design and printing costs of a new brochure. For small firms, using e-procurement can have similar costs to large firms and so increase their competitiveness.

Advantest America Inc. supplies measuring instruments, semiconductor test systems and related equipment. It outsourced its delivery of its replacement parts, e-commerce and supply chain management services to FedEx Corporation, which provides transport. Using FedEx's sophisticated, integrated systems it was able to reduce its delivery times by more than 50 per cent, to 48 hours in Asia and 24 hours for customers in America and Europe. Previously, starting from the time the order was taken, it could take between 25 and 42 hours even to get through customs and on to a commercial aeroplane. Extending the system to the firm's customised printed circuit boards would avoid the need for the customer to hold stock on site, thus considerably reducing their inventory.

Every element in the logistics process must be tackled in order to improve performance and an example of this appears in Illustration 12.4. In service callcentres the cost of employing a person capable of dealing with service calls in India is about one-tenth of the cost of employing a person in the UK for an equivalent level of performance. Very often service centre calls are routine and technology can be used to make further savings by replacing people-based transactions with 'intelligent' computer-based responses.

Value chain integration

The key question is how effectively the individual supply chain members around the world work in partnership to maximise the effectiveness of their contributions towards improving efficiency and adding value across the entire value chain, so-called value chain integration. Success is then likely to be dependent on the effectiveness of the working relationship between the members of the supply chain, the speed and openness of information sharing and the degree of collaboration between each company, its suppliers and customers, with the objective of adding value and removing transaction costs.

So, for example, a supermarket chain will allow its hundreds of suppliers to have access to its data warehouse, so they will know how their particular product is selling in each individual store, and to the inventory system to ensure that the supermarket never runs out of stock. This system makes it easier for additional suppliers to be included and managed at low additional cost, allowing consumers more choice and more competitive prices.

Virtual enterprise networks

The possibility for Internet technology-supported collaboration between supply chain members is being extended and applied to SMEs and individuals with

ILLUSTRATION 12.4

Toyota supply chain challenges in Bangalore

The challenge for Transport Corporation of India (TCI) is to deliver parts to Toyota's factory near Bangalore. Toyota operates a just in time delivery system at its factories, where suppliers usually deliver to a staging post near the factory often run by a logistics partner, from where the parts are taken directly to the production line, when and where they are needed. Toyota expects deliveries to be made every two hours with a reliability level in excess of 99 per cent.

PHOTO CREDIT: DANITA DELIMONT/ALAMY

However, the conditions are far worse for just in time delivery in Bangalore than the locations of many of Toyota's other factories around the world. Roads are in poor condition and congested with traffic. Crossing from one state to another can involve hours of queues at the border and endless red tape. With average speeds of around 30–40 km per hour components from the most distant supplier 2000 km away could take a week to deliver.

Toyota taught TCI how to do it. TCI set up a joint venture logistics partnership with Mitsui, a Japanese trading group (*Sogo shosha*) and have cut stocks, saving US$100 million a year in financing costs. Whilst technology is essential for efficient supply chain management some more basic management actions were needed. For example, drivers were trained to look after the load, wear seat belts and drive less aggressively.

Supply chain management provides considerable scope for cost saving and technology and logistics innovation have contributed to this. Logistics costs represented 13 per cent of GDP in India, compared with 21 per cent in China, down from 25 per cent in 1991, and 11 per cent in Europe. It is in the US where the greatest efficiencies have been made. In 1982 logistics represented 14.5 per cent of GDP but now it is down to 8 per cent and inventory costs are estimated to have been reduced by 60 per cent.

QUESTION *Explain how cost savings can be made through using an international supply chain.*

SOURCE: ADAPTED FROM 'CARGO CULTS', *THE ECONOMIST*, 15 JUNE, 2006

complementary expertise that form themselves into a virtual enterprise network to bid for and carry out projects and routine business. Snyder (2005) explains that the Internet has reduced transaction costs and outsourcing risks, enabling the individuals and organisations to form a more efficient form of organisation, based on virtually integrated collaborative networks rather than hierarchical bureaucracies. Virtual enterprise networks are expected to become more common, international in nature and focused on international marketing opportunities.

Customer relationship management

Customer relationship management (CRM) is the process of identifying, attracting, differentiating and retaining customers (Hoffman 2003). It allows a firm to focus its efforts on its most lucrative customers, no matter where they are from, and is based on the 'rule' that 80 per cent of a firm's profits come from 20 per cent of its customers. It is also designed to achieve efficient and effective customer management. As pressures on costs and prices increase firms must manage customers as inexpensively as they can without losing customer loyalty. To answer a customer query with an automatic Web-based service can be less than a tenth of the cost of a person handling it by telephone through a service call centre, but the question is whether it can be as responsive to customer queries.

CRM allows customers to be categorised on the basis of their past profitability. The most profitable customers will be recognised and will be routed to the area that will handle calls fastest. For example, this can be done automatically by transferring telephone calls with a particular number. The profitable customers can then be targeted with attractive deals. The information is shared throughout the company to ensure integration of the firm's activities so that profitable customers get priority service throughout the firm and also from partner firms.

To deliver a CRM strategy the key component is the database of customer information. Techniques and systems are used to manage and extract data (data mining) to identify trends and analyse customer characteristics that enable the targeting to be carried out. Javalgi, Radulovich, Pendelton and Scherer (2005) have developed a framework for providing managerial insights into building and sustaining a competitive advantage using a consumer-centric approach, coupled with CRM technology on a global scale.

There are some limitations with CRM. Customers may well find out that they are not a priority customer and may resent not receiving 'first class' treatment. The system involves the retention of large amounts of detailed information about individual customers in a firm database. Customers often resent firms holding information about them and in some countries it would infringe privacy laws. Companies analyse the data that they have but only past behaviour has been recorded and so this data may not be an accurate predictor of future behaviour. Finally, there is an assumption that customers want a 'relationship' with suppliers and that in some way they will benefit from it. If the benefit is not clear, then customers will not remain loyal.

Customisation

As we have suggested on a number of occasions, customers increasingly want to be treated as individuals and not simply be the unwilling targets of mass market advertising. The Internet allows companies to mass customise their offering and a variety of firms are exploiting the flexibility of online communication. A number of firms are providing software applications that are designed to personalise or more individually target the firm's interactions. For example, Lindgren (2003) explains how Poindexter (US) uses statistical analysis to identify the shared characteristics of online advertising viewers, and be able to cluster those customers who respond to websites and online advertisements in a similar way. The clusters can then be offered a customised marketing mix and customised promotions and product offers. For example, an online shopper who puts products in an online basket but does not go through with the purchase might be offered a discount by the online retailer, as an incentive to go through with the purchase. As more viewers are analysed the system learns the best response and so delivers better performance. A potential customer of insurance group Norwich Union (UK) might complete an online application for car insurance but not buy online. The customer might receive a cash-back offer by email and, if this does not work, a further cash-back offer by post with a prompt to phone the call centre to confirm the service.

Customers can be targeted and made aware of special deals being offered in their own neighbourhood, perhaps on travel, at a restaurant or at the wine shop. Global positioning systems coupled with mobile telephony enable firms to text consumers about deals available in the shop that they are just passing.

THE IMPACT ON INTERNATIONAL MARKETING STRATEGY

Having discussed the central role of the Internet as a technology enabler of international marketing and highlighted the various elements of the electronic marketplace, we now turn to how these can both influence and support the much more dynamic approach to international marketing strategy development that we mentioned at the start of this chapter.

The impact of technology on analysis

Demand patterns are now changing more quickly because of changes in the environment, customer needs and wants and competition, and so it is increasingly vital for firms to be able to track changes through an effective marketing information system. Much of the data that must be gathered from around the world can be more effectively collected, managed and communicated through integrated Web-based systems. Firms can track political, economic and legal changes and new product launches by competitors as they are announced by using search engines and sites that provide up to date expert analysis. Point of sale information can be collected and analysed by retailers on a daily basis to provide information about what products are selling and not selling so that appropriate action can be taken to avoid unnecessary inventory, and build a supply chain that is flexible and responsive. For example, for clothing products sourced from Asia to sell in the US, the fabric production, garment making and logistics must be fast, flexible and quickly adaptable to changing fashion needs to avoid stock write-offs or write-downs.

In the past fashion magazines and newspaper articles provided information about the latest trend and images of celebrities wearing the next 'cool' brand or 'must have' product. Now social networking websites provide the response from customers that are likely to affect their purchasing habits. Because of the informal, non-regulated nature of the websites firms can influence their perceptions of the products, as we discuss later in this section.

The Internet provides not only general information about the firm's products but also information that can be used for promotion and product development by providing direct and indirect indications of consumer behaviour. It is easier and faster to apply questionnaires to existing and potential customers around the world by using the Internet. Customer behaviour can be monitored on websites by tracking navigation through the site to provide new insights, thought processes and predict likely purchasing intentions.

The Internet provides some negative information as well, from blogs and social networking sites, as Dilemma 12.2 shows. Firms can suffer considerable damage at the hands of such sites and Dell suffered badly in 2005, prompting the company to set up its own blog, www.dell2one.com to try to explain and counteract the damage.

As we discussed in Part 1, organisations are collecting this type of information in a much more systematic way. For example, Procter & Gamble and Unilever have a database of observed behaviour accessible to staff worldwide through an intranet.

The impact of technology on international strategy development

For some firms their international marketing strategy is inextricably linked to technology either because of the nature of the business, in the case of firms such as IBM, Microsoft and Acer, or because it is the route to market in the case of Expedia, Dell and CDWow.

DILEMMA 12.2

SOURCE: ADAPTED FROM D. RUSCHE 'ONLINE OPINION GIVES POWER TO THE PEOPLE', SUNDAY TIMES, 18 FEBRUARY, 2007

Social networking sites can make or break product marketing

Social networking is having a significant effect on the way that consumers now search for information about products and services they wish to buy. Consequently, this has implications for the international marketing strategies of firms.

Research by Yahoo in 2006 showed that 77 per cent of consumers are influenced by Internet research and on average customers spent 12 hours researching a potential purchase online but 15 hours on research of more expensive products, such as a television.

Increasingly significant in acting as sources of information are social networking websites such as Digg.com, Reddit, Newsvine and Stumbleupon, which rely on users to create content by sending in their own stories or links to stories they have found on the Web. Users vote for the stories they most like and add their own content. The most voted for stories end up on the front page, where they attract more attention and so the snowball effect continues.

Whilst on the one hand complainers from the US on the Digg website, a site claiming 20 million visitors per month, were saying that 'Steve Jobs and Apple don't produce good tech, they produce good marketing', other contributors were more positive. Smaran Dayal, an 18-year-old from Pune, India was observing that Apple's computers and iPods were revolutionary products. Dayal has 500 'friends' who track his Apple stories, so any recommendations he makes carry

500 votes and this provides a good start towards getting a story on the front page. The different aspect of this type of site from other sites, such as Google and Yahoo, that also aggregate stories is that they rank stories and also recognise the vocal nature of their users and that some are regarded as opinion formers.

There are many implications for marketing. For example, a casual remark by a senior company executive will be pounced upon by users. When he dismissed a rival product, Wii, as 'an impulse buy', a Sony senior executive attracted 270 comments, generally criticising Sony as arrogant and complaining about the high cost of Sony's Playstation 3. These individual stories may seem insignificant but they add up.

In 2005 a blogger and media commentator, Jeff Jarvis, complained about his problems with online computer seller, Dell, and this triggered an avalanche of similar complaints which led to a drop in Dell's share price. This does not illustrate the power the Internet gives to one person, rather it provides a focus for many similar individual complaints from other users to gather together.

Of course, marketing companies may see the opportunity to exploit this grass roots marketing by providing the 'seed' stories, but the risks if they were to do so are potentially huge because of the backlash if consumers found out. They see these websites as their own and not part of traditional media, and object if they are invaded by big marketing firms.

The dilemma is how can firms use social networking websites for their advantage without alienating the users?

For firms in most industry sectors technology, business and marketing innovations are a major source of international competitive advantage. As we discussed earlier, organisations in developed countries cannot compete against the low labour and other associated costs, operational scale benefits and lower research and development costs of firms from developing countries, such as India and China.

Their source of competitive advantage in the future, therefore, is likely to come from technological, business process and marketing innovation, from knowledge management of the organisation's intellectual property and assets, its ability to manage effectively and the contributions of the supply chain to maximise the customer value. For these reasons technological competence and capability, understanding the competitive market position and gaining in-depth customer insights will become key success criteria in the future.

Firms using e-marketing as a key element of their strategy are prioritising customers that are part of a segment that receive online and mobile communications are part of the social networking community and are willing and able to do business over the Internet. These organisations segment suppliers in the same way because of the lower cost of doing business with firms that are effective e-businesses. Of course, this puts firms from emerging economies that are competing to be a member of a major MNE's supply chain at a severe disadvantage if their local country infrastructure does not support e-business.

Internet-based market entry

The Internet provides a market entry method that is particularly suitable for smaller, widespread niche markets. Whilst the website might be accessible worldwide, however, the firm may need to select markets to focus on, possibly excluding those where there may be particular barriers, such as language, legal, payment and over-fulfilment problems. The cost of organising to serve certain markets might outweigh the possible benefits. For firms that already have a strong presence in many markets the Internet supports all aspects of their activity.

Web-based services will be successful if firms develop a global strategy based upon the integrated value chain. As this is a pervasive method of entry, based on global communications, it can facilitate lower-risk access to difficult markets. By building online delivery capability it is possible to serve markets profitably where there might be limited demand. Of course, an e-commerce strategy is limited in scope simply because it appeals to a very specific transnational segment – those that are able to gain access to the firm's website – but as Internet access, particularly high speed access, continues to grow this is a diminishing problem.

The impact of technology on strategy implementation and control

PRODUCT AND SERVICE MANAGEMENT

Technology supports the delivery and control of all the elements of the augmented product and service offer (Figure 8.2) and integrates the worldwide members of the supply chain, as discussed earlier in this chapter. It is also used to speed up innovation and facilitate worldwide contributions to new product and service development activity.

In doing this, technology is increasingly supporting, on the one hand, the standardisation of the components of the product, and creating worldwide product 'platforms'. For example, car firms such as VW, and household appliance manufacturers such as Whirlpool, use a common platform and make minor adaptations for different models and markets. On the other hand, however, it is enabling firms to offer increased customisation of products and services and one-to-one marketing.

PRICING

As we discussed earlier in the chapter, technology is driving down costs and prices through supply chain efficiencies, economies of scale, the experience curve effect and greater price transparency. Price transparency for customers and other stakeholders is created because of the ease with which it is now possible to compare prices offered by competing potential suppliers across borders by searching through the information on their websites. Some sites such as Expedia in travel and Kelkoo on a range of products in B2C markets and the sector and function e-hubs in B2B provide the opportunity for customers to compare prices on one site. The sophistication and usefulness of Web search activity is improving as competition between firms such as Google and Microsoft increases.

The Internet makes grey marketing easier and also makes it much more difficult for firms to operate specific geographic territories and price differentials across country borders, so grey marketing may become less of an issue in international markets as firms give up hope of trying to control it. Price transparency has the effect of driving mature products towards commoditisation in which products become less differentiated and competition is based largely on price. When there are many competitors, price transparency forces down prices as suppliers have to respond by cutting the costs of their products and services. This usually forces them to find ever-lower cost sources. The alternative is to innovate and develop new products and services or add additional services, many of which, such as loyalty reward schemes, are operated online. However, these strategies will only work if customers around the world perceive the additional services to be valuable and of additional benefit over the commodity product alternative.

Customisation is clearly the opposite of commoditisation and therefore can be used partially to counter price transparency. Because international pricing embraces both pricing and financing the transaction, technology allows pricing to be customised. It can enable complex calculations to be made to facilitate the negotiation of mutually beneficial deals between supplier and customer with flexible pricing and financing and also control non-standard repayment schedules that ensure that the transaction is ultimately profitable. An example of this from personal finance is that it is possible to offset longer-term loans, such as a mortgage to buy a house, against savings in a current account and pay interest daily on the balance outstanding.

CHANNEL MANAGEMENT

Electronic marketing has encouraged disintermediation, or the removal of intermediaries from the supply chain, as suppliers market directly to customers. Technology now enables firms to efficiently manage thousands of small transactions that previously would have been left for a local intermediary to undertake. This is possible now because e-marketing has typically lower transaction costs and is capable of managing large inventories, logistics, ordering and payments but also allows the virtual bundling of products that might be sourced from different partner suppliers. Disintermediation provides the manufacturer with stronger control of its activities in the market and avoids being so reliant on third parties. It also enables the distribution channels to be customised to the specific needs of the customers.

For those firms that are maintaining intermediaries within their distribution channel, technology allows much closer cooperation through sharing of market information but also greater control of intermediaries by making it easier to check on a daily basis that they are fulfilling their commitments to the supplier.

COMMUNICATIONS

The main advantage of e-marketing communications is that they are targeted and are often based on one-to-one communications. The most important aspect is that they are interactive. Customers are required to do something rather than being passive recipients of untargeted advertising or other promotion. As customers become more involved, so they are more likely to buy. The increase in eBay's business is quite probably due to customers spending a lot of time on the site and becoming hooked.

Clearly the attractiveness and functionality of websites is key to success but the site must make it easy for customers to buy. Siegel (1999) explains that many firms build 'introvert websites' from the inside. They reflect how the firm or an existing product range is organised in the firm rather than 'extrovert websites' which reflect the customer groups that the firm intends to attract. This is particularly important in international markets where customers must feel that the website is built for them.

Marketing through websites, even interactive ones, is reactive, because potential customers must take the initiative and locate the site first typically by using search, which as we indicate in ILA 3 is critically important. It is essential that the firm features high on the list of search results. Word of mouth referral or viral marketing is important in building traffic to the website, but to gain a large market in unexciting business sectors it is not enough just to have a web site. It is also necessary to proactively market and promote the brand and the site in the traditional media. The fundamental questions of marketing need to be asked, such as who are we targeting, where will we find the target customers on the Internet and how will we get them directed to our site? How best can we then communicate our message to them globally and at low cost? The key is to deliver the right message to the right people at the right time in the right place using the right e-based communication channels.

CONTROL, EVALUATION AND LEARNING

Technology enables firms to collect, transfer and analyse vast amounts of data from anywhere in the world. Using Enterprise Resource Planning (ERP) software they are able to control the use of resources and improve the efficiency of their operations. Financial management and control can be more immediate and more detailed. Firms use other processes and systems to control the supporting operations to ensure quality and efficiency of the manufacturing, distribution operations, and measure the effectiveness of the marketing processes and programmes.

These techniques can be applied in worldwide operations because they can be supported by information technology and systems. Underpinning all these techniques is the need to develop a learning organisation that follows good practice, shares new ideas and creates greater confidence in the abilities of its staff so that they can be empowered to take decisions in their own area of expertise and knowledge. Whilst many MNEs would claim to have developed a learning organisation within a country, few have yet genuinely achieved cross-border learning that enables them to evaluate and improve their programmes and processes based on knowledge shared worldwide.

Some limitations of e-commerce for international marketing strategy

There may be some limitations of e-commerce, for example, there may be a limit to online retailing, as Illustration 12.5 suggests, unless firms embark on new innovation.

There are some disadvantages in operating e-business globally, including the high cost of providing a global website with 24-hour service for customers who expect interactive capability, wherever possible, in their own language and culture and adapted to their own environment. There are also some significant perceived and real dangers associated with e-commerce. Customers are concerned with data security and the risks, for example, of credit card fraud. Customers are also concerned with identity theft, data protection and the use, storage and passing on to third parties of personal information to firms anywhere in the world. Of course technology is being continually developed and improved to try to overcome these difficulties.

Firms basing their business on e-commerce must recognise that there are typically low entry barriers and competitors have greater and easier access to

ILLUSTRATION 12.5

SOURCE: ADAPTED FROM 'ONLINE SALES BOOM FOR UK', SUNDAY TIMES, 22 OCTOBER, 2006

PHOTO CREDIT: RICHARD LEVINE/ALAMY

The future development of online sales

Since online retailing started in volume there has been continuing debate about what the limit might be. For example, in the UK it still only represented about 3 per cent of retail sales in 2006 but was predicted by Verdict Research to continue growing fast at least until 2010. Fast growth experienced by a few retailers has caused them problems, including consumer concern about poor levels of after-sales service, a high rate of product returns when products prove not to be what the customer expected and, particularly, pressure to make websites a more exciting experience for consumers, given the growth of broadband. Like all other forms of selling, online retail will continue to be the victim of fraud, security and other transactional problems.

The challenge for retailers has been to maintain growth by moving customers from low-priced items such as DVDs and books to more expensive items. Cars and holidays are already bought in significant numbers over the Web. Trusted retailers that have a traditional shop chain as well appear to be benefiting with consumers having the ability to view products in store before buying over the Internet. This includes food and household products. Greater interactivity in the website is essential for a generation of buyers used to combining leisure activities, work and shopping on their computer. The first steps are being taken, including the facility to have different views and close ups of clothes, paint a 'virtual room' using a brand of paint, design a car or, perhaps, read the first three pages of a novel before buying.

QUESTION *What innovations are required to accelerate online sales? Do you expect customers around the world to want the same thing?*

information that can be used to challenge the existing supplier. For example, Yell the business directory company blamed a decline in profits on a rival business set up by ex sales staff made redundant in the US by the company. Computer systems are still prone to system failure and corruption and it is still alarmingly easy for computer hackers and computer viruses to cause severe damage to multinational enterprises. Often MNEs, particularly banks, do not publicise such difficulties as it may well deter customers. There is also a proliferation of anti-MNE Web sites that can publicise damaging stories – true or not – virtually without challenge. This is possible, of course, simply because of the relatively uncontrolled nature of the Internet.

The decisions of customers in e-commerce are strongly affected by cultural issues and the patterns of growth in different cultures will continue to be different.

International e-business marketing businesses face some challenges:

1 Customers from some countries, typically low-context countries, embrace the Internet in different ways to those in high-context cultures, because of the lower emphasis placed on implicit interactions when building relationships and purchasing products.

2 Brand values often depend on the different communication methods that people use, both explicit and implicit, such as image, reputation, word of mouth and continual exposure online and offline. This emphasises the need for an integrated communications approach involving virtual and physical media.

3 By being global, e-commerce still favours global players. Consumers expect high quality of performance and image but these can be severely tarnished by a low-cost, poorly performing website and slow or inaccurate order fulfilment. One of the most important issues facing Internet advertisers is still the degree to which customers will purchase from an international company rather than a domestic company.

4 The effectiveness of websites is influenced by such factors as the ease of navigation, company and products information, shipping details and sensitivity to language and culture.

5 The barriers to entry must be significant if the defenders of domestic or limited country niches wish to retain their market share. It must be recognised by marketers that the marketing skills to ensure success in e-business are different from traditional skills, in that success depends on attracting consumers to sites and this is typically more difficult because of the increased media 'noise'.

6 The development of intelligent agents that search for specific pieces of information on markets and potential suppliers means that marketers cannot base their appeal to customers on traditional marketing-mix factors but must find a new sustainable competitive advantage.

Legislation

The aspect of the Internet that seems to raise most concern is the fact that there is very little control exerted and consequently the Internet is used for unethical and illegal purposes and to circumvent the law. The Internet has grown extremely rapidly and the application of existing law and introduction of legislation to control activities has lagged behind. Governments do not want to stifle development and so legislation is being developed not in anticipation but only as problems arise.

Problems of application of existing law to the Internet

The Internet removes traditional geographic boundaries, so that virtually anyone anywhere in the world can access a website. Zugelder, Flaherty and Johnson (2000) explain that a particular difficulty, of course, is the fact that websites are subject to the laws of individual countries, both home and host country, where customers are based. Websites are also subject to regional trade agreements (e.g. EU and NAFTA) and regulations of organisations such as the WTO, the World International Property Organisation (WIPO) and the Berne Convention on copyright law. Many countries either do not conform or interpret many conventions differently. For example, half the world nations (including China, India, Brazil and Taiwan) do not adhere to the Berne Convention.

The result is a chaotic situation in which multiple and contradictory laws apply to the same transaction, leaving a marketer open to the possibility of unintentionally violating the laws of a foreign country. A whole series of issues arise in e-marketing, including what constitutes a contract in cyberspace, how international tax can be harmonised and how tax should be collected for online transactions.

There are many issues of intellectual property protection, including copyright infringement, inappropriate linking to information from another website and trademark infringement, such as the registering of existing trademarks as domain names for the website. Because of the demand for domain names, second-level (for example .co, .org and .com) and third-level country names (.uk and .de) have been added. Countries, including the UK, Mexico and Russia, have taken a 'first come, first served' approach to this, and companies such as Nike, Chrysler and Sony initially failed to register as widely as they should have and have suffered as a consequence.

Consumer protection for international consumer clients must be provided to avoid unfair and deceptive trading practices, such as unsubstantiated advertising claims and false endorsements. Relationship marketing is based, especially for small firms, on building substantial data on customers in order to retain their loyalty, but in a number of countries gathering such information is illegal as laws exist to protect consumer privacy.

Marketers must also know the difference between what is considered free speech and what is defamation and disparagement. In 1997 McDonald's won a court case against two self-proclaimed anarchists who had published leaflets defaming McDonald's but the case cost McDonald's US$15 million. At the time a rogue website, McSpotlight, run by volunteers in 22 countries added further derogatory material about McDonald's. Hundreds of rogue websites have been set up, such as I Hate McDonald's page and ToysRUs Sucks, and firms have considerable difficulty controlling the negative publicity that these sites create.

The problems of the Internet

The problems discussed so far have related to the application of largely existing legislation to the new medium and the fact that the Internet crosses country borders indiscriminately. Other issues are the ease of access and lack of control of illegal activity. It has been estimated that a large percentage of international consumer e-commerce is devoted to pornography and a worrying part of this traffic is illegal and supporting paedophilia. It requires close cooperation between country law enforcement agencies to catch the culprits.

The ease of communicating with many recipients makes it easy to send out 'junk mail' (spam). Millions of messages can be sent out worldwide in the hope of getting just a few responses. Many firms sell to potential customers through emails and text messages. However, if this is overused it degenerates into spam. Spam is the intrusive, offensive and often pornographic junk email that fills up the inboxes of email systems. It threatens to create gridlock on the Internet if it is not controlled. The US has proposed opt-out legislation so that spam would be legal unless the receiver has opted out of receiving it. The EU legislation is opt-in – spam could not be sent unless the receiver had given consent to receive it – and would be more effective in controlling spam. In the UK, the British Computer society reported that 94 per cent of emails in December 2006 were spam.

MOVING TO A CUSTOMER-LED STRATEGY

E-business has revolutionised business and changed the fundamental principles of marketing for ever by allowing anyone anywhere in the world to buy online from anyone else. The range of communication methods has increased significantly as a result of technological advances and entrepreneurialism. The growth in social networking has transformed communications. Sometimes blogging is well informed and sometimes it is completely incorrect and often malicious, but it is strongly influencing consumer purchasing and usage decisions. The technology advances were expected to level the playing field between small and large firms so that the most innovative firms, small or large, would become the winners. It was thought that the technologists rather than the marketers would be in control. In reality consumers have become more sophisticated in their use of technology and used it to their advantage. As a result consumers are increasingly in control of events and so even greater customer insights are needed and marketing expertise has never been more vital.

Seybold (1998) has concluded by explaining the need to focus on the existing customers, figure out what they want and need, and work out how you can make life easier for them.

At the start of the chapter we proposed the idea that technology is an enabler, and Hamill and Stevenson (2003) suggest that technology facilitates cost-effective relationship building, but does not automatically achieve a customer-focused approach. Ritter and Walter (2006) examine the impact of information technology on customer relationships in the B2B context. They conclude that whilst IT competence can replace parts of relationship management, it cannot do so totally.

Technology has shifted the balance of power from suppliers to customers. Consequently, customer dominance must be accepted and those arrogant firms that take customers for granted will suffer. Organisations must adopt a customer-led approach. This means that they must develop innovative approaches to sales, marketing and overall corporate strategy that are driven by what customers need and want. Smaller players, such as publishers, as Illustration 12.6 shows, must find a new niche and new ways to generate income.

The objective of being customer-led is to identify, acquire, retain and grow 'quality' customers. Nykamp (2001) suggests that organisations must achieve competitive differentiation by building impermeable customer relationships and the challenge is to use the interactive power of the Internet to facilitate this by helping the organization to build close one-to-one relationships with their most valuable and growable customers.

Many firms have recognised the need to be customer-led and have responded by implementing sophisticated and expensive customer relationship management systems. Hamill and Stevenson suggest that many of these systems have failed to produce the expected return because they have been technology driven rather than customer-led. The term CRM has been hijacked by software vendors promising 'out-of-the-box' solutions to complex strategic, organisational and human resources problems. They claim that technology has a part to play but customer-led is not about software, database marketing, loyalty programmes, customer bribes or hard selling. It is about building strong one-to-one relationships with quality customers, achieving customer loyalty, maximising customer lifetime earnings and re-engineering the firm towards satisfying the needs of 'quality' customers on a customised and personalised basis. The most convincing reason for a customer to buy from any company in the world is that they are totally satisfied, have no reason to complain about the service they receive and are surprised and delighted by some of the firm's innovative actions.

To deliver this requires a more fundamental reinvention of the firm if it wishes to really succeed in the future. A new mindset is needed together with an innovative approach to the strategy. In practice firms will need to:

- Focus not on markets but on quality customers from anywhere in the world. By quality customers it is the strategically significant, most valuable and 'growable' customers that should be given the highest priority. The suggestion is that, over time, firms have moved from supplying markets to serving market segments, and are now focusing on serving individual customers one at a time.

- Focus on one-to-one relationships. To do this firms must learn about customers and deliver personalised and customised products, services and support in order to maximise the up- and cross-selling opportunities. The implications of this are that at one level firms must be sensitive to the customer's business and social culture and the customer's business dynamics. At another level the firm must be able to form supply and value chain alliances that enable the up- and cross-selling to be developed for the customer's benefit.

- Increasing both lifetime and short-term revenue from customers. Firms must focus on the delivery of exceptional value by developing an effective worldwide supply chain, building ever-closer relationships both with customers and partners and finding ways to erect barriers to entry by competitor firms.

ILLUSTRATION 12.6

Specialist publishers have their finger on the pulse

Many traditional publishers of specialist trade magazines have been hit by online websites that carry out many of their knowledge transfer activities and revenue raising activities more effectively and efficiently. Publishers recognise that traditional media, such as newspaper and journals, are useful for advertisers for raising general awareness but not so good for generating sales leads.

These publishers used to earn revenue from advertising targeted at professionals, but they have been hit by the growth of online job sites and pay per click advertising. One such publisher, Pulse, a weekly paper for General Practitioners has tried to fight back with the launch of Searchmedia, a specialist

doctor's Internet search engine, which aims to provide more authoritative and reliable help than could be obtained from search engines such as Google and Yahoo. The website aims to eliminate 'noise' that comes from Google searches, which includes possible unreliable information from user groups or from Wikipedia, the online encyclopaedia, and provide doctors with clinical evidence, treatment guidelines and information to be passed to patients.

Because doctors find the website useful, it attracts advertising from firms marketing to doctors, such as pharmaceutical companies.

QUESTION *What are the marketing challenges of developing a business based on a specialist professional niche and then internationalising it?*

SOURCE: ADAPTED FROM P. DURMAN 'PUBLISHER PUTS ITS FINGER ON THE PULSE', *SUNDAY TIMES*, 22 OCTOBER, 2006

■ Win-win. The long-term business relationships must be valuable for both supplier and provider and so long-term value for the customer and firm must be maximised. This could require some compromises by both parties to achieve this.

■ Integrated and coordinated approach. The success of a customer-led relationship building approach is that it requires commitment at all levels, creating, communicating and delivering value. For all businesses, but particularly global businesses, this is clearly a major challenge.

Most firms would claim to be customer led but the real test for them is whether they would be willing to change their strategy radically because of the trends that are being perceived in the marketplace. Lindstrom and Seybold (2003) reports on research that suggests that marketing strategies in the future may need to be changed radically in order to be customer led. Very young, computer literate child consumers have a large influence on family purchasing decisions. They are extremely well-informed through online networking sites that influence their behaviour. It is necessary to ask just how far firms should change their international marketing strategy to respond to these changes.

TECHNOLOGY ENABLING

It is evident that information technology and management systems are critical to the successful implementation of such an approach and the key challenge is to manage and integrate the customer-facing systems with the operational and management systems internal to the firm and its supply chain. Even here, however, the major challenge is not that of setting up the systems and processes but rather obtaining total commitment from staff, no matter what their cultural background, to implement the systems.

Technology provides the mechanisms by which strategic planning of a customer-led approach can be effectively managed. The elements include customer mapping and developing an integrated, coordinated, multichannel approach to planning in order to answer the questions on a worldwide basis: who should we serve, what should we serve to them and how should we serve them?

SUMMARY

■ Technology is creating new market opportunities and continually changing the way business is done in international markets. New technology provides new possible solutions to solve old problems but also sets new challenges for international marketing management. Firms will underperform or even fail if they are not able to exploit the global opportunities offered by the new technology or if they take the wrong decisions about how new technology might affect their industry sector.

■ Consumer e-marketing, and especially innovative business models, such as online auctions, attract the interest of global consumers and facilitate new routes to market. Consumers have developed new ways of communicating, collecting information about products and services and making purchase and usage decisions.

■ Although the Internet and advances in telecommunications have had the most dramatic effect on international marketing, other technologies and software to support integrated marketing solutions have been part of this change. They have substantially changed the way consumers live their lives and this will have an increasing effect on company performance.

- Business-to-business e-commerce models, however, are perhaps having the greatest effect on international marketing. For example, e-procurement through e-hubs enables purchasing to be more efficiently managed worldwide.

- Greater cooperation because of improvements in communication and the ease of information sharing make supply chains more effective. Excess capacity and increased competition mean that the power in the supply chain is increasingly favouring the customer, however.

- Because of this, firms will need to work ever harder to find new customers and retain the loyalty of existing customers. To achieve this their international marketing strategies will have to be customer led. But technology must be embraced to make this happen.

KEYWORDS

Business to business	E-commerce	Legislation
Business to consumer	E-procurement	Knowledge management
Customer-led	Enabling technologies	Online auction
Customer relationship management	Function-specific hubs	Supply chain management
Customise	Industry-specific hubs	Telecommunications
Customised	Information technology	Websites
	Internet	

CASE STUDY

India showing IBM the way?

Three decades ago IBM left India because of the difficult nationalistic policies. Only in 1992 did it return, but by 2007 it was holding its annual investors' day in Bangalore Palace rather than in New York. Why? Because it wanted to show that the firm's 'centre of gravity' was moving towards the big developing countries such as Brazil, China and Russia. By 2007 IBM employed 53 000 staff in India, one of the fastest grow-ing markets for IBM, with revenues rising by 40–50 per cent per year. IBM announced that it was investing US$6 billion in India between 2007 and 2010 in addition to any planned acquisitions and it is expected to double its workforce there by 2010.

IBM's challenges

IBM faced a number of challenges. Firstly, emerging countries have posed threats and opportunities, because Indian services firms, such as Infosys, Wipro, Tata and Cognizant have been able to compete more aggressively with IBM and its rivals Accenture, EDS and Hewlett Packard. Now they are all increas-ing their Indian workforce. Secondly, IBM has to decide what makes a successful multinational company in a global market

and as a result what the company must do to generate the growth its shareholders demand.

IBM's boss, Sam Palmisano, explained in a speech at Insead in 2006 that the model of an international company had passed through three stages. The first was the nineteenth-century international model where firms were based in one country and sold goods through sales offices in their international markets. The classic multinational followed in which the parent company created smaller versions of itself in its various country markets. The latest model is the 'globally integrated enterprise' in which the strategy, management and operations are devel-oped as a single entity. It is based on having the right cost, the right skills and the right business environment, so that work flows to places where it is done best.

IBM's investment in India is not solely about cheaper workers but was about leading edge research and development in 19 offices across India, writing software and running low cost call centres. It was also about flexibility. Its financing back office is in Rio de Janeiro and call centres are placed around the world. When rioting disrupted activities in Bangalore in April 2006, IBM moved data centre services to facilities in Brazil and Colombia. In line with building a globally integrated enterprise IBM has replaced its separate supply chains, set up in different markets, with a centralised supply chain and the chief procurement officer John Paterson has relocated to Shenzhen in China in an effort to improve the quality of IBM's purchasing staff in the region.

But what will be the basis of IBM's future growth? Cutting costs will be crucial. Globalising the supply chain has already saved IBM US$8 billion a year. But IBM is a mature business with 330 000 staff in 170 countries and getting them to make the changes to implement the next strategy will be difficult.

IBM's recent history

IBM built its business on computer hardware but when a previous boss, Lou Gerstner, took over in 1993 it was on the point of selling itself off in parts as a response to a huge corporate loss, as its mainframe computer business on which it had built its past declined, and to personal computers becoming commodities. The mainframe computer business was stabilised and the business direction changed to focus not on selling hardware but on the fast-growing IT services market including outsourcing. Between 1992 and 2001 hardware declined as a percentage of revenues from 55 per cent to 30 per cent and services increased from 25 per cent to 42 per cent.

In 2002 IBM bought the consulting arm of Pricewaterhouse Coopers apparently to complete the services strategy by providing consultancy expertise and relationships with some key global firms, in theory enabling IBM to focus on higher value work solving complex business process problems. But as IBM moved upmarket Indian IT firms started to compete strongly at the lower end. Infosys with a market vale of US$28 billion is still less than a quarter of the value of IBM but it is growing fast as clients seek to make cost saving in their outsourcing contracts. Indian firms such as Infosys have started to win contracts that previously IBM would have considered their own. The competition is also forcing IBM to quote for contracts at much lower prices than they would previously have done.

Even though IBM signed up outsourcing deals with Vodafone, the German Army and the State of Indiana in 2006, the days of the 'mega deals' (US$1 billion one supplier contracts over several years) are drying up for IBM as clients

realise they gave too much control to one outsourcing company. In future, contracts are likely to be split between a number of suppliers and be rather more aggressively negotiated. Total outsourcing was IBM's strength, being able to manage everything from simple call centres to remote infrastructure management (over 40 000 servers outside India are managed from India) to business transformation, in which the client's business is re-engineered and its staff managed through the process.

Implementing the international strategy

In practice it has been IBM's investment in India and good management of the Daksh operation that IBM acquired in 2004 that has helped. Daksh was encouraged to carry on as it was before rather than try to operate in the IBM way. IBM initially paid the Indian workers too much which created problems in the IT labour market but now it is focusing on tapping into local talent and developing it through training, staff development and career progression to attract and retrain good staff. Cost reduction from its Indian operation is now helping IBM to increase profit margins.

IBM needs to continue to innovate. IBM draws licence fees, about US$1 billion per year, from clients and competitors alike that use its intellectual property such as in mainframe computers and its multi-core semiconductors that are used widely, including the three leading videogames consoles. It owns a patent on one-click purchasing and other patents fundamental to e-commerce. In 2007, for example, Amazon settled for an undisclosed sum IBM's claim that they were infringing patents.

IBM will need to continue to make bold strategic decisions. It seems to have had no regrets about selling off its loss-making personal computer business to Lenovo. It has invested US$16 billion in four years on 50 acquisitions, mainly software companies. Its software revenue in 2006 was 20 per cent of the total but profits from software were 40 per cent of the total and its ambition seems to be to become the next great software company based on 'middleware' that helps a firm's different software to run together.

The real challenge however is to produce synergies from its hardware, software and services to make it a global leader. To do this IBM staff must work together rather than stay in their business unit 'silos'. It has picked 17 industry sectors on which to focus and will use its research labs around the world to focus on specific sectors. In Bangalore the focus will be on developing software for the healthcare and insurance sectors.

QUESTIONS

1　What are key challenges faced by IBM in its global markets?

2　What recommendations would you make to ensure the firm's continued profitable growth?

PHOTO CREDIT: IMAGEBROKER/ALAMY

SOURCE: ADAPTED FROM S HAMM, 'IBM'S PASSAGE TO INDIA', BUSINESS WEEK 8 AUGUST, 20C5, 'HUNGRY TIGER, DANCING ELEPHANT: HOW INDIA IS CHANGING IBM'S WORLD', THE ECONOMIST 4 APRIL 2007, WWW.IBM.COM AND OTHER PUBLICLY AVAILABLE SOURCES

DISCUSSION QUESTIONS

1 The fundamental concerns of international marketing strategy analysis, development and implementation are to add stakeholder value and remove unnecessary costs. How does technology assist in this process?

2 Choose a service firm. Write a report to the management of the firm on the factors that should be considered when developing an e-based international marketing strategy.

3 As a consultant to an electronics component supplier from a central European country, explain how the development of e-hubs to facilitate global business-to-business transactions will affect their business.

4 Write a report to the chief executive of an insurance company critically analysing the effects of the growth of e-commerce on the global channels of distribution.

5 A small firm which provides consultancy in engineering is seeking to develop an e-commerce strategy to enable them to grow substantially from their current base of customers in eight export markets. Develop an international marketing strategy that would enable them to do this.

References

Chaffy, D., Mayer, R., Johnston, K. and Ellis-Chadwick, F. (2006) *Internet marketing*. FT Prentice Hall.

Hamill, J. and Stevenson, A. (2003) 'Customer-led strategic Internet marketing', in S. Hart (ed.) *Marketing changes*. Thomson Learning.

Hoffman, K.D. (2003) 'Services marketing', in *Marketing Best Practice*. Thomson Learning.

Internet World Stats (2007) accessed at www.internetworldstats.com on 10 April 2007.

Javalgi, R., Radulovich, L.P., Pendelton, G. and Scherer, R.F. (2005) 'Sustainable competitive advantage of internet firms: a strategic framework and implications for global marketers', *International Marketing Review* 22 (6): 658–72.

Kaplan, S. and Sawhney, M. (2000) 'E-hubs: the new B2B marketplaces', *Harvard Business Review*, 78 (3): 97–103.

Lindgren, J.H.E. (2003) 'Marketing', in *marketing best practice*. Thomson Learning.

Lindstrom, M. and Seybold, P. (2003) *BRANDchild*. Kogan Page.

Nykamp, M. (2001) *The customer differential*. AMACOM.

Peppers, D. and Rogers, M. (1997) *Enterprise one to one: tools for competing in the interactive age*. Piatkus.

Ritter, T. and Walter, A. (2006) 'Matching high-tech and high-touch in supplier-customer relationships', *European Journal of Marketing*, 40 (3/4): 292–310.

Seigel, D. (1999) *Futurize your enterprise*. John Wiley and Sons.

Seybold, P. (1998) *Customers.com: how to create a profitable business strategy for the Internet and beyond*. Century Business.

Snyder, D.P. (2005) 'Extra-Preneurship', *Futurist*, 39 (4): 47–53.

Sheth, J. and Arma, A. (2005) 'International e-marketing: opportunities and issues', *International Marketing Review*, 22 (6): 611–22.

Timmers, P. (1999) *Electronic commerce strategies and models for business to business trading*. Wiley.

Unctad (2006) 'Trends in information and communications technology', November 2006, available at www.unctad.org.

Weryu, D., Boonghee, Y. and Ma, L. (2003) 'consumer patronage of ethnic portals', *International marketing Review*, 20 (6): 661–77

Zugelder, M.T., Flaherty, T.B. and Johnson, J.P. (2000) 'Legal issues associated with international Internet marketing', *International Marketing Review*, 17 (3).

INTERGRATIVE LEARNING ACTIVITY 3

INTERNATIONAL MARKETING PLANNING: IMPLEMENTATION, CONTROL AND EVALUATION

Introduction

In the previous two special focus sections on planning we explored the dimensions of analysis and strategy development. We now turn to the implementation of the plan through the application of the marketing mix that has been covered in the chapters in Part 3. In practice, of course, some of the content of the previous chapters needs to be revisited because there is no clear distinction between what might be considered strategy development and implementation. This is especially true of product and service strategy, where many decisions can be regarded as operational, and market entry, where many decisions are closely associated with distribution.

The starting point for implementation is planning the international marketing mix. This includes completing the product and service plan and preparing communications, distribution and pricing plans. The plan should explain how relationships with key partners can be built and managed within the supply chain, how customer relationships can be developed and how technology can be used to facilitate the firm's international marketing plan implementation.

The success of the implementation plan is also dependent on the planning ability, management capability and motivation and effectiveness of the firm's staff. Management need to anticipate and plan for potential problems that might arise in managing the implementation stage. Of course, these problems may well originate in topics that were considered in the first two parts of the book.

We also consider how to establish appropriate performance standards and measurement techniques that can be used to maintain control over the plan and the evaluation that will enable corrective action to be taken whenever the firm's performance deviates from the plan (as it surely will).

In this activity the focus is on developing the skills of decision-making in a local business unit at an operational level, whilst still keeping in mind the implication of the firm's global strategy on these local decisions.

Learning objectives

On completing this activity the reader should be able to:

- Appreciate the opportunities for growth in an international business sector and how they are influenced by the strategy implementation

- Use appropriate concepts and an analysis of market factors to develop marketing mix implementation strategies

- Appreciate the benefit of developing better customer relationship management

- Identify the methods that should be used for the management and control of the business

This integrative learning activity can be applied to any multinational organisation, but we have chosen to provide a short case study of Microsoft, largely because its software is so widely used, the company has reached an interesting point in its history and so much information and comment is available online and in the media to support the activity.

Microsoft – getting the best out of computing

Microsoft is the second most valuable brand in the world (page 288). The company has a global revenue of around US$50 billion and has more than 75 000 employees in 102 countries around the world. Microsoft has headquarters in Redmond, Washington, US and develops, manufactures, licenses and provides support for a wide range of software, of which Microsoft Windows, the operating system for computers and Microsoft Office, for carrying out a variety of applications, such as word processing, spreadsheets, powerpoint presentations, Internet exploration and emailing, are perhaps the best known, because they have come to dominate the desk-top computer market. Microsoft's orginal mission was 'a computer on every desk and in every home, running Microsoft software' and this has been almost completely achieved.

With Paul Allen, Bill Gates founded the firm in 1975 and went on to become CEO and chief software architect. He is generally recognised as the world's richest man with a fortune estimated to be US$56 billion.

The Microsoft competitive advantage and strategy

It is estimated that around one billion personal computers are in use worldwide and Microsoft Windows and Office sit on nearly all of them. It is not surprising therefore that they represent nearly 60 per cent of sales and 80–90 per cent of the profits of Microsoft. Microsoft rose to prominence 25 years ago with its operating system for IBM's personal computer. The company unified standards, making it easier for users and software writers to improve their own skills and develop new applications. Since the early years each new development of the operating system has been welcomed, given the prospect of enhanced functionality, greater speed, security, more efficient and effective working and more interesting and fun leisure applications. Software developers used Windows and Office as platforms for their own applications, leading Microsoft's software to become all pervasive in the computing industry.

The introduction of Vista

After a number of versions of Windows (95, 97 and XP) Microsoft launched the latest version, Vista, in 2007, along with an updated version of Office, and Exchange Server 2007 designed to reduce the growing cost and complexity of a corporate messaging system. The development of Vista took 8000 people five years to develop, cost US$6 billion and was two years late in the launch. Vista was launched under the slogan 'Clear, Confident, Connected – Bringing clarity to your world'. Initial figures from Microsoft suggested that in its first month 20 million copies of Vista had been sold, compared with 17 million in the first two months after the launch of its predecessor, XP. The Internet buzzed with complaints from users, however, saying that the system had caused havoc with games, printers, cameras and other peripherals. This was the usual problem with a new version of the operating system and rather vindicated the view of those who decided to wait until the problems had been ironed out.

Professional users and home technology enthusiasts who understand specifications, computer jargon and the functions of the software would be expected to see the benefits of the new Vista software quickly. With personal and technical selling, demonstration events and support from intermediaries in the distribution channel the major B2B customers were expected to make early purchases. Resellers, such as computer retailers (Dell and PCWorld) would also be expected to commit to the new products. However, persuading small business and home users would always be more of an uphill battle.

Home users Many home users would not be prepared to pay a significant amount of money for the new software package, so the main sales for Vista would come as a result of bundling the operating system software in with the purchase of a new laptop or PC, making it a sale to consumers through the resellers. Given the continual advances in the performance of computers and the need to regularly update them, users would probably be inclined to wait to get Vista until they purchased a new PC or laptop. It is very difficult to describe and explain the benefits of intangible items such as software or other gadgets to home users. Apple has addressed this problem by setting up retail stores largely to allow potential customers to 'play' with the products before purchasing or learn how to get the most out of them. Of course this is only possible in areas of high population and potential sales. If Microsoft did something similar it would also have to be careful not to upset its resellers.

Microsoft recognises that its biggest competitor for Vista is Microsoft itself – or at least the previous versions of the Windows operating system. The problem is that many home users do not really know what the Windows and Office brands stand for and what the products actually do for them. Their earlier Microsoft Windows and Office products usually work satisfactorily, so the users are unclear as to why they should purchase an improved version. So marketing and promotion is critical.

Communications Microsoft develops its major communications, standardised advertisements and launch programmes at head office in the US, but the context for running the advertisements in different country markets can be very different. The Vista launch was accompanied by an advertising campaign based around the word 'Wow' in an attempt to get across the exciting new features. The problem with a standardised global campaign is that different cultures receive the message rather differently: the word 'Wow' has different subtle meanings in different languages, and so the impact of the advertising campaign could be lost. An earlier Microsoft campaign suggesting that people that did not use its software were dinosaurs could not even be shown is some countries because it upset potential customers so much.

Other communications activities that surrounded the campaign were tailored to local user expectations by the local staff. However, the principal of integrated marketing communications is that the customer is put at the centre of the communicatons and should not be overloaded or confused by the many and various messages. The customer should receive consistent messages from the various sources of communications – including culturally consistent messages. This should include coordination of the various brands used, as we discuss later.

Legislation In the past Microsoft tied its Windows operating system and Office applications together by 'commingling' the code in order to strengthen its competitive position. This was the reason why it fell foul of the antitrust (anti-competitive) authorities in the US and in Europe. In Europe, for example, three years after Microsoft had been fined €497 million for breaking competition law, it had not paid and the EU threatened to impose further fines at a rate of €3 million per day. Apart from the fine hanging over its head, Microsoft is watched closely and this is affecting the development of its innovative ideas, which are being treated with suspicion by the authorities.

Security As the major provider of operating systems Microsoft software is the obvious target for disaffected people and criminals who carry out fraud and identity theft. Often this is cross-border making it more difficult to track down the perpetrators. Much of the justification for the Vista development was to improve security, due the considerable problem of hackers and viruses. Only time will tell if Microsoft has kept its promise to improve security with Vista.

Piracy Since the early days of computing, software has been copied and sold on. It has been estimated that as much as 95 per cent of the software being used in India and China has been pirated but some attempts are now being made to address this.

Price One of the problems for firms is price transparency and the Internet allows comparisons to be made. For example the price for Vista Home Premium in the US was approximately the same in dollars as it was in pounds. It is rather hard for users to understand why this is so, as the exchange rate at the time was £1 = $2 and particularly as software could be delivered through downloading anyway.

Competition

Competition is changing the face of computing. Software developers are no longer so dependent on Office and Windows due to the availability of open-source software. The code for this is written by volunteers rather than one company, the programmes are offered free to customers and are open to further enhancement by individual users. Companies ranging from start-ups to MNEs like IBM commercialise open-source sofware by selling supporting services. The collaborative nature of open-source software means development is often quicker and features can be added more easily, saving users' money. Open source has some disadvantages, particularly around ease of use, but improvements are being made incrementally and continually. The way that open source software can be commercially viable is by providing it as a service, using advertising alongside to generate income.

Other product and service areas

Microsoft has extended its activities into many other areas, for example, Xbox video games consoles, Zune digital audio, video ad music players, software and online music stores. Indeed the branding of Xbox video gaming consoles competes with Nintendo and Wii and makes only passing reference to the parent Microsoft brand. It is difficult to find consistent brand values that embrace the professional, B2B market in Microsoft and the fun, exciting world of Xbox video gaming. Zune too must compete directly with the more unconventional, 'cool' iPod sub-brand of Apple.

Microsoft has many other services – but in areas where there are already strong competitors. It has a Web-based email product, Hotmail, instant messenger, a blogging site called Spaces and Virtual Earth, a competitor to Google Earth. These are grouped together under the Windows Live brand. Its search engine is Live.com but its former Internet brand MSN still hosts a range of Internet services too, which is confusing to the user.

Future growth strategy

CEO Steve Ballmer believes that search is the key to Microsoft's future growth, given that it is the starting point for most Internet use. It is also the key to the US$580 billion online advertising market. However, according to Media Matrix, Microsoft's share of searches fell by 3 per cent to 11 per cent by early 2007, whilst Google searches gained 6 points to 48 per cent and Yahoo held 28 per cent of the market.

Microsoft has huge resources and capability – enough to dominate again – but it will have to re-evaluate its implementation strategy.

The task

1 Critically evaluate the global marketing implementation strategy of Microsoft, paying particular attention to the changing nature of business-to-business buying of software and the changing needs, expectations and behaviour of the consumer market around the world.

2 Having identified the challenges Microsoft faces, develop an international marketing implementation

strategy in outline both for the consumer and business market. Focus on the marketing mix implementation issues, including an assessment of the key brand, product, service and communications issues. Identify, too, the factors that will influence the pricing strategy.

3 Prepare a plan for the control, management and continuous improvement of the operations, including appropriate measurement, and outline the processes that are required to achieve sustained success. Explain particularly the key dimensions of the marketing culture that is needed.

Getting started

This section focuses on the business-to-business sector and consumer markets for software and services. You should use this case study not only to focus on the implementation issues of the strategy process but also to study in greater depth the particular issues involved in the B2B sector and the service sector.

Clearly the effective marketing of services requires an understanding of customer requirements and service expectation as well as staff motivation and management, customer relationship building and the cultural issues that underpin much of this.

Task 1 requires an analysis of the factors that have led to the growth in software and services in international markets and of the factors that will determine the nature of purchasing in the future – and consequently how important relationship-building with global customers will be in the future. By now you should have a very good understanding of how you can access and analyse research material from libraries and online sources to complete this task. There is a huge amount of information and comment on Microsoft, the market and the competition in the literature and business press to help you complete Tasks 2 and 3 but you must also include your own creative approaches. You require an understanding of the sector and the software and services that must be provided, how they are bought and managed in the markets around the world.

Customer satisfaction is very dependent on the customers' perception of the software and services that are delivered. Consequently, setting realistic customer expectations, motivating and training staff, solving problems effectively and managing a cost-effective service are all critical for success. Task 3 requires you to think about how you would organise and manage this on a global basis.

In completing the tasks you need to consider the issues highlighted in the following framework shown in Figure III.

The way forward

Strategy development and planning is a continuous process. Having completed the tasks in this section, you will have gained a better understanding of the software and services sector that underpins the operation of computing and the value that customers are able to obtain from them, and the approaches adopted by Microsoft on both a strategic and operational (implementation) level. You should now be well informed to revisit the strategy development process.

You should return to the Part 1 planning framework on page 452 to review the current market environment for Microsoft as the basis for their ongoing strategy. The most important issue is to decide where and how the firm can maintain its dominant global position, using an assessment of the market environment, customer demands and competitor activity. Given the fast growth of the sector you should review the firm's ambitions particularly in developing markets, and focus on the market factors in these countries and use the market information and research framework to identify further growth opportunities. You should also consider the more established markets that still dominate Microsoft's business to assess the opportunities to increase market share. Finally, you might reassess the company capability and expertise that will be expected to underpin its continued expansion.

You should then return to Part 2 and, using the framework in Figure 1.3 on page 25, review the firm's vision and objectives as stated on the website and decide if they are still appropriate. You should re-evaluate and restate the firm's competitive advantage and assess how this informs the international positioning of the various Microsoft brands. Using the recent data available online you should assess the market entry methods used and the effectiveness of these methods in delivering the strategy.

Checklist for success

Having completed the integrative learning activities you should think about how comprehensive your work is and whether you really have addressed the fundamental issues that could well make the difference between a failing and a successful strategy. To help you do this we have identified some of the issues you should consider. Clearly you may not be able to answer these in detail because you will not have sufficient detail about the firm's operations, but you should have thought about how you would address the issues given access to the information.

Does the plan contain:

■ Assumptions about the world economy and the environmental trends in the principal markets?

TABLE III

Key factors to consider in evaluating the implementation of the strategy

The element of the plan	Some concepts, models and issues to be addressed
Environmental analysis	• Identify the global trends that have provided the opportunity for growth in the sector • Analyse the nature of customer needs and the nature of competition in the sector • Evaluate the firm's strategy and its regional focus
Marketing mix	• Building the corporate identity and managing the brand • Product differentiation and the three service Ps • Communication to customers and other stakeholders • Managing the delivery to achieve customer satisfaction • Managing costs and the pricing strategy • The use of technology
Relationship marketing	• The methods of identifying current and potential high value customers • Knowledge and database management • Customer relationship management
Control and management	• The organisation and management structure using the 7S framework • Internal communications with its own staff • Financial and marketing measures and controls • Performance management and improvement processes, including benchmarking, balanced scorecard and self-assessment and improvement • Technology-enabled systems

- Details of historical performance (sales, costs, profitability)?
- Forecasts of future performance based on (a) an extrapolation of the past, (b) alternative scenarios?
- Identified opportunities and threats?
- Analysis of the company strengths, weaknesses and future capabilities in comparison with local and international competition?
- Long-term aims and objectives and the strategies to achieve them?
- One-year marketing objectives and individual strategies (for example, budgets, brand objectives and development of personnel)?
- Country-by-country forecasts and targets?

- Country-by-country plans for all marketing activities and coordination with other functions (for example, manufacturing)?
- An explanation of how country plans will be integrated regionally or globally if appropriate?
- A summary of the critical factors for success?
- An assessment of the likely competitor response? If your objective is to increase market share, your competitors will not simply lie down and let you without fighting back!
- A contingency component for when the unexpected happens and things do not go to plan?
- A control process for feedback, evaluation and taking corrective action?

INDEX

Entries in bold are included in the end-of-chapter keywords lists.